Sociology in our times

the essentials

Second Canadian Edition

Diana Kendall
Baylor University

Rick Linden
University of Manitoba

Jane Lothian Murray
University of Winnipeg

NELSON
THOMSON LEARNING™

Australia • Canada • Mexico • Singapore • Spain • United Kingdom • United States

Sociology In Our Times: The Essentials, Second Canadian Edition

by Diana Kendall, Rick Linden, and Jane Lothian Murray

Editorial Director and Publisher:
Evelyn Veitch

Executive Editor:
Joanna Cotton

Marketing Manager:
Don Thompson

Project Editor:
Toni Chahley

Production Editor:
Tracy Bordian

Production Coordinator:
Hedy Sellers

Copy Editor:
Erika Krolman

Proofreader:
Betty Robinson

Art Director:
Angela Cluer

Cover Design:
Peter Papayanakis

Cover Image:
PhotoDisk

Compositor:
Susan Calverley

Printer:
Transcontinental Printing Inc.

Printed and bound in Canada
2 3 4 04 03 02 01

For more information contact Nelson Thomson Learning, 1120 Birchmount Road, Scarborough, Ontario, M1K 5G4. Or you can visit our internet site at http://www.nelson.com

Canadian Cataloguing in Publication Data

Kendall, Diana Elizabeth
Sociology in our times: the essentials

2nd Canadian ed.
Includes bibliographical references and index.
ISBN 0-17-616889-3

1. Sociology. I. Lothian Murray, Jane, 1960– II. Linden, Rick. III. Title.

HM51.K46 2000 301
C00-932697-9

BRIEF CONTENTS

PART 1 STUDYING SOCIETY

PART 2 THE NATURE OF SOCIAL LIFE

PART 3 SOCIAL DIFFERENCES AND SOCIAL INEQUALITY

CONTENTS

PART 1 STUDYING SOCIETY

1 THE SOCIOLOGICAL PERSPECTIVE: THEORY AND METHODS 3

PART 2 THE NATURE OF SOCIAL LIFE

2 CULTURE 37

4 SOCIAL STRUCTURE, SOCIAL INTERACTION, AND COLLECTIVE BEHAVIOUR 101

5 GROUPS AND ORGANIZATIONS 137

6 DEVIANCE AND CRIME 165

PART 3 SOCIAL DIFFERENCES AND SOCIAL INEQUALITY

7 SOCIAL STRATIFICATION AND CLASS 197

8 GLOBAL STRATIFICATION 221

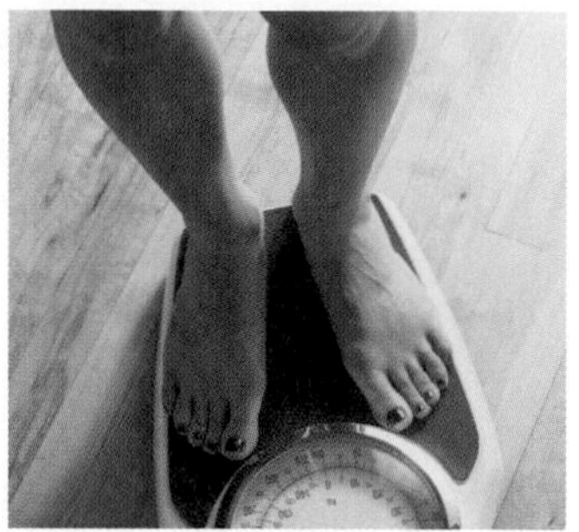

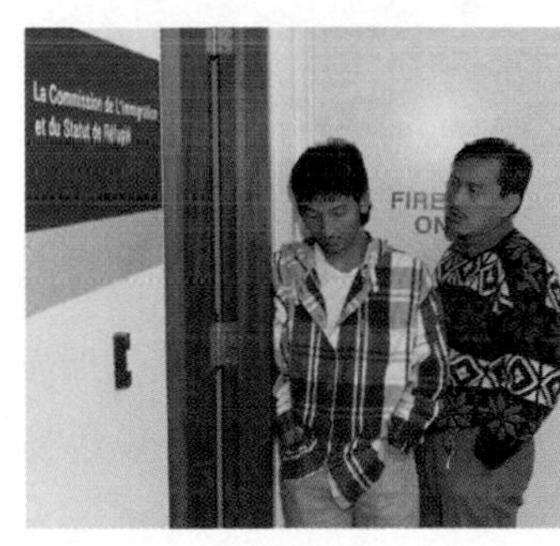

BOXES

Sociology and Technology

Sociology and Everyday Life

Critical Thinking

Sociology and Media

Sociology and Law

Sociology in Global Perspective

PREFACE

Welcome to the second Canadian edition of *Sociology In Our Times: The Essentials*. Because so many students and instructors have highly praised the first edition, we are delighted to bring you this exciting new edition, which highlights the challenges and opportunities that come with living and studying social life in the twenty-first century.

More than ever before, people are interested in the workings not only of their own society, but also of the larger world. We are coming to understand how events in other countries directly affect life in Canada. We wrote *Sociology In Our Times* to capture the excitement of this new era and to help students understand how sociological theory and research can be applied to everyday life and to the pressing social issues we face in a rapidly changing world.

Like the first edition, *Sociology In Our Times: The Essentials* is a cutting-edge book that highlights the relevance of sociology. It does so in at least two ways: (1) by including a diversity of classical and contemporary theory, interesting and relevant research, and lived experiences that accurately mirror the diversity in society itself; and (2) by showing students that sociology involves important questions and issues that they confront both personally and vicariously (for example, through the media). This text speaks to a wide variety of students and captures their interest by taking into account their concerns and perspectives. The text applies the finest research of classical and established contemporary sociologists, and it weaves an inclusive treatment of all people into the examination of sociology throughout the chapters. Although a number of introductory sociology texts give the appearance of inclusion, most are written with class, race, and gender neatly compartmentalized into their "appropriate" chapters, and perhaps an occasional "diversity" box thrown in. Not only does that approach marginalize an increasing proportion of the students in introductory sociology classes, as well as in the broader Canadian population, but it also leads many students to view race, class, and gender as nothing more than variables in sociological research (as found, for example, in statistics on welfare, crime, and homelessness). That approach downplays the significance of the interlocking nature of class, race, and gender in all topics examined by sociologists.

We encourage you to read our text and judge the writing style for yourself. We have sought to make the research accessible and engaging for both students and instructors. Concepts and theories are presented in a straightforward and understandable way, and a wealth of concrete examples and lived experiences are woven throughout. For students, this approach serves to clarify both the relevance and the importance of sociological theory and research.

ORGANIZATION OF THIS TEXT

Sociology In Our Times: The Essentials is divided into fifteen chapters and three parts.

- In Part 1, "Studying Society," Chapter 1, "The Sociological Perspective: Theory and Methods," students are introduced to the sociological imagination and the development of sociological thinking. The chapter sets forth the major theoretical perspectives used by sociologists in analyzing compelling social issues such as suicide, and it provides a thorough description of both quantitative and qualitative methods.

- Part 2, "The Nature of Social Life," focuses on core sociological concepts. Chapter 2, "Culture," spotlights culture as either a stabilizing force or a force that can generate discord, conflict, and even violence in societies. Cultural diversity is discussed as an important contemporary issue. Chapter 3, "Socialization," looks at positive and negative aspects of socialization across the life course and presents an innovative analysis of gender socialization. Chapter 4, "Social Structure, Social Interaction, and Collective Behaviour," examines social structure and social interaction in detail, using homelessness as an example of the dynamic interplay between social structure and interaction. Unique to this chapter are discussions of the sociology of emotions and of personal space as viewed through the lenses of race, class, gender, and age. This chapter also explores the dynamics of collective behaviour as it is expressed in the formation of urban legends, protests, and social movements. Chapter 5, "Groups and Organizations," includes analysis of innovative forms of social organization and ways in which organizational structures may differentially affect people depending on their race, class, gender, and age. Chapter 6, "Deviance and Crime," examines diverse perspectives on deviance, crime, and the criminal justice system. Key issues are dramatized for students through an analysis of recent research on organized crime, gangs, and the experiences of biker gang members.
- Part 3, "Social Differences and Social Inequality," looks at issues of class, race/ethnicity, and sex/gender. Chapter 7, "Social Stratification and Class," addresses systems of stratification and surveys social inequality in Canada. Using child poverty as a recurring theme, the chapter analyzes the causes and consequences of inequality and poverty. Chapter 8, "Global Stratification," extends the discussion by examining differences in wealth and poverty in rich and poor nations around the world. Explanations for these differences are discussed. Chapter 9, "Race and Ethnicity," focuses on the components of racial and ethnic conflict. A thorough analysis of prejudice, discrimination, and the experiences of racial and ethnic groups is presented, along with global, racial, and ethnic issues in the future. Chapter 10, "Sex and Gender," examines the links between gender socialization and contemporary gender inequality, providing lived experiences and perspectives on body image. Chapter 11, "Health, Health Care, and Disability," analyzes these issues in global perspective and in Canada. Chapter 12, "Politics and the Economy," looks at the nature of power and at Canadian and foreign political systems. It also explores topics such as global economic systems and the role of work. Chapter 13, "Families and Intimate Relationships," focuses on the diversity found in Canadian families today. Chapter 14, "Education and Religion," looks at systems of education and highlights issues of race, class, and gender in the schools. The chapter also examines religion in a global perspective, providing a survey of the world's major religions, and shows how religious beliefs affect other aspects of our social lives. Chapter 15, "Population and Urbanization," looks at demography, global population change, and the process and consequences of urbanization.

UNIQUE FEATURES

The following features are specifically designed to reflect the themes of relevance and diversity in *Sociology In Our Times: The Essentials*, as well as to support student learning.

Interesting and Engaging Lived Experiences throughout Chapters

Authentic first-person accounts are used as opening vignettes and throughout each chapter to create interest and to give concrete meaning to the topics discussed. Lived experiences, including experiences of racism, homelessness, child abuse, eating disorders, poverty, and divorce, provide opportunities for students to examine social life beyond their own experiences and to consider class, ethnicity, gender, and age from diverse perspectives. An unusually wide range of diverse experiences—both positive and negative—is systematically incorporated to expose students to multiple viewpoints. These lived experiences were selected for their ability to speak to students, to assist them in learning concepts and theories, and to show them how these examples can be applied to other situations.

Focus on the Relationship between Sociology and Everyday Life

Each chapter has a brief quiz that relates the sociological perspective to the pressing social issues described in the opening vignette. (Answers are provided on the subsequent page.) Do official statistics accurately reflect crime rates in Canada? Does increasing cultural diversity lead to an increasing incidence of hate crimes and racism? Do welfare benefits provide enough income for recipients to live comfortably? Topics such as these will pique the interest of students.

Use of the Media to Encourage Critical Thinking

Like most people in our society, students get much of their information about the social world from the media. A significant benefit of a sociology course is that it encourages students to think critically about such information. Focusing on various types of media depictions—including television news, daytime talk shows, television commercials and magazine advertisements, cartoons, movies, and mainstream and alternative presses—*Sociology and Media* boxes provide an overview of sociological topics as seen through the "eye" of the media. Topics range from racism in the media and an analysis of messages that affect women's body images, to the electronic church and the Internet and news coverage of diverse topics such as advertising and people living with AIDS.

Application of the Sociological Imagination to Contemporary Issues and the Law

Based on the latest legal research, *Sociology and Law* boxes encourage students to think critically about the many ties between the law and sociology and provide a springboard for discussion. Topics include child abuse, immigration law in Canada, and AIDS and public health.

Emphasis on the Importance of a Global Perspective

In our interconnected world, the sociological imagination must extend beyond national borders. The global implications of all topics are examined throughout each chapter and in *Sociology in Global Perspective* boxes. Topics include child abuse in Asia, poverty in Brazil, organized crime in Japan, and the AIDS epidemic in Africa.

Sociology in the Future

In addition to highlighting the contemporary relevance of sociology, students are encouraged to consider the sociological perspective as it might be in the future. The concluding sections of Chapters 2 through 15 look into the future and suggest how our social lives may change in the years to come. Homelessness, technology, population, deviance and crime, and the economy and work are among the topics discussed.

IN-TEXT LEARNING AIDS

Sociology In Our Times: The Essentials includes a number of pedagogical aids to promote students' mastery of sociological concepts and terminology.

- ***Chapter Outlines.*** A concise outline at the beginning of each chapter gives students an overview of major topics and a convenient aid for review.
- ***Questions and Issues.*** After the opening lived experience in each chapter, a series of introductory questions invites students to think about the major topics discussed in the chapter.
- ***Integrated Running Glossary.*** Major concepts and key terms are concisely defined and highlighted in bold print within the text flow to avoid disrupting students' reading. These concepts and

terms are also listed at the end of the chapters and in the glossary at the back of the book.

- ***End-of-Chapter Study Aids.*** The *Chapter Review* provides a concise summary of key points and theoretical perspectives, along with a list of *Key Terms*. *Questions for Critical Thinking* encourage students to assess their knowledge of the chapter and to apply insights they have gained to other issues. The *Suggested Readings* describe recent publications related to the chapter. This list also is a good source for book review suggestions.

NEW CHAPTERS AND FEATURES

- A new chapter, "Global Stratification" (Chapter 8), has been added to the second Canadian edition of *Sociology In Our Times: The Essentials* to provide students with more comprehensive coverage of a significant contemporary issue. In order to keep the text at a manageable length for a one-semester course, we have integrated the discussion of the economy and government into one chapter, "Politics and the Economy" (Chapter 12).

- In addition to the new chapters, we have added several hundred new references that include not only the most current census data, but also new and relevant Canadian research.

- Also new and unique to this text is the acknowledgment of feminist theory as a distinct theoretical perspective. Unlike other texts, the discussion of feminist theory and methodology is not compartmentalized into only gender or family chapters, but instead is fully integrated throughout the text.

New Sociology and Technology and Critical Thinking Boxes

- ***Sociology and Technology.*** As computers become an increasingly important part of our everyday lives, they change how we communicate, how we learn, and how we conceive of ourselves in relationship to others. Topics include seniors in cyberspace, the Internet and social stratification, technology in the classroom, technology and crime, and the Internet and organizations.

- ***Critical Thinking.*** From human rights legislation to reproductive technology to obscenity and women's equality, the Critical Thinking boxes encourage students to use their sociological knowledge to grapple with some of today's most hotly contested issues.

Internet Exercises

Sociology In Our Times: The Essentials not only has its own Web page on the Internet, but it also provides *Internet Exercises* at the end of every chapter. These exercises encourage students to explore the Internet, providing assignments to facilitate the discovery of Web sites that are directly relevant to chapter topics.

What Else Is New in the Second Edition?

- In **Chapter 1** the discussion of feminist theory has been expanded and recognized as a distinct theoretical perspective.
- In **Chapter 2**, the new opening lived experience shows the diversity of Canadian culture and emphasizes how cultural differences may lead to misunderstanding. This chapter includes new information on Aboriginal cultures and languages, highlighting the challenges of attaining the goal of a multicultural society. A new Sociology and Technology box deals with the issue of cyberculture on the Internet, and the new Sociology and Media box provides some amusing examples of cultural misunderstandings.
- **Chapter 3** has a new opening lived experience that illustrates the importance of socialization to children's well-being. It gives an example of a person who was able to overcome childhood abuse.
- In **Chapter 4,** the link between social structure and interaction and the social problem of homelessness has been updated and expanded. A new Critical Thinking box presents many questions about how to deal with homeless people on the street—panhandlers and the young homeless, the squeegee kids.

- In **Chapter 5**, a new chapter theme examines ways in which the bureaucratic form of organizations can lead to rigidity and ineffectiveness, and even to disasters.
- **Chapter 6** includes new material on restorative justice and white-collar crime, as well as a new Sociology and Technology box on the impact of new technology on crime and crime control.
- **Chapter 7** has been substantially rewritten and now focuses primarily on social stratification in Canada. It contains the most current data on poverty in Canada. The new Critical Thinking box includes recommendations for dealing with the problem of poverty and challenges students to think of alternative strategies.
- **Chapter 8** is an exciting new chapter that examines wealth and poverty in global perspective, particularly through the eyes of the world's poor. The chapter presents the major theories of development and describes the ways in which the actions of the wealthiest countries affect the lives of people in the poorest counties. New boxes include a Critical Thinking box on consumption and world poverty and a Sociology and Technology box on the digital Third World. Tables and figures illustrate disparities in wealth, income, and life chances around the globe.
- In **Chapter 9,** new data on race and ethnicity are set forth, and the components of racial and ethnic conflict are examined. Personal narratives from individuals who have been the victims of racism are designed to have an impact on students who may have difficulty understanding concepts such as prejudice, discrimination, and racism in the abstract.
- **Chapter 10** has a new opening lived experience that sparks students' interest in the gender-related issues of body consciousness and eating disorders. The figures, tables, and photographs have been updated throughout. Also included is additional current feminist research in the area of gender-based inequality in Canada.
- **Chapter 11** features a new lived experience describing a young woman's reaction to learning that she was HIV-positive and challenges many of the stereotypes concerning HIV/AIDS. This chapter provides extensive coverage of the sociology of health and medicine, including the social construction of illness and the process of medicalization, as well as the effects on health of social factors such as age, sex, and social class. Health care in Canada is compared and contrasted with health care in the United States. *Sociology In Our Times: The Essentials* is the only current sociology text to incorporate a thorough discussion of health issues of Aboriginal people in Canada. Likewise, it is the only text with a comprehensive discussion of disability.
- **Chapter 12** includes updated statistics and research on the Canadian economy and a new Critical Thinking box on technology and the workforce. It also includes new data on women in politics around the world.
- **Chapter 13** has a new opening lived eperience that calls attention to the changing nature of families and the new demands and challenges of parenting in families of divorce. All figures and tables have been updated with the latest information on such topics as gay and lesbian families, single parenting, and stepfamilies. Feminist theory has been expanded and emphasized as a central theoretical perspective in the study of sociology of the family. The new Critical Thinking box provides a feminist critique of some of the reproductive technologies available to families today.
- **Chapter 14** contains a new opening lived experience that sets the stage for examining the importance of education in a person's life. The chapter highlights ways in which race, class, and gender differentially affect people's access to education and its outcomes. The chapter also includes a new Science and Technology box on the technology revolution in Canadian classrooms. The chapter examines, in addition, the issue of the role of religion in educational institutions, and it contrasts the sociology of religion with theological perspectives on religion. A new Sociology and Technology box looks at the electronic church and the Internet.
- **Chapter 15** examines demography and urban life. Global population projections have been updated, and a Sociology in Global Perspective box examines the immigration policies of Canada and other countries. The chapter includes a discussion of how women experience city life differently from men, and it cites the latest studies on race, class, and gender in city and suburban living.

FULLY INTEGRATED SUPPORT PACKAGE FOR INSTRUCTORS AND STUDENTS

Ancillary materials that enhance teaching and learning are an important feature of a textbook. The supplements offered with *Sociology In Our Times: The Essentials* ensure that the themes of diversity, inclusiveness, and contemporary issues are consistent with the text. These pieces work together as an effective and integrated teaching package.

Instructor's Resource Manual

The Instructor's Resource Manual, written by Anna Lucy Robinson of Lambton College, provides lecture outlines, chapter summaries, and teaching tips, as well as a list of further print and video resources. In addition, guest speaker suggestions, student learning objectives, student projects, and essay questions are included. Instructors wishing to insert their own examples and references can download chapter outlines from our Web site, or they may request them from Nelson Thomson Learning in ASCII format.

Test Bank

A completely revised Test Bank is available with over 2000 multiple-choice and true-false items. Each question is categorized as testing conceptual understanding, concept application, or factual knowledge, and a page reference is provided for each answer. The Test Bank is available in both print and Windows formats to facilitate the creation of your own tests.

PowerPoint Presentation Software

PowerPoint presentation software is available to assist instructors in managing lectures. Nelson Thomson Learning has reproduced chapter objectives, key definitions, and a brief overview of the important concepts in a PowerPoint format. Instructors will have the ability to add, delete, or modify the slides according to their individual requirements.

SocLINK CD-ROM Instructor's Presentation Tool

An exceptional resource, SocLINK contains a wide assortment of photos, figures, maps, and audio and video clips, as well as easy access to the Internet. SocLINK is an ideal in-class instruction tool that allows professors to combine customized multimedia and live video with their lectures.

New Thematic Videos

Nelson Thomson Learning offers two new videotapes featuring 180 minutes of excerpts compiled from the CTV Television Network archives and corresponding to each chapter of the book. The segments were chosen to amplify the concepts of each chapter and to provide further examples of the sociology of everyday life. An accompanying discussion guide offers a synopsis of each segment, suggestions for introducing the videos, and discussion questions.

Sociology on the Web www.sociologytheessentials-2nded.nelson.com

Sociology In Our Times: The Essentials, Second Canadian Edition, features a companion Web site for students. Features of the Web site include an online tutorial, online material linked directly to the text (SocLinks), study resources, and career information. Instructors can find downloadable resources, including Web assignments, on this page.

Study Guide

Created by Diane Symbaluk of Grant MacEwan Community College, the Study Guide to accompany *Sociology In Our Times: The Essentials, Second Canadian Edition*, gives students further opportunity to think sociologically. Each chapter includes a chapter summary, a list of key terms and key people, a list of learning objectives, and multiple-choice and true-false questions.

ACKNOWLEDGMENTS

This edition of *Sociology In Our Times* would not have been possible without the insightful critiques of the following colleagues, who have reviewed some or all of this book. Our profound thanks to each reviewer for engaging in this time-consuming process:

Tulsie Raghubir, Niagara College
Bill Adcock, Sheridan College
Patricia Whaley, Durham College
David English, Durham College
Jock MacKay, Vanier College
Dave Dwyer, Fanshawe College
Laura Pao-Mercier, Vanier College
Tom Callaghan, St. Clair College
Anna Lucy Robinson, Lambton College

We would like to express our appreciation to the many individuals at Nelson Thomson Learning involved in the development and production of the second edition of *Sociology In Our Times: The Essentials*. Among them, Joanna Cotton and Toni Chahley for their motivation, guidance, and encouragement. Tracy Bordian for putting it all together in her usual professional manner. Evelyn Veitch for ensuring that this project ran smoothly. Once again, your creativity, dedication, long hours, and hard work has made this an experience we have enjoyed and a final product that we are extremely pleased with. Thank you also to our research assistant Heather Milne for providing the most current research in a form that students can interpret.

Jane Lothian Murray would like to thank her colleagues at the University of Winnipeg, Doug Skoog, Gillian Balfour, Sandra Kirby, Lesley Murphy, Michael Weinrath, and Harry Rosenbaum, for their encouragement, advice, and resources whenever needed. Rick Linden would like to thank G.N. Ramu and Rod Kueneman for their help with some of the new reference material required for this edition. Finally, we would once again like to thank our families for tolerating us when we got a little "cranky" from meeting deadlines and for inspiring us to finish so that we could spend more time with them.

We invite your comments and suggestions. Send them to us care of:

Nelson Thomson Learning
1120 Birchmount Rd.
Scarborough, Ontario
M1K 5G4

We also welcome e-mail messages at:

jane.murray@uwinnipeg.ca
rlinden@cc.umanitoba.ca

Jane Lothian Murray
University of Winnipeg

Rick Linden
University of Manitoba

CHAPTER 1

"There is an impossible situation. There is no way it can be worked out. There is no reason I can see to drain & strain my children's and my friends' strength & lives, in order to maintain for me a 'life'... My 'life' revolves around a worn-out undependable body that is only a burden to me & others....

"Later—Have made up my mind. God, please let this work. 6:45 pm—I took the toast & glass of water an hour ago.... Can you believe that I spent a long time searching for the damn tea kettle to get boiling water into which to dissolve the pills? Couldn't find it. Ever resourceful, I got hot water from the coffee maker by not putting in coffee.

"I spent an hour cracking open those damn capsules with a knife, to get the powder. I have probably lost 1/3 of the stuff.

"Clea the cat is racing around. I guess she knows something is going on." (King, 1997:387–388)

The above excerpts are from the diary of Margaret Laurence, one of Canada's greatest writers, whose best-known works are *The Stone Angel* and *The Diviners*. At the age of sixty-one and suffering from terminal cancer, Laurence took her own life. Biographer James King continues the story:

"There is a hiatus in the journal and then she made this final entry while waiting for death to arrive: 'Please, my near & dear ones, forgive me & understand. I hope this potion works. My spirit is already in another country, & my body has become a damn nuisance. I have been so fortunate.'" (King, 1997: 388)

Why do people commit suicide? Can sociological research help us understand the very individualistic act of taking one's own life? Do individuals (at least under some circumstances) have a right to end their own lives? Given who we are, what we know, and what we believe, our individual answers to these questions may vary. Along with others posed in this book, the questions may produce strong responses. In this chapter, suicide is used as an example of a problem that sociologists examine. We also will see

THE SOCIOLOGICAL PERSPECTIVE: THEORY AND METHODS

how sociological research methods might be used to answer complex questions, and we wrestle with some of the difficulties in attempting to study human behaviour.

People in various occupations may have different perspectives on suicide. A journalist may wonder whether a suicide is "newsworthy." Is either the deceased or the family well known? Did the suicide occur at an unusual time or location? A physician might assess the nature and extent of the physical injuries that caused death to occur. A psychiatrist might evaluate the mental state of the deceased prior to the suicide. A minister or a social worker might consider the appropriate counselling for the family. Law enforcement officers might want to determine if the death was in fact a suicide or whether charges should be brought against someone for causing or assisting in the death.

What, then, is the sociologist's perspective on the problem of suicide? The sociological perspective is a point of view that helps us understand human behaviour in the larger social context in which it occurs. Accordingly, sociologists would focus on the social environment in which suicide occurs, seeking explanations by analyzing why and under what circumstances that behaviour takes place. Using existing sociological theories and methods of inquiry, sociologists would sort out probable answers from unlikely ones in their search for recurring patterns of social behaviour (see Wilson and Selvin, 1980).

Not all sociologists would apply the same theory or methods to study the issue of suicide. Some would be most interested in the demographic profiles of persons who commit suicide: their age, marital status, occupation, and any of hundreds of other statistical categories. Others might seek to document the factors that contribute to societal breakdown and result in high incidences of suicide. Sociologists constantly debate issues such as suicide, asking about its causes and effects. Both the sociological study and the related debate help society articulate and deal with a multitude of such problems.

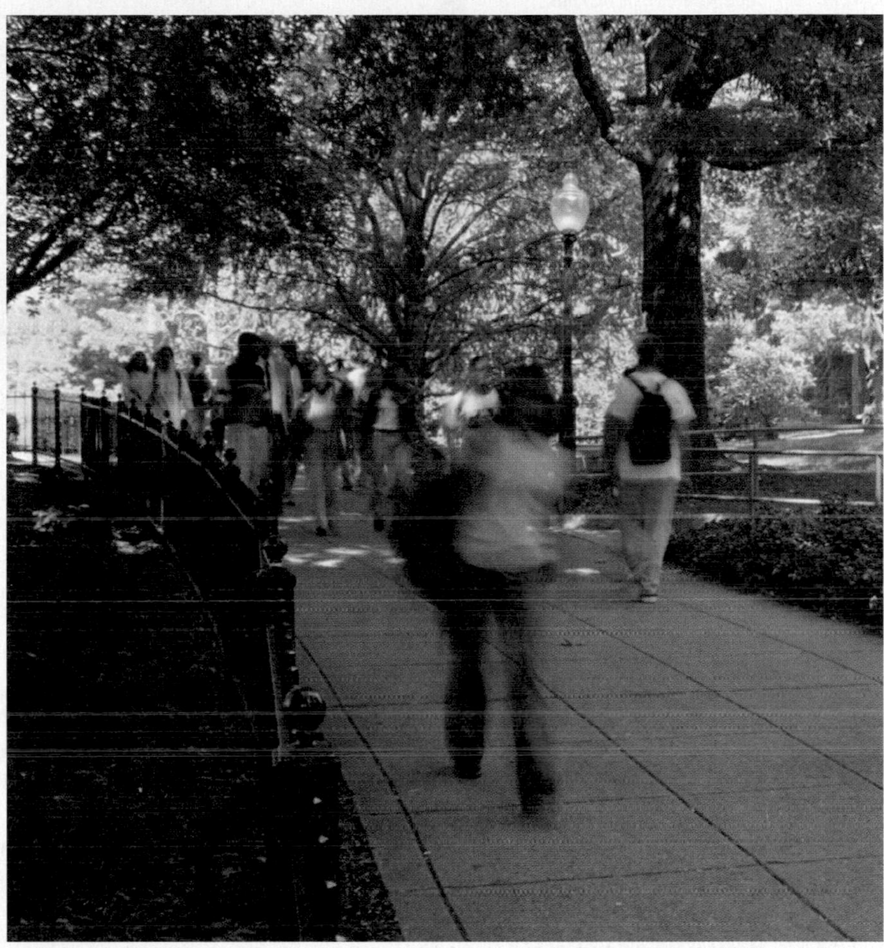

Questions and Issues

CHAPTER FOCUS QUESTION: Why is it important to use the sociological imagination when studying issues such as suicide?

How do you form a sociological perspective on issues such as suicide?

Why were early thinkers concerned with social order and stability?

Why were later social thinkers concerned with change?

What are the assumptions behind each of the contemporary theoretical perspectives?

How do sociologists conduct their research?

Events around the world affect us all. These demonstrators outside the Chinese consulate in Toronto are protesting the 1989 massacre at Tiananmen Square in Beijing, China.

PUTTING SOCIAL LIFE INTO PERSPECTIVE

***Sociology* is the systematic study of human society and social interaction.** It is a systematic study because sociologists apply both theoretical perspectives and research methods to examinations of social behaviour. Sociologists study human societies and their social interactions in order to develop theories of how human behaviour is shaped by group life and how, in turn, group life is affected by individuals.

Why Study Sociology?

Sociology helps us gain a better understanding of ourselves and our social world. It enables us to see how behaviour is largely shaped by the groups to which we belong and the society in which we live.

Sociology helps us look beyond our personal experiences and gain insights into society and the larger world order. A ***society* is a large social grouping that shares the same geographical territory and is subject to the same political authority and dominant cultural expectations.** Examples include the societies of Canada, the United States, and Mexico. Examining the world order helps us understand that each of us is affected by ***global interdependence*—a relationship in which the lives of all people are closely intertwined and any one nation's problems are part of a larger global problem.**

Individuals can make use of sociology on a more personal level. Sociology enables us to move beyond established ways of thinking, thus allowing us to gain new insights into ourselves and to develop a greater awareness of the connection between our own "world" and that of other people. According to sociologist Peter Berger (1963:23), sociological inquiry helps us see that "things are not what they seem." Sociology provides new ways of approaching problems and making decisions in everyday life. Sociology promotes understanding and tolerance by enabling each of us to look beyond our personal experiences.

SOCIOLOGY AND COMMON SENSE Many of us rely on intuition or common sense gained from personal experience to help us understand our daily lives and other people's behaviour. ***Commonsense knowledge* guides ordinary conduct in everyday life.**

Many commonsense notions actually are myths. A *myth* is a popular but false notion that may be used, either intentionally or unintentionally, to perpetuate certain beliefs or "theories" even in the light of conclusive evidence to the contrary. Before reading on, take the quiz in Box 1.1, which includes a number of commonsense notions about suicide.

By contrast, sociologists use scientific standards, not popular myths or hearsay, in studying society and social interaction. They use systematic research

BOX 1.1 SOCIOLOGY AND EVERYDAY LIFE

HOW MUCH DO YOU KNOW ABOUT SUICIDE?

TRUE	FALSE	
T	F	1. For people thinking of suicide, it is difficult, if not impossible, to see the bright side of life.
T	F	2. People who talk about suicide don't do it.
T	F	3. Once people contemplate or attempt suicide, they must be considered suicidal for the rest of their lives.
T	F	4. In Canada, there is a suicide every two hours.
T	F	5. Accidents and injuries sustained by teenagers and young adults may indicate suicidal inclinations.
T	F	6. Alcohol and drugs are outlets for anger and thus reduce the risk of suicide.
T	F	7. Older men have higher rates of both attempted and completed suicide than do older women.
T	F	8. Children don't know enough to be able to intentionally kill themselves.
T	F	9. Suicide rates for Aboriginal peoples are the highest in Canada.
T	F	10. Suicidal people are fully intent on dying.

Answers on page 6.

techniques and are accountable to the scientific community for their methods and the presentation of their findings. While some sociologists argue that sociology must be completely ***objective*—free from distorting subjective (personal or emotional) bias**—others do not think that total objectivity is an attainable or desirable goal when studying human behaviour. However, all sociologists attempt to discover patterns or commonalities in human behaviour. For example, when they study suicide, they look for recurring patterns of behaviour, even though *individual* people usually commit the acts and *other individuals* suffer as a result of these actions.

Consequently, sociologists seek out the multiple causes and effects of suicide or other social issues. They analyze the impact of the problem not only from the standpoint of suicide victims or perpetrators but also from the standpoint of the effects of such behaviour on all people.

The Sociological Imagination

Sociologist C. Wright Mills (1959) described sociological reasoning as the ***sociological imagination*—the ability to see the relationship between individual experiences and the larger society.** This awareness enables us to understand the link between our personal experiences and the social contexts in which they occur. The sociological imagination helps us distinguish between personal troubles and social (or public) issues. *Personal troubles* are private problems of individuals and the networks of people with whom they associate regularly. As a result, those problems must be solved by individuals within their immediate social settings. For example, one person being unemployed may be a personal trouble. *Public issues* are matters beyond an individual's own control that are caused by problems at the societal level. Widespread unemployment as a result of economic changes such as plant closings is an example of a public issue. The sociological imagination helps us place seemingly personal troubles, such as contemplating suicide or losing one's job, into a larger social context, where we can distinguish whether and how personal troubles may be related to public issues.

SUICIDE AS A PERSONAL TROUBLE Many of our individual experiences may be largely beyond our own control. They are determined by society as a whole—by its historical development and its organization. In

BOX 1.1

Answers to the Sociology Quiz on Suicide

1. **True.** To people thinking of suicide, an acknowledgment that there is a bright side only confirms and conveys the message that they have failed; otherwise, they, too, could have a bright side of life. Being told that "things will look better tomorrow" may cause a depressed person to feel more isolated and alone.
2. **False.** Some people who talk about suicide do kill themselves. Warning signals of possible suicide attempts include talk of suicide, the desire not to exist anymore, despair, and hopelessness.
3. **False.** Most people think of suicide for only a limited amount of time. When the crisis is over and the problems leading to suicidal thoughts are resolved, people usually cease to think of suicide as an option. However, if in the future problems arise with which the individual cannot cope, suicide may once again be an option.
4. **True.** A suicide occurs an average of every two hours in Canada; however, the rate of suicide differs with respect to the sex, race/ethnicity, and age of the individual. For example, men kill themselves more than three times as often as do women.
5. **True.** Accidents and injuries may be signs that a person is on a course of self-destruction. One study concluded that the incidence of suicide was twelve times higher among adolescents and young adults who previously had been hospitalized because of an injury.
6. **False.** Excessive use of alcohol or drugs may enhance a person's feelings of anger and frustration, making suicide a greater possibility. This risk appears to be especially high for men who abuse alcohol or drugs.
7. **True.** In Canada, as in other countries, suicide rates are highest among men over the age of 70. One theory of why this is true asserts that older women may have a more flexible and diverse coping style than older men.
8. **False.** Children do know how to intentionally hurt or kill themselves. They may learn the means and methods from television, movies, and other people. However, the Division of Health Statistics Canada (the agency responsible for compiling suicide statistics) does not recognize suicides under the age of 10; they are classified as accidents, despite evidence that young children have taken their own lives.
9. **True.** The rate of suicide among Aboriginal peoples in Canada for all age groups is 2 to 3 times higher than the rate among non-Aboriginal people. It is 5 to 6 times higher among Aboriginal youth than among non-Aboriginal youth.
10. **False.** Suicidal people often have an ambivalence about dying—they want to live and to die at the same time. They want to end the pain or problems they are experiencing, but they also wish that something or someone would remove the pain or problem so that life can continue.

Sources: Based on Levy and Deykin, 1989; Patros and Shamoo, 1989; Wickett, 1989; Leenaars, 1991, 1998; Health Canada, 1994; and Royal Commission on Aboriginal Peoples, 1995.

everyday life, we do not define personal experiences in these terms. If a person commits suicide, many people consider it to be the result of his or her own personal problems.

Suicide as a Public Issue We can use the sociological imagination to look at the problem of suicide as a public issue—a societal problem. For example, we may use our sociological imagination to understand why suicide rates are so high in some Aboriginal communities in Canada. Early sociologist Emile Durkheim related suicide to the issue of cohesiveness (or lack of cohesiveness) in society rather than viewing it as an isolated act.

BOX 1.2 SOCIOLOGY IN GLOBAL PERSPECTIVE

A Look at International Trends in Suicide

Researchers have difficulty making global comparisons regarding certain kinds of behaviour. Suicide is no exception. Frequently, suicide is discussed in Canada as if the patterns for this country are typical of all countries; however, this assumption generally is invalid.

In Canada, the two most discussed trends in suicide are the increasing suicide rate with age and the rising adolescent suicide rate among young men. How do these trends compare with other nations? Worldwide, there are three basic patterns in the variation of suicide rates:

1. an incline where the suicide rate increases regularly with age;
2. the two-peak model, where the suicide rate increases slightly in young adulthood and increases dramatically in old age;
3. one that peaks in middle age and has an inverted U-shaped curve.

Table 1 on the following page lists some countries that generally meet each of these criteria. Note that the trends for men and women are different within a number of the countries.

As Table 1 shows, several countries have suicide rates that rise with age for both sexes. In Austria and France, the peak in old age is particularly striking. For example, in Austria, the suicide rate for men aged 75 and older in 1989 was 96.0 per 100,000; in France, it was 109.0 per 100,000. In 1989 Japan had one of the highest rates of suicide for women aged 75 and older—51.6 per 100,000. Among developed nations, the second pattern—a slight peak in young adulthood and a major peak in old age—primarily describes male suicide patterns. Other nations have peak suicide rates in the middle-aged years. In Canada, the peak suicide rate for men is at age 75 and older, while 45 to 54 is the peak age range for women.

What reasons can you think of that might cause the differences discussed here? How would you analyze the data and what conclusions might you draw on the basis of these international comparisons of suicide data?

In Japan, the suicide rate peaks for both men and women at the age of 75 and over. By contrast, in France the peak suicide rate for men is 75 and over, but the peak rate for women occurs between 45 and 54 years of age. Do these patterns provide us with insights about the intertwining of attitudes regarding gender and aging in these societies?

Sources: Lester, 1992; Health Canada, 1994; and Leenaars et al., 1998.

BOX 1.2

CONTINUED

TABLE 1 GLOBAL TRENDS IN SUICIDE

Pattern	Country: Males	Country: Females
1. Rate increases regularly with age.	Austria France Italy Japan Germany	Austria Italy Japan Germany
2. Rate peaks twice: once in young adulthood (ages 15–24, 25–34, or 35–44) and once in old age.	Australia Canada England and Wales Netherlands United States	
3. Rate peaks in middle age (ages 45–54 or 55–64).	Denmark Poland Sweden	Australia Canada France Netherlands Poland Sweden United States

The Importance of a Global Sociological Imagination

Although existing sociological theory and research provide the foundation for sociological thinking, we must reach beyond past studies that have focused primarily on North America to develop a more comprehensive global approach for the future. We must do so because in the twenty-first century, we face important challenges in a rapidly changing world.

The world's most ***developed nations*** **are countries with highly industrialized economies, technologically advanced industrial, administrative, and service occupations, and relatively high levels of national and per capita (per person) income.** Examples are New Zealand, Japan, Canada, and the United States. Compared with other countries of the world, people in the most developed nations typically have a high standard of living and a lower death rate due to advances in nutrition and medical technology. As discussed in Box 1.2, developed nations tend to differ among themselves in their patterns of suicide.

Developing nations **are countries undergoing transformation from agrarian to industrial economies.** People living in these countries are more likely to work the land, and national income and per capita income remain relatively low. However, generalizations are difficult to make about developing nations because these nations vary widely in levels of economic development and standards of living. Nations such as Mexico, Brazil, and South Korea are industrializing rapidly, but some countries in Africa and Asia remain much less developed and are among the poorest in the world. Suicide patterns in these countries vary widely from those in the most developed nations. For example, some social analysts suggest the recent increase in suicides among the Kaiowá Indians in Brazil can be linked to the loss of their land (which previously was used to grow crops to feed their families) to large, foreign-owned agribusinesses. With loss of land has come loss of culture because to the Kaiowá, land is more than a means of surviving; it is the support for a social life that is directly linked to their system of belief and knowledge (Schemo, 1996).

Throughout this text, we will examine social life in other countries—as well as in Canada—because the future of this country is deeply intertwined with the future of all nations of the world on economic,

The opening ceremonies of Expo 1986 in Vancouver reflected the increasing diversity of the Canadian population and reminded Canadians of the need to take all people's experiences into account as we confront public issues.

political, and humanitarian levels. We buy many goods and services that were produced in other nations, and sell much of what we produce to the people of other nations. Peace in other nations is important if we are to ensure peace within our own borders. Famine, unrest, and brutality in other regions of the world must be of concern to people in Canada. Global problems such as these contribute to the large influx of immigrants who arrive in this country annually. They bring with them a rich diversity of language, customs, religions, and previous life experiences. They also contribute to dramatic population changes that will have long-term effects on this country. Developing a better understanding of diversity and tolerance for people who are different from us is important for our personal, social, and economic well-being.

Whatever your race/ethnicity, class, sex, or age, are you able to include in your thinking the perspectives of people with quite dissimilar experiences and points of view? Before answering this question, a few definitions are in order. ***Race* is a term used by many people to specify groups of people distinguished by physical characteristics such as skin colour;** in fact, there are no "pure" racial types, and the concept of race is considered by most sociologists to be a myth. ***Ethnicity* refers to the cultural heritage or identity of a group and is based on factors such as language or country of origin. *Class* is the relative location of a person or group within a larger society,** based on wealth, power, prestige, or other valued resources. ***Sex* refers to the biological and anatomical differences between females and males.** By contrast, ***gender* refers to the meanings, beliefs, and practices associated with sex differences,** referred to as *femininity* and *masculinity* (Scott, 1986:1054).

In forming your own sociological imagination and in seeing the possibilities for sociology in this new century, it will be helpful to understand the development of the discipline, beginning about one hundred years ago.

THE DEVELOPMENT OF SOCIOLOGICAL THINKING

Throughout history, social philosophers and religious authorities have made countless observations about human behaviour. However, these early thinkers primarily stated what they thought society *ought* to be like, rather than describing how society actually *was*. The idea of observing how people lived to find out what they thought, and doing so in a systematic manner that could be verified, did not take hold until the nineteenth century with the social upheaval brought about by industrialization and urbanization.

***Industrialization* is the process by which societies are transformed from dependence on agriculture and handmade products to an emphasis on**

Early in the twentieth century, sights like this 14-year-old girl working in a factory caught the attention of social thinkers and brought demands for protective child labour laws.

Auguste Comte

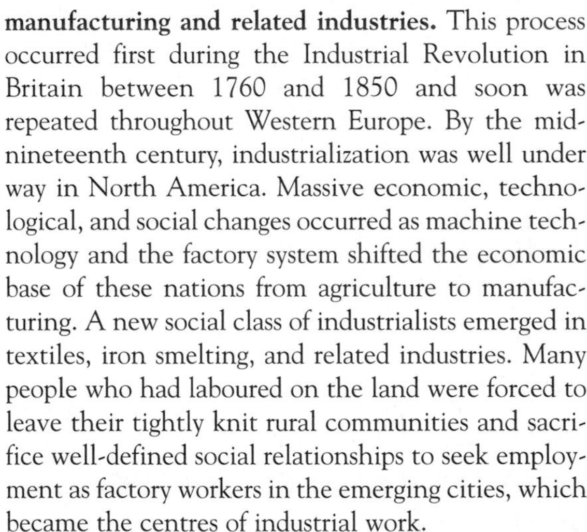

manufacturing and related industries. This process occurred first during the Industrial Revolution in Britain between 1760 and 1850 and soon was repeated throughout Western Europe. By the mid-nineteenth century, industrialization was well under way in North America. Massive economic, technological, and social changes occurred as machine technology and the factory system shifted the economic base of these nations from agriculture to manufacturing. A new social class of industrialists emerged in textiles, iron smelting, and related industries. Many people who had laboured on the land were forced to leave their tightly knit rural communities and sacrifice well-defined social relationships to seek employment as factory workers in the emerging cities, which became the centres of industrial work.

Urbanization **is the process by which an increasing proportion of a population lives in cities rather than in rural areas.** Although cities existed long before the Industrial Revolution, the development of the factory system led to a rapid increase in both the number of cities and the size of their populations. People from very diverse backgrounds worked together in the same factory. At the same time, many people shifted from being *producers* to being *consumers*. For example, families living in the cities had to buy food with their wages because they could no longer grow their own crops to consume or to barter for other resources. Similarly, people had to pay rent for their lodging because they could no longer exchange their services for shelter.

These living and working conditions led to the development of new social problems: inadequate housing, crowding, unsanitary conditions, poverty, pollution, and crime. Wages were so low that entire families—including very young children—were forced to work, often under hazardous conditions and with no job security. As these conditions became more visible, a new breed of social thinkers turned its attention to trying to understand why and how society was changing.

Early Thinkers: A Concern with Social Order and Stability

At the same time as urban problems were growing worse, natural scientists had been using reason, or rational thinking, to discover the laws of physics and the movement of the planets. Social thinkers started to believe that, by applying the methods developed by the natural sciences, they might discover the laws of human behaviour and apply these laws to solve social problems.

The French philosopher Auguste Comte (1798–1857) coined the term *sociology* from the Latin *socius* (social, being with others) and the Greek *logos* (study of) to describe a new science that would

Harriet Martineau

Emile Durkheim

engage in the study of society. Comte is considered by some to be the "founder of sociology." Comte's theory that societies contain *social statics* (forces for social order and stability) and *social dynamics* (forces for conflict and change) continues to be used, although not in these exact terms, in contemporary sociology.

Comte's works were made more accessible for a wide variety of scholars through the efforts of British sociologist Harriet Martineau (1802–1876). Until recently, Martineau received no recognition in the field of sociology, partly because she was a woman in a male-dominated discipline and society. Not only did she translate and condense Comte's work, but she was also an active sociologist in her own right. Martineau studied the social customs of Britain and the United States and analyzed the consequences of industrialization and capitalism. In *Society in America* (1962/1837), she examined religion, politics, child rearing, slavery, and immigration in the United States, paying special attention to social distinctions based on class, race, and gender.

British social theorist Herbert Spencer (1820–1903) used an evolutionary perspective to explain social order and social change. He believed that society, like a biological organism, has various interdependent parts (such as the family, the economy, and the government) that work to ensure the stability and survival of the entire society. According to Spencer, societies developed through a process of "struggle" (for existence) and "fitness" (for survival), which he referred to as the "survival of the fittest." Spencer equated this process of *natural selection* with progress, because only the "fittest" members of society would succeed. As a result of these ideas, he strongly opposed attempts at social reform that might interfere with the natural selection process and, thus, damage society by favouring its least worthy members.

Although Spencer contributed many useful concepts, many of his ideas had serious flaws. For one thing, societies are not the same as biological systems; people are able to create and transform their environment. Moreover, the notion of the survival of the fittest can easily be used to justify class, racial-ethnic, and gender inequalities and to rationalize the lack of action to eliminate harmful practices that contribute to such inequalities.

French sociologist Emile Durkheim (1858–1917) disagreed with many of Spencer's views. Durkheim stressed that people are the product of their social environment and that behaviour cannot be understood fully in terms of *individual* biological and psychological traits. He believed that the limits of human potential are *socially*, not *biologically*, based.

In his work *The Rules of Sociological Method* (1964a/1895), Durkheim set forth one of his most important contributions to sociology: the idea that societies are built on social facts. ***Social facts*** **are patterned ways of acting, thinking, and**

Karl Marx

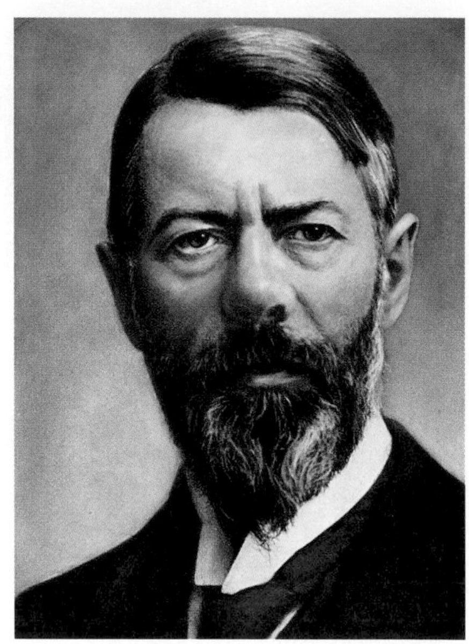

Max Weber

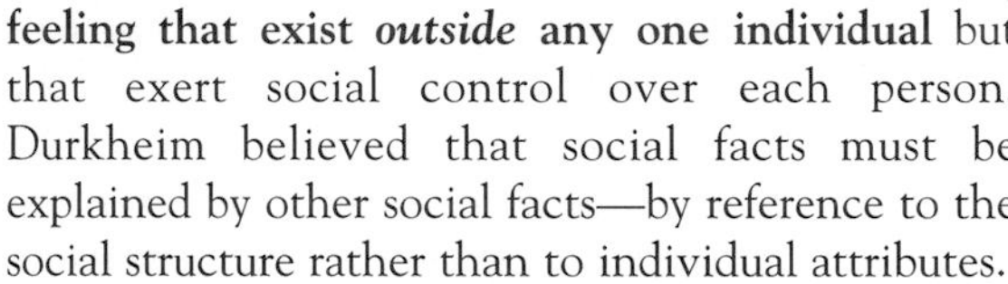

feeling that exist *outside* any one individual but that exert social control over each person. Durkheim believed that social facts must be explained by other social facts—by reference to the social structure rather than to individual attributes.

Durkheim was concerned with social order and social stability because he lived during the period of rapid social changes in Europe resulting from industrialization and urbanization. He observed that rapid social change and a more specialized division of labour produce *strains* in society. These strains lead to a breakdown in traditional organization, values, and authority and to a dramatic increase in ***anomie*—a condition in which social control becomes ineffective as a result of the loss of shared values and of a sense of purpose in society.** According to Durkheim, anomie is most likely to occur during a period of rapid social change. In *Suicide* (1964b/1897), he explored the relationship between anomic social conditions and suicide.

Differing Views on the Status Quo: Stability Versus Change

In sharp contrast to Durkheim's focus on the stability of society, German economist and philosopher Karl Marx (1818–1883) stressed that history is a continuous clash between conflicting ideas and forces. He believed that conflict—especially class conflict—is necessary in order to produce social change and a better society. For Marx, the most important changes were economic. He concluded that the capitalist economic system was responsible for the overwhelming poverty that he observed in London at the beginning of the Industrial Revolution (Marx and Engels, 1967/1848).

In the Marxian framework, ***class conflict* is the struggle between the capitalist class and the working class.** The capitalist class, or ***bourgeoisie*, is composed of those who own and control the means of production.** The ***means of production* refers to the tools, land, factories, and money for investment that form the economic basis of a society. The working class, or *proletariat*, is composed of those who must sell their labour because they have no other means to earn a livelihood.** From Marx's viewpoint, the capitalist class controls and exploits the masses of struggling workers by paying less than the value of their labour. This exploitation results in workers' ***alienation*—a feeling of powerlessness and estrangement from other people and from oneself.** Marx predicted that the working class would become aware of its exploitation, overthrow the capitalists, and establish a free and classless society. This is more fullly discussed in Chapter 7 ("Social Stratification and Class").

Marx's social and economic analyses have inspired heated debates among generations of social

Many Canadians work in large-scale bureaucracies, which Max Weber analyzed nearly a hundred years ago.

scientists. Although his evaluation of capitalism and his theories on the process of social change have been criticized, many of his ideas form the foundation of contemporary conflict theory.

German social scientist Max Weber (pronounced VAY-ber) (1864–1920) also was concerned about the changes brought about by the Industrial Revolution. Although he disagreed with Marx's idea that economics is *the* central force in social change, Weber acknowledged that economic interests are important in shaping human action. Even so, he thought that economic systems were heavily influenced by other factors in a society.

Weber was concerned that large-scale organizations (bureaucracies) were becoming increasingly oriented toward routine administration and a specialized division of labour, which he believed were destructive to human vitality and freedom. As we will see in Chapter 5 ("Groups and Organizations"), Weber's work on bureaucracy has had a far-reaching impact.

CONTEMPORARY THEORETICAL PERSPECTIVES

Given the many and varied ideas and trends that influenced the development of sociology, how do contemporary sociologists view society? Some see it as basically a stable and ongoing entity; others view it in terms of many groups competing for scarce resources; still others describe it as based on the everyday, routine interactions among individuals. Each of these views represents a method of examining the same phenomena. Each is based on general ideas as to how social life is organized and represents an effort to link specific observations in a meaningful way. Each utilizes ***theory*****—a set of logically interrelated statements that attempts to describe, explain, and (occasionally) predict social events.** Each theory helps interpret reality in a distinct way by providing a framework in which observations may be logically ordered. Sociologists refer to this theoretical framework as a ***perspective*****—an overall approach to or viewpoint on some subject.** The major theoretical perspectives that have emerged in sociology are the functionalist, conflict, feminist, and interactionist perspectives. These perspectives will be used throughout this book to show you how sociologists try to understand many of the issues affecting Canadian society.

Functionalist Perspectives

Functionalist perspectives **are based on the assumption that society is a stable, orderly system.** This stable system is characterized by ***societal consensus*** **whereby the majority of members share a common set of values, beliefs, and behavioural**

Former MP Roseanne Skoke took a public stand against rights for same-sex couples. Contemporary debates over "family values" reflect the significance of family in society. For functionalists such as Talcott Parsons, families serve important functions that other social institutions cannot perform.

expectations. According to this perspective, a society is composed of interrelated parts, each of which serves a function and (ideally) contributes to the overall stability of the society. Societies develop social structures, or institutions, that persist because they play a part in helping society survive. These institutions include the family, education, government, religion, and the economy. If anything adverse happens to one of these institutions or parts, all other parts are affected and the system no longer functions properly. As Durkheim noted, rapid social change and a more specialized division of labour produce *strains* in society that lead to a breakdown in these traditional institutions.

Talcott Parsons (1902–1979) was perhaps the most influential contemporary advocate of the functionalist perspective. He stressed that all societies must make provisions for meeting social needs in order to survive. For example, in a functional analysis of the U.S. family in the 1950s, Parsons (1955) suggested that a division of labour (distinct, specialized functions) between husband and wife is essential for family stability and social order. The husband/father performs the *instrumental tasks*, which involve leadership and decision-making responsibilities in the home and employment outside the home to support the family. The wife/mother is responsible for the *expressive tasks*, including housework, caring for the children, and providing emotional support for the entire family. Parsons believed that other institutions, including school, church, and government, must function to assist the family and that all institutions must work together to preserve the system over time (Parsons, 1955).

Functionalism was refined further by Robert K. Merton (b. 1910), who distinguished between manifest and latent functions of social institutions. ***Manifest functions* are intended and/or overtly recognized by the participants in a social unit.** In contrast, ***latent functions* are unintended functions that are hidden and remain unacknowledged by participants.** For example, a manifest function of education is the transmission of knowledge and skills from one generation to the next; a latent function is the establishment of social relations and networks. Merton noted that all features of a social system may not be functional at all times; ***dysfunctions* are the undesirable consequences of any element of a society.** A dysfunction of education can be the perpetuation of gender, racial, and class inequalities. Such dysfunctions may threaten the capacity of a society to adapt and survive (Merton, 1968).

Conflict Perspectives

According to ***conflict perspectives,* groups in society are engaged in a continuous power struggle for control of scarce resources.** Conflict theory sharply contrasts with functionalist approaches, which see society as based primarily on consensus. Conflict may take the form of politics, litigation, negotiations, or family discussions about financial matters. Marx and Weber contributed significantly to this perspective by focusing on the inevitability of clashes between social groups. Today, advocates of the conflict perspective view social life as a continuous power struggle among competing social groups.

As previously discussed, Marx focused on the exploitation and oppression of the proletariat (the workers) by the bourgeoisie (the owners or capitalist class). Weber recognized the importance of economic conditions in producing inequality and conflict in society but added *power* and *prestige* as other sources of inequality. Weber (1968/1922) defined power as the ability of a person within a social relationship to carry out his or her own will despite

Margrit Eichler

resistance from others. Prestige ("status group" to Weber) is a positive or negative social estimation of honour (Weber, 1968/1922).

Other theorists have looked at conflict among many groups and interests (such as employers and employees) as a part of everyday life in any society. Ralf Dahrendorf (b. 1929), for example, observed that conflict is inherent in *all* authority relationships, not just that between the capitalist class and the working class. To Dahrendorf, power is the critical variable in explaining human behaviour. People in positions of authority benefit from the conformity of others; those who are forced to conform feel resentment and demonstrate resistance, much as a child may resent parental authority. The advantaged group that possesses authority attempts to preserve the status quo—the existing set of social arrangements—and may use coercion to do so (Dahrendorf, 1959).

C. Wright Mills (1916–1962), a key figure in the development of contemporary conflict theory, encouraged sociologists to get involved in social reform. He contended that value-free sociology was impossible because social scientists must make value-related choices—including the topics they investigate and the theoretical approaches they adopt. Mills encouraged us to look beneath everyday events in order to observe the major resource and power inequalities that exist in society. He believed that the most important decisions in the United States are made largely behind the scenes by the ***power elite*****—a small clique composed of the top corporate, political, and military officials.** Mills's power elite theory is discussed in Chapter 12 ("Politics and Government").

Feminist Perspectives

In the past several decades, feminists have radically transformed the discipline of sociology. Feminist theory first emerged as a critique of traditional sociological theory and methodology. The primary criticism was that sociology did not acknowledge the experiences of women. Written by men, sociology involved the study of men and not humankind, much less women; sociology examined only half of social reality (Fox, 1989). Feminist scholar Dorothy Smith (1974) argued that sociological methods, concepts, and analyses were products of the "male social universe." If women appeared at all, it was as men saw them and not as they saw themselves. In this way, feminist sociologists argued, sociology actually contributed to the subordination and exploitation of women (Anderson, 1996). The first task of feminist sociology was to provide the missing half of social reality by generating research and theory "by, for, and about women" (Smith, 1987). In doing so, feminist sociology brought the personal problems of women, including violence against women, the poverty of women, and the invisibility of women's reproductive labour, into the public forum.

Feminist perspectives **focus on the significance of gender in understanding and explaining inequalities that exist between men and women in the household, in the paid labour force, and in the realms of politics, law, and culture** (Armstrong and Armstrong, 1994; Luxton, 1995; Marshall, 1995). Feminism is not one single unified approach. Rather, there are different approaches among feminist writers, namely the liberal, radical, and socialist strains (discussed in Chapter 10, "Sex and Gender"). Feminist sociology incorporates both microlevel and macrolevel analyses in studying the experiences of women. For example, some feminist theorists, such as Margrit Eichler, have used a structural approach to explain how gender inequality is created and maintained in a society dominated by men (Armstrong and Armstrong, 1994; Eichler, 1988b). Other feminist research has focused on the interpersonal relationships between men and women in terms of verbal and nonverbal communication styles, attitudes, and values in explaining the dynamics of power and social control in the private sphere (Mackie, 1995). All of these approaches share the belief that "women and men are equal and should be equally valued as well as have equal rights" (Basow, 1992). According to feminists (including many men as well as women), we live in a *patriarchy*, a hierarchical system of power in which males possess greater economic and social privilege than females (Saunders, 1999). Feminist perspectives assume that gender roles are socially created rather than determined by one's biological inheritance, and that change is essential in order for people to achieve their human potential without limits based on gender. Feminism assumes that society reinforces social expectations through social learning: what we learn is a social product of the political and economic structure of the society in which we live (Renzetti and Curran, 1995).

Interactionist Perspectives

Both the conflict and the functional perspectives have been criticized for focusing primarily on macrolevel analysis. A ***macrolevel analysis*** **examines whole societies, large-scale social structures, and social systems** instead of looking at important social dynamics in individuals' lives. Our final perspective, interactionism, fills this void by examining people's day-to-day interactions and their behaviour in groups. Thus, interactionist approaches are based on a ***microlevel analysis*****, which focuses on small groups rather than on large-scale social structures.**

According to ***interactionist perspectives*****, society is the sum of the interactions of individuals and groups.** This approach focuses on how people act toward one another and on how they make sense of those interactions. George Herbert Mead, the original force behind this perspective, emphasized that the ability to communicate in symbols is the key feature distinguishing humans from other animals. Although there are a number of loosely linked interactionist approaches, symbolic interaction is the most widely used.

SYMBOLIC INTERACTION For *symbolic interactionists*, people create and change their social worlds through the use of mutually understood symbols. A ***symbol*** **is anything that meaningfully represents something else.** Examples of symbols include signs, gestures, written language, and shared values. Symbolic interaction occurs when people communicate through the use of symbols; for example, a gift of food—a cake or a casserole—to a newcomer in a neighbourhood is a symbol of welcome and friendship.

From this perspective, each person's interpretation or definition of a given situation becomes a *subjective reality* from that person's viewpoint. Individuals generally assume that their subjective reality is the same as that of others; however, this may be incorrect. Subjective reality is acquired and shared through agreed-upon symbols, especially language. If a person shouts, "Fire!" in a crowded movie theatre, for example, that language produces the same response (attempting to escape) in all of those who hear and understand it. When people in a group do not share the same meaning for a given symbol, however, confusion results; for example, people who did not know the meaning of the word *fire* would not know what the commotion was about. How people interpret the messages they receive and the situations they encounter becomes their subjective reality and may strongly influence their behaviour.

Social learning is important in how we define ourselves and our relationship to others. Because interactionist perspectives focus on the microlevel of society, they help us see how individuals interact in their daily lives and interpret their experiences. However, this approach also is limited in that it basically ignores the larger social context in which behaviour takes place. If we focus primarily on the individual and small-group context of behaviour, we may overlook important macrolevel societal forces that are beyond the control of individuals, such as the effects of socially imposed definitions of race-ethnicity, gender, class, and age on people's lives.

Each of the sociological perspectives we have examined involves different assumptions. Consequently, each leads us to ask different questions and to view the world somewhat differently. Different aspects of reality are the focus of each approach. While functionalism emphasizes social cohesion and order, conflict and feminist approaches focus primarily on social tension and change. In contrast, interactionism primarily examines people's interactions and shared meanings in everyday life. Concept Table 1.A reviews the three major perspectives. Throughout this book, we will be using these perspectives as lenses through which to view our social

CONCEPT TABLE 1.A

THE MAJOR THEORETICAL PERSPECTIVES

PERSPECTIVE	ANALYSIS LEVEL	NATURE OF SOCIETY
Functionalist	Macrolevel	Society is composed of interrelated parts that work together to maintain stability within society. This stability is threatened by dysfunctional acts and institutions.
Conflict	Macrolevel	Society is characterized by social inequality; social life is a struggle for scarce resources. Social arrangements benefit some groups at the expense of others.
Feminist	Macrolevel and Microlevel	Society is based on patriarchy—a hierarchical system of power in which males possess greater economic and social privilege than females.
Interactionist	Microlevel	Society is the sum of the interactions of people and groups. Behaviour is learned in interaction with other people; how people define a situation becomes the foundation for how they behave.

world. You will see how sociologists use these perspectives to guide their research.

SOCIOLOGICAL RESEARCH METHODS

Sociologist Ian Robertson describes the process of doing research:

> Research in sociology is really a form of systemic detective work—it poses the same early puzzles and suspicions, the same moments of inspired guessing and routine sifting through the evidence, the same disappointments over false leads and facts that do not fit and perhaps, the same triumph when the pieces finally fall into place and the answer emerges. Research in sociology is where the real action takes place. (1977:29)

In the rest of this chapter, we will see how sociological research methods are used to answer complex questions, and we will address some of the difficulties of studying human behaviour.

Common Sense and Sociological Research

Common sense may tell us that people who threaten suicide will not commit suicide. Sociological research indicates that this assumption is frequently incorrect: people who threaten to kill themselves often are sending messages to others and may indeed attempt suicide. Common sense also may tell us that suicide is caused by despair or depression. However, research suggests that suicide sometimes is also used as a means of lashing out at friends and relatives because of real or imagined wrongs.

Historically, the commonsense view of suicide was that it was a sin, a crime, and the result of mental illness (Evans and Farberow, 1988). Emile Durkheim refused to accept these explanations. In what is probably the first sociological study to use scientific research methods, Durkheim, as men-

BOX 1.3 SOCIOLOGY AND MEDIA

THE HEAVEN'S GATE MASS SUICIDE AND THE INTERNET

On March 27, 1997, people around the globe learned that 39 members (21 women and 18 men) of a religious cult called Heaven's Gate had committed suicide in Rancho Santa Fe, California. Television stations broadcast a video showing law enforcement officers pointing out the bodies—dressed alike in androgynous black clothes and identical running shoes—lying on spartan bunk beds with purple cloths folded in triangles over their heads and shoulders like shrouds. Newspaper and television journalists swarmed outside the house day and night, and television film crews circled overhead in helicopters, shooting photos of the estate and of the bodies being removed by the coroner's office.

Though most people first learned of the mass suicide and of the existence of the Heaven's Gate cult from television, newspapers, and radio, the Internet and the World Wide Web were also information sources for this story. Members of the cult were apparently active in the use of this new form of communication—some supported themselves by creating Web pages for a variety of businesses. In addition, cult members distributed the cult's millennial message that "the end is near" on the Internet. The final message they left on their home page advised the world that the comet streaking across the sky at the time, Hale-Bopp, was "the 'marker' [they had] been waiting for—the time for the arrival of the spacecraft from the Level Above Human to take [them] home to 'Their World' in the literal Heavens." It appears that the cult first came to believe that the comet had special significance for its members as a result of rumours circulating on the Internet according to which an alien spaceship was lurking behind the comet. Some Internet chat groups at locations like **alt.conspiracy** and **sci.astro** had carried discussions about an unidentified flying object from outer space hiding behind the comet. As corrections regarding the comet's predicted trajectory were made, some people began to believe that the comet was under the control of intelligent beings in the spacecraft. To the Heaven's Gate members, who believed that they had been deposited on earth from space and were going to be "picked up" in the very near future in order to be lifted to the Next Level (heaven), this spacecraft was the one for which they had been waiting. They did not believe that they were committing suicide, but rather that they were simply shedding their "earthly containers."

Initial journalistic and sociological explanations of the Heaven's Gate mass suicide focused on (among other things) issues such as how members of the cult behaved and who their leaders were. Although some sociologists might focus on these issues, others would also emphasize what we can learn from Emile Durkheim: that most forms of behaviour, including mass suicide, have certain sociological features in common. Sociologist T.R. Young (1997) has identified several of these features: first, social

tioned earlier in this chapter, did not view suicide as an isolated act that could be understood only by studying individual personalities or inherited tendencies; instead he related suicide to the issue of cohesiveness (or lack of cohesiveness) in society. In *Suicide* (1964b/1897), he documented his contention that a high suicide rate was symptomatic of large-scale societal problems. In the process, he developed an approach to research that influences researchers to this day. As we discuss sociological research, we will focus on the problem of suicide to demonstrate the research process.

Since much of sociology deals with everyday life, we might think that common sense, our own personal experiences, and the media are the best sources of information. However, our personal experiences are subjective, and much of the information provided by the media comes from sources seeking

BOX 1.3

CONTINUED

isolation often contributes to mass suicide. In this case, remaining isolated may have been easier for cult members because they could rely on the Internet and the World Wide Web as sources of communication and employment. Whereas in the past most people with computer skills would have been integrated with the larger community during working hours, today many people lead solitary lives, working alone at a home computer terminal. Second, most cults have a normative structure that is well ordered and tightly configured. If the daily routines of the people involved were charted, we would likely find great regularity and great conformity to norms that mark the cycles of the day. Third, there are socially skewed patterns of power in which one or a few people hold most of the social, economic, moral, and physical power. Fourth, the final hours leading up to a mass suicide typically are tightly orchestrated and engineered by those with authority. If power were democratized in the group, some people might simply walk away.

Other social scientists would focus on the role of the Internet and the World Wide Web in events such as this. According to psychologist Ray Hayman, the Internet aggravates the problem of what he refers to as "information pollution": "Much of the stuff we find is nonsense, but because it comes off the computer, it has the mark of being credible" (Markoff, 1997:A12). It is possible that the members of Heaven's Gate found the "marker" they were looking for to be following comet Hale-Bopp simply because of the fact that it appeared on the Internet. Due to their deep interest in computer technology and the World Wide Web, the rumour of the spacecraft may have appeared to them to be fact.

What do you think? Did the Internet and the World Wide Web play a role in this mass suicide, or was the event something that was destined to occur soon anyway?

The Heaven's Gate Web site describes the group's desire to leave earth and rendezvous with a spacecraft they believed travels behind comet Hale-Bopp.

Source: Markoff, 1997; and Young, 1997 (used with permission from T.R. Young. Director, The Red Feather Institute for Advanced Studies in Sociology).

support for a particular point of view. The content of the media is also influenced by the continuous need for high audience ratings.

We need to be able to evaluate the information we receive. The quantity of information available has grown dramatically as a result of the information explosion brought about by the computer and telecommunications. The need for information evaluation is apparent in the discussion in Box 1.3 of the linkages between the 1997 Heaven's Gate cult mass suicide and the Internet.

Sociology and Scientific Evidence

Sociology often involves *debunking*—the unmasking of fallacies (false or mistaken ideas or opinions) in the everyday and official interpretations of society (Mills, 1959). Since problems such as suicide

BOX 1.4 CRITICAL THINKING

ASSISTING SUICIDE

In a recent Gallup poll, over 75 percent of people surveyed agreed with the statement "When a person has an incurable disease that causes great suffering, competent doctors should be allowed to end the patient's life through mercy killing" (C. Wood, 1994). Although prohibited by law from doing so, many physicians are participating in physician-assisted suicides (Searles, 1995).

Under common law, suicide was a crime. It was also an offence to "aid and abet" suicide—to counsel or to help someone commit suicide. Thus, the government was "reimbursed" for its loss of the individual, through both financial and other penalties imposed on the perpetrator and any "accomplices."

In Canada, suicide is no longer a crime. However, counselling or assisting suicide remains a criminal act in Canada, punishable by a maximum of fourteen years' imprisonment.

People can now be kept alive by machines long after there is any realistic expectation that they will ever again function independently. In such cases, friends and relatives frequently have sought legal authorization to allow the patient to die "in peace and dignity." Also,

Sue Rodriguez battled all the way to the Supreme Court to have physician-assisted suicide decriminalized.

many individuals have chosen to have a living will, which is written in advance and which directs that they not be kept alive past the point when life without the support of medical tech-

involve threats to existing societal values, we cannot analyze the problems without acknowledging the values involved.

Based on your own beliefs, do you think that suicide and/or assisting suicide should be legal? How should society deal with these issues? We often answer questions like this by using either the normative approach or the empirical approach. The ***normative approach*** **uses religion, customs, habits, traditions, and law to answer important questions.** It is based on strong beliefs about what is right and wrong, and what ought to be in society. Issues such as assisted suicide (see Box 1.4) often are analyzed using the normative approach. From a legal standpoint, the consequences of assisting in another person's suicide may be severe.

While these issues are profound, contemporary sociologists, for the most part, discourage the use of the normative approach in their field and advocate instead the use of the empirical approach. The ***empirical approach*** **attempts to answer questions through systematic collection and analysis of data.** This approach is referred to as the "scientific method" and is based on the assumption that knowledge is best gained by direct, systematic observation. Sociologists, then, adhere to two basic scientific standards: (1) "scientific beliefs must be supported by good evidence or information" and

BOX 1.4

CONTINUED

nology is no longer possible. To some people, a living will is still a form of suicide: the individual is directing that life end before the last point at which it can be maintained. In Canada, a person who turns off the life-sustaining treatment under the authority of a living will is not committing an offence.

Still to be resolved, however, is the issue of assisting people who have a terminal illness and who want to end their own (or perhaps their family member's or friend's) agony over an apparently irreversible physical deterioration—and the pain that may accompany it. Should it be up to the courts or the legislatures to decide this issue? This question was pursued all the way to the Supreme Court of Canada by Sue Rodriguez, a 42-year-old woman suffering from Lou Gehrig's disease (a degenerative fatal disease in which the muscles weaken until eating and breathing are no longer possible). Rodriguez requested the legal right to have the assistance of a physician in ending her life. She was told that it is illegal for anyone to assist in a suicide, even if the person wanting to die is too disabled to commit suicide on her or his own. In 1993, in a narrow decision, the Supreme Court declined Rodriguez's challenge and upheld the law prohibiting assisted suicide.

Does a person have a right to die if he or she is physically healthy? Does society have the right to say that such a person does not have that right? If a person has the right to terminate her or his own life, should that person be able to get advice and assistance regarding that decision—just as the person does for any other legal action? If the answer is yes, then does a person have the right to at least request assistance in committing suicide? Does someone else have the right to provide that assistance? Should a perfectly healthy (in a physical sense) person have that right? These are the types of questions sociologists, lawyers, legislatures, courts, and the general public must continue to try to answer. What do you think?

Sources: Based on Humphrey, 1993; Lester and Tallmer, 1993; Health Canada, 1994; Searles, 1995 and C. Wood, 1994.

(2) "beliefs must be open to debate and criticism, and alternative interpretations must be considered" (Cancian, 1992:631).

Sociologists typically use two types of empirical studies: descriptive and explanatory. ***Descriptive studies*** **attempt to describe social reality or provide facts about some group, practice, or event.** Studies of this type are designed to find out what is happening to whom, where, and when. For example, a descriptive study of suicide might attempt to determine the number of people who recently contemplated suicide. Well-known descriptive studies include the reports on the Canadian Census and the Uniform Crime Reports; however, even these "objective" studies have certain biases, as discussed in this chapter and in Chapter 6 ("Deviance and Crime"). By contrast, ***explanatory studies*** **attempt to explain cause-and-effect relationships and to provide information on why certain events do or do not occur.** In an explanatory study of suicide, we might ask, Why do Aboriginal people in Canada have such high suicide rates? or Why do more women than men engage in nonfatal suicidal behaviour? Seeking answers to questions such as these is why sociologists engage in the research process.

The Sociological Research Process

Not all sociologists conduct research in the same manner. Some primarily engage in quantitative research whereas others use qualitative research methods. With ***quantitative research*, the goal is scientific objectivity, and the focus is on data that can be measured numerically.** Quantitative research typically emphasizes complex statistical techniques. Most sociological studies on suicide have used quantitative research. They have compared rates of suicide with almost every conceivable variable, including age, sex, race/ethnicity, education, and even sports participation (see Lester, 1992). One study examined the effects of church membership, divorce, and migration on suicide rates in the United States at various times between 1933 and 1980. It concluded that suicide rates were higher where divorce rates were higher, migration was higher, and church membership was lower (see Breault, 1986).

With ***qualitative research*, interpretive description (words) rather than statistics (numbers) is used to analyze underlying meanings and patterns of social relationships.** A study of suicidal behaviour based on suicide notes is an example of qualitative research. In one study, the researcher examined recurring themes (such as feelings of despair or failure) in such notes to determine if any patterns could be found that would help in understanding why people kill themselves (Leenaars, 1988).

Research designs are tailored to the specific problems being investigated and the focus of the researcher. Both quantitative and qualitative research contribute to our knowledge of society and human social interaction. Whether you are developing your own research project or reading an article in a journal, at some point in the research process, you must take the steps shown in Figure 1.1. We will now trace those steps in the "conventional" research process, which focuses on deduction and quantitative research, using Durkheim's early research on suicide as a model. Then we will contrast them with an alternative approach that emphasizes induction and qualitative research.

1. *Select and define the research problem*. Sometimes, an experience such as knowing someone who committed suicide can trigger your interest in a topic. Other times, you might select topics to fill gaps or challenge misconceptions in existing research or to test specific theory (Babbie, 1995). Durkheim selected suicide because he wanted to demonstrate the importance of society in situations that might appear to be arbitrary acts by individuals.
2. *Reviewing previous research*. Once you have defined your research problem, you need to review the literature (relevant books and scholarly articles). Knowledge of the existing literature is essential for a number of reasons. It helps to refine the research problem, provides possible theoretical approaches, indicates which aspects of the research topic have already been examined and where the gaps are, and identifies mistakes to avoid. When Durkheim began his study, there was very little sociological literature about suicide for him to review; instead, he studied the works of several moral philosophers.
3. *Formulate the hypothesis* (if applicable). After reviewing previous research you may formulate a *hypothesis*—a statement of the expected relationship between two or more variables. A ***variable* is any concept with measurable traits or characteristics that can change or vary from one person, time, situation, or society to another.** The most fundamental relationship in a hypothesis is between a dependent variable and one or more independent variables (see Figure 1.2). The ***independent variable* is presumed to be the cause of the relationship; the dependent variable is assumed to be caused by the independent variable(s).** Durkheim's hypothesis stated that the rate of suicide varies *inversely* with the degree of social integration. In other words, a low degree of social integration (the independent variable) may "cause" or "be related to" a high rate of suicide (the dependent variable).

   Not all social research makes use of hypotheses. If you plan to conduct an explanatory study (showing a cause-and-effect relationship), you likely will want to formulate one or more hypotheses to test theories. If you plan to conduct a descriptive study, however, you will be less likely to do so, since you may desire only to describe social reality or provide facts.
4. *Develop the research design*. During the research design phase, you will decide on one or more of the research methods—including experiments, survey research, field research, and secondary analysis of data, all of which are described in

FIGURE 1.1 Steps in Sociological Research

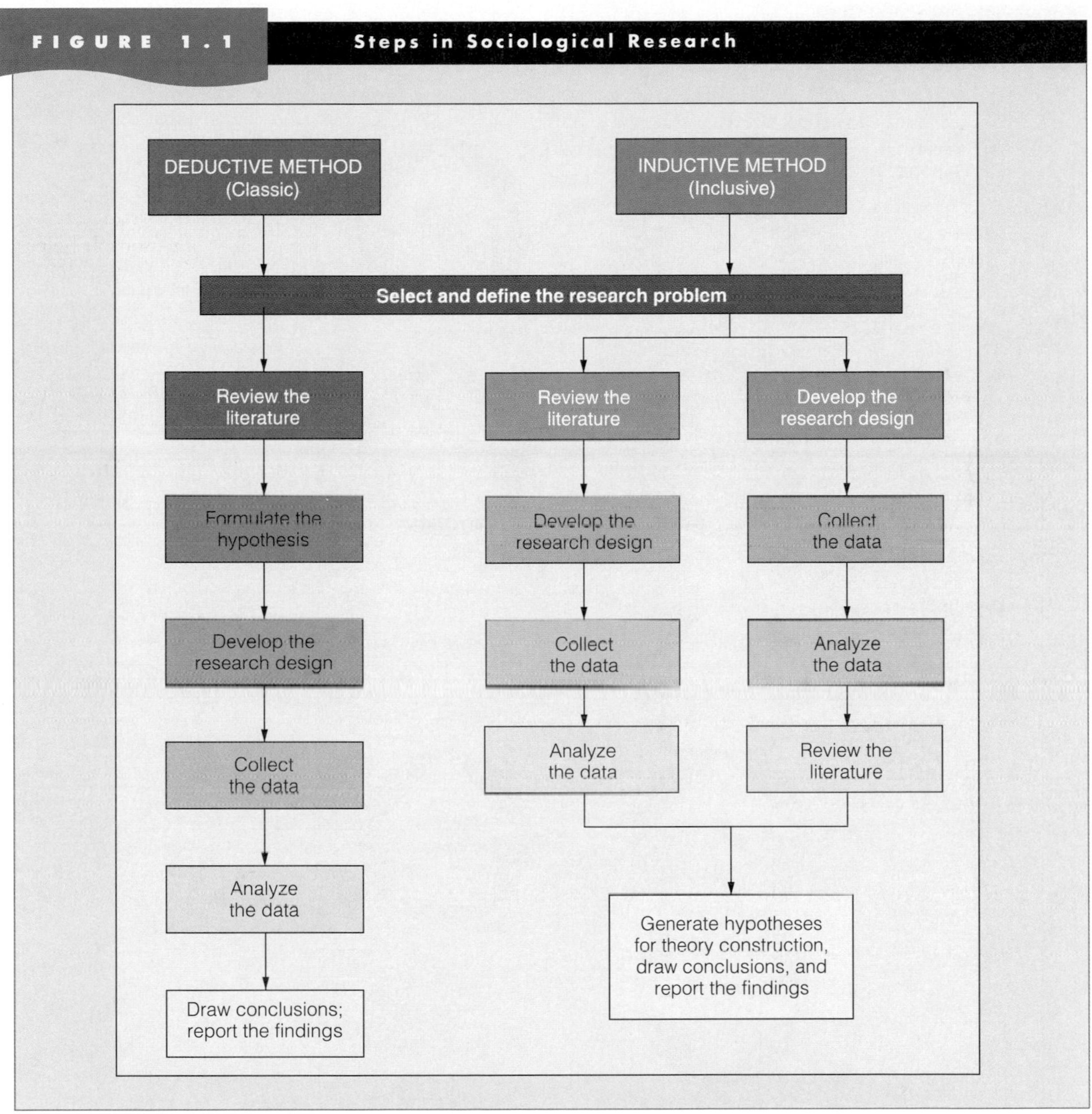

this chapter. In developing the research design, it is important to carefully consider the advantages and disadvantages of each of these methods. Your final research results will be no better than the data on which they are based, so the researcher must take great care in collecting and recording information (Robertson, 1977:43).

You must determine the units of analysis and the time frame of the study. A *unit of analysis* is *what* or *whom* is being studied (Babbie, 1995). In social science research, individuals, social groups (such as families, cities, or geographic regions), organizations (such as clubs, labour unions, or political parties), and social artifacts (such as books, paintings, or weddings) may be units of analysis. Durkheim's unit of analysis was social groups, not individuals, because he believed that the study of individual cases of suicide would not explain the rates of suicide in various European countries.

FIGURE 1.2 Hypothesized Relationships Between Variables

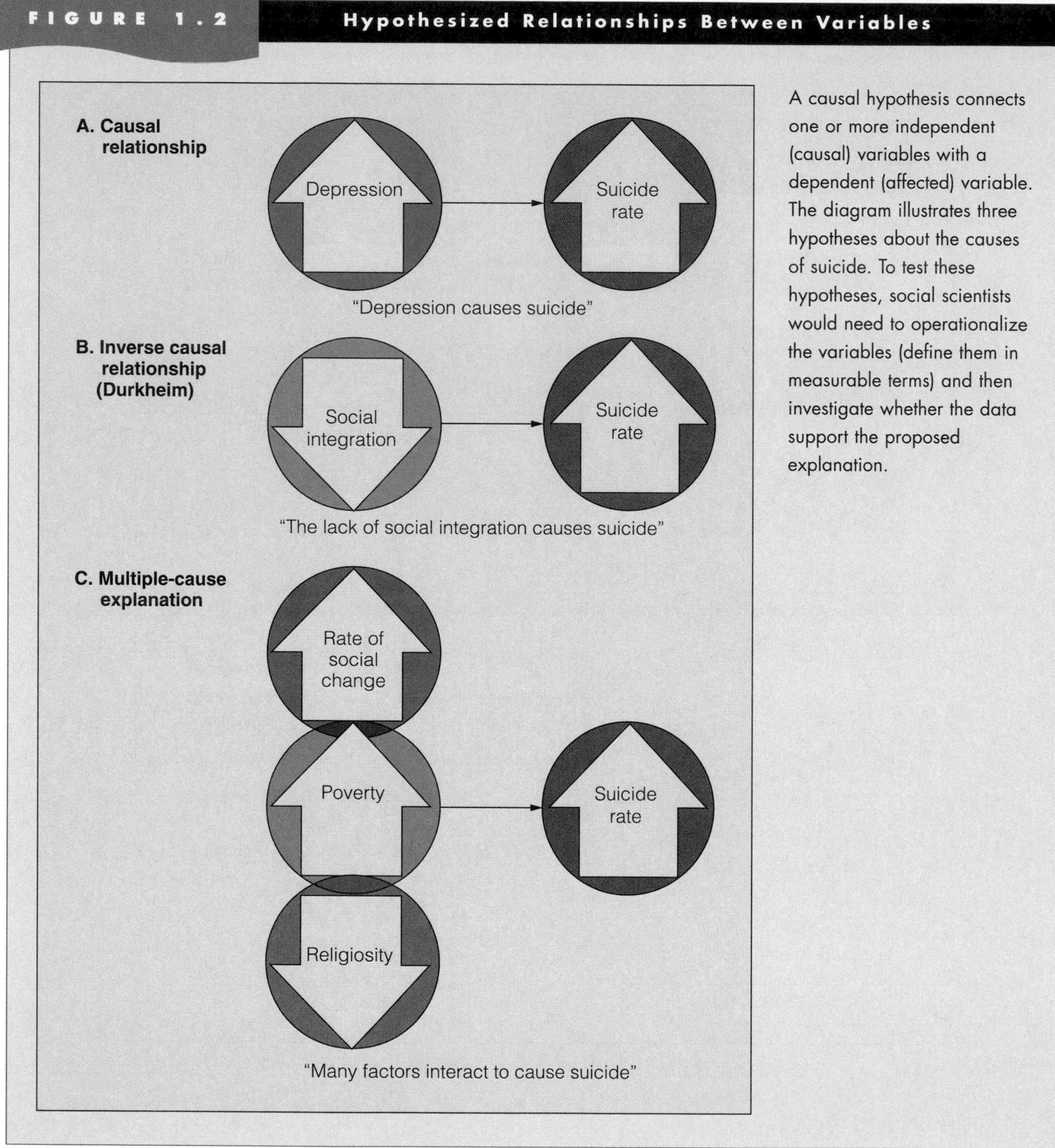

A causal hypothesis connects one or more independent (causal) variables with a dependent (affected) variable. The diagram illustrates three hypotheses about the causes of suicide. To test these hypotheses, social scientists would need to operationalize the variables (define them in measurable terms) and then investigate whether the data support the proposed explanation.

After determining the unit of analysis for your study, you must select a time frame for study: cross-sectional or longitudinal. *Cross-sectional studies* are based on observations that take place at a single point in time; these studies focus on behaviour or responses at a specific moment. *Longitudinal studies* are concerned with what is happening over a period of time or at several different points in time; they focus on processes and social change. Some longitudinal studies are designed to examine the same set of people each time, whereas others look at trends within a general population.

5. *Collect the data.* You must decide what population will be observed or questioned and carefully select a sample. A ***sample* is the people who are selected from the population to be studied; the sample should accurately represent the larger population. A *representative sample* is a selection from a larger population that has the essential characteristics of the total population.** For example, if you were to interview 200 students selected haphazardly from students you met in the halls, they would not be representative of your school's total student body. By contrast, if 200 students were selected from the total student body by a random sample, they would be much more likely to be representative.

   Validity and reliability may be problems in research. ***Validity* is the extent to which a study or research instrument accurately measures what it is supposed to measure.** A recurring issue in studies that analyze the relationship between religious beliefs and suicide is whether "church membership" is an accurate indicator of a person's religious beliefs. One person may be very religious yet not belong to a specific church; another person may be a member of a church yet not hold very deep religious beliefs or even attend church regularly. ***Reliability* is the extent to which a study or research instrument yields consistent results** when applied to different individuals at one time or the same individuals over time. Sociologists have found that different interviewers get different answers from the people being interviewed. For example, how might interviews with college students who have contemplated suicide be influenced by the interviewers themselves?

6. *Analyze the data.* Once you have collected your data it must be analyzed. ***Analysis* is the process through which data are organized so that comparisons can be made and conclusions drawn.** Sociologists use many techniques to analyze data. The process for each type of research method is discussed later in this chapter.

   After collecting data from vital statistics for approximately 26,000 suicides, Durkheim analyzed his data according to four distinctive categories of suicide. *Egoistic suicide* occurs among people who are isolated from any social group. By contrast, *altruistic suicide* occurs among individuals who are excessively integrated into society (e.g., military leaders who kill themselves after defeat in battle). *Anomic suicide* results from a lack of social regulation, whereas *fatalistic suicide* results from excessive regulation and oppressive discipline (e.g., slaves).

7. *Draw conclusions and report the findings.* After analyzing the data, your first step in drawing conclusions is to return to your hypothesis or research objective to clarify how the data relate both to the hypothesis and to the larger issues being addressed. At this stage, you note the limitations of the study, such as problems with the sample, the influence of variables over which you had no control, or variables that your study was unable to measure.

   Reporting the findings is the final stage. The report generally includes a review of each step taken in the research process in order to make the study available for ***replication*—the repetition of the investigation in substantially the same way that it originally was conducted.** Social scientists generally present their findings in papers at professional meetings and publish them in technical journals and books. In reporting his findings in *Suicide* (1964b/1897), Durkheim concluded that the suicide rate of a group is a social fact that cannot be explained in terms of the personality traits of individuals.

We have traced the steps in the "conventional" research process (based on deduction and quantitative research). But what steps might be taken in an alternative approach based on induction and qualitative research?

A Qualitative Approach to Researching Suicide

Do societal beliefs and values have any effect on women's and men's suicides? Why are women more likely to "attempt" suicide but men more likely to "complete" suicide? In studying different rates of suicide among women and men, psychologist Silvia Canetto (1992) questioned whether existing theories and research provided an adequate explanation for gender differences in suicidal behaviour and decided that she would explore alternative explanations. Analyzing previous research, Canetto learned that most studies linked suicidal behaviour in women to problems in their personal relationships, particularly with men. By contrast, most studies of men's suicides linked the behaviour to their performance and found that men are more likely to be suicidal when their self-esteem and independence are threatened. According to Canetto's analysis, gender differences in suicidal behaviour are more closely associated with beliefs about and cultural expectations for men and women rather than purely interpersonal crises.

As in Canetto's study, researchers using a qualitative approach may engage in problem formulation to clarify the research question and to formulate questions of concern and interest to people participating in the research (Reinharz, 1992). To create a research design for Canetto's study, we might start with the proposition that studies have attributed women's and men's suicidal behaviour to the wrong causes. Next, we might decide to interview individuals who have attempted suicide. Our research design might develop a collaborative approach in which the participants are brought into the research design process, not just treated as passive objects to be studied (Reinharz, 1992).

Although Canetto did not gather data in her study, she re-evaluated existing research, concluding that alternative explanations of women's and men's suicidal behaviour are justified from existing data.

In a qualitative approach, the next step is collecting and analyzing data to assess the validity of the starting proposition. Data gathering is the foundation of the research. Researchers pursuing a qualitative approach tend to gather data in natural settings, such as where the person lives or works, rather than in a laboratory or other research setting. Data collection and analysis frequently occur concurrently, and the analysis draws heavily on the language of the persons studied, not the researcher.

Research Methods for Collecting Data

How do sociologists know which research method to use? Which method is best for a particular problem? ***Research methods* are strategies or techniques for systematically conducting research.** We will look at four of these methods: experiments, surveys, analysis of existing statistical data, and field studies.

EXPERIMENTS An ***experiment* is a carefully designed situation in which the researcher studies the impact of certain variables on subjects' attitudes or behaviour.** Experiments are designed to create "real-life" situations, ideally under controlled circumstances, in which the influence of different variables can be modified and measured. Conventional experiments require that subjects be divided into two groups: an experimental group and a control group. The ***experimental group* contains the subjects who are exposed to an independent variable** (the experimental condition) to study its effect on them. The ***control group* contains the subjects who are not exposed to the independent variable.** The members of the two groups are matched for similar characteristics or randomly assigned to each group so that comparisons may be made between the groups. The experimental and control groups are then compared to see if they differ in relation to the dependent variable, and the hypothesis about the relationship of the two variables is confirmed or rejected.

Researchers may use experiments when they want to demonstrate that a cause-and-effect relationship exists between variables. In order to show that a change in one variable causes a change in another, these three conditions must be satisfied:

1. A correlation between the two variables must be shown to exist (**a *correlation* exists when two variables are associated more frequently than could be expected by chance**),
2. the independent variable must have occurred prior to the dependent variable, and
3. any change in the dependent variable must not have been due to an extraneous variable—that is, one outside the stated hypothesis.

The major advantage of the controlled experiment is the researcher's control over the environment and the ability to isolate the experimental variable. Since many experiments require relatively little time and money and can be conducted with limited numbers of subjects, it is possible for researchers to replicate an experiment several times by using different groups of subjects (Babbie, 1995). Replication strengthens claims about the validity and generalizability of the original research findings. Perhaps the greatest limitation of experiments is that they are artificial. Social processes that occur in a laboratory setting often do not occur in the same way in real-life settings.

SURVEYS Survey research is the method of data collection most often associated with the discipline of sociology. In a ***survey* a number of respondents are**

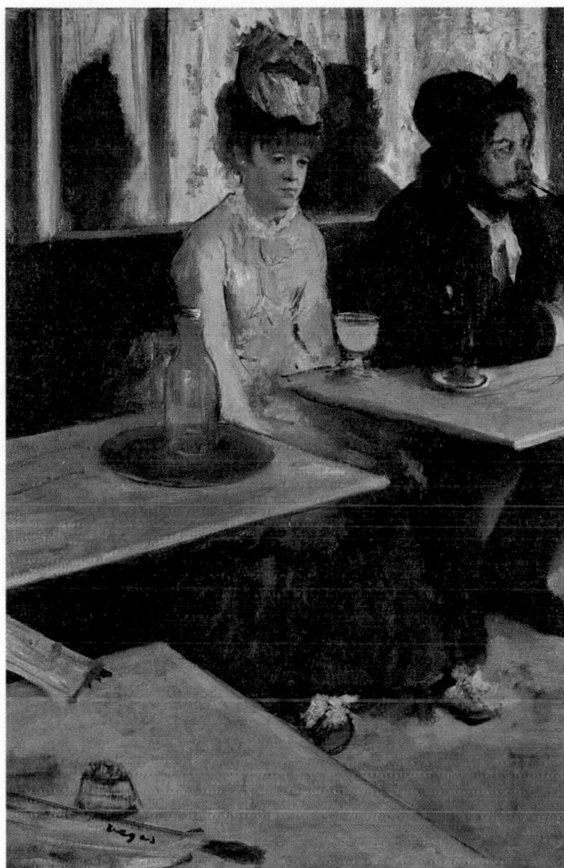

From Emile Durkheim's day to the present, people are more likely to kill themselves when their ties to others are very weak—as shown by two lonely people at L'Absinthe in Paris during Durkheim's time—or when ties are very strong—as shown by the 1994 mass suicide in Cheiry, Switzerland, where forty-eight members of a Canadian-based cult allegedly committed suicide.

asked identical questions through a systematic questionnaire or interview. Researchers frequently select a representative sample (a small group of respondents) from a larger population (the total group of people) to answer questions about their attitudes, opinions, or behaviour. ***Respondents* are persons who provide data for analysis through interviews or questionnaires.** The Gallup and Angus Reid polls are among the most widely known large-scale surveys. Government agencies such as Statistics Canada conduct a variety of surveys as well. Unlike many polls that use various methods of gaining a representative sample of the larger population, the census attempts to gain information from all persons in Canada. Surveys are an important research method in sociology because they make it possible to study things that are not directly observable—such as people's attitudes and beliefs—and to describe a population too large to observe directly (Babbie, 1995).

Survey data are collected by using self-administered questionnaires, personal interviews, and/or telephone surveys. A ***questionnaire* is a printed research instrument containing a series of items to which subjects respond.** Items are often in the form of statements with which the respondent is asked to "agree" or "disagree." Questionnaires may be administered by interviewers in face-to-face encounters or by telephone, but the most commonly used technique is the *self-administered questionnaire*. The questionnaires typically are mailed or delivered to the respondents' homes; however, they also may be administered to groups of respondents gathered at the same place at the same time.

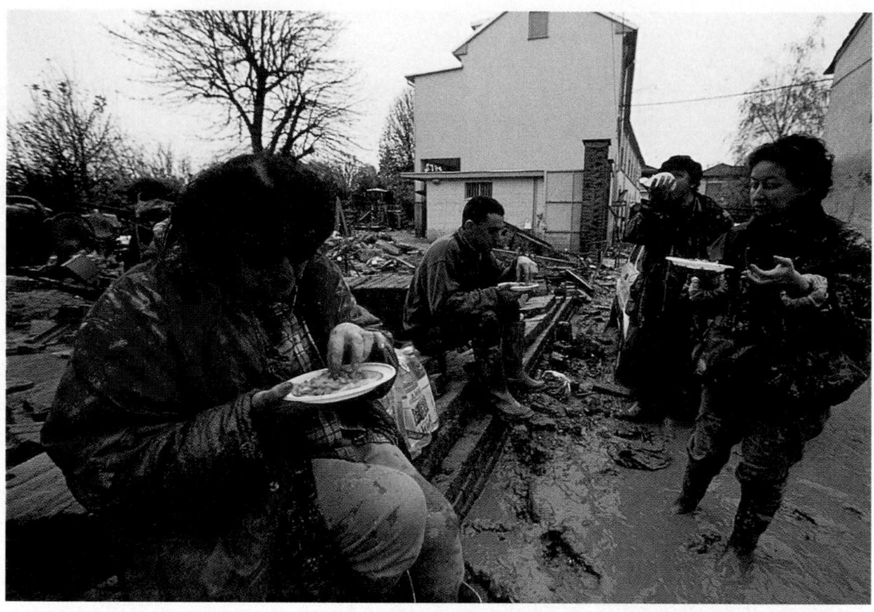

Not all experiments occur in laboratory settings. Natural disasters, such as this flood in Piedmont, Italy, may be "living laboratories" for sociologists.

An ***interview*** **is a data collection encounter in which an interviewer asks the respondent questions and records the answers.** Survey research often uses *structured interviews*, in which the interviewer asks questions from a standardized questionnaire. Structured interviews tend to produce uniform or replicable data that can be elicited time after time by different interviews.

Interviews usually are more effective in dealing with complicated issues and provide an opportunity for face-to-face communication between the interviewer and respondent. When open-ended questions are used, the researcher may gain new perspectives. The major disadvantage of interviews is the cost and time involved in conducting them.

Questionnaires may also be administered by *telephone surveys*, which are becoming an increasingly popular way to collect data for a number of reasons. Telephone surveys save time and money compared to self-administered questionnaires or face-to-face interviews. Some respondents may be more honest than when they are facing an interviewer. Telephone surveys also give greater control over data collection and provide greater personal safety for respondents and researchers than do personal encounters.

Some scholars have criticized the way survey data are sometimes used. The data collected are not always the "hard facts" some researchers claim they are. For example, survey statistics may over- or underestimate the extent of a problem, as shown in Table 1.1.

Survey research is useful in that it allows the researcher to describe a large population without having to interview each person in that population. It also enables the researcher to search for causes and effects and to assess the relative importance of a number of variables. Survey research can also be useful in analyzing social change or documenting the existence of a social problem. Contemporary scholars have used survey research to document that some problems—such as racial discrimination, sexual harassment, and sex-based inequality in employment—are more widespread than previously thought (Reinharz, 1992).

Survey research, however, has several weaknesses. One is that the use of standardized questions tends to force respondents into categories in which they may or may not belong. Another weakness concerns validity. People's opinions on issues seldom take the form of a standard response ranging from "strongly agree" to "strongly disagree." Moreover, as in other types of research, people may be less than truthful, especially on emotionally charged issues or on issues such as suicide that have a strong element of social undesirability. This can make reliance on self-reported attitudes and behaviour problematic.

Secondary Analysis of Existing Data In *secondary analysis,* **researchers use existing material and analyze data originally collected by others.** Existing data sources include public records, official reports of organizations or government agencies, and surveys conducted by researchers in universities and private corporations. Other sources of data for secondary analysis are books, magazines, newspapers, radio and television programs, and personal documents. Secondary analysis is referred to as *unobtrusive research* because it includes a variety of nonreactive research techniques—that is, techniques that have no impact on the people being studied. In Durkheim's study of suicide, for example, his analysis of existing statistics on suicide did nothing to increase or decrease the number of people who *actually* committed suicide.

One strength of secondary analysis is that data are readily available and are often inexpensive to obtain. Another is that, because the researcher often does not collect the data personally, the chances of bias may be reduced. In addition, the use of existing sources makes it possible to analyze longitudinal data to provide a historical context within which to locate original research. However, secondary analysis has inherent problems. For one thing, the data may be incomplete, inauthentic, or inaccurate. Also, as Durkheim found in his study of suicide records (that did not include religious affiliation), secondary data are often collected for administrative purposes, so the categories may not reflect variables of interest to the researcher.

Field Research *Field research* **is the study of social life in its natural setting: observing and interviewing people where they live, work, and play.** Some kinds of behaviour can be studied best by "being there"; a fuller understanding can be developed through observations, face-to-face discussions, and participation in events. Researchers use these methods to generate *qualitative* data: observations that are best described verbally rather than numerically. Although field research is less structured and more flexible than the other methods we have discussed, it also places many demands on the researcher. To engage in field research, sociologists must select the method or combination of methods that will best reveal what they want to know. For example, they must decide how to approach the target group, whether to identify themselves as researchers, and whether to participate in the events they are observing.

Sociologists who are interested in observing social interaction as it occurs may use either complete observation or participant observation. In *complete observation,* **the researcher systematically observes a social process but does not take part in it.** Observational research can take place just about anywhere. For example, sociologists David Karp and William Yoels (1976) became interested in why many students do not participate in discussions in university classrooms. Observers sat in on various classes and took notes that included the average number of students who participated, the number of times they talked during one class session, and the sex of the instructor and of the students who talked in class. From their observational data, Karp and Yoels found that, on average, a very small number of students are responsible for the majority of all discussion that occurs in class on any given day.

Suppose you wanted to study your own class to identify the "talkers" and the "silent ones." You would need to develop a game plan before you

TABLE 1.1 STATISTICS: WHAT WE KNOW (AND DON'T KNOW)

	TOPIC HOMELESSNESS IN CANADA	GAY MEN IN CANADA	SUICIDE IN CANADA
Research Finding	Over 200,000 people in this country are homeless.	At least 1 percent of Canadian men are exclusively homosexual.	At least 3941 Canadians committed suicide in 1996.
Possible Problem	Does that badly underestimate the total number of homeless people?	Does this underestimate the gay population? Is the actual percentage higher?	Are suicide rates recorded in the official death certificates?
Explanation	The homeless are difficult to count. They may avoid interviews with census takers. The 1996 census was the first attempt to count the number of homeless in Canada. However, these numbers will not be released by Statistics Canada.	As one analyst noted, many people lie about their sexuality; people often are hesitant to report their sexual orientation. This may result in estimates being too low; however, gay rights organizations may overstate percentages to gain political clout.	Suicides for children under 10 are not recorded in Canada. Some accidental deaths may in fact be suicides.

started to observe. A game plan typically is guided by a research question, such as, "Why don't more university students participate in class discussions?" Subjects in observation studies may not realize that they are being studied, especially if the researcher remains unobtrusive. Observations help us view behaviour as it is taking place; however, they provide limited opportunities to learn why people do certain things. One way for researchers to remain unobtrusive is through ***participant observation*—collecting systematic observations while being part of the activities of the group they are studying.** Participant observation generates more "inside" information than simply asking questions or observing from the outside. As sociologist William Whyte noted in his classic participant observation study of a Boston low-income neighbourhood: "As I sat and listened, I learned the answers to questions I would not have had the sense to ask" (1988/43:303).

Most participant observation research takes the form of a ***case study*, an in-depth, multifaceted investigation of a single event, person, or social grouping** (Feagin, Orum, and Sjoberg, 1991). Case studies often involve more than one method of research, such as participant observation, unstructured or in-depth interviews, and life histories.

An ***ethnography* is a detailed study of the life and activities of a group of people by researchers who may live with that group over a period of years** (Feagin, Orum, and Sjoberg, 1991). Although this approach is similar in some ways to participant observation, these studies typically take place over much longer periods of time. For example, researcher Anastasia Shkilnyk (1985) lived in an Ojibwa community in Grassy Narrows, in northwestern Ontario, for several years. As a result, she was able to describe the destruction and human suffering brought about by mercury contamination and by the relocation of the residents of Grassy Narrows to a new reserve.

Ethical Issues in Sociological Research

The study of people ("human subjects") raises vital questions about ethical concerns in sociological research. Because of past abuses, researchers are now required by a professional code of ethics to weigh the

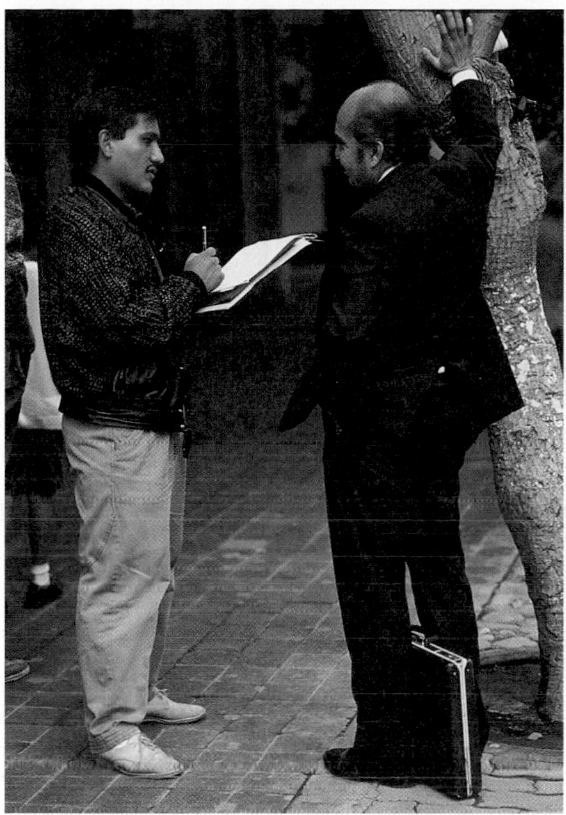

Conducting surveys or polls is an international means of gathering data. This investigator is conducting his research in Mexico City.

societal benefits of research against the potential physical and emotional costs to participants. Researchers are required to obtain written "informed consent" statements from the persons they study. However, these guidelines have produced many new questions, such as, What constitutes "informed consent"? What constitutes harm to a person? How do researchers protect the identity and confidentiality of their sources?

The Canadian Sociology and Anthropology Association has outlined the basic standards sociologists must follow in conducting research. Social research often involves intrusions into people's lives—surveys, interviews, field observations, and participation in experiments all involve personally valuable commodities: time, energy, and privacy. Participation in research must be voluntary. No one should be enticed, coerced, or forced to participate. Researchers must not harm the research subjects in any way—physically, psychologically, or personally. For example, the researcher must be careful not to reveal information that would embarrass the participants, or damage their personal relationships. Researchers must respect the rights of research subjects to anonymity and confidentiality.

A respondent is *anonymous* when the researcher cannot identify a given response with a given respondent. Anonymity is often extremely important when obtaining information on "deviant" or illegal activities. For example, in a study on physician-assisted suicides conducted by the Manitoba Association of Rights and Liberties (Searles, 1995), ensuring the anonymity of the physicians responding to the survey was crucial because the doctors were being asked about their participation in illegal acts (see Box 1.4, "Assisting Suicide").

Maintaining *confidentiality* means that the researcher is able to identify a given person's responses with that person but essentially promises not to do so. Whether the researcher should reveal his or her identity is also a difficult issue. In some cases, it is useful to identify yourself as a researcher to obtain cooperation from respondents. However, there are other instances when revealing your identity can affect the content and quality of your research. Deception should not be used where another methodology would accomplish the same research objectives. Furthermore, it is not acceptable to use deception to obtain informed consent. For example, not informing a research subject of potential risk or harm constitutes deception. Finally, researchers have an obligation to report all of their research findings in full, including unexpected or negative findings and limitations of the research.

Sociologists are committed to adhering to these ethical considerations and to protecting research participants; however, many ethical issues arise that cannot be resolved easily. Ethics in sociological research is a difficult and often ambiguous topic. However, ethical issues cannot be ignored by researchers, whether they are sociology professors, graduate students conducting investigations for their dissertations, or undergraduates conducting a class research project.

In this chapter, we have looked at the research process and the methods used to pursue sociological knowledge. We also have critiqued many of the existing approaches and suggested alternative ways of pursuing research. The important thing to realize is that research is the lifeblood of sociology. Without

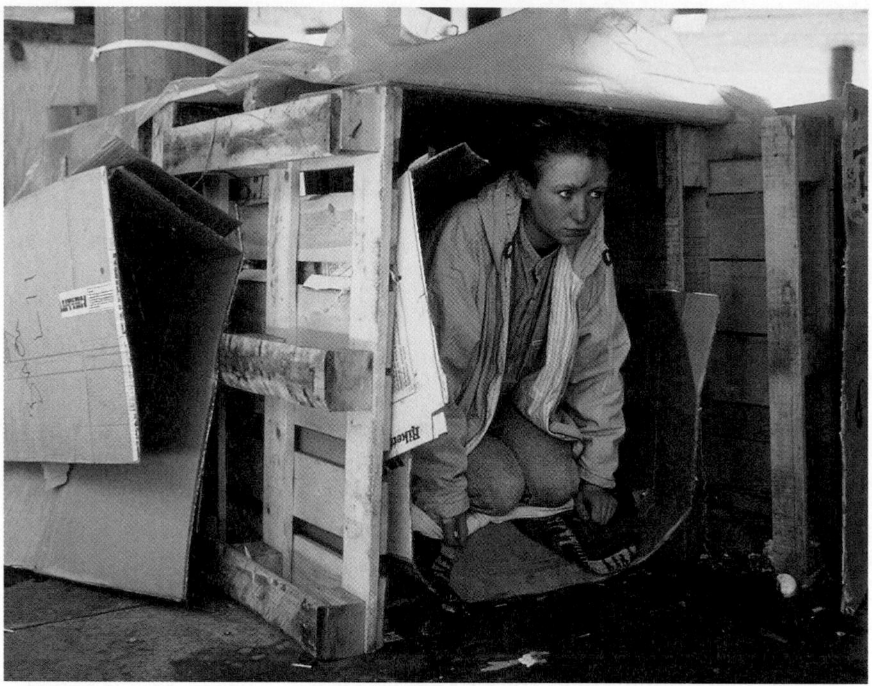

Case studies of homeless persons have added to our insights on the causes and consequences of this major social concern.

research, sociologists would be unable to test existing theories and develop new ones. Research takes us beyond common sense and provides opportunities for us to use our sociological imagination to generate new knowledge.

Our challenge today is to understand how to determine what is useful for enhancing our knowledge, to find new ways to integrate knowledge and action, and to encourage the inclusion of all people in the research process. This inclusion would be on two levels: (1) as active participants in research, to give voice to previously excluded people's experiences, and (2) as researchers, to help fill some of the gaps in our existing knowledge of how the research process is shaped by gender, race, class, and sexual orientation of the researcher and by the broader social and cultural context (Cancian, 1992).

CHAPTER REVIEW

What is sociology and how can it help us to understand ourselves and others?

Sociology is the systematic study of human society and social interaction. We study sociology to understand how individual behaviour is largely shaped by the groups to which we belong and the society in which we live. Sociology also makes us aware of global interdependence.

What is the sociological imagination?

According to C. Wright Mills, the sociological imagination helps us understand how seemingly personal troubles, such as suicide, actually are related to larger social forces. It is the ability to see the relationship between individual experience and the larger society.

What factors contributed to the emergence of sociology as a discipline?

Industrialization and urbanization increased rapidly in the late eighteenth century, and social thinkers began to examine the consequences of these powerful forces.

What are the major contributions of the early sociologists Durkheim, Marx, and Weber?

The ideas of Emile Durkheim, Karl Marx, and Max Weber helped lead the way to contemporary sociology. Durkheim argued that societies are built on social facts, that rapid social change produces strains in society, and that the loss of shared values and purpose can lead to a condition of anomie. Marx stressed that within society there is a continuous clash between the owners of the means of production and the workers who have no choice but to sell their labour to others. According to Weber, it is necessary to acknowledge the meanings that individuals attach to their own actions.

What are the major contemporary sociological perspectives?
Functionalist perspectives assume that society is a stable, orderly system characterized by societal consensus. Conflict perspectives argue that society is a continuous power struggle among competing groups, often based on class, race, ethnicity, or gender. Feminist perspectives focus on the significance of gender in understanding and explaining inequalities that exist between men and women in the household, in the paid labour force, and in politics, law, and culture. Interactionist perspectives focus on how people make sense of their everyday social interactions, which are made possible by the use of mutually understood symbols.

How does quantitative research differ from qualitative research?
Quantitative research focuses on data that can be measured numerically (comparing rates of suicide, for example). Qualitative research uses interpretive description rather than statistics to analyze underlying meanings and patterns of social relationships.

What are the key steps in a conventional research process?
A conventional research process based on deduction and the quantitative approach has these key steps: (1) selecting and defining the research problem, (2) reviewing previous research, (3) formulating the hypothesis, which involves constructing variables, (4) developing the research design, (5) collecting, (6) analyzing the data, and (7) drawing conclusions and reporting the findings.

What steps are typically taken by researchers using the qualitative approach?
A researcher taking the qualitative approach might (1) formulate the problem to be studied instead of creating a hypothesis, (2) collect and analyze the data, and (3) report the results.

What are the major sociological research methods?
Research methods are systematic techniques for conducting research. Through experiments, researchers study the impact of certain variables on their subjects. Surveys are polls used to gather facts about people's attitudes, opinions, or behaviours; a representative sample of respondents provides data through questionnaires or interviews. In secondary analysis, researchers analyze existing data, such as a government census, or cultural artifacts, such as a diary. In field research, sociologists study social life in its natural setting through participant and complete observation, case studies, unstructured interviews, and ethnography.

Key Terms

power elite 15
proletariat 12
qualitative research 22
quantitative research 22
questionnaire 27
race 9
reliability 25
representative sample 25
research methods 26
respondents 27
sample 25
secondary analysis 29
sex 9
social facts 11
societal consensus 13
society 4
sociological imagination 5
sociology 4
survey 26
symbol 16
theory 13
urbanization 10
validity 25
variable 22

Internet Exercises

1. Several good search engines exist on the Web. Some of the most popular are:

   www.lycos.com
   www.altavista.ca
   www.yahoo.ca

   You can use these search engines to further research the topics discussed in these chapters or to complete the exercises. Yahoo! offers a search engine specifically for Canadian-based Web sites.

   For your first exercise, go to the Yahoo! Canada uniform resource locator (URL) listed above and find the sociology section. Look at some of the sociology links. Based on these links, how do the perceptions of "what sociology is" differ from what you think sociology is, or should be? Follow some links that are not explicitly sociological. Do the authors of these Web sites seem to have an underlying sociological theory for their work (regardless of whether or not they realize it)? What connections can you draw between some of these links and the theorists you have just read about?

   Professor Craig McKie of Carleton University has developed an excellent source of links for information about sociology and anthropology at:

   www.socsciresearch.com/r7.html

2. Try this URL:

   www.runet.edu/~lridener/DSS/DEADGALL.HTML

   This is the Dead Sociologists' Society Web site. Many of the sociologists discussed in this chapter are also on this site. How are Professor Ridener's views on these theorists different from those in this chapter? How are they the same? How does the view presented on the various theorists at the Dead Sociologists' Society compare with those found on SocioWeb, which may be found at:

   www.socioweb.com/~markbl/socioweb

   How are the differences in viewpoints among these sites useful to understanding the works of these theorists? How are they detrimental to this understanding? In what ways does the World Wide Web limit or expand a person's ability to relay ideas, and how does it limit the ability to communicate?

3. A basic source of statistical information about Canadian society is Statistics Canada:

   www.statcan.ca

   You can use this Web site to search for data on a wide range of topics including births, deaths, crime, marriage, and employment. Just click "Daily News" to find a page that gives you the latest news from Statistics Canada. Near the bottom of this page click "Search the Daily Archive." This page will allow you to search for a wide range of statistical information. On the Statistics Canada home page, clicking on "Links to other sites" and then "Other statistical Web sites" will enable you to find statistical information about the provinces, territories, and other countries. The home page also has a quiz that will enable you to test your knowledge and learn about Canada and Canadians.

Net Links

For more Web links related to the topic of this chapter, see the Nelson sociology Web site: **www.sociologyessentials-2nded.nelson.com**.

Carleton University sociologist Craig McKie has designed a Web site that has a rich variety of Internet links for researchers:

www.socsciresearch.com

The Web site for Statistics Canada's Data Liberation Initiative gives you access to other Statistics Canada data as well as providing links to statistical agencies in many other parts of the world:

http://www.statcan.ca/english/Dli/contents.htm

The code of ethics of the Canadian Sociology and Anthropology Association is published on their Web site:

www.unb.ca/web/anthropology/csaa/csaa.html

One of Canada's leading social research organizations is the Institute for Social Research at York University:

www.isr.yorku.ca

Questions for Critical Thinking

1. What does C. Wright Mills mean when he says the sociological imagination helps us "to grasp history and biography and the relations between the two within society" (Mills, 1959:6)?
2. As a sociologist, how would you remain objective and yet see the world as others see it? Would you make subjective decisions when trying to understand the perspectives of others?
3. Early social thinkers were concerned about stability in times of rapid change. In our more global world, is stability still a primary goal? Or is constant conflict important for the well-being of all humans? Use the conflict and functionalist perspectives to support your analysis.
4. The agency that funds the local suicide clinic has asked you to study the clinic's effectiveness in preventing suicide. What would you need to measure? What can you measure? What research method(s) would provide the best data for analysis?
5. Together with a group of students, perform a content analysis on the photographs in your textbooks. First, determine whether to sample texts from various fields of study or just one field. Try to follow the steps in the sociological research process.

Suggested Readings

The following books provide in-depth information about research methods:

Earl Babbie. *The Practice of Social Research* (6th ed.). Belmont, Cal.: Wadsworth, 1992.

Therese L. Baker. *Doing Social Research* (2nd ed.). New York: McGraw-Hill, 1994.

Margrit Eichler. *Nonsexist Research Methods: A Practical Guide*. Boston: Allen & Unwin, 1988.

Sandra Kirby and Kate McKenna. *Experience, Research, and Social Change: Methods from the Margins*. Toronto: Garamond, 1989.

Shulamit Reinharz. *Feminist Methods in Social Research*. New York: Oxford University Press, 1992. (Provides excellent information and examples of qualitative research using methods such as oral histories, content analysis, case studies, action research, and multiple-method research.)

Janice L. Ristock and Joan Pennell. *Research as Empowerment: Feminist Links, Postmodern Interruptions*. Don Mills, Ont.: Oxford University Press, 1996.

To find out more about writing a sociology term paper or report, see:

Richard Floyd. *Success in the Social Sciences: Writing and Research for Canadian Students*. Toronto: Harcourt Brace, 1995.

Margot Northey. *Making Sense: A Student's Guide to Research, Writing and Style*. Don Mills, Ont.: Oxford University Press, 1993. (Takes the reader from the initial steps of choosing a topic to doing research and writing the final paper. Describes existing types of social science literature and makes suggestions about writing a research paper and preparing an oral presentation.)

INFOTRAC® COLLEGE EDITION

Either from the *Sociology In Our Times: The Essentials* Web site (**www.sociologyessentials-2nded.nelson.com**) or directly from your Web browser, you may access InfoTrac® College Edition, an online university library that includes over 600 popular and scholarly journals in which you can find articles related to the topics in this chapter.

CHAPTER 2

Crown attorney and author Rupert Ross describes the difficulties he had in learning to understand and accept the cultural traditions of the Ojibway. According to Ross this story demonstrates how easy it is to misread people who have a "different understanding" of the world (1996:51):

"My own cultural eyes have often tricked me into seeing things that Aboriginal people did not—or completely missing things they thought too obvious to point out. One of the most significant came one day when I was having coffee with an Ojibway friend. I asked her about something I often saw in the North: older couples walking along with the man twelve paces out in front, his wife bringing up the rear. I asked her how that behaviour fit with what I was being taught about equality between men and women in traditional times. She laughed, then said something like 'Rupert, Rupert, that's only your eyes again! You have to look at it the way we do!'

"She began by asking me to remember where those old people had spent their lives, to imagine walking a narrow trail through the bush with my own family. She asked me to think about who I would prefer to have out in front, my wife or myself, to be the first to face whatever dangers the bush presented. In one way, she said, it could be compared to wartime. 'Where,' she asked, 'do you put your general? Are they out in front or are they in the rear, where they have time to see and plan and react?'

"Viewed in that way, things appeared to be the opposite of what I had first supposed. Instead of occupying an inferior position, the woman was seen as the organizer and director, while the man out front was counted on for his capacity to take action under her direction. Instead of remembering the bush context in which they had lived their lives, I had put them in my own urban context where such a formation might indicate the opposite. 'So,' I said, 'she's really the general and her husband is just the footsoldier!'

"There was a pause then, and she chuckled again, shaking her head. 'Not really,' she said. 'The problem is ... you see everything in terms of hierarchies, don't you? Why do you do that?' ... She tried to express her way then, the way she understood from the teaching of her people.

CULTURE

In those teachings, all things have a purpose, and unless these are fulfilled, the strength of the whole is weakened. The jobs of the husband and of the wife were just that, their jobs, assumed on the basis of their having different skills and capacities—different *gifts*—none of which had to be compared with each other in terms of worth or importance. Comparison itself was seen as a strange thing to do.

"As she spoke, I was flooded with recollections of other events that raised the issue of our Western dependence on hierarchies of worth and power." (Ross, 1996:52–53)

C*ulture* is the knowledge, language, values, customs, and material objects that are passed from person to person and from one generation to the next in a human group or society. As previously defined, a society is a large social grouping that occupies the same geographic territory and is subject to the same political authority and dominant cultural expectations. While a society is made up of people, a culture is made up of ideas, behaviour, and material possessions. Society and culture are interdependent; neither could exist without the other.

To what extent does our own culture "blind" us, that is, keep us from understanding, accepting, or learning from other unique cultures? Is intolerance toward "outsiders"—people who are viewed as being different from one's own group or way of life—accepted by some people in Canada?

Culture can be an enormously stabilizing force for a society, and it can provide a sense of continuity. However, culture also can be a force that generates discord and conflict between different groups. How people view culture is intricately related to their location in society with regard to their ethnicity, class, sex, and age. From one perspective, Canadian culture does not condone or tolerate attacks against people because of their religion, colour, disability, sexual orientation, ethnic origin, or ancestry. From another perspective, however, intolerance may be the downside of some "positive" cultural values—such as individualism, competition, and materialism—found in Canadian society. Just as attitudes of love and tolerance may be embedded in societal values and teachings, beliefs that reinforce intolerance may also be embedded in culture.

In this chapter, we examine society and culture, with special attention to the components of culture and the relationship between cultural change and diversity. We will also analyze culture from functionalist, conflict, and interactionist perspectives. Before reading on, test your knowledge of the relationship between culture and intolerance toward others by answering the questions in Box 2.1.

QUESTIONS AND ISSUES

CHAPTER FOCUS QUESTION: To what extent are Canadians accepting and tolerant of cultural diversity?

What are the essential components of culture?

How do subcultures and countercultures reflect diversity within a society?

How do the various sociological perspectives view culture?

CULTURE AND SOCIETY

Understanding how culture affects our lives helps us develop a sociological imagination. When we meet someone from a culture vastly different from our own, or when we travel in another country, it may be easier to perceive the enormous influence of culture in people's lives. However, when we turn our sociological lens on our own society, it is more difficult to examine culture because we take our own way of life for granted.

The Importance of Culture

How important is culture in determining how people think and act on a daily basis? Simply stated, culture is essential for our individual survival and our communication with other people. We rely on culture because we are not born with the information we need to survive. We do not know how to take care of ourselves, how to behave, how to dress, what to eat, which gods to worship, or how to make or spend money. We must learn about culture through interaction, observation, and imitation in order to participate as members of the group (Samovar and Porter, 1991a). Sharing a common culture with others simplifies day-to-day interactions. However, as our society becomes more diverse, and communication among members of international cultures more frequent, the need to appreciate diversity and to understand how people in other cultures view their world also increases (Samovar and Porter, 1991b:65).

Just as culture is essential for individuals, it is also fundamental for the survival of societies. Culture has been described as "the common denominator that makes the actions of individuals intelligible to the group" (Haviland, 1993:30). Some system of rule

BOX 2.1 SOCIOLOGY AND EVERYDAY LIFE

HOW TOLERANT ARE CANADIANS OF OTHER CULTURES?

TRUE	FALSE	
T	F	1. In recent years, the number of reported attacks in Canada against persons because of their race, religion, or ethnic origin has increased.
T	F	2. It is illegal to be a member of a racist organization.
T	F	3. Some people are born with hatred for people who are different from themselves.
T	F	4. As the rate of immigration to Canada has increased in recent years, anti-immigrant feelings have risen.
T	F	5. The majority of hate crimes in Canada are directed against racial minorities.
T	F	6. Incidents of violence targeted toward African Canadians and Jews have declined in recent years.
T	F	7. Communities with greater proportions of visible-minority immigrants are generally more tolerant of racial and ethnic differences.
T	F	8. A recent Toronto survey found most multicultural groups felt generally well accepted.
T	F	9. A recent national survey found that the majority of respondents accept the concept of Canada as a multicultural mosaic.
T	F	10. Canadians generally see themselves as tolerant of other cultures and intolerant of racism.

Answers on page 39.

BOX 2.1

Answers to the Sociology Quiz on Other Cultures

1. **True.** Even though such incidents are seriously underreported in Canada, statistics indicate that the number of reported hate or bias crimes has increased in recent years.
2. **False.** As provided for in the Charter of Rights and Freedoms, individuals have the right to belong to any organization they choose to join.
3. **False.** Sociologists agree that hatred and intolerance are learned attitudes and behaviours, not genetic by-products.
4. **True.** Polls show that high rates of immigration, combined with a tightening in the economy, are related to an increase in anti-immigrant sentiment.
5. **True.** Recent statistics indicate that in one year, 61 percent of hate crime incidents reported to police were directed against racial minorities, 23 percent against religious minorities, 11 percent against gays or lesbians, and 5 percent against ethnic minorities.
6. **False.** Despite Canada's record of tolerance, a 1999 report showed that violent incidents directed at these two groups are on the rise.
7. **True.** According to the Economic Council of Canada's report on changing attitudes toward prejudice, the communities with more visible minorities expressed the most tolerant attitudes.
8. **False.** In a survey conducted in Toronto in which respondents were asked how well their racial or cultural group was accepted, 80 percent of those surveyed in the African Canadian community, 63 percent in the Chinese community, and 62 percent in the East Indian–Pakistani Canadian community felt there was some prejudice toward them.
9. **False.** Nearly 73 percent of 1200 Canadians surveyed in a recent poll rejected the concept of Canada as a multicultural mosaic.
10. **True.** Canadians generally see themselves as tolerant of other cultures. Yet they are also aware that racism is a serious problem in Canada. Sociologists identify this as a paradox of Canadian society.

Sources: Based on Levin and McDevitt, 1993; Gilmour, 1994; Roberts, 1995; Henry et al., 1996; and Galloway, 1999.

making and enforcing necessarily exists in all societies. What would happen, for example, if *all* rules and laws in Canada suddenly disappeared? At a basic level, we need rules in order to navigate our bicycles and cars through traffic. At a more abstract level, we need laws to establish and protect our rights.

In order to survive, societies need rules about civility and tolerance toward others. We are not born knowing how to express kindness or hatred toward others, although some people may say, "Well, that's just human nature," when explaining someone's behaviour. Such a statement is built on the assumption that what we do as human beings is determined by *nature* (our biological and genetic makeup) rather than *nurture* (our social environment)—that is, that our behaviour is instinctive. An *instinct* is a biologically determined behaviour pattern common to all members of a species that predictably occurs whenever certain environmental conditions exist. For example, spiders do not learn to build webs. They build webs because of instincts that are triggered by basic biological needs such as protection and reproduction.

Humans do not have instincts. What we most often think of as instinctive behaviour can be attributed to reflexes and drives. A *reflex* is a biologically determined involuntary response to some physical stimulus (such as a sneeze after breathing some pepper through the nose or the blinking of an eye when a speck of dust gets in it). *Drives* are biologically determined impulses common to all members of a species that satisfy needs such as sleep, food, water, or sexual gratification. Reflexes and drives do not determine how people will behave in human societies; even the expression of these biological characteristics is channelled by culture. For example, we may be taught that the "appropriate" way to sneeze (an involuntary response) is to use a

Shelter is a universal type of material culture, but it comes in a wide variety of shapes and forms. What might some of the reasons be for the similarities and differences you see in these cross-cultural examples?

tissue or turn our head away from others (a learned response). Similarly, we may learn to sleep on mats or in beds. Most contemporary sociologists agree that culture and social learning, not nature, account for virtually all of our behaviour patterns.

Since humans cannot rely on instincts in order to survive, culture is a "tool kit" for survival. According to sociologist Ann Swidler (1986:273), culture is a "tool kit of symbols, stories, rituals, and world views, which people may use in varying configurations to solve different kinds of problems." The tools we choose will vary according to our own personality and the situations we face. We are not puppets on a string; we make choices from among the items in our own "tool box."

Material and Nonmaterial Culture

Our cultural tool box is divided into two major parts: *material* and *nonmaterial* culture (Ogburn, 1966/1922). ***Material culture*** **consists of the physical or tangible creations that members of a society make, use, and share.** At the most basic level, material culture is important because it is our buffer against the environment. For example, we create shelter to protect ourselves from the weather and to provide ourselves with

The customs and rituals associated with weddings are one example of nonmaterial culture. What can you infer about beliefs and attitudes concerning marriage in the societies represented by these photographs?

privacy. Beyond the survival level, we make, use, and share objects that are interesting and important to us. Why are you wearing the particular clothes you have on today? Perhaps you're communicating something about yourself, such as where you attend school, what kind of music you like, or where you went on vacation.

***Nonmaterial culture* consists of the abstract or intangible human creations of society that influence people's behaviour.** Language, beliefs, values, rules of behaviour, family patterns, and political systems are examples of nonmaterial culture. A central component of nonmaterial culture is *beliefs*—the mental acceptance or conviction that certain things are true or real. Beliefs may be based on tradition, faith, experience, scientific research, or some combination of these. Faith in a supreme being, that education is the key to success, and that smoking causes cancer are examples of beliefs. We also have beliefs in items of material culture. For example, most students believe that computers are the key to technological advancement and progress.

Cultural Universals

Because all humans face the same basic needs (such as food, clothing, and shelter), we engage in similar activities that contribute to our survival. Anthropologist George Murdock (1945:124) compiled a list of over seventy ***cultural universals*—customs and practices that occur across all societies.** His categories included appearance (such as bodily adornment and hairstyles), activities (such as sports, dancing, games, joking, and visiting), social institutions (such as family, law, and religion), and customary practices (such as cooking, folklore, gift giving, and hospitality). These general customs and practices may be present in all cultures, but their specific forms vary from one group to another and from one time to another within the same group. For example, while telling jokes may be a universal practice, what is considered a joke in one society may be an insult in another.

How do sociologists view cultural universals? In terms of their functions, cultural universals are useful because they ensure the smooth and continuous operation of society (Radcliffe-Brown, 1952). A society must meet basic human needs by providing food, shelter, and some degree of safety for its members so that they will survive. Children and other new members (such as immigrants) must be taught the ways of the group. A society also must settle disputes and deal with people's emotions. All the while, the self-interest of individuals must be balanced with the needs of society as a whole. Cultural universals help to fulfil these important functions of society.

From another perspective, however, cultural universals are not the result of functional necessity; these practices may have been *imposed* by members of one society on members of another. For example, although religion is a culture universal, traditional religious practices of indigenous peoples (those who first live in an area) often have been repressed and even stamped out by subsequent settlers or conquerors who hold political and economic power over them.

COMPONENTS OF CULTURE

Even though the specifics of individual cultures vary widely, all cultures have four common nonmaterial cultural components: symbols, language, values, and norms. These components contribute to both harmony and conflict in a society.

Symbols

A *symbol* is anything that meaningfully represents something else. Culture could not exist without symbols because there would be no shared meanings among people. Symbols can simultaneously produce loyalty and animosity, and love and hate. They help us communicate ideas such as love or patriotism because they express abstract concepts with visible objects.

For example, flags can stand for patriotism, nationalism, school spirit, or religious beliefs held by members of a group or society. They also can be a source of discord and strife among people, as evidenced by recent controversies over the Canadian flag. In 1996, a retired Canadian couple, vacationing in a Florida trailer park, decided to fly the Canadian flag on their trailer. Their neighbours, patriotic Americans, objected so strenuously that the Canadians were forced to take their flag down. One of the neighbours even claimed (mistakenly) that it was against the law to fly a foreign flag on American soil. In 1992, a U.S. marine inadvertently held the Canadian flag upside down during the singing of "O Canada" at a World Series game. Although baseball administrators immediately apologized, Canadians were outraged and insulted by the improper display of our national symbol. This incident had a happy ending for some enterprising individuals who did a booming business at the next World Series game, selling ... you guessed it—upside-down American flags.

Symbols can stand for love (a heart on a valentine), peace (a dove), or hate (a Nazi swastika), just as words can be used to convey these meanings. Symbols also can transmit other types of ideas. A siren is a symbol that denotes an emergency situation and sends the message to clear the way immediately. Gestures also are a symbolic form of communication—a movement of the head, body, or hands can express our ideas or feelings to others. For example, in Canada, pointing toward your chest with your thumb or finger is a symbol for "me." We are also all aware of how useful our middle finger can be in communicating messages to inconsiderate drivers.

Symbols affect our thoughts about gender. The colour of clothing, for example, has different symbolic meaning for females and males. In a study of baby clothing, sociologist Madeline Shakin and her associates (1985) found that 90 percent of the infants they observed were dressed in colours indicating their sex. The colour of the clothing sends implicit messages about how the child should be treated. If a female infant is wearing a pink dress, the message is, "I'm a girl. Say that I'm pretty, not that I'm handsome." Such messages about gender have long-term effects on individual and societal perceptions about how women and men should think and act.

Language

***Language* is a set of symbols that express ideas and enable people to think and communicate with one another.** Verbal (spoken) and nonverbal (written or gestured) language help us describe reality. One of our most important human attributes is the ability to use language to share our experiences, feelings, and knowledge with others. Language can create visual

Symbols are powerful sources of communication. What messages do these two pictures communicate to you?

images in our head, such as "the kittens look like little cotton balls" (Samovar and Porter, 1991a). Language also allows people to distinguish themselves from outsiders and maintain group boundaries and solidarity (Farb, 1973).

Language is not solely a human characteristic. Other animals use sounds, gestures, touch, and smell to communicate with one another, but they use signals with fixed meanings that are limited to the immediate situation (the present) and cannot encompass past or future situations. For example, chimpanzees can use elements of Standard American Sign Language and manipulate physical objects to make "sentences," but they are not physically endowed with the vocal apparatus needed to form the consonants required for verbal language. As a result, nonhuman animals cannot transmit the more complex aspects of culture to their offspring. Humans have a unique ability to manipulate symbols to express abstract concepts and rules and thus to create and transmit culture from one generation to the next.

Language and Gender What is the relationship between language and gender? What cultural assumptions about women and men does language reflect? Scholars have suggested several ways in which language and gender are intertwined:

- The English language ignores women by using the masculine form to refer to human beings in general (Basow, 1992). For example, the word *man* is used generically in words like *chairman* and *mankind*, which allegedly include both men and women. However, *man* can mean either "all human beings" or "a male human being" (Miller and Swift, 1993:71).
- Use of the pronouns *he* and *she* affects our thinking about gender. Pronouns show the gender of the person we *expect* to be in a particular occupation. For instance, nurses, secretaries, and schoolteachers usually are referred to as *she*, while doctors, engineers, electricians, and presidents are referred to as *he* (Baron, 1986).
- A language-based predisposition to think about women in sexual terms reinforces the notion that women are sexual objects. Women often are described by terms such as *fox*, *broad*, *bitch*, *babe*, or *doll*, which ascribe childlike or even petlike characteristics to them. By contrast, men have performance pressures placed on them by being defined in terms of their sexual prowess, such as *dude*, *stud*, and *hunk* (Baker, 1993).

Gender in language has been debated and studied extensively in recent years, and greater awareness and some changes have been the result. For example, the desire of many women to have Ms. (rather than *Miss* or *Mrs.*, which indicated their marital status) precede their names has received a degree of acceptance in public life and the media (Tannen, 1995). Many organizations and publications have established guidelines for the use of nonsexist language and have changed titles such as *chairman* to *chair* or *chairperson*. "Men Working" signs in many areas have been replaced with ones that say "People Working" (Epstein, 1988:227). Some occupations have been given "genderless" titles, such as *firefighter* and *flight attendant* (Maggio, 1988). Yet many people resist change, arguing the English language is being ruined (Epstein, 1988).

Unlike English, in which nouns can be feminine, masculine, and sometimes neuter, the Aboriginal language Ojibwa is not preoccupied with gender and divides nouns into two classes—the animate and inanimate. In addition, only one pronoun is used for *he* or *she*. To develop a more inclusive and equitable society, many scholars suggest that a more inclusive language is needed (see Basow, 1992). Perhaps we can to look to our First Nations languages for examples of how to create a more gender-inclusive English language.

LANGUAGE, RACE, AND ETHNICITY Language may create and reinforce our perceptions about race and ethnicity by transmitting preconceived ideas about the superiority of one category of people over another. Let's look at a few images conveyed by words in the English language in regard to race/ethnicity.

- Words may have more than one meaning and create and reinforce negative images. Terms such as *blackhearted* (malevolent) and expressions such as "a black mark" (a detrimental fact) and "Chinaman's chance of success" (unlikely to succeed) give the words *black* and *Chinaman* negative associations and derogatory imagery. By contrast, expressions such as "That's white of you" and "The good guys wear white hats" reinforce positive associations with the colour white.
- Overtly derogatory terms such as *nigger*, *kike*, *gook*, *honkey*, *chink*, *squaw*, *savage*, and other racial/ethnic slurs have been "popularized" in movies, music, comedy routines, and so on. Such derogatory terms often are used in conjunction with physical threats against persons.
- Words frequently are used to create or reinforce perceptions about a group. For example, native peoples have been referred to as "savages" and described as "primitive," while blacks have been described as "uncivilized," "cannibalistic," and "pagan."

In addition to these concerns about the English language, problems also arise when more than one language is involved.

Language Diversity in Canada

Language has been referred to as the keystone to culture because it is the chief vehicle for understanding and experiencing one's culture (McVey and Kalbach, 1995). In recent decades, Canada has experienced rapid changes in language and culture.

BILINGUALISM In 1969 the federal government passed the Official Languages Act, making both French and English official languages. In doing so, Canada officially became a bilingual society. However, this action by no means resolved the very complex issues regarding language in our society. Canada is a linguistically diverse society consisting of Aboriginal languages, French and English, and heritage languages. Canada's two charter language groups are often referred to as "two solitudes" (Hiller, 1995). How is it possible to have a unified country when groups of people within a society cannot talk to each other? According to a recent census, 67 percent of Canadians speak English only, another 14 percent speak French only, and slightly more than 17 percent are bilingual. Only 2 percent, or 473,475 Canadians, indicated they lacked the skills to converse in either French or English (Statistics Canada, 1997d). Although French-versus-English language issues have been a significant source of conflict, bilingualism remains a distinct component of Canadian culture. As one Canadian said to the Citizen's Forum on Canada's Future:

> Most people I talk to do not want a divided country. Nor do they deny the right of Québécois to preserve their language and culture ... having two languages doesn't split up the country, it *makes* it. Without Quebec and their French language I would feel lost as a Canadian. (1991:55)

Although it may be easy for members of the English-speaking majority to display such acceptance and tolerance of bilingualism, francophones are concerned that this policy is not enough to save their culture. Efforts to protect French language and culture have resulted in some exclusionary policies. For example, Quebec's controversial Bill 178 specifies that exterior signs on stores, restaurants, and offices are to be in French only. As the following incident demonstrates, this law has increased the tension between our two charter linguistic groups:

> I went to meet some friends at a downtown bar ... As I arrived, a solemn middle-aged man was taking photographs of the blackboard mounted on the outside steps. He was intent on a notice scrawled in chalk on the board: Today's Special—Ploughman's Lunch. This notice happened to be a blatant violation of Quebec's Bill 178 ... and the photographer was one of a number of self-appointed vigilantes who ... dutifully search the downtown streets for English language or bilingual commercial signs ... They photograph the evidence and then lodge an official complaint with the Commission de Protection de la Langue Française. (Richler, 1992:1)

Plainly, Québécois feel that their language and culture are threatened and that defensive strategies such as Bill 178 are essential to the survival of both.

Aboriginal Languages Canada's Aboriginal languages are many and diverse. These languages, tangible symbols of Aboriginal culture and group identity, are tremendously important to Canada's indigenous people. Aboriginal people's cultures are *oral cultures*, that is, cultures that are transmitted through speech rather than the written word. Many Aboriginal stories can be passed on only in the Aboriginal language in which they originated. Language is not only a means of communication, but also a link that connects people with their past and grounds their social, emotional, and spiritual vitality. Although loss of language doesn't necessarily lead to the death of a culture, it can severely handicap the transmission of that culture (Norris, 1998:8). For Aboriginal people, huge losses have already occurred as a result of the assimilist strategies of missionaries and Jesuit priests running residential schools. At these schools Aboriginal children were forbidden to speak their language. An Ojibway woman from northwestern Ontario describes her experience:

> Boarding school was supposed to be a place where you forgot everything about being Anishinabe. And our language too. But I said, "I'm going to talk to myself"—and that's what I did, under my covers—talked to myself in Anishinabe. If we were caught, the nuns would make us stand in a corner and repeat over and over, "I won't speak my language." (Ross, 1996:122)

Despite the efforts of Canadian Aboriginal peoples to maintain their languages, these languages are among the most endangered in the world. Only three of the approximately fifty Aboriginal languages in Canada are in a healthy state; many have already disappeared or are near extinction. In the 1996 census, only 26 percent of Aboriginal persons reported an Aboriginal language as their first language and even fewer spoke it at home (Norris, 1998). Loss of their languages will have a profound effect on the cultural survival of Aboriginal peoples. According to Eli Taylor, a Dakota-Sioux from Manitoba:

> Our native language embodies a value system about how we ought to live and relate to each other ... Now if you destroy our language, you not only break down these relationships, but you also destroy other aspects of our Indian way of life and culture, especially those that describe man's connection with nature, the Great Spirit, the order of things. Without our language, we will cease to exist as a separate people. (Fleras and Elliott, 1992:151)

Aboriginal elders, teachers, and other leaders are well aware of the gravity of the language situation and have taken steps to preserve the few remaining indigenous languages. These include the introduction of Aboriginal language courses in schools and universities, Aboriginal media programming, and the recording of elders' stories, songs, and accounts of history in Aboriginal languages (Ponting, 1997). According to social analyst Mary Jane Norris, if these languages vanish, "they take with them unique ways of looking at the world, explaining the unknown and making sense of life" (Norris, 1998:8).

Heritage Language Groups The term *heritage language groups* refers to those groups whose language is not English, French, or one of the Aboriginal languages. In recent decades Canada has experienced a number of significant changes in the composition of its heritage languages, largely as a result of increased immigration. For example, the number of speakers of Asian languages has increased sharply (Statistics Canada, 1997f).

Theoretical Interpretations of Language Diversity

How do the many new languages introduced into Canada via increased immigration affect Canadian culture? From the functionalist perspective, a shared language is essential to a common culture; language is a stabilizing force in society and is an important means of cultural transmission. Through language, children learn about their cultural heritage and develop a sense of personal identity in relation to their group. Functionalists would therefore view language diversity as potentially detrimental to Canadian culture.

Conflict theorists view language as a source of power and social control; it perpetuates inequalities between people and between groups because words are used (intentionally or not) to "keep people in their place." For example, derogatory messages such as the rap lyrics "Beat that bitch with a bat" on T-shirts may devalue women and desensitize people toward violence (Gelman, 1993). As linguist Deborah Tannen (1993:B5) has suggested, "The devastating group hatreds that result in so much suffering in our own country and around the world are related in origin to the small intolerances in our everyday conversations—our readiness to attribute good intentions to ourselves and bad intentions to others." Furthermore, different languages themselves are associated with inequalities. Consider this Aboriginal language instructor's comments on the lure of the English language, "It's to do with the perception of power. People associate English with prestige and power. We don't have movies in [native language], we don't have hardcover books ... or neon signs in our language" (Martin, 1996:A8). Language, then, is a reflection of our feelings and values.

Values

***Values* are collective ideas about what is right or wrong, good or bad, and desirable or undesirable in a particular culture** (Williams, 1970:27). Values do not dictate which behaviours are appropriate and which ones are not, but they provide us with the criteria by which we evaluate people, objects, and events. Values typically come in pairs of positive and negative values, such as being brave or cowardly, hardworking or lazy. Since we use values to justify our behaviour, we tend to defend them staunchly (Kluckhohn, 1961).

Core Canadian Values Do we have shared values in Canada? Sociologists disagree about the extent to which all people in this country share a core set of values. Functionalists tend to believe that shared values are essential for societies and have conducted most of the research on core values. Between November 1990 and July 1991, approximately 400,000 Canadians participated in the Citizen's Forum on Canada's Future. The participants focused a great deal on what it meant to be Canadian. The following list summarizes the core values that emerged most strongly from participants in all regions of Canada:

1. *Equality and fairness in a democratic society*. Equality and fairness were not seen as mutually exclusive values.
2. *Consultation and dialogue*. Canadians view themselves as people who settle their differences peaceably and in a consultative rather than confrontational manner. The view was widely held that Canadians must work together to solve their problems and remedy the apparent lack of understanding between different groups, regions, and provinces.
3. *Accommodation and tolerance*. The forum participants recognized the existence of different groups in Canadian society and their need to sustain their own culture while attaching themselves to the country's society, values, and institutions.
4. *Support for diversity*. This diversity has a number of facets, including linguistic, regional, ethnic, and cultural differences. Again, the respondents spoke of the difficulty of achieving a balance between a multicultural Canada and a secure sense of a Canadian identity.
5. *Compassion and generosity*. Forum participants deeply valued Canada's compassion and generosity as exemplified in our universal and extensive social services, health-care and pension systems, immigration policies, and commitment to regional economic equalization.
6. *Canada's natural beauty*. Canada's unspoiled natural beauty was identified as very important. The forum also recognized that this may be threatened by inadequate attention to environmental protection issues.

7. *Canada's world image: Commitment to freedom, peace, and nonviolent change*. Canada's role as a nonviolent, international peacekeeper was summed up in one respondent's comments: "Canada should not try to be a world power like the U.S.A. We should be the same kind of nation that we have always been, a peaceful and quiet nation" (1991:44).

More recently, sociologist and pollster Michael Adams examined Canadian social values as we entered the new millennium. According to Adams, the consensus on social values is breaking down as Canadians focus more on personal freedom and self-fulfilment and less on demographic factors such as age, gender, and social class.

According to Adams, when Canadians are divided according to their social values, twelve distinct social value groups emerge: three groups among those over 50, four groups among the baby boomers (aged 30 to 49), and five groups of Canadians under 30 (Generation X). The fact that there are more social value groups among the Generation Xers reflects a trend toward increasingly diverse Canadian values. Adams (1998) attributes this trend largely to the effects of advances in technology such as computers and the Internet, which allow Canadians to cross cultural boundaries and explore a diverse spectrum of values.

VALUE CONTRADICTIONS All societies have value contradictions. ***Value contradictions* are values that conflict with one another or are mutually exclusive** (achieving one makes it difficult, if not impossible, to achieve another). For example, core values of morality and humanitarianism may conflict with values of individual achievement and success. In the 1990s, for example, humanitarian values reflected in welfare and other government aid programs have come into conflict with values emphasizing hard work and personal achievement. Similarly, despite the fact that 84 percent of Canadians feel that "people who are poor have a right to an adequate income to live on" (Bibby, 1995), they have also shown strong support for governments that have dramatically cut budgets in order to reduce financial deficits. Can you identify the value contradictions in the list of Canadian core values proposed by the Citizen's Forum?

IDEAL VERSUS REAL CULTURE What is the relationship between values and human behaviour? Sociologists stress that a gap always exists between ideal culture and real culture in a society.

***Ideal culture* refers to the values and standards of behaviour that people in a society profess to hold. *Real culture* refers to the values and standards of behaviour that people actually follow.** For example, we may claim to be law-abiding (ideal cultural value) but smoke marijuana (real cultural behaviour), or we may regularly drive over the speed limit but think of ourselves as "good citizens."

Most of us are not completely honest about how well we adhere to societal values. In a study known as the "Garbage Project," household waste was analyzed to determine the rate of alcohol consumption in a U.S. city. People were asked about their level of alcohol consumption, and in some areas of the city, very low levels of alcohol use were reported. However, when household garbage was analyzed, researchers found that in more than 80 percent of these households some beer had been consumed, and in more than half occupants threw out eight or more empty beer cans a week (Haviland, 1993:11–12). Obviously, this study shows a discrepancy between ideal cultural values and people's actual behaviour.

Norms

Values provide ideals or beliefs about behaviour but do not state explicitly how we should behave. Norms, on the other hand, do have specific behavioural expectations. ***Norms* are established rules of behaviour or standards of conduct.** *Prescriptive norms* state what behaviour is appropriate or acceptable. For example, persons making a certain amount of money are expected to file a tax return and pay any taxes they owe. Norms based on custom direct us to open a door for a person carrying a heavy load. By contrast, *proscriptive norms* state what behaviour is inappropriate or unacceptable. Laws that prohibit us from driving over the speed limit and "good manners" that preclude reading a newspaper during class are examples. Prescriptive and proscriptive norms operate at all levels of society, from our everyday actions to the formulation of laws.

FORMAL AND INFORMAL NORMS Not all norms are of equal importance; those that are most crucial are formalized. *Formal norms* are written down and involve

BOX 2.2 SOCIOLOGY AND TECHNOLOGY

INTERNET CYBERCULTURE

> So I was talking on the phone with my mother out in Minnesota the other day, and she sounded upset. "What's wrong, Mom?" I asked. "Well," she said, "I've been playing bridge on the Internet with three Frenchmen and they keep speaking French to each other and I can't understand them." When I chuckled at the thought of my card-shark mom playing bridge on the net, she took a little umbrage. "Don't laugh," she said. "I was playing bridge with someone in Siberia the other day." (Friedman, 1998:A10)

Is there a new culture developing in cyberspace? Apparently so. The term *cyberculture* has been coined to describe this new form of popular culture. Cyberculture, which makes up a large portion of the World Wide Web, has been described as the melting pot of the world's diversity. The Internet links the world as never before, creating a global village where people from around the world can communicate with a simple click of the mouse. Through various Internet services such as chat rooms, newsgroups, and e-mail, people can connect with anyone, almost anywhere in the world. This allows for the sharing of ideas and the exchange of both material and nonmaterial cultural products.

Recent surveys report that Canada is at the leading edge of technology adoption. Among North American and European countries, Canada has the highest level of home PC use, and Canadians and Americans lead the pack for the rate of acquiring home Internet access. As a result of these advances in communication technologies, people can travel *virtually* in a cyberculture made up of networks, projects, and communities with people they have never met, in cultures they have never visited.

specific punishments for violators. Laws are the most common type of formal norms; they have been codified and may be enforced by sanctions. ***Sanctions* are rewards for appropriate behaviour or penalties for inappropriate behaviour.** Examples of *positive sanctions* include praise, honours, or medals for conformity to specific norms. *Negative sanctions* range from mild disapproval to life imprisonment.

Norms considered to be less important are referred to as *informal norms*—unwritten standards of behaviour understood by people who share a common identity. When individuals violate informal norms, other people may apply informal sanctions. *Informal sanctions* are not clearly defined and can be applied by any member of a group (such as frowning at someone or making a negative comment or gesture).

FOLKWAYS Norms are also classified according to their relative social importance. ***Folkways* are informal norms or everyday customs that may be violated without serious consequences within a particular culture** (Sumner, 1959/1906). They provide rules for conduct but are not considered to be essential to society's survival. In Canada, folkways include using underarm deodorant, brushing one's teeth, and wearing appropriate clothing for a specific occasion. Folkways can vary considerably from one society to another and are not often enforced; when they are enforced, the resulting sanctions tend to be informal and relatively mild.

MORES Other norms are considered highly essential to the stability of society. ***Mores*** (pronounced MOR-ays) **are strongly held norms with moral and ethical connotations that may not be violated without serious consequences in a particular culture.** Since mores are based on cultural values and are considered crucial for the well-being of the group, violators are subject to more severe negative sanctions (such as ridicule, loss of employment, or imprisonment) than

BOX 2.2

CONTINUED

According to sociologist Michael Adams, "Thanks to virtual travel through the globalization of culture, teenagers in Toronto, Miami and Kiev often have more in common with each other than they do with their own parents" (1998:32).

Is this universal cultural connection a good thing? What possible effects do you foresee for Canadian culture? On the positive side, this new Internet culture allows for the exchange of ideas and makes foreign cultures seem familiar. This can only serve to increase global cultural understanding and tolerance.

However, on the negative side, chances are we can expect the significant influence of U.S. culture on Canadian culture to become even more pronounced through this new form of popular culture. Furthermore, the Internet is a virtually uncensored forum for free speech. Anyone with Internet access can publish their own personal views—some of which may be racist, sexist, exploitative, or destructive. These ideas can be disseminated quickly and easily in cyberspace.

Does cyberculture open up the world? Experts on Internet culture remind us that although cyberculture may be an increasingly significant part of mainstream popular culture in Canada, we may be thinking in ethnocentric terms when assuming that this resource is readily available in all cultures. While industrialized countries are exploring sophisticated uses of the Internet, more than half of the world's population has never used a telephone.

Sources: Buckler, 1996; Hansen, 1995; and Adams, 1998.

are those who fail to adhere to folkways. The strongest mores are referred to as taboos. ***Taboos* are mores so strong that their violation is considered to be extremely offensive and even unmentionable.** Violation of taboos is punishable by the group or even, according to certain belief systems, by a supernatural force. The incest taboo, which prohibits sexual or marital relations between certain categories of kin, is an example of a nearly universal taboo.

LAWS ***Laws* are formal, standardized norms that have been enacted by legislatures and are enforced by formal sanctions.** Laws may be either civil or criminal. *Civil law* deals with disputes among persons or groups. Persons who lose civil suits may encounter negative sanctions such as having to pay compensation to the other party or being ordered to stop certain conduct. *Criminal law*, on the other hand, deals with public safety and well-being. When criminal laws are violated, fines and prison sentences are the most likely negative sanctions.

Changes in law often reflect changes in culture. In the 1990s, increasing awareness of hate crimes based on racial/ethnic, religious, or sexual-orientation biases has led to increasing pressure on the federal government to establish uniform reporting requirements and to increase penalties for hate crimes.

While culture may contribute to permanence and stability, changes in material and nonmaterial culture also tend to bring about dramatic changes in society.

CULTURAL CHANGE AND DIVERSITY

We have examined the nature of culture within society, the defining components of culture, and the

BOX 2.3 SOCIOLOGY AND MEDIA

CULTURAL CONFUSION: ADVERTISING—THE GLOBAL MARKETING HALL OF SHAME

Selling a product in a foreign culture requires that attention be paid to cultural differences. The world's smartest advertising minds have sometimes forgotten to do so and, as the examples below demonstrate, they have consequently come off as village idiots. Costly—often amusing—mistakes have been made by advertisers who have misread cultural attitudes, sensitivities, or superstitions, or something has simply been lost in the translation to the global marketplace. Here are a few examples:

- When the makers of Coca-Cola were launching their drink in China, they found a phrase that sounded perfect: "Ko-kou-ke-la." After printing thousands of signs, the Coke masterminds discovered that they had christened their drink "Bite the wax tadpole."
- Carmaker Ford has faced several problems playing the name game. Sales of the Pinto petered out in Brazil because it turns out the word is slang for "tiny male genitals." When this was discovered, Ford pried all the nameplates off and substituted Corcel, which means "horse."
- Ford also introduced a low-cost truck to some less-developed countries named the Fiera, a word that means "ugly old woman" in Spanish.
- General Motors introduced its Chevy Nova in South America unaware that "no va" means "It won't go" in Spanish.
- Most North Americans know the slogan for Kentucky Fried Chicken as "Finger-lickin' good." In China, after translation, the slogan became "Eat your fingers off."
- The American Dairy Council ran a "Got milk?" campaign that featured celebrities sporting milk moustaches. In converting the message to Spanish, the Council ended up asking its Mexican consumers, "Are you lactating?"

forcefulness of popular culture. Cultures do not generally remain static, however. There are many forces working toward change and diversity. (For example, the Internet links material and nonmaterial cultures throughout the world, thus accelerating cultural change; see Box 2.2.) Some societies and individuals adapt to this change, while others suffer culture shock and succumb to ethnocentrism.

Cultural Change

Societies continually experience cultural change, at both material and nonmaterial levels. Moreover, a change in one area frequently triggers a change in other areas. For example, the personal computer has changed how we work and how we think about work; today, many people work at home—away from the immediate gaze of a supervisor. Ultimately, computer technology may change the nature of boss–worker relations. Such changes are often set in motion by discovery, invention, and diffusion.

***Discovery* is the process of learning about something previously unknown or unrecognized.** Historically, discovery involved unearthing natural elements or existing realities, such as "discovering" fire or the true shape of the earth. Today, discovery most often results from scientific research. For example, discovery of a polio vaccine virtually eliminated one of the major childhood diseases. A future discovery of a cure for cancer or the common cold could result in longer and more productive lives for many people.

As more discoveries have occurred, people have been able to reconfigure existing material and nonmaterial cultural items through invention. ***Invention* is the process of reshaping existing cultural items into a new form.** Guns, video games, airplanes, and the Charter of Rights and Freedoms

BOX 2.3

CONTINUED

- "Come alive with the Pepsi Generation" was a perfectly good slogan—until it got translated into Taiwanese as: "Pepsi will bring your ancestors back from the dead."
- The makers of Coors Light beer hired an agency to develop promotional materials aimed at Hispanics in the United States. In trying to translate the ad's catchphrase "Turn it loose" into Spanish, a copywriter ended up inviting customers to "Drink Coors and get diarrhea."

The lack of cultural awareness of corporate North America is obvious in the following blunders:

- When Coca-Cola introduced its two-litre bottles in Japan, it was unaware of the fact that few Japanese refrigerators are roomy enough to store such a large bottle.
- Trying to market its cake mixes in Japan in the 1960s, Betty Crocker discovered that most Japanese homes were missing a necessary ingredient: an oven.
- When McDonald's ventured into China, corporate mascot Ronald McDonald was in tow to clown around at the launch. Talk about a bozo move: to the Chinese, the clown is a symbol of death.
- A toothpaste company ran a commercial in Southeast Asia proclaiming that its product helped whiten teeth. The problem was that the people in the local target market were in the habit of chewing betel nut in order to achieve darkly stained teeth—a social sign of prestige.

are examples of inventions that positively or negatively affect our lives today.

When diverse groups of people come into contact, they begin to adapt one another's discoveries, inventions, and ideas for their own use. ***Diffusion* is the transmission of cultural items or social practices from one group or society to another** through such means as exploration, military endeavours, the media, tourism, and immigration. To illustrate, consider the comments of former Indian cabinet minister I.K. Gujral:

> My granddaughter is 4, she is always talking about bubble gum, not Indian food, or she says, "I don't like Pepsi, I like Coke." She even speaks English more than Hindi. I asked her one day why she doesn't speak to me in Hindi, and then she went to her mother and asked: "Doesn't grandfather speak English?" The other day my granddaughter said she wanted pizza. So her grandmother said she would make her a pizza. My granddaughter said, "No, no, I want Pizza Hut." (Friedman, 1998:A10)

As this example demonstrates, in today's "shrinking globe," cultural diffusion moves at a very rapid pace as countries continually seek new markets for their products (Friedman, 1998:A10). (See Box 2.3.)

When a change occurs in the material culture of a society, nonmaterial culture must adapt to that change. Frequently, this rate of change is uneven, resulting in a gap between the two. Sociologist William F. Ogburn (1966/1922) referred to this disparity as ***cultural lag*—a gap between the technical development of a society and its moral and legal institutions** (G. Marshall, 1994). The failure of nonmaterial culture to keep pace with material culture is linked to social conflict and problems in society. In Canada, medical treatment is a right of Canadian citizenship. In contrast, although the United States has some of the most advanced medical technology in the world, there is a lack of consensus regarding to whom it should be available. The debate centres on whether medical care is a privilege for which people must pay or a right of U.S. citizenship (or noncitizen residency). The number of Americans *not* covered by medical insurance (about 35 million) exceeds the entire population of Canada. (See Chapter 10, "Health and Health Care.")

Cultural Diversity

Cultural diversity refers to the wide range of cultural differences found between and within nations. Cultural diversity between countries may be the result of natural circumstances (such as climate and geography) or social circumstances (such as level of technology and composition of the population). Some countries—such as Sweden—are referred to as *homogeneous societies*, meaning they include people who share a common culture and are typically from similar social, religious, political, and economic backgrounds. By contrast, other countries—including Canada—are referred to as *heterogeneous societies*, meaning they include people who are dissimilar in regard to social characteristics such as nationality, race, ethnicity, class, occupation, or education (see Figure 2.1).

Christmas trees and other holiday symbols exemplify the way in which elements from diverse cultures take on new meanings through the process of diffusion. For instance, notice the European-looking Joseph and Mary, as well as the Greek columns, in this depiction of a manger in Bethlehem. Even the traditional date chosen to celebrate the birth of Jesus (to Christians, the "light of the world") is an adaptation of an ancient pagan celebration of the winter solstice (when the light of the returning sun conquers the darkness of winter).

Immigration contributes to cultural diversity in a society. Throughout its history, Canada has been a nation of immigrants. Over the past 150 years, more than 13 million immigrants have arrived here. Immigration can cause feelings of frustration and hostility, especially in people who feel threatened by the changes that large numbers of immigrants may produce (Fleras and Elliott, 1996). Often, people are intolerant of those who are different from themselves. When societal tensions rise, people may look for others on whom they can place blame—or single out persons because they are the "other," the "outsider," the one who does not "belong." Sociologist Adrienne Shadd described her experience of being singled out as an "other":

> Routinely I am asked, "Where are you from?" or "What nationality are you?" as if to be Black, you have to come from somewhere else. I respond that I'm "Canadian." ... I play along. The scenario usually unfolds as follows:
>
> "But where are you *originally* from?"
>
> "Canada."
>
> "Oh, *you* were born here. But where are your parents from?"
>
> "Canada"
>
> "But what about your grandparents?"
>
> As individuals delve further into my genealogy to find out where I'm "really" from, their frustration levels rise.
>
> "No, uh, I mean ... your *people*. Where do your people come from?"
>
> At this point, questioners are totally annoyed and/or frustrated. After all, Black people in Canada are supposed to come from "the islands," aren't they? For those of us living in large urban centres, there are constant reminders that we are not regarded as truly "Canadian." (1994:11)

FIGURE 2.1 Heterogeneity of Canadian Society

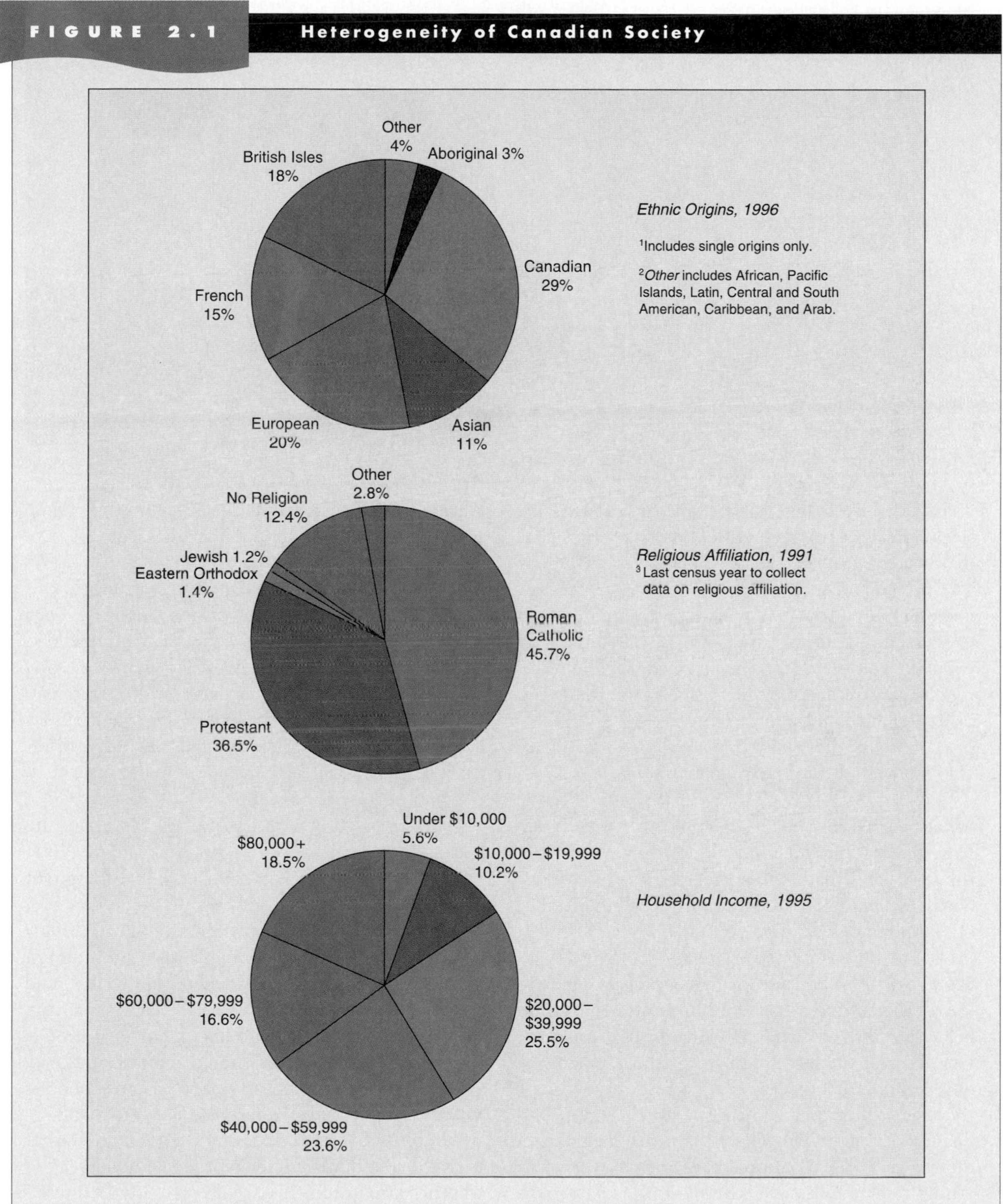

Throughout history, Canada has been heterogeneous. Today, Canada is represented by a wide variety of social categories, including our religious affiliations, income levels, and ethnic origins.

Sources: "Ethnic Origins, 1996," adapted with permission from "Total Population by Ethnic Categories and Sex, for Canada, Provinces, Territories and Census Metropolitan Areas, 1996 Census," Cat. no. 930026XDB96002; "Household Income, 1995," adapted with permission from the Statistics Canada Web site at www.statcan.ca/english/census96/may12/t6can.htm.

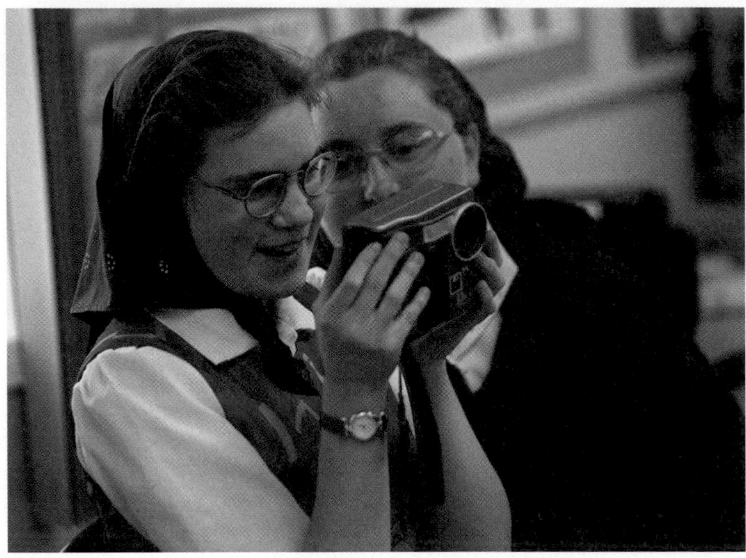

Technology and tradition meet at the Fairholme Hutterite Colony as these young women try out a new digital camera at school.

Have you ever been made to feel like an "outsider"? Each of us receives cultural messages that may make us feel good or bad about ourselves or may give us the perception that we "belong" or "do not belong." However, in heterogeneous societies such as Canada, cultural diversity is inevitable. In Canada, this diversity has created some unique problems in terms of defining and maintaining our distinct Canadian culture.

Canadian Culture

It has been suggested that complex societies are more likely to produce subcultures. This is certainly the case in Canada where regional, ethnic, class, language, and religious subcultures combine to produce a highly diverse society.

SUBCULTURES A ***subculture*** **is a group of people who share a distinctive set of cultural beliefs and behaviours that differ in some significant way from that of the larger society.** Although members of subcultures participate in the mainstream society, they tend to associate with one another more frequently and more personally than with members of other groups. Occupational groups such as lawyers; ethnic populations such as Italian Canadians; religious groups such as Orthodox Jews; people living in small rural communities: all of these are examples of subcultures. All of these groups will develop unique beliefs, norms, and values. We next look at one subculture—the Hutterites—to see how this group interacts with the dominant Canadian culture.

The Hutterites This subculture has fought for many years to maintain its distinct identity. They are the largest family-type communal grouping in the Western world, with over 20,000 members living in approximately 200 settlements (Curtis and Lambert, 1994). The Hutterites live on farms in Western Canada and the United States where they practise their religious beliefs and maintain a relatively closed social network.

The Hutterites are considered a subculture because their values, norms, and appearance differ significantly from those of members of the dominant culture. They have a strong faith in God and reject worldly concerns. Their core values include the joy of work, the primacy of the home, faithfulness, thriftiness, tradition, and humility. Hutterites hold conservative views of the family, believing that women are subordinate to men, birth control is unacceptable, and wives should remain at home. Children are cherished and seen as an economic asset: they help with the farming and other work.

Hutterite life is centred on the community rather than the individual. Significant life decsions such as whether a high school graduate will attend university are made on the basis of what is best for the entire community. All aspects of day-to-day life—right down to eating every meal in a community hall—are based on sharing. Members of this group

Members of white extremist countercultures such as these neo-Nazi skinheads in Germany speak an international language of intolerance about those who are different from themselves.

have communal rather than private property; nobody is permitted to individually own as much as a pair of shoes (Curtis and Lambert, 1994). The Hutterites also have a distinctive mode of dress which makes this subculture readily identifiable in Canadian society.

The Hutterites are aware that their values are distinct from those of most other Canadians and that they look different from other people; these differences, though, provide them with a collective identity and make them feel close to one another (Peter, 1987). However, the Hutterites do not attempt to achieve complete social isolation from the wider society. Although this subculture strictly adheres to centuries-old traditions, the Hutterites don't hesitate to take advantage of the twentieth century (Lyons, 1998). They are successful farmers who trade with people in the surrounding communities and buy modern farm machinery from outsiders. They also read newspapers, use home computers, and utilize the services of non-Hutterite professionals (Curtis and Lambert, 1994).

COUNTERCULTURES Some subcultures actively oppose the larger society. A ***counterculture* is a group that strongly rejects dominant societal values and norms and seeks alternative lifestyles** (Yinger, 1960, 1982). Young people are most likely to join countercultural groups, perhaps because younger persons generally have less invested in the existing culture. Examples of countercultures include the beatniks of the 1950s, the flower children of the 1960s, the drug enthusiasts of the 1970s, and members of nonmainstream religious sects, or cults.

One of the countercultures closely associated with hate crimes is the skinheads, sometimes referred to as "neo-Nazi skinheads," who have been present in North America since the early 1980s. Skinheads primarily are young, white, working-class males who express group identity by wearing boots, jeans, suspenders, green flight jackets, and chains, and by shaving their heads or sporting "burr" haircuts. Core values of "hard-core" skinheads include racial group superiority, patriotism, a belief in the traditional roles of women and men, and justification of physical violence as a means of expressing anger toward immigrants, gay men and lesbians, people of colour, and Jews (Wooden, 1995). Some skinhead groups tend to engage in relatively spontaneous outbursts of violence; others are highly organized and motivated. These groups select leaders, hold regular meetings, distribute racist propaganda, and attend rallies sponsored by groups like the Ku Klux Klan and the White Aryan Resistance (Barrett, 1987).

Culture Shock

***Culture shock* is the disorientation that people feel when they encounter cultures radically different from their own** and believe they cannot depend on their own taken-for-granted assumptions about life. When people travel to another society, they may not know how to respond to that setting. For example, Napoleon Chagnon (1992) described his initial shock at seeing the Yanomamö (pronounced yah-noh-MAH-mah) tribe of South America for the first time in 1964.

The Yanomamö (also referred as the "Yanomami") are a tribe of about 20,000 South American Indians who live in the rain forest. Although Chagnon travelled in a small aluminum motorboat for three days to reach these people, he was not prepared for the sight that met his eyes when he arrived:

> I looked up and gasped to see a dozen burly, naked, sweaty, hideous men staring at us down the shafts of their drawn arrows. Immense wads of green tobacco were stuck between their lower teeth and lips, making them look even more hideous, and strands of dark-green slime dripped from their nostrils—strands so long that they reached down to their pectoral muscles or drizzled down their chins and stuck to their chests and bellies. We arrived as the men were blowing *ebene*, a hallucinogenic drug, up their noses. As I soon learned, one side effect of the drug is a runny nose. The mucus becomes saturated with the drug's green powder, and the Yanomamö usually just let it dangle freely from their nostrils to plop off when the strands become too heavy.
>
> Then the stench of decaying vegetation and filth hit me, and I was almost sick to my stomach. I was horrified. What kind of welcome was this for someone who had come to live with these people and learn their way of life—to become friends with them? But when they recognized Barker [a guide], they put their weapons down and returned to their chanting, while keeping a nervous eye on the village entrances. (Chagnon, 1992:12–14)

The Yanomamö have no written language, system of numbers, or calendar. They lead a nomadic lifestyle, carrying everything they own on their backs. They wear no clothes and paint their bodies; the women insert slender sticks through holes in the lower lip and through the pierced nasal septum.

Ethnocentrism

To Canadians, the life of the Yanomamö seems very strange. Many of us tend to make judgments about other cultures in terms of our own culture. ***Ethnocentrism* is the assumption that one's own culture and way of life are superior to all others** (Sumner, 1959/1906). From a functionalist viewpoint, ethnocentrism can serve a positive function in societies by promoting group solidarity and loyalty and by encouraging people to conform to societal norms and values. For example, nationalism and patriotism encourage people to think of their own nation as "the best." International sports competitions, such as the Olympic Games, help to foster this idea.

On the other hand, ethnocentrism can be problematic for societies. Historically, people have regarded outsiders as "barbarians" or "primitive" because they were different. Until recently, for example, few people in the more developed nations have been interested in what indigenous peoples such as the Yanomamö might know; after all, what could nations with high levels of technology possibly learn from tribal cultures? Yet people in such cultures have devised ways to survive and flourish that constitute an important source of knowledge. Some have created methods of farming without irrigation; others hunt, fish, and gather food in the rain forest without destroying the delicate balance that maintains the ecosystem. Ethnocentrism is counterproductive when it blinds us to what other groups have to offer or when it leads to conflict, hostility, and war.

Ethnocentrism can be a problem within societies as well as between them when it leads to social isolation, prejudice, discrimination, and oppression of one group by another. People who have recently arrived in a country where their customs, dress, eating habits, or religious beliefs differ markedly from those of existing residents often find themselves the object of ridicule. Indigenous groups, such as Canada's Aboriginal peoples, also have been the target of ethnocentrism by other groups.

Cultural Relativism

An alternative to ethnocentrism is ***cultural relativism*—the belief that the behaviours and customs of a society must be viewed and analyzed within the context of its own culture.** Cultural relativism is a part of the sociological imagination; researchers

The distinctiveness of the Yanomamö is evident in this picture of tribe members making bread for guests. Do you think you would experience culture shock upon encountering these people for the first time?

must be aware of the customs and norms of the society they are studying and then spell out their background assumptions so that others can spot possible biases in their studies.

Anthropologist Marvin Harris (1974, 1985) uses cultural relativism to explain why cattle, which are viewed as sacred, are not killed and eaten in India, where widespread hunger and malnutrition exist. From an ethnocentric viewpoint, we might conclude that cow worship is the cause of the hunger and poverty in India. However, Harris demonstrates that the Hindu taboo against killing cattle is very important to their economic system. Live cows are more valuable than dead ones because they have more important uses than as a direct source of food. As part of the ecological system, cows consume grasses of little value to humans. Then they produce two valuable resources—oxen (the neutered offspring of cows), to power the ploughs, and manure (for fuel and fertilizer)—as well as milk, floor covering, and leather. As Harris's study reveals, culture must be viewed from the standpoint of those who live in a particular society.

SOCIOLOGICAL ANALYSIS OF CULTURE

Sociologists regard culture as a central ingredient in human behaviour. Although all sociologists share a similar purpose, they typically see culture through somewhat different lenses as they are guided by different theoretical perspectives in their research. What do these perspectives tell us about culture?

Functionalist Perspective

As previously discussed, functionalist perspectives are based on the assumption that society is a stable, orderly system with interrelated parts that serve specific functions. Anthropologist Bronislaw Malinowski (1922) suggested that culture helps people meet their *biological needs* (including food and procreation), *instrumental needs* (including law and education), and *integrative needs* (including religion and art). Societies in which people share a common language and core values are more likely to have consensus and harmony. However, all societies have dysfunctions that produce a variety of societal problems. Inequalities along class, racial, and gender lines often contribute to many of these problems. When a society contains numerous subcultures, discord results from a lack of consensus about core values and a failure to educate everyone about the positive value of cultural diversity. Resolution of such problems must come from families, schools, and other organizations charged with teaching the young and maintaining order and peace.

A strength of the functionalist perspective on culture is its focus on the needs of society and the fact that stability is essential for society's continued survival. A shortcoming is its overemphasis on harmony and cooperation and a lack of acknowledgment of societal factors that contribute to conflict and strife.

Many people in our society face the challenge of preserving a subcultural heritage while sharing in many of the values and norms of the dominant culture. The powwow is a means through which Aboriginal peoples can celebrate their unique culture and pass on cultural traditions to future generations.

Conflict Perspective

Conflict perspectives are based on the assumption that social life is a continuous struggle in which members of powerful groups seek to control scarce resources. Values and norms help create and sustain the privileged position of the powerful in society while excluding others. As early conflict theorist Karl Marx stressed, ideas are cultural creations of a society's most powerful members. According to conflict theorists, most people are not aware that they are being dominated because they have ***false consciousness*, which means that they hold beliefs they think promote their best interests when those beliefs actually are damaging to their interests.** For example, when hate groups "blame" people located at the margins of society for society's problems, they shift attention away from persons in positions of political and economic power. Extremist groups may perpetuate the very "problem" they think exists. Thus, hate crimes may maintain the status quo by protecting the people who are responsible for making important decisions at the highest levels of society (Levin and McDevitt, 1993:234).

A strength of the conflict perspective is that it stresses how cultural values and norms may perpetuate social inequalities. It also highlights the inevitability of change and the constant tension between those who want to maintain the status quo and those who desire change. A limitation is its focus on societal discord and the divisiveness of culture.

Interactionist Perspective

Unlike functionalists and conflict theorists, interactionists do not examine the functions of culture or the ways in which culture helps maintain the status of privileged groups while excluding others from society's benefits. Interactionists instead focus on a microlevel analysis that views society as the sum of all people's interactions. From this perspective, people create, maintain, and modify culture as they go about their everyday activities. Symbols make communication with others possible because they provide us with shared meanings.

According to interactionist theory, people continually negotiate their social realities. Values and norms are not independent realities that automatically determine our behaviour. Instead, we reinterpret them in each social situation we encounter. Hard-core skinheads defy dominant group norms and accept alternative norms of violence as an appropriate response to groups they consider "inferior." This interpretation of reality is reinforced by continual interaction with other hard-core skinhead groups (Farley, 1993a). Canada and the United States are not the only countries to experience these problems; as Box 2.4 points out, Western Europe is experiencing an upswing in hate crimes against "foreigners" by neo-Nazi skinheads and others.

An interactionist approach highlights how people maintain and change culture through their interactions with others. However, interactionism does not provide a systematic framework for analyzing how we shape culture and how it, in turn, shapes us. It also does not provide insight into how shared meanings are developed among people, and it does not take into account the many situations in which there is disagreement on meanings. Where the functional and conflict approaches tend to overemphasize the macrolevel workings of society, the interactionist viewpoint often fails to take into account these larger social structures.

In viewing culture from any of these perspectives, the impact of ethnicity, class, gender, religion, and age must be taken into account in examining people's experiences. In Canada, people have a wide array of experiences because they come from diverse backgrounds. However, simply by living in this country, most of us share some aspects of the dominant culture. This shared culture may be as basic as our use of Canadian currency or postage stamps. It may involve a core curriculum of subjects all children are required to take in elementary school. Shared culture for many individuals is framed at the subcultural level, where, for example, members of a particular church, private club, or other organization may have similar lifestyles and hold values in common with other members of the group.

CULTURAL PATTERNS FOR THE FUTURE

As we have discussed in this chapter, many changes are occurring in our Canadian culture. Increasing cultural diversity can either cause long-simmering racial and ethnic antagonisms to come closer to a boiling point or result in the creation of a truly multicultural society in which diversity is respected and encouraged. According to our ideal culture, Canada will "prosper in diversity." The Multicultural Act has legislated "cultural freedom." However, it has been suggested that this freedom is more "symbolic" than real (Roberts and Clifton, 1990). In the real culture, anti-immigration sentiment has risen in response to the estimated one and a half million newcomers who have arrived in Canada over the past decade. Cultural diversity and global immigration are affecting economic and employment perceptions. Many people accuse newcomers of stealing jobs and overutilizing the social service safety net at the Canadian taxpayer's expense.

In the decades ahead the issue of cultural diversity will increase in importance, especially in schools. Multicultural education that focuses on the contributions of a wide variety of people from different backgrounds will continue to be an issue from kindergarten through university. Public schools have incorporated a number of heritage languages into their curriculum. These schools will face the challenge of embracing widespread cultural diversity while conveying a sense of community and national identity to students.

Culture and Technology

In the twenty-first century, technology will continue to profoundly affect culture. Television and radio, films and videos, and electronic communications (including the telephone, electronic mail, and fax) will continue to accelerate the flow of information and expand cultural diffusion throughout the world. Global communication devices will move images of people's lives, behaviour, and fashions instantaneously among almost all nations (Petersen, 1994). Increasingly, television may become people's window on the world and, in the process, promote greater integration or fragmentation among nations.

BOX 2.4 SOCIOLOGY IN GLOBAL PERSPECTIVE

Hostility Toward Immigrants

Hate crimes have increased in the nations of Western Europe as well as in North America in recent years. Hundreds of thousands of people fleeing economic depression or political oppression in African and Southeast Asian countries have migrated to Western Europe, where attitudes toward immigrants have changed dramatically as their numbers have grown. In many countries, immigrants were previously seen as a source of cheap labour for jobs like ditch digging or street cleaning. Today, however, in many countries (including Canada) some people see immigrant workers as competing for scarce jobs in tough economic times and as draining the welfare, education, and health-care systems. Many immigrants do not have anywhere to go, as indicated by a Liberian man who stowed away on a freighter from Nigeria to get to Western Europe: "I don't know what to do. I can't go back [to Liberia, where civil wars have continued for a number of years]. I walk the street and I'm a dead man" (Darnton, 1993:A1).

In recent years, several political candidates in Western European nations have promised, if they are elected, to expel these "foreigners." A rising tide of racism and hate crimes waged by neo-Nazi skinheads against persons believed to be recent immigrants has bolstered their political claims that something must be done very soon. Hate speech often is based on nostalgia for a bygone era alleged to have been "comfortable, orderly, and virtually all white" (Darnton, 1993:A6). In actuality, changes in the ethnic makeup of Western European nations occurred years ago; Turks, for instance have lived for generations in Germany, as have Pakistanis in Britain.

With dramatic increases in immigration, hate speech and crimes have skyrocketed. In Britain, the increase in tension has been particularly sharp in inner-city neighbourhoods, where most nonwhite immigrants have settled and where unemployment and recession have taken their greatest toll. The grandson of Winston Churchill publicly complained about the "relentless flow of immigrants" and noted that in the future, England would by characterized by "the muezzin ... calling Allah's faithful to the high street mosque for Friday prayers" (Schmidt, 1993:A2).

Other Western European countries, including Spain, Italy, and France, also have seen an increase in hate speech and crimes. For example, in Aravaca, a suburb of Madrid, *rapadas* (urban gang members) have shot undocumented Dominican immigrants living in abandoned buildings. Likewise, in Rome, "Nazi-skins" seek out Africans who sleep in the parks at night and beat them up, as well as burning down the residences of foreigners (Darnton, 1993:A6).

The tide of people crossing borders to flee war, drought, and economic misery "could become the human crisis of our age" (quoted in Darnton, 1993:A6). Globally, then, it is very likely that immigration pressures will continue and that hate crimes will increase.

Integration occurs when there is a widespread acceptance of ideas and items—such as democracy, rock music, blue jeans, and McDonald's hamburgers—among cultures. By contrast, fragmentation occurs when people in one culture disdain the beliefs and actions of other cultures, such as the rejection by fundamentalist Muslims of Western cultural values, especially as shown in North American–based television shows, music, films, and videos. As a force for both cultural integration and

Multiculturalism has been described as a policy that is more symbolic than real. In recent years, Canada has experienced increasing conflict and intergroup hostility as reflected in Aboriginal peoples' struggles to gain recognition as a unique society within Canadian culture and increasing anti-immigrant sentiments among Canadians.

fragmentation, technology will continue to revolutionize communications, but most of the world's population will not participate in this revolution (Petersen, 1994).

A Global Culture?

Some scholars have suggested that a single *global culture*—a worldwide interconnection of material and nonmaterial culture without regard for national identities or boundaries—may emerge in the twenty-first century (see Featherstone, 1990). Others note that global subcultures, such as those of science, business, and diplomacy, already exist and that people are "more at home in these placeless subcultures than in any traditional culture or nation or tribe" (Anderson, 1990:23). If this assumption is correct, these subcultures would create linkages around the world with "communities of shared interest, ideology, and information" (Anderson, 1990:23). However, some analysts do not believe that such widespread acceptance of a single culture will occur.

Critics argue that the world is not developing a homogeneous global culture; rather, other cultures are becoming Westernized. Political and religious leaders in some nations oppose this process, which they view as ***cultural imperialism*, or the extensive infusion of one nation's culture into other nations.** Some view the widespread infusion of the English language into countries that speak other languages as a form of cultural imperialism. A number of countries or states within them have sought to prevent English from overtaking their native language. For example, several of India's largest states have ordered that all official government work and correspondence must be conducted in Hindi (the dominant language of northern India) (McCarroll, 1993: 53). In Canada, conflict over the use of English in French-speaking Quebec is ongoing.

Perhaps the concept of cultural imperialism fails to take into account various cross-cultural influences. For example, Japanese management styles and cars are widely known in North America, and cultural diffusion of literature, music, clothing, and food has occurred on a global scale. A global culture, if it comes into existence, most likely will include components from many societies and cultures. It has been suggested that the "global culture is going to be one with a thin, fragile, and ever-shifting web of common ideas and values, and within that, incredible diversity—more diversity than there has ever been" (Anderson, 1990:25).

However, predictions of a global culture may be premature. Currently, a resurgence of *nationalism*, an ethnocentric belief that the political and economic rights of one's own nation morally supersede those of other nations, has occurred throughout the nations of Eastern Europe and the former Soviet Union. As these nations have experienced rapid change and economic decline, many people have identified more strongly with their original nationalities

Is this Japanese amusement park a sign of a homogeneous global culture or of cultural imperialism?

(as Russians, Armenians, Azerbaijanis, Georgians, or another of the hundreds of nationalities and ethnic groups in that part of the world) than as citizens of a single nation.

From a sociological perspective, the study of culture helps us not only understand our own "tool kit" of symbols, stories, rituals, and world views but also expand our insights to include those of other people of the world who, like us, seek strategies for enhancing their lives. If we understand how culture is used by people, how cultural elements constrain or facilitate certain patterns of action, what aspects of our cultural heritage have enduring effects on our actions, and what specific historical changes undermine the validity of some cultural patterns and give rise to others, we can apply our sociological imagination not only to our own society but also to the entire world (see Swidler, 1986).

CHAPTER REVIEW

What is culture?

Culture encompasses the knowledge, language, values, and customs passed from one generation to the next in a human group or society. Culture may be either material or nonmaterial. Material culture consists of the physical creations of society. Nonmaterial culture is more abstract and reflects the ideas, values, and beliefs of a society.

What are cultural universals?

Cultural universals are customs and practices that exist in all societies and include activities and institutions such as storytelling, families, and laws. Specific forms of these universals vary from one cultural group to another, however.

What are the four nonmaterial components of culture that are common to all societies?

These components are common to all cultures: symbols, language, values, and norms. Symbols express shared meanings; through them, groups communicate cultural ideas and abstract concepts. Language is a set of symbols through which groups communicate. Values are a culture's collective ideas about what is or is not acceptable. Norms are the specific behavioural expectations within a culture.

What causes culture change?

Culture change takes place in all societies. Change occurs through discovery and invention and through diffusion, which is the transmission of culture from one society or group to another.

How is cultural diversity reflected in society?
Cultural diversity is reflected through race, ethnicity, age, sexual orientation, religion, occupation, and so forth. A diverse culture also includes subcultures and countercultures. A subculture has distinctive ideas and behaviours that differ from the larger society to which it belongs. A counterculture rejects the dominant societal values and norms.

What are culture shock, ethnocentrism, and cultural relativism?
Culture shock refers to the anxiety people experience when they encounter cultures radically different from their own. Ethnocentrism is the assumption that one's own culture is superior to others. Cultural relativism counters culture shock and ethnocentrism by viewing and analyzing another culture in terms of its own values and standards.

How do the major theoretical perspectives view culture?
A functional analysis of culture assumes that a common language and shared values help to produce consensus and harmony. According to some conflict theorists, culture may be used by certain groups to maintain their privilege and exclude others from society's benefits. Symbolic interactionists suggest that people create, maintain, and modify culture as they go about their everyday activities.

Key Terms

counterculture 55
cultural imperialism 61
cultural lag 51
cultural relativism 56
cultural universals 41
culture 37
culture shock 56
diffusion 51
discovery 50
ethnocentrism 56
false consciousness 58
folkways 48
ideal culture 47
invention 50
language 42
laws 49
material culture 40
mores 48
nonmaterial culture 41
norms 47
real culture 47
sanctions 48
subculture 54
symbol 42
taboos 49
values 46
value contradictions 47

Internet Exercises

1. To find out which Canadian cultural "tribe" you belong to, visit

   www.environics.net/surveys/socialvalues

   and plot your position on the sociocultural map.

2. Go to the Alta Vista search engine

   www.altavista.com

   and do a search for the terms *hacker* and *warez*. Some people consider hackers to be a counterculture. Compare what you have read in this chapter about counterculture to what you find on the *hacker* and *warez* pages. What criteria of a counterculture do hackers fit? In what ways don't they fit?

3. This chapter looks at culture from functionalist, conflict, and interactionist perspectives. Visit the Postmodern Culture Journal home page

   jefferson.village.Virginia.EDU/pmc

   and configure your newsreader software to read the newsgroup **alt.postmodern**. The postmodern perspective has its roots in the three perspectives you have been reading about; however, it can also be vastly different. What are some of the differences between functionalist/conflict/interactionist perspectives and the postmodern perspective?

Net Links

For more Web links related to the topic of this chapter, see the Nelson sociology Web site: **www.sociologyessentials-2nded.nelson.com**.

The federal government has a Web site called "Facts on Canada" that contains information related to society and culture, including multiculturalism, French language and identity, and national cultural institutions. Its address is:

www.cio-bic.gc.ca/facts

The Department of Heritage has a site entitled "Multiculturalism" that includes current research on hate-motivated activities in Canada. To see it, go to:

www.pch.gc.ca/multi/publi/links.htm

Ethnocentrism Online has two insightful stories that demonstrate the concept of ethnocentrism at:

www.geocities.com/CapitolHill/Lobby/8506

To read some interesting ideas about modern culture and the ideas of Marshall McLuhan, see:

R **www.cios.org/encyclopedia/mcluhan/probe/probe.html**

Questions for Critical Thinking

1. Would it be possible today to live in a totally separate culture in Canada? Could you avoid all influences from the mainstream popular culture or from the values and norms of other cultures? How would you be able to avoid any change in your culture?
2. In Chapter 1, we examined sociological research and various studies on suicide. Suppose you wanted to find out why rates of suicide were higher in some cultures than in others. What might you examine in each culture? Symbols, language, values, or norms? The amount of diversity in a culture? What would be the best way to conduct your research?
3. In the future, will there be many separate cultures in Canada, or will there be one large, diverse culture?

Suggested Readings

An interesting functionalist analysis of culture is provided by this anthropologist:

Marvin Harris. *Cannibals and Kings: The Origins of Cultures*. New York: Random House, 1977.

Marvin Harris. *Good to Eat: Riddles of Food and Culture*. New York: Simon & Schuster, 1986.

These authors analyze aspects of culture from diverse perspectives:

Michael Adams. *Sex in the Snow: Canadian Social Values at the End of the Millennium*. Toronto: Penguin, 1998.

Reginald W. Bibby. *Mosaic Madness: The Poverty and Potential of Life in Canada*. Toronto: Stoddart Publishing, 1990.

bell hooks. *Outlaw Culture: Resisting Representations*. New York: Routledge, 1994.

These books provide interesting insights on culture and demonstrate how fieldwork can be carried out in a wide variety of settings:

Napoleon A. Chagnon. *Yanamamö: The Last Days of Eden*. San Diego: Harcourt Brace Jovanovich, 1992.

Stephen M. Fjellman. *Vinyl Leaves: Walt Disney World and America*. Boulder, Colo.: Westview Press, 1992.

To find out more about subcultures, countercultures, and hate crimes, see the following:

Stanley R. Barrett. *Is God a Racist? The Right Wing in Canada*. Toronto: University of Toronto Press, 1987.

William M. Kephart and William W. Zellner. *Extraordinary Groups: An Examination of Unconventional Life-Styles* (5th ed.). New York: St. Martin's Press, 1994.

INFOTRAC® COLLEGE EDITION

Either from the *Sociology In Our Times: The Essentials* Web site (**www.sociologyessentials-2nded.nelson.com**) or directly from your Web browser, you may access InfoTrac® College Edition, an online university library that includes over 600 popular and scholarly journals in which you can find articles related to the topics in this chapter.

CHAPTER 3

Dave Pelzer, public speaker and author of *A Child Called "It,"* describes the physical and emotional abuse he suffered at the hands of his mother during childhood:

"Before the station wagon comes to a complete stop, I dash out of the car. Mother yells for me to return. I have forgotten my crumpled lunch bag, which has always had the same menu for the last three years—two peanut butter sandwiches and a few carrot sticks. Before I bolt out of the car again, she says, 'Tell 'em ... Tell 'em you ran into the door.' Then in a voice she rarely uses with me, she states, 'Have a nice day.'

"Moments later, the school nurse leads me into her office, where we go through the normal routine. First, she examines my face and arms. 'What's that above your eye?' she asks.

"I nod sheepishly. 'Oh, I ran into the hall door ... by accident.' Again she smiles and takes a clipboard from the top of the cabinet. She flips through a page or two then bends down to show me. 'Here,' she points to the paper, 'You said that last Monday. Remember?'

"I quickly change my story, 'I was playing baseball and I got hit with the bat. It was an accident.' Accident. I am always supposed to say that. But the nurse knows better. She scolds me so I tell the truth. I always break down in the end and confess, even though I feel I should protect my mother ...

"'Oh no!' I tell myself, 'I've done something wrong ... again.' The nurse must have seen the concern in my eyes. She puts the clipboard down and hugs me. 'God,' I tell myself, 'She is so warm.' I don't ever want to let go. I want to stay in her arms forever. I hold my eyes tightly shut, and for a few moments nothing else exists. She pats my head. I flinch from the swollen bruise Mother gave me this morning. The nurse then breaks the embrace and leaves the room. I rush to put my clothes back on. She doesn't know it, but I do everything as fast as possible." (Pelzer, 1995:5–7)

SOCIALIZATION

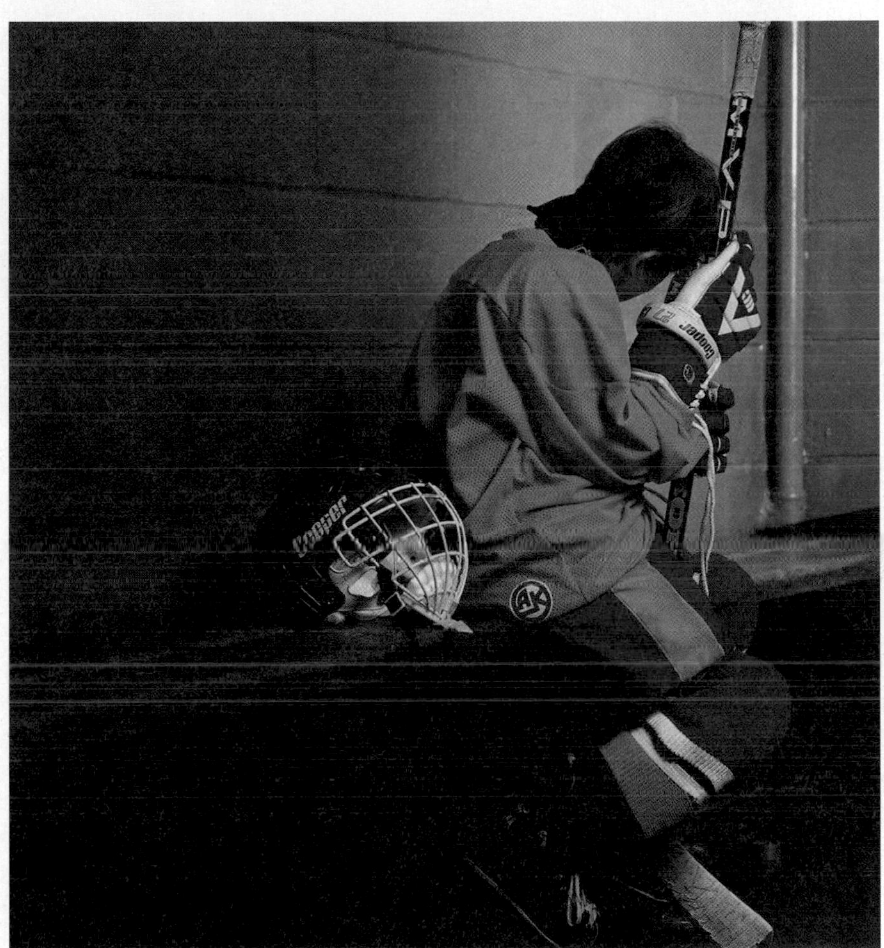

The process of socialization is of major significance to sociologists. Although most children are nurtured, trusted, and loved by their parents, Pelzer's experience of child abuse and neglect is not an isolated incident: large numbers of children experience maltreatment at the hands of family members or other caregivers such as babysitters or day-care workers. Child maltreatment includes physical abuse, sexual abuse, physical neglect, and emotional mistreatment of children and young adolescents (Zuravin, 1991). Such maltreatment has a serious impact on a child's social growth, behaviour, and self-image—all of which develop within the process of socialization. Children who are abused rather than treated with respect by their parents find it difficult to develop a positive self-image and learn healthy conduct because the appropriate models of behaviour that parents normally provide are absent. In some abusive families, children may be socialized to think that maltreatment is normal interactive behaviour.

In this chapter, we examine why socialization is so crucial, and we discuss both sociological and psychological theories of human development. We look at the dynamics of socialization—how it occurs and what shapes it. Throughout the chapter, we focus on child abuse and its impact on socialization. Before reading on, test your knowledge of child abuse by taking the quiz in Box 3.1.

Questions and Issues

Chapter Focus Question: What purpose does socialization serve?

How do individuals develop a sense of self?

What happens when children do not have an environment that supports positive socialization?

How does socialization vary throughout the different stages of our lives?

How does age determine a person's roles and statuses?

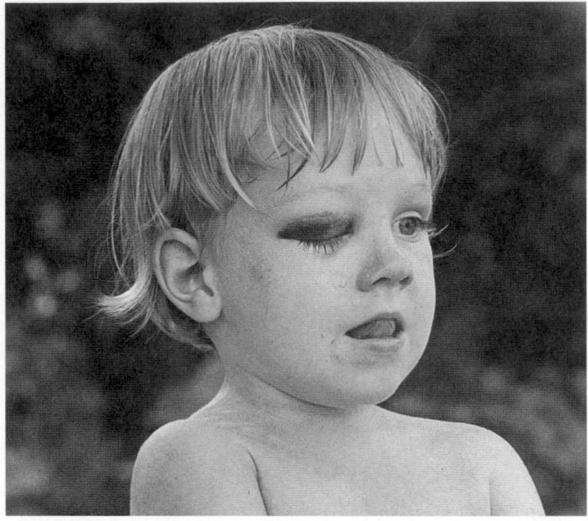

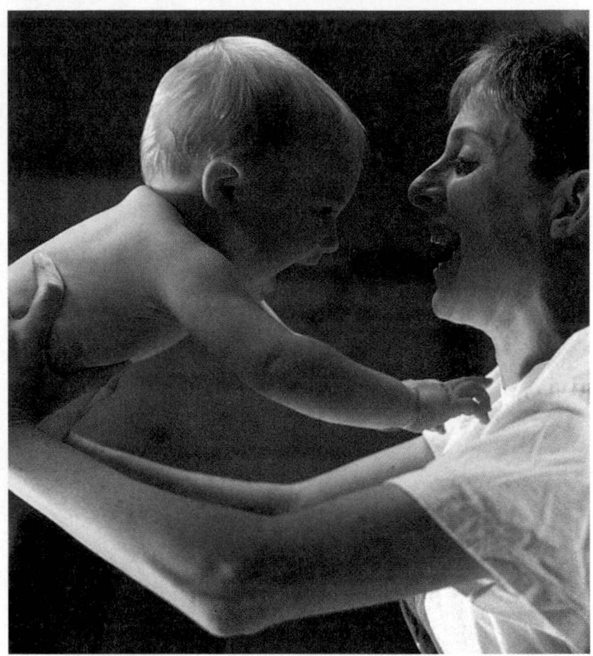

Human interaction is essential to the development of a positive self-concept; in abusive families, however, children may come to view abuse as "normal" everyday behaviour.

WHY IS SOCIALIZATION IMPORTANT?

***Socialization* is the lifelong process of social interaction through which individuals acquire a self-identity and the physical, mental, and social skills needed for survival in society.** It is the essential link between the individual and society (Robertson, 1989). Socialization enables each of us to develop our human potential and learn the ways of thinking, talking, and acting that are essential for social living.

Socialization is essential for the individual's survival and for human development. The many people who met the early material and social needs of each of us were central to our establishing our own identity. During the first three years of our life, we begin to develop a unique identity and the ability to manipulate things and to walk. We acquire sophisticated cognitive tools for thinking and for analyzing a wide variety of situations, and we learn effective communication skills. In the process, we begin a relatively long socialization process that culminates in our integration into a complex social and cultural system (Garcia Coll, 1990).

Socialization also is essential for the survival and stability of society. Members of a society must be socialized to support and maintain the existing social structure. From a functionalist perspective, individual conformity to existing norms is not taken for granted; rather, basic individual needs and desires must be balanced against the needs of the social structure. The socialization process is most effective when people conform to the norms of society because they believe this is the best course of action. In Chapter 2, we saw how people shape and are shaped by the knowledge, language, values, and customs within their cultures. Socialization enables a society to "reproduce" itself by passing on this cultural content from one generation to the next.

Although the techniques used to teach beliefs, values, and rules of behaviour are somewhat similar in many countries, the content of socialization differs greatly from society to society. How people walk, talk, eat, make love, and wage war are all functions of the culture in which they are raised. At the same time, we also are influenced by our exposure to subcultures of class, ethnicity, religion, and gender. In addition, each of us has unique experiences in our families and friendship groupings. The kind of human being that we become depends greatly on the particular society and social groups that surround us at birth and during early childhood. What we believe about ourselves, our society, and the world is largely a product of our interactions with others.

BOX 3.1 SOCIOLOGY AND EVERYDAY LIFE

How Much Do You Know about Child Abuse?

TRUE	FALSE	
T	F	1. Research suggests that older children are at greater risk of sexual abuse than younger children.
T	F	2. Child abuse only occurs in lower-class families.
T	F	3. Men are always the perpetrators of sexual abuse and very seldom the victims.
T	F	4. Infants are Canada's most likely homicide victims.
T	F	5. Neglect is not a form of child abuse.
T	F	6. In a family in which child abuse occurs, all of the children are likely to be victims.
T	F	7. It is against the law to fail to report child abuse.
T	F	8. In most cases of sexual abuse, the perpetrator is known to the child.
T	F	9. People who are the victims of child abuse are more likely than those who are not to become abusers themselves.
T	F	10. Some people are "born" abusers while others learn abusive behaviour from their family and friends.

Answers on page 70.

Human Development: Biology and Society

What does it mean to be "human"? To be human includes being conscious of ourselves as individuals with unique identities, personalities, and relationships with others. As humans, we have ideas, emotions, and values. We have the capacity to think and to make rational decisions. But what is the source of "humanness"? Are we born with these human characteristics, or do we develop them through our interactions with others?

When we are born, we are totally dependent on others for our survival. We cannot turn ourselves over, speak, reason, plan, or do many of the things that are associated with being human. Although we can nurse, wet, and cry, most small mammals also can do those things. As discussed in Chapter 2, we humans differ from nonhuman animals because we lack instincts and must rely on learning for our survival. Human infants have the potential for developing human characteristics if they are exposed to an adequate socialization process.

Every human being is a product of biology, society, and personal experiences—that is, of heredity and environment or, in even more basic terms, "nature" and "nurture." How important is social influence, or "nurture," in human development? There is hardly a behaviour that is not influenced socially. Except for simple reflexes, such as dilation of the pupils and knee-jerk responses, most human actions are social, either in their causes or in their consequences. Even solitary actions such as crying or brushing our teeth are ultimately social. We cry because someone has hurt us. We brush our teeth because our parents (or a dentist) told us it was important. Social environment probably has a greater effect than heredity on the way we develop and the way we act. However, heredity does provide the basic material from which other people help to mould an individual's human characteristics.

Our biological and emotional needs are related in a complex equation. Children whose needs are met in settings characterized by affection, warmth, and closeness see the world as a safe and comfortable place and other people as trustworthy and helpful. By contrast, infants and children who receive less-than-adequate care or who are emotionally rejected or abused often view the world as hostile and have feelings of suspicion and fear.

BOX 3.1 SOCIOLOGY AND EVERYDAY LIFE

Answers to the Sociology Quiz on Child Abuse

1. **False.** Based on Uniform Crime Report Survey results, 56 percent of reported child sexual abuse victims were 10 and under.
2. **False.** Child abuse occurs in families from all social classes.
3. **False.** Men are not always the perpetrators of sexual abuse, and they may indeed be the victims. Many male victims of sexual abuse are abused by male abusers. However, in about 92 percent of reported sexual abuse cases, young girls and women are the victims; and in 98 percent of the cases, men are the perpetrators.
4. **True.** Between 1993 and 1997, far more infants under the age of one were victims of homicide than were the members of any other age category of children, youth, and adults. Family members committed 93 percent of these homicides.
5. **False.** Child abuse and child neglect are both types of child abuse. Neglect refers to the failure of a parent to provide minimally adequate care in terms of health, nutrition, shelter, education, supervision, affection, attention, or protection. Neglect may be as physically and mentally damaging as physical abuse.
6. **False.** In some families, one child repeatedly may be the victim of abuse while others are not. This is especially true with incest, whereby one daughter may be singled out for abuse by a father, stepfather, uncle, or other male relative.
7. **True.** In Canada, all of the provinces have mandatory reporting requirements. However, there has been inconsistent compliance with these legal mandates. All adults who believe or suspect that a child is in need of protection have a duty to report this to the authorities. Some provinces specify that professionals who are in contact with children must report suspected abuse cases or face a fine of up to $1000.
8. **True.** Data from police departments across Canada show that 81 percent of the child sexual assault victims knew their abuser. The largest group of offenders is fathers.
9. **True.** Although scholars disagree on this point, a number of studies have found that adults who were abused as children have a greater tendency to be violent and abusive compared with those who were not abused.
10. **False.** No one is "born" to be an abuser. People learn abusive behaviour from their family and friends.

Sources: Based on Wolfe, 1987; Knudsen, 1992; Jackson, 1993; Begin, 1994; Wachtel, 1994; Gunn and Linden, 1994; Rodgers and Kong, 1996; Durrant and Rose-Krasnor, 1995; and Statistics Canada, 1999c.

Social Isolation

Social environment, then, is a crucial part of an individual's socialization. Even nonhuman primates such as monkeys and chimpanzees need social contact with others of their species in order to develop properly. As we will see, appropriate social contact is even more important for humans.

ISOLATION AND NONHUMAN PRIMATES Researchers have attempted to demonstrate the effects of social isolation on nonhuman primates raised without contact with others of their own species. In a series of laboratory experiments, psychologists Harry and Margaret Harlow (1962, 1977) took infant rhesus monkeys from their mothers and isolated them in

As this birthday celebration attended by four generations of family members illustrates, socialization enables society to "reproduce" itself.

separate cages. Each cage contained two nonliving "mother substitutes" made of wire, one with a feeding bottle attached and the other covered with soft terry cloth but without a bottle. The infant monkeys instinctively clung to the cloth "mother" and would not abandon it until hunger drove them to the bottle attached to the wire "mother." As soon as they were full, they went back to the cloth "mother" seeking warmth, affection, and physical comfort.

The Harlows' experiments show the detrimental effects of isolation on nonhuman primates. When the young monkeys later were introduced to other members of their species, they cringed in the corner. Having been deprived of social contact with other monkeys during their first six months of life, they never learned how to relate to other monkeys or to become well-adjusted adult monkeys—they were either fearful of or hostile toward other monkeys (Harlow and Harlow, 1962, 1977).

Because humans rely more heavily on social learning than do monkeys, the process of socialization is even more important for us.

ISOLATED CHILDREN Social scientists have documented cases of children who were deliberately raised in isolation. A look at the life of one child who suffered such emotional abuse provides important insights into the effect of social isolation on human beings.

Anna Born in 1932 to an unmarried, mentally impaired woman, Anna was an unwanted child. She was kept in an attic-like room in her grandfather's house. Her mother, who worked on the farm all day and often went out at night, gave Anna just enough care to keep her alive; she received no other care. Sociologist Kingsley Davis (1940) described her condition when she was found in 1938:

> [Anna] had no glimmering of speech, absolutely no ability to walk, no sense of gesture, not the least capacity to feed herself even when the food was put in front of her, and no comprehension of cleanliness. She was so apathetic that it was hard to tell whether or not she could hear. And all of this at the age of nearly six years.

When she was placed in a special school and given the necessary care, Anna slowly learned to walk, talk, and care for herself. Just before her death at the age of 10, Anna reportedly could follow directions, talk in phrases, wash her hands, brush her teeth, and try to help other children (Davis, 1940).

Cases like that of Anna are important to our understanding of the socialization process because they show that social isolation and neglect are extremely detrimental to young children. When infants are deprived of human contact, they do not develop the characteristics most of us think of as "human."

Child Abuse

What do the words "child abuse" mean to you? Many people first think of cases that involve severe physical injuries or sexual abuse. However, "child abuse" is a general term used to describe a variety of injuries inflicted by a parent or caregiver. There are three types of abuse: physical abuse or battering; neglect; and sexual abuse. It is estimated that neglect is the most common form of child abuse (Wachtel, 1994). Child neglect occurs when a child's basic needs—including emotional warmth and security, adequate shelter, food, health care, education, clothing and protection—are not met, regardless of cause (Dubowitz et al., 1993:12). The case of Anna demonstrates the devastating effect that parental neglect can have on a child's development.

What acts constitute child abuse or neglect? Throughout history and across cultures, perceptions of what constitutes abuse or neglect have differed. What might have been considered appropriate disciplinary action by parents in the past (such as following the adage "Spare the rod, spoil the child") today is viewed by many as child abuse. Still, many Canadian parents choose to use spanking as a form of discipline. Recent research on the use of corporal punishment has revealed that approximately 70 percent of Canadian parents have used physical punishment, although the majority indicate that it is ineffective to do so (Durrant and Rose-Krasnor, 1995).

As the debate surrounding Section 43 of the Criminal Code demonstrates (see Box 3.2), there is little agreement within Canadian society with regard to what constitutes child abuse.

SOCIALIZATION AND THE SELF

Without social contact, we cannot form a sense of self or personal identity. The *self* represents the sum total of perceptions and feelings that an individual has of being a distinct, unique person—a sense of who and what one is. This sense of self (also referred to as *self-concept*) is not present at birth; it arises in the process of social experience. ***Self-concept* is the totality of our beliefs and feelings about ourselves** (Gecas, 1982). Four components comprise our self-

Our self-concept continues to be influenced by our interactions with others throughout our lives.

concept: (1) the *physical* self ("I am tall"), (2) the *active* self ("I am good at soccer"), (3) the *social* self ("I am nice to others"), and (4) the *psychological* self ("I believe in world peace"). Between early and late childhood, a child's focus tends to shift from the physical and active dimensions of self toward the social and psychological aspects (Lippa, 1994). Self-concept is the foundation for communication with others; it continues to develop and change throughout our lives (Zurcher, 1983).

Our *self-identity* is our perception about what kind of person we are. As we have seen, socially isolated children do not have typical self-identities because they have had no experience of "humanness." According to interactionists, we do not know who we are until we see ourselves as we believe others see us. We gain information about the self largely through language, symbols, and interaction with others. Our interpretation and evaluation of these messages is central to the social construction of our identity. However, we are not just passive reactors to situations, programmed by society to respond in fixed ways. Instead, we are active agents who develop plans out of the pieces supplied by culture

BOX 3.2 SOCIOLOGY AND LAW

CHILD ABUSE THEN AND NOW

Historically, society has viewed children as the property of their parents—to be treated as the parents wished. In the United States in the early 1600s, the "Stubborn Child Act" specified that the parents of a rebellious or stubborn child could petition the court for permission to put the child to death (Wolfe, 1987). Even without such a law, physical beatings often have been considered appropriate discipline for children. In fact, parents who did not beat their children were considered to be neglecting their parental duties. Parents had absolute power and control over their children. An early Roman law, referred to as *patria potestas,* included the right of the father to give a child away or have the child put to death.

The first legal challenge to the absolute rights of parents occurred in 1870 in New York when a social worker was forced to turn to the American Society for the Prevention of Cruelty to Animals as a means of obtaining legal sanctions against the parents of a neglected child. In response, the American Society for the Prevention of Cruelty to Children was founded. Shortly thereafter, in 1891, the Children's Aid Society was established in Toronto.

One of the most contentious current issues pertaining to child abuse revolves around Section 43 of the Criminal Code, which states:

> Every school teacher, parent or person standing in the place of a parent is justified in using force by way of correction toward a pupil or child, as the case may be, who is under his care, if the force does not exceed what is reasonable under the circumstances.

The original intention of Section 43 was the protection of the child from unreasonable force, not to sanction physical punishment by parents. However, those lobbying for the repeal of Section 43 argue that this provision gives parents the legal right to assault their children with impunity. Others argue that removing Section 43 would remove the protection that parents now have against criminal prosecution if they physically discipline their children.

Source: Durrant and Rose-Krasnor, 1995; Mitchell, 1995.

and attempt to execute these plans in social encounters (McCall and Simmons, 1978).

Sociological Theories of Human Development

The perspectives of symbolic interactionists Charles Horton Cooley and George Herbert Mead help us understand how our self-identity is developed through our interactions with others.

THE LOOKING-GLASS SELF According to sociologist Charles Horton Cooley (1864–1929), the ***looking-glass self*** **refers to the way in which a person's sense of self is derived from the perceptions of others.** Our looking-glass self is not who we actually are or what people actually think about us; it is based on our *perception* of how other people think of us (Cooley, 1922/1902). Cooley asserted that we base our perception of who we are on how we think other people see us and on whether this seems good or bad to us.

FIGURE 3.1 How the Looking-Glass Self Works

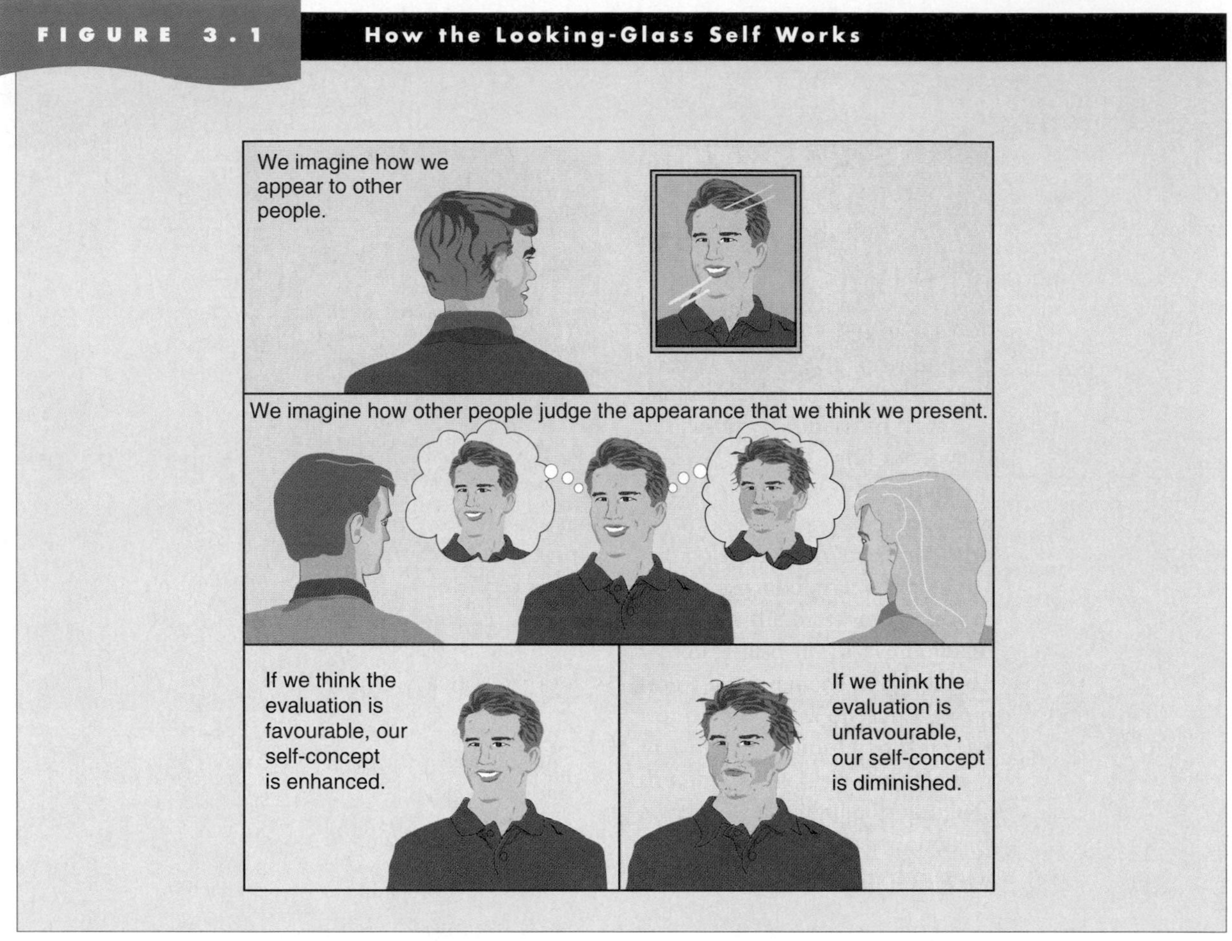

As Figure 3.1 shows, the looking-glass self is a self-concept derived from a three-step process:

1. We imagine how our personality and appearance will look to other people. We may imagine that we are attractive or unattractive, heavy or slim, friendly or unfriendly, and so on.
2. We imagine how other people judge the appearance and personality that we think we present. This step involves our *perception* of how we think they are judging us. We may be correct or incorrect!
3. We develop a self-concept. If we think the evaluation of others is favourable, our self-concept is enhanced. If we think the evaluation is unfavourable, our self-concept is diminished (Cooley, 1922/1902).

According to Cooley, we use our interactions with others as a mirror for our own thoughts and actions; our sense of self depends on how we interpret what they do and say. Consequently, our sense of self is not permanently fixed; it is always developing as we interact with others.

Role-Taking George Herbert Mead (1863–1931) extended Cooley's insights by linking the idea of self-concept to ***role-taking*****—the process by which a person mentally assumes the role of another person in order to understand the world from that person's point of view.** Role-taking often occurs through play and games, as children try out different roles (such as being mommy, daddy, doctor, or teacher) and gain an appreciation of them.

According to Mead (1934), in the early months of life, children do not realize that they are separate from others. They do, however, begin early on to see a mirrored image of themselves in others. Shortly after birth, infants start to notice the faces of those

According to sociologist George Herbert Mead, the self develops through three stages. In the preparatory stage, children imitate others; in the play stage, children pretend to take the roles of specific people; and in the game stage, children become aware of the "rules of the game" and the expectations of others.

around them, especially the significant others whose faces start to have meaning because they are associated with experiences such as feeding and cuddling. ***Significant others* are those persons whose care, affection, and approval are especially desired and who are most important in the development of the self.** Gradually, we distinguish ourselves from our caregivers and begin to perceive ourselves in contrast to them. As we develop language skills and learn to understand symbols, we begin to develop a self-concept. When we can represent ourselves in our own minds as objects distinct from everything else, our self has been formed.

Mead divided the self into the "I" and the "me." The "I" is the subjective element of the self that represents the spontaneous and unique traits of each person. The "me" is the objective element of the self, which is composed of the internalized attitudes and demands of other members of society and the individual's awareness of those demands. Both the "I" and the "me" are needed to form the social self. The unity of the two constitutes the full development of the individual. According to Mead, the "I" develops first, and the "me" takes form during the three stages of self development:

1. During the *preparatory stage*, up to about the age of 3, interactions lack meaning, and children largely imitate the people around them. Children may mimic family members or others nearby, but they lack understanding of the meaning of their behaviour and are simply copying others. At this stage, children are *preparing* for role-taking.
2. In the *play stage*, from about ages 3 to 5, children learn to use language and other symbols, thus enabling them to pretend to take the roles of specific people. At first, children tend to model

themselves on significant others, typically members of their families, teachers, and other caregivers with whom they spend substantial amounts of time. Later, children may play at taking the roles of others, such as "doctor, "superhero," or "bad guy." At this stage, children begin to see themselves in relation to others, but they do not see role-taking as something they have to do.

3. During the *game stage*, which begins in the early school years, children understand not only their own social position but also the positions of others around them. In contrast to play, games are structured by rules, often are competitive, and involve a number of other "players." Children now learn a system of interdependent roles and ways of relating to many people and groups. At this time, they become concerned about the demands and expectations of others and of the larger society. Mead used the example of a baseball game to describe this stage because children, like baseball players, must take into account the roles of all the other players at the same time. They must plan their responses to the predicted actions of other players based on the "big picture" of the entire situation. Mead's concept of the ***generalized other*** **refers to the child's awareness of the demands and expectations of the society as a whole or of the child's subculture.** To return to Mead's baseball analogy, for instance, think of the 7-year-old's abstract ability to *simultaneously* consider the roles of other team members when the ball is hit to centre field.

Evaluating Interactionist Theories How useful are interactionist perspectives such as Cooley's and Mead's in enhancing our understanding of the socialization process? Certainly, this approach contributes to our understanding of how the self develops. Cooley's idea of the looking-glass self makes us aware that our perception of how we *think* others see us is not always correct. Mead extended Cooley's ideas by emphasizing the cognitive skills acquired through role-taking. He stressed the importance of play and games, as children try out different roles and gain an appreciation of them. His concept of the generalized other helps us see that the self is a social creation. According to Mead (1934:196), "Selves can only exist in definite relations to other selves. No hard-and-fast line can be drawn between our own selves and the selves of others."

As with any theoretical approach, the viewpoints of interactionists such as Cooley and Mead have certain limitations. Some conflict theorists have argued that these theories are excessively conservative because they assume that what is good for dominant group members is good for everyone. For example, sociologist Anne Kaspar (1986) suggests that Mead's ideas about the social self may be more applicable to men than women. According to Mead's theory, both the "I" and the "me" are needed to form the social self, and there is no inherent conflict between the two. By contrast, Kaspar asserts that women experience inherent conflicts between the meanings they derive from their *personal experience* and those they take from the *culture*. She notes that "ideals of motherhood" that derive from culture may be in sharp contrast to the actual experiences of women as mothers. For many women, it is difficult to balance the idealized view of a mother as selfless, nurturing, and devoted to family with the realities of their own needs for autonomy, independence, and valued work in and outside the home (Kaspar, 1986).

Psychological Theories of Human Development

Up to this point, we have discussed sociologically oriented theories; we now turn to psychological theories that have influenced contemporary views of human development.

Psychoanalytic Perspective Sigmund Freud (1856–1939) is known as the founder of psychoanalytic theory. He lived in the Victorian era, during which biological explanations of human behaviour were prevalent. It also was an era of extreme sexual repression and male dominance when compared to contemporary North American standards. Freud's theory was greatly influenced by these cultural factors, as reflected in the importance he assigned to sexual motives in explaining behaviour.

Freud divided the mind into three interrelated parts: id, ego, and superego. The ***id*** **is the component of personality that includes all of the individual's basic biological drives and needs that demand immediate gratification.** The new-born child's personality is all id, and from birth, the child finds that urges for self-gratification—such as wanting to be held, fed, or changed—are not going to be satisfied immediately.

FIGURE 3.2 **Freud's Theory of Personality**

This illustration shows how Freud might picture a person's internal conflict over whether to commit an antisocial act such as stealing a candy bar. In addition to dividing personality into three components, Freud theorized that our personalities are largely unconscious—hidden away outside our normal awareness. To dramatize his point, Freud compared conscious awareness (portions of the ego and superego) to the visible tip of an iceberg. Most of our personality—including all of the id, with its raw desires and impulses—lies submerged in our unconscious.

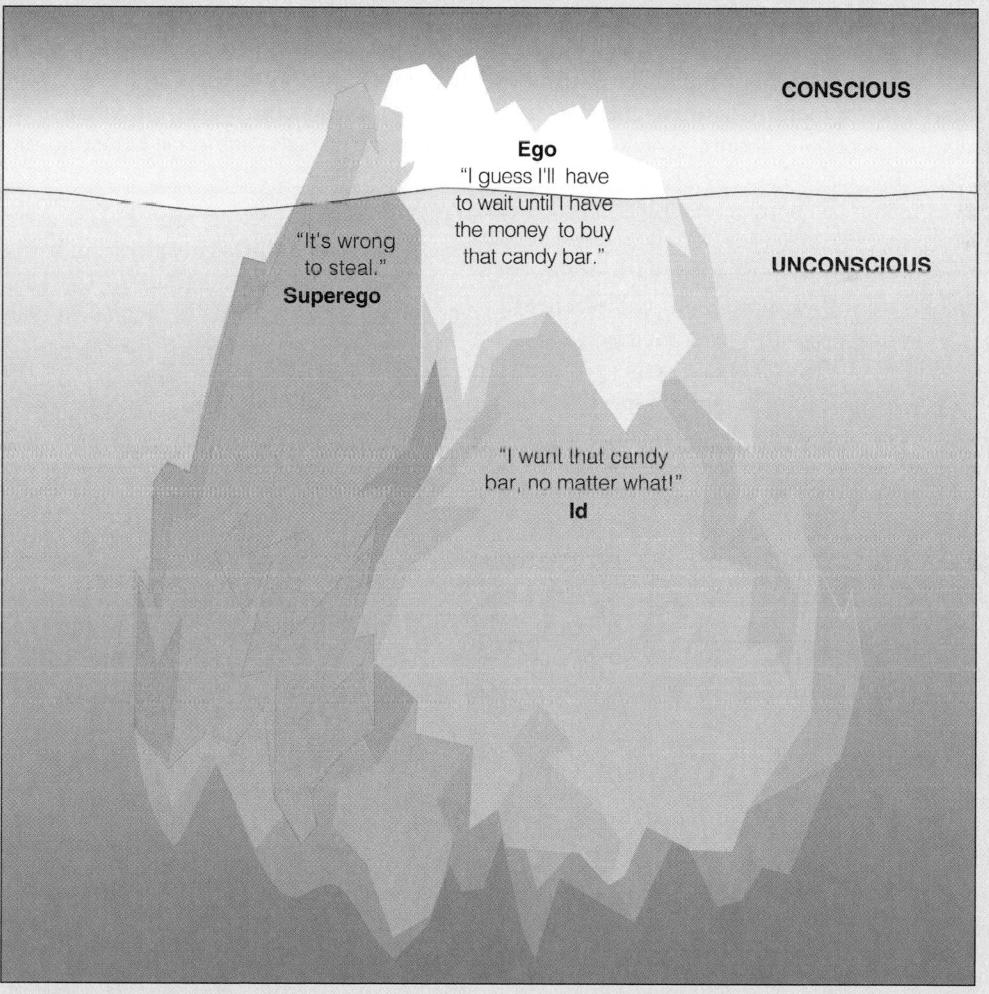

The ***ego* is the rational, reality-oriented component of personality that imposes restrictions on the innate pleasure-seeking drives of the id.** The ego channels the desire of the id for immediate gratification into the most advantageous direction for the individual. The ***superego*, or conscience, consists of the moral and ethical aspects of personality.** It is first expressed as the recognition of parental control and eventually matures as the child learns that parental control is a reflection of the values and moral demands of the larger society. When a person is well adjusted, the ego successfully manages the opposing forces of the id and the superego. Figure 3.2 illustrates Freud's theory of personality.

Freud's theory has been heavily criticized by many scholars. One criticism is that his work was based on unprovable assertions. For example, according to Freud's psychoanalytic theory, most incest reports represent the sexual fantasies of alleged victims (Roth, 1993). Freud assumed that his female patients' accounts of incest were figments of their imaginations, based on their own sexual desires. Sociologist Diana E.H. Russell (1986) has argued that this assumption discounts the reality of incestuous abuse.

COGNITIVE DEVELOPMENT Jean Piaget (1896–1980), a Swiss psychologist, was a pioneer in the field of cognitive (intellectual) development. Cognitive theorists are interested in how people obtain, process, and use information—that is, in how we think. Cognitive development relates to changes over time in how we think.

Piaget (1954) believed that in each stage of development (from birth through adolescence), children's activities are governed by their perception of the world around them. His four stages of cognitive development are organized around specific tasks that, when mastered, lead to the acquisition of new mental capacities, which then serve as the basis for the next level of development. Piaget emphasized that all children must go through each stage in sequence before moving on to the next one, although some children move through them faster than others.

1. *Sensorimotor stage* (birth to age 2). During this period, children understand the world only through sensory contact and immediate action because they cannot engage in symbolic thought or use language.
2. *Preoperational stage* (age 2–7). In this stage, children begin to use words as mental symbols and to form mental images. However, they still are limited in their ability to use logic to solve problems or to realize that physical objects may change in shape or appearance while still retaining their physical properties. For example, they do not realize that the same amount of water appears at a different level in a narrow glass than it does in a wide glass.
3. *Concrete operational stage* (age 7–11). During this stage, children think in terms of tangible objects and actual events. They can draw conclusions about the likely physical consequences of an action without always having to try it out.
4. *Formal operational stage* (age 12 through adolescence). By this stage, adolescents are able to engage in highly abstract thought and understand places, things, and events they have never seen. They can think about the future and evaluate different options or courses of action.

STAGES OF MORAL DEVELOPMENT Lawrence Kohlberg (b. 1927) elaborated on Piaget's theories of cognitive reasoning by conducting a series of studies in which respondents were presented with a moral dilemma. Based on the responses, Kohlberg classified moral reasoning into three levels, each containing two specific stages. He argued that people must pass through each stage before going on to the next (Kohlberg, 1969, 1981).

1. *Preconventional level* (age 7–10). At this level, children give little consideration to the views of others. Kohlberg referred to the first stage of moral development as *punishment and obedience orientation* (punishment avoidance). Here, the child's judgment as to what is right or wrong is simply based on a fear of punishment. Stage 2 of moral development is *naive instrumental hedonism* (need satisfaction). Here, the child believes that good conduct produces pleasure and bad conduct results in unwanted consequences.
2. *Conventional level* (age 10 through adulthood). At this level, individuals are most concerned with how they are perceived by their peers. Stage 3 of moral development involves *"good-boy/nice-girl" morality* in which children believe that behaviour is good (or right) if it receives wide approval from significant others, including peers. Stage 4, *law-and-order orientation*, is based on how one conforms to rules and laws. Conforming to rules and laws is seen as being important in maintaining societal approval.
3. *Postconventional level* (few adults reach this stage). At this level, people view morality in terms of individual rights. In stage 5, *social contract orientation*, ideals and principles are seen as having value that does not depend on the approval of others; rather, rights are seen as part of a social contract. Stage 6, the final moral stage, is *universal ethical principles*, and "moral conduct" is judged by principles based on human rights that transcend government and laws.

Critics have challenged Kohlberg's concept of stages of moral development and his belief that these stages are linked to cognitive development. They also have questioned whether these stages are universal.

GENDER AND MORAL DEVELOPMENT One of the major criticisms of Kohlberg's work came from psychologist Carol Gilligan (b. 1936), a former colleague. According to Gilligan (1982), Kohlberg's research has key weaknesses. Because all of his subjects were male, his model was based solely on male responses. Gilligan stated that there is evidence of male–female differences with regard to morality. The difference in responses does not indicate a "moral deficiency" on the part of either gender; rather, it results from different socialization and life experiences.

To correct what she perceived to be a male bias in Kohlberg's research, Gilligan (1982) examined morality in women by interviewing twenty-eight pregnant women who were contemplating having an abortion. Based on her research, Gilligan concluded that Kohlberg's stages do not reflect the ways many women think about moral problems. As a result, Gilligan identified three stages in female moral development. In stage 1, the woman is motivated primarily by selfish concerns ("This is what I want ... this is what I need"). In stage 2, she increasingly recognizes her responsibility to others. In stage 3, she makes her decision based on her desire to do the greatest good for both herself and others. Gilligan argued that men are socialized to make moral decisions based on abstract principles of justice ("What is the fairest thing to do?") while women are socialized to make such decisions from a responsibility and care perspective ("Which option will cause the least amount of pain?").

Subsequent research that directly compared women's and men's reasoning about moral dilemmas has supported some of Gilligan's assertions but not others. Most studies have found that both men and women use care-based reasoning *and* justice-based reasoning. Nevertheless, Gilligan's argument that people make moral decisions according to both abstract principles of justice and principles of compassion and care is an important contribution to our knowledge about moral reasoning. Studies have not confirmed, however, that women are more compassionate than men (Tavris, 1993). One study concluded that a person's level of education is a better predictor of moral reasoning than gender (Walker, 1989).

Although the sociological and psychological perspectives we have examined often have been based on different assumptions and have reached somewhat different conclusions, an important theme emerges from these models of cognitive and moral development—through the process of socialization, people learn how to take into account other people's perspectives.

AGENTS OF SOCIALIZATION

Agents of socialization **are the persons, groups, or institutions that teach us what we need to know in order to participate in society.** We are exposed to many agents of socialization throughout our lifetime. Here, we look at the most pervasive ones in childhood—the family, the school, peer groups, and the mass media.

The Family

The family is the most important agent of socialization in all societies. The love and nurturance we receive from our families are essential to normal cognitive, emotional, and physical development. Furthermore, our parents are our first teachers. From infancy, our families transmit cultural and social values to us. As discussed in Chapter 13 ("Families and Intimate Relationships"), families in Canada vary in size and structure. Some families consist of two parents and their biological children, while others consist of a single parent and one or more children. Still other families reflect changing patterns of divorce and remarriage, and an increasing number are made up of same-sex partners and their children.

Functionalists emphasize that families are the primary locus for the procreation and socialization of children in industrialized nations. Most of us form an emerging sense of self and acquire most of our beliefs and values within the family context. We also learn about culture (including language, attitudes, beliefs, values, and norms) as it is interpreted by our parents and other relatives.

Day-care centres have become important agents of socialization for increasing numbers of children. Today, more than 50 percent of all Canadian pre-school children are in day care of one kind or another.

Families also are the primary source of emotional support. Ideally, people receive love, understanding, security, acceptance, intimacy, and companionship within families (Benokraitis, 1997:6). The role of the family is especially significant because young children have little social experience beyond its boundaries; they have no basis for comparison or for evaluating how they are treated by their own family.

Conflict theorists stress that socialization reproduces the class structure in the next generation. Children in poor and low-income families, for example, may be unintentionally socialized to believe that acquiring an education and aspiring to lofty ambitions are pointless because of existing economic conditions in the family (Ballantine, 1997). By contrast, middle- and upper-income families typically instil ideas of monetary and social success in children, as well as emphasizing the necessity of thinking and behaving in "socially acceptable" ways.

The School

As the amount of specialized technical and scientific knowledge has expanded rapidly and the amount of time children are in educational settings has increased, schools have come to play an enormous role in the socialization of young people. For many people, the formal education process is an undertaking that lasts up to twenty years.

The number of one-parent families and families in which both parents work outside the home has increased dramatically in the past two decades. With this change the number of children in day care and preschool programs has grown rapidly. Currently, more than 50 percent of Canadian preschool children are in day care, either in private homes or institutional settings, and this percentage continues to climb (Burke et al., 1994). Studies generally have found that day care and preschool programs may have a positive effect on the overall socialization of children (Silverstein, 1991). These programs are especially beneficial for children from less-advantaged backgrounds in that they provide these children with valuable learning experiences not available at home. Many scholars also have found that children from all social classes and family backgrounds may benefit from learning experiences in early childhood education programs that they have not had in their homes.

Schools teach specific knowledge and skills; they also have a profound effect on children's self-image, beliefs, and values. As children enter school for the first time, they are evaluated and systematically compared with one another by the teacher. A permanent, official record is kept of each child's personal behaviour and academic activities. From a functionalist perspective, schools are responsible for (1) socialization, or teaching students to be productive members of society, (2) transmission of culture,

The pleasure of hanging out with friends is not the only attraction of adolescent peer groups. Peer groups contribute to our sense of belonging and self-worth regardless of our age.

(3) social control and personal development, and (4) the selection, training, and placement of individuals on different rungs in the society (Ballantine, 1997).

In contrast, conflict theorists assert that students have different experiences in the school system, depending on their social class, ethnic background, the neighbourhood in which they live, their gender, and other factors. According to sociologist Stephen Richer (1988), much of what happens in school amounts to teaching a *hidden curriculum* in which children learn to value competition, materialism, work over play, obedience to authority, and attentiveness. Richer's study of Ottawa classrooms indicated that success in school may be based more on students' ability to conform to the hidden curriculum than their mastery of the formal curriculum. Therefore, students who are destined for leadership or elite positions acquire different skills and knowledge than those who will enter working-class and middle-class occupations (see Cookson and Persell, 1985).

Peer Groups

As soon as we are old enough to have acquaintances outside the home, most of us begin to rely heavily on peer groups as a source of information and approval about social behaviour (Lips, 1989). A ***peer group* is a group of people who are linked by common interests, equal social position, and (usually) similar age.** In early childhood, peer groups often are composed of classmates in day care, preschool, and elementary school. In adolescence, these groups typically are people with similar interests and who take part in the same social activities. As adults, we continue to participate in peer groups of people with whom we share common interests and comparable occupations, income, or social position.

Peer groups function as agents of socialization by contributing to our sense of "belonging" and our feelings of self-worth. Unlike families and schools, peer groups provide children and adolescents with some degree of freedom from parents and other authority figures (Corsaro, 1992). Peer groups also teach and reinforce cultural norms while providing important information about "acceptable" behaviour. The peer group is both a product of culture and one of its major transmitters (Elkin and Handel, 1989). In other words, peer groups simultaneously reflect the larger culture and serve as a conduit for passing on culture to young people.

Is there such a thing as "peer pressure"? Individuals must *earn* their acceptance with their peers by conforming to a given group's *own* norms, attitudes, speech patterns, and dress codes. When we conform to our peer group's expectations, we are rewarded; if we do not conform, we may be ridiculed or even expelled from the group. Conforming to the demands of peers frequently places children and adolescents at

BOX 3.3 SOCIOLOGY AND MEDIA

Public Awareness of Child Abuse

The media have the potential for socializing large numbers of people regarding important social problems such as child abuse. In 1992, for example, *Scared Silent: Exposing and Ending Child Abuse,* hosted by Oprah Winfrey, was the first non-news event ever to be shown simultaneously on prime-time television by three broadcast networks.

The purpose of the film was to inform people about the nature of child abuse and to encourage them "to break the silence, to speak out, and stop further pain, injury, and death" (Rowe, 1992:11). Information about sexual, physical, and emotional abuse was provided through six true stories of intergenerational child abuse in which the victims and the perpetrators both were profiled.

The documentary, viewed by over 45 million people in North America, generated more than 112,000 telephone calls on the National Child Abuse Hotline in the five days following its airing. Local child abuse organizations also received thousands of calls.

In 1997 former NHL player Sheldon Kennedy drew widespread media attention when he announced he had been sexually abused over a period of several years by junior hockey coach Graham James. In the summer of 1998 Kennedy continued to raise public awareness by in-line skating across Canada to raise money for sexual abuse victims. In the fall of 1998 Kennedy attended a memorial service at Maple Leaf Gardens for a young man who had committed suicide shortly after exposing the existence of a pedophile ring at the Gardens.

"When you get a prominent building like Maple Leaf Gardens and a prominent figure like Ken Dryden [Toronto Maple Leafs president] talking about an issue that's not talked about much, it's good," says Sheldon Kennedy (Hendley, 1998:10).

Public response to both Sheldon Kennedy and *Scared Silent* shows the media's immense capacity for bringing important issues such as child abuse to our attention and providing us with information about how to prevent such violence and neglect.

"There's no question that celebrities—and sports celebrities in general—bring people in," says Sue Hunter, executive director of the Toronto Child Abuse Centre. "There's a tremendous response in our society to celebrities."

cross purposes with their parents. Sociologist William A. Corsaro (1992) notes that children experience strong peer pressure even during their preschool years. For example, children frequently are under pressure to obtain certain valued material possessions (such as toys, videotapes, clothing, or athletic shoes); they then pass this pressure on to their parents through emotional pleas to purchase the desired items. In this way, adult caregivers learn about the latest fads and fashions from children, and they may contribute to the peer culture by purchasing the items desired by the children (Corsaro, 1992). Socialization is not a one-way process from adults to children. Adults also learn from children.

Mass Media

An agent of socialization that has a profound impact on both children and adults is the *mass media*, which is composed of large-scale organizations that use print or electronic means (such as radio, television, or film) to communicate with large numbers of people. The media function as socializing agents in several ways: (1) they inform us about events, (2) they introduce us to a wide variety of people, (3) they provide an array of viewpoints on current issues, (4) they make us aware of products and services that, if we purchase them, supposedly will help us be accepted by others, and (5) they entertain us by providing the opportunity to live vicariously

BOX 3.3

CONTINUED

In addition to providing information about social problems, the media also have the potential for sensationalizing (and perhaps trivializing) cases of alleged child abuse. In 1993, for example, Michael Jackson, the superstar pop singer, was accused of sexual abuse by a 13-year-old boy. Instantly, the media sensationalized the case under the guise of providing the public with the latest information. The allegations regarding Jackson were discussed on network news programs and television talk shows. Among the newfound (although temporary) celebrities to be interviewed were two of Jackson's other young male friends, whose interviews received global coverage. They defended Jackson and stated that the accusations against him were false. They were instant celebrities because they each admitted that they had slept with Jackson without being molested (McGuigan, 1993).

When other stories such as this arise in the future, the media no doubt will continue to publicize (and perhaps sensationalize) allegations of child abuse because it is assumed that this is what people want to read about and see. As psychologist Melvin Guyer noted, "The public gets to be puritanical and voyeuristic at the same time. Their attitude is basically, 'This food is terrible, and there's not enough of it'" (Corliss, 1993:56).

Do highly publicized cases make us more aware of child abuse, or do they trivialize the genuine problem of child abuse in our society?

Sheldon Kennedy takes a donation from a little girl in support of his skate across Canada to raise funds to build a haven for sexually abused children.

(through other people's experiences). Although most of us take for granted that the media play an important part in contemporary socialization, we frequently underestimate the enormous influence this agent of socialization may have on children's attitudes and behaviour.

Recent estimates indicate that close to 100 percent of Canadian households have at least one television. Canadian viewers watch an average of 3.3 hours of television per day (Adams, 1998). This means that the average sixteen-year-old will have spent more time watching television than attending school.

Parents, educators, social scientists, and public officials have widely debated the consequences for young people of watching television. Television has been praised for offering numerous positive experiences to children. Some scholars suggest that television (when used wisely) can enhance children's development by improving their language abilities, concept formation skills, and reading skills and by encouraging prosocial development (Winn, 1985). On the other hand, television has been criticized for sensationalizing and trivializing violence (Adams, 1998).

Most children who watch television and movies have seen thousands of people injured or killed as a result of the aggressive behaviour of others. The increasing level of violence in movies and television

FIGURE 3.3 Socialization Through Television

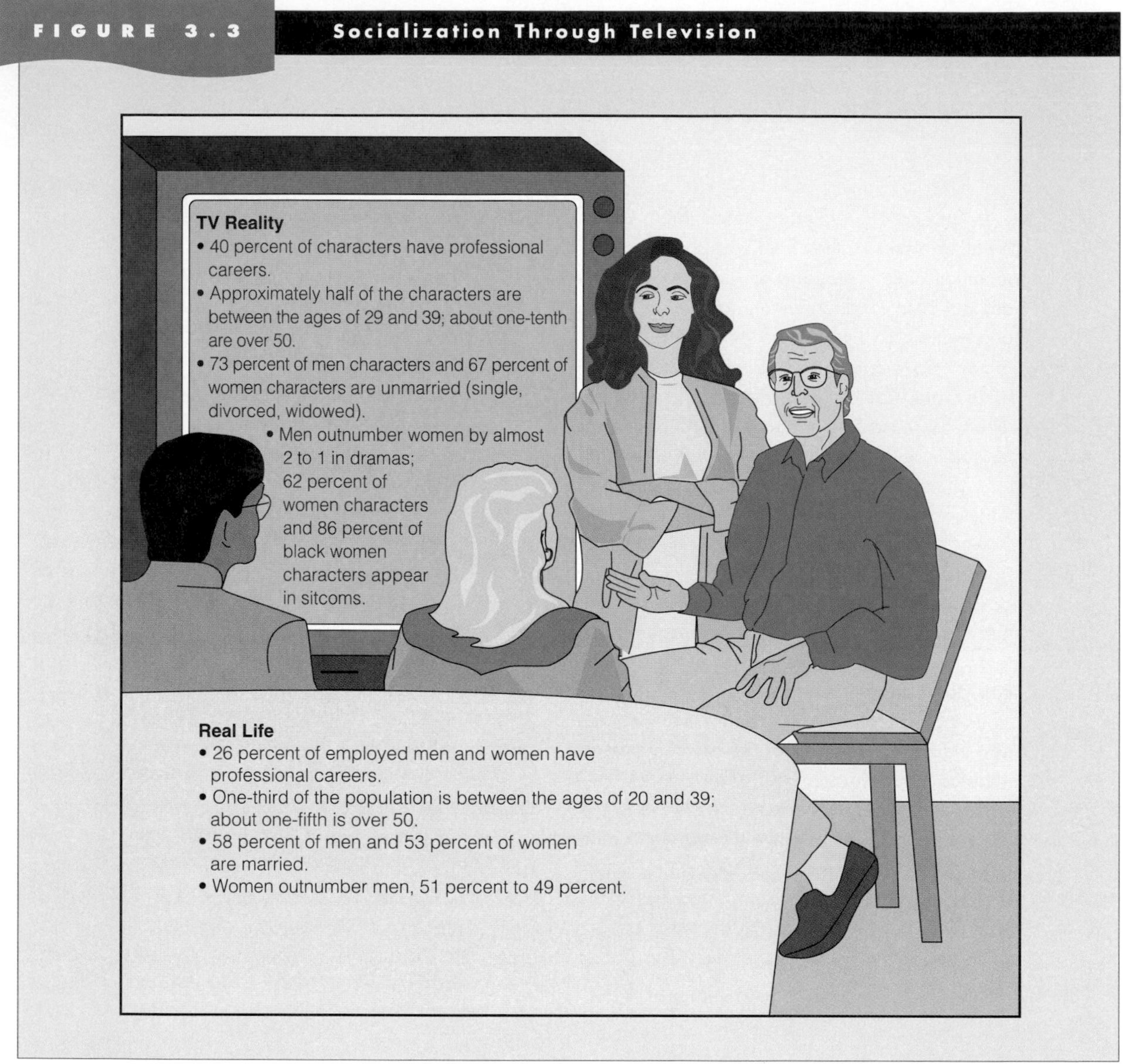

has been mirrored in virtually all the mass media. For example, taboos about what can be said and what can be shown on television newscasts are collapsing. From automobile accidents, to homicide victims, to airplane crash survivors, no scene is too grisly or traumatic to show viewers in the name of ratings.

TV Reality
• 40 percent of characters have professional careers.
• Approximately half of the characters are between the ages of 29 and 39; about one-tenth are over 50.
• 73 percent of men characters and 67 percent of women characters are unmarried (single, divorced, widowed).
• Men outnumber women by almost 2 to 1 in dramas; 62 percent of women characters and 86 percent of black women characters appear in sitcoms.
Real Life
• 26 percent of employed men and women have professional careers.
• One-third of the population is between the ages of 20 and 39; about one-fifth is over 50.
• 58 percent of men and 53 percent of women are married.
• Women outnumber men, 51 percent to 49 percent.

What we see on television and in films can influence our behaviour. For example, the Walt Disney Company removed a scene from one of its films, *The Program* (in which several drunken college football players lie in the middle of a busy road to prove their toughness), after three teenagers apparently attempted to imitate the scene. Unlike the movie hero, they did not walk away unharmed: one was killed, another paralyzed, and the third critically injured when hit by passing vehicles. Whether or not we are aware of it, television, films, and other forms of mass media—including newspapers, magazines, radio, musical recordings, and books—have a profound influence on how we are socialized. Figure 3.3 contrasts television "reality" with its real-life counterpart.

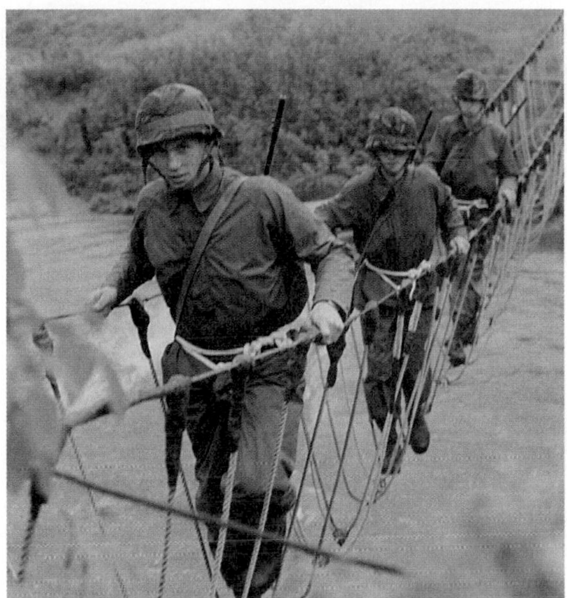

Recruits in this Canadian Armed Forces training exercise are resocialized through extensive, gruelling military drills and manoeuvres. What types of new values and behaviours do you think they are expected to learn?

RESOCIALIZATION

Resocialization **is the process of learning a set of attitudes, values, and behaviours that is new and different from those in one's previous background and experience.** It may be voluntary or involuntary. In either case, people undergo changes that are much more rapid and pervasive than the gradual adaptations that socialization usually involves.

Voluntary Resocialization

Resocialization is voluntary when we assume a new status (such as becoming a student, an employee, or a retiree) of our own free will. Sometimes, voluntary resocialization involves medical or psychological treatment or religious conversion, in which case the person's existing attitudes, beliefs, and behaviours must undergo strenuous modification to a new regime and a new way of life. For example, resocialization for adult survivors of emotional/physical child abuse includes extensive therapy in order to form new patterns of thinking and action, somewhat like Alcoholics Anonymous's twelve-step program, which has become the basis for many other programs dealing with addictive behaviour (Parrish, 1990).

Involuntary Resocialization

Involuntary resocialization occurs against a person's wishes and generally takes place within a ***total institution*****—a place where people are isolated from the rest of society for a set period of time and come under the control of the officials who run the institution** (Goffman, 1961). Military boot camps, jails and prisons, concentration camps, and some mental hospitals are total institutions. In these settings, people are totally stripped of their former selves—or depersonalized—through a *degradation ceremony* (Goffman, 1961). Inmates entering prison, for example, are required to strip, shower, and wear assigned institutional clothing. In the process, they are searched, weighed, fingerprinted, photographed, and given no privacy even in showers and restrooms. Their official identification becomes not a name but a number. In this abrupt break with their former existence, they must leave behind their personal possessions and their family and friends. The depersonalization process continues as they are required to obey rigid rules and to conform to their new environment.

After stripping people of their former identities, the institution attempts to build a more compliant person. A system of rewards and punishments (such as providing or withholding cigarettes and television or exercise privileges) encourages conformity to institutional norms. Some individuals may be rehabilitated; others become angry and hostile toward the system that has taken away their freedom. Although the assumed purpose of involuntary resocialization is to reform persons so that they will conform to societal standards of conduct after their release, the ability of total institutions to modify offenders' behaviour in a meaningful manner has been widely questioned. In many prisons, for example, inmates may conform to the norms of the prison or of other inmates, but little relationship exists between those norms and the laws of society.

GENDER SOCIALIZATION

If you had only one child, would you prefer for the child to be a boy or a girl? In most societies, parents

BOX 3.4 SOCIOLOGY IN GLOBAL PERSPECTIVE

CHILD ABUSE IN ASIA

How child abuse is viewed may depend on cultural values. Based on North American values, child treatment in many other nations would be defined as abuse. For example, child labour conditions in India are considered intolerable in Canada. In India, children as young as 4 may work at looms weaving carpets for up to 15 hours a day (without a break) to earn 5 rupees, or about 15 cents. In North America, this practice would be viewed as parents "selling" their children as "child labour." In Pakistan and Bangladesh, 4- to 8-year-old boys are sold as jockeys for camel races in Saudi Arabia. Bangladeshi girls aged 8 to 10 are auctioned into sexual slavery in the slums of Karachi. Many parents consider a pretty daughter or a strong son to be a financial asset. If a girl is considered to be pretty, she is sold into prostitution; if not, she is sold to a sweatshop. Overall, millions of children live in virtual slavery, toiling for little or no pay in brothels, fields, factories, mines, or stone quarries, or as domestic help.

In cross-cultural terms, is this child abuse? In societies where poverty is endemic, the answer to this question is intertwined with the constant struggle with hunger. Cultural relativism, as discussed in Chapter 2, tells us that we should view this question from viewpoints other than our own. Some critics of child labour state that it perpetuates poverty, illiteracy, adult unemployment, and overpopulation. Others point out, however, that not working often means not eating. For example, Mohammad Sohrab, age 8, carries heavy loads of fish, rice, and vegetables from the market to shoppers' homes in Dhaka, the capital of Bangladesh, to earn the equivalent of $1 a day to support himself and

prefer male children to female children based on cultural assumptions about sex differences (Steinbacher and Holmes, 1987). Is this because males inherently are superior to females? Not at all; parents acquire these gender preferences through ***gender socialization*****, the aspect of socialization that contains specific messages and practices concerning the nature of being female or male in a specific group or society.** Gender socialization is important in determining what we *think* the "preferred" sex of a child should be and in influencing our beliefs about acceptable behaviours for males and females.

Parents may respond differently toward male and female infants; they often play more roughly with boys and talk more lovingly to girls (Eccles, Jacobs, and Harold, 1990). Throughout childhood and adolescence, boys and girls typically are assigned different household chores and given different privileges (such as how late they may stay out at night).

Like the family, schools, peer groups, and the media contribute to our gender socialization. From kindergarten through college, teachers and peers reward gender-appropriate attitudes and behaviour. Sports reinforce traditional gender roles through a rigid division of events into male and female categories. The media also are a powerful source of gender socialization; from an early age, children's books, television programs, movies, and music provide subtle and not-so-subtle messages about "masculine" and "feminine" behaviour. Gender socialization is discussed in more depth in Chapter 10 ("Sex and Gender").

Scholars may be hesitant to point out differences in socialization practices among diverse ethnic and social class groupings because such differences typically have been interpreted by others to be a sign of inadequate (or inferior) socialization practices. Beliefs as to what is, and what is not, proper treatment of children vary from society to society around the world, as Box 3.4 explains.

BOX 3.4

CONTINUED

his four younger brothers and sisters. Sohrab describes his life: "My mother is ill, my father is dead. The family will starve if I don't work. I hate to work. I want to play like other children."

Although all countries of South Asia have enacted laws against child labour, enforcement is lax. The ban on child labour does not cover agriculture, where about 75 percent of the child labourers are found. Officials in India estimate 20 million children, most of them below the age of 13, work in hazardous industries such as making matches, quarrying, tanning, fireworks-making, and carpet weaving. Child rights activists estimate the figure is closer to 55 million.

External pressures against child labour in Asia are rising. The United Nations International Labor Organization is attempting to force governments to acknowledge that child labour is a problem in their countries. Canadian child rights activist Craig Kielburger, founder of a group called Free The Children, toured Asia to speak out against child labour. This 13-year-old schoolboy from Ontario met with the prime minister in order to convince Mr. Chrétien that Canada should make a long-term commitment to protect child rights and ensure that goods imported by Canada were not the products of child labour and exploitation. Canada is exploring the possibility of "confronting the menace of child labour" by imposing restrictions on selected imports of products made by children.

Sources: Based on Moorhead, 1992; Schmetzer, 1992; Joshi, 1993; and Hauser, 1996.

SOCIALIZATION THROUGH THE LIFE COURSE

Why is socialization a lifelong process? Throughout our lives, we continue to learn. Each time we experience a change in status (such as becoming a university student or getting married), we learn a new set of rules, roles, and relationships. Even before we achieve a new status, we often participate in ***anticipatory socialization*—the process by which knowledge and skills are learned for future roles.**

"How old are you?" is one of the most frequently asked questions in our society. Beyond indicating how old or young a person is, age is socially significant because it defines what is appropriate for or expected of people at various stages. Moreover, while it is an ascribed status, age is one of the few ascribed statuses that changes over time.

When we hear the word age, most of us think of ***chronological age*—a person's age based on date of birth** (Atchley, 1994). In everyday life, however, we gain a general idea of a person's age based on ***functional age*—observable individual attributes such as physical appearance, mobility, strength, coordination, and mental capacity that are used to assign people to age categories** (Atchley, 1994). Because we typically do not have access to other people's birth certificates to learn their chronological age, we often use visible characteristics—such as youthful appearance or grey hair and wrinkled skin—as our criteria for determining whether someone is "young" or "old." As historian Lois W. Banner (1993:15) suggests, "Appearance, more than any other factor, has occasioned the objectification of aging. We define someone as old because he or she looks old." Feminist scholars have noted that functional age works differently for women and men—as they age, men may be viewed as distinguished

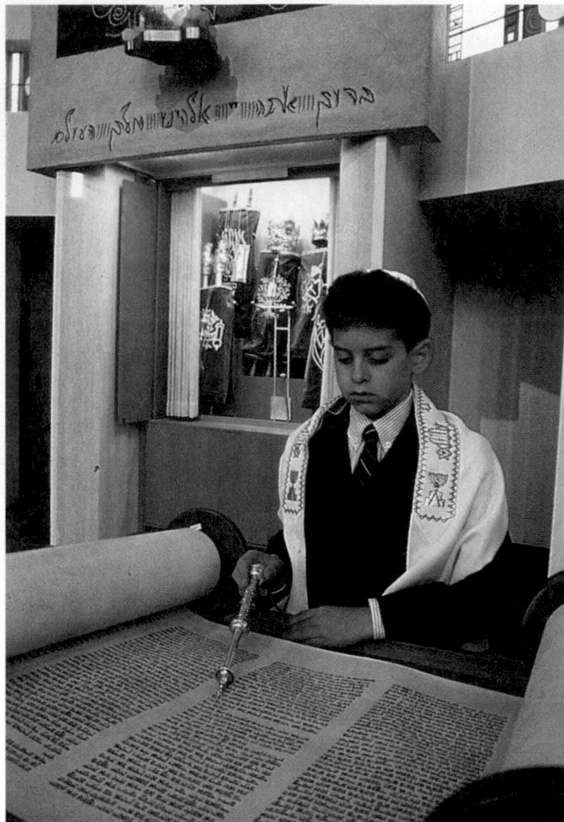

A Jewish boy's bar mitzvah is an outward manifestation of his attainment of the age of religious responsibility. Many societies have similar rites of passage that publicly dramatize changes in a person's status.

or powerful while women may be viewed as old or grandmotherly.

Many societies organize social experience according to age. Some have distinct *rites of passage*, based on age or other factors, that publicly dramatize and validate changes in a person's status. In Canada and other industrialized societies, the most common categories of age are infancy, childhood, adolescence, and adulthood (often subdivided into young adulthood, middle adulthood, and older adulthood).

Infancy and Childhood

Some social scientists believe that a child's sense of self is formed at a very early age and that it is difficult to change this view later in life. Interactionists emphasize that during infancy and early childhood, family support and guidance are crucial to a child's developing self-concept. In some families, children are provided with emotional warmth, feelings of mutual trust, and a sense of security. These families come closer to our ideal cultural belief that childhood should be a time of carefree play, safety, and freedom from economic, political, and sexual responsibilities. However, other families reflect the discrepancy between cultural ideals and reality—children grow up in a setting characterized by fear, danger, and risks that are created by parental neglect, emotional abuse, or premature economic and sexual demands (Knudsen, 1992).

Abused children often experience low self-esteem, an inability to trust others, feelings of isolation and powerlessness, and denial of their feelings. However, the manner in which parental abuse affects children's ongoing development is subject to much debate and uncertainty. For example, some scholars and therapists assert that the intergenerational hypothesis—the idea that abused children will become abusive parents—is valid, but others have found little support for this hypothesis (Knudsen, 1992).

Adolescence

In industrialized societies, the adolescent (or teenage) years represent a buffer between childhood and adulthood. In Canada, no specific rites of passage exist to mark children's move into adulthood; therefore, young people have to pursue their own routes to self-identity and adulthood (Gilmore, 1990). Anticipatory socialization often is associated with adolescence, whereby many young people spend much of their time planning or being educated for future roles they hope to occupy. However, other adolescents (such as 15- and 16-year-old mothers) may have to plunge into adult responsibilities at this time. Adolescence often is characterized by emotional and social unrest. In the process of developing their own identities, some young people come into conflict with parents, teachers, and other authority figures who attempt to restrict their freedom. Adolescents also may find themselves caught between the demands of adulthood and their own lack of financial independence and experience in the job market. The experiences of individuals during adolescence vary according to their ethnicity, class, and gender. Based on their family's economic situation, some young people move directly into the adult world of work. However, those from upper-middle- and upper-class families may extend adolescence into their late twenties or early thirties by attending graduate or professional school and then receiving additional advice and financial support from their parents as they start their own families, careers, or businesses.

Adulthood

One of the major differences between child and adult socialization is the degree of freedom of choice. If young adults are able to support themselves financially, they gain the ability to make more choices about their own lives. In early adulthood (usually until about age 40), people work toward their own goals of creating meaningful relationships with others, finding employment, and seeking personal fulfillment. Of course, young adults continue to be socialized by their parents, teachers, peers, and the media, but they also learn new attitudes and behaviours. For example, when we marry or have children, we learn new roles as partners or parents. Adults often learn about fads and fashions in clothing, music, and language from their children. Parents in one study indicated that they had learned new attitudes and behaviours about drug use, sexuality, sports, leisure, and ethnic issues from their university-aged children (Peters, 1985).

Workplace, or *occupational*, *socialization* is one of the most important types of adult socialization. Sociologist Wilbert Moore (1968) divided occupational socialization into four phases: (1) career choice, (2) anticipatory socialization (learning different aspects of the occupation before entering it), (3) conditioning and commitment (learning the ups and downs of the occupation and remaining committed to it), and (4) continuous commitment (remaining committed to the work even when problems or other alternatives may arise). This type of socialization tends to be most intense immediately after a person makes the transition from school to the workplace; however, this process continues throughout our years of employment. Today, many people will experience continuous workplace socialization as a result of individuals having more than one career in their lifetime (Lefrançois, 1993).

LATE ADULTHOOD: AGING IN CANADA

As you will read in Chapter 15 ("Population and Urbanization") Canada's population is steadily aging. As a result, aging has become an important social issue and research on aging has grown dramatically in the past fifty years. *Gerontology* is the study of aging and older people. A subfield of gerontology, ***social gerontology* is the study of the social (nonphysical) aspects of aging**, including such topics as the societal consequences of an aging population and the personal experience of aging (Novak, 1993). According to gerontologists, age is viewed differently from society to society and changes over time.

As in the other stages of the life course, late adulthood involves transitions that require a new set of rules, roles, and relationships. Events such as retirement, widowhood, chronic illness and preparing for death all involve major changes in an individual's life.

Late adulthood is generally considered to begin at age 65—the "normal" retirement age. *Retirement* is the institutionalized separation of an individual from an occupational position, with continuation of income through a retirement pension based on prior years of service (Atchley, 1994). Retirement means the end of a status that long has been a source of income and a means of personal identity. Perhaps the loss of a valued status explains why many retired persons introduce themselves by saying, "I'm retired now, but I was a (banker, lawyer, plumber, supervisor, and so on) for forty years."

Some gerontologists subdivide late adulthood into three categories: (1) the "young-old" (ages 65–74), (2) the "old-old" (ages 75–85), and (3) the "oldest-old" (over age 85) (see Moody, 1994). Although these are somewhat arbitrary divisions, the "young-old" are less likely to suffer from disabling illnesses, while the "old-old" are more likely to suffer such illnesses (Belsky, 1990). A recent study found, however, that the prevalence of disability among those 85 and over decreased during the 1980s due to better health care.

The rate of biological and psychological changes in older persons may be as important as their chronological age in determining how they are perceived by themselves and others. As adults grow older, they actually become shorter, partly because bones that have become more porous with age develop curvature. As bones become more porous, they also become more brittle; simply falling may result in broken bones that take longer to heal. With age, arthritis increases, and connective tissue stiffens

BOX 3.5 SOCIOLOGY AND TECHNOLOGY

SENIORS AND CYBERSPACE

Do you know a grandparent or other older person who will not use a bank machine or who can't understand why there is so much fuss about computers? If so, this fits the stereotype many of us hold that seniors are far behind the rest of us in their use of technology. While older people are not usually among the first to adopt new technology, recent studies concerning their use of computers and the Internet have shown that they are rapidly catching up to other age groups. In fact, seniors are the fastest growing group of Internet users (Philbeck, 1997).

In the early days of personal computing few seniors used computers. Because many of them had retired by the time computers became common in the workplace, they did not learn to use computers on the job and the early technology was difficult to use. However, computers are now much more user-friendly, requiring neither lengthy training nor consultants on stand-by. There is even technology that enables older persons with disabilities such as blindness or arthritis to use computers.

Many seniors start using the Internet in order to communicate by e-mail with children and grandchildren living in other parts of the country. However, the Internet has many other uses. Chat rooms and other forms of e-mail can help to replace friends who have died and keep in touch with those who have moved away. Internet shopping can help those who have difficulty going out. Surfing the Internet can help to alleviate the boredom felt by some older persons. One senior describes her experience with the Internet:

> From my desk chair I now tracked elephants in Africa, listened to the national anthem of Greece, read the *New York Times* ... But most of all, the people. Relatives and long-time, long-distance friends who used to be in touch only on holidays, were now "talking" with me

joints. Wrinkled skin, "age spots," grey (or white) hair, and midriff bulge appear.

Older persons also have increased chances of heart attacks, strokes, and cancer, and some diseases affect virtually only persons in late adulthood. Alzheimer's disease (a progressive and irreversible deterioration of brain tissue) is an example; about 55 percent of all organic mental disorders in the older population are caused by Alzheimer's (Atchley, 1994). Persons with this disease have an impaired ability to function in everyday social roles; eventually, they cease to be able to recognize people they have always known and lose all sense of their own identity. Finally, they may revert to a speechless, infantile state such that others must feed them, dress them, sit them on the toilet, and lead them around. The disease has no known cause and, currently, there is no cure. Over a quarter of a million Canadians suffer from Alzheimer's disease and related dementias. By the year 2030, it is estimated that this number will grow to three-quarters of a million.

The time and attention needed to care for someone who has Alzheimer's disease or who simply no longer can leave home without help can be staggering. Daniel Heinrichs, a full-time caregiver for his wife, explains what caring for Norah was like:

> My wife Norah was afflicted with Alzheimer's disease. She could no longer function as a person in our marriage. Slowly I had to take over the various duties she had performed. After that I took over her financial affairs. Then I had to care for her personally: choosing, buying, and looking after clothing, dressing and undressing her, combing her hair, and feeding her. Slowly our conversation ceased. She could not think rationally anymore. She could not understand the words that were being used, and she did not know the names of objects she saw. She no longer knew

BOX 3.5

CONTINUED

regularly on the computer. I soon made myself at home in a chat-room for seniors only and met people from all over the United States and beyond—"senior-netters" ... who also had exchanged their typewriters for cyberspace.

What a zany, caring bunch! It was obvious that the Internet was rescuing many seniors from what otherwise would be isolated lives. Some were house-bound due to illness or the illness of a spouse. Others sought relief from boredom, or relished just plain fun and good conversation. Friendships (yes, real ones), blossomed through this medium and, with appropriate precautions, I dared travel to meet in person some of those whom I had met online.

My mother, nearing 90, remains convinced that the folks I meet via computer all belong to the Mafia and warns me regularly about "those Internet people." I try to break the news gently that I am one of "those Internet people." (Patterson, 1998)

Recent research has shown that Internet use may even have health benefits: a psychological study found that Internet-using older persons showed gains in a cognitive ability test that is part of the Geriatric Depression Scale (Philbeck, 1997).

Some Web sites for seniors are:
www.seniornet.org
www.hc-sc.gc.ca/seniors-aines

Sources: Patterson, 1998; and Philbeck, 1997.

who I was either. "Norah is gone, there is nothing left of your marriage. You need to look after yourself again," is advice that I have heard and felt. Fortunately, I did not yield to this advice. Despite all of Norah's disabilities, we continued to have a rich and enjoyable experience together. I learned to communicate with Norah in other ways. How I spoke the words said more than their actual meaning. She watched for the smile on my face and the fun in my voice. My disposition had more effect on her than my words. She let me put my arm around her and hold her hands whenever I desired, or needed to do so ... Now Norah is gone, but I'm glad that I stayed with her "... till death do us part." (Heinrichs, 1996:48)

Fortunately, most older people do not suffer from Alzheimer's and are not incapacitated by their physical condition. Only about 5 percent of older people live in nursing homes, about 10 percent have visual impairment, and about 50 percent have some hearing loss (Naeyaert, 1990; Novak, 1993). Although most older people experience some decline in strength, flexibility, stamina, and other physical capabilities, much of that decline does not result simply from the aging process and is avoidable; with proper exercise, some of it is even reversible (Lefrançois, 1993).

Along with physical changes come changes in the roles played by older adults. One that most people enjoy is being a grandparent. An extended family is a great source of pleasure for many older Canadians. Grandparenting is an interesting role because it "has no clearly defined responsibilities, expectations, or rights" (McPherson, 1998:209). This gives members of younger and older generations the opportunity to build relationships that are to their mutual benefit. Some of the benefits of having grandparents are described in the following comments by Grade 3 students about the role of a grandmother (Huyck, cited in McPherson, 1998:213):

> When they read to us they don't skip words and they don't mind if it is the same story.
>
> They don't have to be smart, only answer questions like why dogs hate cats, and how come God isn't married.
>
> Grandmas are the only grownups who have got time—so everybody should have a grandmother, especially if you don't have television.

The physical and psychological changes that come with increasing age can cause stress. According to Erik Erikson (1963), older people must resolve a tension of "integrity versus despair." They must accept that the life cycle is inevitable, that their lives are nearing an end, and that achieving inner harmony requires accepting both one's past accomplishments and past disappointments. Mark Novak interviewed several older people about what he termed "successful aging." One respondent, Joanne, commented:

> For me getting older was very painful at first because I resisted change. Now I'm changed, and it's okay. I would say I have a new freedom ... I thought I had no limits, but for me a great learning [experience] was recognizing my limits. It was a complete turnover, almost like a rebirth. I guess I've learned we're all weak really. At least we should accept that—being weak—and realize, "Hey, I'm only a fragile human being." (Novak, 1995:125)

Like many older people, Joanne has worked to maintain her dignity and autonomy. Despite its negative aspects, aging has many positive dimensions and most older people are quite content with their lives. Many are financially secure with home mortgages paid off and no children remaining at home. This gives them a great deal of personal freedom. Most report they are in good or excellent health (Norland, 1994). Northcott found that older Edmonton residents were actually happier with their lives than younger respondents (1984). A national study conducted by Health and Welfare Canada (1998) found that older people were much less likely than younger people to report that their lives were stressful and the vast majority (92 percent) reported that they were pretty happy or very happy.

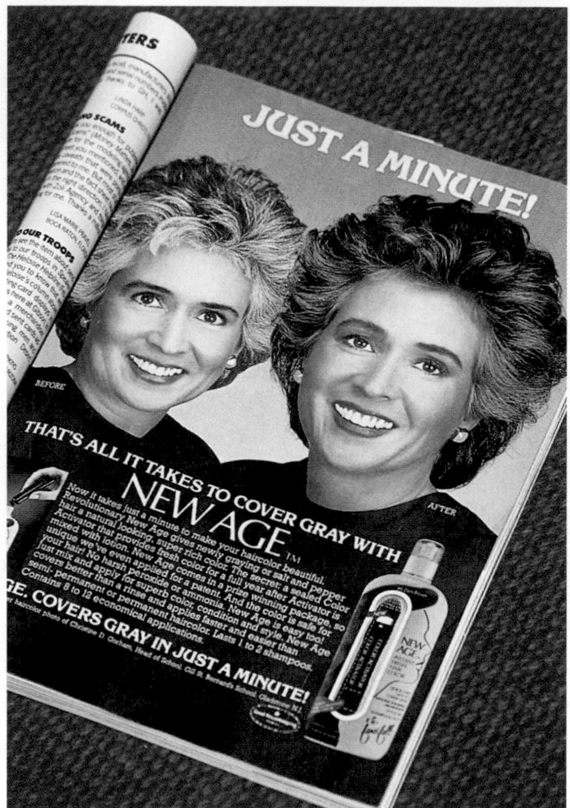

For many years, advertisers have bombarded women with messages about the importance of a youthful appearance. Increasingly, men, too, are being targeted by advertising campaigns that play on fears about the "ravages" of aging.

Ageism

In previous chapters, we have seen how prejudice and discrimination may be directed toward individuals based on ascribed characteristics—such as ethnicity or gender—over which they have no control. The same holds true for age.

In some respects, older people are treated very well in Canada. Most have adequate incomes and all have access to publicly funded medical care. Housing for older people is often subsidized, and many businesses offer discounts to people who are over 65. At the same time, however, many older people feel their biggest problem is that other people have negative views of aging and of the capabilities of older people.

Stereotypes regarding older persons reinforce ***ageism*—prejudice and discrimination against people on the basis of age, particularly when they**

are older persons (Butler, 1975). Ageism against older persons is rooted in the assumption that people become unattractive, unintelligent, asexual, unemployable, and mentally incompetent as they grow older (Comfort, 1976).

Ageism is reinforced by stereotyping, whereby people have narrow, fixed images of certain groups. One-sided and exaggerated images of older people are used repeatedly in everyday life. Older persons often are stereotyped as thinking and moving slowly; as bound to themselves and their past, unable to change and grow; as being unable to move forward and often moving backward (Belsky, 1990). They are viewed as cranky, sickly, and lacking in social value (Atchley, 1994); as egocentric and demanding; as shallow and enfeebled; and as aimless and absent-minded (Belsky, 1990).

The media contribute to negative images of older persons, many of whom are portrayed as doddering, feebleminded, wrinkled, and laughable men and women, literally standing on their last legs (Lefrançois, 1993). This is especially true with regard to advertising. In one survey, 40 percent of respondents over the age of 65 agreed that advertising portrays older people as unattractive and incompetent (Pomice, 1990). According to the advertising director of one magazine, "Advertising shows young people at their best and most beautiful, but it shows older people at their worst" (quoted in Pomice, 1990:42). Of older persons who do appear on television, most are male; only about one in ten characters appearing to be 65 or older is a woman, conveying a subtle message that older women especially are unimportant (Pomice, 1990).

Stereotypes also contribute to the view that women are "old" ten or fifteen years sooner than men (Bell, 1989). The multibillion-dollar cosmetics industry helps perpetuate the myth that age reduces the "sexual value" of women but increases it for men. Men's sexual value is defined more in terms of personality, intelligence, and earning power than physical appearance. For women, however, sexual attractiveness is based on youthful appearance. By idealizing this "youthful" image of women and playing up the fear of growing older, sponsors sell thousands of products that claim to prevent the "ravages" of aging.

Fortunately, in recent years there appears to have been a change in the media coverage of older persons. Analysis of books, magazines, advertisements, and television shows has shown that media images of older people have recently become more positive (Chen and Zhou, 1994; Novak, 1997). Features such as the "Aging Dangerously" segment on CBC radio's *This Morning* program draw attention to the contributions, talents, and stamina of older persons rather than offering stereotypical and negative portrayals.

Despite some changes in media coverage of older people, many younger individuals still hold negative stereotypes of "the elderly." In one study, William C. Levin (1988) showed photographs of the same man (disguised to appear as 25, 52, and 73 years of age in various photos) to a group of college students and asked them to evaluate these (apparently different) men for employment purposes. Based purely on the photographs, the "73-year-old" was viewed by many of the students as being less competent, less intelligent, and less reliable than the "25-year-old" and the "52-year-old."

Although not all people act on appearances alone, Patricia Moore, an industrial designer, found that many do. At the age of 27, Moore disguised herself as an 85-year-old woman by donning age-appropriate clothing and placing baby oil in her eyes to create the appearance of cataracts. With the help of a makeup artist, Moore supplemented the "aging process" with latex wrinkles, stained teeth, and a grey wig. For three years, "Old Pat Moore" went to various locations, including a grocery store, to see how people responded to her:

> When I did my grocery shopping while in character, I learned quickly that the Old Pat Moore behaved—and was treated—differently from the Young Pat Moore. When I was 85, people were more likely to jockey ahead of me in the checkout line. And even more interesting, I found that when it happened, I didn't say anything to the offender, as I certainly would at age 27. It seemed somehow, even to me, that it was okay for them to do this to the Old Pat Moore, since they were undoubtedly busier than I was anyway. And further, they apparently thought it was okay, too! After all, little old ladies have plenty of time, don't they? And then when I did get to the checkout counter, the clerk might start yelling, assuming I was deaf, or becoming immediately testy, assuming I would take a long time to get my money out, or would ask to have the price repeated, or somehow become confused about the transaction. What it all added up to was that people feared I

> would be trouble, so they tried to have as little to do with me as possible. And the amazing thing is that I began almost to believe it myself. … I think perhaps the worst thing about aging may be the overwhelming sense that everything around you is letting you know that you are not terribly important any more. (Moore with Conn, 1985:75–76)

If we apply our sociological imagination to Moore's study, we find that "Old Pat Moore's" experiences reflect what many older persons already know—it is other people's *reactions* to their age, not their age itself, that places them at a disadvantage.

Many older people buffer themselves against ageism by continuing to view themselves as being in middle adulthood long after their actual chronological age would suggest otherwise. In one study of people aged 60 and over, 75 percent of the respondents stated that they thought of themselves as middle-aged and only 10 percent viewed themselves as being old. When the same people were interviewed again ten years later, one-third still considered themselves to be middle-aged. Even at age 80, one out of four men and one out of five women said that the word *old* did not apply to them; this lack of willingness to acknowledge having reached older age is a consequence of ageism in society (Belsky, 1990).

Wealth, Poverty, and Aging

How have older people as a group fared economically in recent decades? There is no easy answer to this question. The elderly comprise an extremely heterogeneous group. Some of Canada's wealthiest individuals are old. There is also a significant number of this country's older citizens who are poor or nearly poor. The image of our elderly population living the "high life" on the backs of our younger population is a myth that only serves to perpetuate ageism.

In order to accurately assess the economic situation of older people, it is necessary to ask two questions. First, has the economic situation of older Canadians improved? Yes—rather dramatically. The income of people over the age of 65 has improved in the past two decades. In fact, the income for Canadians aged 65 and over has risen faster than that of the rest of the population since the early 1970s (Statistics Canada, 2000).

The second question is, do older Canadians maintain a satisfactory standard of living? The answer to this question is more complex. If we compare wealth (all economic resources of value, whether they produce cash or not) with income (available money or its equivalent in purchasing power), we find that older people tend to have more wealth but less income than younger people. For example, older people are more likely to own a home that has increased substantially in market value; however, some may not have the available cash to pay property taxes, to buy insurance, and to maintain the property (Moody, 1994). In short, although some older Canadians are able to maintain a reasonable standard of living, they do not have higher incomes than the rest of the population.

Changes to government income transfer programs, expansion of tax-sheltered RRSPs, and increased investment returns have reduced the incidence of low income among older people in Canada since the early 1970s (Ng, 1994). Yet, it is important to remember that although the economic situation of seniors has improved, 15 percent of all people over the age of 65 have low incomes. Furthermore, while income has risen in the past few years for older people in general, certain groups of older people still have incomes below the poverty line. Older people from lower-income backgrounds are people who cannot speak English or French, people with limited education, Aboriginal people, and people in small towns. In addition, very old people, women, and unattached individuals often live below the poverty line (Novak, 1993).

The Feminization of Poverty

> One conclusion stands out from all the facts and figures [about aging and poverty]: Poverty in old age is largely a woman's problem, and is becoming more so every year. (National Council of Welfare, quoted in Novak, 1993:239)

The poverty rate for elderly women is double the poverty rate for elderly men. *Unattached* elderly women are at the greatest risk of poverty with a rate that is double that of married elderly women. Why do women have such low incomes in old age? According to the National Council of Welfare, "after a lifetime spent taking care of their spouses and children, these women who had no opportunity to become financially self-sufficient are now abandoned by the generation that benefited most from their work" (quoted in Novak, 1993:239).

Although middle-aged and older women make up an increasing portion of the workforce, they are paid substantially less than men their age, receive raises at a slower pace, and still work largely in gender-segregated jobs (see Chapter 10). As a result, women do not garner economic security for their retirement years at the same rate that men do. These factors have contributed to the economic marginality of the current cohort of older women (Novak, 1993).

In a recent study, gerontologists Melissa A. Hardy and Lawrence E. Hazelrigg (1993) found that gender was more directly related to poverty in older persons than was ethnicity, educational background, or occupational status. Hardy and Hazelrigg (1993) suggested that many women who are now age 65 or over spent their early adult lives as financial dependents of husbands or as working nonmarried women trying to support themselves in a culture that did not see women as either the heads of households or the sole providers of family income. Because they were not viewed as being responsible for the family's financial security, women were paid less. Therefore, older women may now be relying on inadequate income replacement programs originally designed to treat them as dependents. Furthermore, women tend to marry men who are older than themselves, and women live longer than men. Consequently, nearly half of all women over the age of 65 are widowed and living alone on fixed incomes. The result? According to the National Council of Welfare, "after fifty years or so of unpaid, faithful service a women's only reward is likely to be poverty" (quoted in Novak, 1993:241).

Young women today will be much better equipped to deal with the financial pressures of old age as a result of a number of structural changes in Canadian society. The majority of women are working in the paid labour force, and more of them have begun to enter male-dominated professions and to belong to private pension plans (Connelly and MacDonald, 1990).

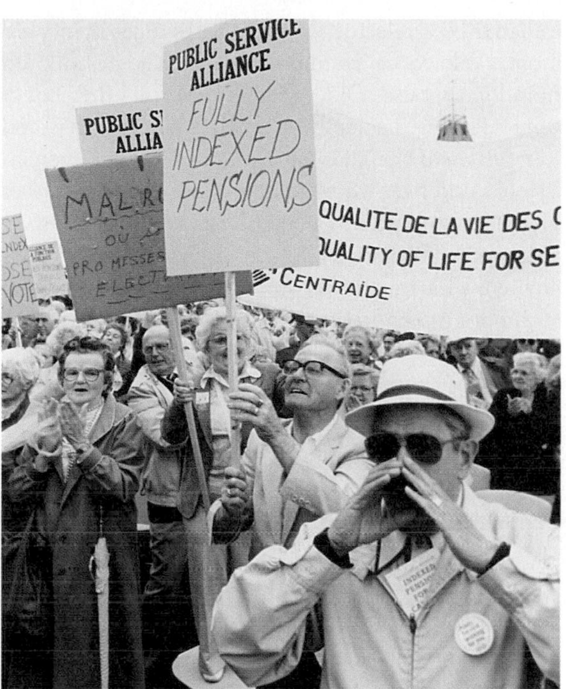

Older persons seek to be fully accepted as participants in everyday life, as this seniors protest demonstrates.

Elder Abuse

Abuse and neglect of older persons has received increasing public attention in recent years, due both to the increasing number of older people and to the establishment of more vocal groups to represent their concerns. ***Elder abuse*** **refers to physical abuse, psychological abuse, financial exploitation, and medical abuse or neglect of people aged 65 or older** (Patterson and Podnieks, 1995).

The elderly are often referred to as "hidden victims" of intimate violence (DeKeseredy, 1996). It is difficult to determine the extent of the abuse of older persons. Many victims are understandably reluctant to talk about it. One study used a cross-Canada telephone survey of elderly persons living in private houses (Podnieks, 1989). Four percent of a randomly selected sample reported some form of abuse. Although this may appear to be a small percentage, 4 percent of all seniors living in private dwellings translates into 98,000 Canadians. Many cases of abuse are chronic or repetitive. Podnieks reported that only 25 percent of the victims of elder abuse had reported the incident to the police. In only one case was a criminal charge laid. The most common reasons for not reporting the incident were that it was not serious enough to report to the police or it was a private family matter. The research indicates that elder abuse tends to be concentrated among those over the age of 75 (Steinmetz, 1987). In most cases the abuse is inflicted by a relative. In these cases older men were more likely to be victimized by their adult children than by a spouse. Older women, on the other hand, were victimized equally by both adult children and spouses. As is the case with younger women, women aged 65 and over were more frequently the victims of violence committed by family members than were older men (Statistics Canada, 1999c). Abusers usually live with the victim and have often cared for the victim for a long time.

Death and Dying

Historically, death has been a common occurrence at all stages of the life course. Until the twentieth century, the chances that a newborn child would live to adulthood were very small. Poor nutrition, infectious diseases, accidents, and natural disasters took their toll on men and women of all ages. In contemporary industrial societies, however, death is looked on as unnatural because it has largely been removed from everyday life. Most deaths now occur among older persons and in institutional settings. The association of death with the aging process has contributed to ageism in our society; if people can deny aging, they feel they can deny death (Atchley, 1994).

How do people cope with dying? To answer this question, psychiatrist Elisabeth Kübler-Ross (1969) proposed five stages: (1) denial ("Not me!"), (2) anger ("Why me?"), (3) bargaining ("Yes me, but ... "—negotiating for divine intervention), (4) depression and sense of loss, and (5) acceptance. She pointed out that these stages are not the same for all people; some of them may exist at the same time. Kübler-Ross (1969:138) also stated that "the one thing that usually persists through all these stages is hope."

Kübler-Ross's stages were attractive to the general public and the media because they provided common responses to a difficult situation. On the other hand, her stage-based model also generated a great deal of criticism. Some have pointed out that these stages have never been conclusively demonstrated or comprehensively explained. Others have noted that there are many ways in which people cope with dying, not just five.

Criticisms notwithstanding, Kübler-Ross's perspective made the process of dying an acceptable topic for public discussion and helped facilitate the hospice movement in the 1970s (Weitz, 1995). A ***hospice*** **is a homelike facility that provides supportive care for patients with terminal illnesses.** The hospice philosophy asserts that people should participate in their own care and have control over as many decisions pertaining to their life as possible. Pain and suffering should be minimized, but artificial measures should not be used to sustain life. This approach is family based and provides support for family members and friends, as well as for the person who is dying (see Corr, Nabe, and Corr, 1994). Although the hospice movement has been very successful, critics claim that the movement has exchanged much of its initial philosophy and goals for social acceptance and financial support (Finn Paradis and Cummings, 1986; Weitz, 1995).

SOCIALIZATION IN THE FUTURE

In the twenty-first century, the family is likely to remain the institution that most fundamentally shapes and nurtures personal values and self-identity. However, parents increasingly may feel overburdened by this responsibility, especially without societal support—such as high-quality, affordable child care—and more education in parenting skills. Some analysts have suggested that there will be an increase in known cases of child abuse and in the number of children who experience delayed psychosocial development, learning difficulties, and emotional and behavioural problems. They attribute these increases to the dramatic changes occurring in the size, structure, and economic stability of families.

A central value-oriented issue facing parents and teachers as they attempt to socialize children is the growing dominance of the mass media and other forms of technology. For example, interactive television and computer networking systems will enable children to experience many things outside their own homes and schools and to communicate regularly with people around the world. If futurists are correct in predicting that ideas and information and access to them will be the basis for personal, business, and political advancement in the twenty-first century, people without access to computers and other information technology will become even more disadvantaged. This prediction raises important issues about the effects of social inequality on the socialization process. In this new century, socialization—a lifelong learning process—can no longer be viewed as a "glance in the rearview mirror" or a reaction to some previous experience. With the rapid pace of technological change, we must not only learn about the past but learn how to anticipate—and consider the consequences of—the future (Westrum, 1991).

CHAPTER REVIEW

What is socialization and why is it important?

Socialization is the lifelong process through which individuals acquire their self-identity and learn the physical, mental, and social skills needed for survival in society. The kind of person we become depends greatly on what we learn during our formative years from our surrounding social groups and social environment.

How many of our unique human characteristics come from heredity and how many from our social environment?

Each of us is a product of two forces:
(1) heredity, referred to as "nature," and
(2) the social environment, referred to as "nurture."
While biology dictates our physical makeup, the social environment largely determines how we develop and behave.

How do sociologists understand the development of self-concept?

Charles Horton Cooley developed the image of the looking-glass self to explain how people see themselves through the perceptions of others. Our initial sense of self is typically based on how families perceive and treat us. George Herbert Mead linked the idea of self-concept to role-playing and to learning the rules of social interaction. According to Mead, the self is divided into the "I" and the "me." The "I" represents the spontaneous and unique traits of each person. The "me" represents the internalized attitudes and demands of other members of society.

What are the main psychological theories of human development?

Sigmund Freud divided the self into three interrelated forces: the id, the ego, and the superego. When a person is well adjusted, the three forces act in balance. Jean Piaget identified four cognitive stages of development; at each stage, children's activities are governed by how they understand the world around them. Lawrence Kohlberg classified moral development into six stages and said that certain levels of cognitive development are essential before corresponding levels of moral reasoning may occur. Carol Gilligan suggested that there are male–female differences regarding morality and identified three stages in female moral development.

What are the most important agents of socialization?

The people, groups, and institutions that teach us what we need to know in order to participate in society are called agents of socialization. The most important of these are the family, schools, peer groups, and the media.

When does socialization end?

Socialization is ongoing throughout the life course. We learn knowledge and skills for future roles through anticipatory socialization. Parents are socialized by their own children, and adults learn through workplace socialization. Resocialization is the process of learning new attitudes, values, and behaviours, either voluntarily or involuntarily.

What is gerontology? What are ageism and elder abuse?

Ageism is prejudice and discrimination against people on the basis of age, particularly when they are older persons. Ageism is reinforced by stereotypes of older people. Elder abuse includes physical abuse, psychological abuse, financial exploitation, and medical abuse or neglect of people aged 65 or older. Passive neglect is the most common form of abuse.

Key Terms

ageism 92
agents of socialization 79
anticipatory socialization 87
chronological age 87
ego 77
elder abuse 95
functional age 87
gender socialization 86
generalized other 76
hospice 96
id 76
looking-glass self 73
peer group 81
resocialization 85
role-taking 74
self-concept 72

significant others 75
social gerontology 89
socialization 68
superego 77
total institution 85

Internet Exercises

1. Have you ever wondered what type of personality you have? Visit the Keirsey Temperament Sorter (**www.davideck.com/links/keirsey1.html**) and take the personality test. How well do the results agree with what you think of yourself? Compare Keirsey's test to any of the personality tests given at The Personality Test Corner (**www.signet.com.sg/~tangs/Test/test.html**). Which are more accurate?
2. The World Wide Web is a form of mass media that allows one person or group to communicate a message to any number of people. Unlike most forms of mass media, there are no restrictions on what a person can say or do on a Web page. To demonstrate this, pick a prominent political figure who has been in the news lately. Go to Yahoo!'s Canadian Newspaper links page (**www.yahoo.ca/Regional/Countries/Canada/News_and_Media/Newspapers**) and read about this person in any of Canada's newspapers. Then do a search for this figure using the Lycos search engine (**www.lycos.com**). How is the media's depiction of this figure the same as, and different from, the way this person is portrayed on various Web sites? How do the depictions of this person differ from page to page? How would reading only one of these pages bias your opinion? What are the positive and negative effects of having such a wide variety of viewpoints and interpretations of individuals and events on the World Wide Web?
3. Much of the Internet seems to revolve around people in their twenties or thirties. However, there are some sites and chat rooms maintained by and devoted to people who are older. Use Yahoo! (**www.yahoo.com**) to find sites aimed at older people. How do these sites differ from those geared toward a younger audience?

Net Links

For more Web links related to the topic of this chapter, see the Nelson sociology Web site: **www.sociologyessentials-2nded.nelson.com**.

The International Society for the Prevention of Child Abuse and Neglect works toward the prevention and treatment of child abuse, neglect, and exploitation. To view its site, go to:

www.ispcan.org

For current and expert knowledge about healthy socialization and development, visit the Voices for Children site at:

www.voices4children.org

To see an Internet journal on the development, care, and education of young children, go to:

www.ecrp.uiuc.edu

Several universities, including the University of Manitoba, have research centres focusing on aging. See how sociologists approach aging and pick up other Net links at:

www.umanitoba.ca/centres/aging

For data about Canada's seniors, see the Canada's Seniors at a Glance Web site:

www.hc-sc.gc.ca/seniors-aines/pubs/poster/seniors/page1e.htm

Questions for Critical Thinking

1. Consider the concept of the looking-glass self. How do you think others perceive you? Do you think most people perceive you correctly?
2. What are some different ways you might study the effect of toys on the socialization of children? How could you isolate the toy variable from other variables that influence children's socialization?
3. How can individuals who were abused as children be resocialized toward nurturing behaviour as adults?
4. Is it necessary to have a mandatory retirement age?
5. How will the size of the older population in Canada affect society in the twenty-first century?

Suggested Readings

These books provide in-depth information on various aspects of socialization:

Carol Gilligan. *In a Different Voice: Psychological Theory and Women's Development*. Cambridge, Mass.: Harvard University Press, 1982.

Erving Goffman. *Asylums: Essays on the Social Situation of Mental Patients and Other Inmates*. Chicago: Aldine, 1961.

Bernice Lott. *Women's Lives: Themes and Variations in Gender Learning* (2nd ed.). Pacific Grove, Cal.: Brooks/Cole, 1994.

George Herbert Mead. *Mind, Self, and Society from the Standpoint of a Social Behaviouralist*. Charles W. Morris (ed.). Chicago: University of Chicago Press, 1962; orig. pub. 1934.

To find out more about the problem of child abuse:

Sylvia Fraser. *My Father's House: A Memoir of Incest and Healing*. Toronto: Doubleday, 1987.

Connie Guberman and Margie Wolfe (eds.). *No Safe Place: Violence Against Women and Children*. Toronto: Women's Press, 1985.

Dave Pelzer. *A Child Called "It."* Deerfield Beach, Fla.: Health Communications, 1995.

David A. Wolfe. *Child Abuse: Implications for Child Development and Psychopathology*. Newbury Park, Cal.: Sage, 1987.

INFOTRAC® COLLEGE EDITION

Either from the *Sociology In Our Times: The Essentials* Web site (**www.sociologyessentials-2nded.nelson.com**) or directly from your Web browser, you may access InfoTrac® College Edition, an online university library that includes over 600 popular and scholarly journals in which you can find articles related to the topics in this chapter.

CHAPTER 4

Twenty-year-old David moved to Vancouver looking for a job. He rented a bachelor apartment in the downtown core with most of his savings and set out to find a job. One evening he was robbed of all his belongings, including the rest of his life savings, which as meagre as they were, he had not bothered to deposit in a bank. David found himself without a place to stay, with his dreams in ruins. When he was interviewed, David had been homeless for three months. He was unable to go out to look for work. Demoralized, victimized, and too embarrassed to go to his family for assistance, he spent his days wandering the downtown areas of Vancouver. David describes his "drift" into homelessness:

"When I walked across the threshold of the shelter it was like someone had just hit me in the guts. I felt sick to my stomach. I'd read about homeless people but they were different, bums, and that wasn't me. Now, here I was just like them, one of them, a bum. It was a shock that has left me numb ever since. You know you're at rock bottom but you just can't shake it. You're homeless, a homeless person, that's your identity now, everything else just drops away. It's like the rest of your life never happened ... It'll probably take me months more to get out of this rut. I know I will, but it gets harder every day, you get used to it." (O'Reilly-Fleming, 1993:56)

David's activities reflect a specific pattern of social behaviour. All activities in life—including living in shelters, hostels, or "on the streets"—are social in nature. Homeless persons and domiciled persons (those with homes) live in social worlds that have predictable patterns of social interaction. ***Social interaction* is the process by which people act toward or respond to other people and is the foundation for all relationships and groups in society.** In this chapter, we look at the relationship between social structure and social interaction. In the process, homelessness is used as an example of how social problems occur and may be perpetuated within social structures and patterns of interaction.

***Social structure* is the stable pattern of social relationships that exists within a particular group or society.**

SOCIAL STRUCTURE, SOCIAL INTERACTION, AND COLLECTIVE BEHAVIOUR

This structure is essential for the survival of society and for the well-being of individuals because it provides a social web of familial support and social relationships that connects each of us to the larger society. Many homeless people have lost this vital linkage. As a result, they often experience a loss of both personal dignity and a sense of moral worth because of their "homeless" condition (Snow and Anderson, 1993).

In the years since 1987, the International Year of Shelter for the Homeless, there has been little improvement in the homelessness situation in Canada. In fact, a 1998 United Nations report was highly critical of Canada for failing to take care of its poor, highlighting crisis levels of homelessness, inadequate funding for women's shelters, and grossly substandard living conditions in many Aboriginal communities. Governments are now being asked to declare homelessness a national disaster.

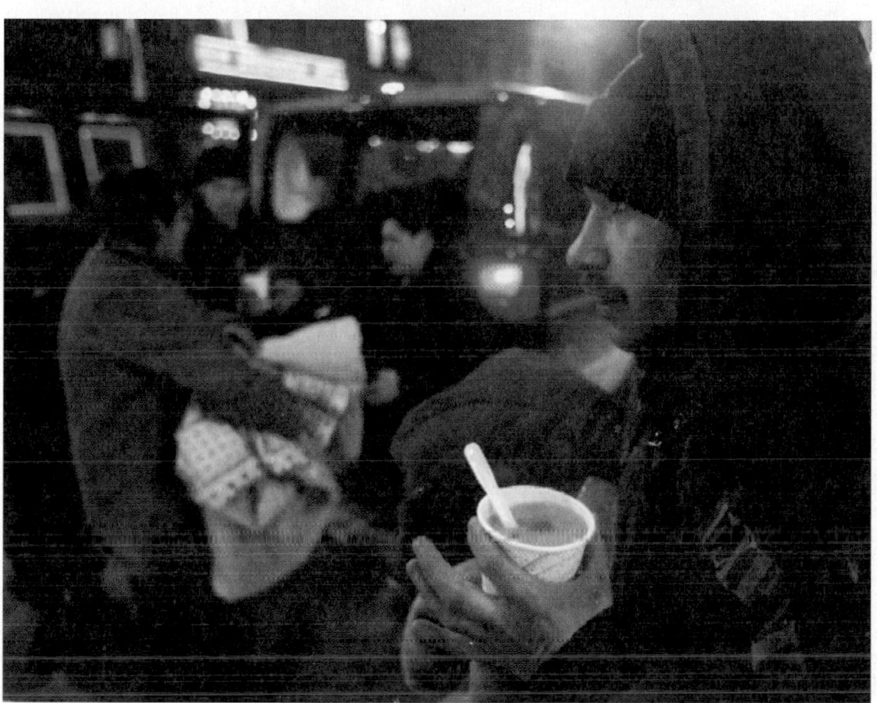

Who are the homeless? Before reading on, take the quiz on homelessness in Box 4.1. The profile of Canada's homeless has changed dramatically in recent years. Our stereotypical image of single, alcoholic, or drug-using males "down on their luck" is far from an accurate reflection of our country's homeless population. Now included in the category of homeless are people who have never before had to depend on social assistance for food, clothing, and a roof over their heads. Today's homeless include increasing numbers of women and children, adolescents, and Aboriginal people. One of the most disturbing changes among the homeless has been the rapid growth in the numbers of homeless women and children. For example, in Toronto an average of 3600 people a day stay in emergency shelters—50 percent of whom are families with children (Canadian Public Health Association, 1997).

Also startling is the overrepresentation of Aboriginal people in Canada's homeless population. ***Relative homelessness*—being housed in a dwelling that fails to meet basic living standards**—is disturbingly common in both the urban and rural Aboriginal population. Although most of the research has been done in Western Canada, large numbers of Aboriginal homeless also populate Eastern cities such as Toronto and Montreal (Beavis et al., 1997). Refugees and visible minorities are also overrepresented among the homeless (O'Reilly-Fleming, 1993).

Homeless people come from all walks of life. They live in cities, suburbs, and rural areas. Contrary to popular myth, most of the homeless are not on the streets by choice or because they were deinstitutionalized by mental hospitals (Canadian Public Health Association, 1997).

Questions and Issues

CHAPTER FOCUS QUESTION: How is homelessness related to the social structure of a society?

What are the components of social structure?

How do societies maintain social solidarity and continue to function in times of rapid change?

Why do societies have shared patterns of social interaction?

Do changes in society occur through individual or institutional efforts?

What causes people to engage in collective behaviour?

What are some common forms of collective behaviour?

Although eating from a dumpster may appear to be an individual act, this behaviour—like all other activities in life—is affected by the larger patterns of social interaction and social structure found in society.

SOCIAL STRUCTURE: THE MACROLEVEL PERSPECTIVE

Social structure provides the framework within which we interact with others. This framework is an orderly, fixed arrangement of parts that together make up the whole group or society (see Figure 4.1). At the macrolevel, the social structure of a society has several essential elements: social institutions, groups, statuses, roles, and norms.

Functional theorists emphasize that social structure is essential because it creates order and predictability in a society (Parsons, 1951). Social structure also is important for our human development. As we saw in Chapter 3, we develop a self-concept as we learn the attitudes, values, and behaviours of the people around us. When these attitudes and values are part of a predictable structure, it is easier to develop that self-concept.

Social structure gives us the ability to interpret the social situations we encounter. For example, we expect our families to care for us, our schools to educate us, and our police to protect us. When our circumstances change dramatically, most of us feel an acute sense of anxiety because we do not know what to expect or what is expected of us. For example, newly homeless individuals may feel disoriented because they do not know how to function in their new setting. The person is likely to wonder, "How will I survive on the streets?" "Where do I go to get help?" "Should I stay at a shelter?" and "Where can I get a job?" Social structure helps people make sense out of their environment, even when they find themselves on the streets.

In addition to providing a map for our encounters with others, social structure may limit our options and place us in arbitrary categories not of our own choosing. Conflict theorists maintain that there is more to the social structure than is readily visible and that we must explore the deeper, underlying structures that determine social relations in a society. Karl Marx suggested that the way economic production is organized is the most important structural aspect of any society. In capitalistic societies where a few people control the labour of many, the social structure reflects a system of relationships of domination among categories of people (for example, owner–worker and employer–employee).

Social structure creates boundaries that define which persons or groups will be the "insiders" and which will be the "outsiders." ***Social marginality* is the state of being part insider and part outsider in the social structure.** Sociologist Robert Park (1928) coined this term to refer to persons (such as immigrants) who simultaneously share the life and traditions of two distinct groups. Social marginality can result in stigmatization. A ***stigma* is any physical or social attribute or sign that so devalues a person's social identity that it disqualifies that person from full social acceptance** (Goffman, 1963b). A convicted criminal, wearing a prison uniform, is an example of a person who has been stigmatized; the uniform says that the person has done something wrong and should not be allowed unsupervised outside the prison walls.

COMPONENTS OF SOCIAL STRUCTURE

The social structure of a society includes its social positions, the relationships among those positions, and the kinds of resources attached to each of the positions. Social structure also includes all of the groups that make up society and the relationships

BOX 4.1 SOCIOLOGY AND EVERYDAY LIFE

How Much Do You Know about Homelessness?

TRUE	FALSE	
T	F	1. Many homeless people choose to be homeless.
T	F	2. There are an estimated 20,000 homeless people in Canada.
T	F	3. Homeless people do not work.
T	F	4. Most homeless people are mentally ill.
T	F	5. Older men over the age of 50 make up most of Canada's homeless population.
T	F	6. Most homeless people are alcoholics and substance abusers.
T	F	7. The number of homeless adolescents has increased in the past decade.
T	F	8. Homelessness is a relatively new social problem in Canada.
T	F	9. One out of every four homeless people is a child.
T	F	10. Some homeless people have attended university.

Answers on page 104.

among those groups (Smelser, 1988). We begin by examining the social positions that are closest to the individual.

Status

A ***status*** **is a socially defined position in a group or society characterized by certain expectations, rights, and duties.** Statuses exist independently of the specific people occupying them (Linton, 1936); the statuses of professional athlete, rock musician, professor, university student, and homeless person all exist exclusive of the specific individuals who occupy these social positions. For example, although thousands of new students arrive on university campuses each year to occupy the status of first-year student, the status of university student and the expectations attached to that position have remained relatively unchanged for most of the past hundred years.

Does the term *status* refer only to high-level positions in society? No, not in a sociological sense. Although many people equate the term *status* with high levels of prestige, sociologists use it to refer to *all* socially defined positions—high and low rank.

Take a moment to answer the question, "Who am I?" To determine who you are, you must think about your social identity, which is derived from the statuses you occupy and is based on your status set. A ***status set*** **is made up of all the statuses that a person occupies at a given time.** For example, Marie may be a psychologist, a professor, a wife, a mother, a Catholic, a school volunteer, an Alberta resident, and a French Canadian. All of these socially defined positions constitute her status set.

ASCRIBED AND ACHIEVED STATUS Statuses are distinguished by the manner in which we acquire them. An ***ascribed status*** **is a social position conferred at birth or received involuntarily later in life, based on attributes over which the individual has little or no control,** such as ethnicity, age, and gender. Marie, for example, is a female born to French Canadian parents; she was assigned these statuses at birth. An ***achieved status*** **is a social position a person assumes voluntarily as a result of personal choice, merit, or direct effort.** Achieved statuses (such as occupation, education, and income) are thought to be gained as a result of personal ability or successful competition. Most occupational positions in modern societies are achieved statuses. Not all achieved statuses, however, are positions most people would want to attain; being a criminal, a drug addict, or a homeless person, for example, are negative achieved statuses.

Ascribed statuses have a significant influence on the achieved statuses we occupy. Ethnicity, gender, and age affect each person's opportunity to acquire certain achieved statuses. Those who are privileged by their positive ascribed statuses are more likely to

BOX 4.1 SOCIOLOGY AND EVERYDAY LIFE

Answers to the Sociology Quiz on Homelessness

1. **False.** This myth is an example of "blaming the victim." Homelessness is the result of a number of social factors—namely, poverty, changes in the housing market, and growing rates of unemployment.
2. **False.** Recent estimates place the number of homeless Canadians at approximately 200,000, 25 percent of whom live in Toronto. It is very difficult to get an accurate estimate of the total number of homeless individuals in Canada given the transient status of these individuals.
3. **False.** Many homeless people are among the working poor. Minimum-wage jobs do not pay enough for an individual to support a family and pay for housing.
4. **False.** Approximately 20 percent of homeless people are mentally ill.
5. **False.** Men over the age of 50 no longer represent the majority of the homeless. The composition of the homeless population has changed significantly in the past twenty years. Now, young men, teenagers, and families with children are predominant among homeless Canadians.
6. **False.** Most homeless people are not heavy drug users. Estimates suggest that about one-fourth of the homeless are substance abusers. Many of these individuals are also mentally ill.
7. **True.** The growth in this population of "street youth" has significantly altered the population of homeless Canadians. Over 70 percent of these youth report leaving home because of physical and sexual abuse.
8. **False.** Homelessness has always existed in Canada. However, the problem has grown to such proportions that the mayors of Canada's ten largest cities have declared homelessness a national disaster.
9. **True.** Children also make up the fastest growing category of homeless people in North America.
10. **True.** Some homeless people have attended university, and some have gone to graduate school. Many have completed high school.

Sources: Based on Harman, 1989; Liebow, 1993, O'Reilly-Fleming, 1993; Corelli, 1996; Canadian Public Health Association, 1997; and Branswell, 1998.

achieve the more prestigious positions in a society. Those who are disadvantaged by their ascribed statuses may more easily acquire negative achieved statuses.

MASTER STATUS If we occupy many different statuses, how can we determine which is the most important? Sociologist Everett Hughes has stated that societies resolve this ambiguity by determining master statuses. A ***master status* is the most important status a person occupies;** it dominates all of the individual's other statuses and is the overriding ingredient in determining a person's general social position (Hughes, 1945). Being poor or rich is a master status that influences many other areas of life, including health, education, and life opportunities. Historically, the most common master statuses for women have related to positions in the family, such as daughter, wife, and mother. For men, occupation usually has been the most important status, although occupation increasingly is a master status for many women as well. "What do you do?" is one of the first questions many people ask when meeting one another. Occupation provides important clues to a person's educational level, income, and family background. An individual's ethnicity also may constitute a master status in a society in which dominant group members single out members of other groups as "inferior" on the basis of real or alleged physical, cultural, or nationality characteristics (see Feagin and Feagin, 1996).

Master statuses are vital to how we view ourselves, how we are seen by others, and how we interact with others. Beverley McLachlin is both the chief justice of the Supreme Court and a mother. Which is her master status? Can you imagine how

FIGURE 4.1 Social Structure Framework

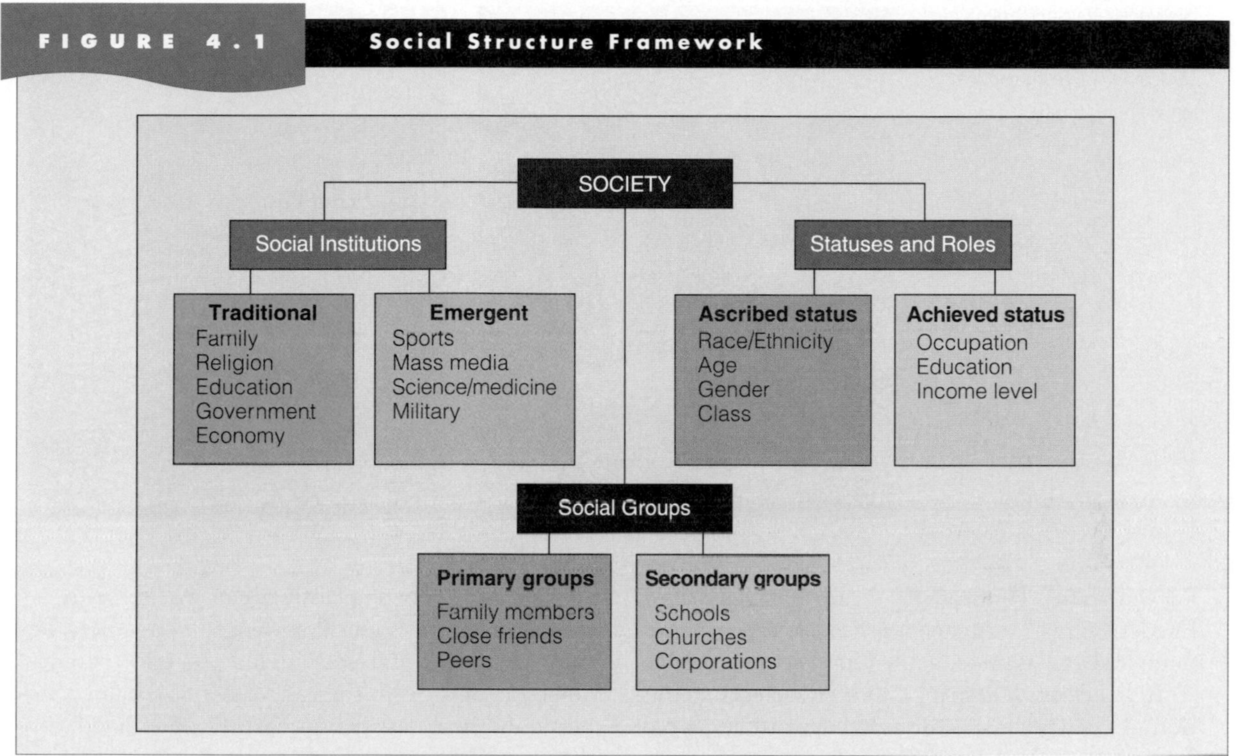

she would react if attorneys arguing a case before the Supreme Court of Canada treated her as if she were a mother rather than the chief justice? Lawyers wisely use "Honourable Madam Justice" as her master status and act accordingly.

Master statuses confer high or low levels of personal worth and dignity on people. Those are not characteristics that we inherently possess; they are derived from the statuses we occupy. For those who have no residence, being a homeless person readily becomes a master status regardless of the person's other attributes. Homelessness is a stigmatized master status that confers disrepute on its occupant because domiciled people often believe a homeless person has a "character flaw." The circumstances under which someone becomes homeless determine the extent to which that person is stigmatized. For example, individuals who become homeless as a result of natural disasters (such as floods or ice storms) are not seen as causing their homelessness or as being a threat to the community. Thus, they are less likely to be stigmatized. However, in cases in which homeless persons are viewed as the cause of their own problems, they are more likely to be stigmatized and marginalized by others.

STATUS SYMBOLS When people are proud of a particular social status they occupy, they often choose to use visible means to let others know about their position. ***Status symbols*** **are material signs that inform others of a person's specific status.** For example, just as wearing a wedding ring proclaims that a person is married, owning a Rolls-Royce announces that one has "made it." In North American society, people who have "made it" frequently want symbols to inform others of their accomplishments.

In our daily lives, status symbols both announce our statuses and facilitate our interactions with others. For example, medical students wear white lab jackets with plastic name tags identifying their status to all hospital personnel, patients, or visitors they encounter (Haas and Shaffir, 1995). The length and colour of a person's uniform in a hospital may indicate the individual's status within the medical centre.

Roles

Role is the dynamic aspect of a status. While we *occupy* a status, we *play* a role (Linton, 1936). A ***role*** **is a set of behavioural expectations associated with**

How does your perception of Sheila Copps's master status change when you compare these photographs?

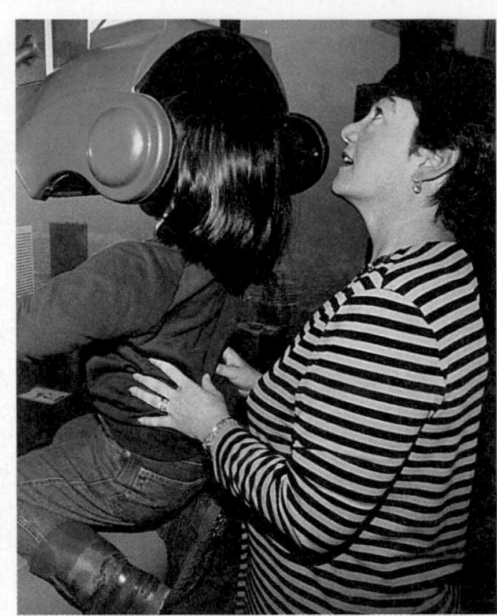

a given status. For example, a carpenter (employee) hired to remodel a kitchen is not expected to sit down uninvited and join the family (employer) for dinner.

***Role expectation* is a group's or society's definition of the way a specific role ought to be played.** By contrast, ***role performance* is how a person *actually* plays the role**. Role performance does not always match role expectation. Some statuses have role expectations that are highly specific, such as that of surgeon or university professor. Other statuses, such as friend or significant other, have less structured expectations. The role expectations tied to the status of student are more specific than those for being a friend. Role expectations typically are based on a range of acceptable behaviour rather than on strictly defined standards.

Our roles are relational (or complementary); that is, they are defined in the context of roles performed by others. We can play the role of student because someone else fulfils the role of professor. Conversely, to perform the role of professor, the teacher must have one or more students.

Role ambiguity occurs when the expectations associated with a role are unclear. For example, it is not always clear when the provider–dependent aspect of the parent–child relationship ends. Should it end at the age of 18 or 21? When a person is no longer in school? Different people will answer these questions differently depending on their experiences and socialization, as well as on the parents' financial capability and psychological willingness to continue contributing to the welfare of their adult children.

Role ambiguity frequently occurs when a status is relatively new or is unacknowledged by a society. In Canada, such statuses include single parent, domestic partner (in the case of gay or lesbian couples), and homeless person. On the one hand, for the homeless, the role of "street person" and the activities associated with it (such as day labour, panhandling, or scavenging) are devalued by society. On the other hand, some of the skills needed by the homeless for day-to-day survival (such as "street smarts") are valued in other contexts, such as a "wilderness survival course," where a person must be able to live in an unfamiliar and sometimes harsh environment with very limited resources. Such problems of role ambiguity often are closely linked with role conflict and role strain.

ROLE CONFLICT AND ROLE STRAIN Most people occupy a number of statuses, each of which has numerous role expectations attached. For example, Charles is a student who attends morning classes at the university, and an employee at a fast-food restaurant where he works from 3 to 10 p.m. He also is Stephanie's boyfriend, and she would like to see him more often. On December 7, Charles has a final exam at 7 p.m., when he is supposed to be working. Meanwhile, Stephanie is pressuring him to take her to a movie. To top it off, his mother calls, asking him to fly home because his father is going to have emergency surgery. How can Charles be in all of these places at once? Such experiences of role conflict can be overwhelming.

***Role conflict* occurs when incompatible role demands are placed on a person by two or more statuses held at the same time.** When role conflict occurs, we may feel pulled in different directions. To deal with this problem, we may prioritize our roles and first complete the one we consider to be most important. Or we may *compartmentalize* our lives and "insulate" our various roles (Merton, 1968). That is, we may perform the activities linked to one role for part of the day, and then engage in the activities associated with another role in some other time period or elsewhere. For example, under routine circumstances, Charles would fulfil his student role for part of the day and his employee role for another part of the day. In his current situation, however, he is unable to compartmentalize his roles.

Role conflict may occur as a result of changing statuses and roles in society. Research has found that women who engage in behaviour that is gender-typed as "masculine" tend to have higher rates of role conflict than those who engage in traditional "feminine" behaviour (Basow, 1992). According to sociologist Tracey Watson (1987), role conflict sometimes can be attributed not to the roles themselves but to the pressures people feel when they do not fit into culturally prescribed roles. In her study of women athletes in college sports programs, Watson found role conflict in the traditionally incongruent identities of being a woman and being an athlete. Even though the women athletes in her study wore makeup and presented a conventional image when they were not on the basketball court, their peers in school still saw them as "female jocks," thus leading to role conflict.

Whereas role conflict occurs between two or more statuses (such as being homeless and being a temporary employee of a social services agency), role strain takes place within one status. ***Role strain* occurs when incompatible demands are built into a single status that a person occupies** (Goode, 1960). For example, many women experience role strain in the labour force because they hold jobs that are "less satisfying and more stressful than men's jobs since they involve less money, less prestige, fewer job openings, more career roadblocks, and so forth" (Basow, 1992:192). Similarly, married women may experience more role strain than married men, because of work overload, marital inequality with their spouse, exclusive parenting responsibilities, unclear expectations, and lack of emotional support.

Recent social changes may have increased role strain in men. In the family, men's traditional position of dominance has eroded as more women have entered the paid labour force and demanded more assistance in child-rearing and homemaking responsibilities. High rates of unemployment have produced problems for many men whose major role in the past was centred on their occupation.

Individuals frequently distance themselves from a role they find extremely stressful or otherwise problematic. People use distancing techniques when they do not want others to take them as the "self" implied in a particular role, especially if they think the role is "beneath them." While Charles is working at the fast-food restaurant, for example, he does not want people to think of him as a "loser in a dead-end job." He wants them to view him as a university student who is working there just to "pick up a few bucks" until he graduates.

Role distancing is most likely to occur when people find themselves in roles in which the social identities implied are inconsistent with how they think of themselves or how they want to be viewed by others. Snow and Anderson found that role distancing was common among the homeless—especially the recently homeless. One 24-year-old man who had been homeless for only a few weeks commented:

> I'm not like the other guys who hang down at the Sally [Salvation Army]. If you want to know about the street people, I can tell you about them; but you can't really learn about street people from studying me, because I'm different. (1993:349)

These individuals often pursue employment opportunities in an effort to exit their role as a homeless person as quickly as possible.

ROLE EXIT ***Role exit* occurs when people disengage from social roles that have been central to their self-identity** (Ebaugh, 1988). Sociologist Helen Rose Fuchs Ebaugh studied this process by interviewing ex-convicts, ex-nuns, retirees, divorced men and women, and others who had exited voluntarily from significant social roles. According to Ebaugh, role exit occurs in four stages. The first stage is doubt, in which people experience frustration or burnout when they reflect on their existing roles. The second stage involves a search for alter-

For many years, capitalism has been dominated by powerful "old-boy" social networks.

natives; here, people may take a leave of absence from their work or temporarily separate from their marriage partner. The third stage is the turning point at which people realize that they must take some final action, such as quitting their job or getting a divorce. The fourth and final stage involves the creation of a new identity.

Groups

Groups are another important component of social structure. To sociologists, a ***social group* consists of two or more people who interact frequently and share a common identity and a feeling of interdependence.** Throughout our lives, most of us participate in groups, from our families and childhood friends, to our university classes, to our work and community organizations, and even to society.

Primary and secondary groups are the two basic types of social groups. A ***primary group* is a small, less specialized group in which members engage in face-to-face, emotion-based interactions over an extended period of time.** Typically, primary groups include our family, close friends, and school or work-related peer groups. By contrast, a ***secondary group* is a larger, more specialized group in which members engage in more impersonal, goal-oriented relationships for a limited period of time.** Schools, churches, the military, and corporations are examples of secondary groups. In secondary groups, people have few, if any, emotional ties to one another. Instead, they come together for some specific, practical purpose, such as getting a degree or a paycheque. Secondary groups are more specialized than primary ones; individuals relate to one another in terms of specific roles (such as professor and student) and more limited activities (such as course-related endeavours).

***Social solidarity*, or cohesion, relates to a group's ability to maintain itself in the face of obstacles.** Social solidarity exists when social bonds, attractions, or other forces hold members of a group in interaction over a period of time (Jary and Jary, 1991). For example, if a local church is destroyed by fire and congregation members still worship together, in a makeshift setting, then they have a high degree of social solidarity.

Many of us build social networks from our personal friends in primary groups and our acquaintances in secondary groups. A ***social network* is a series of social relationships that link an individual to others.** Social networks work differently for men and women, for different ethnic groups, and for members of different social classes. Traditionally, visible minorities and women have been excluded from powerful "old-boy" social net-

Whose interests are served when residential and commercial properties in a city become more upscale? How might functionalists and conflict theorists differ in their interpretations of scenes like this one?

works (Kanter, 1977; McPherson and Smith-Lovin, 1982, 1986). At the middle- and upper-class levels, individuals tap social networks to find employment, make business deals, and win political elections. However, social networks typically do not work effectively for poor and homeless individuals. Snow and Anderson (1993) found that homeless men have fragile social networks that are plagued with instability. They often do not even know each other's "real" names.

Sociological research on the homeless largely has emphasized the social isolation experienced by people on the streets. Sociologist Peter H. Rossi (1989) found that a high degree of social isolation exists because the homeless are separated from their extended family and former friends. Rossi noted that among the homeless who did have families, most either did not wish to return to them or believed that they would not be welcome. Most of the avenues for exiting the homeless role and acquiring housing are intertwined with the large-scale, secondary groups that sociologists refer to as formal organizations.

A ***formal organization*** **is a highly structured group formed for the purpose of completing certain tasks or achieving specific goals.** Many of us spend most of our time in formal organizations, such as universities, corporations, or the government. In Chapter 5 ("Groups and Organizations"), we analyze the characteristics of bureaucratic organizations; however, at this point, we should note that these organizations are a very important component of social structure in all industrialized societies. We expect such organizations to educate us, solve our social problems (such as crime and homelessness), and provide work opportunities.

Social Institutions

At the macrolevel of all societies, certain basic activities routinely occur—children are born and socialized, goods and services are produced and distributed, order is preserved, and a sense of purpose is maintained (Aberle et al., 1950; Mack and Bradford, 1979). Social institutions are the means by which these basic needs are met. A ***social institution*** **is a set of organized beliefs and rules that establish how a society will attempt to meet its basic social needs.** In the past, these needs have centred around five basic social institutions: the family, religion, education, the economy, and the government or politics. Today, mass media, sports, science and medicine, and the military also are considered to be social institutions.

What is the difference between a group and a social institution? A group is composed of specific, identifiable people; an institution is a standardized way of doing something. The concept of "family" helps to distinguish between the two. When we talk about your family or my family, we are referring to *a* family. When we refer to *the* family as a social institution, we are talking about ideologies and standardized patterns of behaviour that organize family life. For example, the family as a social institution contains certain statuses

BOX 4.2 CRITICAL THINKING

The Ethics of Legislating against Panhandling

Are homeless people in Canada allowed to sleep in parks and other public areas? Should homeless people be permitted to support themselves by panhandling on the street? Legal ethicist Arthur Schafer discusses the ethics of legally prohibiting homeless persons from panhandling on the street.

Beginning in the 1980s, and continuing into the 1990s, the centre of many Canadian cities experienced a dramatic increase in the number of down-and-out individuals living on the street: bag-ladies sitting in doorways or pushing their worldly goods in supermarket carts, homeless men and women huddled over heating grates during the winter, scruffy teenagers with their hands outstretched for a donation, "squeegee kids" wiping auto windshields without invitation in the expectation of payment from embarrassed motorists, beggars outside hotels and shopping malls.

Twenty years ago, an encounter with a beggar was not a common occurrence in Toronto or Winnipeg or Vancouver. Today, however, in the downtown centre of large and medium-sized Canadian cities, panhandlers seem to be ubiquitous. One is likely to encounter them on the sidewalks, on the streets, in city parks.

Cities across Canada are now moving swiftly to ban or to severely restrict panhandling. They are legislating the use of legal coercion not only against aggressive begging (which is already covered by the Criminal Code of Canada) but also against passive (peaceful) begging. For example, the city of Vancouver recently passed a law that targets squeegee kids by making it illegal to ask anyone in a stopped car for money. Violators could face fines of up to $2000. Winnipeg enacted a citywide ban on squeegee kids, with fines of up to $1000. In Toronto, police handed out hundreds of tickets after motorists complained about aggression and topless squeegee girls.

A constitutional test-case is about to come to trial, in which the National Anti-Poverty Association challenges the validity of the City of Winnipeg's anti-panhandling by-law. If this challenge is successful, cities across Canada will be forced to rethink their enthusiasm for using legal coercion against panhandlers.

Is it good public policy to use legal coercion against peaceful panhandlers? Can it be morally right in a democratic society to prevent

organized into well-defined relationships, such as husband–wife, parent–child, brother–sister, and so forth. Specific families do not always conform to these ideologies and behaviour patterns.

Functional theorists emphasize that social institutions exist because they perform five essential tasks:

1. *Replacing members*. Societies and groups must have socially approved ways of replacing members who move away or die. The family provides the structure for legitimated sexual activity—and thus procreation—between adults.
2. *Teaching new members*. People who are born into a society or move into it must learn the group's values and customs. The family and the education system are essential in teaching new members.
3. *Producing, distributing, and consuming goods and services*. All societies must provide and distribute goods and services for their members. The economy is the primary social institution fulfilling this need; the government often is involved in the regulation of economic activity.
4. *Preserving order*. Every group or society must preserve order within its boundaries and protect

BOX 4.2

CONTINUED

one person from publicly saying to another "I'm in trouble and need help"?

There is no denying that panhandling sometimes causes problems for the rest of the community. But the question that must be answered is: Are the negative consequences of peaceful panhandling so seriously harmful that they justify legal coercion that may contravene other basic social values? Is the cure (legal coercion) worse than the disease (passive panhandling)?

To defend the right to beg peacefully is not to deny that panhandling is a serious negative symptom of a deep social problem. But sweeping the existence of beggars under a coercive legal carpet is the wrong way to go about dealing with this problem.

Do we, as a society, really want to rely upon still more laws to deal with the serious social problems of poverty, homelessness, and panhandling? Are we convinced that legal coercion, with its use of physical force backed by weapons, lawyers, courts and jails, will be effective in addressing what is essentially a social problem? Are we prepared to violate fundamental rights to freedom of expression and add further burdens to the least advantaged members of our society?

We cannot expect much success if we treat panhandling as an isolated problem to be dealt with by police action. Legal prohibition may sound as if it would be a cheap and easy solution, but the messy truth is that it would, at best, provide a temporary cosmetic cover-up. To ban or to severely restrict a person's right to peacefully ask others for help would jeopardize some of the most cherished rights of a democratic society.

Passive panhandling is a nuisance, not a menace. The top-down passage of anti-panhandling legislation is neither good ethics nor good social policy. It should be rejected in favour of a more complex, possibly more expensive (in the short run), bottom-up approach involving such measures as income redistribution and appropriate provision of housing and social services. A social approach to passive panhandling would be more just, more humane, and ultimately more effective.

Source: Adapted with permission from Schafer, A. 1998. *Down and Out in Winnipeg and Toronto. The Ethics of Legislating Against Panhandling*. Ottawa: Caledon Institute of Social Policy (August).

itself from attack by outsiders. The government legitimates the creation of law enforcement agencies to preserve internal order and some form of military for external defence.

5. *Providing and maintaining a sense of purpose.* In order to motivate people to cooperate with one another, a sense of purpose is needed.

Although this list of functional prerequisites is shared by all societies, the institutions in each society perform these tasks in somewhat different ways depending on their specific cultural values and norms.

Conflict theorists agree with functionalists that social institutions are organized to meet basic social needs. They do not agree, however, that social institutions work for the common good of everyone in society. The homeless, for example, lack the power and resources to promote their own interests when they are opposed by dominant social groups. From the conflict perspective, social institutions such as the government maintain the privileges of the wealthy and powerful while contributing to the powerlessness of others (see Domhoff, 1983, 1990). For example, government policies in urban areas have benefited

BOX 4.3 You Can Make a Difference!

Helping the Homeless

Each of us can make a difference for the homeless. We can contribute hands-on knowledge and experience by tutoring children at homeless shelters, or we can donate funds so that volunteers can provide the children with clothing, toiletries, school supplies, and toys.

The Salvation Army home page for Canada can be found at:

www.salvationarmy.org

This site provides addresses to Salvation Army locations across Canada.

The Web site for The Mission, a homeless shelter in Ottawa, has links to other shelters across the country:

www.ottawamission.com

Another organization that can give you information about helping the homeless is the United Way:

www.uwc-cc.ca

some people but exacerbated the problems of others. Urban renewal and transportation projects caused the destruction of low-cost housing and put large numbers of people "on the street" (Katz, 1989). Similarly, the shift in governmental policies toward the mentally ill and welfare recipients resulted in more people struggling—and often failing—to find affordable housing. Meanwhile, many wealthy and privileged bankers, investors, developers, and builders benefited at the expense of the low-income casualties of those policies.

Functionalist and conflict perspectives provide a macrosociological overview because they concentrate on large-scale events and broad social features. For example, sociologists using the macrosociological approach to study the homeless might analyze how social institutions have operated to produce current conditions. By contrast, the interactionist perspective takes a microsociological approach, asking how social institutions affect our daily lives.

SOCIAL INTERACTION: THE MICROLEVEL PERSPECTIVE

So far in this chapter, we have focused on society and social structure from a macrolevel perspective. We have seen how the structure of society affects the statuses we occupy, the roles we play, and the groups and organizations to which we belong. We will now look at society from the microlevel perspective, which focuses on social interactions among individuals, especially in face-to-face encounters.

Social Interaction and Meaning

When you are with other people, do you often wonder what they think of you? If so, you are not alone! Because most of us are concerned about the meanings others ascribe to our behaviour, we try to interpret their words and actions so that we can plan how we will react toward them (Blumer, 1969). We know that others have expectations of us. We also have certain expectations about them. For example, if we enter an elevator that has only one other person in it, we do not expect that individual to confront us and stare into our eyes. As a matter of fact, we would be quite upset if the person did so.

Social interaction within a given society has certain shared meanings across situations. For instance, our reaction would be the same regardless of *which* elevator we rode in *which* building. Sociologist Erving Goffman (1963b) described these shared meanings in his observation about two pedestrians approaching each other on a public sidewalk. He

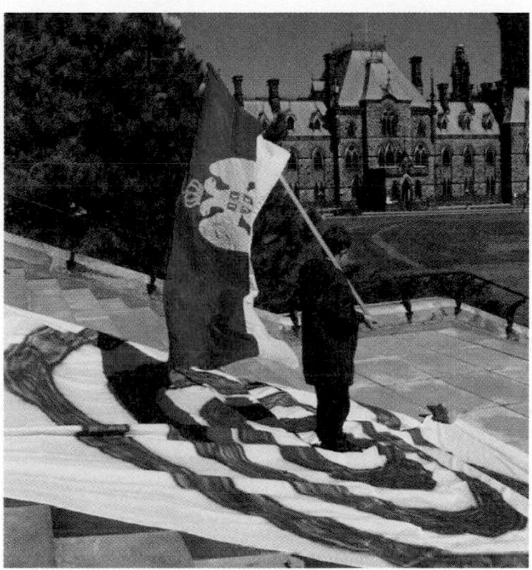

Sharply contrasting views of the same reality are evident in these people's views about NATO's bombing of Yugoslavia. *Right:* A Serbian Canadian protests. *Left:* A Kosovar refugee shows support for the Kosovo Liberation Army.

noted that each will tend to look at the other just long enough to acknowledge the other's presence. By the time they are about eight feet away from each other, both individuals will tend to look downward. Goffman referred to this behaviour as *civil inattention*—the ways in which an individual shows an awareness that others are present without making them the object of particular attention. The fact that people engage in civil inattention demonstrates that interaction does have a pattern, or *interaction order*, which regulates the form and processes (but not the content) of social interaction.

Does everyone interpret social interaction rituals in the same way? No. Ethnicity, gender, and social class play a part in the meanings we give to our interactions with others, including chance encounters on elevators or on the street. Our perceptions about the meaning of a situation vary widely based on the statuses we occupy and our unique personal experiences. For example, sociologist Carol Brooks Gardner (1989) found that women frequently do not perceive street encounters to be "routine" rituals. They fear for their personal safety and try to avoid comments and propositions that are sexual in nature when they walk down the street.

In another example, members of the dominant classes regard the poor, unemployed, and working class as less worthy of attention, frequently subjecting them to subtle yet systematic "attention deprivation" (Derber, 1983). The same can certainly be said about how members of the dominant classes "interact" with the homeless. A recent survey of Canadians' attitudes toward the homeless showed that over 60 percent of respondents felt uncomfortable when they encountered homeless people (Canada Mortgage and Housing Corporation, 1998).

The Social Construction of Reality

If we interpret other people's actions so subjectively, can we have a shared social reality? Some interaction theorists believe that there is very little shared reality beyond that which is socially created. Interactionists refer to this as the ***social construction of reality*—the process by which our perception of reality is shaped largely by the subjective meaning that we give to an experience** (Berger and Luckmann, 1967). This meaning strongly influences what we "see" and how we respond to situations.

Our perceptions and behaviour are influenced by how we initially define situations: We act on reality as we see it. Sociologists describe this process as the *definition of the situation*, meaning that we analyze a social context in which we find ourselves, determine what is in our best interest, and adjust our attitudes and actions accordingly. This can result in a ***self-fulfilling prophecy*—a false belief or prediction that produces behaviour that makes the originally false**

belief come true (Thomas and Thomas, 1928:72). An example would be a person who has been told repeatedly that she or he is not a good student; eventually, this person might come to believe it to be true, stop studying, and receive failing grades.

People may define a given situation in very different ways, a tendency demonstrated by sociologist Jacqueline Wiseman (1970) in her study of "Pacific City's" skid row. She wanted to know how people who live or work on skid row (a run-down area found in all cities) felt about it. Wiseman found that homeless people living on skid row evaluated it very differently from the social workers who dealt with them there. On the one hand, many of the social workers "saw" skid row as a smelly, depressing area filled with men who were "down-and-out," alcoholic, and often physically and mentally ill. On the other hand, the men who lived on skid row did not see it in such a negative light. They experienced some degree of satisfaction with their "bottle clubs [and a] remarkably indomitable and creative spirit"—at least initially (Wiseman, 1970:18). Also consider Lesley Harman's initial reaction to her field research site, a facility for homeless women in an Ontario city:

> The initial shock of facing the world of the homeless told me much about what I took for granted ... The first day I lasted two very long hours. I went home and woke up severely depressed, weeping uncontrollably. (Harman, 1989:42)

In contrast, many of the women who lived there defined the situation of living in a hostel in very different terms. For example, one resident commented, "This is home to me because I feel so comfortable. I can do what I really want, the staff are very nice to me, everybody is good to me, it's home, you know?" (1989:91). As these studies show, we define situations from our own frame of reference, based on the statuses we occupy and the roles we play.

Dominant group members with prestigious statuses may have the ability to establish how other people define "reality" (Berger and Luckmann, 1967:109). For example, the media often set the tone for our current opinions about homelessness, either with negative stories about the problems the homeless "cause" or with "human interest" stories, as discussed in Box 4.4.

Dramaturgical Analysis

Erving Goffman suggested that day-to-day interactions have much in common with being on stage or in a dramatic production. ***Dramaturgical analysis* is the study of social interaction that compares everyday life to a theatrical presentation.** Members of our "audience" judge our performance (Goffman, 1959, 1963a). Consequently, most of us attempt to play our role as well as possible and to control the impressions we give to others. *Impression management*, or ***presentation of self*, refers to people's efforts to present themselves to others in ways that are most favourable to their own interests or image.**

For example, suppose that a professor has returned graded exams to your class. Will you discuss the exam and your grade with others in the class? If you are like most people, you probably play your student role differently depending on whom you are talking to and what grade you received on the exam. In a study at the University of Manitoba, Daniel and Cheryl Albas (1988) analyzed how students "presented themselves" or "managed impressions" when exam grades are returned. Students who all received high grades ("Ace–Ace encounters") willingly talked with one another about their grades and sometimes engaged in a little bragging about how they had "aced" the test. However, encounters between students who had received high grades and those who had received low or failing grades ("Ace–Bomber encounters") were uncomfortable. The Aces felt as if they had to minimize their own grade. Consequently, they tended to attribute their success to "luck" and were quick to offer the Bombers words of encouragement. On the other hand, the Bombers believed that they had to praise the Aces and hide their own feelings of frustration and disappointment. Students who received low or failing grades ("Bomber–Bomber encounters") were more comfortable when they talked with one another because they could share their negative emotions. They often indulged in self-pity and relied on face-saving excuses (such as an illness or an unfair exam) for their poor performances (Albas and Albas, 1988).

In Goffman's terminology, *face-saving behaviour* refers to the strategies we use to rescue our performance when we experience a potential or actual loss of face. When the Bombers made excuses for their

BOX 4.4 SOCIOLOGY AND MEDIA

The Homeless and the Holidays

Why do newspaper and television stories on the homeless proliferate in November, December, and January, as shown in the figure below? Journalists may find the plight of the homeless more newsworthy during the cold winter months and the holiday season because of the stark contrast between their situation and that of the domiciled. Homeless people constitute "human interest" stories for the holiday season. Members of the press barrage service providers at "soup kitchens" and homeless shelters for interviews and stories about "Jimmy G." or "Sherry P.," and volunteers are shown as they serve turkey dinners to the homeless on Thanksgiving.

From one viewpoint, the media serve an important function by keeping the public aware of the plight of homeless people. From another viewpoint, however, the media perpetuate negative images and myths about the homeless. In some articles and news stories, the homeless are depicted as drug addicts, alcoholics, or con artists who choose to be homeless. Photographs of homeless women and men in alcohol- or drug-induced stupors lying on park benches, heat grates, and the street reinforce these stereotypes.

What do you think about the media's coverage of the homeless? Does extensive coverage during the holiday season perhaps appeal to the "guilty conscience" of individuals who have a place to live while the homeless do not?

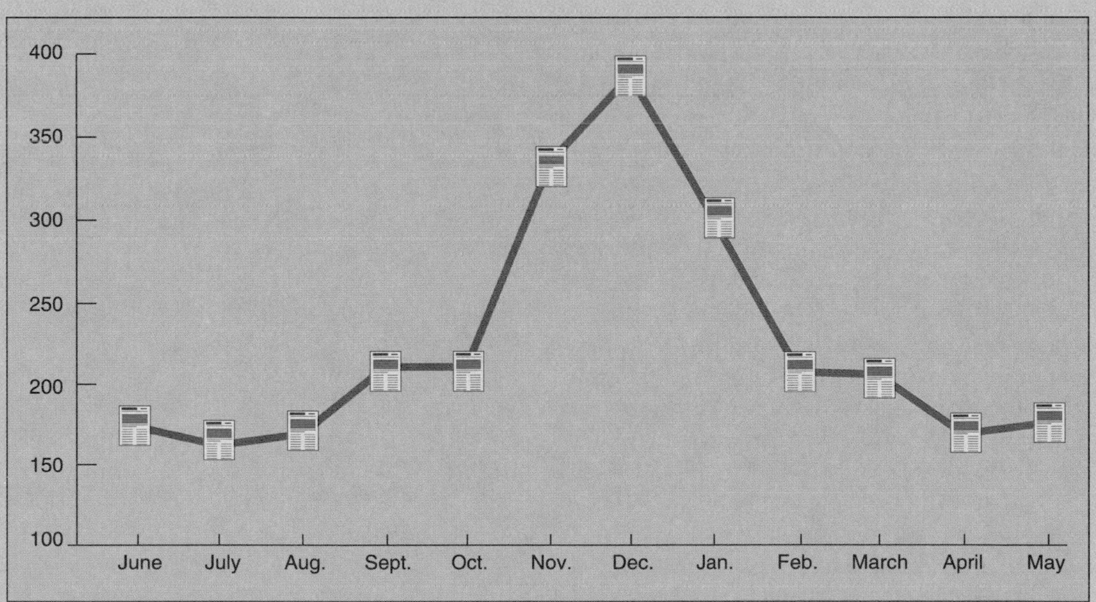

***New York Times* Stories on the Homeless, by Month, 1975–1993**

Source: Snow and Anderson, 1993; and Bunis, Yancik, and Snow, 1996.

low scores, they were engaged in face-saving; the Aces attempted to help them save face by asserting that the test was unfair or that it was only a small part of the final grade. Why would the Aces and Bombers both participate in face-saving behaviour? In most social interactions, all role players have an interest in keeping the "play" going so that they can maintain their overall definition of the situation in which they perform their roles.

Social interaction, like a theatre, has a front stage and a back stage. The *front stage* is the area where a player performs a specific role before an audience. The *back stage* is the area where a player is not required to perform a specific role because it is out of view of a given audience. For example, when the Aces and Bombers were talking with each other at school, they were on the "front stage." When they were in the privacy of their own residences, they were in "back stage" settings—they no longer had to perform the Ace and Bomber roles and could be themselves.

For face-saving purposes, many homeless individuals create justifications to give meaning to their actions or to the settings in which they find themselves. To "salvage the self," the homeless often use one of three adages: "I'm down on my luck"; "What goes around, comes around"; and "I've paid my dues" (Snow and Anderson, 1993: 204). "I'm down on my luck" means that the role does not really fit the person: as one homeless man stated: "It ain't my fault I'm on the streets. I didn't choose to become homeless. I just had a lot of bad luck. And that ain't my fault. ... It can happen to anyone, you know!" (Snow and Anderson, 1993:205). Others may salvage the self by embellishing stories about past or current occupational and financial accomplishments or sexual and drinking exploits. They may fantasize about the future regarding employment, money, material possessions, and women. One of the most prominent role fantasies is of becoming rich (Snow and Anderson, 1993). However, the homeless do not passively accept the roles into which they are cast. For the most part, they attempt—as we all do—to engage in impression management in their everyday life.

The dramaturgical approach helps us think about the roles we play and the audiences who judge our presentation of self. Like all other approaches, it has its critics. Sociologist Alvin Gouldner (1970) criticized this approach for focusing on appearances and not on the underlying substance. Others have argued that Goffman's work reduces the self to "a peg on which the clothes of the role are hung" (see Burns, 1992) or have suggested that this approach does not place enough emphasis on the ways in which our everyday interactions with other people are influenced by occurrences within the larger society. For example, if a political official belittles the homeless as being lazy and unwilling to work, it may become easier for people encountering them as they walk down the street to do likewise. Goffman's defenders counter that he captured the essence of society because social interaction "turns out to be not only where most of the world's work gets done, but where the solid buildings of the social world are in fact constructed" (Burns, 1992:380).

Biker gangs like the Hell's Angels are very good at impression management. How do you think their front and back stage roles differ?

Nonverbal Communication

In a typical stage drama, the players not only speak their lines but also convey information by nonverbal communication. In Chapter 2, we discussed the importance of language; now we will look at the messages we communicate without speaking. ***Nonverbal communication* is the transfer of information between persons without the use of speech.** It includes not only visual cues (gestures, appearances) but also vocal features (inflection, volume, pitch) and environmental factors (use of space, position) that affect meanings (J. Wood, 1994). Facial expressions, head movements, body positions, and other gestures carry as much of the total *meaning* of our communication with others as our spoken words do (J. Wood, 1994:151).

Nonverbal communication may be intentional or unintentional. Actors, politicians, and salespersons may make deliberate use of nonverbal communication to convey an idea or "make a sale." We also may send nonverbal messages through gestures or facial expressions or even our appearance without intending to let other people know what we are thinking.

Functions of Nonverbal Communication Nonverbal communication often supplements verbal communication (J. Wood, 1994). Head and facial movements may provide us with information about other people's emotional states, as others receive similar information from us (Samovar and Porter, 1991a). We obtain first impressions of others from various kinds of nonverbal communication, such as the clothing they wear and their body positions.

Our social interaction is regulated by nonverbal communication. Through our body posture and eye contact, we signal that we do or do not wish to speak to someone. For example, we may look down at the sidewalk or off into the distance when we pass homeless persons who look as if they are going to ask for money.

Nonverbal communication establishes the relationship between people in terms of their responsiveness to and power over one another (J. Wood, 1994). For example, we show that we are responsive toward or like another person by maintaining eye contact and attentive body posture and perhaps by touching and standing close. By contrast, we signal to others that we do not wish to be near them or that we dislike them by refusing to look them in the eye or stand near them. We can even express power or control over others through nonverbal communication. Goffman (1956) suggested that *demeanour* (how we behave or conduct ourselves) is relative to social power. People in positions of dominance are allowed a wider range of permissible actions than are their subordinates, who are expected to show deference. *Deference* is the symbolic means by which subordinates give a required permissive response to those in power; it confirms the existence of inequality and reaffirms each person's relationship to the other (Rollins, 1985).

Facial Expression, Eye Contact, and Touching Deference behaviour is important in regard to facial expression, eye contact, and touching. This type of nonverbal communication is symbolic of our relationships with others. Who smiles? Who stares? Who makes and sustains eye contact? Who touches whom? All of these questions relate to demeanour and deference; the key issue is the status of the person who is *doing* the smiling, staring, or touching relative to the status of the recipient (Goffman, 1967).

Facial expressions, especially smiles, also reflect gender-based patterns of dominance and subordination in society. Women typically have been socialized to smile and frequently do so even when they are not actually happy (Halberstadt and Saitta, 1987). Jobs held predominantly by women (including flight attendant, secretary, elementary school teacher, and nurse) are more closely associated with being pleasant and smiling than are "men's jobs." In addition to smiling more frequently, many women tend to tilt their heads in deferential positions when they are talking or listening to others. By contrast, men tend to display less emotion through smiles or other facial expressions and instead seek to show that they are "reserved and in control" (J. Wood, 1994:164).

Women are more likely to sustain eye contact during conversations (but not otherwise) as a means of showing their interest in and involvement with others. By contrast, men are less likely to maintain prolonged eye contact during conversations but are more likely to stare at other people (especially men) in order to challenge them and assert their own status (Pearson, 1985).

Eye contact can be a sign of domination or deference. For example, in a participant observation study of domestic (household) workers and their employers, sociologist Judith Rollins (1985) found that the domestics were supposed to show deference by averting their eyes when they talked to their employers. Deference also required that they present an "exaggeratedly subservient demeanour" by standing less erect and walking tentatively.

Nonverbal communication may be thought of as an international language. What message do you receive from the facial expression, body position, and gestures of each of these people? Is it possible to misinterpret their messages?

Touching is another form of nonverbal behaviour that has many different shades of meaning. Gender and power differences are evident in tactile communication from birth. Studies have shown that touching has variable meanings to parents: boys are touched more roughly and playfully, while girls are handled more gently and protectively (Condry, Condry, and Pogatshnik, 1983). This pattern continues into adulthood, with women touched more frequently than men. Sociologist Nancy Henley (1977) attributed this pattern to power differentials between men and women and to the nature of women's roles as mothers, nurses, teachers, and secretaries. Clearly, touching has a different meaning to women than to men (Stier and Hall, 1984). Women may hug and touch others to indicate affection and emotional support, while men are more likely to touch others to give directions, assert power, and express sexual interest (J. Wood, 1994:162). The "meaning" we give to touching is related to its "duration, intensity, frequency, and the body parts touching and being touched" (J. Wood, 1994:162).

Personal Space Physical space is an important component of nonverbal communication. Anthropologist Edward Hall (1966) analyzed the physical distance between people speaking to one another and found that the amount of personal space people prefer varies from one culture to another. ***Personal space* is the immediate area surrounding a person that the person claims as private.** Our personal space is contained within an invisible boundary surrounding our body, much like a snail's shell. When others invade our space, we may retreat, stand our ground, or even lash out, depending on our cultural background (Samovar and Porter, 1991a). Hall (1966) observed that North Americans have different "distance zones" ranging from about *intimate distance* (from contact to half a metre) to *public distance* (beyond 4 metres).

Hall makes the distinction between "contact" and "noncontact" cultures and emphasizes that people from different cultures have different distance zones. *Contact cultures* are characterized by closer physical distance in interaction, more frequent eye contact and touch, and greater voice volume. Representatives of contact cultures include Arabs, Southern Europeans, and the French. Canadians, Asians, and the British are examples of *noncontact cultures* who typically interact at greater distances with less eye contact and touch, and lower voice volume (Hall, 1966).

What happens to personal distance when individuals from contact and noncontact cultures interact? This question is particularly important in our multicultural society where members of different ethnic subcultures interact on a regular basis. One study examined this question by observing members of a contact culture (Franco-Manitobans) with a noncontact culture (Anglo-Manitobans) interacting in their natural setting. Albas and Albas (1989) reported that the subjects, in an attempt to comply with the expectations of others, would adjust their "distance zone" when interacting with someone from a different cultural group.

Power differentials are also reflected in personal space and privacy issues. Adults generally do not hesitate to enter the personal space of a child (Thorne, Kramarae, and Henley, 1983). The need for personal space appears to increase with age (Baxter, 1970; Aiello and Jones, 1971), although it may begin to decrease at about the age of 40 (Heshka and Nelson, 1972).

In sum, all forms of nonverbal communication are influenced by gender, ethnicity, social class, and the personal contexts in which they occur.

COLLECTIVE BEHAVIOUR

In the first two sections of this chapter we looked at the impact of social structure on behaviour and at patterns of social interaction among individuals. In this section, we will consider ***collective behaviour,* which is relatively spontaneous, unstructured activity that typically violates established social norms.** Unlike the *organizational behaviour* found in corporations and voluntary associations (such as labour unions and environmental organizations), collective behaviour lacks an official division of labour, hierarchy of authority, and established rules and procedures. Unlike institutional behaviour (in education, religion, or politics, for example), it lacks institutionalized norms to govern behaviour. Collective behaviour can take various forms, including crowds, mobs, riots, panics, fads, fashions, public opinion, and social movements.

Conditions for Collective Behaviour

Collective behaviour occurs as a result of some common influence or stimulus that produces a response from a collectivity. A *collectivity* is a relatively large number of people who mutually transcend, bypass, or subvert established institutional patterns and structures. Collectivities in which people are in physical proximity to one another (such as a crowd or a riot) are referred to as *localized collectivities;* those in which people are some distance apart from one another (such as with rumours, fashions, and public opinion) are referred to as *dispersed collectivities* (Turner and Killian, 1993).

Three major factors contribute to the likelihood that collective behaviour will occur: (1) structural factors that increase the chances of people responding in a particular way, (2) timing, and (3) a breakdown in social control mechanisms and a corresponding feeling of normlessness (McPhail, 1991; Turner and Killian, 1993). A common stimulus is an important factor. For example, in 1993 hundreds of people were arrested during a demonstration against clear-cut logging in British Columbia's Clayoquot Sound. In this instance, the issue of clear-cutting was part of the larger issue of environmental destruction. In the words of one commentator, "Clayoquot is a symbol, a cause, one of those local battles that becomes a flashpoint of a larger war" (Fulton and Mather, 1993:20). The clear-cut logging issue came at a time when people were becoming more concerned about social issues and beginning to see that they could empower themselves through grassroots activism.

Timing and a breakdown in social control mechanisms also are important in collective behaviour. Since the 1960s, most urban riots in Canada and the United States have begun in the evenings or on weekends when most people are off work (McPhail, 1971). For example, the 1992 Los Angeles riots erupted in the evening of the day the verdict in the Rodney King beating trial was announced. As rioting, looting, and arson began to take a toll on certain areas of Los Angeles, a temporary breakdown in formal social control mechanisms occurred. In some areas of the city, law enforcement was inadequate to quell the illegal actions of rioters, some of whom began to believe that the rules had been suspended. In the aftermath of the Montreal riot following the 1993 Stanley Cup victory, the Montreal Canadiens were protected by hundreds of police officers and a riot squad in an effort to prevent any further breakdown of social control.

Dynamics of Collective Behaviour

To better understand the dynamics of collective behaviour, let us briefly examine three basic questions. First, how do people come to transcend, bypass, or subvert established institutional patterns and structures? Prior to the Clayoquot logging protest, a group called the Friends of Clayoquot Sound initially tried to work within established means through provincial government environment officials. However, they quickly learned that their problems were not being solved through these channels; as the problems appeared to grow worse, organizational responses became more defensive and obscure. Accordingly, some activists began acting outside of established norms by holding protests, establishing blockades, and (on one occasion) storming the B.C. legislature and almost breaking into the assembly. Some situations are more conducive to collective behaviour than others. When people can communicate quickly and easily with one another, spontaneous behaviour is more likely (Turner and Killian, 1993). When people are gathered together in one general location (whether lining the streets or assembled in a stadium), they are more likely to respond to a common stimulus.

Second, how do people's actions compare with their attitudes? People's attitudes (as expressed in public opinion surveys, for instance) are not always reflected in their political and social behaviour. Issues pertaining to the environment are no exception. The National Opinion Survey of Canadian Public Opinion on Forestry Issues showed that a majority of Canadians believed that "too many trees are being logged." In fact, 71 percent of Canadians disapproved of clear-cut logging and 61 percent indicated that they "get personally upset" when they see the results of clear-cutting (Harding, 1993:456). However, when the Friends of Clayoquot held their first protest session, only 200 people attended. Nevertheless, they assured the media that 1000 people would gather at Clayoquot on Canada Day. Their confidence was unfounded: only 150 supporters appeared (Brunet, 1993). According to sociologist William A. Gamson (1990), the thousands of people who agreed with the cause but never made it to Clayoquot were *free riders*—people who enjoy the benefits produced by some group even though they have not helped support it.

Third, why do people act collectively rather than singly? Sociologists Ralph H. Turner and Lewis M. Killian (1993:12) say one reason is that "the rhythmic stamping of feet by hundreds of concert-goers in unison is different from isolated, individual cries of 'bravo.'" Likewise, people may act as a collectivity when they believe it is the only way to fight those with greater power and resources. Collective behaviour is not just the sum of a large number of individuals acting at the same time; rather, it reflects people's joint response to some common influence or stimulus.

Distinctions Regarding Collective Behaviour

People engaging in collective behaviour may be divided into crowds and masses. A ***crowd*** **is a relatively large number of people who are in one another's immediate vicinity** (Lofland, 1993). In contrast, a ***mass*** **is a number of people who share an interest in a specific idea or issue but who are not in one another's immediate vicinity** (Lofland, 1993). To further distinguish between crowds and masses, think of the difference between a riot and a rumour: people who participate in a riot must be in the same general location; those who spread a rumour may be thousands of miles apart, communicating by telephone or online computer networks.

Collective behaviour also may be distinguished by the dominant emotion expressed. According to sociologist John Lofland (1993:72), the *dominant emotion* refers to the "publicly expressed feeling perceived by participants and observers as the most prominent in an episode of collective behaviour." Lofland suggests that fear, hostility, and joy are three fundamental emotions found in collective behaviour; however, grief, disgust, surprise, or shame also may predominate in some forms of collective behaviour.

Types of Crowd Behaviour

When we think of a crowd, many of us think of ***aggregates*, previously defined as a collection of people who happen to be in the same place at the same time but who have little else in common.** However, the presence of a relatively large number of people in the same location does not necessarily produce collective behaviour. Sociologist Herbert Blumer (1946) developed a typology in which crowds are divided into four categories: casual, conventional, expressive, and acting. Other scholars have added a fifth category, protest crowds.

CASUAL AND CONVENTIONAL CROWDS ***Casual crowds* are relatively large gatherings of people who happen to be in the same place at the same time; if they interact at all, it is only briefly.** People in a shopping mall or a bus are examples of casual crowds. Other than sharing a momentary interest, such as a watching a busker perform on the street or observing the aftermath of a car accident, a casual crowd has nothing in common. The casual crowd plays no active part in the event—such as the car accident that would have occurred whether or not the crowd was present; it simply observes.

***Conventional crowds* are made up of people who specifically come together for a scheduled event and thus share a common focus.** Examples include religious services, graduation ceremonies, concerts, and university lectures. Each of these events has established schedules and norms. Because these events occur regularly, interaction among participants is much more likely; in turn, the events would not occur without the crowd, which is essential to the event.

EXPRESSIVE AND ACTING CROWDS *Expressive crowds* provide opportunities for the expression of some strong emotion (such as joy, excitement, or grief). People release their pent-up emotions in conjunction with other persons experiencing similar emotions. Examples include worshippers at religious revival services; mourners lining the streets when a celebrity, public official, or religious leader has died; and nonrioting crowds at a sporting event.

Acting crowds are collectivities so intensely focused on a specific purpose or object that they may erupt into violent or destructive behaviour. Mobs, riots, and panics are examples of acting crowds, but casual and conventional crowds may become acting crowds under some circumstances. **A *mob* is a highly emotional crowd whose members engage in, or are ready to engage in, violence against a specific target—a person, a category of people, or physical property.** Mob behaviour in this country has included fire bombings, effigy hangings, and hate crimes. Mob violence tends to dissipate relatively quickly once a target has been injured, killed, or destroyed. Sometimes, actions such as effigy hanging are used symbolically by groups that otherwise are not violent; for example, during the 1990 Oka Crisis on the Kanehsatake reserve in Quebec, local non-Aboriginal residents burned an effigy of a Mohawk to emphasize their displeasure with the blockade of the Mercier Bridge to Montreal.

Riots may be of somewhat longer duration than mob actions. **A *riot* is violent crowd behaviour that is fuelled by deep-seated emotions but not directed at one specific target.** Riots often are triggered by fear, anger, and hostility. This was true of the previously mentioned 1992 Los Angeles riots, which resulted from the announcement of the acquittal of the white police officers involved in the brutal beating of Rodney King, a black. These especially destructive riots caused millions of dollars worth of damage and thousands of injuries, and left more than fifty people dead. These riots were followed days later by race riots on the streets of Toronto. However, not all riots are caused by deep-seated hostility and hatred; people may be expressing joy and exuberance when rioting occurs. Examples include celebrations after sports victories such as those that

This crowd is made up of thousands of Canadians from across the country who gathered in Montreal in October 1995 to demonstrate their strong emotions against Quebec separation.

occurred in Montreal following a Stanley Cup win and in Vancouver following a playoff victory.

Panic **is a form of crowd behaviour that occurs when a large number of people react to a real or perceived threat with strong emotions and self-destructive behaviour.** The most common type of panic, known as *entrapment panic*, occurs when people seek to escape from a perceived danger, fearing that few (if any) of them will be able to get away from that danger. For example, in 1994 a firebomb on a New York City subway engulfed a car in flames. Many people were knocked to the ground by the crush of people (Gonzales, 1994).

Panic sometimes occurs, however, when people attempt to gain access to an event or a location, as was the case at a concert by the British rock group The Who in Cincinnati in 1979. Seating was on a first-come, first-served basis, and when the doors opened, people surged into the arena and began to fall over one another. Unaware of the press of bodies in front of them, those farther back heard the band warming up and began to panic for fear that they would not get a seat. This type of panic is referred to as *exclusion panic*. When people started to realize what was happening, they experienced an overwhelming emotion of fear. Eleven people were killed in the ensuing pile-up.

Panic also can arise in response to events that people believe are beyond their control—such as a major disruption in the economy. Although instances of panic are relatively rare, they receive massive media coverage because they provoke strong feelings of fear in readers and viewers, and because the number of casualties may be large.

PROTEST CROWDS Sociologists Clark McPhail and Ronald T. Wohlstein (1983) added protest crowds to the four types of crowds identified by Blumer. ***Protest crowds*** **engage in activities intended to achieve specific political goals.** Examples include sit-ins, marches, boycotts, blockades, and strikes. These sometimes take the form of ***civil disobedience*****—nonviolent action that seeks to change a policy or law by refusing to comply with it.** Sometimes, acts of civil disobedience become violent, as in a confrontation between protesters and police officers; in this case, a protest crowd becomes an *acting crowd*. Such was the case during the Oka Crisis, when a police officer was shot and killed and several persons on both sides of the blockade were injured. Some protests can escalate into violent confrontations even though that is not the intent of the organizers.

As you will recall, collective action often puts individuals in the position of doing things as a group that they would not do on their own. Does this mean that people's actions are produced by some type of "herd mentality"? Some analysts have

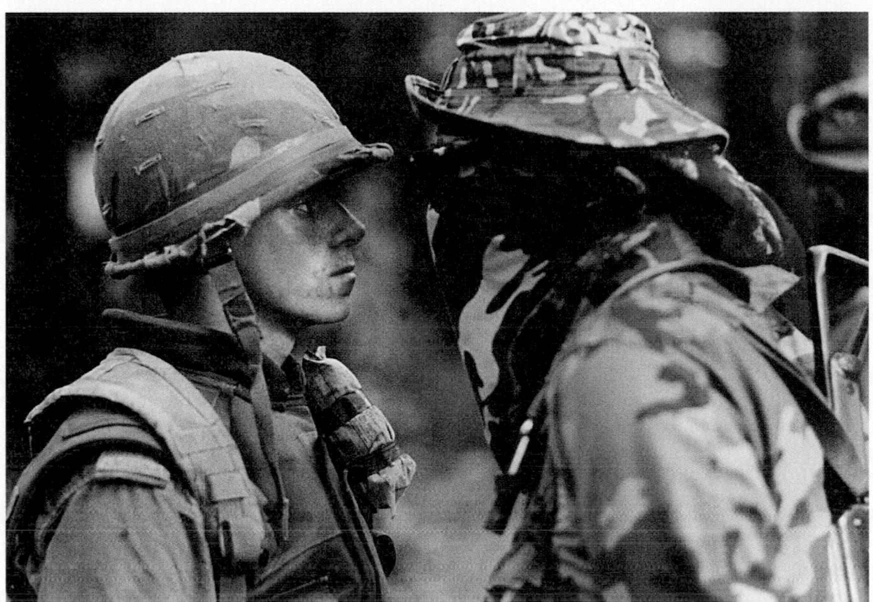

Sometimes acts of civil disobedience become violent even though it is not the intent of the parties involved. During what is referred to as the Oka Crisis, a police officer was shot and killed and several people on both sides of the blockade were injured.

answered this question affirmatively; however, sociologists typically do not agree with that assessment.

Explanations of Crowd Behaviour

What causes people to act collectively? How do they determine what types of action to take? One of the earliest theorists to provide an answer to these questions was Gustave Le Bon, a French scholar who focused on crowd psychology in his contagion theory.

CONTAGION THEORY *Contagion theory* focuses on the social-psychological aspects of collective behaviour; it attempts to explain how moods, attitudes, and behaviour are communicated rapidly and why they are accepted by others (Turner and Killian, 1993). Gustave Le Bon (1841–1931) argued that people are more likely to engage in antisocial behaviour in a crowd because they are anonymous and feel invulnerable. Le Bon (1960/1895) suggested that a crowd takes on a life of its own that is larger than the beliefs or actions of any one person. Because of its anonymity, the crowd transforms individuals from rational beings into a single organism with a collective mind. In essence, Le Bon asserted that emotions such as fear and hate are contagious in crowds because people experience a decline in personal responsibility; they will do things as a collectivity that they would never do when acting alone.

Le Bon's theory is still used to explain crowd behaviour. However, critics argue that the "collective mind" has not been documented by systematic studies.

CONVERGENCE THEORY *Convergence theory* focuses on the shared emotions, goals, and beliefs many people bring to crowd behaviour. Because of their individual characteristics, many people have a predisposition to participate in certain types of activities (Turner and Killian, 1993). From this perspective, people with similar attributes find a collectivity of like-minded persons with whom they can express their underlying personal tendencies. For example, the 1996 riots at the National Assembly in Quebec City on St. Jean Baptiste Day were believed to have been started by "professional agitators" who were members of the Northern Hammer Skins, a right-wing extremist organization associated with the neo-Nazi Heritage Front. Such groups are known to publish hate propaganda that glorifies rioting and violence against the government. These individuals may have been present at the St. Jean Baptiste Day celebrations with the intent of participating in violence or instigating a riot. Although people may reveal their "true selves" in crowds, their behaviour is not irrational; it is highly predictable to those who share similar emotions or beliefs.

Convergence theory has been applied to a wide array of conduct, from lynch mobs to environmental movements. In social psychologist Hadley Cantril's (1941) study of one lynching in the United States, he found that the participants shared certain common attributes: they were poor and working-class whites who felt that their own status was threatened by the presence of successful African Americans. Consequently, the characteristics of these individuals made them susceptible to joining a lynch mob even if they did not know the target of the lynching.

Convergence theory adds to our understanding of certain types of collective behaviour by pointing out how individuals may have certain attributes—such as racial hatred or fear of environmental problems that directly threaten them—that initially bring them together. However, this perspective does not explain how the attitudes and characteristics of individuals who take some collective action differ from those who do not.

Emergent Norm Theory Unlike contagion and convergence theories, *emergent norm theory* emphasizes the importance of social norms in shaping crowd behaviour. Drawing on the interactionist perspective, sociologists Ralph Turner and Lewis Killian (1993:12) asserted that crowds develop their own definition of a situation and establish norms for behaviour that fit the occasion:

> Some shared redefinition of right and wrong in a situation supplies the justification and coordinates the action in collective behaviour. People do what they would not otherwise have done when they panic collectively, when they riot, when they engage in civil disobedience, or when they launch terrorist campaigns, because they find social support for the view that what they are doing is the right thing to do in the situation.

According to Turner and Killian (1993:13), emergent norms occur when people define a new situation as highly unusual or see a long-standing situation in a new light.

Mass Behaviour

Not all collective behaviour takes place in face-to-face collectivities. ***Mass behaviour* is collective behaviour that takes place when people (who often are geographically separated from one another) respond to the same event in much the same way.** For people to respond in the same way, they typically have common sources of information, and this information provokes their collective behaviour. The most frequent types of mass behaviour are rumours, gossip, mass hysteria, public opinion, fashions, and fads. Under some circumstances, social movements constitute a form of mass behaviour. However, we will examine social movements separately because they differ in some important ways from other types of dispersed collectivities.

Rumours and Gossip ***Rumours* are unsubstantiated reports on an issue or subject** (Rosnow and Fine, 1976). Rumours may spread through an assembled collectivity, but they may also be transmitted among people who are dispersed geographically. Although they may initially contain a kernel of truth, as they spread, rumours may be modified to serve the interests of those repeating them. Rumours thrive when tensions are high and little authentic information is available on an issue of great concern.

People are willing to give rumours credence when no offsetting information is available. Once rumours begin to circulate, they seldom stop unless compelling information comes to the forefront that either proves the rumour false or makes it obsolete.

In industrialized societies with sophisticated technology, rumours come from a wide variety of sources and may be difficult to trace. Print media (newspapers and magazines) and electronic media (radio and television), fax machines, cellular networks, satellite systems, and the Internet facilitate the rapid movement of rumours around the globe. In addition, modern communications technology makes anonymity much easier. In a split second, messages (both factual and fictitious) can be disseminated to thousands of people through e-mail, computerized bulletin boards, and newsgroups on the Internet. (See Box 4.5.)

Whereas rumours deal with an issue or a subject, ***gossip* refers to rumours about the personal lives of individuals.** Charles Horton Cooley (1962/1909) viewed gossip as something that spread among a small group of individuals who personally knew the person who was the object of the rumour. Today, this often is not the case; many people enjoy gossiping about people they have never met. Tabloid newspapers and magazines such as the *National Enquirer* and *People*, and television "news" programs that purport to provide "inside" information on the lives of celebrities are sources of contemporary gossip, much of which has not been checked for authenticity.

MASS HYSTERIA AND PANIC ***Mass hysteria*** **is a form of dispersed collective behaviour that occurs when a large number of people react with strong emotions and self-destructive behaviour to a real or perceived threat.** Does mass hysteria actually occur? Although the term has been widely used, many sociologists believe this behaviour is best described as panic with a dispersed audience.

FADS AND FASHIONS A ***fad*** **is a temporary but widely copied activity enthusiastically followed by large numbers of people.** Some examples of fads are pet rocks, Tickle Me Elmo dolls, Pokémon cards, Teenage Mutant Ninja Turtles, Hula Hoops, and mood rings. Can you think of others? A recent fad among college and university students is body piercing, in which the ears, nose, navel, cheeks, nipples, and genitals are pierced and the resulting cavities are usually adorned with jewellery. Another college fad—one especially remembered by faculty who have been on campus for several decades—was the 1970s "streaking" craze. Students chose highly visible occasions for these nude escapades. Fads can be embraced by widely dispersed collectivities; news networks such as CNN may bring the latest fad to the attention of audiences around the world.

Fashion **may be defined as a currently valued style of behaviour, thinking, or appearance that is longer lasting and more widespread than a fad.** Fashion can apply to many areas, including child rearing, education, sports, clothing, music, and art. Sociologist John Lofland (1993) found that language is subject to fashion trends. He examined the terms used to express approval during different decades and found: "Neat!" in the 1950s, "Right on!" in the 1960s, "Really!" in the 1970s, "Awesome!" in the 1980s, and of course, "Cool!" in the 1990s.

Most sociological research on fashion has focused on clothing, especially women's apparel (Davis, 1992). In preindustrial societies, clothing styles remained relatively unchanged. With the advent of industrialization, however, items of apparel became readily available at low prices because of mass production. Fashion became more important as people embraced the "modern" way of life and advertising encouraged "conspicuous consumption."

Georg Simmel (1904) viewed fashion as a means of status differentiation among members of different social classes. He suggested a classic "trickle-down" theory (although he did not use those exact words) to describe the process by which members of the lower classes emulate the fashions of the upper class. As the fashions descend through the status hierarchy, they are watered down and "vulgarized" so that they are no longer recognizable to members of the upper class, who then regard them as unfashionable and in bad taste (Davis, 1992).

Perhaps one of the best refutations of the trickle-down approach is the way in which fashion today often originates among people in the lower social classes and is mimicked by the elites. The mid-1990s so-called grunge look is a prime example of this.

PUBLIC OPINION ***Public opinion*** **consists of the political attitudes and beliefs communicated by ordinary citizens to decision makers** (Greenberg and Page, 1996). It is measured through polls and surveys, which utilize research methods such as interviews and questionnaires, as described in Chapter 1. Many people are not interested in all aspects of public policy but are concerned about issues they believe are relevant to themselves. Even on a single topic, public opinion will vary widely based on race/ethnicity, religion, region, social class, education level, gender, age, and so on.

As the masses attempt to influence elites and vice versa, a two-way process occurs with the dissemination of ***propaganda*****—information provided by individuals or groups that have a vested interest in furthering their own cause or damaging an opposing one.** For example, in the Clayoquot Sound protest, the B.C. government and the logging industry used slogans such as "forest renewal," "world-class logging," and "getting greener all the time" (Lam, 1995:24). On the other hand, environmental activists referred to Clayoquot Sound as "the Brazil of the North." Although many of us think of propaganda in negative terms, the information provided can be correct and can have a positive effect on decision making.

BOX 4.5 SOCIOLOGY AND TECHNOLOGY

URBAN LEGENDS—DON'T BELIEVE EVERYTHING YOU READ

Consider the following story:

> I wish to warn you about a new crime that is targeting business travellers. This ring is well organized, well funded, has very skilled personnel, and is currently in most major cities and recently very active in New Orleans.
>
> The crime begins when a business traveller goes to a lounge for a drink at the end of a work day. A person in the bar walks up to the traveller who is sitting alone and offers to buy them a drink.
>
> The last thing the traveller remembers before waking up in a hotel room bathtub is their body submerged to their neck in ice, sipping that drink. There is a note taped to the wall instructing them not to move and to call 911. A phone is on a small table next to the bathtub for them to call.
>
> The business traveller calls 911 and is told this has become a quite familiar crime. The business traveller is instructed by the 911 operator to very slowly and carefully reach behind them and feel if there is a tube protruding from their lower back.
>
> The business traveller finds the tube and answers yes. The 911 operator tells the business traveller to remain still, adding that paramedics are on their way. The operator knows that both of the business traveller's kidneys have been harvested.
>
> This is not a scam or out of a science fiction novel, it is real. It is documented and confirmable. If you travel or someone close to you travels, please be careful.

This story is often accepted as accurate because most people aren't aware of the intricate surgical procedures involved in organ harvesting. The story originated in New Orleans during one Mardi Gras celebration, and there were so many calls to the police that a Web site was put up to dispel any more rumours. This rumour is an example of an *urban legend*—an unsubstantiated story, containing a sensational or unusual plot, that is widely circulated and believed. The stories in urban legends are either completely false, or if they do have some basis in fact, the events occurred in the distant past. Urban legends are believed because they call up fears or concerns that are real, because they describe embarrassing situations that we can all imagine ourselves in,

SOCIAL MOVEMENTS

While collective behaviour is short-lived and relatively unorganized, social movements are longer lasting and more organized and have specific goals or purposes. A ***social movement* is an organized group that acts consciously to promote or resist change through collective action** (Goldberg, 1991). Because social movements have not become institutionalized and are outside the political mainstream, they offer "outsiders" an opportunity to have their voices heard.

Social movements are more likely to develop in industrialized societies than in preindustrial societies, where acceptance of traditional beliefs and practices makes such movements unlikely. Diversity and a lack of consensus (hallmarks of industrialized nations) contribute to demands for social change, and people who participate in social movements typically lack power and other resources to bring about change without engaging in collective action.

BOX 4.5

CONTINUED

or because they relate to some aspect of modern life that we accept but find somewhat disturbing. Often, like true stories, they contain a moral.

The urban legend described above is one of the more famous urban legends making its way around the world via the Internet. The Internet has been described as the perfect environment for fostering urban legends. Through e-mail, newsgroups, and the World Wide Web, the Internet provides the medium to share stories with more people, faster than ever before.

Why do we believe these outrageous stories? Paul Gilster, author of *Digital Literacy,* explains that for many Internet users any information provided via the computer has instant credibility:

> There's lingering public perception ... of the computer's ferocious accuracy: computers don't make mistakes. Couple that with the general public's sense of the Internet as having been developed by the academic–scientific community, under government auspices, as a high level information source, and you do indeed have some people accepting far too quickly, any information that appears on a computer screen simply because it does appear on a screen. (cited in Ferrell, 1997:4)

Have you received any urgent e-mail lately warning of a deadly virus, or telling you of free Nike shoes in exchange for your dirty, old runners, or free copies of Windows 98 from Bill Gates? These are all Internet urban legends. Some are so believable that they get passed around endlessly. In fact, the world of urban legends is growing so rapidly via the Internet that there are now dozens of Web sites devoted just to debunking these stories. To read about some of the more common urban legends or verify whether the e-mail you received about the $250 Nieman Marcus cookie recipe is true, explore some of the following urban legend sites:

www.urbanmyths.com
www.scambusters.org/legends.html
urbanlegends.miningco.com/library/blhoax.htm
www.snopes.com

Sources: Lanford and Lanford, 1998; and Ferrell 1997.

Social movements are most likely to spring up when people come to see their personal troubles as public issues that cannot be solved without a collective response.

Social movements make democracy more available to excluded groups (see Greenberg and Page, 1993). Historically, people in North America have worked at the grassroots level to bring about changes even when elites sought to discourage activism (Adams, 1991). For example, in the United States the civil rights movement brought into its ranks African Americans who had never been allowed to participate in politics (see Killian, 1984). The women's suffrage movement gave a voice to women who had been denied the right to vote (Rosenthal et al., 1985). Disability rights advocates brought together a "hidden army" of supporters without disabilities who had friends or family members with a disability (Shapiro, 1993). Similarly, a grassroots environmental movement gave the working-class residents of Clayoquot Sound a way to "fight city hall" and a huge corporation—MacMillan Bloedel.

Social movements provide people who otherwise would not have the resources to enter the game of politics a chance to do so. We are most familiar with those movements that develop around public policy issues considered newsworthy by the media, ranging from abortion and women's rights to gun control and environmental justice. However, a number of other types of social movements exist as well.

Types of Social Movements

Social movements are difficult to classify; however, sociologists distinguish among movements on the basis of their *goals* and the *amount of change* they seek to produce (Aberle, 1966; Blumer, 1974). Some movements seek to change people while others seek to change society.

Reform Movements Grassroots environmental movements are an example of *reform movements*, which seek to improve society by changing some specific aspect of the social structure. Members of reform movements usually work within the existing system to attempt to change existing public policy so that it more adequately reflects their own value system. Examples of reform movements (in addition to the environmental movement) include labour movements, animal rights movements, antinuclear movements, Mothers Against Drunk Driving, and the disability rights movement.

Revolutionary Movements Movements seeking to bring about a total change in society are referred to as *revolutionary movements*. These movements usually do not attempt to work within the existing system; rather, they aim to remake the system by replacing existing institutions with new ones. Revolutionary movements range from utopian groups seeking to establish an ideal society to radical terrorists who use fear tactics to intimidate those with whom they disagree ideologically (see Alexander and Gill, 1984; Berger, 1988; Vetter and Perlstein, 1991).

***Terrorism* is the calculated unlawful use of physical force or threats of violence against persons or property in order to intimidate or coerce a government, organization, or individual for the purpose of gaining some political, religious, economic or social objective.** Movements based on terrorism often use tactics such as bombings, kidnappings, hostage taking, hijackings, and assassinations (Vetter and Perlstein, 1991). Over the past thirty years, terrorism has become a global phenomenon. For example, the Irish Republican Army has set off dozens of bombs in England; mafia terrorists have targeted judges, prosecutors, and politicians in Italy; and right-wing militia members are suspected in the 1995 bombing of the Alfred P. Murrah Federal Building, a large government office building, in Oklahoma City.

Canada is not immune to terrorist activity. In the late 1960s, the Front de Libération du Québec (FLQ), a small group of extremists on the fringe of the separatist movement, carried out 200 bombings. These incidents ranged from mail bombs to the bombing of the Montreal Stock Exchange, where 27 people were injured. In addition, Sikh separatists are believed to be responsible for the 1985 bombing of an Air India jet that was travelling to India from Canada. This disaster was the biggest mass killing in Canadian history. Of the 329 people who died, 278 were Canadians.

Religious Movements Social movements that seek to produce radical change in individuals typically are based on spiritual or supernatural belief systems. Also referred to as *expressive movements*, *religious movements* are concerned with renovating or renewing people through "inner change." Fundamentalist religious groups seeking to convert nonbelievers to their belief system are an example of this type of movement. Some religious movements are *millenarian*—that is, they forecast that "the end is near" and assert that an immediate change in behaviour is imperative. Relatively new religious movements in industrialized Western societies have included Hare Krishnas, the Unification Church, Scientology, and the Divine Light Mission, all of which tend to appeal to the psychological and social needs of young people seeking meaning in life that mainstream religions have not provided for them.

Alternative Movements Movements that seek limited change in some aspect of people's behaviour are referred to as *alternative movements*. For example, in the early twentieth century, the Women's Christian Temperance Union attempted to get people to abstain from drinking alcoholic beverages. Some analysts place "therapeutic social movements" such as Alcoholics Anonymous in this category; however, others do not, due to their belief that people must

These "pro-lifers" demonstrating outside the Morgentaler clinic in Toronto are members of a resistance movement. They are seeking to prevent or undo change advocated by another social movement: the "pro-choice" movement.

change their lives completely in order to overcome alcohol abuse (see Blumberg, 1977). More recently, a variety of "New Age" movements have directed people's behaviour by emphasizing spiritual consciousness combined with a belief in reincarnation and astrology. Such practices as vegetarianism, meditation, and holistic medicine often are included in the self-improvement category. In the 1990s, some alternative movements include the practice of yoga (usually without its traditional background in the Hindu religion) as a means by which the self can be liberated and union can be achieved with the supreme spirit or universal soul.

RESISTANCE MOVEMENTS Also referred to as *regressive movements*, *resistance movements* seek to prevent change or to undo change that already has occurred. Virtually all of the proactive social movements previously discussed face resistance from one or more reactive movements that hold opposing viewpoints and want to foster public policies that reflect their own viewpoints. Examples of resistance movements are groups organized to oppose free trade, gun control, gay rights, and restrictions on smoking. Perhaps the most widely known resistance movement, however, is made up of those who label themselves "pro-life" advocates—such as the members of Operation Rescue, who seek to close abortion clinics and make abortion illegal under all circumstances (Gray, 1993; Van Biema, 1993a). Protests by some radical anti-abortion groups in Canada and the United States have become violent and have resulted in the deaths of several doctors and clinic workers, thus creating fear among health professionals and patients seeking abortions (Belkin, 1994).

Stages in Social Movements

Do all social movements go through similar stages? Not necessarily, but there appear to be identifiable stages in virtually all movements that succeed beyond their initial phase of development.

In the *preliminary* (or incipiency) *stage*, widespread unrest is present as people begin to become aware of a problem. At this stage, leaders emerge to agitate others into taking action. In the *coalescence stage*, people begin to organize and to publicize the problem. At this stage, some movements become formally organized at local and regional levels. In the *institutionalization* (or bureaucratization) *stage*, an organizational structure develops, and paid staff (rather than volunteers) begin to lead the group. When the movement reaches this stage, the initial zeal and idealism of members may diminish as administrators take over management of the organization. Early grassroots supporters may become disillusioned and drop out; they also may start another movement to address some as yet unsolved aspect of the original problem. For example, some environmental organizations—such as the Sierra Club, the Canadian Nature Federation, and the National Audubon Society—that started as grassroots conservation movements currently are viewed by many people as being unresponsive to local environmental problems (Cable and Cable, 1995). As a result, new movements have arisen.

Social movements may be an important source of social change. Most movements initially develop innovative ways to get their ideas across to decision makers and the public. Some have been successful in achieving their goals; others have not. As historian Robert A. Goldberg (1991) has suggested, gains made by social movements may be fragile, acceptance brief, and benefits minimal and easily lost. For this reason, many groups focus on preserving their gains while simultaneously fighting for those they believe they still deserve.

CHANGING SOCIAL STRUCTURE AND INTERACTION IN THE FUTURE

The social structure in North America has been changing rapidly in recent decades. Currently, there are more possible statuses for persons to occupy and roles to play than at any other time in history. Although achieved statuses are very important today, ascribed statuses still have a significant impact on the options and opportunities people have.

Ironically, at a time when we have more technological capability, more leisure activities and types of entertainment, and more quantities of material goods available for consumption than ever before, many people experience high levels of stress, fear for their lives because of crime, and face problems such as homelessness. Homelessness is not just a problem in Canada and the United States, however. As discussed in Box 4.5, other industrialized nations share the problem.

Individuals and groups often show initiative in trying to solve some of our pressing problems. However, individual initiative alone will not solve all our social problems. Large-scale, formal organizations must become more responsive to society's needs.

At the microlevel, we need to regard social problems as everyone's problem; if we do not, they have a way of becoming everyone's problem anyway. When we think about "the homeless," for example, we are thinking in a somewhat misleading manner. "The homeless" suggests a uniform set of problems and a single category of poor people. Jonathan Kozol (1988:92) emphasizes that "their miseries are somewhat uniform; the squalor is uniform; the density of living space is uniform. [However, the] uniformity is in their mode of suffering, not in themselves."

Tom Allen provides this view of the issue:

> Solutions to homelessness are contained within the solutions to hunger, poor health, educational deprivation, violence and victimization, and slum housing conditions, and must address issues of power, social justice and privilege ... Short-term solutions, such as more shelters and correctionalist policies, will only further institutionalize the situation and end up costing more in the long run. Government policy must be directed towards long-term solutions, such as the construction of more affordable, low-cost housing for those persons being threatened with the increasing gentrification of our cities and towns, and safe and secure housing with supportive services for those marginalized by the drive to create profit. (Allen, 2000)

What can be done about homelessness in the future? We must first become dissatisfied with explanations that see personal problems as the cause of homelessness (Burt, 1992). Only changes in structural factors can explain why we have a homelessness crisis in Canada today. Unless these factors are addressed, homelessness will continue to flourish and be a national disgrace.

In sum, the future of this country rests on our collective ability to deal with major social problems at both the macrolevel and the microlevel of society.

BOX 4.6 SOCIOLOGY IN GLOBAL PERSPECTIVE

HOMELESSNESS IN JAPAN AND FRANCE

Homelessness is a problem not only in Canada and the United States but also in virtually all industrialized nations. Homeless people sleep on the sidewalks and warm air vents in Tokyo and Paris, as well as in Vancouver, Toronto, and Chicago. While many people in Canada feel fear, resentment, or compassion fatigue regarding the homeless, the Japanese and French are just becoming aware of the problem.

In Japan, volunteers feed many of the homeless to make up for the absence of any type of governmental assistance. Recently, the number of homeless people has increased significantly, even with Japan's high per capita income of over $28,000 annually. However, the Japanese economy has dipped into its deepest slump since World War II, and this recession has forced many Japanese companies to do away with their previous guarantee of lifetime employment for their workers. Layoffs and so-called voluntary retirement have produced many unemployed workers who are over the age of 50. Although the Japanese government does not keep records of the homeless, some experts estimate that persons over the age of 50 account for more than half of the homeless population. In order to have a roof over their heads, many near-homeless men rent cheap hotel rooms for as long as they can afford them. In the short term, the extremely high cost of housing in Japan makes the homeless problem even worse. If homelessness becomes a long-term problem, government initiatives will be inevitable.

Although this scene would be familiar in any major North American city, this homeless person is sleeping in front of a Tokyo shop patronized by wealthy Japanese.

Like Japan, France has experienced a high rate of homelessness caused at least in part by a downturn in the economy and massive immigration by refugees from war-torn countries. Paris has set up camps for the homeless in two underground subway stations and offers free showers in public baths. Charity groups have mobilized soup vans and expanded their shelters. A group of social workers known as the Companions of the Night has set up a meeting place where homeless people can meet and talk all night if they so desire.

Do you think volunteers and charities alone can solve major problems such as homelessness?

Sources: Based on Greenwald, 1993; and Simons, 1993a.

CHAPTER REVIEW

How does social structure shape our social interactions?

The stable patterns of social relationships within a particular society make up its social structure. Social structure is a macrolevel influence because it shapes and determines the overall patterns in which social interaction occurs. Social interaction refers to how people within a society act and respond to one another. This interaction is a microlevel dynamic—between individuals and groups—and is the foundation of meaningful relationships in society. Social structure provides an ordered framework for society and for our interactions with others.

What are the main components of social structure?

Social structure comprises statuses, roles, groups, and social institutions. A status is a specific position in a group or society and is characterized by certain expectations, rights, and duties. Ascribed statuses, such as gender, class, and ethnicity, are acquired at birth or involuntarily later in life. Achieved statuses, such as education and occupation, are assumed voluntarily as a result of personal choice, merit, or direct effort. We occupy a status, but a role is a set of behavioural expectations associated with a given status. A social group consists of two or more people who interact frequently and share a common identity and sense of interdependence. A formal organization is a highly structured group formed to complete certain tasks or achieve specific goals. A social institution is a set of organized beliefs and rules that establish how a society attempts to meet its basic needs.

What are the functionalist and conflict perspectives on social institutions?

According to functionalist theorists, social institutions perform several prerequisites of all societies: replace members; teach new members; produce, distribute, and consume goods and services; preserve order; and provide and maintain a sense of purpose. Conflict theorists, however, note that social institutions do not work for the common good of all individuals. Institutions may enhance and uphold the power of some groups but exclude others, such as the homeless.

What is collective behaviour and when is it most likely to occur?

Collective behaviour is relatively spontaneous, unstructured activity that typically violates established social norms. Collective behaviour occurs when some common influence or stimulus produces a response from a relatively large number of people.

What is a crowd and what causes crowd behaviour?

A crowd is a relatively large number of people who are in one another's immediate vicinity. Social scientists have developed several theories to explain crowd behaviour. Contagion theory asserts that a crowd takes on a life of its own as people are transformed from rational beings into part of an organism that acts on its own. Convergence theory asserts that people with similar attributes find other like-minded persons with whom they can release underlying personal tendencies. Emergent norm theory asserts that, as a crowd develops, it comes up with its own norms that replace more conventional norms of behaviour.

What are the major types of social movements, and what are their goals?

A social movement is an organized group that acts consciously to promote or resist change through collective action; such movements are most likely to be formed when people see their personal troubles as public issues that cannot be resolved without a collective response. Reform movements seek to improve society by changing some specific aspect of the social structure. Revolutionary movements seek to bring about a total change in society—sometimes by the use of terrorism. Religious movements seek to produce radical change in individuals based on spiritual or supernatural belief systems. Alternative movements seek limited change to some aspect of people's behaviour. Resistance movements seek to prevent change or to undo change that already has occurred.

Key Terms

achieved status 103
ascribed status 103
casual crowd 121
civil disobedience 122
collective behaviour 119
conventional crowd 121
crowd 120
dramaturgical analysis 114
fad 125
fashion 125
formal organization 109
gossip 124
mass 120
mass behaviour 124
mass hysteria 125
master status 104
mob 121
nonverbal communication 117
panic 122
personal space 119
presentation of self 114
primary group 108
propaganda 125
protest crowd 122
public opinion 125
relative homelessness 101
riot 121
role 105
role conflict 107
role exit 107
role expectation 106
role performance 106
role strain 107
rumours 124
secondary group 108
self-fulfilling prophecy 113
social construction of reality 113
social group 108
social institution 109
social interaction 100
social marginality 102
social movement 126
social network 108
social structure 100
status 103
status set 103
status symbols 105
stigma 102
terrorism 128

Internet Exercises

1. Using the Lycos search engine **(www.lycos.com)**, set the search to "all of the words" and do a search for "homeless Canada." Visit five of the sites it identifies and try to fit the theme of the pages you choose into one of the perspectives used in the book (e.g., conflict, functionalist, interactionist). With which perspective do you feel the most comfortable?
2. Societies find ways to censure those who act outside of their norms. In addition to **alt.sci.sociology** and **alt.feminism**, also start reading **alt.psi.psychology**. How do people in these newsgroups deal with those who act outside of the norms of the group? What ways seem to work best? How does someone become familiar with the norms of a newsgroup?
3. This chapter discusses nonverbal communication. Most people who use e-mail or post to newsgroups will use emoticons—which are symbols such as ;-) and :) — to indicate emotions without having to type them out. Go to the PC Webopaedia page listing emoticons **(webopedia.internet.com/TERM/e/emoticon.html)** to familiarize yourself with the most popular emoticons. Do you think these symbols would qualify as nonverbal symbols? How easy is it to determine the meaning of these symbols? Why do you think that emoticons are in widespread use online, while they are at the same time rarely if ever used in other types of written communication?
4. Does collective behaviour exist on the Internet? Monitor the newsgroup **alt.feminism** and watch for behaviours that may be considered to be "collective." Do a search for the term "chat site" using any of the search engines, and monitor a chat site watching for signs of collective behaviour in this setting as well. Are the behaviours you have noted similar to or different from those described in this book? If they are different, would you still consider them collective behaviours?

Questions for Critical Thinking

1. Think of a person you know well who often irritates you or whose behaviour grates on your nerves (it could be a parent, friend, relative, teacher). First, list that person's statuses and roles. Then, analyze his or her possible role expectations, role performance, role conflicts, and role strains. Does anything you find in your analysis help to explain his or her irritating behaviour? (If not, change your method of analysis!) How helpful are the concepts of social structure in analyzing individual behaviour?
2. Are structural problems responsible for homelessness, or are homeless individuals responsible for their own situation?
3. You are conducting field research on gender differences in nonverbal communication styles. How are you going to account for variations among age, ethnicity, and social class?
4. What types of collective behaviour in Canada do you believe are influenced by inequalities based on race/ethnicity, class, gender, age, or disabilities? Why?

Net Links

For more Web links related to the topic of this chapter, see the Nelson sociology Web site: **www.sociologyessentials-2nded.nelson.com**.

To learn more about Erving Goffman's book *The Presentation of Self in Everyday Life*, go to:

R **www.cfmc.com/adamb/writings/goffman.htm**

What changes can we expect to see in our everyday social interactions as a result of new electronic technologies? The paper "The Presentation of Self in Electronic Life: Goffman on the Internet" addresses this question:

www.ntu.ac.uk/soc/psych/miller/goffman/htm

The Canada Mortgage and Housing Corporation has current research on homeless women and homelessness among Aboriginal peoples, as well as a 1998 survey of Canadians' attitudes toward homelessness. To see it, go to:

www.cmhc-schl.gc.ca/cmhc.html

Raising the Roof is a national charity that funds long-term solutions to homelessness in Canada. Its primary activities involve developing, finding, and/or maintaining homes for homeless people. Questions and answers, as well as current articles on homelessness, are available at this site:

www.communitygates.com/raisetheroof/under.htm

Suggested Readings

These books provide interesting insights on social interaction and the social construction of reality:

Peter L. Berger and Thomas Luckmann. *The Social Construction of Reality: A Treatise in the Sociology of Knowledge*. Garden City, N.Y.: Doubleday/Anchor Books, 1967.

Erving Goffman. *The Presentation of Self in Everyday Life*. New York: Doubleday, 1959.

David A. Karp and William C. Yoels. *Sociology and Everyday Life*. Itasca, Ill.: Peacock, 1986.

The process of leaving a significant role and establishing a new identity is examined in this book:

Helen Rose Fuchs Ebaugh. *Becoming an EX: The Process of Role Exit*. Chicago: University of Chicago Press, 1988.

To find out more about the problem of homelessness:

Lars Eighner. *Travels with Lizbeth*. New York: St. Martin's Press, 1993.

David A. Snow and Leon Anderson. *Down on Their Luck: A Case Study of Homeless Street People*. Berkeley: University of California Press, 1993.

Lesley D. Harman. *When a Hostel Becomes a Home: Experiences of Women*. Toronto: Garamond Press, 1989.

Thomas O'Reilly-Fleming. *Down and Out in Canada: Homeless Canadians*. Toronto: Canadian Scholars Press, 1993.

INFOTRAC® COLLEGE EDITION

Either from the *Sociology In Our Times: The Essentials* Web site (**www.sociologyessentials-2nded.nelson.com**) or directly from your Web browser, you may access InfoTrac® College Edition, an online university library that includes over 600 popular and scholarly journals in which you can find articles related to the topics in this chapter.

CHAPTER 5

Kenneth Payne describes his journey through a bureaucratic maze:

"Since November, I have spent six to eight hours a day trying to persuade the authorities to accommodate me, but it just goes around in a circle ... It's George Orwell's Big Brother, 14 years after his book *1984* ... The bureaucracy is making me prove a negative and it turns 'innocent until proven guilty' on its head ... There's no common sense here. It's an inflexible bureaucracy where nobody takes any responsibility." (Reed, 1998:A11)

What is Mr. Payne's problem? The former carpenter wants to be a school teacher. He has a degree in education and has taught as a substitute. However, he is unable to get a permanent job teaching because he has a skin disease that causes the skin on his hands to blister and peel. Why should this disqualify Mr. Payne from teaching? Because the disease has removed his fingerprints and legislators in his home state of California have passed a law requiring that all teachers be fingerprinted so their criminal records can be checked. Of course, because Mr. Payne has never had proper fingerprints, there would be nothing on file to check against even if they could read his prints. But this has not discouraged the bureaucrats. He has appealed to the state and offered to prove in other ways that he has no criminal record, but he has been unable to get an exemption from the rule.

GROUPS AND ORGANIZATIONS

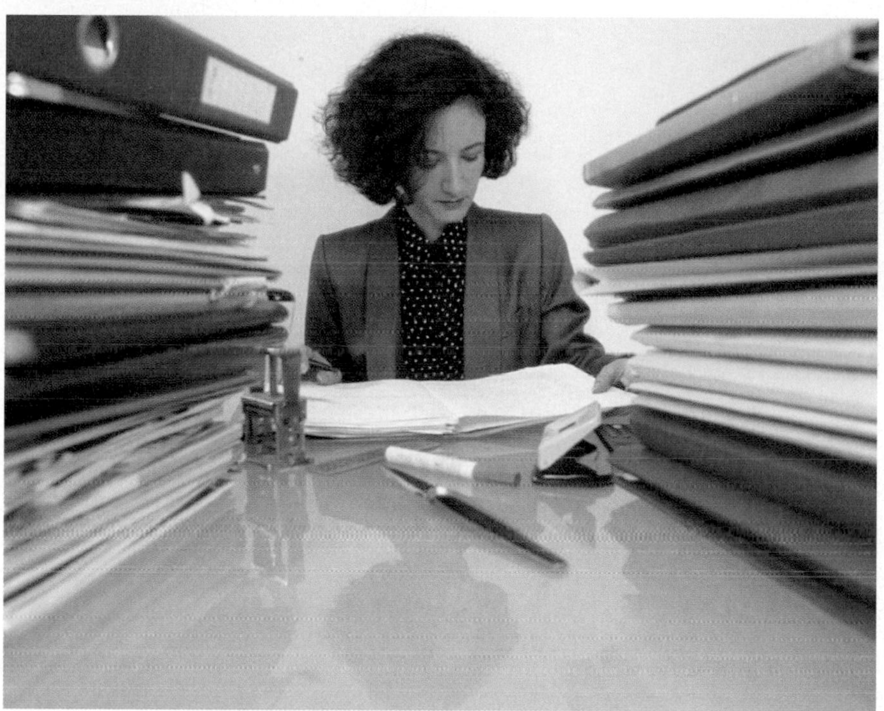

We have all been treated badly by some bureaucracy—though not perhaps to the degree of this unusual case. In fact many of us think of bureaucracies in a very negative way because of their red tape and impersonal nature. However, while bureaucracies can be inflexible and inhumane, they are also a very powerful type of social organization and are essential to modern life. Bureaucracies are the best way of managing large numbers of people who must accomplish a common task, so they are an essential part of our industrialized global society. Much of our lives is spent dealing with bureaucratic organizations. Most of us are born in hospitals, educated in schools, fed by restaurants and supermarket chains, entertained by communications companies, employed by corporations, and buried by funeral companies.

In this chapter, you will learn about different types of groups and organizations including bureaucracies. As social beings, we live our lives in groups and they constantly affect our behaviour. Before reading on, test your knowledge about bureaucracies by taking the quiz in Box 5.1.

Questions and Issues

CHAPTER FOCUS QUESTION: How can we explain the behaviour of people who work in bureaucracies?

What constitutes a social group?

How are groups and their members shaped by group size, leadership style, and pressures to conform?

What purposes does bureaucracy serve?

What are some of the characteristics of bureaucracies?

How might an alternative form of organization differ from existing ones?

Napoleon's defeat at Waterloo in 1815 showed that massive armies could not be led in the traditional way, by a single commander responsible for everything. Subsequently, armies developed more effective organizational structures.

SOCIAL GROUPS

Three strangers are standing at a street corner waiting for a traffic light to change. Do they constitute a group? Five hundred women and men are first-year students at a university. Do they constitute a group? We use the word *group* to mean any collection of people. According to sociologists, however, the answer to these questions is no; individuals who happen to share a common feature or to be in the same place at the same time do not constitute social groups.

Types of Groups

As you will recall from Chapter 4, groups have varying degrees of social solidarity and structure. This structure is flexible in some groups and more rigid in others. Some groups are small and personal; others are large and impersonal. We more closely identify with the members of some groups than we do others.

PRIMARY AND SECONDARY GROUPS Sociologist Charles H. Cooley (1962/1909) used the term *primary group* to describe a small, less specialized group in which members engage in face-to-face, emotion-based interactions over an extended period of time. We have primary relationships with other individuals in our primary groups—that is, with our *significant others*, who frequently serve as role models.

In contrast, you will recall, a *secondary group* is a larger, more specialized group in which the members engage in more impersonal, goal-oriented relationships for a limited period of time. The size of a secondary group may vary. Twelve students in a university seminar may start out as a secondary group but eventually become a primary group as they get to know one another and communicate on a more personal basis. Formal organizations are secondary groups, but they also contain many primary groups within them. For example, how many primary groups do you think there are within the secondary group setting of your university?

INGROUPS AND OUTGROUPS All groups set boundaries by distinguishing between insiders who are members and outsiders who are not. Sociologist William Graham Sumner (1959/1906) coined the terms *ingroup* and *outgroup* to describe people's feelings toward members of their own and other groups. An ***ingroup* is a group to which a person belongs and with which the person feels a sense of identity.** An ***outgroup* is a group to which a person does not belong and toward which the person may feel a sense of competitiveness or hostility.** Distinguishing between our ingroups and our outgroups helps us establish our individual identity and self-worth. Likewise, groups are solidified by ingroup and outgroup distinctions; the presence of an enemy or hostile group may bind members more closely together (Coser, 1956).

Group boundaries may be formal, with clearly defined criteria for membership. For example, a country club that requires applicants for membership to be recommended by four current members, to pay a $25,000 initiation fee, and to pay $1,000 per month membership dues has clearly set requirements

BOX 5.1 SOCIOLOGY AND EVERYDAY LIFE

HOW MUCH DO YOU KNOW ABOUT BUREAUCRACY?

TRUE	FALSE	
T	F	1. Large bureaucracies have existed for about a thousand years.
T	F	2. Because of the efficiency and profitability of the new factory bureaucracies, people were eager to leave the farms to work in the factories.
T	F	3. Bureaucracies are deliberately impersonal.
T	F	4. In addition to their formal structure, bureaucracies also have an "other face"—an informal structure that is also important in analyzing their operation.
T	F	5. The rise of Protestantism helped create the social conditions favourable to the rise of modern bureaucracies.
T	F	6. Because people in bureaucracies follow the direction of their superiors, bringing about change in large organizations is easy.
T	F	7. One of the first modern bureaucratic organizations was the Prussian army.
T	F	8. Businesses in Japan have developed an organizational model that is different from the one prevalent in North America.
T	F	9. The Internet company that calls itself "the Earth's Biggest Bookstore" keeps only a small stock of books.
T	F	10. The comic strip *Dilbert* has become popular because it is a reflection of the way many people feel about the bureaucracies in which they work.

Answers on page 140.

for its members. The club may even post a sign at its entrance that states "Members Only," and use security personnel to ensure that nonmembers do not encroach on its grounds. Boundary distinctions often are reflected in symbols such as emblems or clothing. These symbols denote that the bearer/wearer is a member of the ingroup; they are status symbols.

Group boundaries are not always as formal as they are in a private club. Friendship groups, for example, usually do not have clear guidelines for membership. Rather, the boundaries tend to be very informal and vaguely defined.

Ingroup and outgroup distinctions may encourage social cohesion among members, but they also may promote classism, racism, sexism, and ageism. Ingroup members typically view themselves positively and members of outgroups negatively. These feelings of group superiority, or *ethnocentrism*, are somewhat inevitable. However, members of some groups feel more free than others to act on their beliefs. If groups are embedded in larger groups and organizations, the large organization may discourage such beliefs and their consequences (Merton, 1968). Conversely, organizations covertly may foster these ingroup/outgroup distinctions by denying their existence or by failing to take action when misconduct occurs. For example, take the case of sexual harassment in a Winnipeg plant:

> In Winnipeg, Manitoba, recently two male employees were fired from a Canada Safeway bread plant for accusations of sexual harassment against female employees. One of the men allegedly exposed himself, stalked, and gave photographs of his anatomy to a female employee. Accusations against the other man included repeatedly making lewd and suggestive comments to female employees and inappropriately touching them. The female employee said that 10 or 12 women on the work floor have taken stress leave from work over the last five years because of the abuse. Men outnumber women on the shop floor by about eight to one. ... Female employees say that the atmosphere at the plant discouraged women from coming forward to report incidents of harassment. One stated "we were terrified ... they told us not to

BOX 5.1

Answers to the Sociology Quiz on Bureaucracy

1. **False.** While not all sociologists agree on the specific origins of bureaucracies, many feel that modern bureaucracies began with the development of large factories in England during the nineteenth century. Large-scale organizations had existed prior to this time, but they were not organized on bureaucratic principles. As organizations grew in size, they became difficult to manage, so new organizing principles were required.
2. **False.** Commenting on the eighteenth-century factory, Charles Perrow has observed that "the unnaturalness of working for someone else's profit twelve hours a day, seven days a week was so pronounced that the early factories had to rely on criminals and paupers to do the work" (1986:49).
3. **True.** Bureaucracies are designed to be efficient and productive. In order to do this, they take a detached approach to clients and employees so that personal feelings do not interfere with organizational decisions.
4. **True.** All bureaucracies have an informal structure that is composed of activities and interactions that do not correspond with the official rules and procedures of the bureaucracy.
5. **True.** According to Max Weber, Protestantism, with its emphasis on worldliness and commitment to long-term goals, helped create the social conditions that led to the rise of the modern bureaucracy.
6. **False.** It is extremely difficult to bring about change in bureaucracies because people become comfortable with the way things have been done in the past.
7. **True.** Napoleon's defeat at Waterloo in 1815 by the allied armies of Prussia (now part of Germany), Britain, Austria, and Russia showed that mass armies could not be led in the traditional way, by a single commander responsible for everything (Stark, 1998). The Prussian military, having learned from observing Napoleon's defeat, set about designing a more effective organization. Field Marshal Helmuth von Moltke, who took command of the Prussian army in 1857, was responsible for two major innovations. He developed a general staff made up of carefully selected and trained officers who could carry out the leader's commands and he divided his army into standard-sized "divisions" that could be detached to fight as self-sufficient units. These innovations, which still guide contemporary armies, also influenced the development of industrial bureaucracies.
8. **True.** The main differences between Japanese and North American corporations are that Japanese employees can expect lifetime employment and are encouraged to participate in management decisions. This may change, however, as the recession of the 1990s has led some Japanese companies to rethink their guarantee of lifetime employment.
9. **True.** While you can order over a million titles from Amazon.com, the company does not stock all of these titles. The rest are ordered and delivered from traditional book wholesalers.
10. **True.** Thousands of workers have posted *Dilbert* cartoons on their cubicle and office walls, and many of the ideas you see in *Dilbert* actually come from their suggestions.

Sources: Based on Perrow, 1986; and Stark, 1998.

do it and we didn't know any better … they kept saying they'll deal with it, but they never did. And we didn't know anything about our rights." (Owen, 1996)

In this case, male co-workers, it seems, had developed an ingroup from which the female employees were not only categorically excluded, but were also made the object of the group's ridicule. In a work

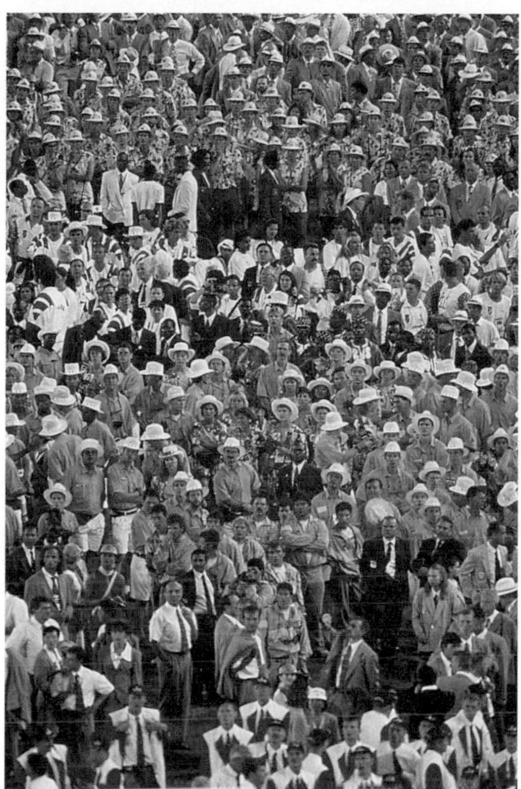

These Olympic teams graphically illustrate the concept of ingroups and outgroups. Each Olympic team can be seen as an ingroup that helps to give its members a sense of belonging and identity—feelings that are strengthened by the presence of clearly defined outgroups (competing teams).

environment, ingroups can provide support for group members. Those who are denied membership in the group, however, may find it impossible to perform their job effectively.

Reference Groups Ingroups provide us not only with a source of identity but also with a point of reference. A ***reference group*** **is a group that strongly influences a person's behaviour and social attitudes, regardless of whether that individual is an actual member.** When we attempt to evaluate our appearance, ideas, or goals, we automatically refer to the standards of some group. Sometimes we will refer to our membership groups, such as family or friends. Other times, we will refer to groups to which we do not currently belong but that we might wish to join in the future, such as a social club or a profession. We also may have negative reference groups. For many people, the Ku Klux Klan and neo-Nazi skinheads are examples of negative reference groups because most people's racial attitudes compare unfavourably with such groups' blatantly racist behaviour.

Reference groups help explain why our behaviour and attitudes sometimes differ from those of our membership groups. We may accept the values and norms of a group with which we identify rather than one to which we belong. We also may act more like members of a group we want to join than members of groups to which we already belong. In this case, reference groups are a source of anticipatory socialization. Many people have more than one reference group and often receive conflicting messages from them about how they should view themselves. For most of us, our reference group attachments change many times during our life course, especially when we acquire a new status in a formal organization.

GROUP CHARACTERISTICS AND DYNAMICS

What purpose do groups serve? Why are individuals willing to relinquish some of their freedom to participate in groups? According to functionalists, people form groups to meet instrumental and expressive needs. *Instrumental*, or task-oriented, needs cannot always be met by one person, so the group works cooperatively to fulfil a specific goal. Think, for example, of how hard it would be to function as a one-person football team or to single-handedly build a skyscraper. Groups help members do jobs that are impossible to do alone or that would be very difficult and time consuming at best. In addition to instrumental needs, groups also help people meet their *expressive*, or emotional, needs, especially for self-expression and support from family, friends, and peers.

While not disputing that groups ideally perform such functions, conflict theorists suggest that groups also involve a series of power relationships whereby the needs of individual members may not be equally served. Symbolic interactionists focus on questions such as how the size of a group influences the kind of interaction that takes place among members.

We now will look at certain characteristics of groups, such as how size affects group dynamics.

Group Size

The size of a group is one of its most important features. Interactions are more personal and intense in a ***small group,*** **a collectivity small enough for all members to be acquainted with one another and to interact simultaneously.**

Sociologist Georg Simmel (1950/1917) suggested that small groups have distinctive interaction patterns that do not exist in larger groups. According to Simmel, in a ***dyad*****—a group composed of two members**—the active participation of both members is crucial for the group's survival. If one member withdraws from interaction or "quits," the group ceases to exist. Examples of dyads include two people who are best friends, married couples, and domestic partnerships. Dyads provide members with a more intense bond and with a sense of unity not found in most larger groups.

When a third person is added to a dyad, a ***triad,*** **a group composed of three members,** is formed. The nature of the relationship and interaction patterns changes with the addition of the third person. In a triad even if one member ignores another or declines to participate, the group can still function. In addition, two members may unite to create a coalition that can subject the third member to group pressure to conform. A *coalition* is an alliance created in an attempt to reach a shared objective or goal. If two members form a coalition, the other member may be seen as an outsider or intruder.

As the size of a group increases beyond three people, members tend to specialize in different tasks, and everyday communication patterns change. For instance, in groups of more than six or seven people, it becomes increasingly difficult for everyone to take part in the same conversation; therefore, several conversations likely will take place simultaneously. Members also are likely to take sides on issues and form a number of coalitions. In groups of more than ten or twelve people, it becomes virtually impossible for all members to participate in a single conversation unless one person serves as moderator and facilitates the discussion. As shown in Figure 5.1, when the size of the group increases, the number of possible social interactions also increases.

Our most intense relationships occur in dyads—groups composed of two members. How might the interaction of these two people differ if they were with several other people?

Group Leadership

What role do leaders play in groups? Leaders are responsible for directing plans and activities so that the group completes its task or fulfils its goals. Primary groups generally have informal leadership. For example, most of us do not elect or appoint leaders in our own families. By comparison, leadership in secondary groups (such as colleges, government agencies, and corporations) involves a clearly defined chain of command with written responsibilities assigned to each position in the organizational structure.

LEADERSHIP FUNCTIONS Both primary and secondary groups have some type of leadership or positions that enable certain people to be leaders, or at least to wield power over others. From a functionalist perspective, if groups exist to meet the instrumental and expressive needs of their members, then leaders are responsible for helping the group meet those needs. ***Instrumental leadership*** **is goal- or task-oriented;** this type of leadership is most appropriate when the group's purpose is to complete a task or reach a particular goal. ***Expressive leadership*** **provides emotional support for members;** this type of leadership is most appropriate when the group is dealing with emotional issues, and harmony, solidarity, and high morale are needed. Both kinds of leadership are needed for groups to work effectively.

LEADERSHIP STYLES Three major styles of leadership exist in groups: authoritarian, democratic, and

FIGURE 5.1 Growth of Possible Social Interactions Based on Group Size

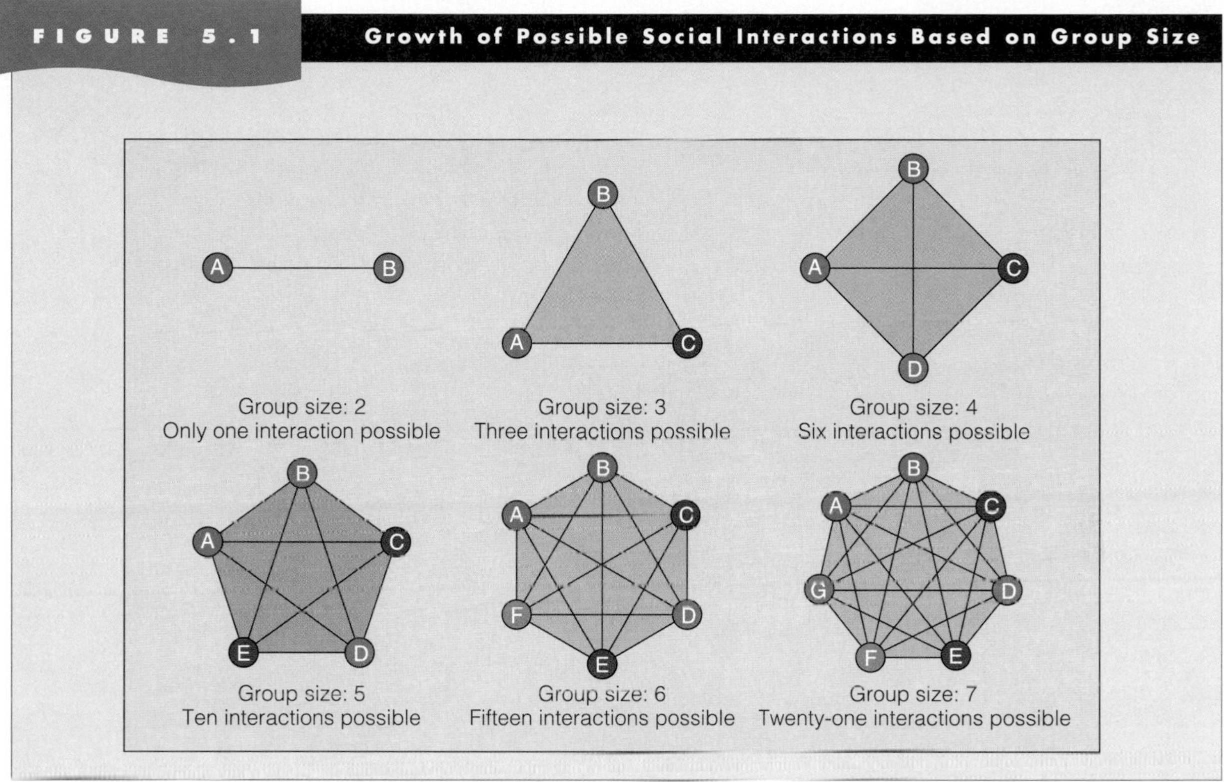

laissez-faire. ***Authoritarian leaders* make all major group decisions and assign tasks to members.** These leaders focus on the instrumental tasks of the group and demand compliance from others. In times of crisis, such as a war or natural disaster, authoritarian leaders may be commended for their decisive actions. In other situations, however, they may be criticized for being dictatorial and for fostering intergroup hostility. By contrast, ***democratic leaders* encourage group discussion and decision making through consensus building.** These leaders may be praised for their expressive, supportive behaviour toward group members, but they also may be blamed for being indecisive in times of crisis.

Laissez-faire means "to leave alone." ***Laissez-faire leaders* are only minimally involved in decision making and encourage group members to make their own decisions.** On the one hand, laissez-faire leaders may be viewed positively by group members because they do not flaunt their power or position. On the other hand, a group that needs active leadership is not likely to find it with this style of leadership, which does not work vigorously to promote group goals (White and Lippitt, 1953, 1960).

Group Conformity

To what extent do groups exert a powerful influence in our lives? Groups have a significant amount of influence over our values, attitudes, and behaviour. In order to gain and then retain our membership in groups, most of us are willing to exhibit a high level of conformity to the wishes of other group members. ***Conformity* is the process of maintaining or changing behaviour to comply with the norms established by a society, subculture, or other group.** We often experience powerful pressure from other group members to conform. In some situations, this pressure may be almost overwhelming.

In several studies (which would be impossible to conduct today for ethical reasons), researchers found that the pressure to conform may cause group members to say they see something that is contradictory to what they actually are seeing or to do something

FIGURE 5.2 Asch's Cards

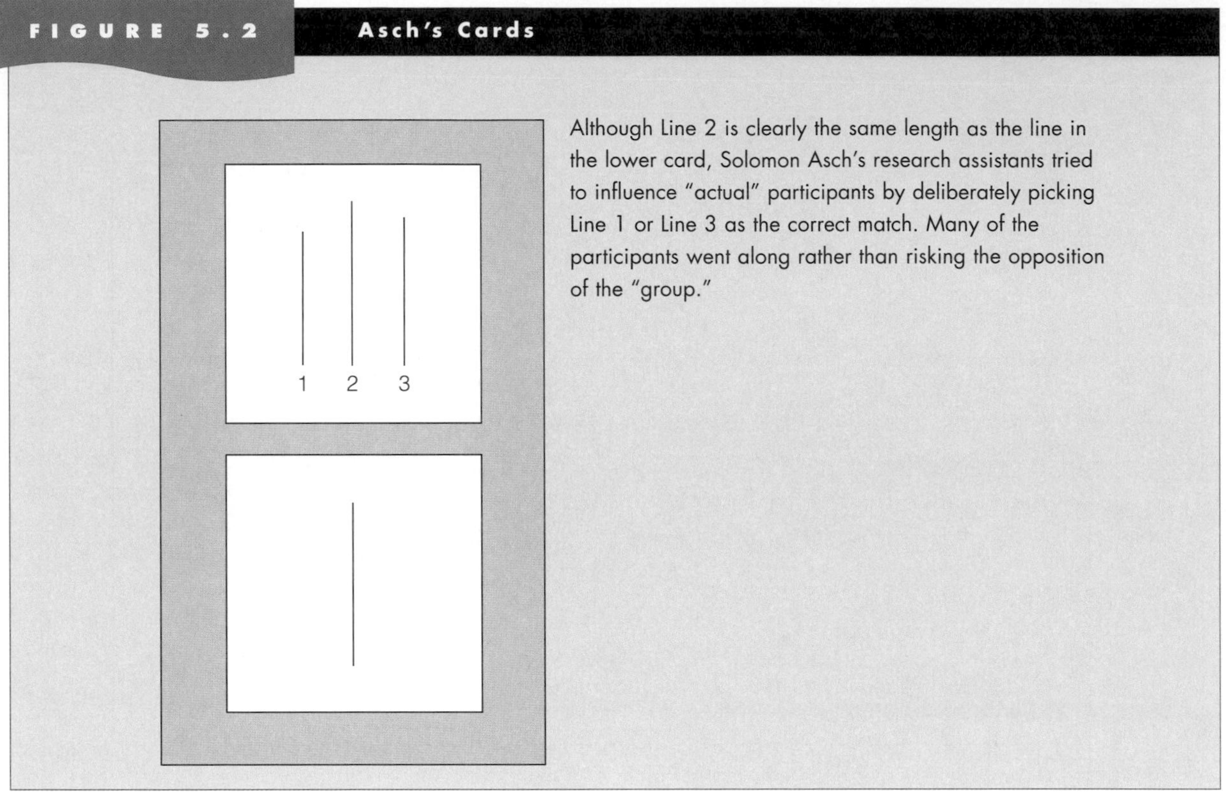

Although Line 2 is clearly the same length as the line in the lower card, Solomon Asch's research assistants tried to influence "actual" participants by deliberately picking Line 1 or Line 3 as the correct match. Many of the participants went along rather than risking the opposition of the "group."

Source: Asch, 1955.

they otherwise would be unwilling to do. As we look at two of these studies, ask yourself what you might have done if you had been involved in this research.

Asch's Research Pressure to conform is especially strong in small groups in which members want to fit in with the group. In a series of experiments conducted by Solomon Asch (1955, 1956), the pressure toward group conformity was so great that participants were willing to contradict their own best judgment if the rest of the group disagreed with them.

One of Asch's experiments involved groups of undergraduate men (seven in each group) who allegedly were recruited for a study of visual perception. All the men were seated in chairs. However, the person in the sixth chair did not know that he was the only actual subject; all the others were assisting the researcher. The participants were first shown a large card with a vertical line on it and then a second card with three vertical lines (see Figure 5.2). Each of the seven participants was asked to indicate which of the three lines on the second card was identical in length to the "standard line" on the first card.

In the first test with each group, all seven men selected the correct matching line. In the second trial, all seven still answered correctly. In the third trial, however, the subject became very uncomfortable when all of the others selected the incorrect line. The actual subject could not understand what was happening and became even more confused as the others continued to give incorrect responses on eleven out of the next fifteen trials.

If you had been in the position of the subject, how would you have responded? Would you have continued to give the correct answer, or would you have been swayed by the others? When Asch (1955) averaged the responses of the fifty actual subjects who participated in the study, he found that about 33 percent routinely chose to conform to the group by giving the same (incorrect) responses as Asch's assistants. Another 40 percent gave incorrect responses in about half of the trials. Although 25 percent always gave correct responses, even they felt very uneasy and "knew that something was wrong." In discussing the experiment afterwards, most of the subjects who gave incorrect responses indicated that they had known the answers were wrong but decided to go along with the group in order to avoid ridicule or ostracism.

In later studies, Asch found that if even a single assistant did not agree with the others, the subject was reassured by hearing someone else question the accuracy of incorrect responses and was much less likely to give a wrong answer himself.

One contribution of Asch's research is the dramatic way in which it calls our attention to the power that groups have to produce conformity among members. *Compliance* is the extent to which people say (or do) things so that they may gain the approval of other people. Certainly, Asch demonstrated that people will bow to social pressure in small-group settings.

Milgram's Research How willing are we to do something because someone in a position of authority has told us to do it? How far are we willing to go in following the demands of that individual? Stanley Milgram (1963, 1974) conducted a series of controversial experiments to find answers to these questions about people's obedience to authority.

Milgram's subjects were men who had responded to an advertisement for participants in an experiment. When the first (actual) subject arrived, he was told that the study concerned the effects of punishment on learning. After the second subject (an assistant of Milgram's) arrived, the two men were instructed to draw slips of paper from a hat to get their assignments as either the "teacher" or the "learner." Because the drawing was rigged, the actual subject always became the teacher, and the assistant the learner. Next, the learner was strapped into a chair with protruding electrodes that looked something like an electric chair. The teacher was placed in an adjoining room and given a realistic-looking but nonoperative shock generator. The "generator's" control panel showed levels that went from "Slight Shock" (15 volts) on the left, to "Intense Shock" (255 volts) in the middle, to "DANGER: SEVERE SHOCK" (375 volts), and finally "XXX" (450 volts) on the right.

The teacher was instructed to read aloud a pair of words and then to repeat the first of the two words. At that time, the learner was supposed to respond with the second of the two words. If the learner could not provide the second word, the teacher was instructed to press the lever on the shock generator so that the learner would be punished for forgetting the word. Each time the learner gave an incorrect response, the teacher was supposed to increase the shock level by 15 volts. The alleged purpose of the shock was to determine if punishment improves a person's memory.

What was the maximum level of shock that a teacher was willing to inflict on a learner? The learner had been instructed (in advance) to beat on the wall between himself and the teacher as the experiment continued, pretending that he was in intense pain. The teacher was told that the shocks might be "extremely painful" but that they would cause no permanent damage. At about 300 volts, when the learner quit responding at all to questions, the teacher often turned to the experimenter to see what he should do next. When the experimenter indicated that the teacher should give increasingly painful shocks, 65 percent of them administered shocks all the way up to the "XXX" (450-volt) level (see Figure 5.3). By this point in the process, the teachers frequently were sweating, stuttering, or biting on their lip. According to Milgram, the teachers (who were free to leave whenever they wanted to) continued in the experiment because they were being given directions by a person in a position of authority (a university scientist wearing a white coat).

What can we learn from Milgram's study? The study provides evidence that obedience to authority may be more common than most of us would like to believe. None of the "teachers" challenged the process before they had applied 300 volts. Almost two-thirds went all the way to what could have been a deadly jolt of electricity if the shock generator had been real.

This research once again raises some of the questions originally posed in Chapter 1 concerning research ethics. As in Asch's research, Milgram's subjects were deceived about the nature of the study in which they were being asked to participate. Many of them found the experiment extremely stressful. Such conditions cannot be ignored by social scientists because subjects may receive lasting emotional scars from this kind of research. It would be virtually impossible today to obtain permission to replicate this experiment in a university setting.

FIGURE 5.3 Results of Milgram's Obedience Experiment

Even Milgram was surprised by subjects' willingness to administer what they thought were severely painful and even dangerous shocks to a helpless "learner."

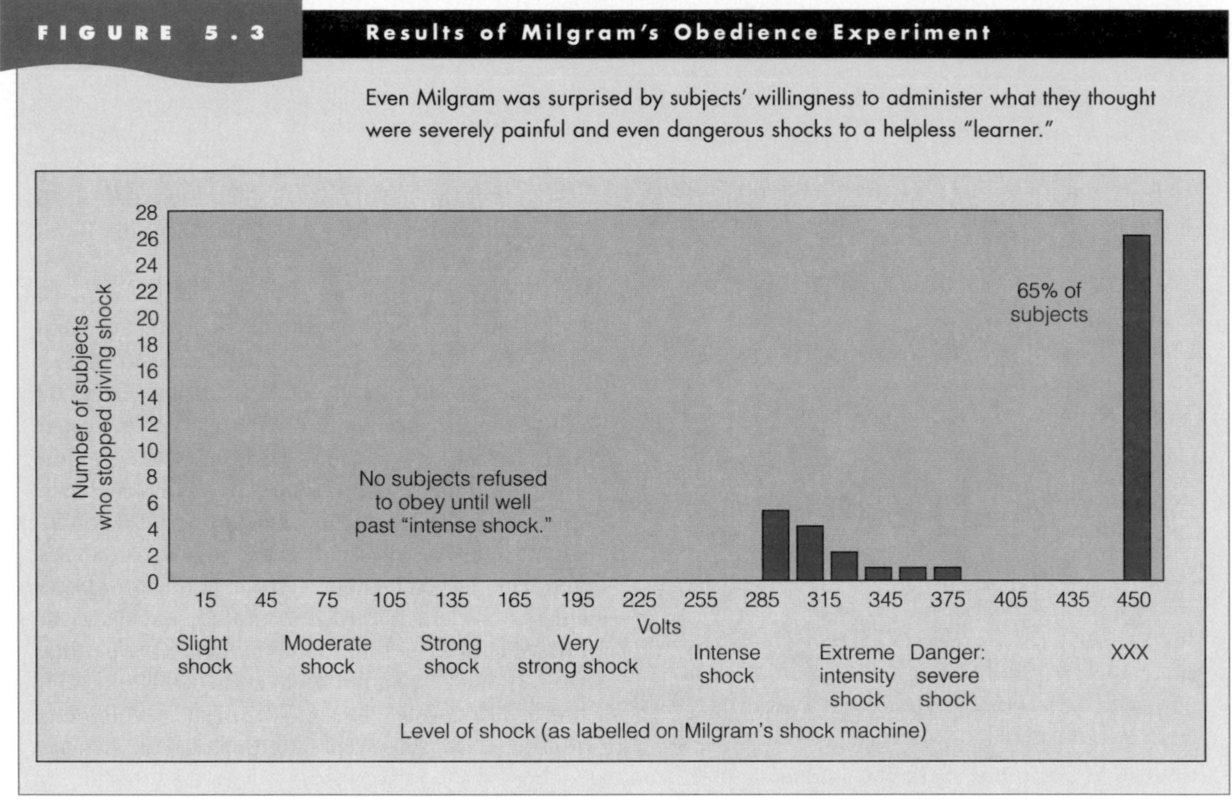

Graph is based on Table 2 in Stanley Milgram's "Behavioural Study of Obedience," *Journal of Abnormal and Social Psychology* (1963), Vol. 67, No. 4, p. 376. Used by permission.

Group Conformity and Sexual Harassment Psychologist John Pryor (*PBS*, 1992) has conducted behavioural experiments on university campuses to examine the social dynamics of sexual harassment. In one of his studies, a graduate student (who actually was a member of the research team) led research subjects to believe that they would be training undergraduate women to use a computer. The actual purpose of the experiment was to observe whether the trainers (subjects) would harass the women if given the opportunity and encouraged to do so. By design, the graduate student purposely harassed the women (who also were part of the research team), setting an example for the subjects to follow.

Pryor found that when the "trainers" were led to believe that sexual harassment was condoned and then were left alone with the women, they took full advantage of the situation in 90 percent of the experiments. Shannon Hoffman, one of the women who participated in the research, felt vulnerable because of the permissive environment created by the men in charge:

> It was very uncomfortable for me. I realized that had it been out of the experimental setting that, as a woman, I would have been very nervous with someone that close to me and reaching around me. So it kind of made me feel a little bit powerless as far as that goes because there was nothing I could do about it. But I also realized that in a business setting, if this person really was my boss, that it would be harder for me to send out the negative signals or whatever to try to fend off that type of thing. (*PBS*, 1992)

This research suggests a relationship between group conformity and harassment. Behaviour such as sexual harassment or racism is more likely to occur when it is encouraged (or at least not actively discouraged) by others. When people think they can be rewarded by it or get away with it, they are more likely to engage in such behaviour.

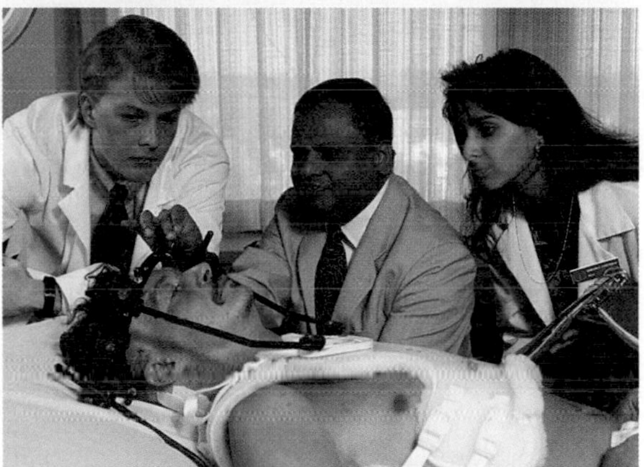

Normative organizations rely on volunteers to fulfil their goals; these volunteers (left) make Red Cross work possible in Honduras, Central America. Coercive organizations rely on involuntary recruitment; these young men (upper right) were remanded to this juvenile correctional centre (a total institution). Utilitarian organizations provide material rewards to participants; in teaching hospitals such as this (lower right), physicians, medical students, and patients all hope they may benefit from involvement with the organization.

FORMAL ORGANIZATIONS

Over the past century, the number of formal organizations has increased dramatically in Canada and other industrialized nations. Everyday life previously was centred in small, informal, primary groups, such as the family and the village. With the advent of industrialization and urbanization (as discussed in Chapter 1), people's lives became increasingly dominated by large, formal, secondary organizations. A ***formal organization* is a highly structured secondary group formed for the purpose of achieving specific goals in the most efficient manner.** Formal organizations (such as corporations, schools, and government agencies) usually keep their basic structure for many years in order to meet their specific goals.

Types of Formal Organizations

We join some organizations voluntarily and others out of necessity. Sociologist Amitai Etzioni (1975) classified formal organizations into three categories—normative, coercive, and utilitarian—based on the nature of membership in each.

Normative Organizations We voluntarily join normative organizations when we want to pursue some common interest or gain personal satisfaction or prestige from being a member. Voluntary membership is one of the central features of normative associations. The majority (56 percent) of these volunteers were women (Vanier Institute of the Family, 1994). A widely diverse range of normative organizations exists in Canada. These include political

Although telephone- and computer-based procedures have streamlined the registration process at many schools, for many students registration exemplifies the worst aspects of academic bureaucracy. Yet students and other members of the academic community depend upon the "bureaucracy" to establish and administer procedures that enable the complex system of the university to operate smoothly.

parties, activist groups, religious organizations, and educational associations.

People join normative organizations for a number of reasons, some of which may be to advance a particular cause the group represents; to gain a sense of purpose and identity; or to promote social change. Many women have joined together to form women's interest groups across the country and were influential in establishing what was formerly called the National Action Committee on the Status of Women. Anti-racist coalitions are another example of an organization that fights for a particular cause, in this case to eradicate racism. Normative organizations have also formed to address gay rights, nuclear disarmament, environmental pollution, ozone depletion and many other issues.

There are several well-known humanitarian voluntary organizations in Canada, including the Red Cross, Easter Seals, Shriners, Big Brothers and Big Sisters, and the Canadian Cancer Society. Members volunteer their time for the good of helping others.

Since participation in the organization is voluntary, few formal control mechanisms exist for enforcing norms on members. As a result, people tend to change affiliations rather frequently. They may change groups when personal objectives have been fulfilled or when other groups might better meet their individual needs.

Coercive Organizations Unlike normative organizations, people do not voluntarily become members of *coercive organizations*—associations people are forced to join. Total institutions, such as boot camps, prisons, and some mental hospitals, are examples of coercive organizations. As discussed in Chapter 3, the assumed goal of total institutions is to resocialize people through incarceration. These environments are characterized by restrictive barriers (such as locks, bars, and security guards) that make it impossible for people to leave freely. When people leave without being officially dismissed, their exit is referred to as an "escape."

Utilitarian Organizations We voluntarily join *utilitarian organizations* when they can provide us with a material reward we seek. To make a living or earn a university degree, we must participate in organizations that can provide these opportunities. Although we have some choice regarding where we work or attend school, utilitarian organizations are not always completely voluntary. For example, most people must continue to work even if the conditions of their employment are less than ideal.

Bureaucracies

The bureaucratic model of organization is the most universal organizational form in government, business, education, and religion. A ***bureaucracy*** **is an**

organizational model characterized by a hierarchy of authority, a clear division of labour, explicit rules and procedures, and impersonality in personnel matters.

When we think of a bureaucracy, we may think of "buck-passing," such as occurs when we are directed from one office to the next without receiving an answer to our question or a solution to our problem. We also may view a bureaucracy in terms of "red tape" because of the situations in which there is so much paperwork and so many incomprehensible rules that no one really understands what to do. However, the bureaucracy originally was not intended to be this way; it was seen as a way to make organizations *more* productive and efficient.

German sociologist Max Weber (1968/1922) was interested in the historical trend toward bureaucratization that accelerated during the Industrial Revolution. To Weber, the bureaucracy was the most "rational" and efficient means of attaining organizational goals because it contributed to coordination and control. According to Weber, ***rationality* is the process by which traditional methods of social organization, characterized by informality and spontaneity, are gradually replaced by efficiently administered formal rules and procedures.**

FORMAL CHARACTERISTICS OF BUREAUCRACY Weber set forth several characteristics of bureaucratic organizations. Although bureaucratic realities often differ from these formal characteristics, Weber's model highlights the organizational efficiency and productivity that bureaucracies strive for.

Division of Labour Bureaucratic organizations are characterized by specialization, and each member has a specific status with certain assigned tasks to fulfil. This division of labour requires the employment of specialized experts who are responsible for the effective performance of their duties. In a university, for example, a distinct division of labour exists between the faculty and administration.

Hierarchy of Authority Weber described a hierarchy of authority, or chain of command, in which each lower office is under the control and supervision of a higher one. Sociologist Charles Perrow (1986) has noted that all groups with a division of labour are hierarchically structured. Although the chain of command is not always followed, "in a crunch, the chain is there for those higher up to use it." Authority that is distributed hierarchically takes the form of a pyramid. Those few individuals at the top have more power and exercise more control than do the many at the lower levels. Hierarchy inevitably influences social interaction. Those who are lower in the hierarchy report to (and often take orders from) those above them in the organizational pyramid. Persons at the upper levels are responsible not only for their own actions but also for those of the individuals they supervise.

Rules and Regulations Weber asserted that rules and regulations establish authority within an organization. These rules are typically standardized and provided to members in a written format. In theory, written rules and regulations offer clear-cut standards for determining satisfactory performance. They also provide continuity so that each new member does not have to reinvent the necessary rules and regulations.

Qualification-Based Employment Bureaucracies hire staff members and professional employees based on specific qualifications. Favouritism, family connections, and other subjective factors not relevant to organizational efficiency are not acceptable criteria for employment. Individual performance is evaluated against specific standards, and promotions are based on merit as spelled out in personnel policies.

Impersonality A detached approach should prevail toward clients so that personal feelings do not interfere with organizational decisions. Officials must interact with subordinates based on their official status, not on their personal feelings about them.

INFORMAL STRUCTURE IN BUREAUCRACIES When we look at an organizational chart, the official, formal structure of a bureaucracy is readily apparent. In practice, however, a bureaucracy has patterns of activities and interactions that cannot be accounted for by its organizational chart. These have been referred to as *bureaucracy's other face* (Page, 1946).

An organization's ***informal structure* is composed of those aspects of participants' day-to-day activities and interactions that ignore, bypass, or do not correspond with the official rules and procedures of the bureaucracy.** An example is an informal "grapevine" that spreads information (with varying degrees of accuracy) much faster than do official channels of communication, which tend to be slow and unresponsive. The informal structure also includes the ideology and practices of workers on the job. It is the "informal, customary values and rules [that] mediate the formal authority structure of the workplace and distance workers from its impact" (Benson, 1983:185). Workers create this work culture in order to confront, resist, or adapt to the constraints of their jobs, as well as to guide and interpret social relations on the job (Zavella, 1987).

Positive and Negative Aspects of Informal Structure Is informal structure good or bad? Should it be controlled or encouraged? Two schools of thought have emerged with regard to these questions. One approach emphasizes control (or eradication) of informal groups; the other suggests that they should be nurtured. Traditional management theories are based on the assumption that people basically are lazy and motivated by greed. Consequently, informal groups must be controlled (or eliminated) in order to ensure greater worker productivity.

By contrast, the other school of thought asserts that people are capable of cooperation. Thus, organizations should foster informal groups that permit people to work more efficiently toward organizational goals. Chester Barnard (1938), an early organizational theorist, focused on the functional aspects of informal groups. He suggested that organizations are cooperative systems in which informal groups "oil the wheels" by providing understanding and motivation for participants. In other words, informal networks serve as a means of communication and cohesion among individuals, as well as protecting the integrity of the individual (Barnard, 1938; Perrow, 1986).

More recent studies have confirmed the importance of informal networks in bureaucracies. While some scholars have argued that women and visible minorities receive fairer treatment in larger bureaucracies than they do in smaller organizations, others have stressed that they may be categorically excluded from networks that are important for survival and advancement in the organization (Kanter, 1977; South et al., 1982; Benokraitis and Feagin, 1986; Feagin, 1991). A female firefighter describes how detrimental, and even hazardous, it is for workers to be excluded from such informal networks because of ethnicity, gender, or other attributes:

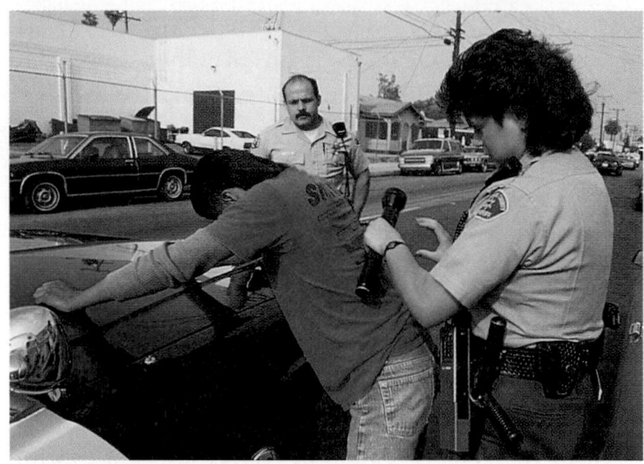

Sociologists have found that women in law enforcement are less likely than men to be included in informal networks and more likely to be harassed on the job. Are these two factors related? What steps could be taken to reduce the problems of harassment and lack of networks?

> I had sort of a "Pollyanna" view of how long it would take before women were really accepted in these non-traditional, very male-dominated jobs [such as being a firefighter]. One always thinks that once I and the other women prove that we can do the job well, people will just accept us and we'll all fit in ... [However,] I went to a firehouse where the men refused to eat with me. They would not talk to me. On one occasion my protective gear had been tampered with. It was always a big question as to whether in fact you have anyone there to back you up when you needed them. (*PBS*, 1992b)

White women and visible minorities who are employed in positions traditionally held by white men (such as firefighters, police officers, and factory workers) often experience categoric exclusion from the informal structure. Not only do they lack an informal network to "grease the wheels," but they also may be harassed and endangered by their co-workers. In sum, the informal structure is critical for employees—whether they are allowed to participate in it or not.

Shortcomings of Bureaucracies

Weber's description of bureaucracy was intentionally an idealized model of a rationally organized institution. However, the very characteristics that make up this "rational" model have a dark side that frequently has given this type of organization a bad name (see Figure 5.4). Three of the major problems of bureaucracies are (1) inefficiency and rigidity, (2) resistance to change, and (3) perpetuation of ethnic, class, and gender inequalities (see Blau and Meyer, 1987).

Inefficiency and Rigidity Bureaucracies experience inefficiency and rigidity at both the upper and lower levels of the organization. The self-protective behaviour of officials at the top may render the organization inefficient. One type of self-protective behaviour is the monopolization of information in order to maintain control over subordinates and outsiders. Information is a valuable commodity in organizations. Budgets and long-range plans theoretically are based on relevant information, and decisions are made based on the best available data. However, those in positions of authority may guard information because it is a source of power for them—others cannot "second-guess" their decisions without access to relevant (and often "confidential") information (Blau and Meyer, 1987).

This information blockage is intensified by the hierarchical arrangement of officials and workers. While those at the top tend to use their power and authority to monopolize information, they also fail to communicate with workers at the lower levels. As a result, they are often unaware of potential problems facing the organization and of high levels of worker frustration. Meanwhile, those at the bottom of the structure hide their mistakes from supervisors, a practice that ultimately may result in disaster for the organization.

Policies and procedures also contribute to inefficiency and rigidity. Sociologists Peter M. Blau and Marshall W. Meyer (1987) have suggested that bureaucratic regulations are similar to bridges and buildings in that they are designed to withstand far greater stresses than they will ever experience. Accordingly, bureaucratic regulations are written in far greater detail than is necessary, in order to ensure that almost all conceivable situations are covered. ***Goal displacement* occurs when the rules become an end in themselves rather than a means to an end, and organizational survival becomes more important than achievement of goals** (Merton, 1968). Administrators tend to overconform to the rules because their expertise is knowledge of the regulations, and they are paid to enforce them. They also fear that if they bend the rules for one person, they may be accused of violating the norm of impersonality and engaging in favouritism (Blau and Meyer, 1987).

Bureaucrats may also be inflexible because they fear criticism or liability if they do not follow the rules closely. In the case of Kenneth Payne, the aspiring teacher you read about at the beginning of this chapter, bureaucrats were afraid to waive the need for fingerprints because they were wary of public concern about the possibility of sexual offenders working in the schools. Even though it made no sense to demand fingerprints from a man who had none, and even though Mr. Payne offered other ways of demonstrating he did not have a criminal record, bureaucrats were not willing to bend the rules to enable him to teach. These bureaucrats were also able to avoid taking responsibility for their stupid decision by saying that they were "just following the rules." Mistakes can be blamed on the bureaucracy rather than on the individuals who run it.

Inefficiency and rigidity occur at the lower levels of the organization as well. Workers often engage in ritualism; that is, they become most concerned with "going through the motions" and "following the rules." According to Robert Merton (1968), the term ***bureaucratic personality* describes those workers who are more concerned with following correct procedures than they are with getting the job done correctly.** Such workers usually are able to handle routine situations effectively but frequently are incapable of handling a unique problem or an emergency. Thorstein Veblen (1967/1899) used the term *trained incapacity* to characterize situations in which workers have become so highly specialized, or have been given such fragmented jobs to do, that they are unable to come up with creative solutions to problems. Workers who have reached this point also tend to experience bureaucratic alienation—they really do not care what is happening around them.

Sociologists have extensively analyzed the effects of bureaucracy on workers. While some may become alienated, others may lose any identity apart from the organization. Sociologist William H. Whyte, Jr. (1957) coined the term *organization man* to identify an individual whose life is controlled by the corporation. C. Wright Mills (1959) suggested that employees become "cheerful robots" when they are controlled by an organization. Other scholars have argued that most workers do not reach these extremes.

FIGURE 5.4 Characteristics and Effects of Bureaucracy

The very characteristics that define Weber's idealized bureaucracy can create or worsen the problems that many people associate with this type of organization.

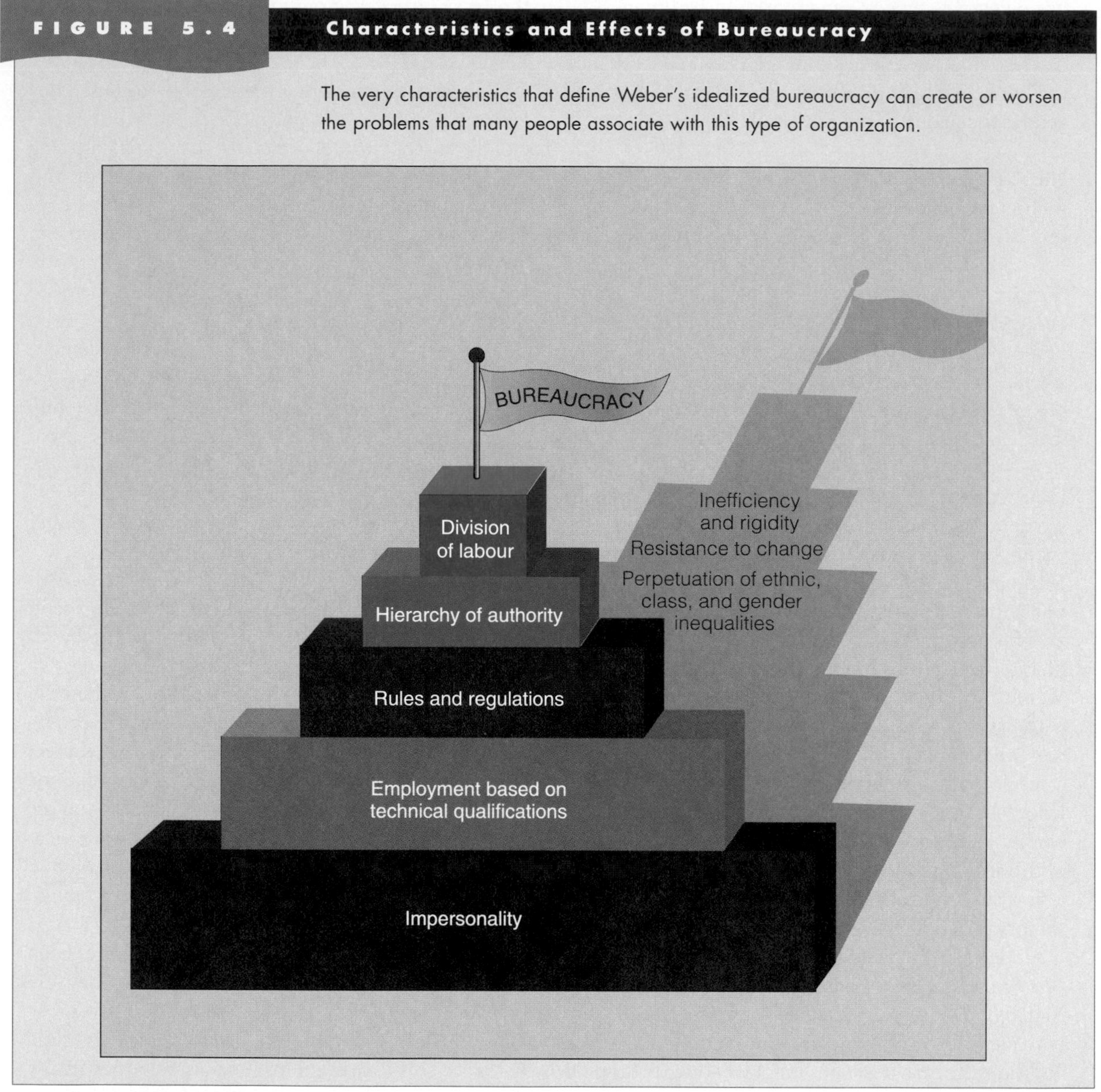

Resistance to Change Resistance to change occurs in all bureaucratic organizations. This resistance can make it very difficult for organizations to adapt to new circumstances. Many workers are reluctant to change because they have adapted their professional and personal lives to the old way of doing their jobs. Also, workers in some fields have seen previous change efforts fail, and may not want to make a commitment to the latest effort at transforming their organization. Those trying to implement change can have a difficult task breaking through this resistance.

The structure of bureaucracies can make this situation worse. The traditional bureaucracy has a very hierarchical structure with many layers of authority and reporting lines that run from bottom to top. Management is separated from labour, clerical workers from professional workers, and people doing

The "organization man" of the computer age varies widely in manner and appearance, as shown in the contrast between the blue-suited chief executive officer of IBM, Louis V. Gerstner, Jr., and the casually clad employee (at left) at Apple Computer.

one function from those doing another function. This structure creates structural barriers to communication and to joint problem solving. People become defined by their positions. Information is restricted and problems are dealt with in a segmented way that may have more to do with the goals of a subunit than of the organization as a whole. People are rewarded for not taking risks and punished when they try to make changes. There is often no structural way of getting innovative ideas from the bottom to the top, so people give up trying. Writing about a textile company that for decades had been putting up with frequent and costly yarn breakages, Rosabeth Moss Kanter provides an example of this kind of blockage:

> A new plant manager interested in improving employee communication and involvement discovered a foreign-born worker with an ultimately successful idea for modifying the machine to reduce breakage—and was shocked to learn that the man had wondered about the machine modification for thirty-two years. "Why didn't you say something before?" the manager asked. The reply: "My supervisor wasn't interested and I had no one else to tell it to." (Kanter, 1983:70)

Organizations that resist change, rather than adapt to it, are not likely to survive and certainly will not flourish. Thus leaders of many different organizations face the task of developing new organizational models that are better suited to today's environment. Consider the challenges faced by leaders of corporations such as those discussed in Box 5.2, "The Internet and the Organization."

Perpetuation of Ethnic, Class, and Gender Inequalities Some bureaucracies perpetuate inequalities of ethnicity, class, and gender because this form of organizational structure creates a specific type of work or learning environment. This structure typically was created for middle- and upper-middle-class white men, who for many years were the predominant organizational participants.

BOX 5.2 SOCIOLOGY AND TECHNOLOGY

THE INTERNET AND THE ORGANIZATION

Do you enjoy going to the grocery store, standing in line at the checkout counter, and carrying your groceries to the car? What if you could order your groceries on the Internet and have them delivered to your home for less than what it would cost to buy them at the store? The Internet may have a major impact on the organizational structure of many businesses, including the food industry, by simplifying product distribution. One company, Peachtree, already sells groceries over the Internet (in Ontario and Quebec), and other Canadian companies including Loblaws are considering the idea. If large numbers of people begin to shop on the Internet, we may see what some analysts have called *disintermediation*—or removing the middleman. An Internet transaction can be made directly between the producer and the consumer. The Internet will allow manufacturers to sell their products faster and more cheaply without going through wholesalers and retailers. This may have a major impact on the structure of organizations that deal with consumer goods.

The greeting card business shows us how the Internet can provide new ways of serving customer needs. For the past century, companies have designed and produced greeting cards and have sold the cards to wholesalers who distributed them to retail outlets. Customers bought the cards, bought stamps, and mailed them to the recipient through Canada Post. A new approach has been taken by E-Greetings (**www.egreetings.com**) that eliminates the need for printers and wholesalers and retailers. Rather than using the mail, E-Greetings designs are sent electronically over the Internet. If this method of sending greetings becomes popular, several bureaucracies will be significantly affected. Can you think through some of the consequences of such a change?

Electronic commerce has become common in areas such as banking, travel services, selling stocks, and selling goods such as automobiles, flowers, and pizza. It is much cheaper for these organizations to transact business over the Internet. What do you think will happen to the jobs of those who sell stocks and work in banks and travel agencies? How will the change affect the bureaucracies in which they work?

If disintermediation because of Internet commerce becomes a trend, there will also be a new need for electronic intermediaries who can provide guidance and assistance for consumers and provide marketing services and transaction assistance for producers. Are such intermediaries likely to work within traditional bureaucratic organizations? One clue to the future may come from currently successful intermediary organizations such as Amazon.com, the Internet bookseller. Amazon.com is an intermediary between publisher and consumer, but rather than being a large, formal bureaucracy, it is a virtual company with little presence outside of cyberspace. Despite calling itself "The Earth's Biggest Bookstore" with its list of over a million titles, Amazon.com keeps only a very

Ethnic Inequalities Many people have experienced an internal conflict between the bureaucratic ideals of equal opportunity and fairness and the prevailing norms of discrimination and hostility that exist in many organizations. Harish Jain has done extensive research on employment discrimination in Canada. His findings indicate that racial minorities encounter both entry-level (hiring) discrimination and post-employment (on the job) discrimination in the workplace, including lack of promotions, transfers, salary increases, and job ghettoization (Jain, 1985). Other research has found that visible minorities are more adversely impacted than dominant-group members by hierarchical bureaucratic

BOX 5.2

CONTINUED

small stock of books on hand. The rest are ordered electronically and shipped from traditional book wholesalers. Because of its low overhead costs, it can sell books more cheaply than traditional retailers. This means that many of these businesses may be in jeopardy.

Internet commerce now represents only a small portion of consumer sales. However, several factors suggest that Internet commerce will continue to expand very rapidly: use of the Internet is growing; those who use the Internet tend to be well-educated people with high incomes who are attractive to marketers; and secure payment mechanisms are making people more comfortable about providing their credit card numbers to Internet vendors. Because of this growth, we should soon be able to get a better indication of how Internet commerce will develop and of how it will affect the structure of traditional bureaucracies.

The Internet also provides opportunities for illegal transactions. For example, the music industry is threatened by the development of technology that allows people to download music from the Internet without paying royalties to the companies or musicians. The MP3 (**www.mp3.com**) program can be used to download the music, which can then be played on conventional stereo systems, stored on players designed to hold MP3 music, or recorded on a custom CD. While some people use MP3 technology to purchase music online or to record songs that are in the public domain, many others use it to record illegally. The major record companies have established a consortium with IBM to try to establish a mechanism for secure Internet sales, but it will be difficult to stop those who wish to pirate music.

The rock group Metallica is suing the developer of another copying service, Napster (**www.napster.com**), to try to stop computer users from illegally copying its songs. However, the development of other software such as Freenet and Gnutella suggests that even a successful lawsuit will not stop the illegal copying. Ian Clarke, the developer of Freenet, has said he thinks that in twenty to forty years people will "look at the idea that you can own information in the same way as gold or real estate the way we look at witch burning today" (Markoff, 2000:B14).

Even if there were no illegal copying, the music industry is still threatened by the fact that Internet technology allows artists to sell their music directly to the public without going through the intermediary of the music companies.

Source: Markoff, 2000.

structures. These studies have been conducted in a number of organizational settings, ranging from medical schools to canning factories to corporations (see Kendall and Feagin, 1983; Zavella, 1987; and S. Collins, 1989). We will continue our discussion of the impact of organizations on visible minorities in Chapter 9 ("Race and Ethnicity").

Social Class Inequalities Like racial inequalities, social class divisions may be perpetuated in bureaucracies (Blau and Meyer, 1987). Sociologists have explored the impact of labour market conditions on the kinds of jobs and wages available to workers. The theory of a "dual labour market" has been developed to explain how social class distinctions

BOX 5.3 SOCIOLOGY AND MEDIA

DILBERT AND THE BUREAUCRACY

Sociologist Robert Merton has pointed out that successful bureaucracies must attain a high degree of reliability of behaviour. Thus, bureaucratic structures exert pressure on officials to be "methodical, prudent, disciplined" (1968:198) and follow the rules in order to accomplish the goals of the organization. However, Merton has also shown that goal displacement can occur and for some bureaucrats the rules become an end in themselves rather than just a means to an end. When this occurs, organizations become rigid and inflexible.

Our experiences with red tape and other bureaucratic inefficiencies have been satirized by cartoonist (and disillusioned bureaucrat) Scott Adams. In the late 1980s Adams began passing his humorous scribbles and doodles around the office at Pacific Bell. Since then his cartoon *Dilbert* has become a phenomenal success and is read in over 1700 papers in 39 countries. *Dilbert* ridicules many of the worst features of bureaucracy including stupid bosses, reliance on technology instead of people, cubicles, management consultants, pointless meetings, and inflexibility. (For examples of the cartoon, go to: **www.unitedmedia.com/comics/dilbert**).

Readership is not the only sign that *Dilbert* strikes a responsive chord with workers. The cartoons are posted on doors, walls, and desks in thousands of offices, and many of Adams's ideas come from readers' suggestions. The British magazine *The Economist* attributes *Dilbert's* popularity to the fact that the comic strip taps into three currents that are troubling workers:

are perpetuated through different types of employment. Middle- and upper-middle-class employees are more likely to work in industries characterized by higher wages, more job security, and opportunities for advancement. By contrast, poor and working-class employees work in industries characterized by low wages, lack of job security, and few opportunities for promotion. Even though the "dual economy" is not a perfect model for explaining class-based organizational inequalities, it does illuminate how individuals' employment not only reflects their position in the social class but also perpetuates it. Peter Blau and Marshall Meyer (1987:160–161) conclude that "over time, then, organizational conditions reinforce social stratification … Bureaucracies create profound differences in the life chances of the people working in them."

Gender Inequalities Gender inequalities also are perpetuated in bureaucracies. Sociologist Rosabeth Moss Kanter (1977) analyzed how the power structure of bureaucratic hierarchies can negatively impact white women and visible minorities when they are underrepresented within an organization. In such cases, they tend to be more visible ("on display") and to feel greater pressure not to make mistakes or stand out too much. They also may find it harder to gain credibility, particularly in management positions. As a result, they are more likely to feel isolated, to be excluded from informal networks, and to have less access both to mentors and to power through alliances. By contrast, affluent white men generally are seen as being "one of the group." They find it easier to gain credibility, to join informal networks, and to find sponsorships (Kanter, 1977:248–249).

Gender inequality in organizations has additional consequences. People who lack opportunities for integration and advancement tend to be pessimistic and to have lower self-esteem. They seek satisfaction away from work and are less likely to promote change at work. Believing they have few opportunities, they resign themselves to staying put and surviving at that level. By contrast, those who enjoy full access to organizational opportunities tend to

BOX 5.3

CONTINUED

1. The obsession with work as employees are forced to labour harder to compensate for the effects of downsizing;
2. Fear in the workplace as workers are laid off or see their wage increases falling far behind those of their managers; and
3. A growing cynicism about new management fads that have led to constant reorganization but that seem to have had little impact on efficiency or on job satisfaction.

Ironically, while many workers feel *Dilbert* says what they feel about stupid and uncaring managers, the leaders of many of North America's largest corporations have used the cartoons for training and corporate communications.

Sources: *The Economist*, 1997; Merton, 1968; and Whitaker, 1997. DILBERT reprinted by permission of United Features Syndicate, Inc.

have high aspirations and high self-esteem. They feel loyalty to the organization and typically see their job as a means for mobility and growth.

An Alternative Form of Organization

Many organizations have sought new and innovative ways to organize work more efficiently than those based on the traditional hierarchical model have.

The company that employs Dilbert (see Box 5.3) would not likely last very long in the real world. That is why the last two decades have seen many attempts to create new types of complex organizations. In the early 1980s, there was a movement in North America to humanize bureaucracy—to establish an organizational environment that develops rather than impedes human resources. More humane bureaucracies are characterized by (1) less rigid hierarchical structures and greater sharing of power and responsibility by all participants, (2) encouragement of participants to share their ideas and try new approaches to problem solving, and (3) efforts to reduce the number of people in dead-end jobs, train people in needed skills and competencies, and help people meet outside family responsibilities while still receiving equal treatment inside the organization (Kanter, 1977, 1983, 1985). However, this movement may have been overshadowed by the perceived strengths of another organizational model.

For several decades, the Japanese model of organization has been widely praised for its innovative structure. A number of social scientists and management specialists concluded that guaranteed lifetime employment and a teamwork approach to management were the major reasons Japanese workers had been so productive since the end of World War II, when Japan's economy was in shambles. When the North American manufacturing sector weakened in the 1980s, the Japanese system was widely discussed as an alternative to the prevalent North American hierarchical organizational structure. Box 5.4 compares the characteristics of large Japanese corporations with their North American counterparts.

BOX 5.4 SOCIOLOGY IN GLOBAL PERSPECTIVE

THE JAPANESE CORPORATION

How do Japanese corporations differ from their North American counterparts? The main differences are the promise of lifetime employment and the participation of Japanese employees in their company decision making.

Until recently, many large Japanese corporations guaranteed their workers permanent employment after an initial probationary period. Thus, Japanese employees often remained with the same company for their entire career, whereas their North American counterparts often changed employers every few years. Japanese workers felt obligated to remain with their company and not to leave for more pay or a better position elsewhere, as frequently occurred in Canada and the United States. Likewise, Japanese employers in the past had an obligation not to "downsize" by laying off workers or to cut their wages. Unlike top managers in North America who gave themselves pay raises, bonuses, and so on even when their companies were financially strapped and laying off workers, Japanese managers took pay cuts. When financial problems occurred, Japanese workers frequently were reassigned or retrained by their company. Since many people retire in Japan at about age 55, the typical length of employment at one corporation for most workers is about thirty to thirty-five years.

According to advocates, the Japanese system encourages worker loyalty and a high level of productivity. Managers move through various parts of the organization and acquire

LIMITATIONS Will the Japanese organizational structure continue to work? Recently, the notion of lifetime employment has become problematic as an economic recession forced some Japanese factories to close and other companies ran out of subsidiaries willing to take on workers for "reassignment" (Sanger, 1994:E5). Also, sociologist Robert Coles (1979) has suggested that the Japanese model does not actually provide workers with more control over the corporation. While it may give them more control over their own work, production goals set by managers still must be met.

Although the possibility of implementing the Japanese model in North American-based corporations has been widely discussed, its large-scale acceptance is doubtful. Cultural traditions in Japan have focused on the importance of the group rather than the individual. Workers in North America are not likely to embrace this idea because it directly conflicts with the value of individualism so strongly held by many in Canada and the United States (Krahn and Lowe, 1996). North American workers also are unwilling to commit themselves to one corporation for their entire work life.

In spite of these limitations, organizations in North America are increasingly turning to a more participatory style of management. The incentive for this change lies in the fact that many of the corporations adopting this style experience greater worker satisfaction and higher productivity and profits (see Florida and Kenney, 1991).

NEW ORGANIZATIONS FOR THE FUTURE

What kind of "Help Wanted" ad might a company run in the twenty-first century? One journalist has suggested that a want ad in the next century might read something like this: "WANTED: Bureaucracy basher, willing to challenge convention, assume big risks, and rewrite the accepted rules of industrial order" (Byrne, 1993:76). Organizational theorists have suggested a *horizontal* model for corporations in which both hierarchy and functional or depart-

BOX 5.4

CONTINUED

technical knowledge about the workings of many aspects of the corporation, unlike their North American counterparts who tend to become highly specialized (Sengoku, 1985). Clearly, permanent employment has its advantages for workers. They do not have to worry about losing their jobs or having their wages cut. Employers benefit by not having to compete with one another to keep workers.

Small workgroups made up of about five to fifteen workers who meet regularly with one or two managers to discuss the group's performance and working conditions are known as *quality circles*. The purpose of this team approach to management is both to improve product quality and to lower product costs. Workers are motivated to save the corporation money because they, in turn, receive bonuses or higher wages for their efforts. Quality circles have been praised for creating worker satisfaction, helping employees develop their potential, and improving productivity (Krahn and Lowe, 1996). Because quality circles focus on both productivity and worker satisfaction, they (at least ideally) meet the needs of both the corporation and the workers. While many Japanese corporations have utilized quality circles to achieve better productivity, many North American-based corporations have implemented automation in hopes of controlling the quality of their products.

Sources: Krahn and Lowe, 1996; and Sengo Ku, 1985.

The contrasting styles of baseball players in North America and Japan reflect profound differences in organizational culture. People in North America tend to value individualism over the group, while people in Japan focus primarily on the group and deemphasize individual accomplishment in favour of teamwork and collective success.

mental boundaries largely would be eliminated. Seven key elements of the horizontal corporation have been suggested: (1) work would be organized around "core" processes, not tasks; (2) the hierarchy would be flattened; (3) teams would manage everything and be held accountable for measurable performance goals; (4) performance would be measured by customer satisfaction, not profits; (5) team performance would be rewarded; (6) employees would have regular contact with suppliers and customers; and (7) all employees would be trained in how to use available information effectively to make their own decisions (Byrne, 1993:76–79).

In the horizontal structure, a limited number of senior executives would still fill support roles (such as finance and human resources), while everyone else would work in multidisciplinary teams and perform core processes (such as product development or sales generation). Organizations would have fewer layers between company heads and the staffers responsible for any given process. Performance objectives would be related to the needs of customers; people would be rewarded not just for individual performance but for skills development and team performance. If such organizations become a reality, organizational charts of the future will no longer resemble the traditional pyramid-shaped stack of boxes connected by lines.

Currently, most corporations are hybrids of vertical and horizontal organizational structures. However, a number of companies appear to be moving toward the horizontal model. If the horizontal model is widely implemented, this will constitute one of the most significant changes in organizational structure since the Industrial Revolution.

What is the best organizational structure for the future? Of course, this question is difficult to answer because it requires the ability to predict economic, political, and social conditions. Nevertheless, we can make several observations. Ultimately, everyone has a stake in seeing that organizations operate in as humane a fashion as possible and that channels for opportunity are widely available to all people regardless of ethnicity, gender, or class. Workers and students alike can benefit from organizational environments that make it possible for people to explore their joint interests without fear of being harassed or pitted against one another in a competitive struggle for advantage.

CHAPTER REVIEW

How do sociologists define social groups?
Sociologists define a social group as a collection of two or more people who interact frequently, share a sense of belonging, and depend on one another.

How do sociologists classify groups?
Primary groups are small and personal, and members engage in emotion-based interactions over an extended period. Secondary groups are larger and more specialized, and members have less personal and more formal, goal-oriented relationships. Ingroups are groups to which we belong and with which we identify. Outgroups are groups we do not belong to or perhaps feel hostile toward.

What is the significance of group size?
In small groups, all members know one another and interact simultaneously. In groups with more than three members, communication dynamics change and members tend to assume specialized tasks.

What do experiments on conformity show about the importance of groups?
Groups may have a significant influence on members' values, attitudes, and behaviours. In order to maintain ties with a group, many members are willing to conform to norms established and reinforced by group members.

What are the strengths and weaknesses of bureaucracies?
A bureaucracy is a formal organization characterized by hierarchical authority, division of labour, explicit procedures, and impersonality. According to Max Weber, a bureaucracy supplies a rational means of attaining organizational goals because it contributes to coordination and control. A bureaucracy also has an informal structure, that includes the daily activities and interactions that bypass the official rules and procedures.
Bureaucracies, however, may be inefficient, resistant to change, and a vehicle for perpetuating class, gender, and ethnic inequalities.

Key Terms

authoritarian leaders 143
bureaucracy 148
bureaucratic personality 151
conformity 143

Internet Exercises

1. If you belong to any groups, go to Google (**www.google.com**) and search for the name of it to see if this group has a Web page. If it does, visit it. Does the group's projected image differ greatly from the way you experience the group? Visit your university's Web page. How does the projected image of the school differ from your experience?
2. This chapter discusses the works of Max Weber. Visit the Weber section of The Dead Sociologists Page (**www.runet.edu/~lridener/dss/deadsoc.html**). Compare the interpretation of Weber on this page with that in this textbook. A continuation of Weber's themes can be found in the book *The McDonaldization of Society* by George Ritzer. Visit the McDonaldization home page (**www.mcdonaldization.com**). After reading about the theory, think about how McDonaldization differs from Weber's theories. Is it more or less reflective of today than Weber is?
3. In his *Dilbert* comic strip, Scott Adams often satirizes corporate programs designed to make life better for a company's employees. Visit the Dilbert Archives (**www.unitedmedia.com/comics/dilbert/archive**) and read through several weeks of strips. How reflective of a typical office do you think the strip is?

Net Links

For more Web links related to the topic of this chapter, see the Nelson sociology Web site: **www.sociologyessentials-2nded.nelson.com**.

To read about the latest research in the area of formal organizations, see the Web site for the journal *Administrative Science Quarterly* at:

www.gsm.cornell.edu/ASQ/asq.html

Government is a very complex bureaucracy. To see the number of departments in the Canadian federal government, go to:

www.canada.gc.ca

The Public Service Commission of Canada has an extensive bibliography of material on group leadership at:

http://jobs.gc.ca/library/document/leadrspe.htm

Read more about Stanley Milgram's work on obedience and hear audio clips from one of his experiments at:

http://elvers.stjoe.udayton.edu/history/history.asp?RURL=http://elvers.stjoe.udayton.edu/history/people/Milgram.html

To read an interview with George Ritzer concerning his view of the "McDonaldization" of society, go to:

www.mcspotlight.org/people/interviews/ritzer_george.html

Questions for Critical Thinking

1. Who might be more likely to conform in a bureaucracy, those with power or those wanting more power?
2. Although there has been much discussion recently concerning what is and what is not sexual harassment, it has been difficult to reach a clear consensus on what behaviours and actions are acceptable. What are some specific ways both women and men can avoid contributing to an atmosphere of sexual harassment in organizations? Consider team relationships, management and mentor relationships, promotion policies, attitudes, behaviour, dress and presentation, and after-work socializing.
3. Do the insights gained from Milgram's research on obedience outweigh the elements of deception and stress that were forced on its subjects?
4. If you were forming a company based on humane organizational principles, would you base the promotional policies on merit and performance or on affirmative action goals?

Suggested Readings

Organizations are examined from a variety of perspectives in these interesting books:

Harvey Krahn and Graham S. Lowe. *Work, Industry and Canadian Society* (3rd ed.). Toronto: ITP Nelson, 1998.

Wallace Clement. *The Canadian Corporate Elite*. Toronto: McClelland and Stewart, 1975.

Kathy E. Ferguson. *The Feminist Case Against Bureaucracy*. Philadelphia: Temple University Press, 1984.

Richard H. Hall. *Organizations: Structures, Processes, and Outcomes*. Englewood Cliffs, N.J.: Prentice-Hall, 1991.

Rosabeth Moss Kanter. *Men and Women of the Corporation*. New York: Basic Books, 1993; orig. pub. 1977.

Gifford Pinchot and Elizabeth Pinchot. *The End of Bureaucracy and the Rise of the Intelligent Organization*. San Francisco: Berrett-Koehler, 1993.

INFOTRAC® COLLEGE EDITION

Either from the *Sociology In Our Times: The Essentials* Web site (**www.sociologyessentials-2nded.nelson.com**) or directly from your Web browser, you may access InfoTrac® College Edition, an online university library that includes over 600 popular and scholarly journals in which you can find articles related to the topics in this chapter.

CHAPTER

When most of us think of organized crime, we think of biker gangs or perhaps the Italian Mafia. In reality, however, organized crime has many faces. Yet organized crime groups have many things in common, including a willingness to use violence—a willingness that is evident from the following account:

"Constable Peter Yuen, a member of the Metropolitan Toronto Police Service, was working undercover in a gaming house, monitoring off-track betting while police backup units waited outside. During this operation, four hooded Vietnamese gang members burst into the room and ordered the gamblers to hand over their valuables. The robbers found Yuen's police badge and ordered him to kneel with his hands behind his head. Next, Yuen recalled, 'I was kicked in the face until my shirt was soaked in blood.' Then, one of the robbers forced the barrel of a .45 calibre automatic into Yuen's mouth, while another held a .357 magnum to his temple. Said Yuen: 'They were shouting that I was a traitor for serving the white authorities and that I deserved to die.' Yuen then heard a gun click and heard an assailant remark, 'Goodbye copper.' But the assault abruptly ceased when another of the robbers noticed that the building was surrounded by police. Two of the suspects were arrested at the scene, but the police ultimately chased one of Yuen's attackers into a bush area where he hid by burying himself in mud and breathing through a piece of straw. Police found him after 30 minutes using tracking dogs.

"Forensic tests on the pistol showed that the gangster had indeed pulled the trigger, but that the bullet in the chamber had not fired ... Concluded Yuen, who was named Toronto's Policeman of the Year ... for his bravery during the attack: 'I have no doubt that they would have done me in if they had not been interrupted.'" (Kaihla, 1991:21)

DEVIANCE AND CRIME

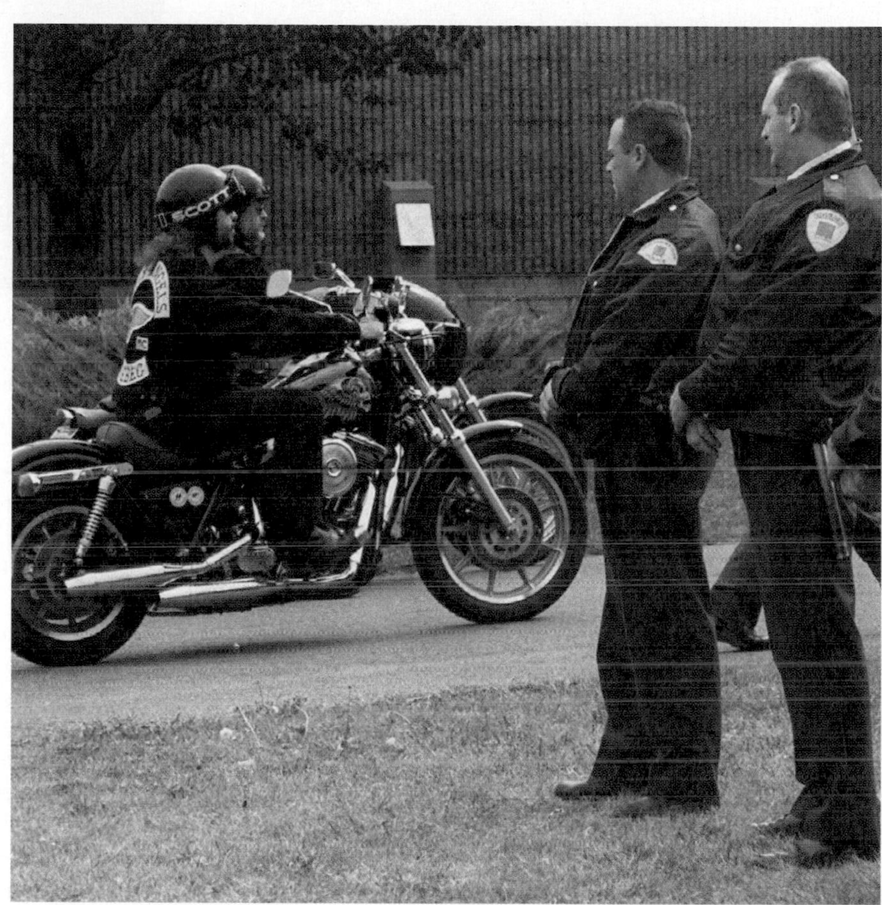

The problem of organized crime is certainly not unique to Canada. This problem has existed for centuries and today such gangs operate around the world. For many years, organized crime and other types of crime and deviance have been of special interest to sociologists. Many of the issues they have examined remain important today: What is deviant behaviour, and how does it differ from criminal behaviour? Why are some people considered to be "deviants" or "criminals" while others are not? In this chapter, we look at the relationship between conformity, deviance, and crime. Before reading on, take the quiz on crime and organized crime in Box 6.1.

Questions and Issues

CHAPTER FOCUS QUESTION: What are the causes and consequences of organized crime in Canada?

What is deviant behaviour?

How do sociologists explain deviant and criminal behaviour?

When is deviance considered a crime?

How do sociologists classify crime?

How does the criminal justice system deal with crime?

How can we begin to solve the crime problem in the future?

WHAT IS DEVIANCE?

How do societies determine what behaviour is acceptable and unacceptable? As discussed in previous chapters, all societies have norms that govern acceptable behaviour. If we are to live and to work with others these rules are necessary. We must also have a reasonable expectation that other people will obey the rules. Think of the chaos that would result if each driver decided which side of the road she would drive on each day, or which stop sign he would decide to obey. Most of us usually conform to the norms our group prescribes. Of course, not all members of the group obey all the time. All of us have broken rules, sometimes even important ones. These violations are dealt with through various mechanisms of ***social control*—systematic practices developed by social groups to encourage conformity and to discourage deviance.** One form of social control takes place through the process of socialization whereby individuals *internalize* societal norms and values. A second form of social control occurs through the use of negative sanctions to punish rule-breakers. Although the purpose of social control is to ensure some level of conformity, all societies still have some degree of ***deviance*—any behaviour, belief, or condition that violates cultural norms** (Adler and Adler, 1994).

We are most familiar with *behavioural* deviance, which is based on a person's intentional or inadvertent actions. For example, a person may engage in intentional deviance by drinking too much or shoplifting or in inadvertent deviance by losing the rent money at a video lottery terminal or laughing during a solemn occasion.

Although we usually think of deviance as a type of behaviour, people may be regarded as deviant if they express *radical* or *unusual beliefs*. For example, members of cults (such as Moonies and satanists) and of far-right- or far-left-wing political groups may be considered deviant when their religious or political beliefs become known to people with more conventional cultural views. For instance, Canadian schoolteachers James Keegstra and Malcolm Ross were removed from their classrooms for expressing anti-Semitic beliefs including denying that the Holocaust actually occurred.

People may be regarded as deviant because of specific *characteristics* or *conditions* that they have had since birth (such as a physical disability or minority status in a racist society) or have acquired (such as contracting AIDS) (Adler and Adler, 1994).

Many different groups are involved in Canadian organized crime. Here Frank Cotroni, a member of one of Montreal's oldest crime networks, is led away in handcuffs after his arrest.

According to sociologists, deviance is *relative*—that is, an act becomes deviant when it is socially defined as such. Definitions of deviance vary widely from place to place, from time to time, and from group to group. For example, you may have played the Pick 3 lottery. To win, you must pick a three-digit number matching the one drawn by the government lottery agency. Television commercials encourage us to risk our money on this game from which the government profits. Several years ago, the same game was called the numbers racket and was the most popular form of gambling in many low-income neighbourhoods. The two main differences between now and then are the game used to be run by organized criminals, and these criminals paid the winners a higher share of the take than the government now does.

Deviance can be difficult to define. Good and evil are not two distinct categories. The two overlap, and the line between deviant and nondeviant can be very *ambiguous*. For example, how do we decide that someone is mentally ill? What if your brother begins to behave in a strange fashion? You notice that he occasionally yells at people for no apparent reason, and keeps changing topics when you talk to him. He begins to wear clothes that don't match and

BOX 6.1 SOCIOLOGY AND EVERYDAY LIFE

HOW MUCH DO YOU KNOW ABOUT CRIME AND ORGANIZED CRIME?

TRUE	FALSE	
T	F	1. Official statistics accurately reflect the amount of crime in Canada.
T	F	2. Most organized criminals are affiliated with the Italian Mafia.
T	F	3. Organized crime exists largely to provide goods and services demanded by "respectable" members of the community.
T	F	4. Rates of murder and other violent crimes have been steadily rising for the past twenty years.
T	F	5. Because of their connection with a variety of charitable causes, biker gangs such as the Hell's Angels have become less of a social threat.
T	F	6. During Canada's great cigarette smuggling epidemic of 1992 and 1993, our major cigarette companies exported cigarettes to the United States that they knew would be smuggled back into Canada.
T	F	7. Canada's most prolific serial killer was a Hell's Angel who killed forty-three people, but served only seven years of a sentence for manslaughter.
T	F	8. Many organized crime groups are made up of people from the same ethnic group.
T	F	9. In Russia, organized crime is so pervasive that it is a threat to the future economic and political life of that country.
T	F	10. Most of the money made by organized criminals comes from gambling and loan-sharking.

Answers on page 168.

phones you in the middle of the night to talk about people on the street who are threatening him. How would you respond to this change in behaviour? Would it make any difference if you knew that your brother was drinking heavily at the time or that he was under a lot of stress at work? Would it make a difference if he behaved this way once a year or twice a week? When would you decide that he had a problem and should seek help? What is the difference between someone who is eccentric and someone who is mentally ill? These questions reflect the difficulty we have in defining deviance.

Deviant behaviour also varies in its degree of seriousness, ranging from mild transgressions of folkways, to more serious infringements of mores, to quite serious violations of the law. Have you kept a library book past its due date or cut classes? If so, you have violated folkways. Others probably view your infraction as relatively minor; at most, you might have to pay a fine or receive a lower grade. Violations of mores—such as falsifying a university application or cheating on an examination—are viewed as more serious infractions and are punishable by stronger sanctions, such as academic probation or expulsion. Some forms of deviant behaviour are officially defined as crimes. A ***crime* is a behaviour that violates criminal law and is punishable with fines, jail terms, and other sanctions.** Crimes range from minor (such as running an illegal bingo game or telling fortunes) to major offences (such as sexual assault and murder). A subcategory, ***juvenile delinquency,* refers to a violation of law by young people under the age of 18.**

In this chapter, we present several sociological explanations of deviance. While each focuses on the role of social groups in creating deviance, these theories are quite different from one another. However, each contributes in its own way to our understanding of deviance. No one perspective is a comprehensive explanation of all deviance, and in many respects the theories presented in this chapter can be considered as complementary.

BOX 6.1

Answers to the Sociology Quiz on Crime and Organized Crime

1. **False.** Although official statistics provide a variety of information about crime in Canada, they reflect only crimes that are *reported* to police, not all the offences that are *committed.* Studies have shown that less than half of all crimes are reported to the police.
2. **False.** The Italian Mafia has a global influence on organized crime. However, it is only one of many organized crime groups.
3. **True.** If not for public demand for illegal drugs, gambling, tax-free liquor and cigarettes, and the other goods and services supplied by organized crime, illegal profits would largely disappear.
4. **False.** While crime rates generally rose through the 1980s, they declined steadily throughout the 1990s.
5. **False.** The Hell's Angels have used high-profile activities like toy runs for children to improve their public image. However, they are one of the most ruthless and profitable criminal organizations in North America.
6. **True.** The vast majority of cigarettes smuggled into Canada were legally manufactured here and exported into the United States. Executives of one of Canada's largest manufacturers, Imperial Tobacco, said explicitly that they wanted to ensure that their cigarettes were the ones smuggled back into Canada.
7. **True.** Yves (Apache) Trudeau was a contract killer who received a lenient sentence in exchange for information about other Montreal underworld figures. (For more on this case, see Box 6.4 on page 188.)
8. **True.** Many different nationalities are involved in Canadian organized crime, including Russian, Iranian, Chinese, Vietnamese, Colombian, Jamaican, and Italian. Restricting membership to one's own group provides a number of advantages. For one thing, interpersonal ties based on ethnic communities and language differences make it difficult for law enforcement to infiltrate the groups. The ethnic ties also facilitate the development of international crime networks.
9. **True.** After the fall of Communism, the lack of meaningful economic institutions and the failure of the criminal justice system created conditions favourable to organized crime. Organized criminals control many of the new businesses in Russia and have powerful links to the government.
10. **False.** The importation and distribution of illegal drugs is the main source of funds for organized crime.

Sources: Based on Evans and Himelfarb, 1996; Lavigne, 1987; and Stamler, 1996.

FUNCTIONALIST PERSPECTIVES ON DEVIANCE

Strain Theory: Goals and the Means to Achieve Them

As discussed in Chapter 1, Durkheim (1964a/1895) introduced the concept of anomie to describe a social condition in which people experience a sense of futility because social norms are weak, absent, or conflicting. Sociologist Robert Merton's (1938, 1968) strain theory is based on Durkheim's assertion that the macrolevel structure of a society can produce social pressures that result in a higher rate of deviant behaviour. According to ***strain theory,*** **people feel strain when they are exposed to cultural goals that they are unable to reach because they do not have access to culturally approved means of achieving those goals.** The goals may be material possessions and money; the approved means may include an education and jobs. When denied legitimate access to these goals, some people seek access through deviant means.

Sociologist Margaret Beare (1996a) has used Merton's strain theory to explain the increased involvement of Canadian Mohawks in the organized crime of smuggling during the early 1990s. In order to raise revenue and to discourage smoking, Canadian governments had for decades imposed high taxes on cigarettes. As a result, the cost of cigarettes had become very high, particularly in comparison with prices in the United States. To save money, many of those addicted to cigarettes turned to the contraband market. By 1993 more than one-quarter of the cigarettes consumed in Canada were purchased illegally. In Ontario and Quebec, residents of some First Nations communities were among the major sources of these contraband cigarettes.

Because of the high unemployment and lack of legitimate opportunities in most First Nations communities, deviance had become an attractive option to some community members who saw smuggling as a means of achieving the goal of financial success. Akwesasne Chief Mike Mitchell described the financial opportunity in a CBC interview:

> The money—it's unbelievable the money you can make and it's so easy ... You can buy a pack of cigarettes on the American side of the reservation for $1.58 and you go across here in Cornwall and you have to buy it for close to $7.00 a pack, same pack, within a short distance of each other, so no one is surprised that all this is happening. (cited in Beare, 1996b:272)

While substantial tax cuts have dramatically reduced the incidence of cigarette smuggling, the networks and expertise developed by the smugglers have remained, and many, having made linkages with other organized criminals, have turned to smuggling other commodities including drugs, alcohol, and firearms. This has helped create illegitimate opportunity structures in some communities that may attract others into the world of organized smuggling.

It is not only the poor who turn to illegal ways of achieving their goals. Some sociologists feel that strain theory can also help explain upper-class deviance. For example, pressure to increase corporate profits may lead executives to turn to illegal ways of doing business. Company documents indicate that the president of Imperial Tobacco knowingly supplied tobacco smugglers, and the federal government has filed a $1 billion lawsuit against RJR-Macdonald Canada and the Canadian Tobacco Manufacturers Council, which alleges their involvement in similar activities. These companies and the council were motivated by their desire to maintain their market share by ensuring that their cigarettes were the ones smuggled back into Canada and by their desire to undermine the government's policy of reducing tobacco use by heavily taxing the price of cigarettes.

Opportunity Theory: Access to Illegitimate Opportunities

Expanding on Merton's strain theory, sociologists Richard Cloward and Lloyd Ohlin (1960) have suggested that for deviance to occur people must have access to ***illegitimate opportunity structures*****—circumstances that provide an opportunity for people to acquire through illegitimate activities what they cannot get through legitimate channels.** For example, members of some communities may have insufficient legitimate means to achieve conventional goals of status and wealth but have much greater access to illegitimate opportunity structures—such as theft, drug dealing, or robbery—through which they can achieve these goals. The situation at Akwesasne provided a very lucrative opportunity structure for the minority of community members who chose to use it. However, more typically, illegitimate opportunities are often situational and small-scale, as the following description an East Coast youth gave of his delinquent behaviour demonstrates:

> We used to break into places. I was drunk on every one of them jobs. We never really planned it, we just broke in. The one I remember most clearly is when we broke into the Lougheed Drive-In. I was drunk then so I can't remember everything. We just wanted to do a break, so we did a break to get more booze for the next day. It was after dark and hardly anybody was there—this was 3:00 in the morning. We busted open the door, because there's no alarm system in it—we checked all that out—we just busted the door with a crowbar. We got in there and we searched everywhere and we didn't find nothing, there wasn't no money there. Then we saw the cigarette machine so we said, "Let's take this." So the six of us picked it

For some people the "information superhighway" is a new avenue of illegitimate opportunity. While "hackers"—those who try and sometimes succeed in infiltrating computer and Internet systems—make up only a small fraction of computer users, this deviant behaviour demonstrates how new opportunity structures can elicit new forms of deviance.

> up and threw it in the back of the trunk—we had an old shitbox of a car—and took off. We got $35.00 out of it and around 200 packs of cigarettes. We dumped it in a field in there by Kmart on Ryerson Road. We bought a bottle of Seagram's—I know it was Seagram's because I drank half—I just drank it all down. You just get drunk, you get blackouts. You're nervous doing breaks. I never really wanted to be involved with them: mostly I just told them I'd be lookout. One time we all broke in this place: I was out watching and the boys went in, and then a cop car and two paddy wagons came down the road. I said, "Boys, the cops are coming," and I beat it. The boys all got caught. (Leyton, 1979:124)

According to Cloward and Ohlin (1960), three different forms of delinquent subcultures—criminal, conflict, and retreatist—emerge based on the type of illegitimate opportunities available in a specific area. The criminal subculture focuses on economic gain and includes acts such as theft, extortion, and drug dealing. Sociologist Elijah Anderson (1990) suggested that the "drug economy [is an] employment agency superimposed on the existing gang network" for many young men who lack other opportunities. For young men who grow up in a gang subculture, running drug houses and selling drugs on street corners becomes a source of illegitimate opportunity. Using the money from these "jobs," they can support themselves and their families as well as purchase material possessions to impress others. When illegitimate economic opportunities are not available, gangs may become conflict subcultures that fight over turf (territory) and adopt a value system of toughness, courage, and similar status-enhancing qualities. Those who lack the opportunity or ability to join one of these gangs may turn to retreatist activities such as drinking and drug use.

Opportunity theory expands strain theory by pointing out the relationship between deviance and the availability of illegitimate opportunity structures. Some recent studies of gangs have supported this premise by pointing out that gang membership provides some women and men in low-income central-city areas with an illegitimate means to acquire money, entertainment, refuge, physical protection, and escape from living like their parents (Jankowski, 1991; Esbensen and Huizinga, 1993).

Control Theory: Social Bonding

Most theories of crime causation ask the question, why do they do it? Control theorists reverse this question, asking, why don't we all do it? That is, why do some people *not* engage in deviant behaviour? In an effort to answer this question, sociologist Walter Reckless (1967) developed a theory of social control, which states that certain factors draw people toward deviance while others "insulate" them from such behaviour. According to Reckless, people are drawn to deviance by poverty, unemployment, and lack of educational opportunity. They also may be influenced by members of deviant subcultures, media depictions of deviant behaviour, and their own feelings of frustration, hostility, or inferiority. However, many people do not turn to deviance because they are insulated by *outer containments* such as supportive family and friends, reasonable social expectations, and supervision by others, and by *inner containments* such as self-control, a sense of responsibility, and resistance to unlawful diversions.

Extending Reckless's containment theory, sociologist Travis Hirschi (1969) developed a theory suggesting that deviant behaviour is minimized when people have strong bonds that bind them to families, school, peers, churches, and other social institutions. ***Social bond theory*** **holds that the probability of deviant behaviour increases when a person's ties to society are weakened or broken.** According to Hirschi, social bonding consists of (1) *attachment* to other people, (2) *commitment* to conventional lines of behaviour such as schooling and job success, (3) *involvement* in conventional activities, and (4) *belief* in the legitimacy of conventional values and norms. Although Hirschi did not include females in his study, others who have replicated it with both females and males have found that the theory appears to explain the delinquency of both (see Linden and Fillmore, 1981).

While Hirschi's theory did not differentiate between bonds to conventional and to deviant others, several researchers have modified the theory and have suggested that the probability of crime or delinquency increases when a person's social bonds are weak and when peers promote antisocial values and deviant behaviour (Linden and Fillmore, 1981). Gang members may bond with one another rather than with persons who subscribe to dominant cultural values. As one gang member explains:

> Before I joined the gang, I could see that you could count on your boys to help in times of need and that meant a lot to me. And when I needed money, sure enough they gave it to me. Nobody else would have given it to me; my parents didn't have it, and there was no other place to go. The gang was just like they said they would be, and they'll continue to be there when I need them. (Jankowski, 1991:42)

INTERACTIONIST PERSPECTIVES ON DEVIANCE

As we discussed in Chapter 3, interactionists focus on how people develop a self-concept and learn conforming behaviour through the process of socialization. According to interactionists, deviance is learned in the same way as conformity—through interaction with others.

Differential Association Theory

More than fifty years ago, sociologist Edwin Sutherland (1939) developed a theory to explain how people learn deviance through social interaction. ***Differential association theory*** **states that individuals have a greater tendency to deviate from societal norms when they frequently associate with persons who favour deviance over conformity.** According to Sutherland, people learn the necessary techniques and the motives, drives, rationalizations, and attitudes of deviant behaviour from people with whom they associate.

An example of this learning of deviance—the acquisition of certain attitudes and the mastery of techniques—is provided in Box 6.2, which discusses how in Japan, younger organized crime gang members serve apprenticeships to older members of their organizations.

Differential association is most likely to result in criminal activity when a person has frequent, intense, and long-lasting interaction with others who violate the law. When there are more factors favouring violation of the law than there are opposing it, the person is more likely to become a criminal. Ties to other deviants can be particularly important in the world of organized crime, where the willingness of peers to stand up for one another can be critical in maintaining power in the face of violent opposition from competitors. Daniel Wolf, an anthropologist who rode with The Rebels, an Edmonton biker gang, describes this solidarity:

> For an outlaw biker, the greatest fear is not of the police; rather, it is of a slight variation of his own mirror image: the patch holder [full-fledged member] of another club. Under slightly different circumstances those men would call each other "brother." But when turf is at stake, inter-club rivalry and war-

BOX 6.2 SOCIOLOGY IN GLOBAL PERSPECTIVE

STREET YOUTHS, *BOSOZOKU*, AND *YAKUZA* IN JAPAN

Criminologists have identified three categories of gangs in Japan: youth gangs, *bosozoku* (hot-rod gangs), and *yakuza* (networks of adult male criminal organizations). In Japanese society, where high levels of conformity are expected, youth groups and gangs deliberately draw public attention to their deviant status.

Youth gang members, who are between the ages of 14 and 20, want to separate themselves from mainstream society. Although these gangs may include females, the focus is on masculinity and male prowess. *Bosozoku* are males (and a very few females) aged 17 to 20, whose activities centre on nightly high-speed, high-noise, and high-risk rides on motorcycles and in customized cars as they are chased by the police. Members who reach the age of 20 are considered too old for the group and must find something else to do or join the *yakuza,* which is made up of adult men, with younger men in apprentice roles. One Japanese man, Hayashi, describes his move from the youth gang to the *yakuza:*

> My life as a *yakuza* [organized crime gang member] began with difficulty, when as a young delinquent I joined a gang ... I wanted to be a gambler, but

> fare completely override any considerations of the common bonds of being a biker—and brother kills brother. None of the outlaws that I rode with enjoyed the prospect of having to break the bones of another biker. Nor did they look forward to having to live with the hate–fear syndrome that dominates a conflict in which there are no rules. I came to realize that the willingness of an outlaw to lay down his life in these conflicts goes beyond a belligerent masculinity that brooks no challenge. When a patch holder defends his colours, he defends his personal identity, his community, his lifestyle. When a war is on, loyalty to the club and one another arises out of the midst of danger, out of apprehension of possible injury, mutilation, or worse. Whether one considers this process as desperate, heroic, or just outlandishly foolish and banal does not really matter. What matters is that, for patch holders, the brotherhood emerges as a necessary feature of their continued existence as individuals and as a group. (1996:11)

Differential association theory contributes to our knowledge of how deviant behaviour reflects the individual's learned techniques, values, attitudes, motives, and rationalizations. However, critics question why many individuals who have had extensive contact with people who violate the law still conform most of the time. They also assert that the theory does not adequately assess possible linkages between social inequality and criminal behaviour.

Labelling Theory

Two complementary processes are involved in the definition of deviance. First, some people act (or are believed to act) in a manner contrary to the expectations of others. Second, others disapprove of and try to control this contrary behaviour. Part of this social control process involves labelling people as deviants. A very important contribution to the study of deviance was made by sociologists who asked the question, "Why are some people labelled as deviants while others are not?" ***Labelling theory*** **suggests that deviants are those people who have been successfully labelled as such by others.** The process of labelling is directly related to the power and status of those persons who *do* the labelling and those who are *being labelled.* Behaviour, then, is not deviant in and of itself; it is defined as such by a social audience (Erikson, 1962). According to sociologist Howard Becker (1963), *moral entrepreneurs* are persons who use their own views of right and wrong to establish rules and label others as deviant. These rules are enforced on persons with less power.

BOX 6.2

CONTINUED

for a long time after joining the family I wasn't allowed to gamble. First I helped with the cooking and cleaning ...

After some months of cleaning duty, I got a position doing *tachiban* [standing guard], but on cold winter days it was difficult. Finally, when new members joined our gang, I was able to do *zoriban* [arranging shoes in order]. These moves were important. For the first time I was not in the house, cleaning. Unless you take these steps, you could not become a card dealer ...

One must pledge total obedience. To do that you must receive sake from the boss, with a third person as a witness. It is a very important ceremony ... *Yakuza* tradition will never cease because we're different from ordinary people. That's why we joined this world. And we share the same idea that if we make one big mistake we die together. (quoted in Kaplan and Dubro, 1987:142–144)

Nearly one-third of the *yakuza's* recruits come from the *bosozuku* (Kersten, 1993).

Robert Rosenhan demonstrated the power of a deviant label in a study in which he and seven other people admitted themselves to mental hospitals. The pseudopatients reported hearing voices saying things like "empty" and "hollow." Other than this faked symptom, which is consistent with a diagnosis of schizophrenia, the "patients" told the truth about their life histories. These histories were distorted by hospital staff to fit the schizophrenia diagnoses. For example, a normal relationship between a man and his parents became psychopathological and was described in this way: "... manifests a long history of considerable ambivalence in close relationships which began in early childhood ... Affective stability is absent ..." (Rosenhan, 1973:254).

Once admitted to hospital, the "patients" acted completely normally. However, their sanity went undetected by hospital staff, though many of their fellow patients realized they were sane. Rosenhan said it was quite common for other patients to make comments such as "You're not crazy. You're a journalist, or a professor ... You're checking up on the hospital" (Rosenhan, 1973:253). The pseudopatients spent an average of nineteen days in hospital before being released. When they were released, it was with the diagnosis "schizophrenic in remission" and not as "sane."

Other research has shown that stigmatizing labels such as "mentally ill" or "criminal" can last a long time and may make it very difficult for the labelled person to reintegrate into society. For example, these labels may hurt one's chances for employment and may affect relationships with friends and acquaintances.

According to sociologist Edwin Lemert (1951), ***primary deviance* is the initial act of rule-breaking. *Secondary deviance* occurs when a person who has been labelled a deviant accepts that new identity and continues the deviant behaviour** (see Figure 6.1). For example, a person may shoplift, not be labelled as deviant, and subsequently decide to forgo such an act in the future. Secondary deviance occurs if the person shoplifts, is labelled a "shoplifter," accepts that label, and then continues to steal. The labelling process actually contributes to the subsequent recurrence of the behaviour it was meant to control.

A major contribution of labelling theory is that it calls attention to the way in which social control and personal identity are intertwined: labelling may contribute to the acceptance of deviant roles and self-images. Critics argue that this theory does not explain what causes the original acts that make up primary deviance. Nor does it provide insight into

FIGURE 6.1 Labelling Theory

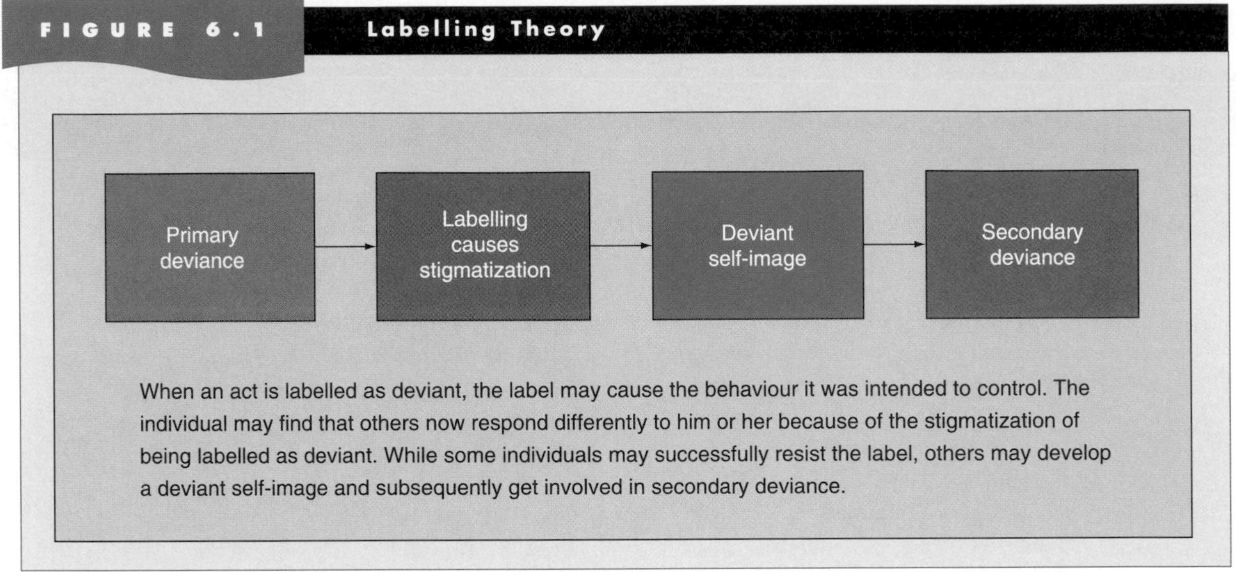

When an act is labelled as deviant, the label may cause the behaviour it was intended to control. The individual may find that others now respond differently to him or her because of the stigmatization of being labelled as deviant. While some individuals may successfully resist the label, others may develop a deviant self-image and subsequently get involved in secondary deviance.

why some people accept deviant labels and others do not (Cavender, 1995).

While interactionist perspectives are concerned with how people learn deviant behaviour, identities, and social roles through interaction with others, conflict theorists are interested in how certain kinds of people and behaviour, and not others, come to be defined as deviant.

CONFLICT PERSPECTIVES ON DEVIANCE

Who determines what kinds of behaviour are deviant or criminal? According to conflict perspectives, people in positions of power maintain their advantage by using the law to protect their own interests. Conflict theorists suggest that lifestyles considered deviant by political and economic elites often are defined as illegal. Conflict theorists note that the activities of poor and lower-income individuals are more likely to be defined as criminal than those of persons from middle- and upper-income backgrounds. For example, those who commit welfare fraud are more likely to face criminal charges than are professionals such as doctors or lawyers whose misconduct is generally dealt with by disciplinary committees of their peers rather than by the criminal courts. The relative degree of social harm caused by either of these groups seems to have little relevance in the determination of who is defined as a criminal. What matters more may be the power of some groups to resist sanctions.

The Conflict Approach

Although Karl Marx wrote very little about deviance and crime, many of his ideas influenced a critical approach that has emerged from earlier Marxist and radical perspectives on criminology. The conflict approach is based on the assumption that the criminal justice system protects the power and privilege of the capitalist class.

As we saw in Chapter 1, Marx based his critique of capitalism on the inherent conflict that he believed existed between the capitalists and the working class. According to Marx, social institutions (such as law, politics, and education) make up a superstructure in society that legitimizes the class structure and maintains the capitalists' superior position in it. Crime is an expression of the individual's struggle against the unjust social conditions and inequality produced by capitalism.

According to sociologist Richard Quinney (1974, 1979, 1980), people with economic and political power define as criminal any behaviour that threatens their own interests. The powerful use the law to control those who are without power. For example, drug laws enacted early in the twentieth century were passed and enforced in an effort to control immigrant workers, particularly the Chinese, who were more inclined than most other residents of Canada to smoke opium. The laws were motivated by racism more than by a real concern over drug use (Cook, 1969). By contrast, while the Canadian government passed anticombines legislation in 1889, in response to concerns expressed by labour and small business people about the growing power of monopoly capitalists, the law had no impact on major companies that engaged in price-fixing and other means of limiting competition. Having symbolic anticombines laws on the books merely shored up the government's legitimacy by making it appear responsive to public concerns about big business (Smandych, 1985).

Why do people commit crimes? Some conflict theorists believe that the affluent commit crimes because they are greedy and want more than they have. Corporate or white-collar crimes often involve huge sums of money and harm many people. By contrast, street crimes such as robbery and aggravated assault generally involve small sums of money and cause harm to limited numbers of victims (Bonger, 1969). According to critical theorists, the poor commit street crimes in order to survive; they find that they cannot afford the necessary essentials such as food, clothing, shelter, and health care. Thus, some crime represents a rational response by the poor to the unequal distribution of resources in society (Gordon, 1973). Further, living in poverty may lead to violent crime and victimization *of the poor by the poor*. For example, violent gang activity may be a collective response of young people to seemingly hopeless poverty (Quinney, 1979).

In sum, the conflict approach argues that criminal law protects the interests of the affluent and the powerful. (See Box 7.2 in the next chapter, "Social Stratification and Class.") The way laws are written and enforced benefits the capitalist class by ensuring that individuals at the bottom of the social class structure do not infringe on the property or threaten the safety of those at the top (Reiman, 1979). While this theory fits some types of laws, it does not fit others. People of all classes share a consensus about the criminality of certain acts. For example, laws that prohibit murder, rape, and armed robbery protect not only middle- and upper-income people but also low-income people, who frequently are the victims of such violent crimes (Klockars, 1979).

Feminist Approaches

Can theories developed to explain male behaviour help us understand female deviance and crime? According to some feminist scholars, the answer is no. The few early studies that were conducted on "women's crimes" focused almost exclusively on prostitution and attributed the cause of this crime to women's biological or psychological "inferiority." As late as the 1980s, researchers were still looking for unique predisposing factors that led women to commit crime, which was often seen as individual psychopathology rather than as a response to their social environment. These theories, which reinforce existing female stereotypes, have had a negative impact on both our understanding and our treatment of female offenders.

A new interest in women and deviance developed in 1975 when two books—Freda Adler's *Sisters in Crime* and Rita James Simons's *Women and Crime*—declared that women's crime rates were going to increase significantly as a result of the women's liberation movement. Although this so-called *emancipation theory* of female crime has been strongly criticized by subsequent analysts (Comack, 2000), Adler's and Simons's works encouraged feminist scholars (both women and men) to examine the relationship between gender, deviance, and crime more closely. While there is no single feminist perspective on deviance and crime, three schools of thought have emerged.

Liberal feminism explains women's deviance and crime as a rational response to gender discrimination experienced in work, marriage, and interpersonal relationships. Some female crimes may be attributed to women's lack of educational and job opportunities and stereotypical expectations about what roles women should have in society. For example, a woman is no more likely to be a big-time drug dealer or an organized crime boss than she is to be a corporate director (see Daly and Chesney-Lind, 1988; Simpson, 1989).

Radical feminism suggests that patriarchy (male domination over females) keeps women more tied to family and home, even if women also work full time. Based on this approach, prostitution might be explained as a reflection of society's sexual double standard, whereby it is acceptable for a man to pay for sex but unacceptable for a woman to accept money for such services. Although prostitution laws in Canada define both the prostitute and the cus-

CONCEPT TABLE 6.A

THEORETICAL PERSPECTIVES ON DEVIANCE

	Theory	Key Elements
Functionalist Perspectives		
Robert Merton	Strain theory	Deviance occurs when access to the approved means of reaching culturally approved goals is blocked.
Richard Cloward/ Lloyd Ohlin	Opportunity theory	For deviance to occur, people must have the opportunity. Access to illegitimate opportunity structures varies, and this helps determine the nature of the deviance in which a person will engage.
Travis Hirschi	Social control/social bonding	Social bonds keep people from becoming criminals. When ties to family, friends, and others become weak, an individual is most likely to engage in criminal behaviour.
Interactionist Perspectives		
Edwin Sutherland	Differential association	Deviant behaviour is learned in interaction with others. A person becomes delinquent when exposure to lawbreaking attitudes is more extensive than exposure to law-abiding attitudes.
Howard Becker	Labelling theory	Acts are deviant or criminal because they have been labelled as such. Powerful groups often label less powerful individuals.
Edwin Lemert	Primary/secondary deviance	Primary deviance is the initial act. Secondary deviance occurs when a person accepts the label of "deviant" and continues to engage in the behaviour that initially produced the label.
Critical Perspectives		
Karl Marx Richard Quinney	Conflict approach	The powerful use law and the criminal justice system to protect their own class interests.
Feminist Perspectives		
Kathleen Daly Meda Chesney-Lind Elizabeth Comack	Feminist approach	Historically, women have been ignored in research on crime. Liberal feminism views women's deviance as arising from gender discrimination; radical feminism focuses on patriarchy; and socialist feminism emphasizes the effects of capitalism and patriarchy on women.

tomer as violating the law, women are far more likely than men to be arrested, brought to trial, convicted, and sentenced for prostitution-related offences.

Socialist feminism notes that women are exploited by capitalism and patriarchy. Because most females have relatively low-wage jobs and few economic resources, crimes such as prostitution and shoplifting become a means to earn money or acquire consumer products. Instead of freeing women from their problems, however, prostitution institutionalizes women's dependence on men and results in a form of female sexual slavery (Vito and Holmes, 1994).

We have examined functionalist, interactionist, and conflict perspectives on deviance and crime (see Concept Table 6.A). These explanations help us to understand the causes and consequences of certain kinds of behaviour; however, they also make us aware of the limitations of our knowledge about deviance and crime.

CRIME CLASSIFICATION AND STATISTICS

How Sociologists Classify Crime

Sociologists categorize crimes based on how they are committed and how society views the offences. We will examine three types: (1) street crime, (2) occupational, or white-collar, and corporate crime, and (3) organized crime. As you read about these types of crime, ask yourself how you feel about them. Should each be a crime? How stiff should the sanctions be against each type?

STREET CRIME When people think of crime, the images that most commonly come to mind are of ***street crime,* which includes offences such as robbery, assault, and break and enter.** These are the crimes that occupy most of the time and attention of the criminal justice system. Obviously, all street crime does not occur on the street; it frequently occurs in the home, workplace, and other locations.

Violent crime consists of actions involving force or the threat of force against others, including murder, sexual assault, robbery, and aggravated assault. Violent crimes are probably the most anxiety-provoking of all criminal behaviour. Victims often are physically injured or even lose their lives; the psychological trauma may last for years after the event (Parker, 1995). Violent crime receives the most sustained attention from law enforcement officials and the media (see Box 6.3). And, while much attention may be given to, and fears aroused by, the violent stranger, the vast majority of violent crime victims actually are injured by someone whom they know: family members, friends, neighbours, or co-workers (Silverman and Kennedy, 1993).

Property crimes include break and enter, theft, motor vehicle theft, and arson. While violent crime receives the most publicity, property crimes are much more common. In most property crimes, the primary motive is to obtain money or some other desired valuable.

Morals crimes involve an illegal action voluntarily engaged in by the participants, such as prostitution, illegal gambling, the private use of illegal drugs, and illegal pornography. Many people assert that such conduct should not be labelled as a crime; these offences often are referred to as "victimless crimes" because they involve exchanges of illegal goods or services among willing adults (Schur, 1965).

However, morals crimes can include children and adolescents as well as adults. Young children and adolescents may unwillingly become child pornography "stars" or prostitutes. Members of juvenile gangs often find selling drugs to be a lucrative business in which getting addicted and/or arrested is merely an occupational hazard.

OCCUPATIONAL AND CORPORATE CRIME Although sociologist Edwin Sutherland (1949) developed the theory of white-collar crime almost fifty years ago, it was not until the 1980s that the public really became aware of its nature. ***Occupational,* or *white-collar,* crime consists of illegal activities committed by people in the course of their employment or financial dealings.**

At the heart of much white-collar crime is a violation of positions of trust in business or government (Shapiro, 1990). These activities include pilfering (employee theft of company property or profits), soliciting bribes or kickbacks, and embezzling. In the past decade, computers have created even greater access to such illegal practices. Some white-collar criminals set up businesses for the sole purpose of victimizing the general public, engaging in activities such as land swindles, securities thefts, and consumer fraud.

BOX 6.3 SOCIOLOGY AND MEDIA

"IF IT BLEEDS, IT LEADS": FEAR OF CRIME AND THE MEDIA

Most Canadians learn about crime through the media rather than from first-hand experience. However, the media do not simply "report" the news. Editors and reporters select the crime news we hear about and construct the way in which this news is presented to us.

Unfortunately, the picture of crime we receive from the media is very inaccurate. For example, while most crime is property crime, most stories in the media deal with violent crime. Typical of research in this area was a review of all the crime-related stories reported over two months in an Ottawa newspaper (Gabor, 1994). Over half the stories focused on violent crimes, particularly murders. However, violent crimes actually made up only 7 percent of reported crimes in Ottawa and the city averaged just six murders per year.

John Rosen, who was Paul Bernardo's lawyer, faces the media during Bernardo's trial.

Why do the media misrepresent crime? The primary goal of the media is to make profits by selling advertising. Stories that attract viewers or readers will boost ratings and circulation

Michael de Guzman (right), a geologist for the Bre-X gold company, is one of those responsible for one of the world's largest stock frauds. It is believed that de Guzman committed suicide while travelling to the Bre-X property in Indonesia.

In addition to acting for their own financial benefit, some white-collar offenders become involved in criminal conspiracies designed to improve the market share or profitability of their companies. This is known as ***corporate crime*—illegal acts committed by corporate employees on *behalf* of the corporation and with its support.** Examples include antitrust violations; false advertising; infringements on patents, copyrights, and trademarks; price fixing; and financial fraud. These crimes are a result of deliberate decisions made by corporate personnel to enhance resources or profits at the expense of competitors, consumers, and the general public.

The cost of white-collar and corporate crimes far exceeds that of street crime. Gabor (1994) reports that tax evasion costs Canadians about $30 billion a year. In one of the world's biggest white-collar crimes, investors in Calgary's Bre-X gold-mining company lost around $5 billion when it was learned that geologist Michael de Guzman had salted core samples with gold to make a worthless mining property look like the world's biggest gold find. At the individual level, while few bank robbers get away with more than a few thousand dollars, Julius

BOX 6.3

CONTINUED

even if these stories do not represent the reality of crime. The informal media rule, "If it bleeds, it leads," reflects the fact that the public are fascinated by sensationalized, bloody stories such as those of mass murders or attacks against helpless senior citizens.

The media's misrepresentation of crime is a major factor in Canadians greatly overestimating the amount of violent crime that is committed and having a fear of crime that is more intense than their risk of victimization justifies. One survey found that the vast majority of Canadians (75 percent) felt that most crimes are accompanied by violence, though the true figure is less than 10 percent (Doob and Roberts, 1983). Crime stories lead us to see Canada as a violent and dangerous place. Our fears are reinforced by the global coverage of violence. Television can instantly bring us events from anywhere and violent crimes such as the bus bombings by Hamas terrorists in Israel and the murder of thirteen people at Columbine High School in Colorado are reported as immediately and as thoroughly as if they had happened in our own communities.

Our fear of crime and our image of the criminal have an impact on government policy toward crime. While crime rates are declining, a combination of increasing media coverage of crime and pressure from a variety of interest groups has led the federal government to tighten several laws including those concerning immigration, young offenders, and firearms.

Sources: Based on Kappeler, Blumberg, and Potter (1996); and McCormick (1995).

Melnitzer, a London, Ontario, lawyer, defrauded Canadian banks of $90 million in order to support his lavish lifestyle.

Corporate crimes can also be very costly in terms of lives lost and injury. Laureen Snider (1988) found that occupational deaths are the third leading cause of death in Canada. She attributes at least half of these deaths to unsafe and illegal working conditions. Working conditions in the mining industry, for example, have been especially dangerous. Decades ago, large numbers of Canadian miners died because their employers failed to protect them from mine hazards. Coal miners died of black lung, a condition caused by inhaling coal dust, and fluorspar miners died from the effects of inhaling silica dust in unventilated mineshafts. Not only did the mine owners fail to provide safe working conditions, but company doctors were also told not to advise the miners of the seriousness of their illnesses. The loss of twenty-six miners in a preventable explosion at Nova Scotia's Westray mine in 1992 suggests some mine owners have yet to put their employees' lives above profits.

One reason many employers have been reluctant to implement required safety measures is because the penalties for violating workplace health and safety laws are so light. Consider the case of Silco, an Edmonton-based construction company. In 1994, a Silco employee fell to his death from a homemade man-basket attached to an unstable crane boom. The company had received three different orders to improve their safety practices earlier that year, but had ignored all of them, including a stop-work order the month of the accident. Despite Silco's obvious negligence, the company received only a fine of $6000 for its part in the employee's death (Ward, 1996).

Although people who commit occupational and corporate crimes can be arrested, fined, and sent to prison, many people do not regard such behaviour as "criminal." People who tend to condemn street crime are less sure of how their own (or their friends') financial and corporate behaviour should be judged. At most, punishment for such offences is usually a fine or a relatively brief prison sentence at a minimum-security facility.

One final point that can be made about white-collar crime is that the concept also fits people who wear blue collars. Because of this, some have suggested that *occupational crime* may be a more accurate term. Many tradespeople defraud the government by doing work "off the books" in order to avoid provincial sales tax and the goods and services tax (GST). Some blue-collar businesses have bad records of consumer fraud. Robert Sikorsky (1990), who travelled across Canada and visited 152 automobile repair shops, documented an appalling degree of misconduct in this business. Before each visit, he disconnected the idle air control in his car, which triggered a warning light on the instrument panel. The repair needed was obvious and simple—reinsert the connector. But, more than half the shops Sikorsky visited performed unnecessary work, overcharged him for work, or lied about the work that had been done. In one case he was presented with an estimate of $570.

ORGANIZED CRIME ***Organized crime*** **is a business operation that supplies illegal goods and services for profit.** Organized crime includes drug trafficking, prostitution, liquor and cigarette smuggling, loan-sharking, money laundering, and large-scale theft, such as truck hijacking (Simon and Eitzen, 1993). No single organization controls all organized crime; rather, many groups operate at all levels of society. Organized crime thrives because there is great demand for illegal goods and services. This public demand has produced illicit supply systems with global connections. These activities are highly profitable, since groups that have a monopoly over goods and services the public strongly desires can set their own prices. Legitimate competitors are excluded because of the illegality; illegitimate competitors are controlled by force.

The deadly nature of organized crime has been shown in Montreal, which has been the scene of a major turf war between two rival biker gangs: the Rock Machine and the Hell's Angels. The two gangs have been engaged in a battle for control of a large segment of the city's illegal drug market. During January and February of 1995, the battle took a particularly bloody turn as rival gang members died at a rate of almost one a week as a result of car bombings, shootings, and stabbings. While the killings declined for several years, three more bikers were killed in one week in April 2000.

Along with their illegal enterprises, organized crime groups have infiltrated the world of legitimate business. Known linkages between legitimate businesses and organized crime exist in banking, hotels and motels, real estate, garbage collection, vending machine businesses, construction, delivery and long-distance hauling, garment manufacturing, insurance, stocks and bonds, vacation resorts, and funeral parlours. In addition, law enforcement and government officials may be corrupted through bribery, campaign contributions, and favours intended to buy them off, although this has been much less of a problem in Canada than in many other countries.

Crime Statistics

While citizens, police, and policy makers all wish to know how much crime there is and what forms this crime takes, those who commit crimes normally try to conceal their actions. It is always difficult to gather statistics about crime and to get access to the social worlds of criminals. Thus our information about crime will always be incomplete and we can never be certain that it is completely accurate. Our main sources of information about crime are police statistics, victimization surveys, and self-reports.

OFFICIAL STATISTICS Our most important source of crime data is the *Canadian Uniform Crime Reports* (CUCR) system, which summarizes crimes reported to all Canadian police departments. Most of our public information about crime comes from the CUCR. When we read that the homicide rate in British Columbia is higher than the national average, or that in 1999, over 2.3 million offences were reported to the police, this information is usually based on CUCR data. Figure 6.2 shows trends in violent and property crimes, and Figure 6.3 shows Canada's homicide rates. While most Canadians think that crime is increasing, these charts show that it has begun to decline in the past decade. The decline is particularly significant in the case of homicide where rates are now the lowest they have been in thirty years.

Crime figures should be interpreted very cautiously. While one can have confidence in homicide statistics, the accuracy of other crime statistics is less certain. Since many policy decisions by governments, as well as decisions by individuals about their personal safety, are based on CUCR statistics, it is important to recognize their limitations.

The major weakness of the CUCR is that police statistics always underreport the actual amount of crime. The vast majority of offences reported in the CUCR come to the attention of the police from the reports of victims of crime, and victims do not report all crimes. Furthermore, reporting of crime is inconsistent from place to place and from time to time. Official crime rates are the result of a criminal act, a complaint by a victim or witness, and a response by the criminal justice system. A change in any of these will lead to an increase or decrease in crime rates. For example, it is likely that much of the increase in violent crime during the late 1980s and early 1990s (see Figure 6.2) was due to the fact that domestic violence is now reported more often than it used to be (Linden, 1994). This makes it very difficult to make sense of crime patterns and trends.

Victimization Surveys The weaknesses of the CUCR have led to other methods of measuring crime, the most important of which is the victimization survey. Because a major problem with the CUCR is the fact that many people do not report their victimization, some governments began to carry out large surveys in which members of the public were directly asked whether they had been victims of crime. In the largest Canadian survey, less than 42 percent of the victimizations reported by respondents had been reported to the police (Evans and Himelfarb, 1996). Thus reported crimes are only the "tip of the iceberg." People told interviewers they did not report crimes because they considered the incident too minor, because they felt it was a personal matter, because they preferred to deal with the problem in another way, or because they did not feel the police could do anything about the crime. Victimization surveys provide us with information about crimes that have not been officially reported, so they provide more accurate statistics of crime than do police records. However, these surveys do have some weaknesses: people may not remember minor types of victimization; they may not report honestly to the interviewer; and they do not provide any information about "victimless crimes" such as drug use and illegal gambling. Despite these flaws, victimization surveys have shed new light on the extent of criminal behaviour and are a valuable complement to other ways of counting crimes.

Street Crimes and Criminals

Given the limitations of official statistics, is it possible to determine who commits crimes? We have much more information available about conventional or street crime than elite crime; therefore, statistics concerning street crime do not show who commits all types of crime. Age, gender, class, and race are important factors in official statistics pertaining to street crime. These are known as *correlates of crime*, that is, they are factors associated with criminal activity. One method of testing theories of crime is to see how well they explain these correlates.

Age and Crime The age of the offender is one of the most significant factors associated with crime. Arrests increase from early adolescence, peak in young adulthood, and steadily decline with age. There is some variation in this pattern—for example, violent crimes peak at a later age than property crimes—but the general pattern is almost always the same. Crime is a young person's game.

Possible explanations for this are the physical effects of aging, which make some criminal activity more difficult, and the realization by older chronic offenders that further arrests will result in very long jail sentences. Perhaps the best explanation for maturational reform, though, is related to the different social positions of youth and adults. Adolescents are between childhood and adult life. They have few responsibilities and no clear social role. Adolescence is also a time when young people are breaking away from the controls of their parents and others and preparing to live on their own. As we age, we begin to acquire commitments and obligations that limit our freedom to choose a lifestyle that includes crime.

Gender and Crime Another consistent correlate of crime is gender. Most crimes are committed by males. Females are more likely to be victims than offenders. As with age and crime, this relationship has existed in almost all times and cultures. However, while the age distribution is remarkably stable, considerably more variation in male/female crime ratios exists in different places, at different times, and for different types of crime.

Men make up over 80 percent of those charged with crimes in Canada (Chard, 1995). As Figure 6.4 shows, the degree of involvement of males and

FIGURE 6.2 Canadian Crime Rates, 1962–1999

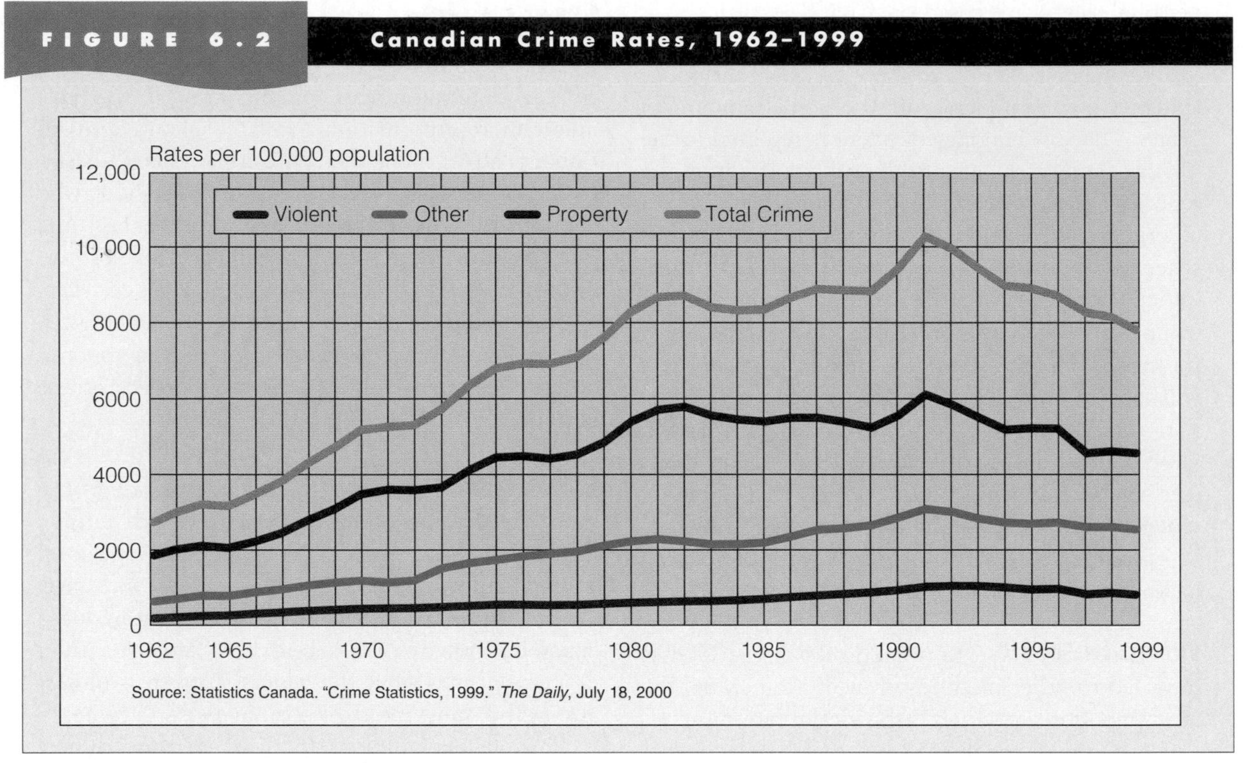

Source: Statistics Canada. "Crime Statistics, 1999." *The Daily*, July 18, 2000

FIGURE 6.3 Canadian Homicide Rates, 1961–1999

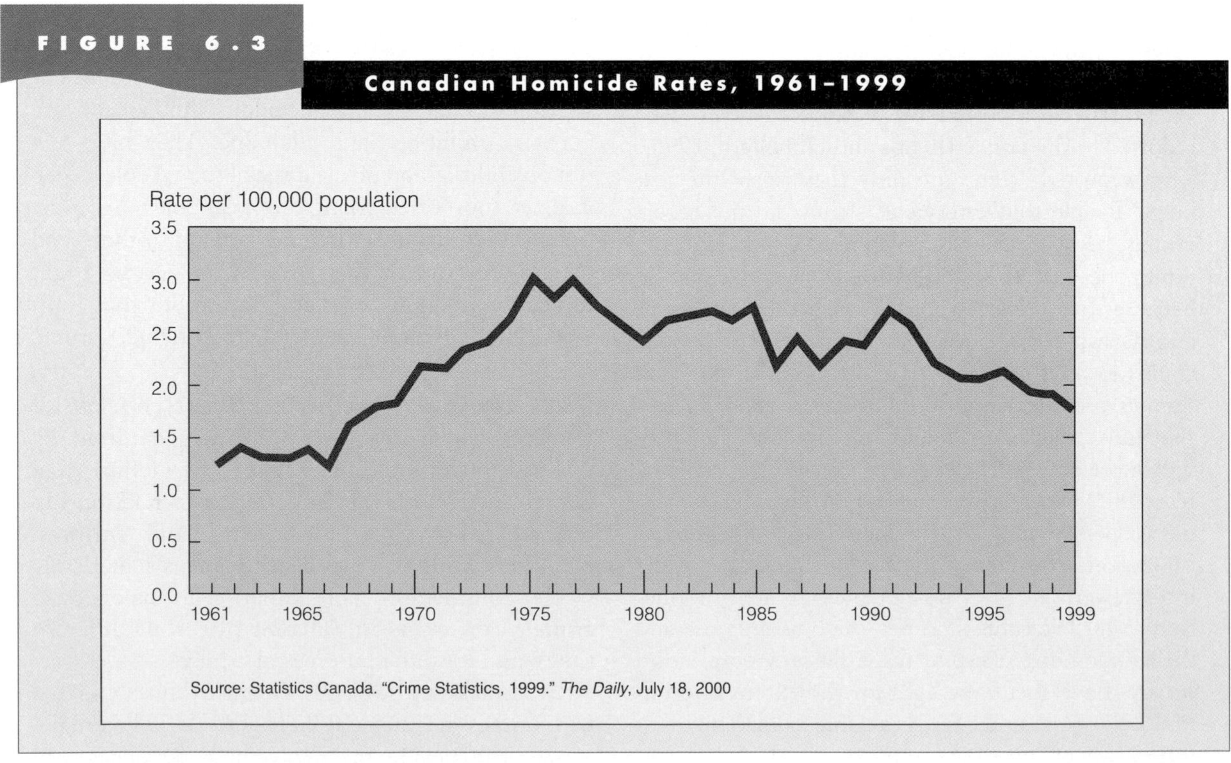

Source: Statistics Canada. "Crime Statistics, 1999." *The Daily*, July 18, 2000

As of 1971, population estimates were adjusted to reflect new methods of calculation.

FIGURE 6.4 Percentages of Adults Charged with Selected Criminal Offences by Sex, 1998

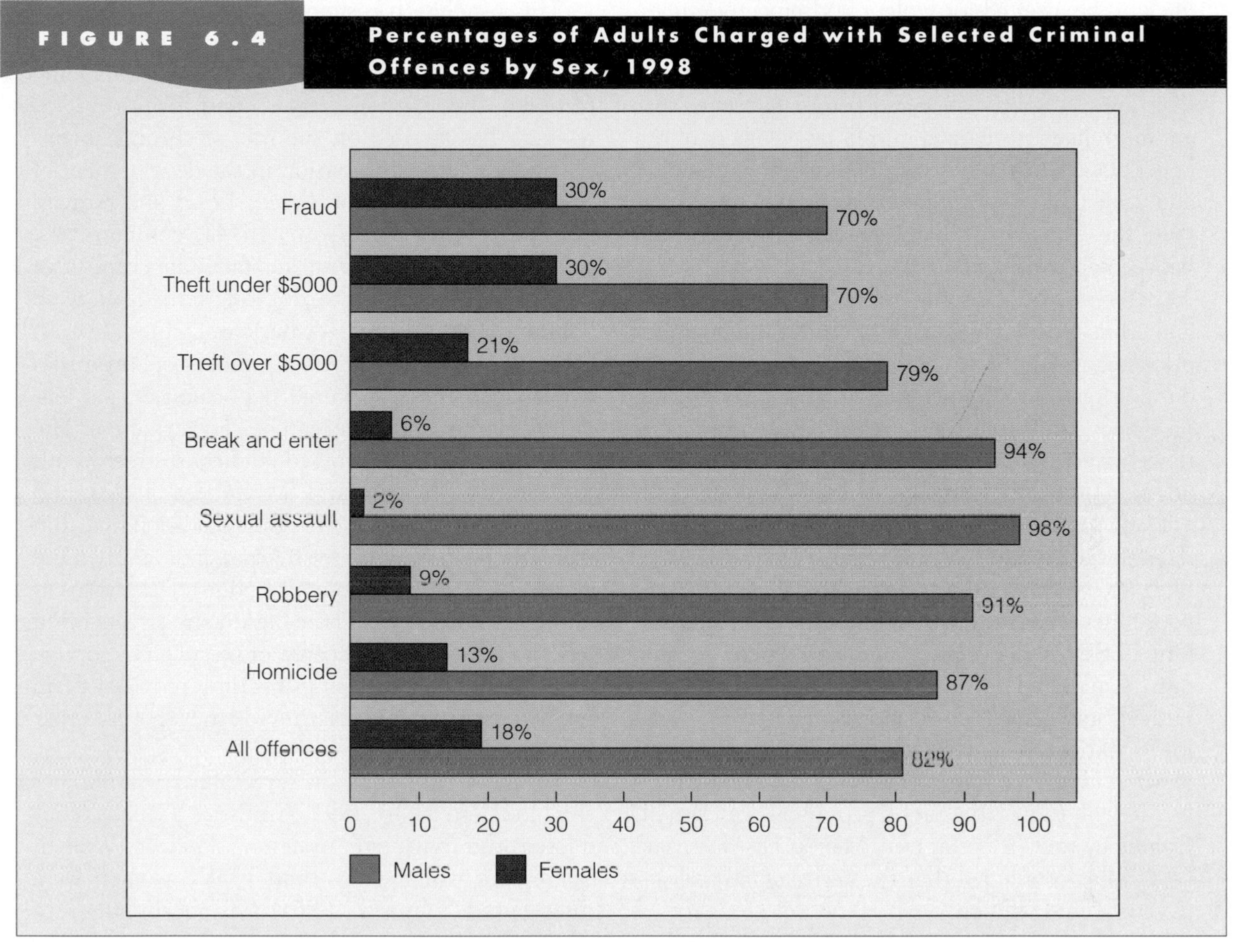

Reproduced by authority of the Minister of Industry, 1999, Statistics Canada, from *Juristat*, Cat. no. 85-0XPE, Vol. 19, No. 9, 1999.

females varies substantially for different crimes. The most important gender differences in arrest rates are reflected in the proportionately greater involvement of men in violent crimes and major property offences.

The difference between male and female crime rates has narrowed over the past three decades. Hartnagel (2000) compared the rate of male and female adults charged with a variety of offences in 1968 and in 1992, and found that crime rates for females increased much more rapidly than for males during this period. The percentage of Criminal Code offences committed by females increased from 9 percent to 18 percent. While there was virtually no change in the proportion of females charged with homicide (11 percent versus 12 percent), the proportion of women charged with serious theft (9 percent to 18 percent), fraud (11 percent to 29 percent,) and minor theft (22 percent to 34 percent) changed substantially.

While female crime rates have increased more rapidly than male crime rates, it is important to remember that the numbers seem more dramatic than they are because the percentage changes are based on very low numbers of female crimes in earlier decades. Women have a long way to go to reach parity in crime with men.

SOCIAL CLASS AND CRIME Criminologists have long debated the relationship between social class and crime. Many theories of crime are based on the assumption that crime is economically motivated and that poverty will lead to criminal behaviour. Unfortunately, the evidence concerning the impact of economic factors on crime is not entirely clear. We do know that persons from lower socioeconomic backgrounds are more likely to be arrested for violent and property crimes. However, we also know that these types of crimes are more likely to come to the attention of the police than are the white-collar and corporate crimes that are more likely to be committed by members of the upper class. Because the vast majority of white-collar and corporate crimes are never reported, we do not have the data to adequately assess the relationship between class and crime.

Before looking at some of the data on social class and crime we do have, let us briefly consider several other economic variables. Does crime increase during times of high unemployment? Do poor cities, provinces, and countries have higher crime rates than richer communities? The answer to both these questions is no. Historically, crime rates are at least as likely to rise during periods of prosperity as during recessionary times (Nettler, 1984). We are also as likely to find high crime rates in rich countries as in poor ones. The world's wealthiest countries, the United States and Japan, have very different crime rates. Compared with other countries, crime in the United States is very high and crime in Japan is very low. Within Canada, the poor provinces of Newfoundland and New Brunswick have crime rates far lower than the rich provinces of British Columbia and Alberta (see Map 6.1). Hartnagel (2000) has concluded that the *degree of inequality*—poverty amid affluence—is a better predictor of crime than is the amount of poverty.

We know that lower-class people are overrepresented in arrest and prison admission statistics. However, we do not know if this is because lower-class people commit more crimes, or because the justice system treats them more harshly. To get closer to actual behaviour, researchers developed the self-report surveys in which people report their own involvement in crime. Some of this research (Elliott and Ageton, 1980; Thornberry and Farnworth, 1982) has supported the view that crime is more frequent in the lower class. Based on the results of these and many other studies, the most likely conclusion is that for the vast majority of people, class and crime or delinquency are not related. People from all classes break the law, at least occasionally. However, those who engage in frequent and serious offending are most likely to come from the very bottom of the class ladder—from an underclass that is severely disadvantaged economically, educationally, and socially.

This conclusion is supported by the work of several researchers who have conducted field studies among street youth in several countries including Canada, the United States, and Britain. U.S. research has focused on the role of chronic unemployment and discrimination in the development of street gangs in Hispanic (Vigil, 1990) and African American (E. Anderson, 1994) communities. Subcultures that encourage and facilitate crime have developed in response to the long-term poverty so common in many American communities. Compared to the bleak legitimate opportunities available to them, criminal opportunities, particularly from the drug trade, can be very attractive. The Canadian research involved studies of street youth in Toronto (Hagan and McCarthy, 1992) and Edmonton (Baron, 1994). These studies found that many street youth were from lower-class families and were on the streets because of poor relationships at home and at school. Their life on the streets often leads to delinquency because of the need to survive and also because engaging in crime provides them with a sense of control they do not get in other facets of their lives.

A unique victimization survey further reinforces this conclusion. In 1993, Statistics Canada conducted the national Violence Against Women Survey, for which more than 12,000 women were interviewed (Johnson, 1996a). Several findings supported the view that violence is greatest in the lower class. First, men with high-school educations assaulted their wives at twice the rate of men with university degrees. Second, men who were out of work committed assaults at twice the rate of men who were employed. Third, men in the lowest income category (less than $15,000 a year) assaulted their wives at twice the rate of men with higher incomes. However, above this $15,000 level, there was no relationship between income and crime. This again suggests that the highest crime rates can be found at the very bottom of the economic ladder.

RACE AND ETHNICITY AND CRIME In societies with culturally heterogeneous populations, some ethnic and racial groups will have higher crime rates than others (Nettler, 1984). For example, in the United States, African Americans and Hispanics are overrepresented in arrest data.

Statistics Canada does not routinely collect data about racial and ethnic correlates of crime, so we know relatively little about the situation in this country. In addition to data about native Canadians, which are discussed below, two relatively recent studies dealt with minorities and crime. The first of these, which examined race and ethnicity in the federal prison system, found that offenders from nonaboriginal, visible ethnic minorities were *underrepresented* in the federal correctional system's population (D. Thomas, 1992). Specifically, the study found that in 1989, 5.2 percent of the federal corrections population were members of ethnic minority groups, while these groups made up over 6.3 percent of the general population. The second study, which examined provincial youth and adult correctional centres in British Columbia, arrived at similar findings. Only 8.2 percent of the prison population were members of nonaboriginal, visible ethnic minorities, yet these groups made up 13.5 percent of the province's population (Gordon and Nelson, 1993).

While statistics on other minorities are limited, there are extensive data on Aboriginal peoples. This is due in part to the documentation that resulted from special inquiries held to find out whether actions toward Aboriginal people by the justice system in several provinces have been discriminatory. Many studies have demonstrated the *overinvolvement* of Aboriginal people (Hartnagel, 2000); a typical finding is that while Aboriginal people made up about 2 percent of the population in 1991, they made up about 24 percent of persons held in custody after being convicted of a crime (Brantingham, Mu, and Verma, 1995). In their study of Canadian homicides, Silverman and Kennedy found that Aboriginal people are involved in homicides in proportions that are at least five times greater than their representation in the population (1993). Hyde and LaPrairie (1987) showed that Aboriginal and non-Aboriginal people had different patterns, as well as different rates, of crime. Aboriginal people had more social disorder offences (many of which were alcohol-related), fewer property offences, and more violent offences. Other researchers found a great deal of variation in Aboriginal crime rates among different communities and parts of the country (Wood and Griffiths, 1996).

What is the reason for these racial and ethnic differences in crime rates? One answer is that there has often been discrimination by the justice system against minority groups. The treatment of blacks in South Africa and in the southern United States throughout much of the nineteenth and twentieth centuries is an obvious example. Discrimination against Aboriginal people in Canada, Australia, and New Zealand has also been well documented by commissions of inquiry. Members of minority groups, who tend to be poor, may go to prison for minor offences if they are unable to pay fines. A report by the Law Reform Commission of Canada (1974) found that in 1970 and 1971 over half of all native people admitted to Saskatchewan jails were incarcerated for nonpayment of fines. While this type of discrimination may be unintentional, it is nonetheless real. Discrimination likely accounts for some, but not all, of the high rates of criminality of some minority groups.

To provide a further explanation, consider the fact that Canada's Aboriginal people have far less power and fewer resources than other Canadians. They must cope with systems of education and religion that are imposed on them from outside their cultural communities and that are not compatible with native customs and traditions. In the past, forced attendance at residential schools and forced adoption outside the community have weakened family ties. Crippling rates of unemployment in many areas mean no job ties, and school curricula that are irrelevant to the lives of native students mean that children do not become attached to their schools. Under these conditions, strong social bonds are difficult to develop and high rates of crime can be predicted.

REGION AND CRIME Crime is not evenly distributed around the globe. Some countries have much higher crime rates than others, and within countries there are often significant differences among regions. The most reliable measure for comparison is homicide rates, which are reported in a reasonably similar fashion in most countries. Canada's homicide rate of about 1.75 per 100,000 people is relatively low by world standards. It is about a quarter of the U.S. rate, but about one and a half times that of the United Kingdom.

Major regional differences in crime rates exist within Canada. As shown in Map 6.1, crime rates are highest in the West and the North and lowest in Atlantic Canada. These interprovincial differences have existed for many years.

MAP 6.1 1999 Crime Rates per 100,000 Population (Criminal Code Excluding Traffic Offences)

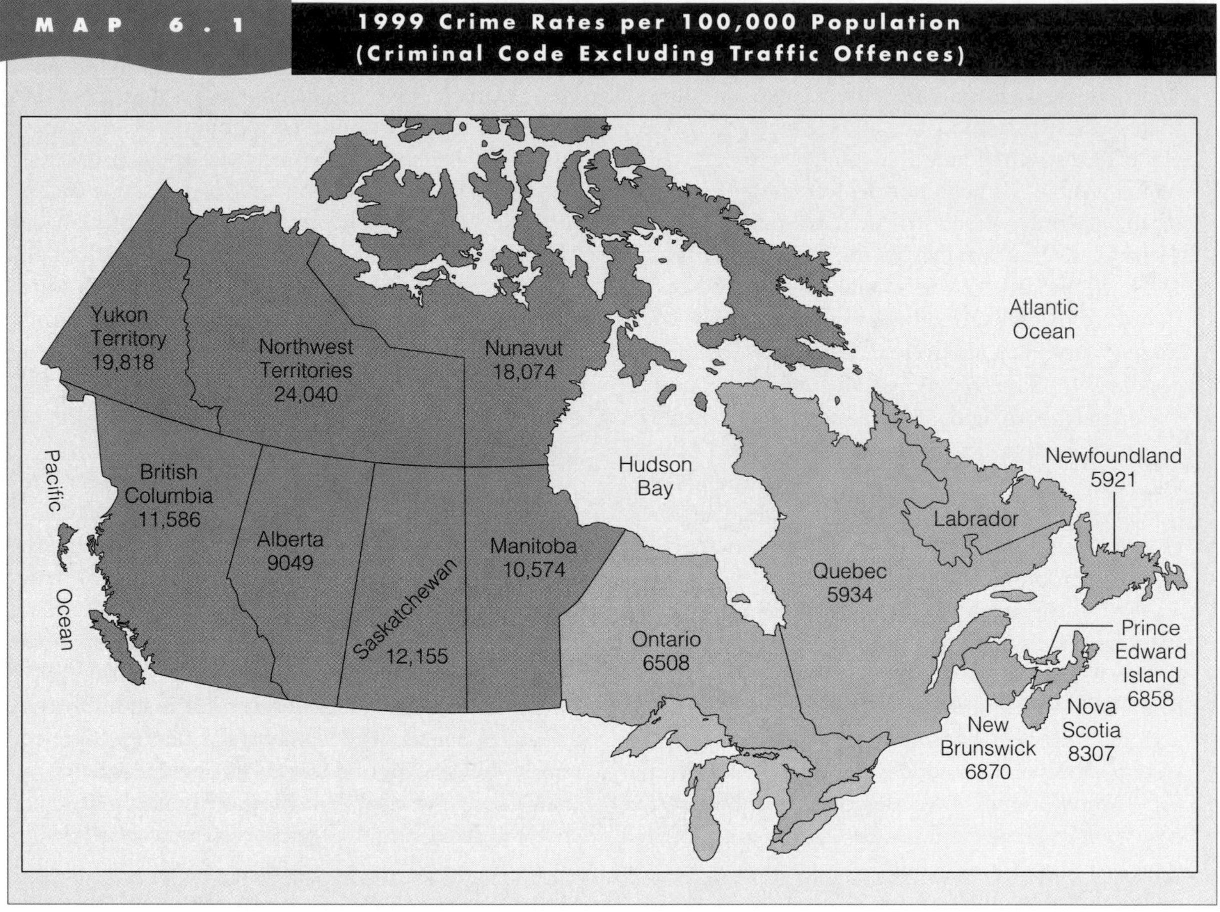

Source: Statistics Canada, *The Daily*, July 18, 2000. "Crime Statistics, 1999."

THE CRIMINAL JUSTICE SYSTEM

The criminal justice system includes the police, the courts, and prisons. However, the term *criminal justice system* is misleading because it implies that law enforcement agencies and courts constitute one large, integrated system, when it is actually a collection of "somewhat interrelated, semi-autonomous bureaucracies," each of which possesses considerable discretion to do as it wishes (Sheley, 1991:334). *Discretion* refers to the use of personal judgment by police officers, prosecutors, judges, and other criminal justice system officials regarding whether and how to proceed in a given situation.

The Police

Most people think the main function of the police is to enforce the law. That is indeed one of their functions, but there are several others including order maintenance and the provision of social services. Order maintenance refers to keeping the peace. Stopping arguments, controlling the areas where skid-row alcoholics drink, and making a group of boisterous teenagers move away from the parking lot of a convenience store are all order maintenance activities. While the main concern in law enforcement is arresting a suspect, the main concern in order maintenance is to restore peace in the community. In difficult situations, arrest may be one means of doing this, but arresting someone may be only a means to an end rather than an end in itself.

The service role is also an important one and consists of many different activities including finding lost children, counselling crime victims, and notifying next of kin in fatal accidents.

Two questions you might ask are: Why do the police have such a broad range of responsibilities? and What, if anything, do these activities have in common? To answer the first question, the following list offers several reasons why the police have the broad responsibilities they do:

1. The police are one of the few public agencies open twenty-four hours a day.
2. In many cases, the police are serving clients that other agencies may not be interested in. The poor, the homeless, and the mentally ill may become police clients almost by default. If no other agency will gather drunks who pass out on downtown streets, the police must do it.
3. The police may not be well informed about, or have access to, other agencies that could handle some of their cases.
4. Historically, the role of the police has been to keep the peace. Sir Robert Peel, the founder of the first municipal police force, in London, England, stressed a service-oriented philosophy, and this tradition has persisted.

Does the justice system discriminate against members of racial minority groups? CITY-TV assignment editor Dwight Drummond attends a public inquiry into his wrongful arrest during a drug bust in October 1993.

The second question—What ties these diverse activities together?—is best answered by looking at two dimensions of the police role. First, the police have the *authority* (and often the duty) to intervene in situations where something must be done immediately. This authority is the same whether the incident is an armed robbery in progress, a naked man standing on a busy street screaming at people, or a complaint that someone's pet boa constrictor has just appeared in someone else's bedroom. Second, the authority is backed up by *non-negotiable force*. If someone refuses to go along with what a police officer suggests, the officer can use force (usually arrest) to back up his or her demands. Even professional caregivers may resort to calling the police when clients refuse to cooperate with them. Once the situation gets into the hands of the police, there may be nobody else to call so the police have to resolve the situation themselves. Egon Bittner has nicely summed up the role of the patrol officer: "What policemen do appears to consist of rushing to the scene of any crisis whatever, judging its needs in accordance with canons of common sense reasoning, and imposing solutions upon it without regard to resistance or opposition" (1980:137).

The Courts

Criminal courts decide the guilt or innocence of those accused of committing a crime. In theory, justice is determined in an adversarial process in which the prosecutor (a lawyer who represents the state) argues that the accused is guilty and the defence lawyer asserts that the accused is innocent. Each side presents its position, the position is debated, and evidence is introduced to support each position. Proponents of the adversarial system feel this system best provides a just decision about guilt or innocence.

The essence of the adversarial system can be seen in the defence lawyer's role, which is to do all he or she can do to help the accused. This role

BOX 6.4 CRITICAL THINKING

Let's Make a Deal: Bargaining for Justice

The image most of us have of the court process is that those who are arrested and charged will go to trial. However, this image is far from the truth. Trials are relatively rare and most cases are decided by guilty pleas. A high proportion, probably the majority, of these guilty pleas result from plea bargaining.

Plea bargaining is the process of negotiating a guilty plea. Informal, private discussions are held between the defence and the prosecution in an attempt to reach a mutually agreeable outcome in which both parties receive concessions. For the accused, plea bargaining may mean that the severity of the penalty will be reduced. For the prosecution, plea bargaining saves time, which is crucial in our overloaded courts. If all cases went to trial, the backlog would be endless. The crown, or prosecuting, attorney may also bargain if the prosecution's case is weak.

Plea bargaining has been widely criticized on the grounds that it subverts the aims of the criminal justice system by rewarding the guilty and penalizing those who elect to maintain their innocence and go to trial.

Plea bargaining has been particularly criticized in cases where guilty people are given light sentences in exchange for testimony against their partners in crime. The twelve-year sentence given to Karla Homolka in exchange for her testimony against Paul Bernardo is an example of this type of bargaining. While the Homolka case was controversial because of her direct involvement with Bernardo's killings, some

was described by Lord Brougham, a British defence lawyer:

> An advocate, in the discharge of his duty, knows but one person in all the world, and that person is his client. To save that client by all means and expedients, and at all hazards and costs to their persons, and amongst them, to himself, is his first and only duty; and in performing this duty he must not regard the alarm, the torments, the destruction which he may bring upon others. Separating the duty of a patriot from that of an advocate, he must go on reckless of the consequences, though it should be his unhappy fate to involve his country in confusion." (cited in Greenspan, 1982:201)

We can add to Lord Brougham's comment that in an adversarial system the defence lawyer is obliged to fulfil this duty to the client without concern for the client's actual guilt or innocence.

Most of those working in the courts strongly defend the adversarial system and see it as one of the cornerstones of a free and democratic society. Many of the procedures that seem to restrict the ability of the court to get at the "truth," such as the rule that accused persons cannot be forced to testify against themselves, were adopted to prevent the arbitrary use of state power against the accused. However, some critics feel that this system does not deal adequately with crime because it places more emphasis on winning than on doing what is best for the accused, for the victim, and for society. Very few people who watched the O.J. Simpson trial could disagree with at least some aspects of this criticism.

Punishment

Punishment **is any action designed to deprive a person of things of value (including liberty) because of some offence the person is thought to have committed** (Barlow, 1987:421). Punishment is seen as serving four functions:

1. *Retribution* imposes a penalty on the offender. Retribution is based on the premise that the punishment should fit the crime: the greater the degree of social harm, the more the offender should be punished.

BOX 6.4

CONTINUED

cases are even more questionable. For example, someone heavily involved in criminal activity can receive a lenient disposition in exchange for information about others who are less involved.

Consider the case of Yves (Apache) Trudeau, for example. A former Hell's Angel, of the notorious Laval, Quebec, chapter, Trudeau is probably the most prolific killer in Canada's history, having admitted to forty-three gang related killings. Yet, he was able to negotiate a plea bargain in which the Crown accepted guilty pleas to forty-three counts of manslaughter and gave a commitment that he would be released with a new identity after serving seven years in jail. Trudeau agreed to cooperate with the police after learning he was the target of other Hell's Angels who had already killed six members of his chapter. In exchange for police protection, a comfortable cell, and a light sentence, Trudeau agreed to tell what he knew about the operation of the Hell's Angels and other Montreal organized crime groups. While the police and prosecutors would argue that plea bargaining was the only way to convict other Hell's Angels and to reduce the influence of the gang, the practice of making deals with killers raises some difficult moral and ethical questions. What are your views about plea bargaining? Do you think that justice is served when deals are made?

Source: Based on Griffiths and Verdun-Jones, 1994; Lavigne, 1987; and Stamler, 1996.

2. *Social protection* results from restricting offenders so they cannot commit further crimes. If someone is in prison, he or she is no longer a threat to those of us on the outside.
3. *Rehabilitation* seeks to return offenders to the community as law-abiding citizens; however, rehabilitation programs are not a priority for governments or prison officials, and the few rehabilitation programs that exist are typically underfunded.
4. *Deterrence* seeks to reduce criminal activity by instilling a fear of punishment. *Specific deterrence* is intended to deter the individual offender from reoffending. For example, a judge may sentence a wife abuser to six months in jail to teach him not to repeat his abuse. *General deterrence* is intended to deter all of us who see the example set by the justice system. For example, a judge may decide that convenience store robberies are getting out of hand and give one offender a severe sentence to set an example for others.

There is no question that the law deters. You do not deliberately park where you know your car will be towed away, and you do not speed if you see a police car behind you. However, the law does not deter as well as we might hope because the *certainty* of being arrested and convicted for most crimes is low. Most crimes do not result in arrests and, perhaps surprisingly, most arrests do not result in convictions. It is difficult to increase the certainty of punishment, so we try to tinker with the severity of punishment instead. Most "law and order" politicians talk about getting tough on crime by increasing penalties rather than by making punishment more certain. However, increasing the average penalty for robbery by a year will not likely reduce robbery rates if most robberies do not result in a conviction and a jail sentence.

We know less about the impact of law as a specific deterrent. That is, does serving a prison sentence make it less likely that a person will commit a crime in the future? While we do know that a large proportion of criminals are *recidivists* (repeat offenders), we do not know how many would repeat if they had not been in prison.

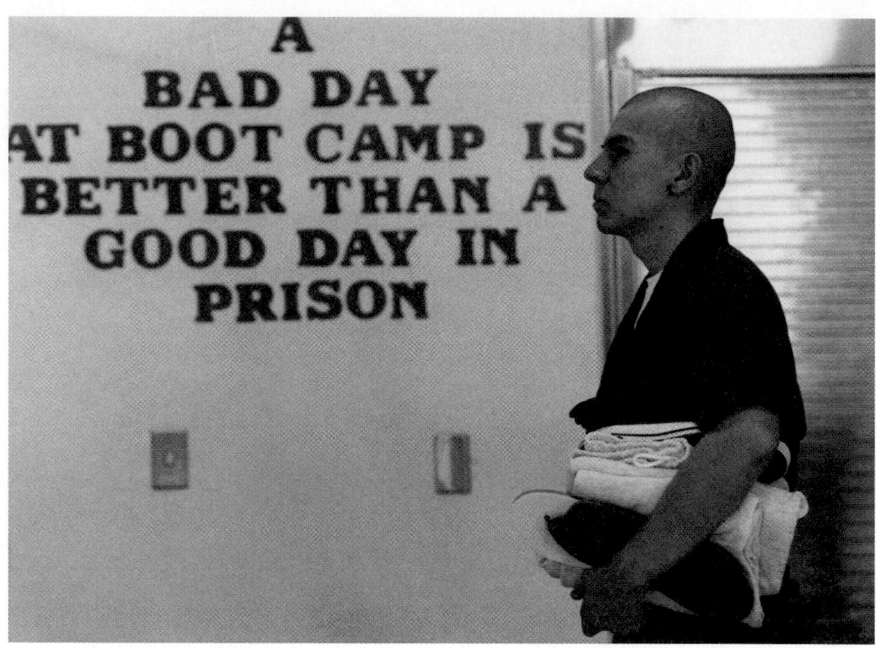

In recent years, military-style boot camps have been used as an alternative to prison and long jail terms, particularly for young offenders. Critics argue that structural solutions—not stop-gap measures—are needed to reduce crime in the future.

Most convicted criminals today are out on either *probation* (supervision of their everyday lives instead of serving a prison term) or *parole* (early release from prison). If offenders violate the conditions of their probation or parole, they may be required to serve their full sentence in prison.

Restorative Justice

For many years, we have relied on the formal justice system to deal with crime. Community members have been discouraged from participating in their own protection and have had little say in the services they received. After the victim called the police dispatcher, the police would soon arrive to take care of the problem, and if an arrest was made, case processing was left in the hands of the formal justice system. Many of those found guilty by the court were removed from the community and sent away to jail. Professionals have controlled each step in the system, and victims and other community members have had little involvement.

While most people have come to accept this as the proper way of dealing with crime, many of those who have been involved with the justice system feel it has failed them. Victims feel left out, as their role as the aggrieved party is forgotten and they are relegated to the role of witnesses. They have no control over the process; often they are not even informed about the disposition of the case. Offenders are also dealt with impersonally. Their crimes become the focus of concern, and their individual circumstances and needs are not considered. Offenders are rarely reminded of the personal harm they have done. Instead, many offenders are sent to costly prisons that result more in alienation than rehabilitation. In addition, the public is often dissatisfied with a justice system that does not respond to their concerns.

Many critics of the present justice system have advocated returning to a fundamentally different way of approaching criminal justice, to a system that is intended to restore social relationships rather than simply to punish (Church Council on Justice and Corrections, 1996). Advocates of *restorative justice* seek to return the focus of the justice system to repairing the harm that has been done to the victim and to the community. A key element of restorative justice is the involvement of the victim and other members of the community as active participants in the process. The focus of the restorative justice approach is to reconcile offenders with those they have harmed and to help communities to reintegrate victims and offenders. Restorative justice has its roots in traditional societies where the restoration of order was crucial to society's survival. In Canada, Aboriginal communities used a variety of different methods, including *circle sentencing*, to resolve disputes. These communities are now leading the way in the return to the use of restorative justice practices with the revival and innovative modification of these traditional practices.

DEVIANCE AND CRIME IN THE FUTURE

Among the questions pertaining to deviance and crime facing us as we enter the twenty-first century are: Is the solution to our "crime problem" more law and order? and, What impact will the global economy have on crime?

Although many Canadians agree that crime is one of our most important problems, they are divided over what to do about it. One thing is clear: the existing criminal justice system cannot solve the "crime problem." If most crimes do not result in arrest, most arrests do not result in convictions, and most convictions do not result in a jail term, the "lock 'em up and throw away the key" approach has little chance of succeeding. Nor does the high rate of recidivism among those who have been incarcerated speak well for the rehabilitative efforts of our existing correctional facilities. We can look to the United States to see a very expensive social experiment. Massive numbers of people are being locked up for very long periods of time and prison populations are increasing much more rapidly than in other countries. Between 1980 and 1990, the American prison population grew by 121 percent, while in Canada the increase was 14 percent (Mihorean and Lipinski, 1992). Since 1990, American prison populations have continued to increase. Many states have passed "three strikes and you're out" laws that impose a mandatory life sentence for anyone convicted of a third felony. Each inmate convicted under these laws will cost about $1.5 million to keep in prison for the rest of his or her life.

An alternative to this approach begins with the realization that the best way to deal with crime is to ensure that it doesn't happen. Instead of longer sentences, military-style boot camps, or other stop-gap measures, *structural solutions*—such as more and better education and jobs, affordable housing, more equality and less discrimination, and socially productive activities—are needed to reduce street crime in the next century. The best approach for reducing delinquency and crime ultimately would be prevention: working with young people *before* they become juvenile offenders, by helping them establish family relationships, build self-esteem, choose a career, and get an education that will give them the foundation for that career.

Perhaps the major trend that will affect the type of crime we will see in the future is the globalization of the economy and of communications. Organized crime has spread from one country to another; the drug trade is a vast international business. With the aid of satellites and computers, financial crimes can be committed from anywhere in the world, and may be almost impossible to punish because of competing jurisdictions and different laws. The reduction of border controls in trading alliances such as the European Community makes it easier for criminals to move from one country to another.

CHAPTER REVIEW

What is deviance?

Deviant behaviour is any act that violates established norms. Deviance varies from culture to culture and in degrees of seriousness. Crime is seriously deviant behaviour that violates written laws and that is punishable by fines, incarceration, or other sanctions.

What is the strain theory of deviance?

Strain theory focuses on the idea that the structure of a society can produce pressures that result in deviant behaviour. When denied legitimate access to cultural goals, such as a good job or nice home, people may engage in illegal behaviour to obtain them. Opportunity theory suggests that access to illegitimate opportunity structures varies, and this access helps determine the nature of the deviance in which a person will engage.

How does social control theory explain crime?

According to social control theory, everyone is capable of committing crimes, but social bonding keeps many from doing so. People bond to society through their attachments to family and to other social institutions such as the church and school. When a person's bonds to society are weakened or broken, the probability of deviant behaviour increases.

BOX 6.5 SOCIOLOGY AND TECHNOLOGY

TECHNOLOGY AND CRIME: ORGANIZED CRIME AND THE INTERNET

For a number of reasons, the fight against organized crime is very difficult. Organized crimes such as drug trafficking and living off the avails of prostitution have no victims who complain, and in others, such as extortion, the victims are too intimidated to go to the police or to testify against those who harm them. Because of the necessity of ethnic ties and the long apprenticeship needed to join organized crime groups, infiltrating these groups is difficult. The very real threat of vengeance makes it unlikely that organized gang members will testify against fellow gang members. One successful method of acquiring evidence has been electronic surveillance. Wiretaps and other listening devices have enabled justice officials to arrest and convict many high-level organized crime leaders including the notorious Mafioso John Gotti, leader of New York's Gambino family.

The rise of the Internet threatens the ability of law enforcement agencies to continue to collect information about organized crime. While the Internet is now not a very private place, new encryption technology now being developed should soon make Internet communication much more secure. Better encryption would speed the development of Internet commerce, as people would be more willing to transact business over the Internet if they knew the information they were sending was secure. However, effective encryption creates an obvious problem for law enforcement: if communications can be securely encrypted, the ability of the police to eavesdrop on organized criminals will be greatly reduced. As a result, police in North America want to restrict the sale of this software and they want the software manufacturers to provide them with the master keys to the encryption codes so that they can freely read Internet communications.

While access to these codes may be helpful for law enforcement agencies, what impact

How do interactionists view the causes of crime?
Differential association theory states that individuals have a greater tendency to deviate from societal norms when they frequently associate with persons who tend toward deviance instead of conformity. According to labelling theory, deviant behaviour is that which is labelled deviant. The process of labelling is related to the relative power and status of those persons who do the labelling and those who are labelled. Those in power may use their power to label the behaviour of others as deviant.

How do conflict and feminist perspectives explain deviance?
Conflict perspectives on deviance examine inequalities in society. According to the critical approach, the legal order protects those with political and economic power and exploits persons from lower classes. Feminist approaches to deviance examine the relationship between gender and deviance. Liberal feminism explains female deviance as a rational response to gender discrimination experienced in work, marriage, and interpersonal relationships. Radical feminism suggests that patriarchy (male domination of females) contributes to female deviance, especially prostitution. Socialist feminism states that exploitation of women by patriarchy and capitalism is related to their involvement in criminal acts such as prostitution and shoplifting.

What are the major types of crime?
Street crime, which includes violent crimes, property crimes, and morals crimes, is a major type of crime. Another is occupational, or white-collar, crime, which consists of illegal activities committed by people in the course of their employment or financial dealings. The two other major types are corporate crime, which includes any illegal acts committed by company employees on behalf of the corporation and with its

BOX 6.5

CONTINUED

would giving this access to them have on society? Bruce Phillips, Canada's privacy commissioner, feels that this would move Canada a step toward becoming a police state. In a report on this issue, Phillips has said it would be like requiring everybody to give the police a key to everybody's homes in case they needed to enter it someday and that it would likely be a violation of the Charter of Rights and Freedoms. Respecting these concerns, the government ultimately decided not to attempt to regulate encryption.

What do you think about this issue? Should there be an absolute right to privacy on the Internet, or does the need for the police to combat organized crime outweigh the individual's right to privacy? Should the police be able to have complete access to encryption keys or should access be regulated by the judiciary in the same way that warrants for searches and wiretaps are now regulated?

In addition to providing a means of communication for organized criminals, the Internet can be used to commit crimes in several other ways. For example, criminals themselves may break encryption programs and use confidential data transmitted by others. The Internet has proved to be a very effective way of distributing pornography, including child pornography. There are also many different types of frauds that can be committed over the Internet. You can look up some of these crimes at **www.scambusters.org** or at **www.ftc.gov/bcp/conline/pubs/alerts/doznalrt.htm.**

Source: Phillips, 1998.

support, and organized crime, which is a business operation that supplies illegal goods and services for profit.

What are our main sources of crime statistics?
Official crime statistics are taken from the Canadian Uniform Crime Reporting survey that lists crimes reported to the police. We also collect information about crime through victimization surveys that interview households to determine the incidence of crimes, including those not reported to police. Studies show that many more crimes are committed than are officially reported.

How are age, sex, and social class related to crime?
Age is a key factor in crime. Persons under 25 have the highest rates of crime. Persons arrested for assault and homicide generally are older, and white-collar criminals usually are older because it takes time to acquire the professional position and skill needed to commit occupational crime. Women have much lower rates of crime than men. Persons from lower socioeconomic backgrounds are more likely to be arrested for violent and property crimes; corporate crime is more likely to occur among upper socioeconomic classes.

How is discretion used in the justice system?
The criminal justice system includes the police, the courts, and prisons. These agencies often have considerable discretion in dealing with offenders. The police often use discretion in deciding whether to act on a situation. Prosecutors and judges use discretion in deciding which cases to pursue and how to handle them.

Key Terms

corporate crime 178
crime 167
deviance 166
differential association theory 171
illegitimate opportunity structures 169
juvenile delinquency 167
labelling theory 172
occupational, or white-collar, crime 177
organized crime 180
primary deviance 173
punishment 188
secondary deviance 173
social bond theory 171
social control 166
strain theory 168
street crime 177

Internet Exercises

1. Go to the Statistics Canada Web pages that list the national crime rate by type of offence (**www.statcan.ca/english/Pgdb/State/Justice/legal02.htm**) and the province-by-province breakdown of crime rates (**www.statcan.ca/english/Pgdb/State/Justice/legal04a.htm**). Compare the province in which you live with other provinces, and then with the national average, with respect to different crimes.
2. Go to the *New York Times* Web site (**www.nytimes.com**) and *The Globe and Mail* Web site (**www.TheGlobeAndMail.com**) and find articles containing the word *hacker*. Read some of the articles and decide which deviance theory (or theories) best describes how reporters from these newspapers view hackers and hacking.
3. Governments in Canada have begun to place a higher priority on the prevention of crime. The Web page of the National Crime Prevention Council (**www.crime-prevention.org/ncpc**) has a section called Prevention Databases. Look at three of the programs in the Urban Safety category. Do you think these programs have the potential to reduce crime in your community? Do you know of any similar activities in your community?

Net Links

For more Web links related to the topic of this chapter, see the Nelson sociology Web site: **www.sociologyessentials-2nded.nelson.com**.

To read about restorative justice issues, visit the site of Transformative Justice Australia at:

www.tja.com.au

Blue Line magazine is intended for police audiences and looks at a variety of issues concerning Canadian policing. Its address is:

www.blueline.ca

Many jurisdictions still have outdated or strange laws on their books. Read some of them at:

www.dumblaws.com

Look at Canada's Criminal Code. You can read the way each offence is defined and look at the maximum penalties at:

http://insight.mcmaster.ca/org/efc/pages/law/cc/cc.html

Read recent news about criminal justice and Canadian research in policing and corrections at the Web site of the Solicitor General of Canada:

www.sgc.gc.ca

Questions for Critical Thinking

1. What factors account for the increase in organized crime throughout the world? How can society best deal with this type of crime?
2. Should so-called victimless crimes, such as prostitution and recreational drug use, be decriminalized? Do these crimes harm society?
3. Several commissions have recommended that Aboriginal people have a separate justice system. Do you agree? How do you think such a system would operate?
4. As a sociologist armed with a sociological imagination, how do you propose to deal with the problem of crime in Canada? What programs would you suggest enhancing? What programs would you reduce?

Suggested Readings

These books provide additional insights into many of the crime and justice issues discussed in this chapter:

Margaret Beare. *Criminal Conspiracies: Organized Crime in Canada*. Toronto: Nelson Canada, 1996.

James Dubro. *Mob Rule: Inside the Canadian Mafia*. Toronto: Macmillan, 1985.

Thomas Fleming. *The New Criminologies in Canada: State, Crime and Control*. Toronto: Oxford University Press, 1985.

Thomas Gabor. *Everybody Does It! Crime by the Public*. Toronto: University of Toronto Press, 1994.

Curt T. Griffiths and Simon N. Verdun-Jones. *Canadian Criminal Justice* (2nd ed.). Toronto: Harcourt Brace and Company, 1994.

James C. Hackler. *Crime and Canadian Public Policy*. Scarborough: Prentice Hall, 1994.

Allen C. Hamilton and C. Murray Sinclair. *Report of the Aboriginal Justice Inquiry of Manitoba, Vol. 1*. Winnipeg: Queen's Printer, 1994.

Holly Johnson. *Dangerous Domains: Violence Against Women in Canada*. Toronto: Nelson Canada, 1996.

Leslie W. Kennedy and Vincent F. Sacco. *Crime Counts: A Criminal Event Analysis*. Toronto: Nelson Canada, 1997.

Yves Lavigne. *Hell's Angels: Taking Care of Business*. Toronto: Ballantine Books, 1987.

Rick Linden. *Criminology: A Canadian Perspective* (4th ed.). Toronto: Harcourt Brace and Company, 2000.

Chris McCormick. *Constructing Danger: The Mis/Representation of Crime in the News*. Halifax: Fernwood Publishing, 1995.

Robert Silverman and Leslie Kennedy. *Deadly Deeds: Murder in Canada*. Scarborough: Nelson Canada, 1993.

Laureen Snider. *Bad Business: Corporate Crime in Canada*. Scarborough: Nelson Canada, 1993.

Daniel Wolf. *The Rebels: A Brotherhood of Outlaw Bikers*. Toronto: University of Toronto Press, 1991.

INFOTRAC® COLLEGE EDITION

Either from the *Sociology In Our Times: The Essentials* Web site (**www.sociologyessentials-2nded.nelson.com**) or directly from your Web browser, you may access InfoTrac® College Edition, an online university library that includes over 600 popular and scholarly journals in which you can find articles related to the topics in this chapter.

CHAPTER 7

Sally is a 29-year-old single mother who lives with her 8-year-old son Sean in Toronto. She is one of many Canadians who has experienced downward mobility—moving from a comfortable middle-class lifestyle to a life of poverty. Sally talks about her life in a motel, her struggle to survive, and the impact of poverty on her young son:

"He just hates it. He's not used to living like this. My son always had the best of everything; now from the best of everything he's got nothing.

"… Every time I look at Sean I think no, I can't let myself down or this kid's even gonna suffer more. This kid's seen more in his eight years. At his age I'd never seen half of this … This is no place for a child at all. There's prostitutes. I hear a lot of fights … I look at myself and Sean and I think at eight years old I'd had no worries … If Sean needs a pair of shoes or boots, well, I got him a pair of boots for $4 over there [the Goodwill Store] and a jacket. I had to say "Well Sean, you need your winter coat, your winter boots so like no, I can't buy this kind of meat and no, I can't buy jam 'cause we need that for your winter boots." (O'Reilly-Fleming, 1993:147–149)

SOCIAL STRATIFICATION AND CLASS

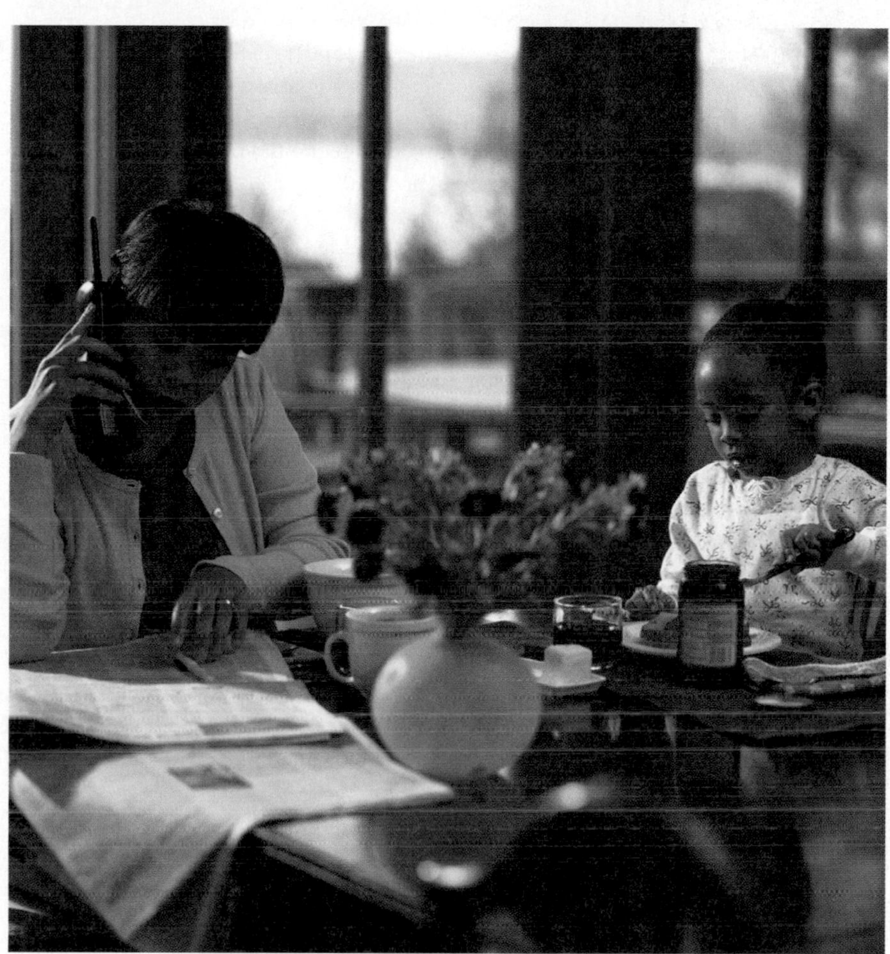

When we examine social stratification and social inequality in Canada, it becomes apparent that Sally and Sean's situation is not unique. Poverty affects people's lives, their sense of self, and their most important relationships with others. The emotional, physical, and social toll that poverty takes is most apparent among children. The evidence suggests that the years spent in childhood poverty will have long term consequences for the life chances of children like Sean. The most recent estimates indicate that 1.4 million of Canada's children were growing up poor (Ross, 1998). Children represent more than one-quarter of our poor and the child poverty rate in Canada is the second highest in the industrialized world, topped only by that of the United States (Duffy and Mandell, 1996). In 1989, the House of Commons unanimously resolved "to seek to achieve the goal of eliminating poverty among Canadian children by the year 2000" (Hughes, 1995:779). At that time, just over 15 percent of Canadian children were living in poverty. Today the child poverty rates have risen to 20 percent. What factors have contributed to this distressing pattern? In this chapter we will attempt to answer this question by examining more closely the relationship between social stratification, social inequality, and child poverty.

Before reading on, test your knowledge of poverty in Canada by taking the quiz in Box 7.1.

QUESTIONS AND ISSUES

CHAPTER FOCUS QUESTION:
How are the lives of Canadians affected by social stratification?

How do prestige, power, and wealth determine social class?

What role does ownership of resources play in a conflict perspective on class structure?

How are social stratification and poverty linked?

What is the extent of social inequality in Canada?

WHAT IS SOCIAL STRATIFICATION?

***Social stratification* refers to the persistent patterns of social inequality within a society, perpetuated by the manner in which wealth, power, and prestige are distributed and passed on from one generation to the next** (Krahn, 1995b). Sociologists examine the social groups that make up the hierarchy in a society and seek to determine how inequalities are structured and persist over time (Jary and Jary, 1991).

Max Weber's term ***life chances* describes the extent to which persons within a particular layer of stratification have access to important scarce resources.** *Resources* are anything valued in a society, ranging from money and property to medical care and education; they are considered to be scarce because of their unequal distribution among social categories. If we think about the valued resources available in Canada, Sally's life chances are readily apparent. As one analyst suggested, "Poverty narrows and closes life chances. The victims of poverty experience a kind of arteriosclerosis of opportunity. Being poor not only means economic insecurity, it also wreaks havoc on one's mental and physical health" (Ropers, 1991:25). Our life chances are intertwined with our class, race, gender, and age.

All societies distinguish among people by age. Young children typically have less authority and responsibility than older persons. Older persons, especially those without wealth or power, may find themselves at the bottom of the social hierarchy. Similarly, all societies differentiate between females and males: women often are treated as subordinate to men. Age and gender are examples of *ascribed status*—that is, a status that is assigned to an individual, typically at birth. Ascribed status is not chosen or earned and cannot be changed. Can you think of other ascribed statuses you may have?

Individuals are also ranked on the basis of *achieved status*—a changeable status that is achieved on the basis of how well an individual performs in a particular role. Examples of achieved statuses are occupational statuses such as accountant, lawyer, professor, as well as other earned roles such as mother, husband, Olympic athlete, or armed robber. There is an element of choice in each of these roles. Can you identify your achieved statuses? The degree of significance of achieved and ascribed statuses will vary in different systems of stratification.

GLOBAL SYSTEMS OF STRATIFICATION

One of the most important characteristics of systems of stratification is their degree of flexibility. Sociologists distinguish among such systems based on the extent to which they are open or closed. In an open system, the boundaries between levels in the hierarchies are more flexible and may be influenced (positively or negatively) by people's achieved statuses. Open systems are assumed to have some degree of social mobility. ***Social mobility* is the movement of individuals or groups from one level in a stratification system to another** (Rothman, 1993). This movement can be either upward or downward. ***Intergenerational mobility* is the social movement experienced by family members from one generation to the next.** By contrast, ***intragenerational mobility* is the social movement of individuals within their own lifetime.** In a *closed system*, the boundaries between levels in the hierarchies of social stratification are rigid, and people's positions are set by ascribed status.

Open and closed systems are ideal-type constructs; no actual stratification system is completely open or closed. The systems of stratification we will examine—caste and class—are characterized by different hierarchical structures and varying degrees of mobility. Let's examine these systems of stratification to determine how people acquire their positions in each and what potential for social movement they have.

The Caste System

Caste is a closed system of social stratification. A ***caste system* is a system of social inequality in which people's status is permanently determined at birth based on their parents' ascribed characteristics.** Vestiges of caste systems exist in contemporary India and South Africa.

In India, caste is based in part on occupation; thus, families typically perform the same type of

BOX 7.1 SOCIOLOGY AND EVERYDAY LIFE

How Much Do You Know about Poverty in Canada?

TRUE	FALSE	
T	F	1. Winning the war on poverty is an unrealistic goal.
T	F	2. Individuals over the age of 65 have the highest rate of poverty.
T	F	3. Men account for two out of every three impoverished adults in Canada.
T	F	4. Most poor children live in female-headed, single-parent households.
T	F	5. The Canadian cities with the highest rates of child poverty are Winnipeg, Montreal, and Saskatoon.
T	F	6. Poverty is predominantly a rural phenomenon.
T	F	7. A large proportion of people receiving social assistance are able to work.
T	F	8. Children living in poverty are more likely to be abused and/or neglected.
T	F	9. A number of people living below the official poverty line have full-time jobs.
T	F	10. Welfare benefits provide enough income for recipients to live comfortably.

Answers on page 200.

work from generation to generation. By contrast, the caste system of South Africa was based on racial classifications and the belief of white South Africans (Afrikaners) that they were morally superior to the black majority. Until the 1990s, the Afrikaners controlled the government, the police, and the military by enforcing ***apartheid*—the separation of the races.** Blacks were denied full citizenship and restricted to segregated hospitals, schools, residential neighbourhoods, and other facilities. Whites held almost all of the desirable jobs; blacks worked as manual labourers and servants.

Cultural beliefs and values sustain caste systems. In India, the Hindu religion reinforced the caste system by teaching that people should accept their fate in life and work hard as a moral duty. Caste systems grow weaker as societies industrialize; the values reinforcing the system break down, and people start to focus on the types of skills needed for industrialization.

"Social stratification" may seem to be an abstract concept, but it is an everyday reality for these individuals, who are spending the night at a shelter.

The Class System

The ***class system* is a type of stratification based on the ownership and control of resources and on the type of work people do** (Rothman, 1993). At least theoretically, a class system is more open than a caste system because the boundaries between classes are less distinct than the boundaries between castes. In a class system, status comes at least partly through achievement rather than entirely by ascription.

In class systems, people may become members of a class other than that of their parents through both

BOX 7.1

Answers to the Sociology Quiz on Poverty

1. **False.** Statistics Canada estimated that the cost of bringing all poor people out of poverty in 1996 would have been $17.8 billion. According to the National Council of Welfare that is a huge but not outrageous amount of money relative to government spending in Canada.
2. **False.** As a group, children have a higher rate of poverty than the elderly. Government programs such as old age security are indexed to inflation, while many of the programs for the young have been scaled back or eliminated. However, many elderly individuals do live in poverty.
3. **False.** Women, not men, account for two out of three impoverished adults in Canada. Reasons for this include lack of job opportunities for women, lower pay for women than men for comparable jobs, lack of affordable day-care for children, and sexism in the workplace.
4. **False.** In 1997, 735,000 poor children were living in two-parent families, compared with 571,000 in female-headed single-parent households. However, the *rate* of poverty is highest for female-headed single-parent families.
5. **True.** In these three cities, one-quarter of preschool-aged children are poor.
6. **False.** Images of poverty as a rural phenomenon are out of date. In 1997, 57 percent of all poor families in Canada lived in a city with a population of 500,000 or more.
7. **False.** According to one widely held stereotype, the poor are lazy and do not want to work. In reality only a fraction of welfare recipients are able-bodied adults who are capable of working. Rather than looking at the structural characteristics of society, people cite the alleged personal attributes of the poor as the reason for their plight.
8. **True.** A literature review on poverty and child abuse concluded that poverty debilitates families and can be a "catalyst and intensifier of child maltreatment" (Volpe, 1989:12).
9. **True.** Many of those who fall below the official poverty line are referred to as the "working poor" because they work full time but earn such low wages that they are considered to be impoverished.
10. **False.** Welfare payments across Canada fall far below the low-income cut-offs.

Sources: Based on Harman, 1995; Lochhead and Shillington, 1996; National Council of Welfare, 1999; and Volpe, 1989.

intergenerational and intragenerational mobility, either upward or downward. *Horizontal mobility* occurs when people experience a gain or loss in position and/or income that does not produce a change in their place in the class structure. For example, a person may get a pay increase and a more prestigious title but still not move from one class to another. In contrast, movement up or down the class structure is *vertical mobility*.

In Canadian society we are socialized to believe that hard work is the key to personal success. Conversely, we are also taught that individuals who fail, who do not achieve success, do so as a result of their own personal inadequacies. Poverty is attributable to personal defect and it is up to the individual to find a way to break the "cycle of poverty." Do you agree? Or do you think structural factors in Canadian society affect the degree of success individuals achieve? We will look at the ideals versus the realities of social mobility as we continue to examine the class structure in Canada.

CLASSICAL PERSPECTIVES ON SOCIAL CLASS

Early sociologists grappled with the definition of class and the criteria for determining people's location within the class structure. Both Karl Marx and Max Weber viewed class as an important determi-

FIGURE 7.1 Marx's View of Stratification

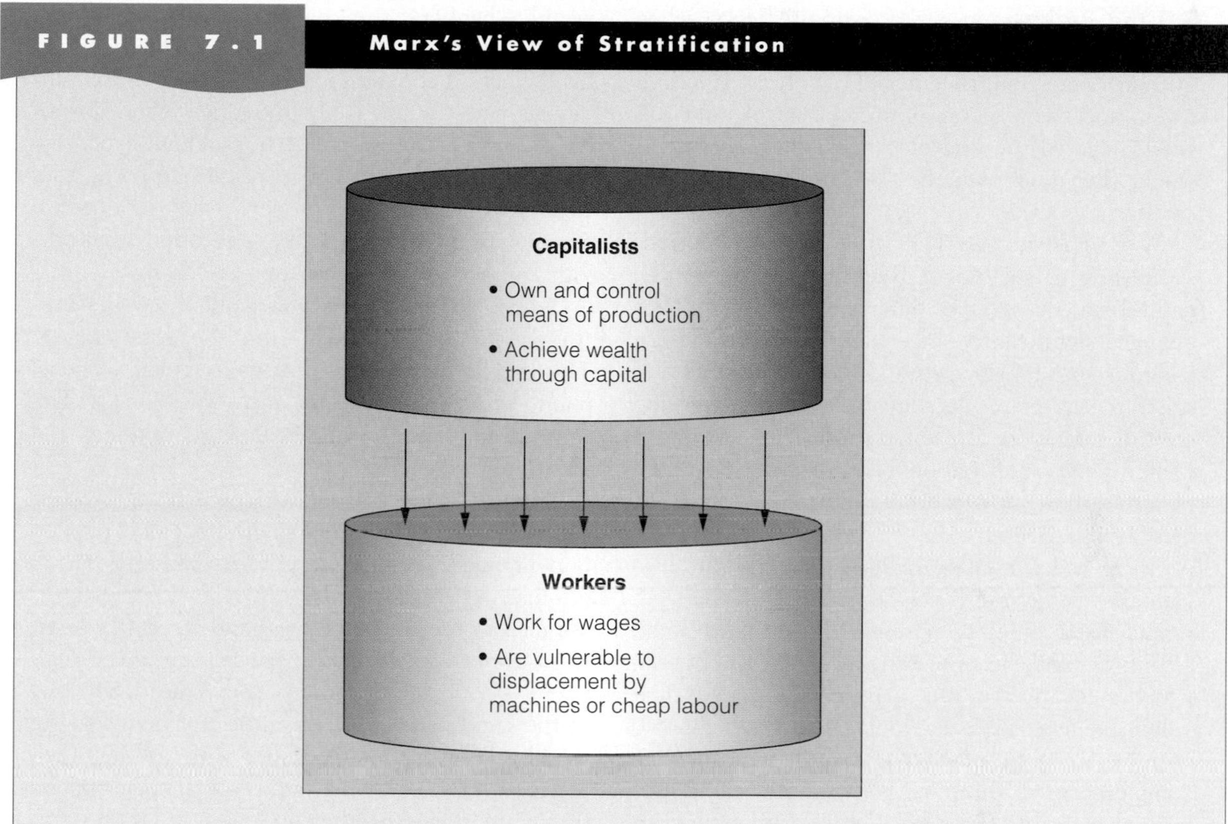

nant of social inequality and social change, and their works have had a profound influence on contemporary class theory.

Karl Marx: Relation to Means of Production

For Karl Marx, class position is determined by people's work situation, or relationship to the means of production. As previously discussed, Marx suggested that capitalistic societies are composed of two classes—the capitalists and the workers. The ***capitalist class,*** or ***bourgeoisie,*** **consists of those who own the means of production**—the land and capital necessary for factories and mines, for example. The ***working class,*** or ***proletariat,*** **consists of those who must sell their labour to the owners in order to earn enough money to survive** (see Figure 7.1).

According to Marx, class relationships involve inequality and exploitation. The workers are exploited as capitalists maximize their profits by paying workers less than the resale value of what they produce but do not own. This exploitation results in workers' ***alienation*****—a feeling of powerlessness and estrangement from other people and oneself.** As mechanization reduces the cost of producing products and machines replace many workers, the newly created surplus of workers becomes a "reserve army." These unemployed workers, who are a readily available source of cheap labour, can be used by capitalists as a "weapon" against employees who demand pay raises or better working conditions. The presence of the reserve army keeps wages low and creates even greater profits for members of the capitalist class.

In Marx's view, the capitalist class maintained its position at the top of the class structure by control of the society's *superstructure*, which is composed of the government, schools, churches, and other social institutions that produce and disseminate ideas perpetuating the existing system of exploitation.

Marx predicted that the exploitation of workers by the capitalist class ultimately would lead to ***class conflict*****—the struggle between the capitalist class**

and the working class. According to Marx, when the workers realized that capitalists were the source of their oppression, they would overthrow the capitalists and their agents of social control, and this would lead to the end of capitalism. The workers would then take over the state and create a more egalitarian society.

Why has no workers' revolution occurred? According to sociologist Ralf Dahrendorf (1959), capitalism may have persisted because it has changed significantly since Marx's time. Individual capitalists no longer own and control factories and other means of production; today, ownership and control largely have been separated. For example, contemporary multinational corporations are owned by a multitude of stockholders but run by paid officers and managers.

Marx had a number of important insights into capitalist societies. First, he recognized the economic basis of class systems (Gilbert and Kahl, 1993). Second, he noted the relationship between people's location in the class structure and their values, beliefs, and behaviour. Finally, he acknowledged that classes may have opposing (rather than complementary) interests. For example, capitalists' best interests are served by a decrease in labour costs and other expenses and a corresponding increase in profit; workers' best interests are served by well-paid jobs, safe working conditions, and job security.

Max Weber: Wealth, Prestige, and Power

Max Weber agreed with Marx's assertion that economic factors are important in understanding individual and group behaviour. However, Weber emphasized that no one factor (such as economic divisions between capitalists and workers) was sufficient for defining people's location within the class structure. As a result, he developed a multidimensional approach to social stratification that focused on the interplay among wealth, prestige, and power in determining a person's class position.

***Wealth* is the value of all of a person's or family's economic assets, including income, personal property, and income-producing property.** Weber placed people who have a similar level of wealth and income in the same class. For example, the privileged commercial class of *entrepreneurs*—wealthy bankers, ship owners, professionals, and merchants who possess similar financial resources—have much in common with *rentiers*—wealthy individuals who live off their investments and do not have to work. Both are able to purchase expensive consumer items, control other people's opportunities to acquire wealth and property, and monopolize costly status privileges (such as education) that provide contacts and skills for their children.

Weber divided those who work for wages into two classes: the middle class and the working class. The middle class consists of white-collar workers, public officials, managers, and professionals. The working class consists of skilled, semiskilled, and unskilled workers.

***Prestige* is the respect with which a person or status position is regarded by others.** Fame, respect, honour, and esteem are the most common forms of prestige. A person who has a high level of prestige is assumed to receive deferential and respectful treatment from others. Weber suggested that individuals who share a common level of social prestige belong to the same status group regardless of their level of wealth. They tend to socialize with one another, marry within their own group of social equals, spend their leisure time together, and safeguard their status by restricting outsiders' opportunities to join their ranks (Beeghley, 1996).

***Power* is the ability of people or groups to achieve their goals despite opposition from others.** The powerful shape society in accordance with their own interests and direct the actions of others (Tumin, 1953). Social power in modern societies is held by bureaucracies; individual power depends on a person's position within the bureaucracy. Weber suggested that the power of modern bureaucracies was so strong that even a workers' revolution (as predicted by Marx) would not lessen social inequality (Hurst, 1992).

Wealth, prestige, and power are separate continuums on which people can be ranked from high to low, as shown in Figure 7.2. Individuals may be high on one dimension and low on another. For example, people may be very wealthy but have little political power. They also may have prestige but not wealth. In Weber's multidimensional approach, people are ranked on all three dimensions.

Although power, wealth, and prestige are independent of one another, one may be used to acquire the others. Wealth, for example, can be used to gain

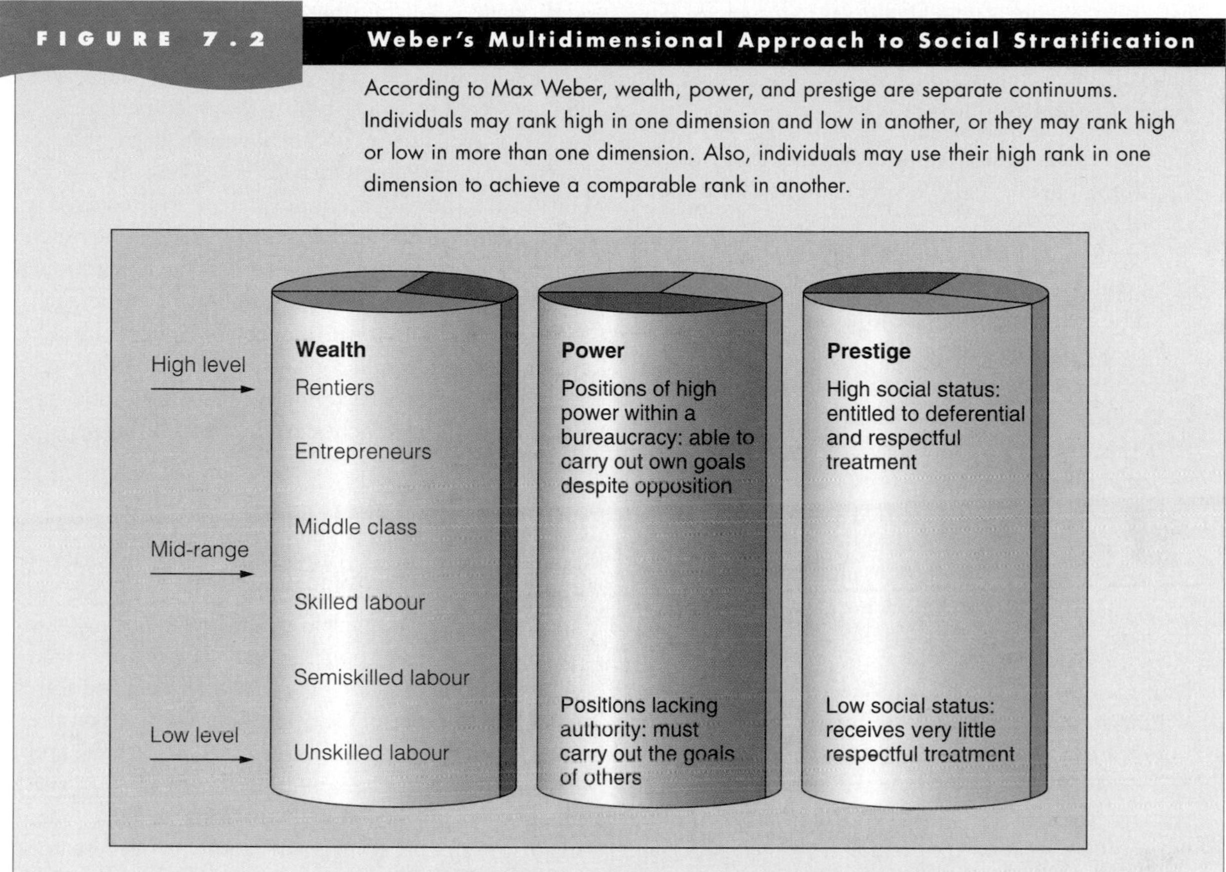

FIGURE 7.2 Weber's Multidimensional Approach to Social Stratification

According to Max Weber, wealth, power, and prestige are separate continuums. Individuals may rank high in one dimension and low in another, or they may rank high or low in more than one dimension. Also, individuals may use their high rank in one dimension to achieve a comparable rank in another.

power or prestige; the "charitable rich" in Canada acquire prestige by their financial contributions to and voluntary activities on behalf of nonprofit groups, such as symphony orchestras, museums, hospitals, and charities (Odendahl, 1990). Similarly, people may use their prestige to gain wealth. For example, celebrity athletes and entertainers often make their fortunes by endorsing products.

Weber's analysis of social stratification contributes to our understanding by emphasizing that people behave according to both their economic interests and their values. He added to Marx's insights by developing a multidimensional explanation of the class structure and identifying additional classes. Both Marx and Weber emphasized that capitalists and workers are the primary players in a class society, and both noted the importance of class to people's life chances. However, they saw different futures for capitalism and the social system. Marx saw these structures being overthrown; Weber saw the increasing bureaucratization of life even without capitalism.

SOCIOLOGICAL EXPLANATIONS OF SOCIAL INEQUALITY

Why are all societies stratified? The functionalist perspective sees inequality as an inevitable and even necessary feature of society. The conflict perspective, influenced by Karl Marx, sees inequality as avoidable, unnecessary, and the source of most human conflict. Gerhard Lenski (1966) has offered a third approach that combines elements of both functionalism and conflict theory.

Functionalist Perspectives

Fifty years ago, Kingsley Davis and Wilbert Moore developed a theory of social stratification that has been debated ever since. Davis and Moore (1945) suggested that social inequality is not only universal but also functionally necessary for all societies. How can social inequality be beneficial to a society? The *Davis–Moore thesis*, which has become the definitive functionalist explanation for social inequality, can be summarized as follows:

1. All societies have important tasks that must be accomplished and certain positions that must be filled.
2. Some positions are more important for the survival of society than others.
3. The most important positions must be filled by the most qualified people.
4. The positions that are the most important for society and that require scarce talent, extensive training, or both, must be the most highly rewarded.
5. The most highly rewarded positions should be those that are functionally unique (no other position can perform the same function) and on which other positions rely for expertise, direction, or financing.

Davis and Moore use the physician as an example of a functionally unique position. Doctors are very important to society and require extensive training, but individuals would not be motivated to go through years of costly and stressful medical training without incentives to do so. The Davis–Moore thesis assumes that social stratification results in ***meritocracy*—a hierarchy in which all positions are rewarded based on people's ability and credentials.**

An important contribution of the Davis–Moore thesis is that it directs attention to the distribution of social prestige based on occupation. Yet occupational prestige rankings may not actually be based on the importance of a position to society. The highest ratings may be given to professionals—such as physicians and lawyers—because they have many years of training in their fields and some control of their own work, not because these positions contribute the most to society. According to some scholars, members of the medical profession have created a professional monopoly that has contributed significantly to their income and prestige throughout most of the past hundred years (see Freidson, 1970, 1986; Starr, 1982).

Critics have suggested that the Davis–Moore thesis ignores inequalities based on inherited wealth and intergenerational family status (Rossides, 1986). The thesis assumes that economic rewards and prestige are the only effective motivators for people and fails to take into account other intrinsic aspects of work, such as self-fulfillment (Tumin, 1953). It also does not adequately explain how such a reward system guarantees that the most qualified people will gain access to the most highly rewarded positions.

What about people who have not been able to maximize their talents and skills because they were born in impoverished circumstances and received a substandard education (see Kozol, 1991)? The functionalist approach generally ignores such questions because it does not consider structural factors (such as racial discrimination, lack of job opportunities, and inadequate funding of many schools) that may contribute to the persistence of inequality in society. Some conflict approaches attempt to fill this gap.

Conflict Perspectives

Conflict approaches, especially those based on Marxist theories, identify ownership or nonownership of the means of production as the distinguishing feature of classes. From this perspective, classes are social groups organized around property ownership and control of the workplace. Conflict theory is based on the assumption that social stratification is created and maintained by one group in order to protect and enhance its own economic interests. Societies are organized around classes in conflict over scarce resources. Stratification exists only because the rich and powerful are determined to hang on to more than their share of scarce resources. Inequality results from the more powerful exploiting the less powerful.

From a conflict perspective, people with economic and political power are able to shape and distribute the rewards, resources, privileges, and opportunities in society for their own benefit. Conflict theorists do not believe that inequality serves as a motivating force for people; they argue that powerful individuals and groups use ideology to maintain their favoured positions at the expense of others. A stratified social system is accepted because of the dominant ideology of the society, the set of beliefs that explain and justify the existing social order (Marchak, 1975). Core values in Canada emphasize the importance of material possessions, hard work, individual initiative to get ahead, and behaviour that supports the existing social structure. These same values support the prevailing resource distribution system and contribute to social inequality.

Conflict theorists note that laws and informal social norms also support inequality in Canada. For the first half of the twentieth century, for example, both legalized and institutionalized segregation and discrimination reinforced employment discrimination and produced higher levels of economic inequality. Although laws have been passed to make these overt acts of discrimination illegal, many forms of discrimination still exist in educational and employment opportunities.

The Evolutionary Approach

Gerhard Lenski (1966) developed a theory of power and privilege to explain social stratification and inequality. Lenski's theory, referred to as the *evolutionary approach*, combined elements from both conflict theory and functionalism. Lenski focused on the concept of ruling elites in society and how they managed to maintain control over society's wealth and power (Krahn, 1995b).

Lenski begins with the idea that people generally are more rewarded by fulfilling their own wants and ambitions rather than by addressing the needs of others. He acknowledged that it may be possible to socialize human beings so that they do not behave in this way, but he also pointed out that it remains an almost universal feature of social life. Most of the things that people want (wealth, power, prestige) are scarce. Therefore, some conflict over how these limited resources are distributed is inevitable. The result is social inequality. Sometimes this inequality is functional for a society. However, Lenski points out, forms of stratification persist long after their functional benefit has ended. As a result, most societies are much more stratified than they need to be (Robertson, 1977).

Lenski traced the evolution of social stratification and argued that the type and form it takes is related to the society's means of economic production or technological base. Lenski shows how the nature of stratification varies from one type of society to another.

Hunting and Gathering Societies People in these societies depend on materials taken directly from nature for their food, clothing, and shelter. Their technology consists of primitive tools and members of these societies are nomadic—as soon as local resources are used up, they move on in pursuit of more. In simple hunting and gathering societies, the few resources of the society were distributed primarily on the basis of need. There is no surplus wealth, and therefore no opportunity for some people to become wealthier than others. Consequently, hunting and gathering societies are the least stratified, especially in the dimensions of property and power. The main criteria for inequality in these societies are age and sex. But the overall stratification system is simple and fairly egalitarian.

Simple Horticultural Societies As societies became more technologically complex, more resources were produced than were needed to fulfil the basic needs of the society. It is possible to accumulate property in horticultural societies because people are not having to move when resources are depleted. In these societies "specialists," such as producers of harpoons, canoes, drums, or art, appear for the first time. With increasing specialization comes increased inequality as some roles are assigned more prestige or power than others. In horticultural and pastoral societies a surplus product is available and chieftainships emerge as powerful families obtain control over surplus—an advantage also known as *resources privilege*. As a result, differences in property, power, and prestige among members are marked.

Agricultural Societies These societies are much larger and richer, and much more specialized and stratified than are simple horticultural societies. The primary reason for these differences is related to technological advancement—specifically the production of metal tools. The metal plough dramatically increased yields from farming. Because a small number of farmers can produce enough food to support a large number of people, a relatively small portion of the population needs to be involved in food production. The most important consequence of increased productivity is the creation of permanent armies and elaborate governmental structures. A number of governmental levels are created—from the king down to the local village headman. In simple horticultural societies a great deal of wealth is based on the accumulation of wives. With advances in production, it becomes profitable to own people in order to gain the surplus wealth from their labour. It is in these societies that slavery first appears. Cattle, land, slaves, and even primitive forms of money can be passed from one generation to another. Therefore, each generation can accumulate more wealth through inheritance. These societies are the first to exhibit hereditary classes and very marked inequalities of power, property, and prestige. The more complex agricultural societies developed highly structured governing and tax collecting systems through which the ruling elites accumulated wealth at the expense of the less privileged, resulting in increasing social stratification (Robertson, 1977).

Industrial Societies In their earliest form, industrial societies had similar stratification systems to that of agricultural societies. However, as the result of industrialization and increasingly complex technology, the trend toward increasing inequality was reversed (Lenski, 1966). Industrial societies became less stratified than agricultural societies and this trend has continued. This is because the owners of the means of production, the ruling elite, could no longer control the production process directly and were forced to rely on educated managers and specialized technical workers to maintain production. This change reduced the power of the ruling classes. Individuals and groups were introduced to ideas of democracy, which led them to demand a larger share of the profits they were helping to produce (Krahn, 1995b). The ruling elite gave in to these demands because they could not produce without the educated, skilled workers. Furthermore, industrialized societies are much more productive—therefore there is more wealth to divide (Lenski, 1966; Robertson, 1977). In industrial societies the importance of ascribed status is diminished while achieved status is emphasized.

INEQUALITY IN CANADA

Throughout human history, people have argued about the distribution of scarce resources in society. Disagreements often centre on whether the share we get is a fair reward for our efforts and hard work (Braun, 1991). Recently, social analysts have pointed out that the old maxim—the rich get richer—continues to apply in Canada and across North America. To understand how this happens, we first must take a look at the distribution of income and wealth in this country.

Distribution of Income and Wealth

Money is essential for acquiring goods and services. People without money cannot purchase food, shelter, clothing, medical care, legal services, education, and the other things they need or desire. Money—in the form of both income and wealth—is very unevenly distributed in Canada. Among the industrialized nations of North America and Europe, Canada has one of the worst records of income inequality, second only to that of the United States (McQuaig, 1993).

Income *Income* is the economic gain derived from wages, salaries, income transfers (governmental aid such as social assistance, Canada Pension Plan payments), and ownership of property (Beeghley, 1989).

Dennis Gilbert and Joseph Kahl (1993:93) compare the distribution of income to a "national pie that has been sliced into portions, ranging in size from stingy to generous, for distribution among segments of the population." One way of measuring income inequality is to divide the population into five equal groups or *quintiles*, and to indicate the share of total income received by each group. As shown in Figure 7.3, in 1996 the wealthiest 20 percent of households received over 40 percent of the total income "pie," while the poorest 20 percent of households received less than 5 percent of all income (Statistics Canada, 1996f). The top 10 percent had average incomes more than ten times greater than the poorest 10 percent (Campaign 2000, 1998). Figure 7.3 also reveals the remarkable stability of income distribution over time.

There is considerable regional variation in income in Canada. As shown in Map 7.1, the average family income is highest in Ontario, British Columbia, and Alberta and lowest in the Atlantic provinces.

Wealth Income is only one aspect of wealth. Wealth includes property such as buildings, land, farms, houses, factories, and cars, as well as other assets such as money in bank accounts, corporate stocks, bonds, and insurance policies. Wealth is computed by subtracting all debt obligations and converting the remaining assets into cash. For most people in Canada, wealth is invested primarily in property that generates no income, such as a house or a car. In contrast, the wealth of an elite minority often is in the form of income-producing property.

Research on the distribution of wealth in Canada reveals that wealth is more unevenly distributed among the Canadian population than is income. For the upper class, wealth often comes from inheritance. The majority of the wealthiest people in Canada are inheritors, with some at least three or four generations removed from the original fortune (Dyck, 1996). The combined wealth of a small number of Canada's richest individuals and families, shown in

FIGURE 7.3 **Percentage Distribution of Total Income of Families and Unattached Individuals by Quintiles, Canada, 1951–1996**

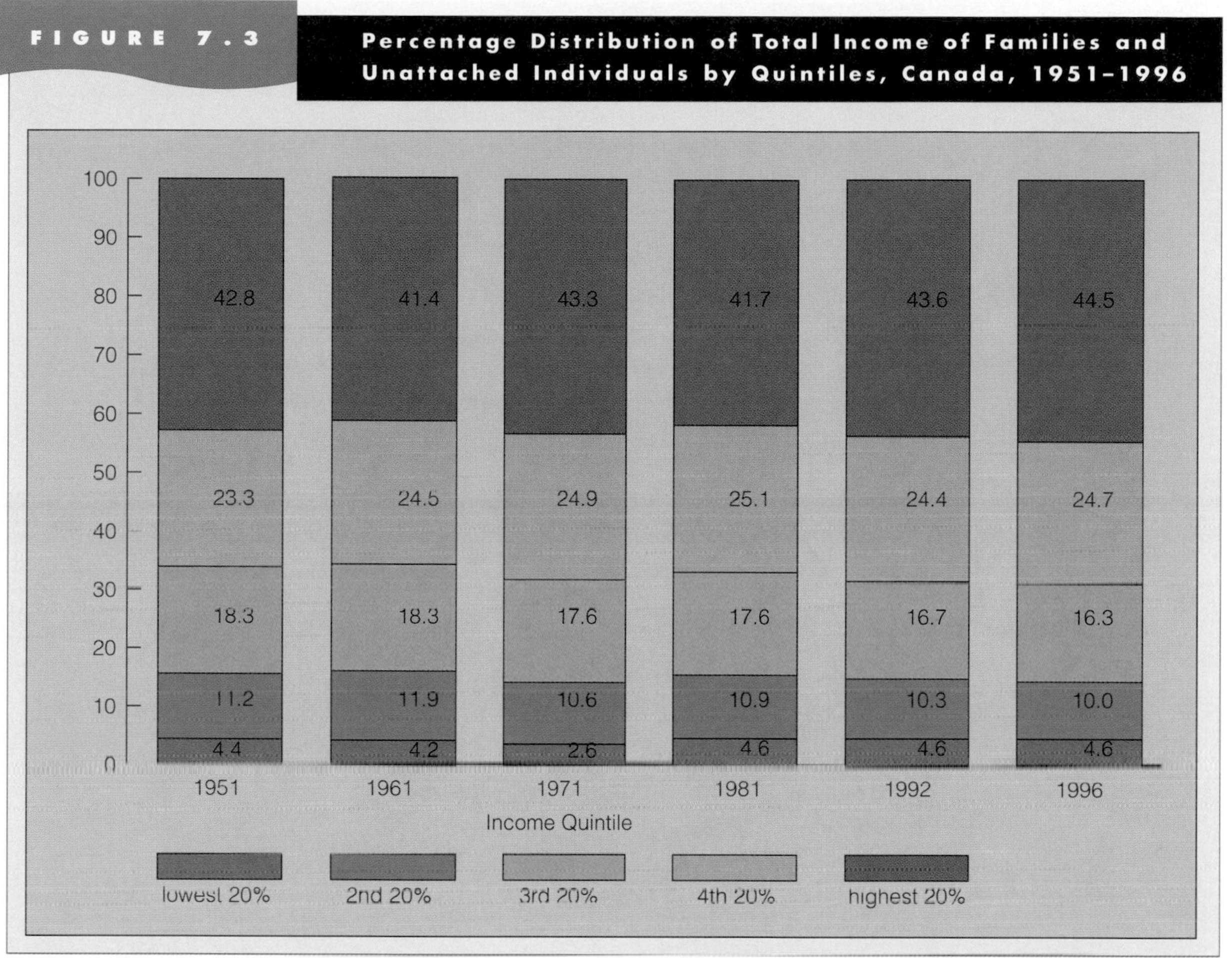

Reproduced by authority of the Minister of Industry, 1996, Statistics Canada, from *Income Distribution by Size in Canada*, Cat. no. 13-207; Centre for International Statistics at the Canadian Council on Social Development, Statistics Canada, *Income Distributions by Size in Canada, 1996*, Cat. no. 13-207.XPB.

Table 7.1, is over $23 billion. Clearly, a limited number of people own or control a very large portion of the wealth in Canada. In fact, the wealthiest quintile accounts for more than 50 percent of the wealth in Canada. Furthermore, Antonious and Crowley (1986) reported that more than two-thirds of the largest Canadian corporations were controlled by a single owner. At least half of these owners were families. Richardson's (1990) analysis of corporate ownership in Canada reported similar findings. He noted that over three-quarters of the assets of Canada's largest nonfinancial corporations were controlled by only 17 large business enterprises. Eleven of the 17 enterprises were controlled by a single owner.

Whether we consider distribution of income or wealth, though, it is relatively clear that social inequality is a real, consistent, and enduring feature of life in Canadian society (Harman, 1995).

Consequences of Inequality

Income and wealth are not simply statistics; they are intricately related to our individual life chances. Persons with a high income or substantial wealth have more control over their lives. They have greater access to goods and services; they can afford better housing, more education, and a wider range of medical services. Similarly, as discussed in Box 7.2, those with greater access to economic resources fare

TABLE 7.1 MAJOR CANADIAN ENTREPRENEURS AMONG THE WORLD'S RICHEST PEOPLE: THEIR PRINCIPAL BUSINESSES AND ESTIMATED WEALTH, 1998

NAME	PRINCIPAL BUSINESS	WEALTH ($ billion)
Kenneth Roy Thomson	Newspapers, Thomson Corp.	14.4
Three Irving brothers	Gas stations, oil refineries	4.0
Charles Bronfman	Seagram Co.	3.3
Israel Asper	CanWest Global Communications	1.8

Reprinted by permission of *Forbes Magazine*. © Forbes Inc., 1998. Figures have been converted to Canadian dollars.

MAP 7.1 Regional Variation in Average Family Income, 1996

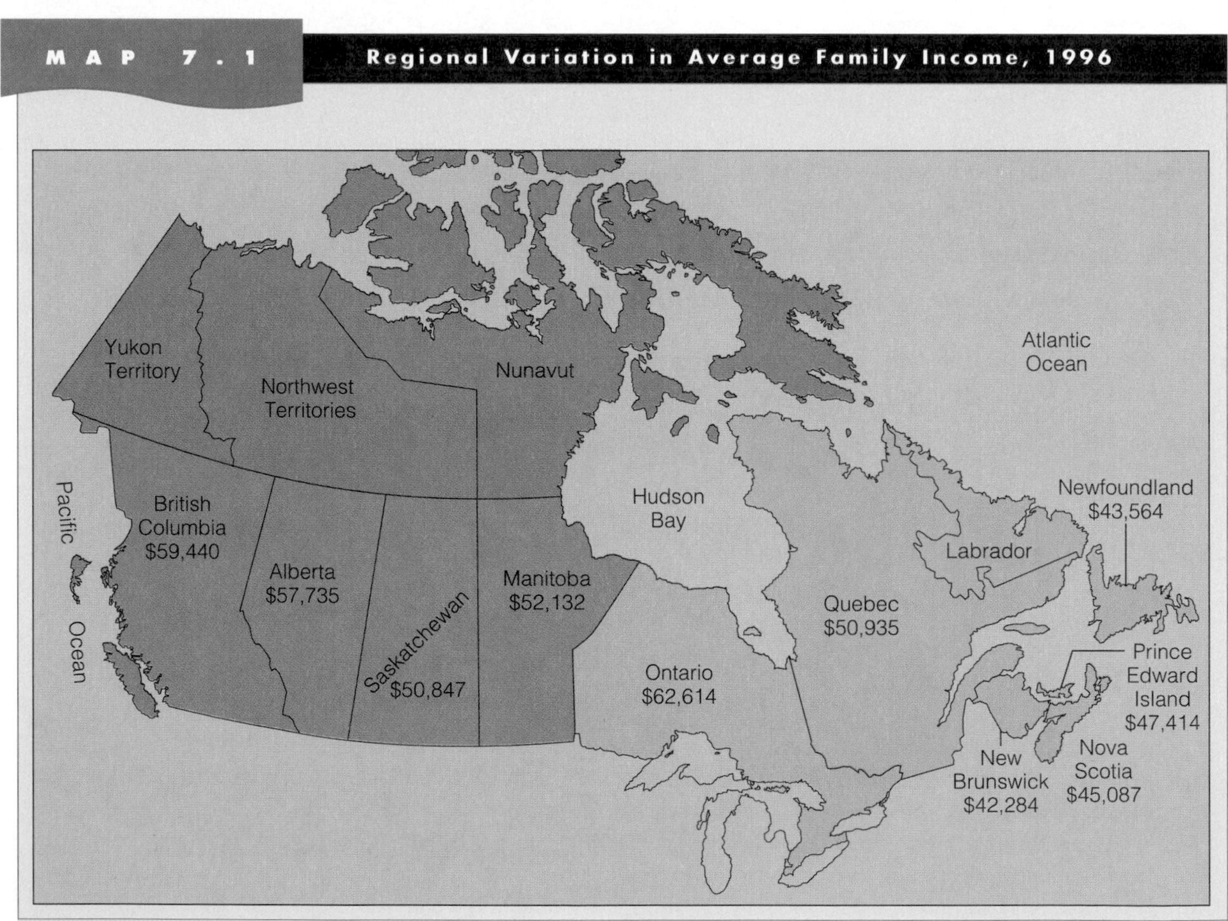

Prepared by the Centre for International Statistics at the Canadian Council on Social Development using data from Statistics Canada, *Income Distributions by Size in Canada, 1996*, Cat. no. 13-207-XPB. Used by permission.

better when dealing with the criminal justice system. Persons with less income, especially those living in poverty, must spend their limited resources to acquire the basic necessities of life.

HEALTH AND NUTRITION People who are wealthy and well educated and who have high-paying jobs are much more likely to be healthy than are poor people. As people's economic status increases, so does their health status. The poor have shorter life expectancies and are at greater risk for chronic illnesses such as diabetes, heart disease, and cancer, as well as for infectious diseases such as tuberculosis.

Children born into poor families are at much greater risk of dying during their first year of life. Some die from disease, accidents, or violence. Others are unable to survive because they are born with low birth weight, a condition linked to birth defects and increased probability of infant mortality (Canadian Institute of Child Health, 1994; Health Canada, 1997). Low birth weight in infants is attributed, at least in part, to the inadequate nutrition received by many low-income pregnant women. Most of the poor do not receive preventive medical and dental checkups; many do not receive adequate medical care after they experience illness or injury. Furthermore, many high-poverty areas lack an adequate supply of doctors and medical facilities. The higher death rates among Aboriginal peoples in Canada are partly attributable to unequal access to medical care and nutrition.

Although the precise relationship between class and health is not known, analysts suggest that people with higher income and wealth tend to smoke less, exercise more, maintain a healthy body weight, and eat nutritious meals than poorer people. As a category, affluent persons also tend to be less depressed and face less psychological stress, conditions that tend to be directly proportional to income, education, and job status (Ross and Roberts, 1997).

EDUCATION Educational opportunities and life chances are directly linked. Some functionalist theorists view education as the "elevator" to social mobility. Improvements in the educational achievement levels (measured in number of years of schooling completed) of the poor, visible minorities, and women have been cited as evidence that students' abilities now are more important than their class, race, or gender. From this perspective, inequality in education is declining, and students have an opportunity to achieve upward mobility through achievements at school (see Hauser and Featherman, 1976).

Functionalists generally see the education system as flexible, allowing most students the opportunity to attend university if they apply themselves (Ballantine, 1993).

In contrast, most conflict theorists stress that schools are agencies for reproducing the capitalist class system and perpetuating inequality in society (Bowles and Gintis, 1976; Bowles, 1977). From this perspective, education perpetuates poverty. Parents with limited income are not able to provide the same educational opportunities for their children as are families with greater financial resources. Author Jonathan Kozol (1991, quoted in Feagin and Feagin, 1996:191) documented the effect of educational inequality on students:

> Kindergartners are so full of hope, cheerfulness, high expectations. By the time they get into fourth grade, many begin to lose heart. They see the score, understanding they're not getting what others are getting ... They see suburban schools on television ... They begin to get the point that they are not valued much in our society. By the time they are in junior high, they understand it. "We have eyes and we can see; we have hearts and we can feel ... We know the difference."

Poverty exacts such a toll that many young people will not have the opportunity to finish high school, much less enter college or university.

POVERTY IN CANADA

When many people think about poverty, they think of people who are unemployed or on welfare. However, many hardworking people with full-time jobs live in poverty. The most common measure used to establish the poverty line is the low-income cut-offs used by Statistics Canada. According to this measure, any individual or family that spends more than 56 percent of their income on the necessities of life—food, clothing, and shelter—is considered to be living in poverty. There is no single cut-off line for all of Canada because living costs vary by family size and place of residence. In 1997, the income cut-offs for a family of four ranged from $22,639 in rural areas to $32,759 in cities of more than 500,000. Based on these low-income cut-offs, nearly 5.2 million children, women, and men—one in every six Canadians—were living in poverty in 1996 (National Council of Welfare, 1998).

When sociologists define poverty, they distinguish between absolute and relative poverty. ***Absolute poverty*** **exists when people do not have the means to secure the most basic necessities of life.** Absolute

BOX 7.2 SOCIOLOGY AND LAW

THE RICH GET RICHER AND THE POOR GET PRISON

How does social class affect the likelihood of being sent to prison? Are there different sets of rules operating in the criminal justice system—one for the rich and one for the poor? According to author Jeffrey Reiman economic power is the central factor in determining whether a person will go to prison for a criminal offence. Reiman supports this premise with data that reveal that in the United States the prison population is comprised overwhelmingly from the ranks of society's disadvantaged. He states:

> For the same criminal behavior, the poor are more likely to be arrested; if arrested, they are more likely to be charged; if charged, more likely to be convicted; if convicted, more likely to be sentenced to prison; and if sentenced, more likely to be given longer prison terms than members of the middle and upper classes. In other words, the image of the criminal population one sees in our nation's jails and prisons is an image distorted by the shape of the criminal justice system itself. It is the face of evil reflected in a carnival mirror, but it is no laughing matter. (1979:97)

According to criminologist Thomas Gabor (1994), the justice system in Canada also favours the middle and upper class—those who have the financial resources to protect their best interests. For example, in the case of young offenders, police are more likely to refer lower-class youths to juvenile court. Youth from wealthier homes are more likely to be dealt with informally. Poor defendants are less likely to be able to afford bail and are therefore more likely to remain in jail until their case goes to trial (this may be several months). The

poverty often has life-threatening consequences, such as when a homeless person freezes to death on a park bench. By comparison, ***relative poverty*** **exists when people may be able to afford basic necessities but are unable to maintain an average standard of living** (Harman, 1995a).

Regardless of how it is defined, poverty is primarily about deprivation, as this woman's comments reveal:

> There are times when I am so scared that I'm not going to find a job, I think, "What the hell is wrong with me?" … I can get scared to death … I have periods of insomnia. I'll get very short tempered with my husband and with the children. (Burman, 1988: 195; cited in Duffy and Mandell, 1996:102)
>
> If I say "no" to the children, they feel very depressed when they see other children taking things to school. The children feel very disappointed. They kind of lose love for you. They think that you don't love them. (Women for Economic Survival, 1984; cited in Duffy and Mandell 1996: 102)

Who Are the Poor?

Poverty in Canada is not randomly distributed, but rather is highly concentrated among certain groups of people—specifically, women, children, persons with disabilities, and Aboriginal peoples. When people belong to more than one of these categories, for example, Aboriginal children, their risk of poverty is even greater.

AGE Today, children are at much greater risk of living in poverty than are adults aged 16 to 64 (National Council of Welfare, 1999). A generation ago, persons over age 65 were at greatest risk of being poor; however, increased government transfer payments and an increase in the number of elderly retiring with personal

BOX 7.2

CONTINUED

poor must rely on legal-aid lawyers who have large caseloads and little time to prepare cases for trial. The state also favours individuals of higher social standing in sentencing. Crimes committed by middle- and upper-class persons (e.g., embezzlement, fraud, income tax evasion) usually earn lighter sentences than those more likely to be committed by the poor (e.g., robbery, burglary).

In short, white-collar criminals have been very successful in ensuring that their interests are reflected in the law and its enforcement. According to Rick Linden, the crimes committed by higher-status persons are much less likely to be labelled criminal:

> A storekeeper who sells a turkey labelled 12 kg which actually weighs 11 kg may not be prosecuted; if he or she actually is, the charge will be breach of a regulatory offence with relatively minor penalties. However, someone caught stealing a kilogram of turkey meat will be charged with the criminal offence of theft. Doctors who fraudulently bill provincial health insurance plans are usually disciplined by their professional body, while someone who fraudulently receives welfare is subject to criminal prosecution. (1994:219)

It is evident that social class plays a significant role in terms of the type of punishment, if any, offenders receive for their crime. However, as Gabor (1994) notes, other factors such as the type and severity of the offence are also important considerations.

Source: Gabor, 1994; Reiman, 1979; and Linden, 1994.

private pension plans has led to a decline in poverty among the elderly. Even so, older women are twice as likely as older men to be poor.

The age category most vulnerable to poverty today is that of the young. While the overall poverty rate in 1996 was about 18 percent, the rate for children under the age of 18 was 21 percent. This means more than 1.4 million Canadian children are living in poverty (Ross, 1998). A large number of children hover just above the official poverty line. The precarious position of Aboriginal children is even more striking. Approximately 51 percent of Aboriginal children (both on and off reserves) are living in poverty.

Children as a group are poorer now than they were at the beginning of the 1980s, and this is true whether they live in one- or two-parent families. The majority of poor children live in two-parent families in which one or both parents are employed. However, children in single-parent households headed by women are much likelier to be living in poverty. Despite the promise to alleviate child poverty by the year 2000 made by the House of Commons in 1989, the future for poor children does not look bright. These children are poor because their parents are poor, and one of the main reasons for poverty among adults is a lack of good jobs. Government cuts to unemployment insurance benefits and employment programs will affect not only those who need these services but also the children of these individuals.

GENDER About two-thirds of all adults living in poverty in Canada are women. As Figure 7.4 shows, in 1997, single-parent families headed by women had a 57 percent poverty rate compared with a rate of almost 12 percent for two-parent families. Furthermore, women are among the poorest of the poor. Poor single mothers with children under 18 are the worst off, living $9604 below the poverty line in 1996. Sociologist Diana Pearce (1978) coined a term to describe this problem: the ***feminization of***

FIGURE 7.4 Poverty Rates by Family Type, 1997

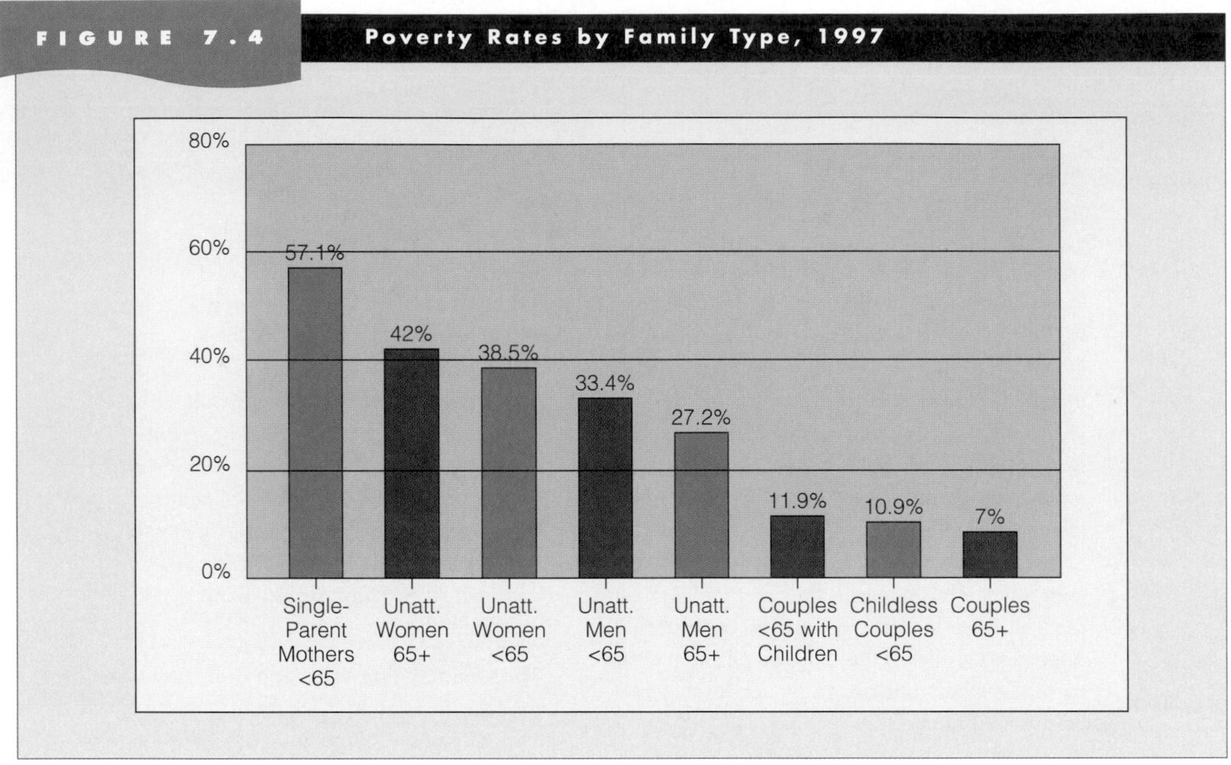

Source: National Council of Welfare, 1999. *Poverty Profile 1997*. Ottawa: Minister of Supply and Services, Fall 1999.

***poverty* refers to the trend in which women are disproportionately represented among individuals living in poverty.** Women have a higher risk of being poor because they bear the major economic burden of raising children as single heads of households but earn only 70 cents for every dollar a male worker earns—a figure that has changed little over four decades. More women than men are unable to obtain regular, full-time, year-round employment, and the lack of adequate, affordable day care exacerbates this problem (Schellenberg and Ross, 1997). As discussed in Box 7.3, the feminization of poverty is a global phenomenon.

While some women are victims of chronic poverty, others are among the "new poor" who have experienced "event-driven poverty" as a result of marital separation, divorce, or widowhood (Bane, 1986). Sociologist Lenore Weitzman (1985) has suggested that no-fault divorce laws have placed many women in financial jeopardy because supposedly "equal" settlements did not take into account women's lesser earning capabilities, especially if they had been out of the workforce, taking care of young children at home. A recent Statistics Canada report indicated that women's incomes (adjusted for family size) dropped by about 23 percent one year after they divorced or separated. Men, on the other hand, reported a 10 percent *gain* in income during the same time period (Statistics Canada, 1997c). Five years after the marriage breakup, women's incomes were still 5 percent *below* their earlier level. In contrast, men's incomes *increased* by an average of 15 percent five years after the breakup (Statistics Canada, 1997c).

Certain groups of women experience "multiple jeopardy," a term used to refer to the even greater risk of poverty faced by women who are immigrants, disabled, visible minorities, or native Canadians (Gerber, 1990).

RACE/ETHNICITY According to some stereotypes, most of the poor and virtually all welfare recipients are visible minorities. Such stereotypes are perpetuated, however, because a disproportionate percentage of the impoverished in Canada are native Canadians and recent immigrants. Aboriginal people in Canada are among the most severely disadvantaged persons. About one-

The "feminization of poverty" refers to the fact that two out of three impoverished adults in North America are women. Should we assume that poverty is primarily a women's issue? Why or why not?

half live below the poverty line, and some live in conditions of extreme poverty. The average income for Aboriginal persons is just over $17,000—34 percent below the national average income of $26,000 (Statistics Canada, 1998e). Also, the unemployment rate for Aboriginal persons in Canada ranges from 40 to 60 percent, while the national average is about 10 percent. In sum, "to be Native in Canada is to face a strong likelihood of poverty" (Harman, 1995a:259).

PERSONS WITH DISABILITIES Awareness that persons with disabilities have been discriminated against in the job market has increased in recent years. As a result, they now constitute one of the recognized "target groups" in efforts to eliminate discrimination in the workplace and have more opportunities to work than they had a decade ago. However, although over 50 percent of people with disabilities are now in the labour force, many continue to be excluded, not because of their disabilities, but because of workplace environmental barriers (Schellenberg and Ross, 1997). The effects of this systemic discrimination continue to be felt by disabled persons as they are still, as a group, vulnerable to poverty (Fawcett, 1996). Adults with disabilities have significantly lower incomes than nondisabled Canadians. Recent estimates indicate that close to half of employed persons with disabilities had incomes below $10,000 (Ross, Shillington, and Lochhead, 1994). Once again, when gender and disability are combined, we find that women with disabilities are doubly disadvantaged (Fawcett, 1996).

Economic and Structural Sources of Poverty

Poverty has both economic and structural sources. The low wages paid for many jobs is the major cause: one-third of all families living in poverty are headed by someone who is employed (National Council of Welfare, 1999). In 1972, minimum-wage legislation meant that a worker who worked 40 hours a week, 52 weeks a year could earn a yearly income that was 20 percent over the poverty line. By today's standards, the same worker would have to earn over $10 per hour simply to reach the poverty line. Minimum wages across Canada range from just over $5 per hour to a high of approximately $7 per hour. In other words, a person with full-time employment in a minimum-wage job cannot keep a family of four above the official poverty line (Campaign 2000, 1998).

Structural problems contribute to both unemployment and underemployment. Automation in the industrial heartland of Quebec and Ontario has made the skills and training of thousands of workers obsolete. Many of these workers have become unemployable and poor. Corporations have been deinvesting in Canada, and millions of people have lost their jobs as a result. Economists refer to this displacement as the *deindustrialization of North America* (Bluestone and Harrison, 1982). Even as they have closed their Canadian factories and plants, many corporations have opened new facilities in other countries where "cheap labour" exists because

BOX 7.3 SOCIOLOGY IN GLOBAL PERSPECTIVE

POVERTY IN BRAZIL: THE EFFECTS ON WOMEN AND CHILDREN

According to the United Nations, most of the roughly 100 million homeless people in the world are women and children, and another 600 million live in impoverished conditions in inadequate and unhealthy shelters. The United Nations Center for Human Settlement published a report indicating that of the 1.3 billion people living in poverty, 70 percent are women and girls. They referred to this as the global feminization of poverty, further indicating that women and girls are also the most rapidly growing group of impoverished people. Some 50,000 people—mostly women and children—die daily because of poor shelter, polluted water, and bad sanitation. The report estimated that if housing could be brought up to a minimum standard, there would be 5 million fewer deaths and 2 million fewer disabilities per year. Women are relegated to homelessness or squatter-status in many parts of the world where they cannot legally own or inherit land, cannot obtain bank loans, receive much lower wages than men, and often are abandoned to raise children on their own. Women are often also the prime targets of political upheavals, making up 70 to 80 percent of the world's 23 million refugees.

What is life like for these women? Persons in all nations have hopes and dreams for their children and grandchildren. Doralice Moreira de Souza is a 47-year-old woman whose hands are gnarled from years of cutting a daily quota of five tons of sugar cane in Conceicao de Macabu, Brazil. She has a dream for Alan, her 10-year-old grandson: "I would like him to study, so that when he grows up, he won't end up like a slave like me." However, Alan's life chances already are seriously limited because of economic conditions and labour exploitation in his country. Today, slavery flourishes in rural and other isolated areas of Brazil—on sugar cane plantations and ranches, in gold mines,

people of necessity will work for lower wages. ***Job deskilling*—a reduction in the proficiency needed to perform a specific job that leads to a corresponding reduction in the wages for that job**—has resulted from the introduction of computers and other technology (Hodson and Parker, 1988). The shift from manufacturing to service occupations has resulted in the loss of higher-paying positions and their replacement with lower-paying and less secure positions that do not offer the wages, job stability, or advancement potential of the disappearing manufacturing jobs. Consequently, there are simply not enough good jobs available in Canada to enable families to lift themselves out of poverty. In addition, the lack of affordable high-quality day care for women who need to earn an income means that many jobs are inaccessible, especially to women who are single parents. The problems of unemployment, underemployment, and poverty-level wages are even greater for visible minorities and young people (Ross, Shillington, and Lochhead, 1994).

SOCIAL STRATIFICATION IN THE FUTURE

Will social inequality in Canada increase in the twenty-first century? Many social scientists predict that existing trends point to an increase. First, the purchasing power of the dollar has stagnated or declined since the early 1970s. As families started to lose ground financially, more family members (especially women) entered the labour force in an attempt to support themselves and their families (Ross, Shillington, and Lochhead, 1994). Economist Robert Reich (1993:145) has noted that the employed have been travelling on two escalators—

BOX 7.3

CONTINUED

and in the charcoal industries of the Amazon. The sugar cane fields in which Doralice works are harvested by farm workers who toil from sunup to sundown and sleep in hammocks strung in cow stalls. Their employer, an alcohol distillery owner, does not pay wages for their work. Workers instead receive scrip, which they can redeem for food. Because landowners need to ensure that they will have a readily available supply of cheap labour, they bind labourers by encouraging them to run up unpayable debts at company-owned stores or canteens. As a Rio de Janeiro prosecutor looking into labour law violations stated, "In the 19th century, the chains were metal. Today, the chains are debt—the worker has to repay his transportation, his tools, his food" (Brooke, 1993b:3).

What is life like for the children living in poverty in Brazil? In the Brazilian slum areas both adults and children rummage through garbage dumps to find enough decaying food to keep themselves alive, and hordes of homeless children roam the streets, begging, stealing, shining shoes—anything to survive. These children are considered by middle- and upper-class Brazilians as part of the "dangerous classes" because they threaten the status quo. Since there are no social institutions in this country to provide for these children, one monstrous "solution" has been to kill them. Each year the Brazilian police and death squads murder about 2000 children. These murders are often preceded by ritual torture.

As these tragic examples demonstrate, poverty is the world's deadliest disease. How should First World nations respond to global world poverty?

Source: Based on Brooke, 1993b; Henslin and Nelson, 1996; and Osterman, 1995.

one going up and the other going down—in recent years. The gap between the earnings of workers and the income of managers and top executives has widened (Feagin and Feagin, 1997).

Second, wealth continues to become more concentrated at the top of the Canadian class structure. As the rich have grown richer, more people have found themselves among the ranks of the poor. Structural sources of upward mobility are shrinking while the rate of downward mobility has increased. The main problem in redistributing wealth and income in Canada is that the middle and upper classes may have to accept less so that others can have more (Krahn, 1995b). This is a tough, if not impossible, sell in a society like that of Canada, in which the ability to acquire material goods is as highly valued as it is.

Are we sabotaging our future if we do not work constructively to eliminate poverty? It has been said that a chain is no stronger than its weakest link. If we apply this idea to the problem of poverty, it is to our advantage to see that those who cannot find work or do not have a job that provides a living wage receive adequate training and employment. Children of today, the adults of tomorrow, need education, health care, and safety as they grow up.

As mentioned at the beginning of this chapter, the House of Commons passed a motion stating a goal of eliminating poverty among children by the year 2000 (Kitcher et al., 1991). Are we getting any closer to reaching these goals? Canada's response to poverty has been contradictory. One would expect that in working toward eliminating poverty action would be taken to address the structural causes of poverty—high unemployment and an inadequate set of child and family social policies. Instead, the federal government has cut federal social supports (such as subsidized day care, unemployment benefits, and

BOX 7.4 CRITICAL THINKING

SOLVING THE POVERTY PROBLEM

In 1996, the International Year for the Eradication of Poverty, the National Council of Welfare made four recommendations to address the issue of poverty in Canada. The Council indicated that in order to achieve any dramatic reductions in poverty, it would be necessary for all levels of government to change their priorities and their attitudes toward poor people. The recommendations, directed at "mounting and winning the war on poverty," were as follows:

1. *Government should make a special effort to promote realistic portraits of poor people.* A faltering economy and family breakups have added greatly to the ranks of the poor in recent years. In this context, it is wrong to condone false and degrading stereotypes of poor people.
2. *Governments should look to tax expenditures rather than cuts in social programs as the prime means for reducing their deficits.* Governments should stop cutting social programs that provide help to the least fortunate members of our society. It is unfair to ask poor people to "pay their share" of the cost of deficit reduction.
3. *Governments should agree to work collectively to fight poverty.* It makes sense for governments to work together rather than passing on their own financial problems to other governments. In the early 1980s the federal government started putting pressure on provincial governments with a series of cuts to cost-shared programs. Many provinces offset the effects of these cuts by reducing funding to local governments, school districts, and hospitals.

family allowance) (Campaign 2000, 1998), leaving families to bear the burden of poverty. Box 7.4 discusses a number of recommendations made by the National Council of Welfare to address the issue of poverty in Canada.

Almost one-fifth of the children in this country continue to grow up poor, in circumstances that seriously jeopardize their chances of becoming happy and productive citizens. As Marsden and Robertson state in their report *Children in Poverty: Toward a Better Future*,

> Children are the future of any society. There is no sounder investment in Canada's future than an investment in our children. It is disturbing ... that the necessity of solving child poverty must be justified in monetary or "bottom line" terms. Nevertheless, if that is required, the figures speak for themselves—but poor children cannot." (Marsden and Robertson, 1991:6)

CHAPTER REVIEW

What is stratification and how does it affect our lives?
Stratification is the hierarchical arrangement of large social groups based on their control over basic resources. People are treated differently based on where they are positioned within the social hierarchies of class, race, gender, and age.

What are the major systems of stratification?
The caste system is a closed system in which people's status is determined at birth based on their parents' position in society. The class system, which exists in Canada, is a type of stratification based on ownership of resources and on the type of work people do. Class systems are characterized by unequal distribution of resources and by movement up and down the class structure through social mobility.

BOX 7.4

CONTINUED

4. *Governments should add fighting poverty to their list of immediate economic priorities.* Given the resources available to governments, there is no reason that fighting poverty should have to wait while governments grapple with reducing the deficit, lowering interest rates, or creating jobs. The reality is that poor people cannot wait five, ten, or twenty years for their concerns to be addressed. (National Council of Welfare, 1996:86)

The question of how to solve the problem of poverty has been debated for the past two decades. A lack of consensus exists regarding both the definition of the problem and the possible solutions for it. While the political debates rage on, many thousands of lives are being unalterably damaged. Sociologist Thomas O'Reilly-Fleming discusses one of these young lives:

> When I interviewed a young homeless family, their daughter ... drew a stark depiction of three figures crowded in a tiny black box. It was her depiction of life for the homeless in a motel ... Leaving the interview, to face a Christmas with no toys, no Christmas tree, and a macaroni dinner, she inquired innocently as she hugged me "Isn't there anyone who looks after little children in Canada?" (O'Reilly-Fleming 1993:178)

Do you think the federal and provincial governments are doing enough to allieviate poverty in Canada? What progress has been made since 1996 in "winning the war on poverty"? To what extent has the government followed through on the recommendations by the National Council of Welfare?

How did classical sociologists Karl Marx and Max Weber view social class?
Karl Marx and Max Weber acknowledged social class as a key determinant of social inequality and social change. For Marx, people's relationship to the means of production determines their class position. Weber developed a multidimensional concept of stratification that focuses on the interplay of wealth, prestige, and power.

What is the functionalist view of social inequality?
According to the Davis–Moore thesis, stratification exists in all societies, and some inequality is not only inevitable but also necessary for the ongoing functioning of society. The positions that are most important within society and that require the most talent and training must be highly rewarded.

What is the conflict view of social inequality?
Conflict perspectives on the Canadian class structure are based on the assumption that social stratification is created and maintained by one group in order to enhance and protect its own economic interests. Conflict theorists measure class according to people's relationships with others in the production process.

What are some of the consequences of inequality in Canada?
The stratification of society into different social groups results in wide discrepancies in income and wealth and in variable access to available goods and services. People with high incomes or wealth have greater opportunity to control their own lives. People with lower incomes have fewer life chances and must spend their limited resources to acquire basic necessities.

Who are the poor in Canada?
Age, gender, race/ethnicity, and disability tend to be factors in poverty. Children have a greater risk of being poor than do the elderly, while women have a higher rate of poverty than do men. Although whites account

for approximately two-thirds of those below the poverty line, native peoples and visible minorities each account for a share of the impoverished in Canada that is disproportionate to their numbers.

Key Terms

absolute poverty 209
alienation 201
apartheid 199
bourgeoisie 201
capitalist class 201
caste system 198
class conflict 201
class system 199
feminization of poverty 211
intergenerational mobility 198
intragenerational mobility 198
job deskilling 214
life chances 198
meritocracy 204
power 202
prestige 202
proletariat 201
relative poverty 210
social mobility 198
social stratification 198
wealth 202
working class 201

Internet Exercises

1. Visit the home page for the Canadian Council on Social Development at: **www.ccsd.ca.**

   From here go to Free Statistics and see what information you can find on the life chances of children in lower-income and higher-income families.
2. There is talk about a widening gap between rich and poor in this country and in the world. Think about the vast amount of information you have been able to gather using the Internet thus far. Some argue that the biggest gap of the twenty-first century will be between the information "haves" and "have nots." What do you think? What aspects of the way in which information is presented on the Internet would lead you to believe that access to the World Wide Web is liberating and empowering? Are there any reasons to believe that access to all of the information on the World Wide Web does little, if anything, to enlighten and educate individuals?

   The most spectacular example of the gap between the information "haves" and "have nots" is Bill Gates, the founder of Microsoft. To see how wealthy Gates is today, go to **webho.com/WealthClock**. Remember, this clock is in American dollars, so you must multiply by 1.5 to get the Canadian value.

Net Links

For more Web links related to the topic of this chapter, see the Nelson sociology Web site: **www.sociologyessentials-2nded.nelson.com**.

The Canadian Council on Social Development is one of the leading organizations speaking for Canada's poor; you can see its Web site at:

www.ccsd.ca

Campaign 2000 is an initiative to end child poverty in Canada; see its Web site at:

www.campaign2000.ca

To see *Forbes's* listing of the world's billionaires, including home country, net worth, source of income, and brief biographies, go to:

www.forbes.com/tool/toolbox/billnew/index99.asp

For a discussion on how families—especially those with low incomes—have fared in the job market in recent years, review the executive summary of *Left Poor by the Market: A Look at Family Poverty and Earnings* by Grant Schellenberg and David P. Ross at:

www.ccsd.ca/es_left.htm 

Does family income affect the healthy development of young children? David P. Ross and Paul Roberts of the Canadian Council on Social Development address this question in their research article, which is available at:

www.ccsd.ca/p211fi.htm 

Questions for Critical Thinking

1. Based on the functionalist model of class structure, what is the class location of each of your ten closest friends or acquaintances? What is their location in relation to yours? to one another? What does their location tell you about friendship and social class?
2. Should employment be based on merit, need, or affirmative action policies?
3. What might happen in Canada in the twenty-first century if the gap between rich and poor continues to widen?

Suggested Readings

These texts provide more in-depth information about social stratification:

Wallace Clement. *The Canadian Corporate Elite: An Analysis of Economic Power*. Toronto: McClelland & Stewart, 1975.

Dennis Forcese. *The Canadian Class Structure*. Toronto: McGraw-Hill Ryerson, 1986.

Charles E. Hurst. *Social Inequality: Forms, Causes, and Consequences*. Boston: Allyn & Bacon, 1992.

John Porter. *The Vertical Mosaic: An Analysis of Social Class and Power in Canada*. Toronto: University of Toronto Press, 1965.

A wide diversity of viewpoints on the intertwining of race, class, and gender in social stratification are found in this reader:

James E. Curtis, Edward Grabb, and Neil Guppy (eds). *Social Inequality in Canada: Patterns, Problems, Policies* (2nd ed.). Scarborough, Ont.: Prentice-Hall, 1993.

For more information on poverty in Canada, see:

David P. Ross, Richard Shillington, and Clarence Lochhead. *The Canadian Fact Book on Poverty*. Ottawa: Canadian Council on Social Development, 1994.

INFOTRAC® COLLEGE EDITION

Either from the *Sociology In Our Times: The Essentials* Web site (**www.sociologyessentials-2nded.nelson.com**) or directly from your Web browser, you may access InfoTrac® College Edition, an online university library that includes over 600 popular and scholarly journals in which you can find articles related to the topics in this chapter.

CHAPTER 8

The following is an excerpt from a letter a mother in the Philippines wrote to her daughters explaining her commitment to political activism:

"Today, both of you are in University. In less than five years, you will join the ranks of the 40–50 percent unemployed and underemployed Filipinos. If you are lucky and do find jobs, you will painfully experience the discrepancy between the daily cost of living at 354 pesos and the minimum wage pegged by the government at 150 pesos. I won't be surprised if you find yourselves in the 70 percent of the population considered below the poverty line and the 40 percent below the food threshold. Even now, that is what we see happening.

"I fear that very soon, even the environment will no longer be a dependable support system. What with biologically dead rivers, contaminated drinking water, and depleted marine resources because of the mine tailings spewed by mining companies, the likes of Marcopper and its Canadian partner, Placer Dome, what with dry rice fields that have to be abandoned due to the lack of water for irrigation brought about by open pit mining operations of giant establishments ... What with 2/3 of the whole Cordillera region apportioned to Australian, American and Canadian mining companies ...

"This government has launched a grandiose plan it calls Philippines 2000. President Fidel Ramos ... wants to take the Philippines down the road to NIC-hood (Newly Industrialized Country) by the year 2000. That is why our agricultural lands which 75 percent of our population was tilling have now been converted into industrial enclaves, called Regional Industrial Centers. Is it any wonder, then, that thousands of peasants have been displaced?

"... The road is long that leads to progress—too long in fact, that hope could easily be snuffed out. But this one thing I can say, Mitzi May and Lily Joyce: I HAVE NOT LOST HOPE. This is why I have opted to leave you for a while—to join the many hopeful Filipinos who have put their lives on the line. And I will continue to put my life on the line for as long as this insensitive government rides roughshod on our people's God-given rights." (Sharon Ruiz-Duremdes, Anglican Church of Canada)

You might be surprised to learn that of all the narratives that we used to open the fifteen chapters in this book, this was the most

GLOBAL STRATIFICATION

difficult to find. The world's poorest people have no voice. Even researchers who study global stratification rarely let them tell their own stories. Books are full of statistics that tell the stories of nations that cannot feed their citizens and of researchers' compassionate descriptions of the lives of people living at the margins of survival. However, the poor themselves remain faceless. If not for the haunting images of famine or civil war that we see on television news programs or the occasional story about problems in low-income countries on the radio or in the newspaper, most of us would know nothing about the over one billion people who live out their lives in abject poverty. They are also invisible to those managing the global corporations and the international organizations whose decisions have life and death consequences for those at the bottom of the global stratification system.

Even the quotation we did select is not really representative of the world's poor. The mother writing to her children is educated, articulate, and a member of an activist political organization. While her country, the Philippines, is poor, it is far wealthier than many other nations. However, her letter does articulate many of the problems of people in poor countries including unemployment, foreign control of resources, environmental degradation, economic restructuring, and political discontent.

Poverty and inequality know no political boundaries or international borders. In this chapter we examine global stratification and inequality, and discuss the perspectives that have been developed to explain this problem. It is often difficult to connect the lives of people living in poverty in distant countries to our own lives in one of the world's wealthiest countries. When television shows us thousands of people starving in Ethiopia or babies being treated for dehydration at aid stations in Rwanda, it is sometimes hard to realize that the people we see are individual human beings just like you and your friends. The global stratification system determines who will live long, prosperous lives and who will live short, miserable lives, eking out a marginal existence in subsistence agriculture and subject to the vagaries of rain, floods, and political instability.

Why do these inequities persist? In this chapter you will learn about some of the reasons the life prospects of billions of people remain so dismal. When you read the explanations of global stratification, you should remember that these are not just dry academic theories. Rather, these are the ideas shaping the way governments and international organizations such as the United Nations deal with this very complex and difficult problem. As you will see, decisions based on the wrong theories can be disastrous for the poor.

Before reading on, test your knowledge of global wealth and poverty by taking the quiz in Box 8.1.

Questions and Issues

Chapter Focus Question: What is global stratification, and how does it contribute to economic inequality?

How are global poverty and human development related?

What is modernization theory, and what are its stages?

How do conflict theorists explain patterns of global stratification?

What is world systems theory?

How is the new system of global trade affecting people in poor countries?

FIGURE 8.1 **Income Gap Between the World's Richest and Poorest People, 1960–1997**

The income gap between the richest and poorest people in the world grew steadily between 1960 and 1997. In 1960 the highest-income 20 percent of the world's population received $30 for each dollar received by the lowest-income 20 percent. By 1997, the disparity had increased, rising to $74 for the richest for every $1 for the poorest.

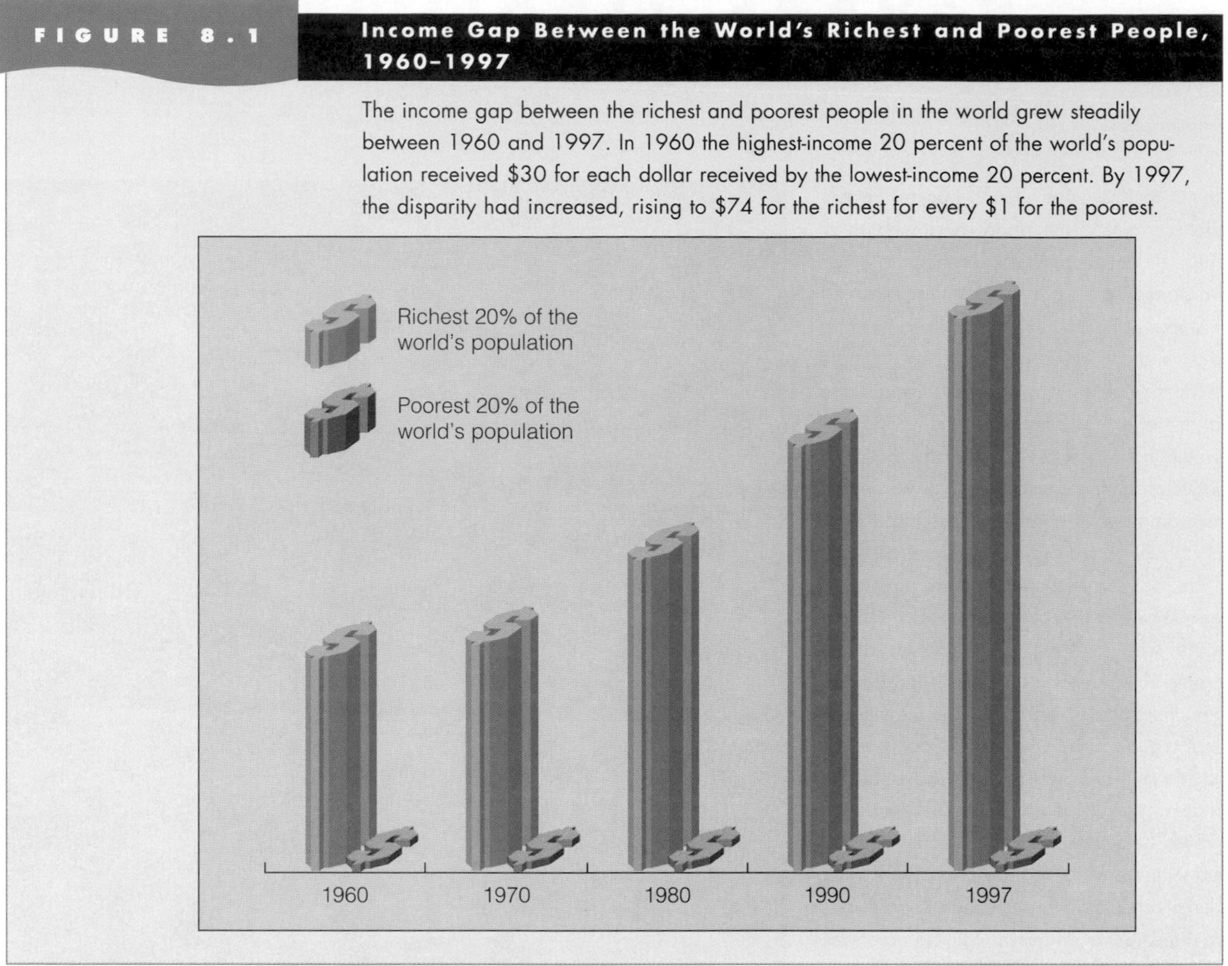

WEALTH AND POVERTY IN GLOBAL PERSPECTIVE

What do we mean by global stratification? *Global stratification* refers to the unequal distribution of wealth, power, and prestige on a global basis, resulting in people having vastly different lifestyles and life chances both within and among the nations of the world. Just as Canada is divided into classes, the world is divided into unequal segments characterized by extreme differences in wealth and poverty. For example, the income gap between the richest and the poorest 20 percent of the world population continues to widen (see Figure 8.1). When we compare social and economic inequality *within* other nations, we find gaps that are more pronounced than they are in Canada. *Developed (high-income) nations* are countries characterized by highly industrialized economies; technologically advanced industrial, administrative, and service occupations; and a relatively high level of national and per capita (per person) income. In contrast, *developing (low-income) nations* are countries that are undergoing the transformation from an agrarian to an industrial economy and have lower levels of income. Within some nations the poorest one-fifth of the population has an income that is only a small fraction of the overall per capita income for that country. For example, in Brazil, Guatemala, and Honduras, less than 3 percent of total national income accrues to the poorest one-fifth of the population (World Bank, 1996).

Between 1960 and 1997, the gap in global income differences between rich and poor countries continued to widen. In 1960, the wealthiest 20 percent

BOX 8.1 SOCIOLOGY AND EVERYDAY LIFE

HOW MUCH DO YOU KNOW ABOUT GLOBAL WEALTH AND POVERTY?

TRUE	FALSE	
T	F	1. Because of foreign aid and the globalization of trade, the gap between the incomes of people in the poorest countries and the richest countries has narrowed over the past several decades.
T	F	2. Although the percentage of the world's people living in absolute poverty has declined over the past decade, the total number of people living in poverty has increased.
T	F	3. The richest fifth of the world's population receives about 50 percent of the total world income.
T	F	4. The political role of governments in policing the activities of transnational corporations has expanded as companies' operations have become more globalized.
T	F	5. Most analysts agree that the World Bank was created to serve the poor of the world and their borrowing governments.
T	F	6. In low-income countries, women are more likely to be poor than men.
T	F	7. Income and standard of living have increased significantly for most Russians as the transition from a centrally planned economy to a market orientation has taken place in recent years.
T	F	8. Poverty levels have declined somewhat in East Asia, the Middle East, and North Africa in recent years.
T	F	9. The majority of people with incomes below the poverty line live in the rural areas of the world.
T	F	10. Poor people in low-income countries meet most of their energy needs by burning wood, dung, and agricultural wastes, which increases health hazards and environmental degradation.

Answers on page 224.

of the world's population had more than 30 times the income of the poorest 20 percent. By 1997, the wealthiest 20 percent of the world's population had 74 times the income of the poorest 20 percent (United Nations Development Programme, 1999).

Many people have sought to address the issue of world poverty and to determine ways in which resources can be used to meet the urgent challenge of poverty. However, not much progress has been made on this front (Lummis, 1992) despite a great deal of talk and billions of dollars in "foreign aid" flowing from high-income to low-income nations. The notion of "development" has become the primary means used in attempts to reduce social and economic inequalities and to alleviate the worst effects of poverty in the less industrialized nations of the world. Often, the nations that have been unable to reduce or eliminate poverty are chastised for not establishing the necessary social and economic reforms to make change possible. However, as other social analysts have suggested,

> The *problem* of inequality lies not in poverty, but in excess. "The problem of the world's poor," defined more accurately, turns out to be "the problem of the world's rich." This means that the solution to the problem is not a massive change in the culture of poverty so as to place it on the path of development, but a massive change in the culture of superfluity in order to place it on the path of counterdevelopment. It does not call for a new value system forcing the world's majority to feel shame at their traditionally moderate consumption habits, but for a new value system forcing the world's rich to see the shame and vulgarity of their overconsumption habits, and the double vulgarity of standing on other people's shoulders to achieve those consumption habits. (Lummis, 1992:50)

BOX 8.1

Answers to the Sociology Quiz on Global Wealth and Poverty

1. **False.** Since 1960, the gap between the incomes of the richest 20 percent of the world's population and the poorest 20 percent has been steadily growing. The ratio of the income of the top 20 percent of the population to that of the poorest 20 percent rose from 30 to 1 in 1960 to 74 to 1 in 1997 (United Nations Development Programme, 1999).
2. **True.** Data from the World Bank indicate that the percentage of the world's people living in absolute poverty has declined since the mid-1980s, particularly in Asia. However, other regions have not reduced the incidence of poverty to the same degree, and the total number of people living in poverty has risen to approximately 1.4 billion by the mid-1990s (World Bank, 1996).
3. **False.** According to the United Nations Development Programme (1996), the richest fifth receive more than 80 percent of total world income.
4. **False.** As companies have globalized their operations, governmental restrictions have become less effective in controlling their activities. Transnational corporations have very little difficulty sidestepping governmental restrictions based on old assumptions about national economies and foreign policy. For example, Honda is able to circumvent import restrictions that the governments of Taiwan, South Korea, and Israel have placed on its vehicles by shipping vehicles made in Ohio to those locations (Korten, 1996).
5. **False.** Some analysts point out the linkages between the World Bank and the transnational corporate sector on both the borrowing and lending ends of its operation. Although the bank is supposedly owned by its members' governments and lends money only to governments, many of its projects involve vast financial dealings with transnational construction companies, consulting firms, and procurement contractors (see Korten, 1996).
6. **True.** In almost all low-income countries (as well as middle- and high-income countries), poverty is a more chronic problem for women due to sexual discrimination, resulting in a lack of educational and employment opportunities (Hauchler and Kennedy, 1994).
7. **False.** Not all Russians have shared equally in the transition to the market economy. In fact, most are worse off than before the change.
8. **True.** These have been the primary regions in which poverty has decreased somewhat and infant mortality rates have fallen. Factors such as economic growth, oil production, foreign investment, and overall development have been credited with the decrease in poverty in East Asia, the Middle East, and North Africa (United Nations DPCSD, 1997).
9. **True.** The majority of people with incomes below the poverty line live in the rural areas of the world; however, the number of poor people residing in urban areas is growing rapidly (United Nations DPCSD, 1997).
10. **True.** Poor people in low-income countries do meet most of their energy needs by burning wood, dung, and agricultural wastes. Although these fuels are inefficient and harmful to health, many low-income people cannot afford appliances, connection charges, and so forth. In some areas, electric hookups are not available (United Nations DPCSD, 1997).

Vast inequalities in income and lifestyle are shown in this photo of slums and nearby upper-class housing in Rio de Janeiro, Brazil. Do similar patterns of economic inequality exist in other nations?

As this statement suggests, the increasing interdependency of all the world's nations was largely overlooked or ignored until increasing emphasis was placed on the global marketplace and the global economy. The linkage between consumption and global poverty is explored in more detail in Box 8.2.

Inequality and Individuals

Nothing illustrates the disparity between rich and poor better than the difference between the wealth amassed by a few individuals and the poverty of the poorest nations. The 225 richest people in the world have a net worth of more than $1.3 trillion. This is equal to the annual incomes of the poorest 2.5 billion people. Only 4 percent of this amount ($53 billion) is required each year to achieve reproductive health care for all women, and basic education, basic medical care, and adequate food, water, and sanitation for all. The wealth of the three richest people (Microsoft owner Bill Gates, investor Warren Buffett, and the oil-rich Sultan of Brunei) is greater than the gross domestic product of the 48 least developed countries (United Nations Development Programme, 1998).

PROBLEMS IN STUDYING GLOBAL INEQUALITY

One of the primary problems encountered by social scientists studying global stratification and social and economic inequality is what terminology should be used to refer to the distribution of resources in various nations. During the past twenty-five years, major changes have occurred in the way that inequality is addressed by organizations such as the United Nations. Most definitions of *inequality* are based on comparisons of levels of economic development.

The Levels of Development Approach

Describing world poverty and global stratification has become quite controversial. Terminology based on levels of development includes concepts such as developed nations, developing nations, less developed nations, and underdevelopment. Let's look first at the contemporary origins of the idea of "underdevelopment" and "underdeveloped nations."

Following World War II, the concepts of *underdevelopment* and *underdeveloped nations* emerged out of the Marshall Plan (named after U.S. Secretary of State George C. Marshall), which provided massive sums of money in direct aid and loans to rebuild the European economic base destroyed during World War II. Given the Marshall Plan's success in rebuilding much of Europe, U.S. political leaders decided that Southern Hemisphere nations that had recently been released from European colonialism could also benefit from a massive financial infusion and rapid economic development. Leaders of the developed nations argued that urgent problems such as poverty, disease, and famine could be reduced through the transfer of finance, technology, and experience from the developed nations to less developed countries. From this viewpoint, economic development is the primary way to solve the poverty problem: hadn't economic growth brought the developed nations to their own high standard of living? Moreover, "self-sustained development" in a nation would require that people in the less developed nations accept the beliefs and values of people

BOX 8.2 SOCIOLOGY IN GLOBAL PERSPECTIVE

CONSUMPTION AND GLOBAL POVERTY

The United Nations *Human Development Report* has played a major role in drawing attention to the need to eradicate poverty. The 1998 edition of the report focused on the way in which some aspects of consumption have affected global stratification. Excessive consumption in developed countries threatens the environment, depletes natural resources, and wastes money that might otherwise provide for the needs of the desperately poor in developing countries.

Global consumption is concentrated among the wealthy. The wealthiest 20 percent of the world's people account for 86 percent of private consumption, while the poorest 20 percent account for only 1.3 percent (see Figure 8.2). While some argue that money now used to buy luxuries might be better spent on the world's poor, others would claim that conspicuous consumption does buy happiness for those who can afford it. Though very limited, the evidence does not support the view that consumption beyond basic needs necessarily makes people happier. According to the *Human Development Report*, the percentage of Americans who describe themselves as "happy" peaked in

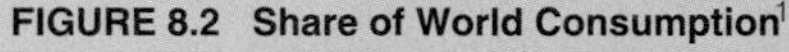

FIGURE 8.2 Share of World Consumption[1]

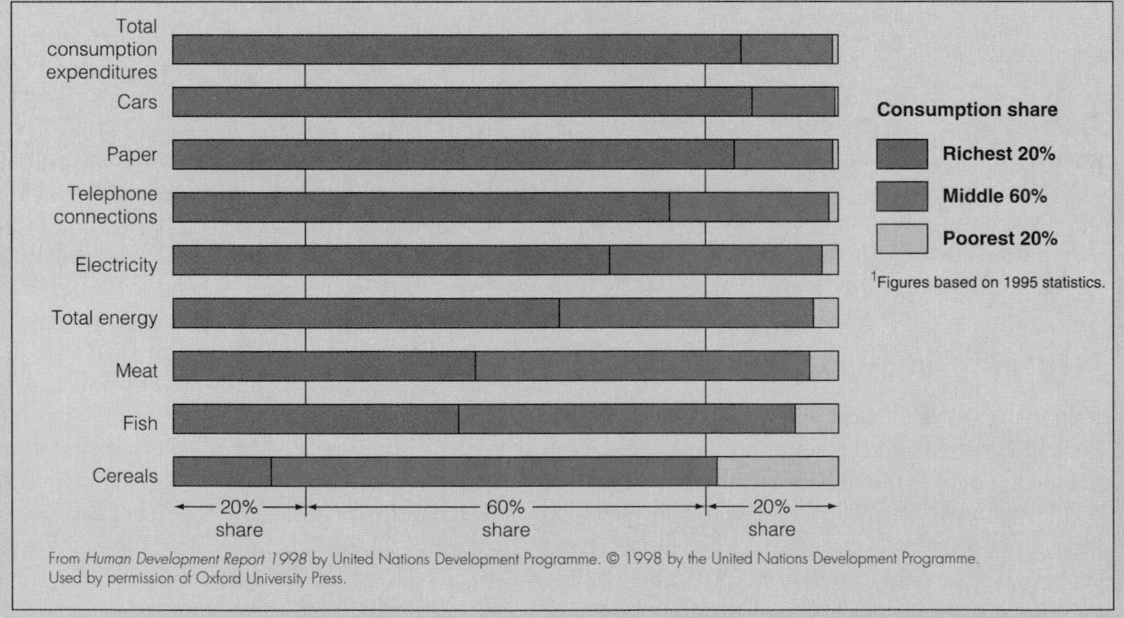

in the developed nations, so the development movement had an explicitly political component.

Ideas regarding *underdevelopment* were popularized by President Harry S. Truman in his 1949 inaugural address. According to Truman, the nations in the Southern Hemisphere were "underdeveloped areas" because of their low *gross national product* (GNP)—a term that refers to all the goods and services produced in a country in a given year, plus the income earned outside the country by individuals or

BOX 8.2

CONTINUED

1957 even though consumption has more than doubled since that time. Unfortunately, as we spend more, we find more things to spend on. If we are able to keep up with the Joneses next door, we shift our horizons to the rich and famous whose lifestyles we know about from newspapers and television. When American consumers were asked in 1986 how much they would need to earn annually to "fulfil all their dreams" the answer was $50,000. By 1994 this had increased to $102,000 (United Nations Development Programme, 1998). Theoretically at least, our wants are limitless.

But surely, some argue, the world's needs are so great that channelling some of the money people in rich nations now spend on excessive consumption would not make a difference in the lives of the world's poor. Surprisingly, the amount of money required to meet some basic human needs is not that great. *The Hindu*, an Indian newspaper, has put these needs in perspective:

> Consumers in Europe and the U.S. spend $17 billion every year on pet foods. Yet, the world cannot find the additional $13 billion that is needed every year to provide basic health services to all people in developing countries. Consumers in Europe and the U.S. annually spend $12 billion on perfumes. This is the additional amount needed to meet the basic reproductive health needs of the women in developing countries. Consumers in Europe spend $11 billion every year buying ice cream, which is more than the extra $9 billion required to provide universal access to drinking water and sanitation in the developing countries. (*The Hindu*, 1998:25)

Excessive consumption hurts the poor in another way. Rising consumption is harmful to the environment, and the poor are more vulnerable than the wealthy to environmental damage. Environmental degradation in high-income countries will hurt some people, particularly those whose incomes depend on agriculture. But in these countries there are many alternative sources of food and money to help restore the environment. However, environmental degradation in countries where people depend on subsistence agriculture can mean malnutrition and starvation for huge numbers of people.

As we consume more, there is less for people in poor countries. Do you think we should continue to increase our consumption at their expense, or should we accept the challenge of setting new directions for future consumption?

Source: United Nations Development Programme, 1998; *The Hindu*, 1998.

corporations. If nations could increase their GNP, then social and economic inequality among the citizens within the country could also be reduced. Accordingly, Truman believed that it was necessary to assist the people of economically underdeveloped areas to raise their *standard of living*, by which he meant material well-being that can be measured by the quality of goods and services that may be purchased by the per capita national income (Latouche, 1992). According to social scientist Serge Latouche

In 1997, people around the world were saddened by the death of Mother Teresa, who had dedicated her life to ministering to the poor and unfortunate in low-income nations, especially India. According to Mother Teresa, people who are not poor could learn much from the poor.

(1992:250–251), measuring social and economic conditions on the basis of standard of living ultimately denigrates the culture and way of life in some societies.

What has happened to the issue of development since the post-World War II era? After several decades of economic development fostered by organizations such as the United Nations and the World Bank, it became apparent by the 1970s that improving a country's GNP did not tend to reduce the poverty of the poorest people in that country. In fact, global poverty and inequality were increasing, and the initial optimism of a speedy end to underdevelopment faded. Although many developing countries had achieved economic growth, it was not shared by everyone in the nation. For example, the poorest 40 percent of the Brazilian population receives less than 7 percent of the total national income, whereas the richest 20 percent of the population receives more than 65 percent (Elliott, 1994).

Why did inequality increase even with greater economic development? Many attribute this to the actions of the industrialized countries. Later in this chapter we will consider the impact of foreign aid programs and policies to control debt on the economies of developing nations. Other analysts in the developed nations began to link growing social and economic inequality on a global basis to relatively high rates of population growth taking place in the underdeveloped nations. Organizations such as the United Nations and the World Health Organization stepped up their efforts to provide family planning services to the populations so that they could control their own fertility.

More recently, however, population researchers have become aware that issues such as population growth, economic development, and environmental problems must be seen as interdependent concerns. This changing perception culminated in the U.N. Conference on Environment and Development in Rio de Janeiro, Brazil (the "Earth Summit"), in 1992; as a result, terms such as *underdevelopment* have been largely dropped in favour of measurements such as *sustainable development*, and economies are now classified by their levels of income (Elliott, 1994).

CLASSIFICATION OF ECONOMIES BY INCOME

An alternative way of describing the global stratification system is simply to measure a country's per capita income. The World Bank classifies nations into three economic categories: *low-income economies* (a GNP per capita of $1100 or less in 1994), *middle-income economies* (a GNP per capita of more than $1100 but less than $13,500 in 1994), and *high-income economies* (a GNP per capita of $13,500 or more in 1994).

Low-Income Economies

About half of the world's population lives in the fifty-one low-income economies where most people engage in agricultural pursuits, reside in nonurban areas, and are impoverished (World Bank, 1996). As shown in Map 8.1, low-income economies are found primarily in countries in Asia and Africa. Included are such nations as Rwanda, Mozambique, Ethiopia, Nigeria, Cambodia, Vietnam, Afghanistan, and Bangladesh. Countries such as Armenia and Bosnia-Herzegovina are among the low-income economies

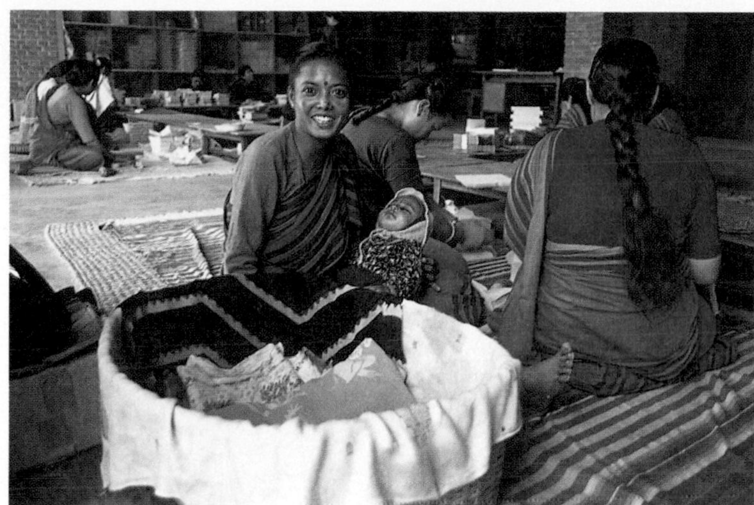

Based on the assumption that economic development is the primary way to reduce poverty in low-income nations, the United Nations has funded projects such as this paper company in Nepal.

in Eastern Europe. Latin American nations with low-income economies include Honduras and Nicaragua.

Women and children are particularly affected by poverty in low-income economies. Many poor women worldwide do not have access to commercial credit and have been trained only in traditionally female skills that produce low wages. All these factors have contributed to the *global feminization of poverty*, whereby women around the world tend to be more impoverished than men (Durning, 1993). Despite the fact that women have made some gains in terms of well-being, the income gap between men and women continues to grow wider in the low-income, developing nations.

Middle-Income Economies

About one-third of the world's population resides in the fifty-seven nations with middle-income economies (a GNP per capita of more than $1100 but less than $13,500 in 1994). The World Bank divides middle-income economies into lower middle-income ($1100 to $4300) and upper middle-income ($4300 to $13,500). Countries classified as lower middle-income include the Latin American nations of Bolivia, Colombia, Guatemala, El Salvador, and Panama. However, even though these countries are referred to as "middle-income," more than half of the people residing in countries such as Bolivia and Guatemala live in poverty, defined as below $90 per month in 1994 dollars (World Bank, 1996).

Other lower middle-income economies include the former Soviet Union, Poland, and Romania. These areas had centrally planned (i.e., socialist) economies until dramatic political and economic changes occurred in the late 1980s and early 1990s. Since then, these nations have been going through a transition to a market economy. Some nations have been more successful than others in implementing key elements of change and bringing about a higher standard of living for their citizens. Among other factors, high rates of inflation, the growing gap between the rich and the poor, low life-expectancy rates, and homeless children have been visible signs of problems in the transition toward a free-market economy in countries such as Russia.

Compared with lower middle-income economies, nations having upper middle-income economies typically have a somewhat higher standard of living and export diverse goods and services, ranging from manufactured goods to raw materials and fuels. Nations with upper middle-income economies include Brazil, South Africa, Chile, Hungary, and Mexico. Although these nations are referred to as middle-income economies, they have extremely high levels of indebtedness, leaving them with few resources for fighting poverty or developing their economies.

MAP 8.1 High-, Middle-, and Low-Income Economies in Global Perspective

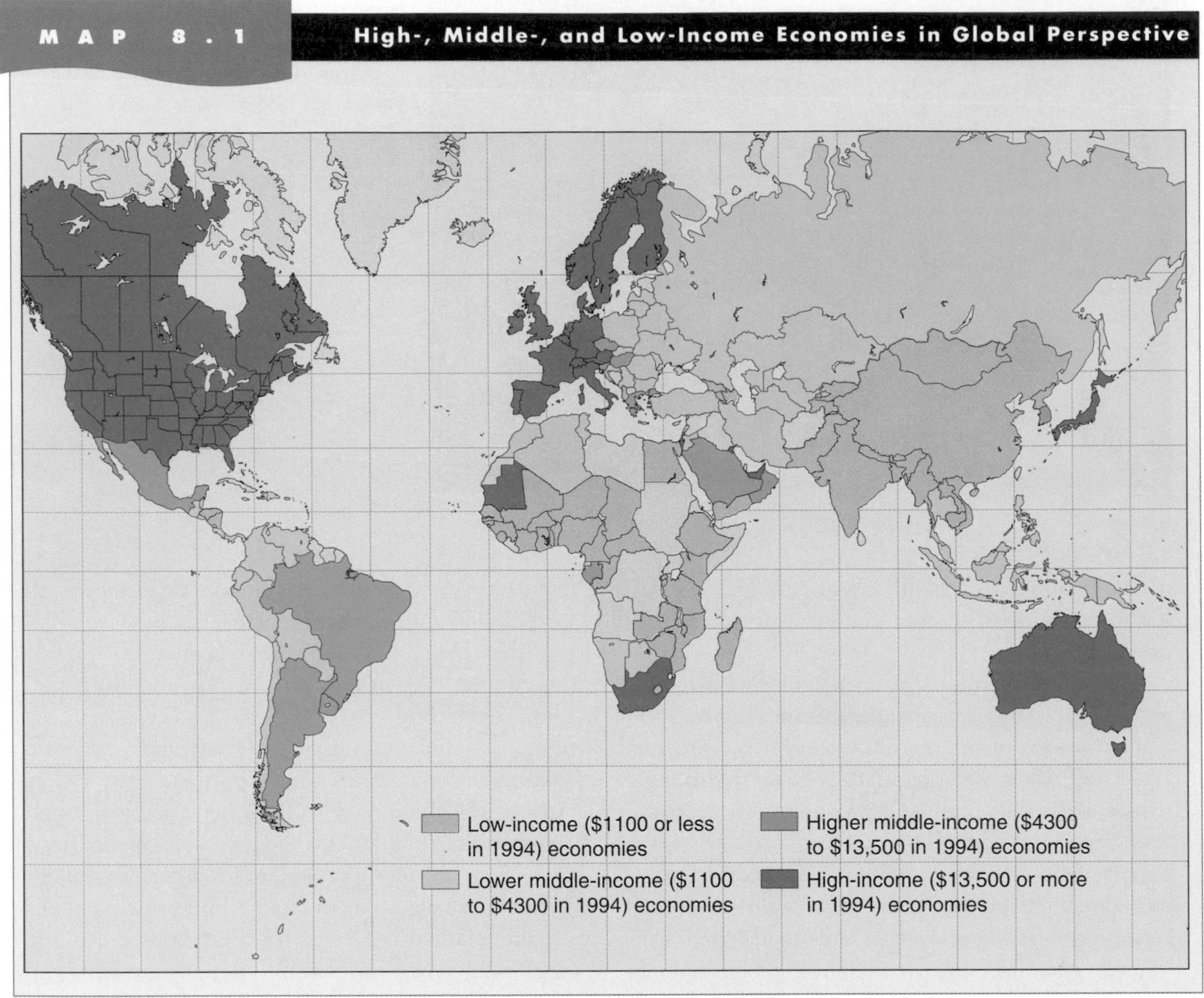

Source: World Bank, *World Development Report 1996: From Plan to Market.* New York: Oxford University Press for the World Bank, 1996. Reprinted by permission.

High-Income Economies

High-income economies are found in twenty-five nations, including Canada, the United States, Japan, Australia, Portugal, Ireland, Israel, Italy, Norway, and Germany. Nations with high-income economies continue to dominate the world economy, despite the fact that shifts in the global marketplace have affected some workers who have found themselves without work due to *capital flight*—the movement of jobs and economic resources from one nation to another—and *deindustrialization*—the closing of plants and factories because of their obsolescence or the fact that workers in other nations are being hired to do the work more cheaply.

The only significant group of middle- and lower-income economies to close the gap with the high-income, industrialized economies over the past few decades have been the nations of East Asia. South Korea has recently been reclassified from a middle-income to a high-income economy. China has experienced a 270 percent increase in per capita income over the past seventeen years. Despite its recent economic growth, however, the East Asian region remains home to approximately 350 million poor people.

Labour protesters march in downtown Seattle as part of a large demonstration near the meetings of the World Trade Organization, on December 3, 1999.

THE IMPACT OF DEBT AND FOREIGN AID

Debt and Global Stratification

The gap between rich and poor countries has grown over the past forty years for many reasons. One is the problem of debt, which has made it virtually impossible for some countries to move out of poverty. Private banks, governments, and international organizations have lent more money to poor countries than these countries can afford to pay back, especially when cyclical reductions in commodity prices have dramatically reduced their incomes. Much of the borrowed money was spent on military hardware and other nonproductive investments, so little went to building the productive capacity that would have allowed the poor countries to develop. As a result of the debt crisis, many countries were forced by the International Monetary Fund and the World Bank to restructure their economies by cutting back on social spending, devaluing their currencies, and reducing the funds spent on economic development. In many respects these governments have lost whatever power they once had to control their own economic destinies because they must follow the dictates of the lenders. This happened to most Latin American economies during the 1980s and to many East Asian and Eastern European economies during the late 1990s.

In many countries, the consequences of this externally imposed structural adjustment have been disastrous. Debt repayment takes money that could otherwise be used to provide social services and health care and to expand the country's economic base. In addition, debt repayment and economic restructuring have caused massive unemployment, reduced incomes, and soaring prices that have led to drastically reduced living standards, declines in investment, and political instability. This has represented a major setback in the progress of development. The problem has been summarized by Michel Chossudovsky:

> The movement of the global economy is "regulated" by "a world wide process of debt collection" which constricts the institutions of the national state and contributes to destroying employment and economic activity. In the developing world, the burden of external debt has reached two trillion dollars: entire countries have been destabilized as a consequence of the collapse of national currencies, often resulting in the outbreak of social strife, ethnic conflicts and civil war (1997:15) ... Internal purchasing power has collapsed, famines have erupted, health clinics and schools have been closed down, hundreds of millions of children have been denied the right to a primary education. In several regions of the developing world, the reforms have been conducive to resurgence of infectious diseases including tuberculosis, malaria, and cholera. (1997:33)

Many countries, particularly those in sub-Saharan Africa, have no chance of progressing economically unless the burden of debt repayment is eased by the richer debtholder countries.

Foreign Aid and Global Stratification

Few of us have not been moved by the compelling images of starving people in developing countries where droughts or floods have destroyed the annual harvest. Most of us support the emergency exports of food to these countries in order to prevent famine. However, some analysts have begun to ask whether this type of aid hurts more than it helps. For example, consider the recent history of Somalia, now one of the world's poorest and the most politically unstable countries. While Somalia's troubles are commonly blamed on drought and clan rivalries, some analysts feel that economic restructuring and food aid are the real causes (Chossudovsky, 1997). Because of droughts and other internal problems, food aid to Somalia increased dramatically from the mid-1970s to the mid-1980s. This donated food was sold into local markets very cheaply and undercut the price of locally grown food. At the same time, a currency devaluation demanded by the International Monetary Fund as a condition for restructuring Somalia's foreign debt made the cost of farm equipment and fuel more expensive. The combined result of the financial restructuring and the lower food prices was the virtual destruction of Somalia's agricultural system. While we normally think that a shortage of food is the cause of starvation, the global oversupply of grain may actually be contributing to famine by destroying the agricultural base of developing countries, making them vulnerable to future food shortages (Chossudovsky, 1997).

Foreign aid can also be damaging to low-income countries in other ways. First, aid can be tied to specific projects or objectives that may meet the interests of the donor country more than the interests of the recipients. For example, military aid will do little to help the lives of the poor and may do them great harm. Similarly, aid devoted to large infrastructure projects such as dams may cause more problems than it solves. Second, aid may be given to achieve political objectives. For example, the Soviet Union provided extensive aid to Cuba to maintain an ally just off the coast of the United States. The United States did the same thing in countries of strategic interest, including several Latin American countries. In these situations, aid is dependent on the low-income country's continuing political support for the activities of the donor country. This can severely constrain the power of governments to make decisions based on their own interests. Third, even when aid is targeted to individuals, it may not filter down to the poor. For example, donor countries may intend food aid to be distributed to the poor without payment, but elites may simply take the food, sell it, and keep the money.

The other problem is that there is not enough aid to help low-income countries solve health, nutrition, and employment problems. According to the head of the United Nations Children's Fund, foreign aid donations from the world's wealthiest countries declined by 30 percent between 1992 and 1997 despite the enormous growth of their economies over that time (Stackhouse, 1999). This has meant major reductions of assistance to the neediest countries. Canada has been one of the countries that have reduced aid donations over the past decade. Although Canada has a target of donating 0.7 percent of its gross domestic product (GDP) to foreign aid, the amount donated in 1998 was only 0.25 percent of GDP.

Thus there is not enough aid, and the aid that is provided is often not spent very effectively. However, there are signs of change. Many aid agencies have changed their focus away from large infrastructure programs such as dams and railroads to programs that focus directly on the poor. New ideas include using labour-intensive technologies and other strategies to create employment; providing basic social services such as health care, nutrition, and education; and giving assistance directly to the poorest people in low-income countries (Martinussen, 1997). Above all, the poor themselves must have a say in aid programs and should be empowered to make decisions about how aid money is spent. Otherwise foreign aid can be a double-edged sword that creates more problems than it solves. Not only do the poorest countries need more help from the industrialized world, but the aid that is provided needs to be administered in a manner that recognizes the needs of the countries receiving aid.

Workers in this toy factory in Zhuhal, China, make toys that are often marketed in high-income nations such as the United States.

GLOBAL POVERTY AND HUMAN DEVELOPMENT ISSUES

Most of the early work on global stratification focused on incomes as a measure of well-being. However, income disparities are not the only factor that defines poverty and its effect on people. Work by prominent economists such as Amaryta Sen and Mahbub ul Haq has led to a shift toward human welfare as a measure of development.

In 1990, the United Nations Development Programme introduced the Human Development Index (HDI), establishing three new criteria—in addition to GDP—for measuring the level of development in a country: life expectancy, education, and living standards. According to the United Nations, human development is "the process of increasing people's options to lead a long and healthy life, to acquire knowledge, and to find access to the assets needed for a decent standard of living" (Pietilä and Vickers, 1994:45).

Table 8.1 shows the difference between Canada and several other countries on the Human Development Index. The World Bank calculates that 37 percent of the population in low- and middle-income countries (1.6 billion people) lack the essentials of well-being, whereas only 21 percent (900 million people) are "income poor," as defined by the bank's poverty line.

While Canadians can be justifiably proud that they have been at the top of the Human Development Index through much of the 1990s, the picture is not completely positive. The United Nations Development Programme also publishes a Human Poverty Index for industrial countries that measures the percentage of people not expected to survive to age 60, the percentage of the population that is functionally illiterate, the population below the poverty line, and the percentage of the labour force that has suffered long-term unemployment. Canada ranks only tenth on this index, because of a high rate of functional illiteracy and a high proportion of the population with incomes below the poverty level. The United Nations has been critical of the quality of life among Canada's Aboriginal people, who rank far below other Canadians on the Human Development Index.

Life Expectancy

Although some advances have been made in middle- and low-income countries regarding life expectancy, major problems still remain (see Figure 8.3a). On the positive side, average life expectancy has increased by about a third in the past three decades and is now more than seventy years in twenty-three countries (United Nations, 1997). On a less positive note, the average life expectancy at birth of people in middle-income countries remains about twelve years less than that of people in high-income countries. Moreover, the life expectancy of people in low-income nations is as much as twenty-three years less than that of people in high-income nations.

One major cause of shorter life expectancy in low-income nations is the high rate of infant mortality (Figure 8.3b). Low-income countries typically have higher rates of illness and disease, and they do not have adequate health care facilities. Malnutrition is a common problem among children, many of whom are underweight, stunted, and have anemia—a nutritional deficiency with serious consequences for child mortality. The world's poorest 600 million people suffer from chronic malnutrition, and over 40 million people die each year from hunger-related diseases (Kidron and Segal, 1995).

TABLE 8.1 **HUMAN DEVELOPMENT INDEX**

COUNTRY	RANK	INDEX	PER CAPITA GDP[1]
Canada	1	0.960	21,916
France	2	0.946	21,176
Norway	3	0.943	22,427
United States	4	0.943	26,977
Japan	8	0.940	21,064
Mexico	49	0.855	6,769
Thailand	59	0.838	7,742
Brazil	62	0.809	5,928
Turkey	69	0.782	5,516
Russia	72	0.769	4,531
China	106	0.650	2,935
Kenya	137	0.463	1,438
India	139	0.451	1,422
Nigeria	142	0.391	1,270
Sierra Leone	174	0.185	625

[1]In comparing GDP, the *Human Development Report* uses purchasing power parities (PPP) in international dollars. PPP is a measure that accounts for different levels of purchasing power within different countries.

To put this figure in perspective, the number of people worldwide dying from hunger-related diseases is the equivalent of over 300 jumbo-jet crashes a day with no survivors, and half the passengers are children (Kidron and Segal, 1995). However, some progress has been made. Since the 1960s life expectancy has increased by sixteen years and infant mortality has been cut in half in the developing world. Basic immunization—a simple measure—saves more than 3 million lives each year (United Nations Development Programme, 1998).

Health

Health is defined by the World Health Organization as "a state of complete physical, mental and social well-being and not merely the absence of disease or infirmity" (Smyke, 1991:2). Because of their poverty, many people in low-income nations are far from having physical, mental, and social well-being. Of the 4.4 billion people who live in developing countries, 2.6 billion lack access to proper sanitation, 1.3 billion do not have safe water, 1 billion do not have adequate shelter, 880 million have no access to modern health services, and 841 million are malnourished (United Nations Development Programme, 1998). About 17 million people die each year from diarrhea, malaria, tuberculosis, and other infectious and parasitic illnesses (Hauchler and Kennedy, 1994). According to the World Health Organization, infectious diseases are far from under control in many nations due to such factors as unsanitary or overcrowded living conditions. Despite the possible eradication of diseases such as poliomyelitis, leprosy, guinea-worm disease, and neonatal tetanus in the near future, at least thirty new diseases—for which there is no treatment or vaccine—have recently emerged. Among these are AIDS and the Ebola virus, both of which were unknown twenty-five years ago (see Chapter 11, "Health, Health Care, and Disability").

FIGURE 8.3 Global Health Trends

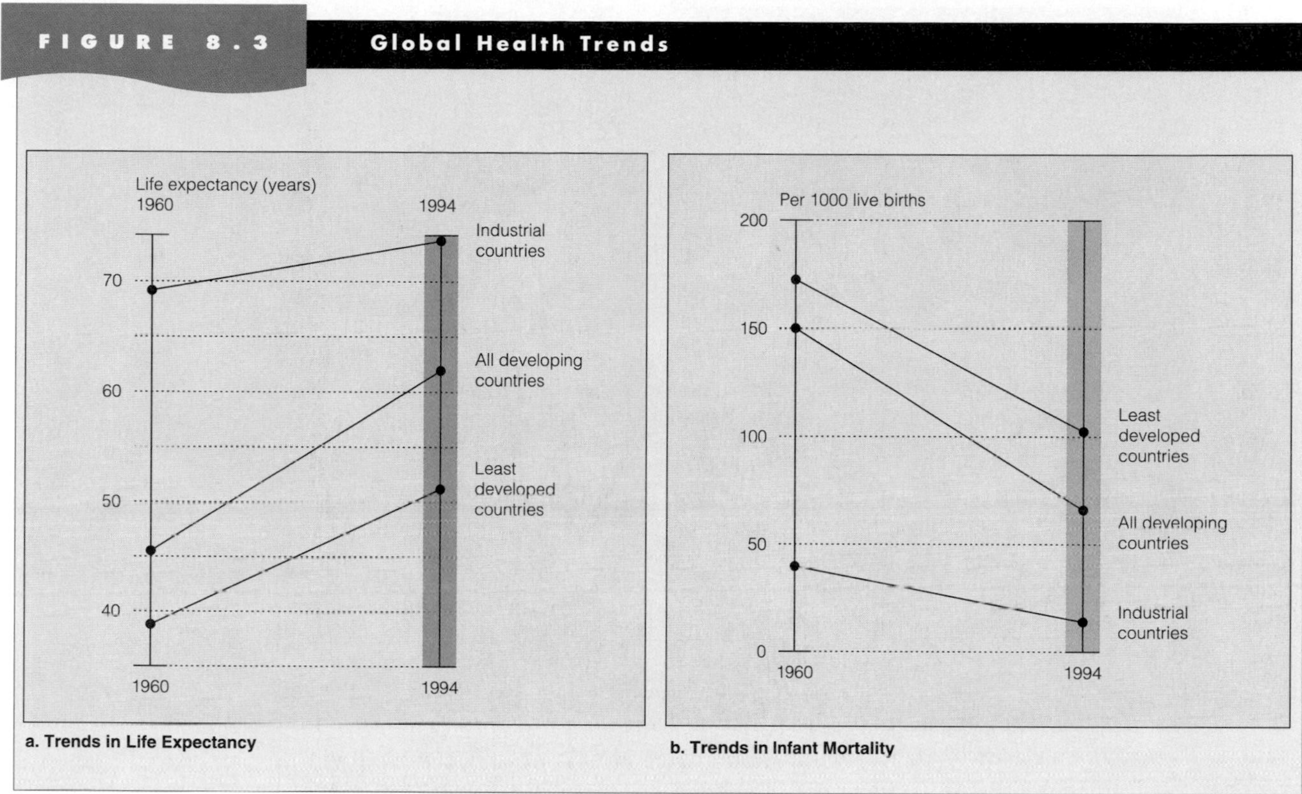

From *Human Development Report 1997* by the United Nations Development Programme. © 1997 by the United Nations Development Programme. Used by permission of Oxford University Press.

Education and Literacy

According to the Human Development Report (United Nations Development Programme, 1997), education is fundamental to reducing both individual poverty and national poverty. As a result, school enrolment is used as one measure of human development. The United Nations Educational, Scientific and Cultural Organization (UNESCO) defines a *literate* person as "someone who can, with understanding, both read and write a short, simple statement on their everyday life" (United Nations, 1997a:89). Based on this definition, people who can write only their name, a memorized phrase, or with figures are not considered literate. The adult literacy rate in low-income countries is about half that of the high-income countries, and for women the rate is even lower (United Nations, 1997a). Women constitute about two-thirds of those who are illiterate: there are approximately 74 literate women for every 100 literate men (United Nations, 1997). Literacy is crucial for women because it has been closely linked to decreases in fertility, improved child health, and increased earnings potential (Hauchler and Kennedy, 1994).

THEORIES OF GLOBAL INEQUALITY

Why is the majority of the world's population growing richer while the poorest 20 percent—over one billion people—are so poor that they are effectively excluded from even a moderate standard of living? Social scientists have developed many theories, which view the causes and consequences of global inequality somewhat differently. We will examine the development approach and modernization theory, dependency theory, world systems theory, and the new international division of labour theory. Modernization theory is part of the functionalist tradition, while the other perspectives are

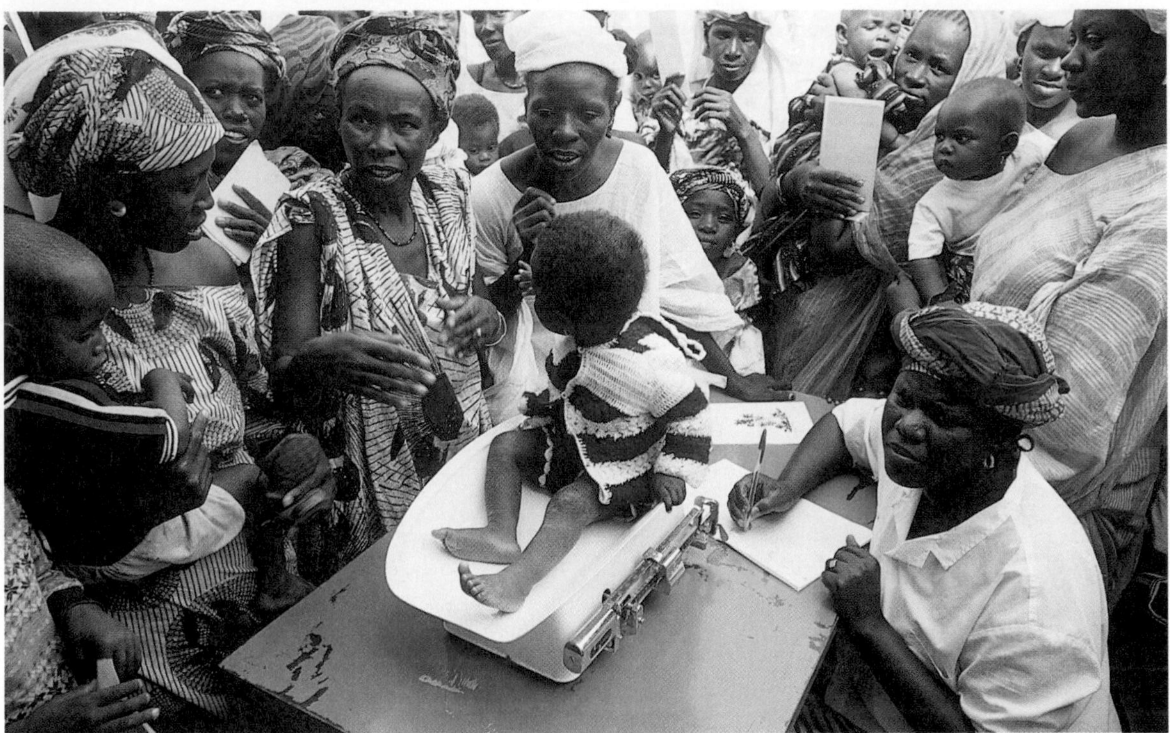

Malnutrition is a widespread health problem in many low-income nations.

rooted in the conflict approach. These approaches are depicted in Figure 8.4.

Development and Modernization Theories

According to some social scientists, global wealth and poverty are linked to the level of industrialization and economic development in a given society. These theorists maintain that low-income nations have progressed less than the wealthier industrial countries. They feel that industrialization and economic development are essential steps that nations must go through in order to reduce poverty and to improve the living conditions of their citizens. These theorists also believe that although the process by which a nation industrializes may vary somewhat, industrialization almost inevitably brings with it a higher standard of living in a nation and some degree of social mobility for individual participants in the society. Family status, race/ethnicity, and gender are said to become less significant in industrialized nations than in agrarian-based societies. As societies industrialize, they also urbanize as workers locate their residences near factories, offices, and other places of work. Consequently, urban values and folkways overshadow the beliefs and practices of the rural areas. Analysts using a development framework typically view industrialization and economic development as essential steps that nations must go through in order to reduce poverty and increase life chances for their citizens.

The most widely known development theory is ***modernization theory*****—a perspective that links global inequality to different levels of economic development and suggests that low-income economies can move to middle- and high-income economies by achieving self-sustained economic growth.** According to modernization theory, the low-income, less-developed nations can improve their standard of living only with a period of intensive economic growth and accompanying changes in people's beliefs, values, and attitudes toward work. As a result of modernization, the values of people in developing countries supposedly become more similar to those of people in high-income nations.

Perhaps the most widely known modernization theory is that of Walt W. Rostow (1971, 1978). To

Rostow, one of largest barriers to development in low-income nations was the traditional cultural values held by people, particularly fatalistic beliefs such as viewing extreme hardship and economic deprivation as inevitable and unavoidable facts of life. Fatalistic people do not see any need to work in order to improve their lot in life: If life is predetermined for them, why bother? According to modernization theory, poverty can be attributed to people's cultural failings, which are further reinforced by governmental policies interfering with the smooth operation of the economy.

Rostow suggested that all countries go through four stages of economic development with identical content, regardless of when these nations started the process of industrialization. He compares the stages of economic development to an airplane ride. The first stage is the *traditional stage*, in which very little social change takes place, and people do not think much about changing their current circumstances. The second stage is the *take-off stage*—a period of economic growth accompanied by a growing belief in individualism, competition, and achievement. During this stage, people start to look toward the future, to save and invest money, and to discard traditional values. According to Rostow's modernization theory, the development of capitalism is essential for the transformation from a traditional, simple society to a modern, complex one. With the financial help and advice of the high-income countries, low-income countries eventually will be able to "fly" and enter the third stage of economic development. In the third stage, the country moves toward *technological maturity*. At this point, the country improves its technology, reinvests in new industries, and embraces the beliefs, values, and social institutions of the high-income, developed nations. In the fourth and final stage, the country reaches the phase of *high mass consumption* and a corresponding high standard of living.

Modernization theory has had both its advocates and its critics. According to proponents of this approach, studies have supported the assertion that economic development occurs more rapidly in a capitalist economy. In fact, the countries that have been most successful in moving from low- to middle-income status typically have been those most centrally involved in the global capitalist economy. For example, many East-Asian nations have successfully made the transition from low-income to higher-income economies through factors such as a high rate of savings, an aggressive work ethic among employers and employees, and the fostering of a market economy.

Critics of modernization theory point out that it tends to be Eurocentric in its analysis of low-income countries, which it implicitly labels as backward (see Evans and Stephens, 1988). In many respects modernization was equated with westernization, as modernization theorists assumed that the problems of low-income countries would only be alleviated once they adopted Western values, culture, and economic models. Modernization theory does not take into account the possibility that all nations do not industrialize in the same manner. For example, Anton Allahar (1989) points out that leading industrial countries such as the United States, Britain, and Japan followed very dissimilar paths to industrialization. Thus we might also assume that the modernization of low-income nations in the late-twentieth and early-twenty-first centuries will require novel policies, sequences, and ideologies that are not accounted for in Rostow's approach (see Gerschenkron, 1962). The theory also does not tell us what actually causes the move from one stage to another, but simply assumes they are natural stages that must be followed as societies advance economically and socially.

One of the most influential critics of modernization theory was Andre Gunder Frank (1969). Frank's research in Latin America convinced him that modernization theory was badly flawed. While Rostow felt that all societies had to move in a linear fashion from underdevelopment to industrialization, Frank pointed out that underdevelopment was not an original stage, but a condition created by the imperial powers that had created dependency through actions such as the deindustrialization of India, the damage incurred by African societies during the years of the slave trade, and the destruction of Indian civilizations in Central and Latin America (Hettne, 1995). All societies were *un*developed at one time, but not all became *under*developed. While some countries moved from being underdeveloped to development, others moved from being undeveloped to a condition of underdevelopment in which they were dependent on other nations. These dependent countries had structures and institutions that effectively blocked any further development (Allahar, 1989).

FIGURE 8.4 **Approaches to Studying Global Inequality**

What causes global inequality? Social scientists have developed a variety of explanations, including the four theories shown here.

Modernization Theory: Low-income, less-developed countries can move to middle- and high-income economies by achieving self-sustained economic growth.

Dependency Theory: Global poverty can at least partially be attributed to the fact that low-income countries have been exploited by high-income economies; the poor nations are trapped in a cycle of dependency on richer nations.

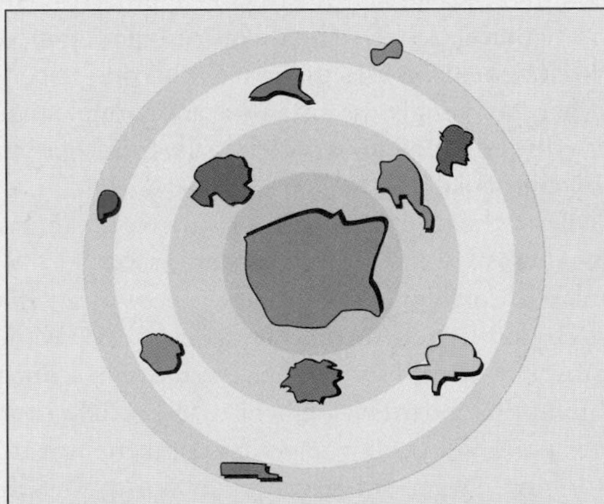

World Systems Theory: How a country is incorporated into the global capitalist economy (e.g., a core, semiperipheral, or peripheral nation) is the key feature in determining how economic development takes place in that nation.

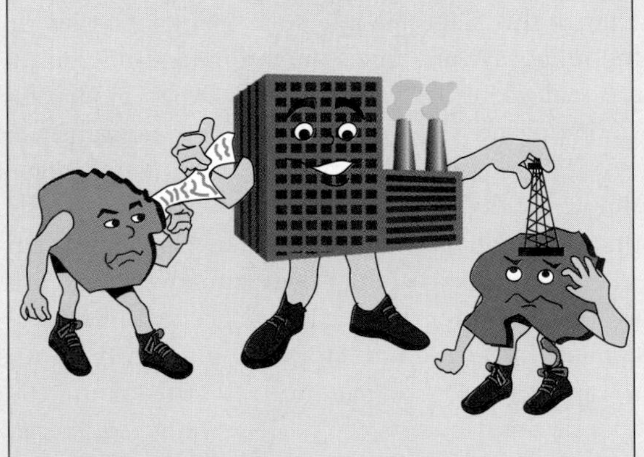

The New International Division of Labour Theory: Commodity production is split into fragments, each of which can be moved (e.g., by a transnational corporation) to whichever part of the world can provide the best combination of capital and labour.

The inadequacies of modernization theory and the political injustices that resulted from policies based on the theory moved the next generation of development theorists to *dependency theory*, an approach that was based on the conflict perspective.

Dependency Theory

According to dependency theorists, rich countries have an interest in maintaining the dependent status of poor countries, since this ensures them a source of raw materials and an essentially captive

A variety of factors—such as foreign investment and the presence of transnational corporations—have contributed to the economic growth of nations such as Singapore.

market for manufactured goods exported to the dependent nations. Business and political leaders in the poor nations find it in their interests to accept dependence and willingly work with the advanced nations to impose policies that maintain the dependent relationship. Any surpluses created in the dependent country will be taken by the affluent capitalist country rather than being used to build up production infrastructure or raise the standard of living in the dependent nations. For these reasons, dependency theorists believe that many countries can never reach the sustained economic growth patterns of the more advanced capitalist economies.

***Dependency theory* states that global poverty can at least partially be attributed to the fact that the low-income countries have been exploited by the high-income countries.** Analyzing events as part of a particular historical process—the expansion of global capitalism—dependency theorists see the greed of the rich countries as a source of increasing impoverishment of the poorer nations and their people. Dependency theory disputes the notion of the development approach—and modernization theory specifically—that economic growth is the key to meeting important human needs in societies. In contrast, the poorer nations are trapped in a cycle of structural dependency on the richer nations due to their need for infusions of foreign capital and external markets for their raw materials, which makes it impossible for the poorer nations to pursue their own economic and human development agendas. Frank and other scholars believed that the best way for low-income countries to move ahead was to break their links with the industrialized countries and to establish independent socialist governments.

Dependency theory has been most often applied to the newly industrializing countries (NICs) of Latin America, whereas scholars examining the NICs of East Asia have found that dependency theory has little or no relevance to economic growth and development in that part of the world. Therefore, dependency theory has had to be expanded to encompass transnational economic linkages that affect developing countries, including foreign aid, foreign trade, foreign direct investment, and foreign loans. On the one hand, in Latin America and sub-Saharan Africa, transnational linkages such as foreign aid, investments by transnational corporations, foreign debt, and export trade have been significant impediments to development within a country. On the other hand, East Asian countries such as Hong Kong, Taiwan, South Korea, and Singapore have also had high rates of dependency on foreign aid, foreign trade, and interdependence with transnational corporations but have nevertheless experienced high rates of economic growth. According to sociologist Gary Gereffi (1994), differences in outcome are probably associated with differences in the timing and sequencing of a nation's relationship with external entities such as foreign governments and transnational corporations.

Dependency theory makes a positive contribution to our understanding of global poverty by pointing out that "underdevelopment" is not necessarily the cause of inequality. Rather, this theory points out that exploitation not only of one country by another but of countries by transnational corporations may limit or retard economic growth and human development in some nations.

What remains unexplained is how some East Asian countries had successful "dependency management" whereas many Latin American countries did not (Gereffi, 1994). In fact, from the mid-1980s to the mid-1990s, the annual economic growth in East Asia (excluding Japan) has averaged 8.5 percent, which is four times the rate of the West (Tanzer, 1996). This growth slowed dramatically at the end of the 1990s and it remains to be seen if the East Asian "economic miracle" will continue.

While dependency theory has made a significant contribution to our understanding of global stratification, even its proponents feel it is no longer adequate. In addition to the problem of explaining the success of the East Asian economies that were closely linked with global capitalist structures, the dependency theorists' faith in development through socialist revolution has been shaken by the failure of many socialist economies including that of the Soviet Union (Frank, 1981). Also, most have concluded that the global economy is so pervasive that it is impossible for low-income countries to disconnect themselves from the industrialized world and proceed with their own development (Martinussen, 1997).

World Systems Theory

Drawing on Karl Marx's ideas about global imperialism and capitalist exploitation, world systems theory suggests that what exists under capitalism is a truly global system held together by economic ties. From this approach, global inequality does not emerge solely as a result of the exploitation of one country by another. Instead, economic domination involves a complex world system in which the industrialized, high-income nations benefit from other nations and exploit the citizens of those nations. This theory is most closely associated with sociologist Immanuel Wallerstein (1979, 1984), who believed that a country's mode of incorporation into the capitalist work economy is the key feature in determining how economic development takes place in that nation. According to ***world systems theory,*** **the capitalist world economy is a global system divided into a hierarchy of three major types of nations—core, semiperipheral, and peripheral—in which upward or downward mobility is conditioned by the resources and obstacles that characterize the international system.**

Core nations **are dominant capitalist centres characterized by high levels of industrialization and urbanization.** Core nations such as the United States, Japan, and Germany possess most of the world's capital and technology. Even more importantly for their position of domination, they exert massive control over world trade and economic agreements across national boundaries.

Most low-income countries in Africa, South America, and the Caribbean are ***peripheral nations*****—nations that are dependent on core nations for capital, have little or no industrialization (other than what may be brought in by core nations), and have uneven patterns of urbanization.** According to Wallerstein (1979, 1984), the wealthy in peripheral nations benefit from the labour of poor workers and from their economic relations with core nation capitalists, whom they uphold in order to maintain their own wealth and position. At a global level, uneven economic growth results from capital investment by core nations. Disparity between the rich and the poor within the major cities in these nations is increased in the process. The United States/Mexico border is an example of disparity and urban growth: transnational corporations have built *maquiladora* plants just over the border in Mexico so that goods can be assembled by low-wage workers to keep production costs down. Because of a demand for a large supply of low-wage workers, thousands of people have moved from the rural regions of Mexico to urban areas along the border in hope of earning a higher wage. This influx has pushed already overcrowded cities far beyond their capacity. Many people live on the edge of the city in shantytowns made from discarded materials or in low-cost rental housing in central-city slums because their wages are low and affordable housing is nonexistent (Flanagan, 1995).

Semiperipheral nations **are more developed than peripheral nations but less developed than core nations.** Nations in this category typically provide labour and raw materials to core nations within the world system. These nations constitute a midpoint between the core and peripheral nations that promotes the stability and legitimacy of the three-tiered world economy. These nations include South Korea and Taiwan in East Asia, Brazil in Latin America, India in South Asia, and Nigeria and South Africa in Africa. According to Wallerstein, semiperipheral nations exploit peripheral nations, just as the core nations exploit both the semiperipheral and the peripheral.

Not all social analysts agree with Wallerstein's (1979, 1984) perspective on the hierarchical position of nations in the global economy. However,

Michael Jordan makes more money for endorsing Nike shoes than the combined salaries of thousands of the workers who manufacture the shoes.

most scholars acknowledge that nations throughout the world are influenced by a relatively small number of cities and transnational corporations that have prompted a shift from an international to a more global economy (see Knox and Taylor, 1995; Wilson, 1997). Even Wallerstein (1991) acknowledges that world systems theory is an "incomplete, unfinished critique" for long-term, large-scale social change that influences global inequality.

The New International Division of Labour Theory

Although the term *world trade* has long implied that there is a division of labour between societies, the nature and extent of this division have been reassessed in the late 1990s based on the changing nature of the world economy. According to the ***new international division of labour theory,*** **commodity production is being split into fragments that can be assigned to whichever part of the world can provide the most profitable combination of capital and labour.** Consequently, the new international division of labour has changed the pattern of geographic specialization between countries, whereby high-income countries have become dependent on low-income countries for labour. The low-income countries provide transnational corporations with a situation in which they can pay lower wages and taxes and face fewer regulations regarding workplace conditions and environmental protection (Waters, 1995).

This new division of labour is part of a global economy based on free trade among countries. Multilateral trade agreements such as the General Agreement on Tariffs and Trade (GATT) and the North American Free Trade Agreement (NAFTA) have allowed the freer transfer of goods and services among countries, and global corporations now view all areas of the world both as potential markets and as potential locations for production.

These trade liberalization agreements would appear to be beneficial for poor countries, as the movement of production into developing countries brings jobs to countries with chronically high unemployment. However, few of the profits remain in these countries. For example, a study of garment manufacturing in Bangladesh found that less than 2 percent of the final value of the product went to production workers and that 1 percent went to the local producer. The rest of the money went to profit those who owned the company and to pay expenses such as shipping and storage costs and customs duties and sales taxes in high-income countries (Chossudovsky, 1997). There is little hope of higher wages for workers, since the jobs are unskilled and can quickly be moved to another poor country if workers begin to put pressure on the companies.

Overall, a global manufacturing system has emerged in which transnational corporations establish labour-intensive, assembly oriented export production, ranging from textiles and clothing to technologically sophisticated exports such as computers, in middle- and lower-income nations (Gereffi, 1994). At the same time, manufacturing technologies are shifting from the large-scale, mass-production assembly lines of the past toward a more flexible production process involving microelectronic technologies. Even service industries—such as processing insurance claims forms—that were formerly thought to be less mobile have become exportable through electronic transmission and the Internet. The global nature of these activities has been referred to as *global commodity chains*, a complex pattern of international labour and production

BOX 8.3 SOCIOLOGY AND TECHNOLOGY

THE DIGITAL THIRD WORLD

There is little doubt that information and communications technologies are changing our world. However, there is considerable debate about the impact of these technologies on the poor. Some feel that the ability to share information from around the globe will hasten the development of low-income countries, as they will be able to become knowledge societies that can compete with the industrialized nations. For example, technology can speed the pace of educational reform and help to build a more participatory civil society through the sharing of information and ideas. However, a more common view is that the move to a world linked by new information and communications technology will lead to a greater polarization between the rich who can exploit the new technologies and the poor who do not even have access to them. In other words, the poor will likely be excluded from the global information society—and this includes the poor in industrialized countries, as the "digital Third World" does not follow international borders. The Internet is accessible to only about 2 percent of the world's people (Hammann, 1998), and these are disproportionately high-income residents of high-income countries. The richest 20 percent of countries have 93 percent of Internet users, while the poorest 20 percent of countries have only 0.2 percent (United Nations Development Programme, 1999).

Why is it unlikely that the information revolution will reduce global stratification? There are many barriers to the spread of information and communications technology. The major obstacle is cost. To become part of the "digital world" low-income countries must build very expensive communications infrastructures. For example, while Canada has 57 phone lines per 100 people, countries such as China, India, Kenya, and Pakistan have just one per 100. The costs of installing a phone line in places like rural Africa are about $5000, and existing phone lines in most low-income countries cannot handle the transmission speeds necessary to use the Internet effectively (Wresch, 1996). In a world in which global communications and access to the Internet are becoming critical to business and trade, countries that cannot afford to build communications networks or to train people in how to use computers will be at a great competitive disadvantage. It is most unlikely that countries that are deeply in debt and have other pressing needs such as health

processes that results in a finished commodity ready for sale in the marketplace.

This type of commodity chain is most common in labour-intensive consumer goods industries such as toys, garments, and footwear (Gereffi, 1994). Athletic footwear companies such as Nike and Reebok and clothing companies like the Gap and Liz Claiborne are examples of this model. Since these products tend to be labour intensive at the manufacturing stage, the factory system is typically very competitive and globally decentralized. Workers in commodity chains are often exploited by low wages, long hours, and poor working conditions. In fact, most workers cannot afford the products they make. Tini Heyun Alwi, who works on the assembly line of the shoe factory in Indonesia that makes Reebok sneakers, is an example: "I think maybe I could work for a month and still not be able to buy one pair" (quoted in Goodman, 1996: F1). Since Tini earns only 2600 Indonesian rupiah ($1.28) per day working a ten-hour shift six days a week, her monthly income would fall short of the retail price of the athletic shoes (Goodman, 1996).

Sociologist Gary Gereffi (1994:225) explains the problem with studying the new global patterns as follows:

BOX 8.3

CONTINUED

care and nutrition will be able to create a communications infrastructure without a great deal of help. It is hard to conceive of the "wired classroom" in a country that cannot afford to build schools or train teachers.

A second reason for the lack of Internet access in most parts of the world is language. The vast majority of content on the Internet is in English. Without multilingual sites, the name, the World Wide Web, will never be accurate. A Web that is dominated linguistically by English and technologically and culturally by the United States will never reflect the point of view of people in low-income countries. (For a rare example of an Internet site that uses several African languages, see the Channel Africa site at **www.channelafrica.org/currenta.html**.)

A final reason for lack of access is government censorship. Most totalitarian countries are afraid of the free flow of information. It is easier to restrict the freedom of people who are unable to share ideas with each other and with people in other countries. As a result, many governments, including China, Algeria, and Afghanistan, have restricted their citizens' access to new forms of communications technology.

While low-income countries continue to fall further behind in the development of information technology, some small steps have been taken to reduce the gap. One model project has been undertaken by Canada's International Development Research Centre (IDRC). Project Acacia is an international effort led by the IDRC to provide sub-Saharan communities with the ability to apply information and communication technologies to their own social and economic development (for more information, go to **www.idrc.ca/acacia/acacia_e.htm**). Its partners in the project include the African Information Society Initiative, which is trying to provide an African perspective on the opportunities and challenges of that continent in an emerging information age. This is important for cultural, as well as for economic, reasons. A global Internet culture controlled by industrialized countries is a great threat to the cultural identity of groups whose perspectives are not represented.

While this project is promising, it is a very small step toward the solution of a very large problem. Much more must be done if low-income countries are to build on-ramps to the information superhighway.

> The difficulty may lie in the fact that today we face a situation where (1) the political unit is *national*, (2) industrial production is *regional*, and (3) capital movements are *international*. The rise of Japan and the East Asian [newly industrializing countries] in the 1960s and 1970s is the flip side of the "deindustrialization" that occurred in the United States and much of Europe. Declining industries in North America have been the growth industries in East Asia.

GLOBAL INEQUALITY IN THE FUTURE

As we have seen, social inequality is a major issue within and among the countries of the world. Even in high-income nations where wealth is highly concentrated, many poor people coexist with the affluent. In middle- and low-income countries, there are small pockets of wealth in the midst of poverty and despair.

What are the future prospects for greater equality across and within nations? Not all social scientists agree on the answer to this question. Depending on their theoretical framework, social analysts may describe either an optimistic or a pessimistic scenario for the future.

In some regions, persistent and growing poverty continues to undermine human development and future possibilities for socioeconomic change. In many poor countries, economic development has stalled. In fact, in about one hundred countries incomes today are lower than they were ten years ago (United Nations Development Programme, 1998). Gross inequality has high financial and quality of life costs to people, even among those who are not the poorest of the poor. In the future, continued population growth, urbanization, and environmental degradation threaten even the meagre living conditions of those residing in low-income nations. From this perspective, the future looks dim not only for people in low- and middle-income countries but also for those in high-income countries, who will see their quality of life diminish as natural resources are depleted, the environment is polluted, and high rates of immigration and global political unrest threaten the elevated standard of living that many have enjoyed over the past fifty years. According to some social analysts, transnational corporations and financial institutions such as the World Bank and the International Monetary Fund will further solidify their control over a globalized economy, which will transfer the power to make significant choices to these organizations and away from the people and their governments. As a result, further loss of resources and means of livelihood will affect people and countries around the globe. Adding to the problem, industrialized countries have cut back on foreign aid despite their increased wealth.

As a result of global corporate domination, there could be a levelling off of average incomes around the world, with wages falling in the high-income countries and increasing significantly in low- and middle-income countries. If this pessimistic scenario occurs, there is likely to be greater polarization of the rich and the poor and more potential for ethnic and national conflicts over such issues as worsening environmental degradation and who has the right to natural resources. For example, pulp-and-paper companies in Indonesia, along with palm oil plantation owners, have continued clearing land for crops by burning off vast tracts of jungle, producing high levels of smog and pollution across seven Southeast Asian nations and creating havoc for millions of people (Mydans, 1997). Whose rights should prevail in situations like this? The smoke from the Indonesian fires has affected agriculture; food shortages and rising prices are inevitable. Reduced sunlight is slowing the growth of crops, and people in record numbers are suffering from respiratory illnesses. The possibility remains that severe, long-term illnesses may also develop over time, especially among the young, the old, and people with respiratory problems (Mydans, 1997). This could be a future scenario if "business as usual" continues to take place around the world.

On the other hand, a more optimistic scenario is also possible. With modern technology and worldwide economic growth, it might be possible to reduce absolute poverty and to increase people's opportunities. Among the trends cited by the Human Development Report (United Nations Development Programme, 1996) that have the potential to bring about more sustainable patterns of development are the socioeconomic progress made in many low- and middle-income countries over the past thirty years as technological, social, and environmental improvements have occurred. For example, technological innovation continues to improve living standards for some people. Fertility rates are declining in some regions (but remain high in others, where there remains grave cause for concern about the availability of adequate natural resources for the future). Health and education may continue to improve in lower-income countries. However, if positive change is to continue, the practices of global corporations, foreign aid donors, and international lending organizations must begin to focus on the needs of low-income countries rather than solely on the perceived demands of the marketplace.

We will continue to focus on issues pertaining to global inequality in subsequent chapters as we discuss such topics as race, gender, education, health and medicine, population, urbanization, social change, and the environment.

CHAPTER REVIEW

What is global stratification, and how does it contribute to economic inequality?

Global stratification refers to the unequal distribution of wealth, power, and prestige on a global basis, which results in people having vastly different lifestyles and life chances both within and among the nations of the world. Today, the income gap between the richest and the poorest 20 percent of the world population continues to widen, and within some nations the poorest 20 percent of the population has an income that is only a slight fraction of the overall per capita income for that country.

How are global poverty and human development related?

Income disparities are not the only factor that defines poverty and its effect on people. The United Nations' Human Development Index measures the level of development in a country through indicators such as life expectancy, infant mortality rate, proportion of underweight children under age five (a measure of nourishment and health), and adult literacy rate for low-, middle-, and high-income countries.

What is modernization theory, and what stages did Rostow believe all societies go through?

Modernization theory is a perspective that links global inequality to different levels of economic development and suggests that low-income economies can move to middle- and high-income economies by achieving self-sustained economic growth. According to Rostow, all countries go through four stages of economic development: (1) the traditional stage, in which very little social change takes place; (2) the take-off stage, a period of economic growth accompanied by a growing belief in individualism, competition, and achievement;
(3) technological maturity, a period of improving technology, reinvesting in new industries, and embracing the beliefs, values, and social institutions of the high-income, developed nations; and (4) the phase of high mass consumption, accompanied by a high standard of living.

How does dependency theory differ from modernization theory?

Dependency theory states that global poverty can at least partially be attributed to the fact that the low-income countries have been exploited by the high-income countries. Whereas modernization theory focuses on how societies can reduce inequality through industrialization and economic development, dependency theorists see the greed of the rich countries as a source of increasing impoverishment of the poorer nations and their people.

What is world systems theory, and how does it view the global economy?

According to world systems theory, the capitalist world economy is a global system divided into a hierarchy of three major types of nations: core nations are dominant capitalist centres characterized by high levels of industrialization and urbanization; peripheral nations are those countries that are dependent on core nations for capital, that have little or no industrialization (other than what may be brought in by core nations), and that have uneven patterns of urbanization; and semiperipheral nations are more developed than peripheral nations but less developed than core nations.

What is the new international division of labour theory?

The new international division of labour theory is based on the assumption that commodity production is split into fragments that can be assigned to whichever part of the world can provide the most profitable combination of capital and labour. This division of labour has changed the pattern of geographic specialization among countries, whereby high-income countries have become dependent on low-income countries for labour. The low-income countries provide transnational corporations with a situation in which they can pay lower wages and taxes and face fewer regulations regarding workplace conditions and environmental protection.

Key Terms

core nations 240
dependency theory 239
modernization theory 236
new international division of labour theory 241
peripheral nations 240
semiperipheral nations 240
world systems theory 240

Internet Exercises

1. Visit the home page for UNICEF (the United Nations Children's Fund): **www.unicef.org**

   What types of issues can you access through this page's links? Click on several of the links. Would some—or even all—of them be helpful in studying the consequences of poverty among the world's children?

2. One of the sites maintained by UNICEF on the Internet is the State of the World's Children:

   www.unicef.org/sowc(plus the last two digits of the most recent year)

   Access this site and its links to lived experiences (under "news features") and data (under "fact sheets"). Compare the status of children in low-income nations as shown on this site's pages with that of children in Canada in terms of absolute, relative, and subjective poverty.

3. Go to the site of the Canadian International Development Agency (CIDA) at:

   www.acdi-cida.gc.ca/index-e.htm

   What are Canada's priorities in giving aid? What regions of the world are most important to those directing aid programs? Do you think CIDA's programs are more concerned with Canada's needs and priorities or with the needs and priorities of the countries receiving the aid?

4. What can be done about the negative consequences of globalization? Go to the site of the 1999 Human Development Report:

   www.undp.org/hdro/report.html

   Look at Chapter 5 of this report for some suggestions.

Net Links

For more Web links related to the topic of this chapter, see the Nelson sociology Web site: **www.sociologyessentials-2nded.nelson.com**.

The United Nations Development Programme has done an excellent job in focusing public attention on global inequality issues. To find out more about the world's poorest people and to learn what can be done to help them, visit the Programme's Web site at:

www.undp.org/index5.html

World Factbook 1999 contains demographic information from around the globe; to see it, go to:

www.odci.gov/cia/publications/factbook

Women's International Net looks at international development issues from a woman's perspective. Its address is:

welcome.to/winmagazine

A number of reports from the World Bank are available at:

www.worldbank.org

Boycotts have been held against Nike and Reebok because of their treatment of workers in low-income countries. Read about boycotts at:

http://boycott-nike.8m.com 

Questions for Critical Thinking

1. You have decided to study global wealth and poverty. How would you approach your study? What research methods would provide the best data for analysis? What might you find if you compared your research data with popular presentations—such as films and advertising—of everyday life in low- and middle-income countries?
2. How would you compare the lives of poor people living in central cities and rural areas of Canada with those of people living in the low-income nations of the world? In what ways are their lives similar? In what ways are they different?
3. Should Canadian foreign policy include provisions for

reducing poverty in other nations of the world? Should our domestic policy include provisions for reducing poverty in Canada? How are these issues similar? How are they different?

4. Using the theories discussed in this chapter, devise a plan to alleviate poverty. Assume that you have the necessary wherewithal, including wealth, political power, and natural resources. Share your plan with others in your class and create a consolidated plan that represents the best ideas and suggestions presented.

Suggested Readings

For more information on issues such as economic development and the global economy, the following books are recommended:

Michel Chossudovsky. *The Globalization of Poverty*. Penang: Third World Network, 1997.

James M. Cypher and James L. Dietz. *The Process of Economic Development*. New York: Routledge, 1997.

David C. Korten. *When Corporations Rule the World*. West Hartford, Conn.: Kumarian Press, 1995.

John Martinussen. *Society, State, and Market: A Guide to Competing Theories of Development*. Halifax: Fernwood Books, 1997.

United Nations Development Programme. *Human Development Report, 1997*. New York: Oxford University Press, 1997.

Malcolm Waters. *Globalization*. New York: Routledge, 1995.

World Bank. *World Development Report 1996: From Plan to Market*. New York: Oxford University Press, 1996.

INFOTRAC® COLLEGE EDITION

Either from the *Sociology In Our Times: The Essentials* Web site (**www.sociologyessentials-2nded.nelson.com**) or directly from your Web browser, you may access InfoTrac® College Edition, an online university library that includes over 600 popular and scholarly journals in which you can find articles related to the topics in this chapter.

CHAPTER 

Race and Ethnicity
- Social Significance of Race and Ethnicity
- Majority and Minority Groups

Components of Racial and Ethnic Conflict
- Prejudice
- Theories of Prejudice
- Discrimination
- Racism

Sociological Perspectives on Race and Ethnic Relations
- Interactionist Perspectives
- Functionalist Perspectives
- Conflict Perspectives
- A Feminist Perspective on Race and Gender

Ethnic Groups in Canada
- First Nations
- Charter Europeans
- Canada's Immigrants

Racial and Ethnic Diversity in Canada in the Future

In the following personal narrative, Valerie Bedassigae Pheasant discusses her experiences with racism and the impact of these experiences on both her mother and herself:

"The cocoon that encased my mother was woven by inside thoughts that constricted her more strongly than anything tangible in the human world. Inside thoughts reacting to outside action generated towards our family's Nativeness. Blatant racist remarks and statements by women who did not care to know us. Each word, each comment diminished her capacity to speak—she moved slower and slower ... My mother liked to play bingo at the church hall occasionally. I went with her ... It was hard to find seats. We found some. We looked around at the other women at the table. Nobody said hello. They looked and I looked back ... The other women talked amongst themselves in what resembled a huddle. They glanced furtively in our direction. We sat and waited—I watched. Whispers. Whispers coming from the huddle. Whispers that called out, too loud, clanging in my ears, 'Smells like Indians!' Instinctively, I breathed in deeply. Did they mean us? I could see them staring at us. My mother's head was down. Tears? I knew it was us. We moved to another table. We do not speak about what was said about us. We do not recognize them. We cannot give them more power. My anger grows. My mother's spirit staggers." (1994:35–36)

RACE AND ETHNICITY

Canada is a diverse and complex society composed of racially and ethnically different groups. It has a reputation as a tolerant and compassionate country whose success in race and ethnic relations has received worldwide admiration. Canadians profess to be colour-blind: the refrain "race doesn't matter here" is widely endorsed (James and Shadd, 1994:47). Is it surprising, therefore, to read this personal narrative, in which it is suggested that Aboriginal people in Canada experience racism as part of their everyday life? As Fleras and Elliott comment, "From afar, Canada looks idyllic; up close, the picture changes. Dig deeper and one can unearth a country that has little to boast about in the treatment of minorities" (1996:17). In this chapter racism will be central to the discussion of race and ethnicity. Before reading on, test your knowledge about racism in Canada by taking the quiz in Box 9.1.

Questions and Issues

CHAPTER FOCUS QUESTION: How significant is race in Canadian society?

How do race and ethnicity differ?

How does discrimination differ from prejudice?

How are racial and ethnic relations analyzed from a sociological perspective?

What are the unique experiences of racial and ethnic groups in Canada?

Golf star Tiger Woods's mother is one-half Chinese and one-half Thai, and his father had one white, one Native, and two black grandparents. Woods calls himself a "Cablinasian" to reflect this diverse background. Racial intermarriage is steadily increasing in Canada, the United States, and Britain. What will this mean for the concept of race in the future?

RACE AND ETHNICITY

What is "race"? Some people think it refers to skin colour (the "Caucasian race"); others use it to refer to a religion (the "Jewish race"), nationality (the "British race"), or the entire human species (the "human race") (Marger, 1997). A ***race* is a category of people who have been singled out as socially different, often on the basis of inherited physical characteristics such as skin colour, hair texture, and eye shape** (Newman, 1995).

Difficulties arise when thinking in terms of race. For example, use of the term *race* implies that racial purity exists. Although we may assume that we can distinguish between people on the basis of racially defined physical characteristics, biology confirms that most Canadians, like people all over the world, are genetically mixed. The combined effects of migration, immigration, and intermarriage have made it impossible to draw a line around human populations, with certain characteristics on one side, but not on the other (Martin and Franklin, 1983). Consider the confusion the concept of race created for one student:

> I am part French, part Cherokee Indian, part Filipino, and part black. Our family taught us to be aware of all these groups, and just to be ourselves. But I have never known what I am. People have asked if I am a Gypsy, or a Portuguese, or a Mexican, or lots of other things. It seems to make people curious, uneasy, and sometimes belligerent. Students I don't even know stop me on campus and ask, "What are you, anyway?" (quoted in Davis, 1991:133)

How do you classify yourself with regard to race? For an increasing number of people, this is a difficult question to answer. What if you were asked about your ethnic origin or your ethnicity? The Canadian census, unlike that of the United States, collects information on ethnic origin rather than race. Race refers only to physical characteristics, but the concept of ethnicity refers to cultural features. These features may include language, religion, national origin, distinctive foods, a common heritage, music, dress, or any other distinctive cultural trait. An ***ethnic group*, then, is a collection of people who, as a result of their shared cultural traits and a high level of interaction, regard themselves and are regarded as a cultural unit** (Robertson, 1977). As Table 9.1 shows, in 1996 over ten million Canadians—roughly 36 percent of all Canadians—reported multiple ethnic origins (Statistics Canada, 1998d). As a result, collecting data on ethnic origin is not a simple task.

Ethnic groups share five main characteristics: (1) *unique cultural traits*, such as language, clothing, holidays, or religious practice, (2) *a sense of community*, (3) *a feeling of ethnocentrism*, (4) *ascribed membership from birth*, and (5) *territoriality, or a tendency to occupy a distinct geographic area by choice or for protection*.

Although the distinction between ethnicity and race appears obvious—one is cultural, the other biological—the terms are often used interchangeably. Many people, for example, believe that Jews constitute a race although their distinctiveness pertains to cultural characteristics, primarily religious beliefs as well as a history of persecution.

BOX 9.1 SOCIOLOGY AND EVERYDAY LIFE

HOW MUCH DO YOU KNOW ABOUT RACISM IN CANADA?

TRUE	FALSE	
T	F	1. There is only one kind of racism in Canada.
T	F	2. The majority of Canadians view racism as a significant social problem.
T	F	3. Racism in Canada is a result of immigration of nonwhites.
T	F	4. Racism occurs only in times of economic decline and recession.
T	F	5. Policies of multiculturalism are insufficient to address the problems of racism.
T	F	6. No civil rights movement has ever existed in Canada.
T	F	7. Affirmative action programs directed at hiring visible minorities are a form of reverse discrimination.
T	F	8. Visible minorities are the likeliest victims of racism.
T	F	9. Incidents of anti-Semitism (racism directed at Jews) have increased in the past decade.
T	F	10. Slavery has never existed in Canada.

Answers on page 252.

Social Significance of Race and Ethnicity

How important are race and ethnicity in Canada? According to sociologists Augie Fleras and Jean Leonard Elliott:

> Most Canadians appear ambivalent about the race concept. The concept carries a negative connotation that conflicts with the virtues of an achievement-oriented, upwardly mobile society. Many dislike the underlying message of race: That is, the most important thing about a person is an accident of birth, something beyond control, and that alone should determine job status, and privilege. (1996:37)

It is easy to suggest that race is insignificant if one is not a member of a racial minority. But, whether we like to acknowledge it or not, race does matter. It matters because it provides privilege and power for some. Fleras and Elliott discuss the significance of being white and enjoying what has sometimes been referred to as *white privilege*:

> Think for a moment about the privileges associated with whiteness, many of which are taken for granted and unearned by accident of birth. Being white means you can purchase a home in any part of town and expect cordial treatment rather than community grumblings about the neighborhood "going to pot." Being white saves you the embarrassment of going into a shopping mall with fears of being followed, frisked, monitored, or finger printed. Being white means you can comment on a variety of topics without someone impugning your objectivity or motives. You can speak your mind with little to lose if things go wrong. Being white enables you to display righteous anger in dealing with colleagues, yet not incur snide remarks about "aggression" or "emotional stability" ... Being white gives you the peace of mind that your actions are not judged as a betrayal or a credit to your race. Finally, being white provides the satisfaction of cruising around late at night without attracting unnecessary police attention (1996:35).

Ethnicity, like race, is a basis of hierarchical ranking in society and an "extremely critical determinant of who gets 'what there is to get' and in what amounts" (Marger, 1994:18). John Porter (1965) described Canada as a "vertical mosaic," made up of different ethnic groups wielding varying degrees of social and economic power, status, and prestige. Porter's extensive analysis of ethnic groups in Canada revealed a significant degree of ethnic stratification with some ethnic groups heavily represented in the upper strata, or elite, and other groups

BOX 9.1

Answers to the Sociology Quiz on Racism

1. **False.** Racism takes many forms. The more subtle forms of racism such as institutional or systemic racism remain prevalent in Canadian society.
2. **True.** A recent poll indicated that 75 percent of Canadians consider racism a serious social problem.
3. **False.** The argument here is that if immigration is curbed, racism will decrease. However, even before Canada began allowing large-scale immigration, racism existed in the relationship between white colonial settlers and Aboriginal peoples.
4. **False.** Racism has been practised systematically in Canada since this country was formed—even in times of economic prosperity. For example, in the early 1950s, despite an economic boom, Chinese and Japanese citizens were regarded as "enemy aliens."
5. **True.** To expect that programs supporting cultural retention can also achieve racial equality and harmony is unrealistic.
6. **False.** In the 1940s and 1950s organizations such as the Windsor Council on Group Relations, the National Unity Association of Chatham-Dresden-North Buxton, and the Negro Citizens' Association of Toronto fought segregation in housing and employment as well as racist immigration laws.
7. **False.** For affirmative action policies to be a form of reverse discrimination, they would have to require employers to discriminate against better-qualified whites and give an unfair advantage to visible minorities. Affirmative action is directed not at discrimination, but at elimination of a long history of employment practices that result in preferential treatment toward white candidates.
8. **False.** In Canada both Aboriginal people and visible minorities are subjected to racism. Which group is victimized more is difficult to measure.
9. **True.** In the past decade, the League for Human Rights of B'nai B'rith has monitored the number and types of anti-Semitic incidents that have occurred in all regions of Canada. They report a significant increase in anti-Semitic incidents of all kinds.
10. **False.** Slavery was introduced in Canada by the French in 1608. Sixteen legislators in the first Parliament of Upper Canada owned slaves. Slavery existed in Quebec, New Brunswick, Nova Scotia, and Ontario until the early nineteenth century.

Source: Henry et al., 1995; and Fleras and Elliott, 1996.

heavily represented in the lower strata. The dominant group holds power over other (subordinate) ethnic groups. Ethnic stratification is one dimension of a larger system of structured social inequality, as examined in Chapter 7.

Majority and Minority Groups

The terms *majority group* and *minority group* are widely used, but what do they actually mean? To sociologists, a ***majority*** **(or** ***dominant*****)** ***group*** **is one that is advantaged and has superior resources and rights in a society** (Feagin and Feagin, 1993). In Canada, whites with northern European ancestry (often referred to as Euro-Canadians, white Anglo-Saxon Protestants, or WASPs) are considered a majority group. A ***minority*** **(or** ***subordinate*****)** ***group*** **is one whose members, because of physical or cultural characteristics, are disadvantaged and subjected to unequal treatment by the dominant group and who regard themselves as objects of collective discrimination** (Wirth, 1945). All visible minorities and white women are considered minority group members in Canada. The term ***visible minority*** **refers to an official government category of nonwhite non-Caucasian individuals.** Included in this category are

TABLE 9.1 SELECTED ETHNIC ORIGINS OF CANADIANS,[1] 1996

	CANADA	
Total population	**28,528,125**	**Percentage**
Single origins[2]	*18,303,625*	*64*
British Isles origins[3]	3,267,520	11
French origins[4]	2,683,840	9
Western European origins	1,126,095	4
Northern European origins	167,285	0.6
Eastern European origins	867,055	3
Southern European origins	1,376,935	5
Other European origins	205,525	0.7
Arab origins	188,435	0.6
West Asian origins	106,870	0.3
South Asian origins	590,145	2
East and Southeast Asian origins	1,217,450	4
African origins	137,315	0.4
Pacific Island origins	5,765	0.002
Latin, Central, and South American origins	118,640	0.4
Caribbean origins	305,290	1
Aboriginal origins[5]	477,630	2
Canadian origins[6]	5,326,995	19
Other origins[7]	80,840	0.2
Multiple origins[8]	*10,224,495*	*36*

1. Ethnic origin refers to the ethnic or cultural group(s) to which the respondent's ancestors belonged. Ethnic origin pertains to the ancestral roots or background of the population, and should not be confused with citizenship or nationality.
2. A single response occurs when the respondent provides only one ethnic origin.
3. British Isles includes single responses of English, Irish, Scottish, Welsh, or other British, as well as multiple "British Isles only" responses—that is, a combination of English, Irish, Scottish, Welsh, or other British.
4. French origins include single responses of French or Acadian, as well as multiple responses of French and Acadian.
5. Aboriginal includes the single response of Inuit, Métis, and North American Indian.
6. Caution should be used in comparing data for "Canadian" ethnic origin between censuses.
7. Includes American, Australian, New Zealander, Québécois, and Other not included elsewhere.
8. A multiple response occurs when the respondent provides two or more ethnic groups.

Source: Statistics Canada, "Single and Multiple Origin Responses, *1996 Census.*" Adapted from "The Nation Series Package No. 6: Ethnic Origin and Visible Minority Population," Cat. no. 93F0026XDB96000. Used by permission.

blacks, Chinese, Japanese, Koreans, Filipinos, Indo-Pakistanis, West Asians and Arabs, Southeast Asians, Latin Americans, and Pacific Islanders (Statistics Canada, 1998d). Aboriginal people form a separate category. The 1996 census was the first census to collect data on persons who are members of visible minorities. This was an important objective due to the increasing number of recent immigrants from China, Asia, and Africa. In 1996, 3.2 million Canadians—over 11 percent of the Canadian population—identified themselves as members of a visible minority (Statistics Canada, 1998h).

Although the terms *majority group* and *minority group* are widely used, their actual meanings are not clear. In the sociological sense, *group* is misleading because people who merely share ascribed racial or ethnic characteristics do not constitute a group. Further, *majority* and *minority* have meanings associated with both numbers and domination. Numerically speaking, *minority* means that a group is smaller in number than a dominant group. However, in countries such as South Africa and India, this has not historically been true. Those running the country were of a race (in South Africa) or caste (in India) with far fewer members than the masses that they ruled. Consequently, the use of these terms from a standpoint of dominance is more accurate. In this context, majority and minority refer to relationships of advantage/disadvantage and power/exploitation.

Many sociologists prefer to use the terms *dominant group* and *subordinate group* because they more precisely reflect the importance of power in the relationships (Feagin and Feagin, 1996).

COMPONENTS OF RACIAL AND ETHNIC CONFLICT

Prejudice

Prejudice **is a negative attitude based on preconceived notions about members of selected groups.** Prejudice partially stems from our attempts to create some order in our lives by classifying others. However, prejudices (pre + judgments) are judgments that are irrational and rigid insofar as they are supported by little or no direct evidence. Prejudice can be directed against a range of social or personal characteristics including social class, gender, sexual orientation, occupation, religion, political affiliation, age, race, or ethnicity. These attitudes may be either felt or expressed. ***Racial prejudices*** **involve beliefs that certain racial groups are innately inferior to others or have a disproportionate number of negative traits.** Prejudice is often reinforced by ***stereotypes*****—overgeneralizations about the appearance, behaviour, or other characteristics of all members of a group.**

Although all stereotypes are hurtful, negative stereotypes are particularly harmful to minorities. As Fleras and Elliott comment, "Power and privilege provide a protective layer. For minorities, however, stereotyping is a problem. Each negative image or unflattering representation reinforces their peripheral position within an unequal society" (1996:69). Consider the following conversation:

> Sabra: So, you think I'm not like the rest of them ...
>
> Alex: Well, when I see you, I don't see your colour. I don't see you as a South Asian. You're not like the rest of them ...
>
> Sabra: Oh, so, I'm more like you and less like, should I say it, "a real South Asian." You see, although you are not saying it, your statement reveals that you have some preconceived ideas of South Asians, the people I'm supposed to be so unlike. This means that whatever your preconceived ideas are of South Asians, they make South Asians less acceptable, less attractive, and less appealing to you than I. Well, this is not just stereotyping, this is racist stereotyping. (Desai, 1994:191)

How do people learn of stereotypes? As Box 9.2 illustrates, the media are a major source of racial and ethnic stereotypes.

Prejudice is often present in ***ethnocentrism*****—the belief in the superiority of one's own culture compared with that of others.** Ethnocentrism involves the evaluation of all groups and cultures in terms of one's own cultural standards and values. What is wrong with believing that your cultural values are preferable to those of others? Such a belief is, after all, a source of pride. The problem with ethnocentrism is that your standards are used as a frame of reference for negatively evaluating the behaviour of other groups. Not surprisingly, these groups will be evaluated negatively as backward, immoral, primitive, or irrational. In short, although ethnocentrism promotes group cohesion and morale, it is also a major source of intergroup hostility and conflict.

Theories of Prejudice

How do people's prejudices develop? Is prejudice a personality characteristic of a select number of individuals or can entire groups or societies collectively display prejudice? Psychologists and sociologists have addressed these questions in their attempts to explain conflicts between groups. Are some people more prejudiced than others? To answer this question, some theories focus on how individuals may transfer their internal psychological problems onto an external object or person (Feagin and Feagin, 1993).

The *frustration-aggression hypothesis* states that people who are frustrated in their efforts to achieve a highly desired goal will respond with a pattern of aggression toward others (Dollard et al., 1939). The object of their aggression becomes the ***scapegoat*—a person or group that is incapable of offering resistance to the hostility or aggression of others** (Marger, 1997). Scapegoats often are used as substitutes for the actual source of the frustration. For example, members of subordinate racial and ethnic groups often are blamed for societal problems (such as unemployment or an economic recession) over which they have no control.

According to some interactionists, prejudice results from *social learning*; in other words, it is learned from observing and imitating significant others, such as parents and peers. Initially, children do not have a frame of reference from which to question the prejudices of their relatives and friends. When they are rewarded with smiles or laughs for telling derogatory jokes or making negative comments about outgroup members, children's prejudiced attitudes may be reinforced.

Do some people have personality patterns that predispose them to prejudice? In the late 1940s, psychologist Theodore W. Adorno and his colleagues (1950) tried to answer this question.

Adorno tested his subjects on three dimensions: fascism, ethnocentrism, and anti-Semitism. The findings indicated that people whose scores on any one of the dimensions were high also tended to have high scores on the others. In other words, if someone was prejudiced against Jews, they were also likely to be prejudiced against other minority groups, to favour strong authoritarian leadership (fascism), and to view their cultural traditions and norms as superior to all others.

Adorno concluded that highly prejudiced individuals tend to have an ***authoritarian personality*, which is characterized by excessive conformity, submissiveness to authority, intolerance, insecurity, a high level of superstition, a propensity for stereotyping, and rigid thinking** (Adorno et al., 1950). This personality, moreover, is most likely to develop in a family environment in which dominating parents who are anxious about status use physical discipline but show very little love in raising their children (Adorno et al., 1950). Other scholars have linked prejudiced attitudes to traits such as being submissive to authority, extreme anger toward outgroups, and conservative religious and political beliefs (Altemeyer, 1981, 1988; Weigel and Howes, 1985).

To measure levels of prejudice, some social scientists use the concept of ***social distance*, which refers to the extent to which people are willing to interact and establish relationships with members of racial and ethnic groups other than their own** (Park and Burgess, 1921). Sociologist Emory Bogardus (1925, 1968) developed a scale to measure social distance in specific situations. Using the scale, he asked respondents to answer yes or no to the following seven statements with regard to members of various racial and ethnic groups:

1. I would marry or accept as a close relative.
2. I would accept as a close friend.
3. I would accept as a next-door neighbour.
4. I would accept in my school or church.
5. I would accept in my community but would not have contact with.
6. I would accept as a resident of my country but not in my community.
7. I would not accept at all, even as a resident of my country.

He found that some groups were consistently ranked as more desirable than others for close interpersonal contact. More recently, analysts have found that whites who accept racial stereotypes desire greater social distance from people of colour than do whites who reject negative stereotypes (Krysan and Farley, 1993). While the Bogardus social distance scale has been used in numerous studies around the world, use of the scale for social distance research in Canada has been limited.

Discrimination

While prejudice refers to attitudes and beliefs, discrimination refers to the process by which these negative attitudes are put into practice. ***Discrimination* involves actions or practices of dominant group members (or their representatives) that have a harmful impact on members of a**

BOX 9.2 SOCIOLOGY AND MEDIA

RACISM IN THE MEDIA

The media are one of the most powerful sources of information in society, tremendously influencing the way we look at the world, how we understand it, and the manner in which we experience and relate to it. For many Canadians, the media are the primary source of information about racial and ethnic groups. For example, the media relay information about who racial minorities are; what they want; and why and how they propose to achieve their goals, and with what consequences for Canadian society. Racial minorities have accused Canada's mass media of slanted coverage; descriptions of the coverage have ranged from unfair and inadequate to racist. The following are examples of how journalist Doug Collins has discussed visible minorities and Aboriginal peoples in his columns in the *North Shore News*:

> The result is that Vancouver is becoming a suburb of Asia; Toronto, once the Queen City of English Canada, has become the tower of Babel, with every race except ours bawling for special rights and receiving them. Montreal is a target for the enlightened folk of Haiti. And the politicians wouldn't care if voodooism became the leading religion.

> What saving the country boils down to is handing out more dough to the French and the ever-squawking Indians who know they are dealing with dummies and never had it so good until we turned up and showed them the wheel.

> The issue is whether the Holocaust took place. In other words, whether the

subordinate group (Feagin and Feagin, 1997). For example, people who are prejudiced toward East Indians, Jews, or Aboriginal people may refuse to hire them, rent an apartment to them, or allow their children to play with children belonging to those groups. In these instances, discrimination involves the differential treatment of minority group members not because of their ability or merit, but because of irrelevant characteristics such as skin colour or language preference. Discriminatory actions vary in severity from the use of derogatory labels to violence against individuals and groups. Discrimination takes two basic forms: *de jure*, or legal discrimination, which is encoded in laws; and *de facto*, or informal discrimination, which is entrenched in social customs and institutions. De jure discrimination has been backed by explicitly discriminatory laws such as the Chinese Exclusionary Act, which restricted immigration to Canada on the basis of race, or the Nuremberg laws passed in Nazi Germany, which imposed restrictions on Jews. The Indian Act provides another example of de jure discrimination. According to the Act, status Indian women lost their "status rights" if they married someone who was not a status Indian, while status Indian men did not. An amendment to the Indian Act in 1985 ended this legalized sex discrimination. Section 15 of the Charter of Rights and Freedom prohibits discrimination on the basis of race, ethnicity, or origin. As a result, many cases of de jure discrimination have been eliminated. De facto discrimination is more subtle and less visible to public scrutiny and, therefore, much more difficult to eradicate.

Prejudice and discrimination do not always go hand in hand. Discrimination can exist without prejudice, and prejudice may flourish without expressing itself in discriminatory actions (Fleras and Elliott, 1996). This was demonstrated in a classic study conducted in the early 1930s. Richard LaPiere travelled around the United States with a Chinese couple, stopping at over 250 restaurants and hotels along the way. The pervasive anti-Oriental prejudice of the

BOX 9.2

CONTINUED

> Hitler regime deliberately set out to kill all the Jews it could get its hands on, and that 6,000,000 died as a result. More and more, I am coming to the conclusion that it [the Holocaust] didn't. (Darling thoughts that could land a guy in jail in this free country of ours!)

The response to these articles has been mixed. Although a complaint against Collins was filed with the British Columbia Press Council, the council dismissed it. In 1993, the British Columbia Organization to Fight Racism (BCOFR) was appalled when it learned that the governor general of Canada had presented Collins with an award that honours Canadians who have made a significant contribution to their fellow citizens, their community, or Canada. Collins was described as a "controversial columnist for the *North Shore News* who forces people to think for themselves and re-evaluate commonly held opinions." Finally, in 1999, the B.C. Human Rights Tribunal ordered Collins to pay a $2000 fine to businessman Harry Abrams for exposing Jews to hatred in contravention of the Human Rigts Act.

What do you think? Is there an effective way to reconcile the apparently contradictory goals of freedom of expression and freedom from discrimination? If not, should we re-examine which of these goals should take priority?

Source: Henry et al., 1996. Doug Collins, quotations from various articles in the *North Shore News*, North Vancouver, B.C. © North Shore News. Reprinted by permission.

time led LaPiere to assume that the travellers would be refused service in most of the hotels and restaurants at which they intended to stop. However, LaPiere was wrong—only one establishment refused service to LaPiere and his friends. Several months later LaPiere sent letters to all the establishments they had visited, asking if they would serve "members of the Chinese race" as guests in their establishments. Ninety-two percent of the establishments that had earlier accepted LaPiere and his guests replied that Chinese people would not be welcome. This study is one of many examples of sociological research that reveals the discrepancy between what people say and what they do (Robertson, 1977).

Racism

Racism is a complex phenomenon that displays itself in a number of different forms. It involves elements of prejudice, ethnocentrism, stereotyping, and discrimination. For example, racism is present in the belief that some racial or ethnic groups are superior while others are inferior; this belief is a prejudice. Racism may be the basis for unfair treatment toward members of a racial or ethnic group. In this case the racism involves discrimination. Fleras and Elliott (1996) developed the most inclusive definition of racism, which incorporates both racial prejudice and discrimination. They define ***racism* as "an organized set of beliefs about the innate inferiority of some racial groups, combined with the power to transform these ideas into practices that deny or exclude equality of treatment on the basis of race"** (1996:98).

Instances of racism are readily available in Canada. Racist, white supremacist groups including the White Aryan Nation, the Western Guard, and the Ku Klux Klan are active in Canada. These groups have relied on violence to create an environment of fear and hatred against minorities throughout Canada and the United States. According to Warren Kinsella (1994), white hate groups disseminate their hate propaganda primarily

BOX 9.3 CRITICAL THINKING

Human Rights Legislation in Action

Human rights legislation is grounded in the premise that all human beings are full and equal persons. As such, all persons have a fundamental right to life and freedom, equality, and dignity in all life pursuits. What legal recourse do individuals have who experience a violation of these basic human rights? How effective is present human rights legislation in curtailing these violations? These questions can be addressed by examining a legal case that was brought forward by a minority claimant under the provisions of human rights legislation in Canada.

The case involves a claim of racial discrimination made against a Victoria restaurant and the Victoria police by a black Canadian. The complainant, born in St. Vincent, holds master's degrees from two Canadian universities and works as a health coordinator in British Columbia. While visiting Victoria, the complainant, a registered guest at a motor inn, went into the restaurant at the inn and sat down at the only available table. All other tables were occupied by nonblack patrons. He placed his order with a waiter, but within five minutes was informed by a waitress that he would have to move so that she could seat two other persons at his table. He refused to move because he could see no other table available and because he had not, as yet, received his order. The police were called. Victoria police questioned him about his citizenship, threatened him with deportation, searched and handcuffed him, and then took him to jail and locked him up for eight hours. The complainant brought his case to the B.C. Human Rights Council, which found that the only reasonable inference that could be drawn was that the complainant was the subject of racial discrimination. The complainant was awarded $2000 for humiliation, embarrassment, and damage to his self-respect in the settlement of his claim against both the restaurant and the police. Do you think the amount awarded is sufficient compensation for the harm done in this case? Do you think this amount will deter future racist actions on the part of the organizations sanctioned? If not, what do you think an appropriate settlement would be?

This case also demonstrates that the onus is on those who control organizations to ensure that their employees respect the human rights of all persons. Do you agree?

Source: Adapted with permission from Kallen, 1991.

through telephone hotlines, the Internet, and disinformation campaigns by hatemongers. White supremacist groups perceive themselves as the "saviours of the White race and Western Christian civilization" (Barrett, 1987:90). They believe that the survival of white society is in jeopardy because of the practice of allowing "non-Aryans" into Canada (see Chapter 2 for more on hate groups).

Although blatant racial slurs may have been acceptable in the past, few people today will tolerate the open expression of racism. Both the Charter of Rights and Freedoms and human rights legislation (see Box 9.3) have served as legal inhibitors to the expression of racist ideology or active racial discrimination. In Canada, overt acts of discrimination are now illegal. While blatant forms of racism have dissipated to some extent, less obvious expressions of bigotry and stereotyping remain prevalent in our society. Although the Charter and human rights legislation were designed to eliminate racism, they may have had the unintentional effect of "moving racism into the closet." As Fleras and Elliott explain,

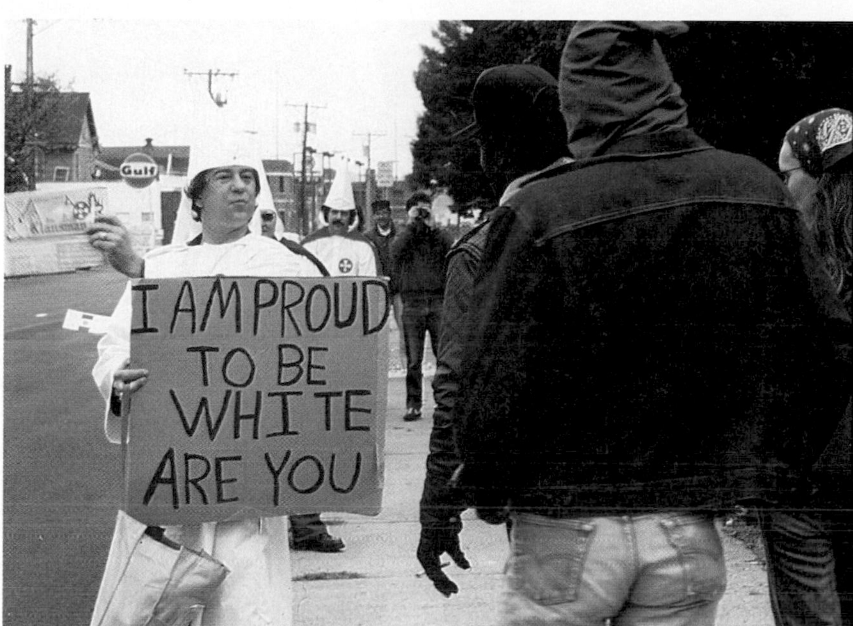

Members of white supremacy groups such as the Ku Klux Klan often use members of subordinate racial and ethnic groups as scapegoats for societal problems over which they have no control.

"Racist slurs ('those kind of people ... ') are now couched in a way that allows us to talk around or disguise our criticism of others by using somewhat more muted (polite) tones" (1996:74). ***Polite racism* is an attempt to disguise a dislike of others through behaviour that appears to be nonprejudicial.** This type of racism may be operating when people of colour are ignored or turned down for jobs or promotions on a regular basis. A number of studies over the past two decades have examined the extent of racial prejudice and discrimination in the workplace. In the well-known study *Who Gets Work?* by Henry and Ginzberg (1984), black and white job seekers with similar job qualifications were sent to apply for entry positions advertised in a major newspaper. After several hundred applications were received and interviews held, the study's results revealed that whites received job offers three times more often than did black job applicants. In addition, telephone callers with accents, particularly those from South Asia and the Caribbean, were often screened out when they phoned to inquire about a job vacancy. This study was replicated in 1989 and the findings were much better. This time, blacks were slightly favoured in job offers: 20 compared with 18 offers to whites. However, individuals with accents were still more likely to be screened out prior to being selected for an interview (Economic Council of Canada, 1991).

***Institutionalized racism* is made up of the rules, procedures, and practices that directly and deliberately prevent minorities from having full and equal involvement in society.** These actions are routinely carried out by a number of dominant group members based on the norms of the immediate organization or community (Feagin and Feagin, 1996).

In 1991, the Canadian Civil Liberties Association (CCLA) examined institutionalized discrimination in employment agencies. The CCLA randomly selected agencies in four cities in Ontario and asked whether the agencies would agree to refer only white people for the jobs that needed to be filled. Eleven of the fifteen agencies surveyed agreed to accept discriminatory job orders. The following are examples of the agencies' responses:

> It is discrimination, but it can be done discreetly without anyone knowing. No problem with that.
>
> That's no problem. It's between you and me. I don't tell anyone; you don't tell anyone.
>
> You are paying to see the people you want to see.
>
> Absolutely—definitely ... that request is pretty standard here.
>
> That's not a problem. Appearance means a lot, whether it's colour or overweight people. (quoted in Henry et al., 1996:142)

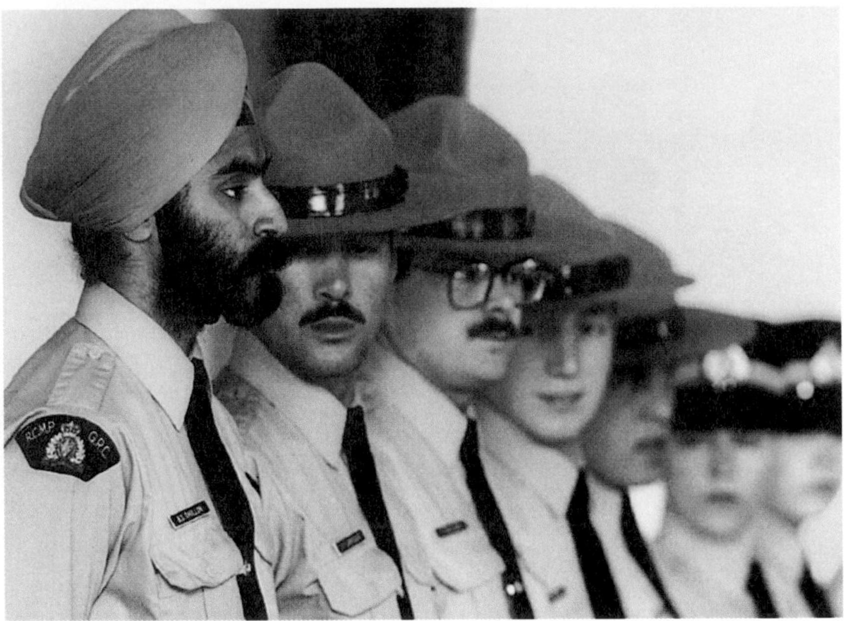

The decision by the RCMP to allow Sikh officers to wear turbans as part of their uniform was an attempt to address potential systemic racism within their own organization. As a result, racist pins and calendars with turban-clad mounties appeared across Canada, and 250,000 Canadians signed a petition protesting that the turbans were "unCanadian."

What happens in actual cases of agencies using such discriminatory employment practices? Recently a complaint laid with the Ontario Human Rights Commission against two employment agencies in Toronto drew public attention to this issue. A settlement was reached in which the agencies agreed to develop policies against accepting discriminatory job requests, and employees received training in race relations and employment equity.

Systemic racism **refers to practices that have a harmful impact on subordinate group members even though the organizationally prescribed norms or regulations guiding these actions initially were established with no intent to harm.** Institutions may have standards that have the unintended effect of excluding members of minority groups (Fleras and Elliott, 1996). For example, occupations such as police officer and firefighter had minimum weight, height, and educational requirements for job applicants. These criteria resulted in discrimination because they favoured white applicants over members of many minority groups, as well as males over females. Though valid reasons may have existed for imposing these restrictions, these criteria remain unfair and exclusionary.

Systemic racism (as well as other forms of systemic discrimination) is normally reflected in statistical underrepresentation of certain groups within an institution or organization. For example, a given group may represent 15 percent of the general population but only 2 percent of those promoted to upper management positions in a large company. Efforts to eliminate this kind of disproportionate representation are the focus of employment equity legislation. The target groups for employment equity in Canada are visible minorities, women, persons with disabilities, and Aboriginal peoples. Strategies may include modified admissions tests and requirements, enhanced recruitment of certain target groups, establishment of hiring quotas for particular minority groups, or specialized training or employment programs for specific target groups. The most recent analysis of employment equity programs indicates that these programs have had the most significant effect on women and Aboriginal peoples, while people with disabilities have made the fewest gains. As for members of visible minorities, although they have higher levels of education on average than do other Canadians and very high labour force participation rates, they continue to be concentrated in low-status, low-paying occupations (Henry et al., 1996). It is important to note that effects of systemic discrimination on specific visible minority groups in Canada vary substantially, with blacks experiencing the greatest disadvantage in income and Asian groups, the least (Boyd, 1992).

SOCIOLOGICAL PERSPECTIVES ON RACE AND ETHNIC RELATIONS

Interactionist, functionalist, and conflict analysts examine race and ethnic relations in different ways. Functionalists focus on the macrolevel intergroup processes that occur between members of majority and minority groups in society. Conflict theorists analyze power and economic differentials between the dominant group and subordinate groups. Interactionists examine how microlevel contacts between people may produce either greater racial tolerance or increased levels of hostility.

Interactionist Perspectives

What happens when people from different racial and ethnic groups come into contact with one another? In the *contact hypothesis*, interactionists point out that contact between people from divergent groups should lead to favourable attitudes and behaviour when certain factors are present. Members of each group must (1) have equal status, (2) pursue the same goals, (3) cooperate with one another to achieve their goals, and (4) receive positive feedback when they interact with one another in positive, nondiscriminatory ways (Allport, 1958; Coakley, 1994). For example, does participation in interracial sports teams promote intergroup cohesion and reduce prejudice? Scholars have found that increased contact may have little or no effect on existing prejudices and, in some circumstances, can even lead to an increase in prejudice and conflict. If racial tension between players on teams is high enough, violence may erupt (Edwards, 1973; Lapchick, 1991). Why might sports contribute to prejudice? Sports events are highly competitive, and prejudice may be aggravated by the actions of players or spectators.

What happens when individuals meet someone who does not conform to their existing stereotype? Frequently, they ignore anything that contradicts the stereotype or interpret the situation to support their prejudices (Coakley, 1994). For example, a person who does not fit the stereotype may be seen as an exception—"You're not like other [persons of a particular race]."

When a person is seen as conforming to a stereotype, he or she may be treated simply as one of "you people." Former Los Angeles Lakers basketball star Earvin "Magic" Johnson (1992:31–32) described how he was categorized along with all other African Americans when he was bused to a predominantly white school:

> On the first day of [basketball] practice, my teammates froze me out. Time after time I was wide open, but nobody threw me the ball. At first I thought they just didn't see me. But I woke up after a kid named Danny Parks looked right at me and then took a long jumper. Which he missed.
>
> I was furious, but I didn't say a word. Shortly after that, I grabbed a defensive rebound and took the ball all the way down for a basket. I did it again and a third time, too.
>
> Finally Parks got angry and said, "Hey, pass the [bleeping] ball."
>
> That did it. I slammed down the ball and glared at him. Then I exploded. "I *knew* this would happen!" I said. "That's why I didn't want to come to this [bleeping] school in the first place!"
>
> "Oh, yeah? Well, you people are all the same," he said. "You think you're gonna come in here and do whatever you want? Look, hotshot, your job is to get the rebound. Let us do the shooting."

The interaction between Johnson and Parks demonstrates that when people from different racial and ethnic groups come into contact with one another, they may treat one another as stereotypes, not as individuals. Eventually, Johnson and Parks were able to work out most of their differences. "There's nothing like winning to help people get along," Johnson explained (1992:32).

Interactionist perspectives make us aware of the importance of intergroup contact and the fact that it may either intensify or reduce racial and ethnic stereotyping and prejudice.

Functionalist Perspectives

How do members of subordinate racial and ethnic groups become a part of the dominant group? To answer this question, early functionalists studied immigration and patterns of majority and minority group interaction.

BOX 9.4 SOCIOLOGY IN GLOBAL PERSPECTIVE

WORLDWIDE RACIAL AND ETHNIC CONFLICTS IN THE TWENTY-FIRST CENTURY

Throughout the world, many racial and ethnic groups are seeking self-determination—the right to choose their own way of life. As many nations currently are structured, however, self-determination is impossible.

The cost of the struggle for self-determination is the loss of life and property in ethnic warfare. In recent years, the Cold War has given way to dozens of small wars over ethnic dominance. In Europe, for example, ethnic violence has persisted in Bosnia-Herzegovina, Croatia, Spain, Britain (between the Protestant majority and the Catholic minority in Northern Ireland), Romania, Russia, Moldova, and Georgia. Hundreds of thousands of people have died from warfare, disease (such as the cholera epidemic in war-torn Rwanda), and refugee migration.

Ethnic wars exact a high price even for survivors, whose life chances can become bleaker after the violence subsides. In the ethnic conflict between Abkhazians and Georgians in the former Soviet Union, for example, as many as two thousand people have been killed and over eighty thousand displaced. Ironically, the Abkhazians previously had been known for their longevity and good mental health—many live into their nineties or more, possibly because of their healthy lifestyle and positive attitudes toward aging (Benet, 1971). More recently, ethnic war has devastated Chechnya, an area attempting to secede from Russia despite Russia's claim of sovereignty.

Conflict between Protestants and Catholics in Northern Ireland has continued for hundreds of years. Here, Londonderry Protestants approach the Catholic Bogside neighbourhood as tensions rose in August 1996.

ASSIMILATION ***Assimilation*** **is a process by which members of subordinate racial and ethnic groups become absorbed into the dominant culture.** To some analysts, assimilation is functional because it contributes to the stability of society by minimizing group differences that otherwise might result in hostility and violence (Gordon, 1964).

Assimilation occurs at several distinct levels, including the cultural, structural, biological, and psychological levels. *Cultural assimilation*, or *acculturation*, occurs when members of an ethnic group adopt dominant group traits, such as language, dress, values, religion, and food preferences. Cultural assimilation in this country initially followed an "Anglo-conformity" model; members of subordinate ethnic groups were expected to conform to the culture of the dominant white Anglo-Saxon population (Gordon, 1964). However, some groups such as Aboriginal peoples and the Québécois refused to be assimilated and sought to maintain their unique cultural identity.

Structural assimilation, or *integration*, occurs when members of subordinate racial or ethnic groups gain acceptance in everyday social interaction with members of the dominant group. This type of assimilation typically starts in large, impersonal settings such as schools and workplaces and only later (if at all) results in close friendships and intermarriage. *Biological assimilation*, or *amalgamation*, occurs when members of one group marry those of other social or ethnic groups.

Psychological assimilation involves a change in racial or ethnic self-identification on the part of an individual. Rejection by the dominant group may prevent psychological assimilation by members of some subordinate racial and ethnic groups, especially those with visible characteristics such as skin colour or facial features that differ from those of the dominant group.

ETHNIC PLURALISM Instead of complete assimilation, many groups share elements of the mainstream culture while remaining culturally distinct from both the dominant group and other social and ethnic groups. ***Ethnic pluralism*** **is the co-existence of a variety of distinct racial and ethnic groups within one society.**

Has Canada achieved equalitarian pluralism? The Canadian Multiculturalism Act of 1988 stated that "[A]ll Canadians are full and equal partners in Canadian society." The Department of Multiculturalism and Citizenship was established in 1991 with the goal of encouraging ethnic minorities to participate fully in all aspects of Canadian life and at the same time maintain their distinct ethnic identities and cultural practices. The objective of multiculturalism is to "promote unity through diversity." Multiculturalism programs provide funding for education, consultative support, and a range of activities including heritage language training, race relations training, ethnic policing and justice, and ethnic celebrations. In recent years multiculturalism policies have been under increasing attack. Neil Bissoondath, author of *Selling Illusions: The Cult of Multiculturalism in Canada* (1994), suggests that multiculturalism does not promote equalitarian pluralism. Rather, he argues, multiculturalism is divisive, because it ghettoizes visible minorities, fosters racial animosity, and detracts from national unity.

INEQUALITARIAN PLURALISM, OR SEGREGATION Segregation exists when specific ethnic groups are set apart from the dominant group and have unequal access to power and privilege (Marger, 1997). ***Segregation*** **is the spatial and social separation of categories of people by race, ethnicity, class, gender, and/or religion.** Segregation may be enforced by law (de jure) or by custom (de facto). An example of de jure segregation was the *Jim Crow laws*, which legalized the separation of the races in all public accommodations (including hotels, restaurants, transportation, hospitals, jails, schools, churches, and cemeteries) in the southern United States after the Civil War (Feagin and Feagin, 1993).

De jure segregation of blacks is also part of the history of Canada. Blacks in Canada lived in largely segregated communities in Nova Scotia, New Brunswick, and Ontario where racial segregation was evident in the schools, government, the workplace, residential housing, and elsewhere. Segregated schools continued in Nova Scotia until the 1960s. Residential segregation was legally enforced through the use of racially restrictive convenants attached to deeds and leases. Separation and refusal of service were common in restaurants, theatres, and recreational facilities (Henry et al., 1995).

One of the most blatant examples of segregation in Canada is the federal government reserve system

Caribana parade marchers exemplify the concept of ethnic pluralism—maintaining their distinct identity even as they share in many elements of mainstream culture.

for status Indians, by which Aboriginal peoples were segregated on reserves in remote areas.

Although legally sanctioned forms of racial segregation have been all but eliminated, de facto segregation, which is enforced by custom, still exists.

Conflict Perspectives

Why do some ethnic groups continue to experience subjugation after many years? Conflict theorists focus on economic stratification and access to power in their analysis of race and ethnic relations.

INTERNAL COLONIALISM Conflict theorists use the term ***internal colonialism*** **to refer to a situation in which members of a racial or ethnic group are conquered or colonized and forcibly placed under the economic and political control of the dominant group.** Groups that have been subjected to internal colonialism often remain in subordinate positions longer than groups that voluntarily migrated to North America.

Aboriginal peoples in Canada were colonized by Europeans and others who invaded their lands and conquered them. In the process, Aboriginal peoples lost property, political rights, aspects of their culture, and often their lives (Das Gupta, 1995). The capitalist class acquired cheap labour and land through this government-sanctioned racial exploitation. The effects of past internal colonialism are reflected today in the number of Aboriginal people who live in extreme poverty on government reserves (Das Gupta, 1995).

The experiences of internally colonized groups are unique in three ways: (1) they have been forced to exist in a society other than their own; (2) they have been kept out of the economic and political mainstream, so that it is difficult for them to compete with dominant group members; and (3) they have been subjected to severe attacks on their own culture, which may lead to its extinction (Blauner, 1972).

THE SPLIT-LABOUR-MARKET THEORY Who benefits from the exploitation of visible minorities? Dual- or split-labour-market theory states that both white workers and members of the capitalist class benefit from the exploitation of visible minorities. ***Split labour market*** **refers to the division of the economy into two areas of employment: a primary sector or upper tier, composed of higher-paid (usually dominant group) workers in more secure jobs, and a secondary sector or lower tier, made up of lower-paid (often subordinate group) workers in jobs with little security and hazardous working conditions** (Bonacich, 1972, 1976). According to this perspective, white workers in the upper tier may use racial discrimination against nonwhites to protect their positions. These actions most often occur when upper-tier workers feel threatened by lower-tier workers hired by capitalists to reduce labour costs and maximize corporate profits. In the past, immigrants were a source of cheap labour that employers could use to break strikes and keep wages down. Agnes Calliste (1987) applied the split-labour-market theory in her study, "Sleeping Car Porters in Canada." Calliste found a doubly submerged split labour market, with three levels of stratification in this area of employment. While "white" trade unions were unable to restrict access to porter positions on the basis of race, they were able to impose differential pay scales. Consequently, black porters received less pay than white porters, even though they were doing the same work. Furthermore, the labour market was doubly submerged because black immigrant workers from the United States received even less pay than both black and white Canadian porters. Throughout history, higher-paid workers have responded with racial hostility and joined movements to curtail immigration and thus do away with the source of cheap labour (Marger, 1997).

A Feminist Perspective on Race and Gender

The term *gendered racism* refers to the interactive effect of racism and sexism in the exploitation of women of colour. According to social psychologist Philomena Essed (1991), women's particular position must be explored within each racial or ethnic group, because their experiences will not have been the same as the men's in each grouping.

All workers are not equally exploited by capitalists. Gender and race or ethnicity are important in this exploitation. For example, jobs are race-typed and gender-typed. Consider a registered nurse and a custodian in a hospital. What race and gender are they likely to be? Did a white woman and a man of colour come to mind? Most jobs have similar race and gender designations. Often, the jobs people hold are linked to their class, race, and gender. Consequently, the effect of class on our life chances is inseparable from the effects of our gender and race or ethnicity. The split labour market, then, involves not only class but also race, ethnicity, and gender (Amott and Matthaei, 1991). Historically, the high-paying primary labour market has been monopolized by white men. People of colour and most white women more often hold lower-tier jobs. Below that tier is the underground sector of the economy, characterized by illegal or quasi-legal activities such as drug trafficking, prostitution, and working in sweatshops that do not meet minimum wage and safety standards. Many undocumented workers and some white women and people of colour attempt to earn a living in this sector (Amott and Matthaei, 1991).

ETHNIC GROUPS IN CANADA

At the turn of the century, the Canadian population was predominantly made up of French Canadians (30.7 percent) and British Canadians (57 percent). As Figure 9.1 indicates, in 1996 approximately one-third of Canada's population claimed ethnic origins other than French or British. Given the diversity of our population, imposing any kind of conceptual order on a discussion of ethnic groups in Canada is difficult. A detailed historical account of the unique experiences of each group is beyond the scope of this chapter. Instead, we will look briefly at some of the unique ethnic groups in Canada. In the process, we will examine a brief history of racism with respect to each group.

First Nations

Canada's Aboriginal peoples are believed to have migrated to North America from Asia an estimated 40,000 years ago (Dyck, 1996). Native peoples are an extremely diverse group. Today, the terms *native*, *First Nations*, and *Aboriginal* refer to approximately fifty-five sovereign peoples including the Inuit, Cree, Micmac, Blackfoot, Iroquois, and Haida. Other categories of Aboriginal peoples are also classified as status Indians (those Indians with legal rights under the Indian Act), nonstatus Indians (those without legal rights), Métis, and Inuit. Those who settled in the southern part of Canada, the Yukon, and the Mackenzie Valley can be termed *North American Indians*. Those located in the eastern Arctic and northern islands, who were formerly referred to as Eskimos, are now referred to as *Inuit*. A third category, *Métis*, who mostly live on the Prairies, are descendants of Indian and non-Indian unions (primarily French settlers and Indian women).

FIGURE 9.1 Percentage Distribution of Population by Ethnic Origin, 1996

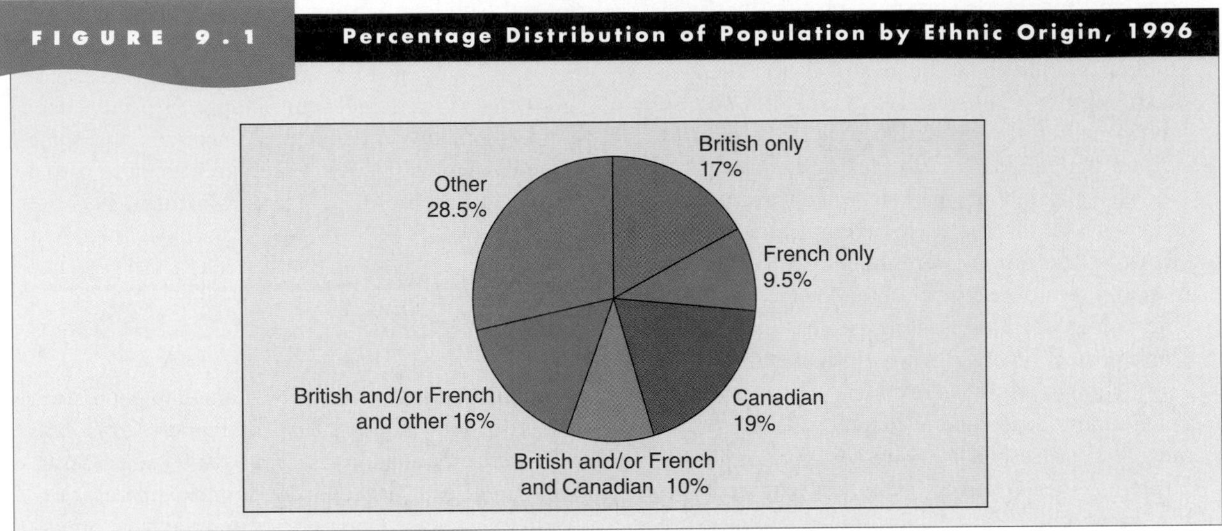

Reprinted by permission of Statistics Canada, "1996 Census: Ethnic Origins, Visible Minorities," *The Daily*, Cat. no. 11-001, February 17, 1998.

When European settlers arrived on this continent, the Aboriginal inhabitants' way of life was changed forever. Experts estimate that between one and twelve million Aboriginal people lived in North America at that time; however, by 1900 their numbers had been reduced to less than 240,000 (Churchill, 1994). What factors led to this drastic depopulation?

GENOCIDE, FORCED MIGRATION, AND FORCED ASSIMILATION Native people have been the victims of genocide and forced migration. Many native Americans either were killed or died from European diseases (such as typhoid, smallpox, and measles) and starvation (Wagner and Stearn, 1945; Cook, 1973). In battle, native people often were no match for the Europeans, who had the latest weaponry (Amott and Matthaei, 1991). Europeans justified their aggression by stereotyping the natives as "savages" and "heathens" (Takaki, 1993).

Entire nations were forced to move in order to accommodate the white settlers. The "Trail of Tears" was one of the most disastrous of the forced migrations to occur in the United States. In the coldest part of the winter of 1832, over half of the Cherokee Nation died during or as a result of their forced relocation from the southeastern United States to the Indian Territory in Oklahoma (Thornton, 1984). The colonization of the native population was far less brutal in Canada than in the United States. However, it is not clear whether this more benign conquest left Aboriginals in Canada any better off than their counterparts in the United States in the long run (Weinfeld, 1995:48).

Indian rights were clearly defined in the Royal Proclamation of 1763, which divided up the territory acquired by Britain. In a large area called Indian Territory, the purchase or settlement of land was forbidden without a treaty. This is sometimes called the principle of "voluntary cession" (Dyck, 1996:154). The government broke treaty after treaty as it engaged in a policy of wholesale removal of indigenous nations in order to clear the land for settlement by Anglo-Saxon "pioneers" (Green, 1977; Churchill, 1994). The Canadian government then passed the Indian Act of 1876, which provided for federal government control of almost every aspect of Indian life. The regulations under the Act included prohibitions against owning land, voting, and purchasing and consuming alcohol. Later provisions prevented Aboriginal people from leaving reserves without permission and a ticket from the agent (Bolaria and Li, 1988).

The Indian Act was designed to promote assimilation; native peoples were to adopt the cultural attitudes and norms of the dominant culture and give up their own cultural traditions (including their values, customs, and language).

Aboriginal children were placed in residential boarding schools to facilitate their assimilation into the dominant culture. The Jesuits and other missionaries

Life chances are extremely limited for Aboriginal peoples who live in Aboriginal communities. These boys are participating in the pole twist—a traditional Inuit game. Despite their athletic prowess, it is unlikely that they will become members of professional sports teams.

who ran these schools believed that Aboriginal peoples should not be left in their "inferior" natural state and considered it their mission to replace Aboriginal culture with Christian beliefs, values, rituals, and practices (Bolaria and Li, 1988). Many of the children who attended these schools were sexually, physically, and emotionally abused. They were not allowed to speak their language or engage in any of their traditional cultural practices. The coercive and oppressive nature of this educational experience is one of the most blatant examples of institutionalized racism (Henry et al., 1995:62).

Aboriginal Peoples Today In 1996, almost 800,000 individuals reported that they were North American Indian, Métis, or Inuit—about 3 percent of Canada's total population (Statistics Canada, 1998).

There are several Indian tribal groups, living in nearly 600 bands. Although the majority of registered Indians live on reserves, the majority of the total Aboriginal population live off reserves. The Aboriginal population is unevenly distributed across Canada, with the heaviest concentrations of Aboriginal Canadians in western and northern Canada.

Aboriginal peoples are the most disadvantaged racial or ethnic group in Canada in terms of income, employment, housing, nutrition, and health. The life chances of Aboriginal peoples who live on reserves are especially limited. They have the highest rates of infant mortality and death by exposure and malnutrition. They also have high rates of tuberculosis, alcoholism, and suicide. The overall life expectancy of Aboriginal Canadians is ten years less than that of non-natives; this is largely due to poor health services and inadequate housing on reserves (Dyck, 1996). Aboriginal peoples also have had very limited educational opportunities (the functional illiteracy of Aboriginal peoples is 45 percent compared with the overall Canadian rate of 17 percent) and they have a very high rate of unemployment (Armstrong, 2000; Tait, 1999).

In spite of the odds against them, many Aboriginal peoples resist oppression. National organizations like the Assembly of First Nations, Inuit Tapirisat, the Native Council of Canada, and the Métis National Council have been instrumental in bringing the demands of those they represent into the political and constitutional arenas. Of these demands, the major ones have been and still are self-government, Aboriginal rights, and the resolution of land claims (see Frideres, 1993).

Charter Europeans

White Anglo-Saxon Protestants (British Canadians) Whereas Aboriginal peoples have been among the most disadvantaged peoples, white Anglo-Saxon Protestants (WASPs) have been the most privileged group in this country. Although many English settlers initially came to North America as indentured servants or as prisoners, they quickly emerged as the dominant group, creating a core culture (including language, laws, and holidays) to which all other groups were expected to adapt. Most WASPs do not think of themselves as having race or ethnicity. As one young woman commented, "I don't think of myself as white, I don't feel superior. I just felt normal" (quoted in Fleras and Elliott, 1996:35). The experience of being a WASP in Canadian society is an experience of privilege. But few Canadians are likely to acknowledge this privileged status—nor that it is derived from skin colour. Even fewer are prepared to concede that whiteness is directly related to the underprivileged status of others (Fleras and Elliott, 1996). The following student's comments, however, reflect a definite awareness of what it means to be a white Anglo-Saxon male:

> I am a member of a majority group that has a great deal of power ... It is White culture that I experience day to day and the very fact that discrimination is rarely an issue for me personally results in my own racial identity becoming an invisible thing. The powerful people within my experience, directly or indirectly—the politician, the employer, the teacher, the social worker—are invariably White. I know that my race will not be an issue with most of the people I must deal with, as I know we will have a commonality from the start. Being in the majority in all three origins [White, English, Canadian], there is also a good chance that either culturally, ethnically or both, our backgrounds will be similar. Neither will I expect my values or behavior to be an issue because I fit into the "norm." (James, 1995:47)

FRENCH CANADIANS The European colonization of Canada began with the exploration and settlement of New France. In 1608, the first permanent settlement in New France was established at Quebec City, by Samuel de Champlain. France's North American empire extended from Hudson Bay to Louisiana.

Following the British conquest of the French in Canada in the Seven Years' War (1756–1763), Canada became a British dominion and the French found themselves in an inferior position (Weinfeld, 1995). The French were able to maintain French civil law, language, and religion; however, the overall economic, social and political power passed to English Canada. Although officially under British control, the competition between French and English Canadians continued until Confederation in 1867.

The British North America Act formally acknowledged the rights and privileges of the French and British as the founding or *charter groups* of Canadian society. With Confederation, it was assumed that in the future French- and English-speaking groups would co-exist and complement one another. However, during the period between Confederation and World War II, the French struggled for cultural survival because English-speaking Canadians controlled the major economic institutions in both English Canada and Quebec.

In the 1960s Quebec nationalism grew and francophones in Quebec began to feel their language and culture were threatened (see Chapter 12, "Politics and the Economy"). In referenda in 1980 and in 1995 Quebeckers rejected sovereignty, but the issue remains contentious.

FRENCH CANADIANS TODAY Today approximately 25 percent of the Canadian population is francophone, 85 percent of which is located in Quebec. Many Quebec nationalists now see independence or separation as the ultimate protection against cultural and linguistic assimilation, as well as the route to economic power. As political scientist Rand Dyck comments,

> [G]iven its geographic concentration in Quebec and majority control of a large province, and given their modern-day self-consciousness and self-confidence, the French fact in Canada cannot be ignored. If English Canada wants Quebec to remain a part of the country, it cannot go back to the easy days of pre-1960 unilingualism." (1996:185)

French Canadians have at least forced Canada to take its second language and culture seriously, which is an important step toward attaining cultural pluralism.

Canada's Immigrants

Home to approximately five million foreign-born immigrants, Canada is well described as a land of immigrants. According to the most recent census, over three-quarters of immigrants arriving in Canada today are members of a visible minority group (Statistics Canada, 1998d). Canada's policies toward some of these groups have been far from exemplary. In fact, initial Canadian immigration policies have been described as essentially racist in orientation, assimilationist in intent, and segregationist in content (Fleras and Elliott, 1996). A "racial pecking order" sorted out potential immigrants on the basis of racial characteristics and capacity for assimilation (Lupul, 1988). As much energy was expended in keeping out certain "types" as was put into encouraging others to settle (Whitaker, 1991). A preferred category was that of *white ethnics*—a term coined to identify immigrants who came from European countries other than England, such as Scotland, Ireland, Poland, Italy, Greece, Germany, Yugoslavia, and Russia and other

As more Chinese Canadians have made gains in education and employment, many have also made a conscious effort to develop a sense of community and cooperation and to increase awareness of Chinese culture. This Chinese Dragon parade exemplifies this desire to increase cultural awareness by maintaining traditional celebrations.

former Soviet republics. Immigration from "white" countries was encouraged to ensure the British character of Canada. With the exception of visa formalities, this category of "preferred" immigrants was virtually exempt from entry restrictions. On the other hand, Jews and Mediterranean populations required special permits for entry, and Asian populations were admitted grudgingly, mostly to serve as cheap labour. The restrictions regarding the Chinese, Japanese, and Jews highlighted the racist dimension of Canada's early immigration policies.

CHINESE CANADIANS The initial wave of Chinese immigration began in the 1850s, when Chinese men were "pushed" from China by harsh economic conditions and "pulled" to Canada by the promise of gold in British Columbia and employment opportunities. Nearly 16,000 Chinese were brought to Canada at this time to lay track for the Canadian Pacific Railway. The work was brutally hard and dangerous, living conditions were appalling, food and shelter were insufficient, and due to scurvy and smallpox there was a high fatality rate. These immigrants were "welcomed" only as long as there was a shortage of white workers. However, they were not permitted to bring their wives and children with them or to have sexual relations with white women because of the fear they would spread the "yellow menace"—a term used to describe individuals with Asian racial origins (Henry et al., 1995). After the railroad was built, the welcome mat was quickly rolled up.

The Chinese were subjected to extreme prejudice and were referred to by derogatory terms such as "coolies," "heathens," and "Chinks." Some were attacked by working-class whites who feared they would lose their jobs to Chinese immigrants. In 1885 the federal government passed its first anti-Chinese bill, the purpose of which was to limit Chinese immigration. Other hostile legislation included a range of racist exclusionary policies including prohibiting the Chinese from voting, serving in public office, serving on juries, participating in white labour unions, and working in the professions of law and pharmacy. In 1888, a head tax was imposed on all Chinese males arriving in Canada. In 1903, the tax was raised to $500 from $100 in a further attempt to restrict entry to Canada (Satzewich, 1991). Not until after World War II were such "objectionable discrimination" policies removed from the Immigration Act. After immigration laws were further relaxed in the 1960s, the second and largest wave of Chinese immigration occurred, with immigrants coming primarily from Hong Kong and Taiwan.

JAPANESE CANADIANS Japanese immigrants began arriving in Canada in large numbers after Chinese immigration tapered off. The Japanese were also viewed as a threat by white workers and became victims of stereotyping and discrimination.

In 1907 an organization known as the Asiatic Exclusion League was formed with the mandate of restricting the admission of Asians to Canada. Following the arrival of a ship carrying over a thousand Japanese and a few hundred Sikhs, the league carried out a demonstration that precipitated a race riot. A "gentlemen's agreement," negotiated in 1908, permitted entry of only certain categories of Japanese on a fixed quota basis.

Japanese Canadians experienced one of the most vicious forms of discrimination ever sanctioned by Canadian law. During World War II, when Canada was at war with Japan, nearly 23,000 people of Japanese ancestry (13,300 of whom were Canadian-born) were placed in internment camps because they were seen as a security threat (Takaki, 1993).

FIGURE 9.2 Place of Birth of Immigrants by Period of Immigration, Before 1961 to 1996

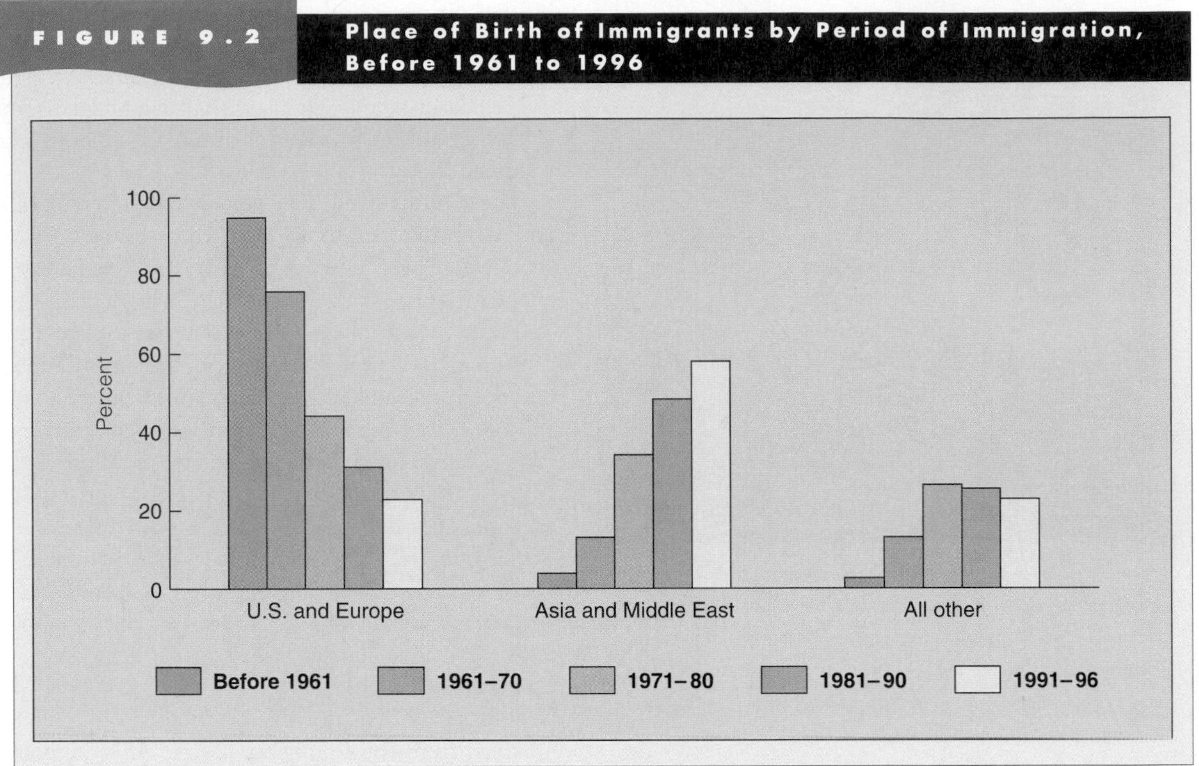

Reprinted by permission of Statistics Canada, "1996 Census: Immigration and Citizenship," adapted from *The Daily*, Cat. no. 11-001. November 4, 1997, p. 3.

They remained in the camps for more than two years despite the total lack of evidence that they posed a danger to this country. Many of the camps were situated in remote locales in British Columbia, Alberta, and Manitoba; they had guard towers, and were surrounded by barbed-wire fences. This action was a direct violation of the citizenship rights of these Japanese who were born in Canada. Ironically, only the Japanese were singled out for such harsh treatment; German immigrants avoided this fate even though Canada was at war with both. After the war, restrictions were placed on where Japanese Canadians could settle and some were forcibly sent back to Japan. Forty years later, the Canadian government issued an apology for its actions and agreed to pay $20,000 to each person who had been placed in an internment camp (Henry et al., 1995).

JEWISH CANADIANS In 1942, Canada closed its doors to Jews fleeing Hitler and the Holocaust. A ship carrying Jewish refugees from Europe attempted to land in Halifax and was denied entrance. During the 1930s Canada admitted fewer Jewish refugees as a percentage of its population than any other Western country. Jews who did immigrate experienced widespread discrimination in employment, business, and education. Other indicators of anti-Semitism included restrictions on where Jews could live, buy property, and attend university. Signs posted along Toronto's beaches warned "No dogs or Jews allowed." Many hotels and resorts had policies prohibiting Jews as guests (Abella and Troper, 1982, quoted in Henry et al., 1995:74). Despite the discrimination and racism to which Jews were subjected, Jewish Canadians today have attained a level of education and income considerably above the Canadian average.

CURRENT IMMIGRATION PATTERNS Changes to the Immigration Act in 1962 opened the door to immigration on a nonracial basis. Education, occupation, and language skills replaced race or national origin as the criteria for admission. In 1967, a *points system* was introduced whereby immigrants were rated according to the totals of points given for the following: job training, experience, skills, level of education, knowledge of English or French, degree of

FIGURE 9.3 Visible Minority Population as a Percentage of Census, Metropolitan Areas, 1996

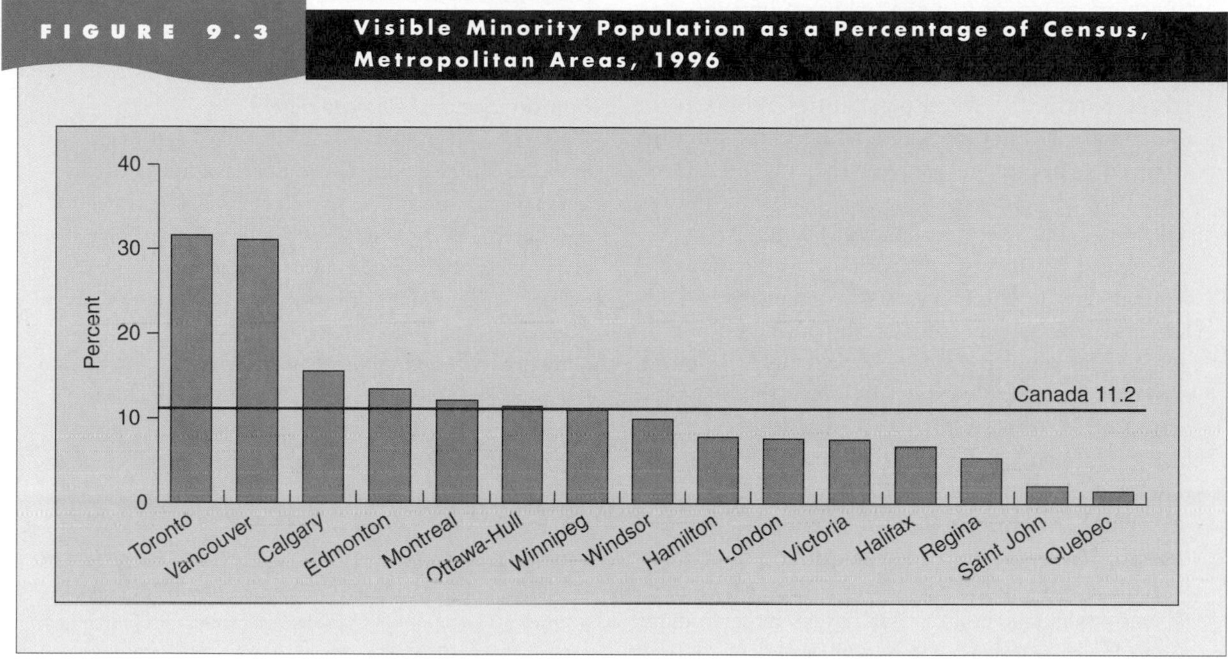

Source: Statistics Canada, "1996 Census: Visible Minority Population."

demand for the applicant's occupation, and job offers. This new act opened the doors to those from previously excluded countries. As Figure 9.2 shows, Canadian immigration patterns changed dramatically because of this new immigration policy. Prior to 1960, the majority of immigrants were from the United States or Europe; by 1996, the percentage of immigrants from these countries had fallen to just over 20 percent. In contrast, prior to 1960, immigrants from Asia and the Middle East accounted for less than 2 percent of immigrants to Canada, but by 1996, this figure had risen to almost 60 percent. However, while changes in Canada's immigration laws altered Canada's ethnic composition, the domination of the Euro-Canadian majority in the stratification system has not significantly changed. While Euro-Canadian and French-Canadian groups have been able to achieve upward mobility into middle- and upper-class social positions, the lower status of many visible minority groups has been virtually unchanged.

RACIAL AND ETHNIC DIVERSITY IN CANADA IN THE FUTURE

Racial and ethnic diversity is increasing in Canada. This changing demographic pattern is largely the result of the elimination of overtly racist immigration policies and the opening up of immigration to Third World countries. Canada has evolved from a country largely inhabited by whites and Aboriginal peoples to a country made up of people from more than seventy countries. Today, almost two-thirds of racial-minority immigrants come from Asia. The number of Latin American immigrants is expected to grow fourfold in the near future (Henry et al., 1996). Almost all immigrants to Canada live in cities. In fact, nearly three-quarters of recent immigrants chose to live in Toronto, Montreal, or Vancouver. As Figure 9.3 shows, in 1996, nearly one-third of the population of Toronto and Vancouver is made up of visible minorities. Visible minorities today make up over 11 percent of the total population of Canada, whereas in 1986 they represented 6.3 percent (Chard and Renaud, 2000).

What effect will these changes have on racial and ethnic relations? Several possibilities exist. On the one hand, conflict between whites and minority groups may become more overt and confrontational. Certainly, the concentration of visible minorities will mean that these groups will become more visible than ever in some Canadian cities. Increasing contact may lead to increased intergroup cohesion and understanding or it may bring on racism or prejudice. The rapid political changes and the global economic recession of the 1990s have made people fearful about their future and may cause some to blame "foreigners" for their problems. Interethnic tensions among members of subordinate groups in urban areas may increase as subordinate groups continue to face economic deprivation and discrimination. People may continue to use *sincere fictions*—personal beliefs that reflect larger societal mythologies, such as "I am not racist" or "I have never discriminated against anyone"—even when these are inaccurate perceptions (Feagin and Vera, 1995). Concerns about violence, crime, welfare, education, housing, and taxes may be encompassed in the larger issue of race (Edsall and Edsall, 1992).

On the other hand, there is reason for cautious optimism. Throughout Canadian history, subordinate racial and ethnic groups have struggled to gain the freedom and rights that previously were withheld from them. Today, employment equity programs are alleviating some of the effects of past discrimination against minority groups as well as addressing systemic and institutional forms of racism that exist in employment. Movements made up of both whites and members of visible minorities continue to oppose racism in everyday life, to seek to heal divisions among racial groups, and to teach children about racial tolerance (Rutstein, 1993). Many groups hope not only to affect their own countries but also to contribute to worldwide efforts to end racism (Ford, 1994).

CHAPTER REVIEW

How do race and ethnicity differ?

A race is a category of people who have been singled out as socially different often on the basis of inherited physical characteristics such as skin colour, hair texture, or eye shape. An ethnic group is a collection of people who, as a result of their shared cultural traits and high level of mutual interaction, regard themselves as a cultural unity.

Why are race and ethnicity important?

Race and ethnicity are ingrained in our consciousness. They often form the basis of hierarchical ranking in society and determine who gets what resources: employment, housing, education, and social services.

What is prejudice?

Prejudice is a negative attitude based on preconceived notions about members of selected groups. Prejudice is often reinforced by stereotypes and is present in ethnocentric attitudes.

Discuss the different theories of prejudice.

According to the frustration-aggression hypothesis of prejudice, people frustrated in their efforts to achieve a highly desired goal may respond with aggression toward others, who then become scapegoats. Another theory of prejudice focuses on the authoritarian personality, which is marked by excessive conformity, submissiveness to authority, intolerance, insecurity, superstition, and rigid thinking. According to social learning theory, prejudice is learned from significant others, such as parents and close friends. From a conflict perspective, prejudice arises as a result of competition among different social groups for scarce and valued resources.

What is discrimination and how does it differ from prejudice?

Discrimination involves actions or practices of dominant group members that have a harmful impact on members of a subordinate group. Whereas prejudice involves attitudes, discrimination involves actions. Discriminatory actions range from name-calling to violent actions. Discrimination can be either de jure (encoded in law) or de facto (informal).

What is racism?
Racism refers to an organized set of beliefs about the innate inferiority of some racial groups combined with the power to discriminate on the basis of race.

How do sociologists view racial and ethnic group relations?
Interactionists suggest that increased contact between people from divergent groups should lead to favourable attitudes and behaviour when members of each group (1) have equal status, (2) pursue the same goals, (3) cooperate with one another to achieve goals, and (4) receive positive feedback when they interact with one another. Functionalists stress that members of subordinate groups become absorbed into the dominant culture. Conflict theorists focus on economic stratification and access to power in race and ethnic relations.

How fair were Canada's early immigration policies?
Canada's early immigration policies were described as racist and included exclusionary policies directed at Asian populations including Chinese and Japanese, and at East Indians and Jews. "White ethnics" who came from European countries comprised the preferred category of immigrants. Changes to the Immigration Act in 1962 involving the implementation of a points system opened the door to immigration on a nonracial basis.

Key Terms

assimilation 263
authoritarian personality 255
discrimination 255
ethnic group 250
ethnic pluralism 263
ethnocentrism 254
institutionalized racism 259
internal colonialism 264
majority (dominant) group 252
minority (subordinate) group 252
polite racism 259
prejudice 254
race 250
racial prejudices 254
racism 257
scapegoat 255
segregation 263
social distance 255
split labour market 264
systemic racism 260

Internet Exercises

1. March 21 is the International Day for the Elimination of Racial Discrimination. Visit the Heritage Canada Web site at **www.march21.com.** What recommendations can you find on how to deal with racial violence?

2. Using the Alta Vista search engine (**altavista.com**), do a search for the term "ethnic struggle." What types of sites do you come to? What are the differences in the way the concept of ethnic struggle is discussed in the textbook and how it is talked about on the Internet?

3. Because of the nature of the Internet, it is possible for anyone with an idea to publish on it, providing he or she has access to a computer. Go to Deja News (**www.dejanews.com**) and run a search on white power. How are the racist arguments on the Internet the same as traditional arguments? How are they different? How do people react to these comments on the Internet?

Net Links

For more Web links related to the topic of this chapter, see the Nelson sociology Web site: **www.sociologyessentials-2nded.nelson.com**.

For highlights from the *Report of the Royal Commission on Aboriginal Peoples*, go to:

www.inac.gc.ca/ch/rcap/rpt/index_e.html

For additional information on First Nations peoples, go to the First Nation Information Project site at:

www.johnco.com/nativel/#13

"The Crosspoint" is the Internet's largest collection of links in the field of human rights, antiracism, and antifacism; see:

www.magenta.nl/crosspoint

For a thorough overview of anti-Semitism in Canada, review Dr. Karen Mock's article "Perspectives on Racism: Anti-Semitism in Canada":

www1.ca.nizkor.org/hweb/people/m/mock-karen/por-02.html

"Hate on the Internet" by Dr. K. Mock and Lisa Armony, B'nai Brith Canada, outlines the growth of hate on the Internet, debates the pros and cons of Internet regulations of hate propaganda, and suggests other responses to the presence of hate on the Internet; to see this site, go to:

www.media-awareness.ca/eng/issues/internet/resource/mock.htm

Questions for Critical Thinking

1. Do you consider yourself defined more strongly by your race or by your ethnicity? Can you explain this choice?
2. Given that minority groups have some common experiences, why is there such deep conflict between certain minority groups?
3. What would need to happen in Canada, both individually and institutionally, for a positive form of ethnic pluralism to flourish in the twenty-first century?

Suggested Readings

For in-depth analyses of race and ethnic relations, these texts are excellent:

W.W. Isajiw. *Understanding Diversity: Ethnicity and Race in the Canadian Context*. Toronto: Thompson Educational Publishing, 1999.

Carl E. James and Adrienne Shadd (eds.). *Talking About Difference: Encounters in Culture, Language and Identity*. Toronto: Between the Lines, 1994.

Peter S. Li (ed.). *Race and Ethnic Relations in Canada*. Toronto: Oxford University Press, 1990.

Martin N. Marger. *Race and Ethnic Relations: American and Global Perspectives*. Belmont, Cal.: Wadsworth, 1994.

These recent books provide excellent discussions on racism in Canada:

Stanley R. Barrett. *Is God a Racist? The Right Wing in Canada*. Toronto: University of Toronto Press, 1987.

Augie Fleras and Jean Leonard Elliott. *Unequal Relations: An Introduction to Race, Ethnic and Aboriginal Dynamics in Canada* (2nd ed.). Scarborough, Ont.: Prentice-Hall, 1996.

Frances Henry, Carol Tator, Winston Mattis, and Tim Rees. *The Colour of Democracy: Racism in Canadian Society*. Toronto: Harcourt Brace, 1995.

Carl James. *Seeing Ourselves: Exploring Race, Ethnicity, and Culture*. Toronto: Thompson Publishing, 1995.

Ormond McKague (ed.). *Racism in Canada*. Saskatoon: Fifth House, 1991.

For additional information on the experiences of specific racial and ethnic groups:

Menno Boldt. *Surviving as Indians: The Challenge of Self-Government*. Toronto: University of Toronto Press, 1993.

James S. Frideres (ed.). *Native Peoples in Canada: Contemporary Conflicts* (4th ed.). Scarborough, Ont.: Prentice-Hall, 1993.

INFOTRAC® COLLEGE EDITION

Either from the *Sociology In Our Times: The Essentials* Web site (**www.sociologyessentials-2nded.nelson.com**) or directly from your Web browser, you may access InfoTrac® College Edition, an online university library that includes over 600 popular and scholarly journals in which you can find articles related to the topics in this chapter.

CHAPTER 10

An estimated 5 percent of Canadian women have an eating disorder. Another 10 to 20 percent have symptoms of eating disorders (Marble, 1995). Approximately 95 percent of those who develop eating disorders are women. Men are not immune to these pressures though they respond in a very different manner than women. An estimated 83,000 Canadian youths—mostly young men—take muscle-building steroids (Nemeth et al., 1994). A recent study of weight and eating disorders indicated that dissatisfaction with weight and shape is a common complaint among many university women (Hesse-Biber, 1996). Consider the story of this young Bishop's University student's struggle with anorexia:

"It was March 1995, I was 17 and in my graduating year of high school when I decided that I wanted to lose weight—10 pounds, maybe 15, certainly not more than 20. I was five eight and 155 pounds. I wanted to impress the boys in university and I thought being thin would help. So I went on a diet.

"People with eating disorders do not wake up one morning and say to themselves, 'I am not going to eat any more' or 'I think I will start bingeing and purging.' Nobody called me fat or told me life would be perfect if I lost 50 pounds. I can't pinpoint one event that directly led to my disorder. I just needed something to depend on, something to think about and to put all my effort into. I just happened to find dieting at the wrong time. It was comforting to take a break from the changes and worries in my life to concentrate on what I was, or wasn't, going to eat that day. It was also nice to pat myself on the back every time I resisted eating.

"By June graduation I was down to 130 pounds. I was satisfied but afraid I might regain weight, so I kept dieting. When I entered university that fall, I weighed 120 pounds. I had heard about the Frosh 15, the 15 pounds on average that university students supposedly gain in the first year. I decided that I, dieter extra ordinaire, would not become part of that statistic ... At Christmas I returned home to a horrified family. I wasn't just thin, I was emaciated. But aside from my looks I still seemed to have it all together. I was an honours student when I entered university and had an 82 percent average after my first semester. I had made lots of friends and had balanced my social and academic obligations. Except for the state of my health, I was a success story.

SEX AND GENDER

"When I went back to university in January, my life dissolved both emotionally and physically. I cried at least twice a day, although never in public. I couldn't get up for class. I couldn't even walk up the stairs without sitting down to take a rest. Every single moment was a fight between me and every cell in my body—cells that were begging me to give in and nourish them ... I know that I could not continue living that way but I saw no alternative. Losing the anorexia nervosa felt like losing everything." (Rutherford, 1998:107–108).

Eating disorders are strongly linked to social and cultural pressures. In our society, thinness is associated with beauty, happiness, and success. We live in a culture in which the body is a means of assessing an individual's value or worth. A person's weight may be "fair game" for jokes even in an era when remarks about race, sex, and religion are considered unacceptable (Wolf, 1990). Discrimination against people on the basis of appearance has been referred to as one of the last acceptable forms of prejudice (Stolker, 1992). People who deviate significantly from existing weight and appearance norms often are devalued and objectified by others. *Objectification* is the process of treating people as if they were objects or things, not human beings. We objectify people when we judge them on the basis of their physical appearance rather than on the basis of their individual qualities or actions (Schur, 1983). In our society, objectification of women is especially common (see Table 10.1).

Studies suggest that both men and women may have negative perceptions about their body size, weight, and appearance (Marble, 1995; Nemeth et al., 1994). Many men compare themselves unfavourably to muscular bodybuilders and believe that they need to gain weight or muscularity, which for some is associated with masculinity and power (Basow, 1992; Klein, 1993). For women, however, body image is an even greater concern. Women may compare themselves unfavourably to slender stars of film and television and believe that they need to lose weight. Men are less likely to let concerns about appearance affect how they feel about their own competence, worth, and abilities; among women, dislike of their bodies may affect self-esteem and feelings of self-worth (Mintz and Betz, 1986).

Why do women and men feel differently about their bodies? Cultural differences in appearance norms may explain women's greater concern; they tend to be judged more harshly, and they know it (Wolf, 1990). Throughout their lives, men and women receive different cultural messages about body image, food, and eating. Men are encouraged to eat while women are made to feel guilty about eating (Basow, 1992). Sociologist Sharlene Hesse-Biber (1996:11) refers to this phenomenon as the *cult of thinness*, in which people worship the "perfect" body and engage in rituals such as dieting and exercise with "obssesive attention to monitoring progress—weighing the body at least once a day and constantly checking calories." The main criterion for the cult of thinness is being female (Hesse-Biber, 1996).

TABLE 10.1 The Objectification of Women

GENERAL ASPECTS OF OBJECTIFICATION	OBJECTIFICATION BASED ON CULTURAL PREOCCUPATION WITH "LOOKS"
Women are responded to primarily as "females," while their personal qualities and accomplishments are of secondary importance.	Women often are seen as the objects of sexual attraction, not full human beings—for example, when they are stared at.
Women are seen as being "all alike."	Women are seen by some as depersonalized body parts—for example, "a piece of ass."
Women are seen as being subordinate and passive, so things can easily be "done to a woman"—for example, discrimination, harassment, and violence.	Depersonalized female sexuality is used for cultural and economic purposes—such as in the media, advertising, fashion and cosmetics industries, and pornography.
Women are seen as easily ignored, dismissed, or trivialized.	Women are seen as being "decorative" and status-conferring objects, to be sought (sometimes collected) and displayed by men and sometimes by other women.
	Women are evaluated according to prevailing, narrow "beauty" standards and often feel pressure to conform to appearance norms.

Source: Edwin M. Schur, *Labeling Women Deviant: Gender, Stigma, and Social Control* © 1983 Temple University Press. Reprinted by permission, The McGraw-Hill Companies.

Body image is only one example of the many socially constructed differences between men and women—differences that relate to gender (a social concept) rather than to a person's biological makeup, or sex. In this chapter, we examine the issue of gender: what it is and how it affects us. Before reading on, test your knowledge about gender and body image by taking the quiz in Box 10.1.

Questions and Issues

CHAPTER FOCUS QUESTION: How do expectations about female and male appearance reflect gender inequality?

How do a society's resources and economic structure influence gender stratification?

What are the primary agents of gender socialization?

How does the contemporary workplace reflect gender stratification?

How do functionalist, conflict, and feminist perspectives on gender stratification differ?

SEX AND GENDER

The word *sex* often is used to refer to the biological attributes of men and women (Epstein, 1988). *Gender* often is used to refer to the distinctive qualities of men and women (masculinity and femininity) that are culturally created (Epstein, 1988; Marshall, 1994).

Sex

***Sex* refers to the biological and anatomical differences between females and males.** At the core of these differences is the chromosomal information transmitted at the moment when a child is conceived. The mother contributes an X chromosome and the father either an X (which produces a female embryo) or a Y chromosome (which produces a male embryo). At birth, male and female infants are distinguished by ***primary sex characteristics:* the genitalia used in the reproductive process.** At puberty, an increased production of hormones results in the development of ***secondary sex characteristics:* the**

BOX 10.1 SOCIOLOGY AND EVERYDAY LIFE

How Much Do You Know about Body Image and Gender?

TRUE	FALSE	
T	F	1. Most people have an accurate perception of their own physical appearance.
T	F	2. Recent studies show that up to 95 percent of men express dissatisfaction with some aspect of their bodies.
T	F	3. Many young girls and women believe that being even slightly overweight makes them less feminine.
T	F	4. Physical attractiveness is a more central part of self-concept for women than for men.
T	F	5. Virtually no men have eating problems such as anorexia and bulimia.
T	F	6. Thinness has always been the "ideal" body image for women.
T	F	7. Women bodybuilders have gained full acceptance in society.
T	F	8. In school, boys are more likely than girls to ridicule people about their appearance.
T	F	9. Canada has laws prohibiting employment discrimination on the basis of weight.
T	F	10. Young girls and women very rarely die as a result of anorexia or bulimia.

Answers on page 280.

physical traits (other than reproductive organs) that identify an individual's sex. For women, these include larger breasts, wider hips, and narrower shoulders; a layer of fatty tissue throughout the body; and menstruation. For men, they include development of enlarged genitals, a deeper voice, greater height, a more muscular build, and more body and facial hair (see Lott, 1994:17–32).

These changes produce an acute awareness of sexuality. During this time, many young people become aware of their ***sexual orientation*—a preference for emotional–sexual relationships with members of the opposite sex (heterosexuality) or the same sex (homosexuality), or no preference for one over the other but an affinity for both (bisexuality)** (Lips, 1993). Some researchers believe that sexual orientation is rooted in biological factors that are present at birth (Pillard and Weinrich, 1986); others believe that sexuality has both biological and social components and is not preordained at birth (Golden, 1987).

Sex is not always clear-cut. Occasionally, a hormone imbalance before birth produces a ***hermaphrodite*—a person in whom sexual differentiation is ambiguous or incomplete** (Renzetti and Curran, 1995). Hermaphrodites tend to have some combination of male and female genitalia. Some people may be genetically of one sex but have a gender identity of the other. That is true for a ***transsexual*, a person who believes that he or she was born with the body of the wrong sex.** Some transsexuals take hormone treatments or have a sex change operation to alter their genitalia in order to achieve a body congruent with their own sense of sexual identity (Basow, 1992).

Western societies acknowledge the existence of only two sexes; some other societies recognize three—men, women, and *berdaches* (or *hijras* or *xaniths*), biological males who behave, dress, work, and are treated in most respects as women. The closest approximation of a third sex in Western societies is a ***transvestite*, a male who lives as a women or a female who lives as a man but does not alter the genitalia.** Although transvestites are not treated as a third sex, they often "pass" for members of that sex because their appearance and mannerisms fall within the range of what is expected from members of the other sex (Lorber, 1994).

Gender

***Gender* refers to the culturally and socially constructed differences between females and males found in the meanings, beliefs, and practices associated with "femininity" and "masculinity."** Although biological differences between women and men are very important, most "sex differences" actually are

BOX 10.1

Answers to the Sociology Quiz on Body Image and Gender

1. **False.** Many people do not have a very accurate perception of their own bodies. For example, many young girls and women think of themselves as fat when they are not. Some young boys and men tend to believe that they need well-developed chest and arm muscles, broad shoulders, and a narrow waist.
2. **True.** In recent studies, up to 95 percent of men believed they needed to improve some aspect of their bodies.
3. **True.** More than half of all adult women in North America are currently dieting, and over three-fourths of normal-weight women think they are too fat. Recently, very young girls have developed similar concerns. For example, 80 percent of Grade 4 girls in one study were watching their weight.
4. **True.** Women have been socialized to believe that being physically attractive is very important. Studies have found that weight and body shape are the central determinants of women's perception of their physical attractiveness.
5. **False.** Some men do have eating problems such as anorexia and bulimia. These problems have been found especially among gay men and male fashion models and dancers.
6. **False.** The "ideal" body image for women has changed a number of times. A positive view of body fat has prevailed for most of human history; however, in the twentieth century in North America, this view has given way to "fat aversion."
7. **False.** Although bodybuilding among women has gained some degree of acceptance, women bodybuilders still are expected to be very "feminine" and not to overdevelop themselves.
8. **True.** Boys are especially likely to ridicule girls whom they perceive to be "unattractive" or overweight.
9. **False.** To date Canada has no laws that specifically prohibit employment discrimination on the basis of weight.
10. **False.** Although the exact number is not known, many young girls and women do die as a result of starvation, malnutrition, and other problems associated with anorexia and bulimia. These are considered life-threatening behaviours by many in the medical profession.

Sources: Based on Lips, 1993; Fallon, Katzman, and Wooley, 1994; Kilbourne, 1994; and Seid, 1994.

socially constructed "gender differences" (Gailey, 1987). According to sociologists, social and cultural processes, not biological "givens," are most important in defining what females and males are, what they should do, and what sorts of relations do or should exist between them (Ortner and Whitehead, 1981; Lott, 1994). Sociologist Judith Lorber (1994:6) summarizes the importance of gender:

> Gender is a human invention, like language, kinship, religion, and technology; like them, gender organizes human social life in culturally patterned ways. Gender organizes social relations in everyday life as well as in the major social structures, such as social class and the hierarchies of bureaucratic organizations.

Virtually everything social in our lives is *gendered:* people continually distinguish between males and females and evaluate them differentially (Mackie, 1995). Gender is an integral part of the daily experiences of both women and men (McDaniel, 1991).

A microlevel analysis of gender focuses on how individuals learn gender roles and acquire a gender identity. ***Gender role*** **refers to the attitudes, behaviour, and activities that are socially defined as appropriate for each sex and are learned through the socialization process** (Lips, 1993). For example, in Canadian society, males traditionally are expected to demonstrate aggressiveness and toughness while females are expected to be passive and nurturing. ***Gender identity*** **is a person's perception**

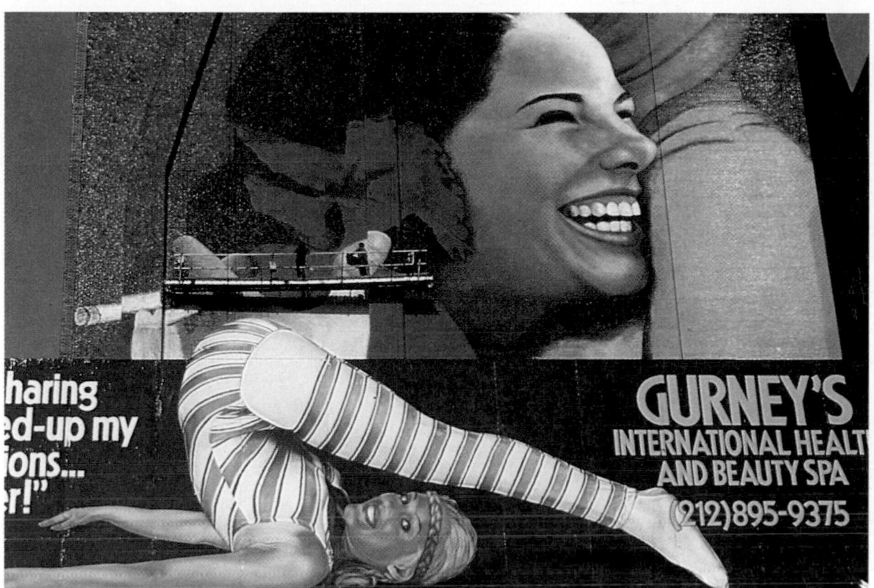

No wonder many women are extremely concerned about body image; even billboards communicate cultural messages about their appearance.

of the self as female or male. Typically established between 18 months and 3 years of age, gender identity is a powerful aspect of our self-concept (Cahill, 1986; Lips, 1993). Although this identity is an individual perception, it is developed through interaction with others. As a result, most people form a gender identity that matches their biological sex: most biological females think of themselves as female, and most biological males think of themselves as male. Body consciousness is a part of gender identity (Basow, 1992). ***Body consciousness* is how a person perceives and feels about his or her body; it also includes an awareness of social conditions in society that contribute to this self-knowledge** (Thompson, 1994). Consider, for example, these comments by Steve Michalik, a former Mr. Universe:

> I was small and weak, and my brother Anthony was big and graceful, and my old man made no bones about loving him and hating me ... The minute I walked in from school, it was, "You worthless little s--t, what are you doing home so early?" His favorite way to torture me was to tell me he was going to put me in a home. We'd be driving along ... and we'd pass a building with iron bars on the windows, and he'd stop the car and say to me, "Get out. This is the home we're putting you in." I'd be standing there sobbing on the curb—I was maybe eight or nine at the time. (quoted in Klein, 1993:273)

As we grow up, we become aware, as Michalik did, that the physical shape of our bodies subjects us to the approval or disapproval of others. While being small and weak may be considered positive attributes for women, they are considered negative characteristics for "real men."

A macrolevel analysis of gender examines structural features, external to the individual, that perpetuate gender inequality. These structures have been referred to as *gendered institutions*, meaning that gender is one of the major ways by which social life is organized in all sectors of society. Gender is embedded in the images, ideas, and language of a society and is used as a means to divide up work, allocate resources, and distribute power. For example, every society uses gender to assign certain tasks—ranging from child rearing to warfare—to females and to males.

These institutions are reinforced by a *gender belief system* that includes all of the ideas regarding masculine and feminine attributes that are held to be valid in a society. This belief system is legitimated by religion, science, law, and other societal values (Lorber, 1994). For example, gendered belief systems may change over time as gender roles change. Many fathers take care of young children today, and there is a much greater acceptance of this change in roles. However, popular stereotypes about men and women, as well as cultural norms about gender-appropriate appearance and behaviour, serve to reinforce gendered institutions in society (Deaux and Kite, 1987).

The way society once viewed women's role in war compared with the way it now views it illustrates how gender belief systems change over time.

The Social Significance of Gender

Like ethnicity, gender is a social construction with important consequences in everyday life. Just as stereotypes regarding race/ethnicity have built-in notions of superiority and inferiority, gender stereotypes hold that men and women are inherently different in attributes, behaviour, and aspirations. Stereotypes define men as strong, rational, dominant, independent, and less concerned with their appearance. Women are stereotyped as weak, emotional, nurturing, dependent, and anxious about their appearance.

The social significance of gender stereotypes is illustrated by eating problems. The three most common eating problems are anorexia, bulimia, and obesity. With *anorexia*, a person has lost at least 25 percent of body weight due to a compulsive fear of becoming fat (Lott, 1994). With *bulimia*, a person binges by consuming large quantities of food and then purges the food by induced vomiting, excessive exercise, laxatives, or fasting (Renzetti and Curran, 1992). With *obesity*, individuals are 20 percent or more above their desirable weight, as established by the medical profession. For a 5-foot-4-inch woman, that is about twenty-five pounds; for a 5-foot-10-inch man, about thirty pounds (Burros, 1994:1).

Sociologist Becky W. Thompson argues that, based on stereotypes, the primary victims of eating problems are presumed to be white, middle-class, heterosexual women. However, such problems also exist among visible-minority women, working-class women, lesbians, and some men. According to Thompson, explanations regarding the relationship between gender and eating problems must take into account a complex array of social factors, including gender socialization and women's responses to problems such as racism and emotional, physical, and sexual abuse (Thompson, 1994; see also, Heywood, 1998).

Bodybuilding is another gendered experience. *Bodybuilding* is the process of deliberately cultivating an increase in mass and strength of the skeletal muscles by means of lifting and pushing weights (Mansfield and McGinn, 1993). In the past, bodybuilding was predominantly a male activity; musculature connoted power, domination, and virility (Klein, 1993). Today, an increasing number of women engage in this activity. As gendered experiences, eating problems and bodybuilding have more in common than we might think. Historian Susan Bordo (1993) has noted that the anorexic body and the muscled body are not opposites; instead, they exist on a continuum because they are united against a "common platoon of enemies: the soft, the loose; unsolid, excess flesh." The *body* is objectified in both compulsive dieting and bodybuilding (Mansfield and McGinn, 1993:53).

Sexism

***Sexism* is the subordination of one sex, usually female, based on the assumed superiority of the other sex.** Sexism directed at women has three components: (1) negative attitudes toward women, (2) stereotypical beliefs that reinforce, complement, or justify the prejudice, and (3) discrimination—acts that exclude, distance, or keep women separate (Lott, 1994).

Can men be victims of sexism? Although women are more often the target of sexist remarks and practices, men can be victims of sexist assumptions. As social psychologist Hilary M. Lips (1993:11) notes, "Sexism cuts both ways; for example, the other side of the prejudiced attitude that [usually bars] women from combat positions in the military is the attitude that it is somehow less upsetting to have male soldiers killed than to have female soldiers killed."

Like racism, sexism is used to justify discriminatory treatment. When women participate in what is considered gender-inappropriate endeavours in the workplace, at home, or in leisure activities, they often find that they are the targets of prejudice and discrimination. Obvious manifestations of sexism are found in the undervaluing of women's work, in hiring and promotion practices that effectively exclude women from an organization or confine them to the bottom of the organizational hierarchy, and in the denial of equal access for women to educational opportunities (Armstrong and Armstrong, 1994). Some people feel that pornography serves to perpetuate sexism by portraying women as objects. Box 10.2 addresses how the law in Canada deals with this rather complex issue. Women who attempt to enter nontraditional occupations (such as firefighting, welding, and steelworking) or professions (such as dentistry and architecture) often encounter hurdles that men do not face. Women may experience discrimination because they are perceived to be "out of place." Consider the following comments from a male steelworker in Hamilton regarding the hiring of female steelworkers:

> It's dirty, heavy, it's no climate for a woman. The men's world is a little rougher than the women's. Physically a man is in better shape. Men are more mechanically minded ... There is nothing wrong with women, it's just that sometimes with heavy work ... if you take the overall picture, masculinity has always been the man's. It doesn't mean that he has more brains because that is not true, but muscularity. I think that women should be outside. It is no place for women. I hate it. (Livingston and Luxton, 1995:190)

Sexism is interwoven with ***patriarchy*—a hierarchical system of social organization in which cultural, political, and economic structures are controlled by men.** By contrast, ***matriarchy* is a hierarchical system of social organization in which cultural, political, and economic structures are controlled by women;** however, few (if any) societies have been organized in this manner (Lengermann and Wallace, 1985). Patriarchy is reflected in the way men may think of their position as men as a given while women may deliberate on what their position in society should be. As sociologist Virginia Cyrus (1993:6) explains, "Under patriarchy, men are seen as 'natural' heads of households, political candidates, corporate executives, university presidents, etc. Women, on the other hand, are men's subordinates, playing such supportive roles as housewife, mother, nurse, and secretary." Gender inequality and a division of labour based on male dominance are nearly universal, as we will see in the following discussion on the origins of gender-based stratification.

GENDER STRATIFICATION IN HISTORICAL PERSPECTIVE

How do tasks in a society come to be defined as "men's work" or "women's work"? Three factors are important in determining the gendered division of labour in a society: (1) the type of subsistence base, (2) the supply of and demand for labour, and (3) the extent to which women's child-rearing activities are compatible with certain types of work. Subsistence refers to the means by which a society gains the basic necessities of life, including food, shelter, and clothing (Nielsen, 1990). The three factors vary according to a society's *technoeconomic base*—the level of technology and the organization of the economy in a given society. Four such bases have been identified: hunting and gathering societies, horticultural and pastoral societies, agrarian societies, and industrial societies, as shown in Table 10.2.

BOX 10.2 CRITICAL THINKING

Obscenity and Women's Equality

Is pornography harmful? If so, who does it harm? Is all pornographic material obscene or just some of it? Does it result in exploitation and further objectification of women in our society? In the Canadian courts, the jury on these issues is still out.

Until recently, judges were responsible for assessing what was decent and what was indecent in obscenity cases. In other words, obscenity was in the eye of the beholder and varied with the times.

This changed in 1992 with the landmark Supreme Court of Canada case R. vs. Butler. David Butler, the owner of a Winnipeg pornography shop, was charged with 250 counts of possessing and trafficking in obscene hardcore videos and magazines. Butler was acquitted on 242 counts and convicted on eight. Unsatisfied with this result, Butler appealed his convictions up to the Supreme Court of Canada, arguing that pornographic material is protected from prosecution because of the guarantee of freedom of expression in the Charter of Rights and Freedoms.

The Women's Legal Education and Action Fund (LEAF) asked the Supreme Court to uphold the obscenity law on the basis that some forms of pornography promoted violence against women. However, as LEAF acknowledged, the research evidence is ambiguous—it neither proves nor disproves this claim.

The Supreme Court agreed with LEAF and in a unanimous decision, upheld the obscenity law and the court's right to censor pornographic material that is defined as obscene.

A more explicit definition of obscenity resulted from Butler's Supreme Court challenge. First, any material that mixes explicit sex and violence, or includes children, should be ruled obscene. Second, materials that involve explicit

Hunting and Gathering Societies

The earliest known division of labour between women and men is in hunting and gathering societies. While the men hunt for wild game, women gather roots and berries (Nielsen, 1990). A relatively equitable relationship exists because neither sex has the ability to provide all of the food necessary for survival. When wild game is nearby, both men and women may hunt (Basow, 1992). When it is far away, hunting becomes incompatible with child rearing (which women tend to do because they breast-feed their young), and women are placed at a disadvantage in terms of contributing to the food supply (Lorber, 1994). In most hunting and gathering societies, women are full economic partners with men; relations between them tend to be cooperative and relatively egalitarian (Chafetz, 1984). Little social stratification of any kind is found because people do not acquire a food surplus.

Horticultural and Pastoral Societies

In horticultural societies, which first developed ten to twelve thousand years ago, a steady source of food becomes available. People are able to grow their own food because of hand tools, such as the digging stick and the hoe. Women make an important contribution to food production because hoe cultivation is compatible with child care. A fairly high degree of gender equality exists because neither sex controls the food supply (Basow, 1992).

When inadequate moisture in an area makes planting crops impossible, *pastoralism*—the domestication of large animals to provide food—develops. Herding primarily is done by men, and women contribute relatively little to subsistence production in such societies. In some herding societies, women have relatively low status; their primary value is their ability to produce male offspring so that the family lineage can be preserved and

BOX 10.2

CONTINUED

sex and degradation are obscene if they are deemed to encourage violence or other harm against women. Finally, other sexually explicit material is permissible.

The ruling in the Butler decision has resulted in increasingly liberal interpretations of obscenity laws. The reason is that now, in order to obtain a conviction on an obscenity charge, the prosecution has to prove that a certain work causes harm. This is a defence counsel's dream; as one Toronto criminal lawyer commented, "Dirty pictures don't cause anything" (Kaihla, 1994:30).

What do you think? In a downtown Toronto shop called "Books," an entire wall is devoted to bondage videos. One of the selections is entitled Women Ruled by Men. On the cover are two nude women strapped back to back by a series of chains. One of them has what looks like a horse's bit in her mouth, held there by a strap around her head. Another selection features a character named Sir Michael, who is pictured in a dungeon in which there are whips and chains hanging from the wall, pulling open the negligee of a young woman who is gagged with a heavy, knotted rope. The cover reads "Join Sir Michael as he teases, torments, humiliates and disciplines some of the most beautiful and submissive women who have fallen under his powerful will" (Kaihla, 1994:30).

Are these videos harmful? If so, how would you go about proving this in a court of law?

Sources: Kaihla, 1994; Verburg, 1994; and Busby, 1999.

enough males will exist to protect the group against attack (Nielsen, 1990).

Social practices contribute to gender inequality in horticultural and pastoral societies. Male dominance is promoted by practices such as menstrual taboos, bridewealth, and polygyny (Nielsen, 1990). *Polygyny*—the marriage of one man to multiple wives—contributes to power differences between women and men. A man with multiple wives can produce many children who will enhance his resources, take care of him in his "old age," and become heirs to his property (Nielsen, 1990). *Menstrual taboos* place women in a subordinate position by segregating them into menstrual huts for the duration of their monthly cycle. Even when women are not officially segregated, they are defined as "unclean." *Bridewealth*—the payment of a price by a man for a wife—turns women into property that can be bought and sold. The man gives the bride's family material goods or services in exchange for their daughter's exclusive sexual services and his sole claim to their offspring.

Agrarian Societies

In agrarian societies, which first developed about eight to ten thousand years ago, gender inequality and male dominance become institutionalized. The most extreme form of gender inequality developed about five thousand years ago in societies in the fertile crescent around the Mediterranean Sea (Lorber, 1994). Agrarian societies rely on agriculture—farming done by animal-drawn or energy-powered ploughs and equipment. Because agrarian tasks require more labour and greater physical strength than horticultural ones, men become more involved in food production. It has been suggested that women are excluded from these tasks because they are viewed as too weak for the work and because childcare responsibilities are considered incompatible

TABLE 10.2 TECHNOECONOMIC BASES OF SOCIETY

	HUNTING AND GATHERING	HORTICULTURAL AND PASTORAL	AGRARIAN	INDUSTRIALIZED
Change from Prior Society	—	Use of hand tools, such as digging stick and hoe	Use of animal-drawn plows and equipment	Invention of steam engine
Economic Characteristics	Hunting game, gathering roots and berries	Planting crops, domestication of animals for food	Labour-intensive farming	Mechanized production of goods
Control of Surplus	None	Men begin to control societies	Men who own land or herds	Men who own means of production
Inheritance	None	Shared—patrilineal and matrilineal	Patrilineal	Patrilineal
Control over Procreation	None	Increasingly by men	Men—to ensure legitimacy of heirs	Men—but less so in later stages
Women's Status	Relative equality	Decreasing in move to pastoralism	Low	Low

Source: Adapted from Lorber, 1994:140.

with the full-time labour that the tasks require (Nielsen, 1990).

Why does gender inequality increase in agrarian societies? Scholars cannot agree on an answer; some suggest that it results from private ownership of property. When people no longer have to move continually in search of food, they can acquire a surplus. Men gain control over the disposition of the surplus and the kinship system, which serves men's interests (Lorber, 1994). The importance of producing "legitimate" heirs to inherit the surplus increases significantly, and women's lives become more secluded and restricted as men attempt to ensure the legitimacy of their children. Premarital virginity and marital fidelity are required; indiscretions are punished (Nielsen, 1990). Other scholars argue that male dominance existed before the private ownership of property (Firestone, 1970; Lerner, 1986).

The division of labour between women and men is very distinct in contemporary agrarian societies in places such as Burma and parts of the Middle East. There, women's work takes place in the private sphere (inside the home) and men's work occurs in the public sphere, providing them with more recognition and greater formal status.

Two practices in agrarian societies contribute to the subordination of women. *Purdah*, found primarily among Hindus and Muslims, requires the seclusion of women, extreme modesty in apparel, and the visible subordination of women to men. Women must show deference to men by walking behind them, speaking only when spoken to, and eating only after the men have finished a meal (Nielsen, 1990).

Genital mutilation is a surgical procedure performed on young girls as a method of sexual control (Nielsen, 1990). The mutilation involves cutting off all or part of a girl's clitoris and labia, and in some cases stitching her vagina closed until marriage (Simons, 1993b). Often justified on the erroneous belief that the Koran commands it, these procedures are supposed to ensure that women are chaste before marriage and have no extramarital affairs after marriage. Genital mutilation has resulted in the maiming of many females, some of whom died as a result of hemorrhaging, infection, or other complications. It is still practised in more that twenty-five countries. Box 10.3 discusses the genital mutilation of women around the world.

In sum, male dominance is very strong in agrarian societies. Women are secluded, subordinated, and mutilated as a means of regulating their sexuality and protecting paternity. Most of the world's population currently lives in agrarian societies in various stages of industrialization.

Gender inequality is intertwined with the tasks that come to be defined as "men's work" or "women's work." In hunting and gathering societies such as the Yanomami of South America, there is a relatively equitable division of labour between women and men. Gender inequality becomes more distinct in pastoral and horticultural societies and increases in agrarian societies, as exemplified by the practice of purdah found primarily among Hindus and Muslims. Gender inequality reaches a peak in industrialized societies, represented here by the "cult of true womanhood" of the late nineteenth century.

Industrial Societies

An *industrial society* is one in which factory or mechanized production has replaced agriculture as the major form of economic activity (Nielsen, 1990:49). As societies industrialize, the status of women tends to decline further. Industrialization in Canada created a gap between the nonpaid work performed by women at home and the paid work that increasingly was performed by men and unmarried girls (Krahn and Lowe, 1993; Armstrong and Armstrong, 1994). When families needed extra money, their daughters worked in the textile mills until they married. Once married, women were expected to leave the paid workforce. In 1931, for example, only 3.5 percent of married Canadian women were in the paid labour force (Baker and Lero, 1996). As it became more difficult to make a living by farming, many men found work in the factories, where their primary responsibility often was supervising the work of women and children. Men began to press for a clear division between "men's work" and "women's work," as well as corresponding pay differentials (higher for men, lower for women).

In Canada, the division of labour between men and women in the middle and upper classes became much more distinct with industrialization (Vanier Institute of the Family, 1994). The men were responsible for being "breadwinners"; the women were seen as "homemakers." In this new "cult of domesticity" (also referred to as the "cult of true womanhood"), the home became a private, personal sphere in which women created a haven for the family (Mandell and Momirov, 1999). Those who

BOX 10.3 SOCIOLOGY IN GLOBAL PERSPECTIVE

WOMEN AND HUMAN RIGHTS: FEMALE GENITAL MUTILATION

> The little girl, entirely nude, is immobilized in the sitting position on a low stool by at least three women. One of them has her arms tightly around the little girl's chest, two others hold the child's thighs apart by force, in order to open the vulva. The child's arms are tied behind her back, or immobilized by two other women guests. Then the old woman takes her razor and excises the clitoris ... The little girl howls and writhes in pain, although strongly held down. The operator wipes the blood from the wound and the mother, as well as the guests, "verify" her work, sometimes putting their fingers in. ... Exhausted, the little girl is then dressed and put on a bed. The operation lasts from 15 to 20 minutes according to the ability of the old woman and the resistance put up by the child. (Tomasevski, 1993:85)

Now in her early thirties, Selma recalls enduring this procedure in Sudan at the age of 8, screaming and resisting to no avail: "They held me down. It was painful. I had some anesthetic, but I felt it all" (Rowley, 1994:A9).

The traditional ritual of female genital mutilation is today performed on more than two million girls and women a year. The World Health Organization estimates that 85 to 115 million women have had their genitals mutilated. Although the practice occurs primarily in twenty-eight African nations and in some areas of Asia, cases of genital mutilation among families of recent immigrants from Africa and Asia have been reported in the United States, Canada, Europe, and Australia.

supported the cult of domesticity argued that women were the natural keepers of the domestic sphere and that children were the mother's responsibility. Meanwhile, the "breadwinner" role placed enormous pressure on men to support their families—being a good provider was considered a sign of manhood. However, this gendered division of labour increased the economic and political subordination of women (Bernard, 1995). As a result, many women focused their efforts on acquiring a husband who was capable of bringing home a good wage. Single women and widows and their children tended to live a bleak existence, crowded into rundown areas of cities, where they were unable to support themselves on their meagre wages.

While industrialization was a source of upward mobility for many whites, most racial and ethnic minorities were left behind. The cult of domesticity, for example, was distinctly white and middle or upper class. White families with the financial means to do so hired domestic servants to do much of the household work. In the early 1900s, many black women (as well as white non-English-speaking European women) were employed as household servants (Das Gupta, 1999).

Today, patriarchy and male dominance remain pervasive. These existing patterns of inequality are perpetuated through the process of gender socialization.

GENDER AND SOCIALIZATION

We learn gender-appropriate behaviour through the socialization process. Our parents, teachers, friends, and the media all serve as gendered institutions that communicate to us our earliest, and often most lasting, beliefs about the social meanings of being male or female and thinking and behaving in masculine or feminine ways. Some gender roles have changed dramatically in recent years; others remain largely unchanged over time.

BOX 10.3

CONTINUED

In 1993, attorney Linda Weil-Curiel made the following statement at the Paris trial of a mother accused of allowing the mutilation of her daughter (a practice brought to France by African immigrants): "This is butchery invented to control women ... It's a form of violence we would never allow here against white girls. If immigrants cut off a girl's ear in the name of tradition, there would be an outcry. But here the sex of a future woman is cut off and people are willing to defend it or turn away" (quoted in Simons, 1993b:A4).

Some view genital mutilation as a deeply embedded ritual that must be understood in terms of the culture involved. These practices may be perpetrated on young girls because of centuries-old customs dictating that girls must be kept chaste and that, without the ritual, they will not get a husband and their family will not get a dowry. A spokesperson for the World Health Organization noted that respect for other cultures is needed but that such practices must be challenged when they threaten people's health. What do you think? Should the United Nations protest the genital mutilation practised by countries belonging to the organization? When this practice occurs in Canada, should the parents be charged with child abuse, or should they be excused because of their cultural background?

Sources: Based on Simons, 1993b; Tomasevski, 1993; Greenhouse, 1994; and Rowley, 1994.

Many parents prefer boys to girls because of stereotypical ideas about the relative importance of males and females to the future of the family and society (Achilles, 1996). Although some parents prefer boys to girls because they believe old myths about the biological inferiority of females, research suggests that social expectations also play a major role in this preference. We are socialized to believe that it is important to have a son, especially as a first or only child. For many years, it was assumed that a male child could support his parents in their later years and carry on the family name.

Across cultures, boys are preferred to girls, especially when the number of children that parents can have is limited by law or economic conditions. For example, in China, which strictly regulates the allowable number of children to one per family, a disproportionate number of female fetuses are aborted (Basow, 1992). In India, the practice of aborting female fetuses is widespread, and female infanticide occurs frequently (Achilles, 1996). As a result, both India and China have a growing surplus of young men who will face a shortage of women their own age (Shenon, 1994).

Gender Socialization by Parents

From birth, parents act toward children on the basis of the child's sex. Baby boys are perceived to be less fragile than girls and tend to be treated more roughly by their parents. Girl babies are thought to be "cute, sweet, and cuddly" and receive more gentle treatment (MacDonald and Parke, 1986). When girl babies cry, parents respond to them more quickly, and parents are more prone to talk and sing to girl babies (Basow, 1992).

Children's clothing and toys reflect their parents' gender expectations. Boys' clothing, for example, is more "masculine" and functional, and features male activities and characters (baseball players and superheros), while girls' clothing is more "feminine" and dainty (floral prints, lace, and bows) and has female

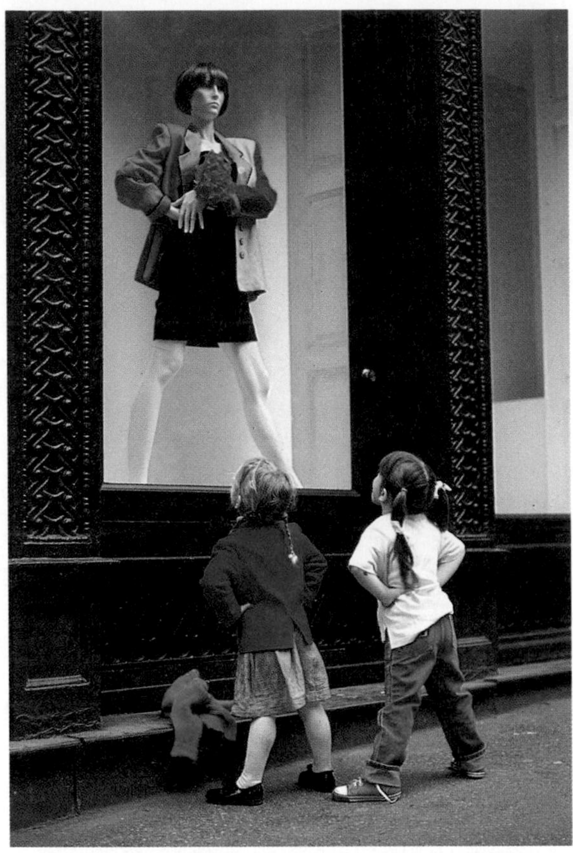

From an early age, a number of societal influences encourage us to learn gender-appropriate behaviour.

characters. Gender-appropriate toys for boys include blocks and building sets, trucks and other vehicles, sports equipment, and war toys such as guns and soldiers (Richardson and Simpson, 1982). Girls' toys include Barbie dolls, play makeup, and homemaking items. Parents' choices of toys for their children are not likely to change in the near future. A group of university students in a recent study was shown slides of toys and asked to decide which ones they would buy for girls and boys. Most said they would buy guns, soldiers, jeeps, carpenter tools, and red bicycles for boys; girls would get baby dolls, dishes, sewing kits, jewellery boxes, and pink bicycles (Fisher-Thompson, 1990).

Differential treatment leads to differential development. A doll or a stuffed animal in a girl's hand calls for "hugging, stroking, and tender loving care"; a ball in a boy's hand "demands bouncing, throwing, and kicking" (Lott, 1994:40). When children are old enough to help with household chores, they often are assigned different tasks. Maintenance chores (such as mowing the lawn) are assigned to boys while domestic chores (such as shopping, cooking, and cleaning the table) are assigned to girls. Chores also may become linked with future occupational choices and personal characteristics. Girls who are responsible for domestic chores such as caring for younger brothers and sisters may learn nurturing behaviours that later translate into employment as a nurse or schoolteacher. Boys may learn about mechanics and other types of technology that lead to different career options.

Many parents are aware of the effect that gender socialization has on their children and make a conscientious effort to provide nonsexist experiences for them. For example, one study found that mothers with nontraditional views encourage their daughters to be independent (Brooks-Gunn, 1986). Many fathers also take an active role in socializing their sons to be thoughtful and caring individuals who do not live by traditional gender stereotypes. However, peers often make nontraditional gender socialization much more difficult for parents and children (see Rabinowitz and Cochran, 1994).

Peers and Gender Socialization

Peers help children learn prevailing gender role stereotypes, as well as gender-appropriate and -inappropriate behaviour. During the school years, same-sex peers have a powerful effect on how children see their gender roles (Maccoby and Jacklin, 1987); children are more socially acceptable to their peers when they conform to gender stereotypes (Martin, 1989).

Male peer groups place more pressure on boys to do "masculine" things than female peer groups place on girls to do "feminine" things (Fagot, 1984). For example, girls wear jeans and other "boy" clothes, play soccer and softball, and engage in other activities traditionally associated with males. But, if a boy wears a dress, plays hopscotch with girls, and engages in other activities associated with being female, he will be ridiculed by his peers. This distinction between the relative value of boys' and girls' behaviours strengthens the cultural message that masculine activities and behaviour are more important and more acceptable (J. Wood, 1994).

During adolescence, peers often are more influential agents of gender socialization than adults. Peers are thought to be especially important in boys' development of gender identity (Maccoby and Jacklin, 1987). Male bonding that occurs during adolescence is believed to reinforce masculine identity (Gaylin, 1992) and to encourage gender-stereotypical attitudes and behaviour (Huston, 1985; Martin, 1989). For example, male peers have a tendency to ridicule and bully others about their appearance, size, and weight. One woman painfully recalled walking down the halls at school when boys would flatten themselves against the lockers and cry, "Wide load!" At lunchtime, the boys made a production of watching her eat lunch and frequently made sounds like pig grunts or moos (Kolata, 1993). Because peer acceptance is so important for both males and females during their first two decades, such actions can have very harmful consequences for the victims.

As young adults, men and women still receive many gender-related messages from peers. Among university students, for example, peers play an important role in career choices and in the establishment of long-term, intimate relationships. Male peers may pressure other men to participate in "male bonding" rituals that are derogatory toward women (DeKeseredy and Kelly, 1995). For example, fraternity initiations may require pledges to participate in behaviour ranging from "showing their manhood" to gang rapes (O'Sullivan, 1993). Some of the research suggests that male peers are often unable to show a man how to effectively interact intimately with other people (Tannen, 1990; DeKeseredy and Kelly, 1995).

Peer groups for both women and men on university campuses are organized largely around gender relations (Holland and Eisenhart, 1990). In a study that followed a number of women students at two universities, anthropologists Dorothy C. Holland and Margaret A. Eisenhart (1990) found that the peer system propelled women into a world of romance in which their attractiveness to men counted most; the women were subjected to a "sexual auction block." While peers initially did not influence the women's choices of majors and careers, they did influence whether the women continued to pursue their initial goals, changed their course of action, or were "derailed" (Holland and Eisenhart, 1981, 1990).

Peer pressure can also strongly influence a person's body consciousness. Women in university often feel pressure to be very thin, as Karen explains:

> "Do you diet?" asked a friend [in my first year of university], as I was stuffing a third homemade chocolate chip cookie in my mouth. "Do you know how many calories there are in that one cookie?"
>
> Stopping to think for a moment as she and two other friends stared at me, probably wanting to ask me the same question, I realized that I really didn't even know what a calorie was …
>
> From that moment, I'd taken on a new enemy, one more powerful and destructive than any human can be. One that nearly fought me to the death—my death …
>
> I just couldn't eat food anymore. I was so obsessed with it that I thought about it every second … In two months, I'd lost thirty pounds … Everyone kept telling me I looked great …
>
> I really didn't realize that anything was wrong with me … There were physical things occurring in my body other than not having my period anymore. My hair was falling out and was getting thinner … I would constantly get head rushes every time I stood up … When my friends would all go out to dinner or to a party I stayed home quite often, afraid that I might have to eat something, and afraid that my friends would find out that I didn't eat. (Twenhofel, 1993:198)

Feminist scholars have concluded that eating problems are not always psychological "disorders" (as they are referred to by members of the medical profession). Instead, eating (or not eating) may be a strategy for coping with problems such as unrealistic social pressures about slenderness (see Orbach, 1978; Chernin, 1981; and Hesse-Biber, 1996) and/or social injustices caused by racism, sexism, and classism in society (Thompson, 1994).

Teacher and Schools and Gender Socialization

From kindergarten through university, schools operate as gendered institutions. Teachers provide important messages about gender through both the formal content of classroom assignments and informal interaction with students. Sometimes, gender-related messages from teachers and other students reinforce gender roles that have been taught at home; however, teachers also may contradict parental socialization. During the early years of a child's schooling, the teachers' influence is very powerful; many children spend more hours per day with their teachers than they do with their parents.

One of the messages teachers may communicate to students is that boys are more important than girls. Research spanning the past twenty years shows that unintentional gender bias occurs in virtually all educational settings. ***Gender bias* consists of showing favouritism toward one gender over the other.** Researchers consistently find that teachers devote more time, effort, and attention to boys than to girls (Sadker and Sadker, 1994). Males receive more praise for their contributions and are called on more frequently in class, even when they do not volunteer. Very often, boys receive attention because they call out in class, demand help, and sometimes engage in disruptive behaviour (Sadker and Sadker, 1994).

The content of teacher–student interaction is very important. In a multiple-year study of more than one hundred Grade 4, Grade 6, and Grade 8 students, education professors Myra and David Sadker (1984) identified four types of teacher comments: praise, acceptance, remediation, and criticism. They found that boys typically received more of all four types of teacher comments than did girls. Teachers also gave more precise and penetrating replies to boys; by contrast, teachers used vague and superficial terms such as "OK" when responding to girls. Because boys receive more specific and intense interaction from teachers, they may gain more insights than girls into the strengths and weaknesses of their answers and thus learn how to improve their responses.

Teacher–student interactions influence not only students' learning but also their self-esteem (Sadker and Sadker, 1985, 1986, 1994). A comprehensive study of gender bias in schools suggested that girls' self-esteem is undermined in school through such experiences as (1) a relative lack of attention from teachers, (2) sexual harassment by male peers, (3) the stereotyping and invisibility of females in textbooks, especially in science and math texts, and (4) test bias based on assumptions about the relative importance of quantitative and visual-spatial ability, as compared with verbal ability, that lessen girls' chances of being admitted to the university of their choice and awarded scholarships.

Most problems that exist in prekindergarten through high school also are found in colleges and universities. University professors often pay more attention to men than women in their classes (Wylie, 1995). Women are also subjected to a number of "exclusionary tactics," such as being called on less frequently and receiving less encouragement than men, or being interrupted, ignored, or devalued (Wylie, 1995). Researchers have found that women university professors (approximately 22 percent of university teachers) encourage a more participatory classroom environment and do a better job of including both women and men in their interactions (Statham, Richardson, and Cook, 1991). However, a study, which has come to be known as the "Chilly Climate Report," conducted at the University of Western Ontario found that the university classroom is a "chilly" climate for women students, who often experience a drop in self-esteem as a result of their academic experiences. One graduate student reported that she felt "totally demoralized ... a failure ... I forget, even now, that I used to be seen as a powerful person. I lost my sense of personal power and self worth in the four years I was there" (Backhouse et al., 1995:127).

Despite these obstacles, women are more likely than men to earn a university degree. In 1996, almost 21 percent of women in their 20s obtained a university degree compared with approximately 16 percent of men in the same age group (Statistics Canada, 1998c). This is a relatively recent trend. It was not until 1988 that women's enrolment in university surpassed men's (Wylie, 1995).

Mass Media and Gender Socialization

The media are a powerful source of gender stereotyping. While some critics argue that the media simply reflect existing gender roles in society, others point out that the media have a uniquely persuasive ability to shape ideas. Think of the impact that television has on children who are estimated to spend one-third of their waking time watching it.

From children's cartoons to adult shows, television programs are sex-typed and white-male oriented. More male than female roles are shown, and male characters act in a strikingly different manner than female ones. Males are typically more aggres-

BOX 10.4 SOCIOLOGY AND MEDIA

"YOU'VE COME A LONG WAY, BABY"

In a television commercial, two little French girls are shown dressing up in the feathery finery of their mothers' clothes. They are exquisite little girls, flawless and innocent, and the scene emphasizes both their youth and the natural sense of style often associated with French women. (The ad is done in French, with subtitles.) One of the girls, spying a picture of the other girl's mother, exclaims breathlessly, "Your mother, she is so slim, so beautiful? Does she eat?" The daughter, giggling, replies, "Silly, just not as much," and displays her mother's helper, a bottle of diet pills. "Aren't you jealous?" the friend asks. Dimpling, shy, yet self-possessed, deeply knowing, the daughter answers, "Not if I know her secrets." (Bordo, 1993:99)

Women are bombarded with such advertisements and commercials for weight-loss products and programs. This ad is especially problematic, however, because it suggests that very young girls should begin learning to control their weight by the use of some "secret" (Bordo, 1993:99). Viewers must use their imagination about how the mother looks, but the message is clear: Her "slim ... beautiful" appearance can belong to any woman who purchases this product. According to media scholar Jean Kilbourne (1994:395):

The current emphasis on excessive thinness for women is one of the clearest examples of advertising's power to influence cultural standards and consequent individual behavior. Body types, like clothing styles, go in and out of fashion, and are promoted by advertising ... The images in the mass media constantly reinforce the latest ideal—what is acceptable and what is out of date ... Advertising and the media indoctrinate us in these ideals, to the detriment of most women.

Today's ideal body type is unattainable except for the thinnest 5 percent of all women. Clearly, the dramatic increase in eating problems in recent years cannot be attributed solely to advertising and the mass media; however, their potential impact on young girls and women in establishing role models with whom to identify is extremely important (Kilbourne, 1994:398).

As women have attempted to gain power and freedom, advertising has worked to reduce the political to the personal. If people buy the right products and get their individual acts together, everything will be fine. As Kilbourne (1994) notes, "The advertisers will never voluntarily change, because it is profitable for women to feel terrible about themselves. Thus, we need to educate everyone to be critical viewers of advertising and the mass media."

Sources: Based on Barthel, 1988; Moog, 1990; Bordo, 1993; and Kilbourne, 1994.

sive, constructive, and direct and are rewarded for their actions. In contrast, females are depicted as acting deferentially toward other people or as manipulating them through helplessness or seductiveness to get their way (Basow, 1992). Because advertisers hope to appeal to boys, who constitute more than half of the viewing audience for some shows, many programs feature lively adventure and lots of loud noise and violence. Even educational programs such as *Barney* may perpetuate gender stereotypes. Most of the characters on these shows have male names and masculine voices and participate in "boys' activities."

While attempts have been made by media watchdogs and some members of the media itself to eliminate sexism in children's programming, adult daytime and prime-time programs (which children frequently watch) have received less scrutiny. Soap operas are a classic example of programs that stereotype gender. In them, women are depicted as emotional, nurturing, and unable to make a decision; men are forceful and more oriented toward problem solving. Daytime talk shows may trivialize important issues of sex and gender under the guise of letting people air their grievances and opinions and of having experts who set the record straight (Basow, 1992).

In prime-time television, a number of significant changes in the past three decades have reduced gender stereotyping; however, men still outnumber women as leading characters. Men, for the most part, have been police officers, detectives, attorneys, doctors, and businessmen. In recent years, women in professional careers have been overrepresented, which may give the erroneous impression that most women in the workforce are in executive, managerial, and professional positions; in the "real world," most employed women work in low-paying, low-status jobs (Basow, 1992). In most programs, women's appearance is considered very important and frequently is a topic of discussion on the program itself.

Advertising—whether on television and billboards or in magazines and newspapers—reinforces the notion that women can never be too young or too thin (see discussion in Box 10.4). Regarding gender generally, the intended message is clear to most people: if they embrace traditional notions of masculinity and femininity, their personal and social success is assured; and if they purchase the right products and services, they can enhance their appearance and gain power over other people. For example, the $20-billion-per-year cosmetics industry uses ads depicting the "truly feminine woman" as needing a "plethora of beauty aids to help her look younger and more attractive to men" (Wolf, 1990). Such ads may play an important role in adult gender socialization.

A knowledge of how we develop a gender-related self-concept and learn to feel, think, and act in feminine or masculine ways is important for an understanding of ourselves. Examining gender socialization makes us aware of the impact of our parents, siblings, teachers, friends, and the media on our own perspectives about gender. However, the gender socialization perspective has been criticized on several counts. Childhood gender-role socialization may not affect people as much as some analysts have suggested. For example, the types of jobs people take as adults may have less to do with how they were socialized in childhood than with how they are treated in the workplace. From this perspective, women and men will act in ways that bring them the most rewards and produce the fewest punishments (Reskin and Padavic, 1994). Also, gender socialization theories can be used to blame women for their own subordination (Eitzen and Baca Zinn, 1995). For example, if we assume that women's problems can all be blamed on women themselves, existing social structures that perpetuate gender inequality will be overlooked. We will now examine a few of those structural forces.

CONTEMPORARY GENDER INEQUALITY

According to feminist scholars, women experience gender inequality as a result of economic, political, and educational discrimination (Luxton, 1980; Smith, 1987; Curtis et al., 1999). Women's position in the Canadian workforce reflects their overall subordination in society.

Gender Segregation in the Paid Workforce

One of the most significant changes in Canadian society in recent decades has been the dramatic rise in the number of women in the paid workforce. As shown in Figure 10.1, in 1951 only 24 percent of all adult women in Canada worked outside of the home for pay. By 1996, this figure had jumped to 57 percent. Among the most significant factors contributing to these changes in the labour force are women's rising educational levels, the rise in single-parent families, and the economic demand for dual-income families (Lowe, 1999).

Not only are more Canadian women working today, but they are also employed in a much wider range of occupations than ever before. In the past two decades women have been successful in breaking down barriers to some of the high-paying, prestigious, traditionally "male" professions such as medicine, law, and corporate management (Creese and Beagan, 1999:202). For example, in 1996, women accounted for 30 percent of general practi-

FIGURE 10.1 Labour Force Participation Rates, Males and Females Aged 15 and Over, 1911–1996

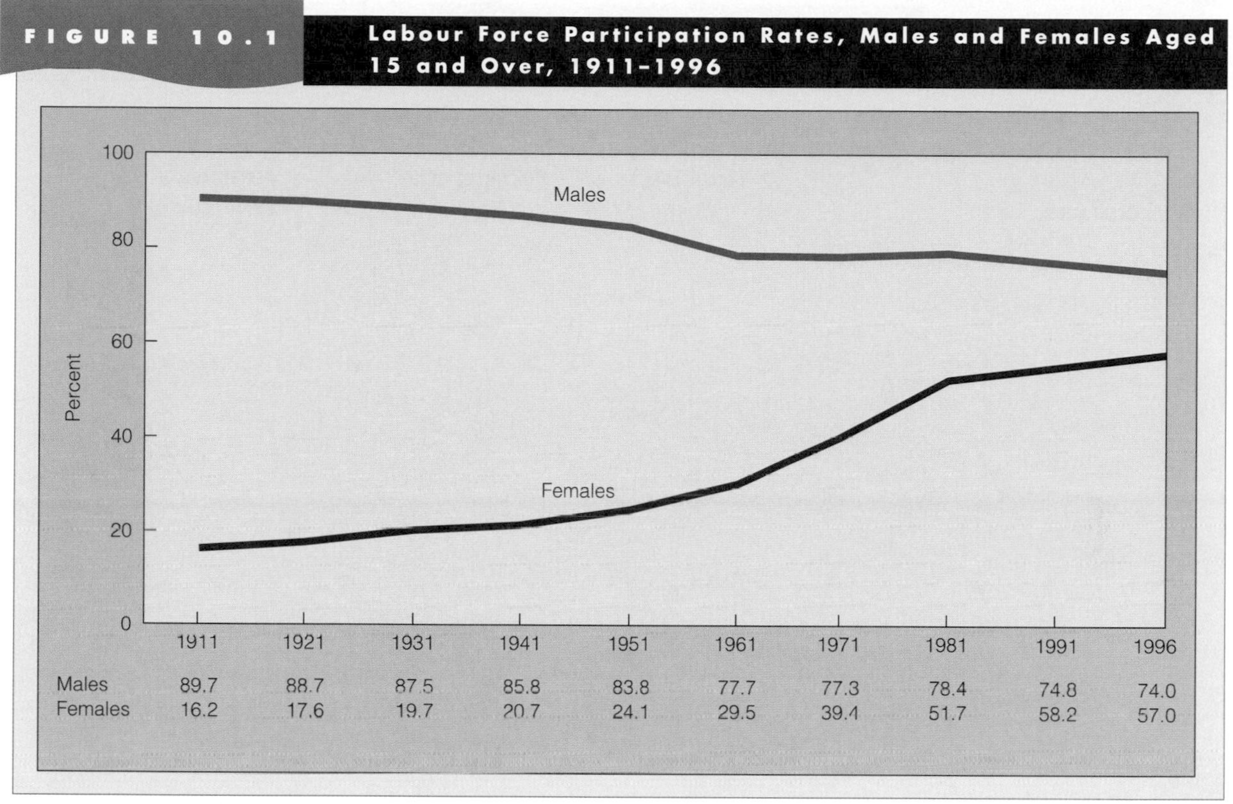

Prepared by the Centre for International Statistics. © The Vanier Institute of the Family. 1996 figures from Akyeampoing, 1996. Used by permission.

tioners and specialist physicians, up from 18 percent in 1982 (Statistics Canada, 1998f). Social analyst John Kettle indicated that women are now filling the majority of new managerial and professional jobs. Using Statistics Canada data, he found that between 1975 and 1996 the Canadian economy produced 1.3 million additional management jobs and 1.2 million professional jobs. Women filled 57 percent of the managerial jobs and 65 percent of the professional jobs (Kettle, 1998). Despite this progress, the majority of Canadian women continue to be employed in a much narrower range of occupations that are lower-paying, low-status, traditionally female jobs. Almost 70 percent of all working women are employed in just five occupational sectors: teaching, nursing and health-related occupations, clerical, sales, and service.

Gender-segregated work refers to the concentration of women and men in different occupations, jobs, and places of work (Lowe, 1999). In 1996, for example, almost 80 percent of all clerical jobs in Canada were held by women (see Table 10.3). In the same year, men were overrepresented in jobs in the natural sciences, engineering, and mathematics, making up 80 percent of the professionals in these fields (Creese and Beagan, 1999). The term *female job ghetto* refers to the unequal rewards and opportunities built into the labour market on the basis of the employee's gender. Women in job ghettos often have limited access to the more challenging, higher-paying occupations dominated by men because many of these professions set up success criteria that are male-biased (Canadian Committee on Women in Engineering, 1992, cited in Lowe, 1999).

Gender-segregated work affects both men and women. Men often are kept out of certain types of jobs. Those who enter female-dominated occupations often have to justify themselves and prove that they are "real men." They have to fight stereotypes ("Is he gay? Lazy?") about why they are interested in such work (Williams, 1993:3). Even if these assumptions do not push men out of female-dominated occupations, they affect how the men manage their gender identity at work. For example, men in occupations

TABLE 10.3 **DISTRIBUTION OF EMPLOYMENT IN CANADA, BY OCCUPATION AND GENDER, 1996**

Occupation	Percentage of Women	Percentage of Men	Women as a Percentage of Employment
Managerial/administrative	12.7	14.0	44.9
Natural sciences/engineering/ mathematics	0.8	5.8	20.2
Social sciences/religion	0.2	2.0	57.5
Teaching	6.6	3.0	64.6
Doctors/dentists	0.5	0.9	32.1
Nursing/other health related	9.1	1.2	86.1
Artistic/literary/recreational	2.3	2.4	44.4
Clerical	25.0	5.3	79.7
Sales	10.2	9.9	46.1
Service	17.5	10.9	57.1
Primary industries	2.2	6.5	21.5
Manufacturing	5.1	18.0	19.0
Construction	0.3	8.9	2.6
Transportation	0.8	6.3	9.3
Material handling/other crafts	1.7	5.1	22.0

Reprinted by permission of Statistics Canada, adapted from *The Labour Force: Annual Averages,* Statistics Canada, 1996, Cat. no. 13-217.

such as nursing emphasize their masculinity, attempt to distance themselves from female colleagues, and try to move quickly into management and supervisory positions (Williams, 1989, 1993).

Although the degree of gender segregation in parts of the professional labour market has declined since the 1970s (Sokoloff, 1992), racial-ethnic segregation has remained deeply embedded in the social structure. However, the relationship between visible minority status and occupational status is complex and varies by gender. Although visible minority males are overrepresented in both lower- and higher-status occupations, nonwhite women are heavily overrepresented in lower-paying, low-skilled jobs (Krahn and Lowe, 1993).

Workplace gender segregation is not unique to Canada. For example, in Sweden, the country with the highest rate of women's paid labour force participation in the world, gender segregation is even greater (Borchorst and Siim, 1987). Across cultures, men are less active than women in crossing the gender barrier in employment (Kauppinen-Toropainen and Lammi, 1993).

Occupational gender segregation contributes to stratification in society. Job segregation is structural; it does not occur simply because individual workers have different abilities, motivations, and material needs. As a result of gender and racial segregation, employers are able to pay many visible minority males and females less money, promote them less often, and provide fewer benefits. If they demand better working conditions or wages, workers often are reminded of the number of individuals (members of Marx's "reserve army") who would like to have their jobs.

What stereotypes are associated with men in female-oriented occupations? With women in male-oriented occupations? Do you think such stereotypes will change in the near future?

The Gender Wage Gap

Occupational segregation contributes to a second form of discrimination—the ***wage gap,* a term that refers to the disparity between women's and men's earnings.** It is calculated by dividing women's earnings by men's to yield a percentage, also known as the *earnings ratio* (Lowe, 1999). Figure 10.2 shows that there has been some improvement in this earnings ratio over the past two decades, but the progress has been slow. In 1996, women who worked full-time for the whole year still earned only 73 cents for each dollar earned by their male counterparts (Statistics Canada, 1999a). Marital status has a dramatic impact on the wage gap. In 1996, *single* women earned 93 cents for every dollar earned by single men. *Married* women, on the other hand, earned only 69 cents for every dollar earned by a married man (Statistics Canada, 1998c). The gender wage gap also exists for all levels of education. Although higher education clearly narrows the wage gap between men and women, a woman with a university degree earns approximately $13,000 less than a man with a university degree. Once again, this gap is attributable to occupation segregation. The majority of female university students enrol in degree programs in education, health professions, fine arts, and the humanities, while males continue to dominate in the fields of science and engineering. Even within occupations that require specialized educational credentials, the wage gap does not disappear—for every dollar earned by men, women earned: 66 cents as dentists, 68 cents as lawyers, and 77 cents as university professors (Statistics Canada, 1998c).

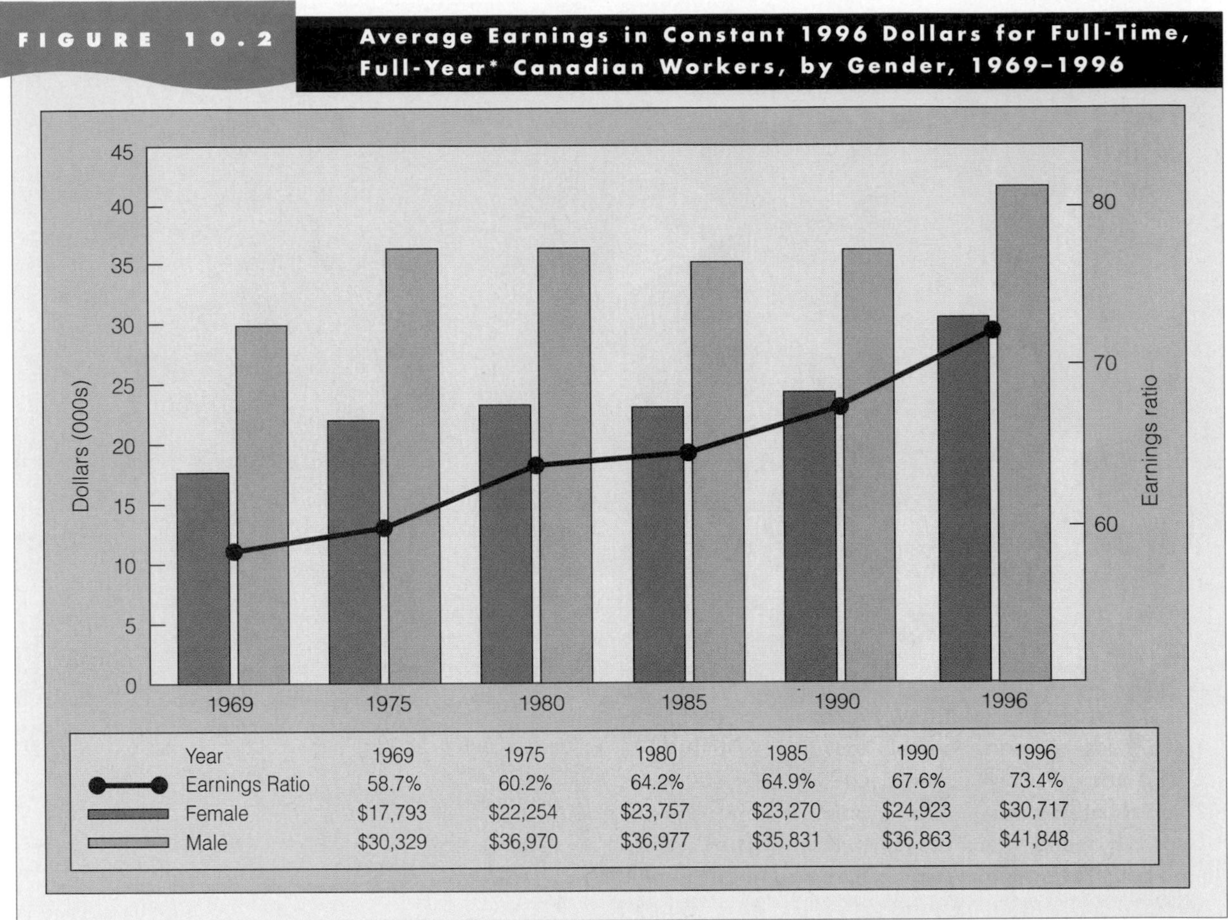

FIGURE 10.2 Average Earnings in Constant 1996 Dollars for Full-Time, Full-Year* Canadian Workers, by Gender, 1969–1996

Year	1969	1975	1980	1985	1990	1996
Earnings Ratio	58.7%	60.2%	64.2%	64.9%	67.6%	73.4%
Female	$17,793	$22,254	$23,757	$23,270	$24,923	$30,717
Male	$30,329	$36,970	$36,977	$35,831	$36,863	$41,848

*Full-time = 30 or more hours weekly; full-year = 49–52 weeks annually (50–52 weeks prior to 1981). Earnings ratio: female earnings as a percentage of male earnings.

Reprinted by permission of Statistics Canada; adapted from *Earnings of Men and Women in 1996*, Cat. no. 13-217.

Because women's overall pay relative to men's has increased by about a penny a year for the past ten years, it might seem that women's earnings have taken a noticeable move upwards. However, this decrease in the wage gap can be partially attributed to the fact that men's earnings have declined since the 1970s while women's have climbed slowly (Krahn and Lowe, 1998).

Pay Equity and Employment Equity

A number of strategies have been implemented in an attempt to achieve greater gender equality in the labour market. *Pay equity* attempts to raise the value of the work traditionally performed by women. *Employment equity* strategies focus on ways to move women into higher-paying jobs traditionally held by men (Creese and Beagan, 1999). Since the 1980s the federal government, some provincial governments, and a number of private companies have implemented pay equity and employment equity policies (Lowe, 1999).

***Pay equity* or, as it is sometimes called—comparable worth—reflects the belief that wages ought to reflect the worth of a job, not the gender or race of the worker** (Kemp, 1994). How can the comparable worth of different kinds of jobs be determined? One way is to compare the actual work of women's and men's jobs and see if there is a disparity in the salaries paid for each. To do this, analysts break a job into components—such as the education, training, and skills required, the extent of responsibility for others'

FIGURE 10.3 Mean Hours of Housework per Week by Gender and Presence of Children

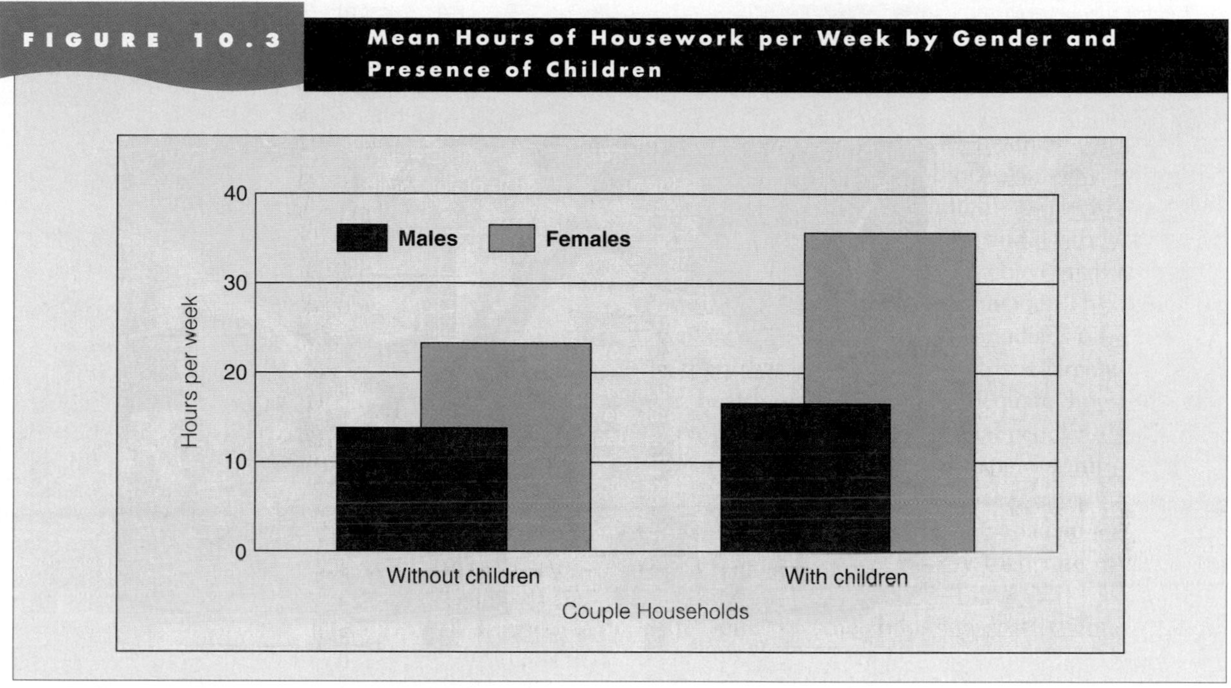

Reprinted by permission of Statistics Canada; adapted from *General Social Survey*, Cat. no. 11-612.

work, and the working conditions—and then allocate points for each (Lorber, 1994). For pay equity to exist, men and women in occupations that receive the same number of points should be paid the same. In short, pay equity promotes the principle of equal pay for work of equal value.

A second strategy for addressing inequality in the workplace is ***employment equity*—a strategy to eliminate the effects of discrimination and to fully open the competition for job opportunities to those who have been excluded historically** (Krahn and Lowe, 1998). The target groups for employment equity are visible minorities, persons with disabilities, Aboriginal peoples, and women. In comparison with pay equity, which addresses wage issues only, employment equity covers a range of employment issues such as recruitment, selection, training, development, and promotion. Employment equity also addresses issues pertaining to conditions of employment such as compensation, layoffs, and disciplinary action (Boyd, 1995). The 1986 Employment Equity Act covers only employers within the federal government, including federal Crown corporations, banks, and companies that have federal government contracts. This represents only about 11 percent of the Canadian labour force (Boyd, 1995:24). Although these policies represent a start in the right direction, male resistance and poor regulation and enforcement have resulted in minimal progress toward gendered employment equity.

Unpaid Work—The Second Shift

As previously discussed, the first big change in the relationship between family and work occurred with the Industrial Revolution and the rise of capitalism. The cult of domesticity kept many middle- and upper-class women out of the workforce during this period. Working-class and poor women primarily were the ones who had to deal with the work/family conflict. Today, however, the issue spans the entire economic spectrum (McQuillan and Belle, 1999). The typical married woman in Canada combines paid work in the labour force and family work as a homemaker.

Even with dramatic changes in women's workforce participation, the sexual division of labour in the family remains essentially unchanged. While most married women now share responsibility for the breadwinner role, many men do not accept their share of domestic responsibilities (Armstrong, 1993; Marshall, 1995; Luxton, 1995, McQuillan and Belle, 1999).

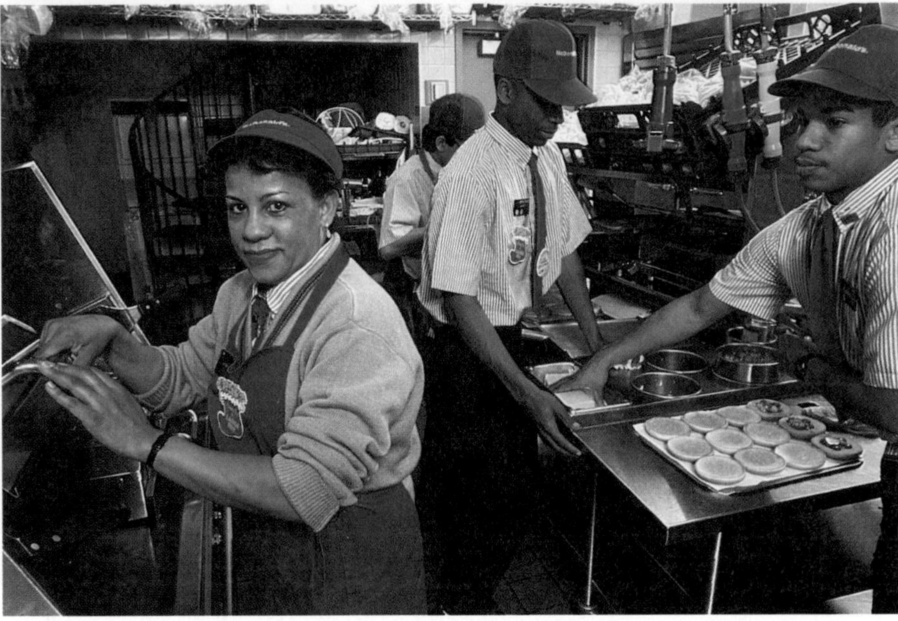
The disparity between women's and men's earnings is even greater for women of colour. Feminists who analyze ethnicity, class, and gender suggest that equality will occur only when all women are treated more equitably.

The 1996 Census was the first census to include questions on unpaid work. The results indicated that even when women work full-time in the paid workforce, most maintain primary responsibility for unpaid work, which includes child care, elder care, housework, shopping, and food preparation (Creese and Beagan, 1999). Among couples without children, the woman does about 60 percent more housework than her male partner (see Figure 10.3). This gap is even more pronounced in families with children. In these households women spend more than twice as much time as men on domestic work. Consequently, many women have a "double day" or "second shift" because of their dual responsibilities for paid and unpaid work (Hochschild, 1989). Working women have less time to spend on housework; if husbands do not participate in routine domestic chores, some chores simply do not get done or get done less often.

Many working women care not only for themselves, their husbands, and their children but also for elderly parents or in-laws. Some analysts refer to these women as "the sandwich generation"—caught between the needs of their young children and elderly relatives. Many women try to solve their time crunch by forgoing leisure time and sleep. When Arlie Hochschild interviewed working mothers, she found that they talked about sleep "the way a hungry person talks about food" (1989:9).

What can be done to address the gendered division of unpaid work? Strategies include improved government supports such as low-cost day care and better maternity and paternity leave provisions. Employers also need to create more "family friendly" programs such as on-site day care, flex-time, and family leave, as well as decreasing demands for overtime. Finally, although men are involved in a greater share of the unpaid work in the home than ever before, the division of labour is still far from equal.

PERSPECTIVES ON GENDER STRATIFICATION

Sociological perspectives on gender stratification vary in their approach to examining gender roles and power relationships in society. Some focus on the roles of women and men in the domestic sphere; others note the inequalities arising from a gendered division of labour in the workplace. Still others attempt to integrate both the public and private spheres into their analyses.

Functionalist Perspectives

As seen earlier, functionalist theory views men and women as having distinct roles that are important for the survival of the family and society. The most basic division of labour is biological: men are physically stronger while women are the only ones able to bear and nurse children. Gendered belief systems foster assumptions about appropriate behaviour for men and women and may have an impact on the types of work women and men perform.

THE IMPORTANCE OF TRADITIONAL GENDER ROLES According to functional analysts such as Talcott Parsons (1955), women's roles as nurturers and caregivers are even more pronounced in contemporary industrialized societies. While the husband performs the *instrumental* tasks of providing economic support and making decisions, the wife assumes the *expressive* tasks of providing affection and emotional support for the family. This division of family labour ensures that important societal tasks will be fulfilled; it also provides stability for family members.

This view has been adopted by a number of conservative analysts. George F. Gilder (1986) argues that traditional gender roles are important not only for individuals but also for the economic and social order of society. He asserts that relationships between men and women are damaged when changes in gender roles occur, and family life suffers as a consequence. According to Gilder, women provide for the socialization of the next generation; if they do not, society's moral fabric will decay, resulting in higher rates of crime, violence, and drug abuse. From this perspective, the traditional division of labour between men and women is the natural order of the universe (Kemp, 1994).

EVALUATION OF FUNCTIONALIST PERSPECTIVES Although Parsons and other functionalists did not specifically endorse the gendered division of labour, their analysis views it as natural and perhaps inevitable. However, critics argue that problems inherent in traditional gender roles, including the personal role strains of men and women and the social costs to society, are minimized by this approach. For example, men are assumed to be "money machines" for their families when they might prefer to spend more time in child-rearing activities. Also, the woman's place is assumed to be in the home, an assumption that ignores the fact that many women hold jobs due to economic necessity.

In addition, the functionalist approach does not take a critical look at the structure of society (especially the economic inequalities) that make educational and occupational opportunities more available to some than to others. Furthermore, it fails to examine the underlying power relations between men and women or to consider the fact that the tasks assigned to women and to men are unequally valued by society (Kemp, 1994).

Conflict Perspectives

According to many conflict analysts, the gendered division of labour within families and in the workplace results from male control of and dominance over women and resources. Differentials between men and women may exist in terms of economic, political, physical, and/or interpersonal power. The importance of a male monopoly in any of these arenas depends on the significance of that type of power in a society (Richardson, 1993). In hunting and gathering and horticultural societies, male dominance over women is limited because all members of the society must work in order to survive (Collins, 1971; Nielsen, 1990). In agrarian societies, however, male sexual dominance is at its peak. Male heads of household gain a monopoly not only on physical power but also on economic power, and women become sexual property.

Although men's ability to use physical power to control women diminishes in industrial societies, men still remain the heads of household and control the property. In addition, men gain more power through their predominance in the most highly paid and prestigious occupations and the highest elected offices. In contrast, women have the ability to trade their sexual resources, companionship, and emotional support in the marriage market for men's financial support and social status; as a result, however, women as a group remain subordinate to men (Collins, 1971; Nielsen, 1990).

All men are not equally privileged; some analysts argue that women and men in the upper classes are more privileged, because of their economic power, than men in lower-class positions and members of some minority groups (Lorber, 1994). In industrialized societies, persons who occupy elite positions in corporations, universities, the mass media, and government or who have great wealth have the most power (Richardson, 1993). Most of these are men, however.

Conflict theorists in the Marxist tradition assert that gender stratification results from private ownership of the means of production; some men not only gain control over property and the distribution of goods but also gain power over women. According to Friedrich Engels and Karl Marx, marriage serves to enforce male dominance. Men of the capitalist class instituted monogamous marriage (a gendered institution) so that they could be certain of the paternity of their offspring, especially sons, whom they wanted to inherit their wealth. Feminist analysts have examined this theory, among others, as they have sought to explain male domination and gender stratification.

Feminist Perspectives

***Feminism*—the belief that women and men are equal and that they should be valued equally and have equal rights**—is embraced by many men as well as women. Gender is viewed as a socially constructed concept that has important consequences in the lives of all people (Craig, 1992). According to sociologist Ben Agger (1993), men can be feminists and propose feminist theories; both women and men have much in common as they seek to gain a better understanding of the causes and consequences of gender inequality.

Feminist perspectives vary in their analyses of the ways in which norms, roles, institutions, and internalized expectations limit women's behaviour. Taken together, they all seek to demonstrate how women's personal control operates even within the constraints of a relative lack of power (Stewart, 1994). We will now look at the main types of feminist theory and examine the focus of each.

LIBERAL FEMINISM In liberal feminism, gender equality is equated with equality of opportunity. The roots of women's oppression lie in women's lack of equal civil rights and educational opportunities. Only when these constraints on women's participation are removed will women have the same chance of success as men. This approach notes the importance of gender-role socialization and suggests that changes need to be made in what children learn from their families, teachers, and the media about appropriate masculine and feminine attitudes and behaviour. Liberal feminists fight for better child-care options, a woman's right to choose an abortion, and the elimination of sex discrimination in the workplace.

RADICAL FEMINISM According to radical feminists, male domination causes all forms of human oppression, including racism and classism (Tong, 1989). Radical feminists often trace the roots of patriarchy to women's childbearing and child-rearing responsibilities, which make them dependent on men (Firestone, 1970; Chafetz, 1984). In the radical feminist view, men's oppression of women is deliberate, and ideological justification for this subordination is provided by other institutions such as the media and religion. For women's condition to improve, radical feminists claim, patriarchy must be abolished. If institutions currently are gendered, alternative institutions—such as women's organizations seeking better health and day care and shelters for victims of domestic violence and sexual assault—should be developed to meet women's needs.

SOCIAL FEMINISM Socialist feminists suggest that women's oppression results from their dual roles as paid *and* unpaid workers in a capitalist economy. In the workplace, women are exploited by capitalism; at home, they are exploited by patriarchy (Kemp, 1994). Women are easily exploited in both sectors; they are paid low wages and have few economic resources. Gendered job segregation is "the primary mechanism in capitalist society that maintains the superiority of men over women, because it enforces lower wages for women in the labour market" (Hartmann, 1976:139). As a result, women must do domestic labour either to gain a better-paid man's economic support or to stretch their own wages (Lorber, 1994). According to socialist feminists, the only way to achieve gender equality is to eliminate capitalism and develop a socialist economy that would bring equal pay and rights to women.

FEMINIST PERSPECTIVES ON EATING PROBLEMS As noted earlier, feminist analysts suggest that eating problems are not just individual "disorders" but relate to the issue of subordination (see Orbach, 1978; Fallon, Katzman, and Wooley, 1994). This analysis focuses on the relationship between eating problems and patriarchy (male dominance) in the labour force and family. Eating problems cannot be viewed solely as psychological "disorders" but rather are symbolic of women's personal and cultural oppression. Anorexia and bulimia reflect women's (and sometimes men's) denial of other problems, disconnection from other people, and disempowerment in society (Peters and Fallon, 1994:353).

Feminist perspectives focus on the prevention of eating problems and a re-evaluation of existing therapies. However, feminist authors Naomi Wolf (1990) and Susan Faludi (1991) have suggested that the current social order may have a vested interest in promoting, rather than preventing, eating problems among women. Wolf (1994) argues that emphasis on thinness is a response to the threat posed by women's efforts to gain courage, self-esteem, and a sense of effectiveness. By contrast, dieting leads to passivity, anxiety, and low self-esteem—traits valued in women by the dominant culture.

Feminists argue that, to prevent eating problems—as well as other mental and physical problems of women—societal changes are needed. These changes relate to work (such as equal pay, and the elimination of sexual harassment and discrimination) and the family (child-care programs and deterrence of sexual violence, for example) (Wolf, 1990; Shisslak and Crago, 1994).

Evaluation of Conflict and Feminist Perspectives Conflict and feminist perspectives provide insights into the structural aspects of gender inequality in society. While functionalist approaches focus on the characteristics of individuals, the conflict and feminist approaches emphasize factors external to individuals that contribute to the oppression of women. These approaches also examine the ways in which the workplace and the home are gendered.

Conflict theory has been criticized for emphasizing the differences between men and women without taking into account their commonalities. Feminist approaches have been criticized for their emphasis on male dominance without a corresponding analysis of the ways in which some men also may be oppressed by patriarchy and capitalism. Some theorists in men's studies have attempted to overcome this deficit by exploring how gender domination includes "men's subordination and denigration of other men as well as men's exploitation of women" (Brod, 1987; Kimmel and Messner, 1992; Lorber, 1994:4).

GENDER ISSUES IN THE FUTURE

In the past thirty years, women have made significant progress in the labour force (Creese and Beagan, 1999). Laws have been passed to prohibit sexual discrimination in the workplace and school. Affirmative action programs have made women more visible in education, government, and the professional world. More women are entering the political arena as candidates instead of as volunteers who "answer the telephone and lick stamps" in the campaign offices of male candidates (Lott, 1994:341).

Many men have joined movements to raise their consciousness not only about men's concerns but also about the need to eliminate sexism and gender bias. Many men realize that what is harmful to women also may be harmful to men. For example, women's lower wages in the labour force suppress men's wages as well.

In the midst of these changes, many gender issues remain unresolved. In the labour force, gender segregation may increase if the number of female-dominated jobs—such as information clerk, nurse's aide, and fast-food restaurant worker—continues to grow. If men lose jobs in the blue-collar sector as factories relocate to other countries or close entirely, they may seek jobs that primarily have been held by women. Although this situation might lead to less gender segregation, the loss of desirable jobs ultimately is not in anyone's interest (Reskin and Padavic, 1994:172). As men see the number and quality of "men's jobs" shrink, they also may become more resistant to women's entry into what have customarily been male jobs (Reskin and Padavic, 1994:172).

The pay gap between men and women should continue to shrink, but this may be due in part to decreasing wages paid to men (Armstrong and Armstrong, 1994). Employers and governments will continue to implement family-leave policies, but these will not relieve women's domestic burden in the family. The burden of the "double day" or "second shift" has led many women to work part-time in an attempt to reconcile family–work contradictions. This choice increases or maintains occupational segregation, low pay with minimal or no benefits, and marginalized treatment (Gee, 1995). The burden of the "second shift" will likely preserve women's inequality at home and in the workplace for another generation.

CHAPTER REVIEW

How do sex and gender differ?
Sex refers to the biological categories and manifestations of femaleness and maleness; gender refers to the socially constructed differences between females and males. In short, sex is what we (generally) are born with; gender is what we acquire through socialization.

What are gender roles and gender identity?
Gender role encompasses the attitudes, behaviours, and activities that are socially assigned to each sex and that are learned through socialization. Gender identity is an individual's perception of his or her self as either female or male.

How does the nature of work affect gender equity in different societies?
In most hunting and gathering societies, fairly equitable relationships exist because neither sex has the ability to provide all of the food necessary for survival. In horticultural societies, a fair degree of gender equality exists because neither sex controls the food supply. In agrarian societies, male dominance is very apparent; agrarian tasks require more labour and physical strength, and women often are excluded from these tasks because they are viewed as too weak or too tied to child-rearing activities. In industrialized societies, a gap exists between nonpaid work performed by women at home and paid work performed by men and women. A wage gap also exists between women and men in the marketplace.

What are the key agents of gender socialization?
The key agents of gender socialization are parents, peers, teachers and schools, sports, and the media, all of which tend to reinforce stereotypes of appropriate gender behaviour.

What causes gender inequality in Canada?
Gender inequality results from economic, political, and educational discrimination against women. In most workplaces, jobs are either gender segregated or the majority of employees are of the same gender.

How is occupational segregation related to the pay gap?
Many women work in lower-paying, less prestigious jobs than men. This occupational segregation leads to a disparity, or pay gap, between women's and men's earnings. Even when women are employed in the same job as men, on average they do not receive the same, or comparable, pay.

How do functionalist and conflict theorists differ in their views of the gendered division of labour?
According to functional analysts, women's roles as caregivers in contemporary industrialized societies are crucial in ensuring that key societal tasks are fulfilled. While the husband performs the instrumental tasks of economic support and decision making, the wife assumes the expressive tasks of providing affection and emotional support to the family. According to conflict analysts, the gendered division of labour within families and the workplace—particularly in agrarian and industrial societies—is caused by male control and dominance over women and resources.

How do the various feminist perspectives explain gender inequality?
Although feminist perspectives vary in their analyses of women's subordination, they all advocate social change to eradicate gender inequality. In liberal feminism, gender equality is connected to equality of opportunity. In radical feminism, male dominance is seen as the cause of oppression. According to socialist feminists, women's oppression is the result of their dual roles as paid and unpaid workers.

KEY TERMS

Internet Exercises

1. Visit the newsgroup **soc.feminism.** What are some of the issues that concern feminists today? What issues seem to be Internet specific? What portion of the people posting to this site are men? How, if at all, do you think the ratio between male and female posters to this group affects the debate? Should men be allowed to post to this newsgroup at all?
2. A famous cartoon shows two dogs sitting at computer keyboards and typing away on the Internet. The caption underneath reads "On the Internet no one knows if you are a dog." It is said that the same rules apply to gender. From Lycos (**www.lycos.com**), do a search on the term *chat room*. Visit a chat room and observe the conversation. Are there differences between the way men and women speak? How easy would it be for you to pass yourself off as a member of the opposite sex? Would you ever consider doing this? Why or why not? Based on your observation of the chat rooms, is there a difference between what can and what does happen in terms of gender-bending activity?
3. Visit the National Organization for Women (NOW) home page (**www.now.org**). Based on your reading there, how closely does the philosophy of this feminist organization fit one of the feminist theory models outlined in this chapter? Visit one of the Canadian feminist organizations listed on the Feminism and Women's Resources page (**www.ibd.nrc.ca/~mansfield/feminism**). How does the philosophy of this organization compare with that of NOW? What model of feminist theory would this organization fit?

Net Links

For more Web links related to the topic of this chapter, see the Nelson sociology Web site: **www.sociologyessentials-2nded.nelson.com**.

Status of Women Canada (SWC) is a federal government agency that promotes gender equality and full participation of women in the economic, social, cultural, and political life of the country. SWC focuses on three areas: improving women's economic autonomy and well-being, eliminating violence against women and children, and advancing women's human rights; to see its Web site, go to:

www.swc-cfc.gc.ca/direct.html

WIN Magazine is an online magazine about women all over the world; to see it, go to:

www.winmagazine.org

Canadian Women's Internet Association (CWIA) contains hundreds of links to sites relevant to women, with a special focus on Canadian content. Its Web address is:

http://herplace.org

What role does gender play in computer culture? Diane Currie of the University of British Columbia addresses this question in "The Construction of Gender at UBC Computing Services"; to see it, go to:

http://www.herplace.org/compgend.html 

Questions for Critical Thinking

1. Do the media reflect societal attitudes on gender, or do the media determine and teach gender behaviour? (As a related activity, watch television for several hours and list the roles women and men play in the shows watched and in the advertisements.)
2. Review the concept of cultural relativism discussed in Chapter 2. To what degree should the Canadian government and human rights groups such as Amnesty International protest genital mutilation in those countries in which it is practised?
3. Examine the various academic departments at your university. What is the gender breakdown of the faculty in selected departments? What is the gender breakdown of undergraduates and graduates in those departments? Are there major differences among the social sciences, sciences, and humanities departments? How can you explain your observations?

Suggested Readings

These well-written books provide in-depth information on various issues raised in this chapter:

Sandra L. Bem. *The Lenses of Gender: Transforming the Debate on Sexual Inequality*. New Haven, Conn.: Yale University Press, 1993.

Michael S. Kimmel and Michael A. Messner (eds.). *Men's Lives*. New York: Macmillan, 1992.

Claire M. Renzetti and Daniel J. Curran. *Women, Men, and Society*. Boston: Allyn & Bacon, 1995.

Women's and men's work is examined in this interesting book:

Pat Armstrong and Hugh Armstrong. *The Double Ghetto: Canadian Women and Their Segregated Work*. Toronto: McClelland & Stewart, 1994.

The unequal treatment of females in schools and universities is explored in these books:

Jane Gaskell and Arlene McLaren. *Women and Education*. Calgary: Detselig, 1992.

Bernice Lott. *Women's Lives: Themes and Variations in Gender Learning* (2nd ed.). Pacific Grove, Cal.: Brooks/Cole, 1994.

Stephen Richer and Lorna Weir. *Beyond Political Correctness: Toward the Inclusive University*. Toronto: University of Toronto Press, 1995.

Bestsellers dealing with feminism, appearance norms, and communication between women and men include these books:

Deborah Tannen. *You Just Don't Understand: Women and Men in Conversation*. New York: Morrow, 1990.

———. *Talking From 9 to 5*. New York: Morrow, 1994.

Naomi Wolf. *The Beauty Myth: How Images of Beauty Are Used Against Women*. New York: Morrow, 1990.

For additional information on the bodybuilding subculture:

Alan M. Klein. *Little Big Men: Bodybuilding Subculture and Gender Construction*. Albany: State University of New York Press, 1993.

Leslea Newman (ed.). *Eating Our Hearts Out: Personal Accounts of Women's Relationship to Food*. Freedom, Cal.: The Crossing Press, 1993.

INFOTRAC® COLLEGE EDITION

Either from the *Sociology In Our Times: The Essentials* Web site (**www.sociologyessentials-2nded.nelson.com**) or directly from your Web browser, you may access InfoTrac® College Edition, an online university library that includes over 600 popular and scholarly journals in which you can find articles related to the topics in this chapter.

CHAPTER 11

Rae Lewis-Thornton describes her experience with HIV/AIDS in the following way:

"The day I found out [I was HIV-positive] I was so calm ... I walked out of the ... Red Cross office and into the ... sunshine, flagged a cab and went back to work. I worked late that night ... I was 24. I'd just been given a death sentence ... I am the quintessential Buppie. I'm young ... Well educated. Professional. Attractive. Smart. I've been drug and alcohol-free all my life. I'm a Christian. I've never been promiscuous. Never had a one-night stand. And I am dying of AIDS.

"I've been living with the disease for nine years, and people still tell me that I am too pretty and intelligent to have AIDS. But I do. I discovered I was HIV-positive when I tried to give blood at the office. I have no idea who infected me or when it happened. Still, there is one thing I am absolutely certain of; I am dying now because I had one sexual partner too many. And I'm here to tell you one is all it takes." (Lewis-Thornton, 1994:63)

As we enter the twenty-first century, AIDS is among the most significant global/human problems we face, taking its toll on individuals, families, cities, and nations. The disease known as AIDS (acquired immunodeficiency syndrome) is caused by HIV, the human immunodeficiency virus, which gradually destroys the immune system by attacking the white blood cells, making the person with HIV more vulnerable to other types of illnesses. While we do not know the actual number of people infected with HIV—some countries do not have adequate diagnostic equipment or centralized reporting systems—the United Nations estimated in 2000 that over 33 million people were infected with HIV and that 2.6 million people died of AIDS in 1999. Some countries are being devastated by HIV/AIDS; in Botswana and Zimbabwe more than 25 percent of the adult population is infected. In Canada an estimated 44,000 people had HIV in 1994 and more than 10,000 had died of AIDS by 1997 (Archibald, 1997). Map 11.1 outlines the global distribution of the HIV virus. The number of victims is growing by about 10 percent each year.

AIDS is also a significant global/human problem because it may be a major species-threatening phenomenon with a potentially devastating impact on the world's population (Robertson, 1992:133). This threat is particularly significant in sub-Saharan Africa. In 1998 the

HEALTH, HEALTH CARE, AND DISABILITY

region experienced 5500 deaths from AIDS each day, and there were four million new cases of the disease (UNAIDS, 1998). Half of all new infections are among 15- to 24-year-olds and many newborns are being infected by their mothers, which means that the disease will destroy much of Africa's hope for the future. The average life expectancy in many countries has dropped by as much as 17 years, and the cost of providing even minimal treatment for the disease is taking away many of the hard-won economic gains some countries have achieved in the past decade.

The problem of AIDS illustrates how sociology can apply to what, at first glance, appears to be a purely medical phenomenon. As sociologist Karen Grant explains, AIDS is a social phenomenon as much as a disease: "AIDS demonstrates that disease not only affects health, but one's definition of self, relations with others, and behaviours. As well, AIDS has had a significant impact on social institutions. The health-care system has been most directly affected, requiring assessments of the adequacy of research, treatment modalities, and health care facilities. Legal scholars and legislators have wrestled with issues of privacy and human rights protections for people with AIDS. AIDS has resulted in social and sexual mores and lifestyles being reassessed. AIDS has challenged stereotypes and forced some people to reconsider their prejudices" (Grant, 1993:395).

In this chapter, we will explore the dynamics of health and health care. In the process, we will periodically focus on HIV/AIDS and on both its present and potential impact on society. While we will use HIV/AIDS as an example throughout this chapter, you should be aware that globally several other causes of death are more common. In 1997, there were 52 million deaths around the world. About 2.5 million of them were due to HIV/AIDS compared with 17.3 million due to infectious and parasitic diseases; 15.3 million were caused by circulatory diseases; 6.2 million were due to cancer; 2.9 million resulted from respiratory diseases; and 3.6 million were due to perinatal conditions (World Health Organization, 1998). Before reading on, test your knowledge about HIV/AIDS by taking the quiz in Box 11.1.

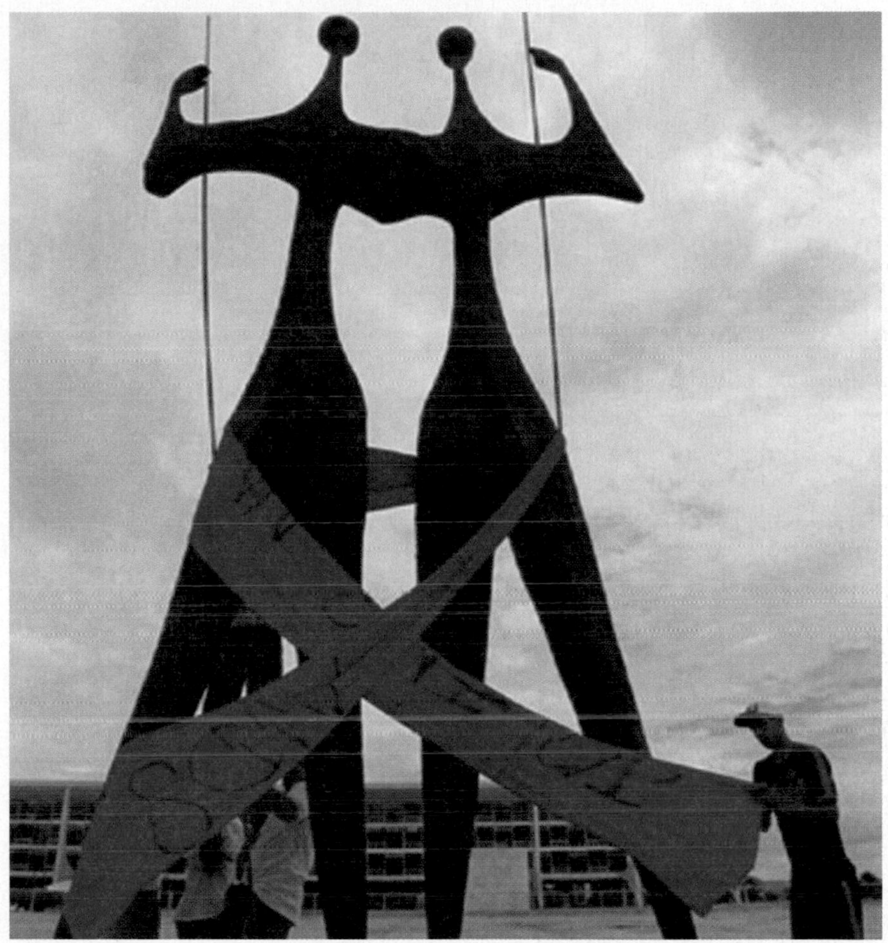

QUESTIONS AND ISSUES

CHAPTER FOCUS QUESTION: What effect has HIV/AIDS had on the health of the global population?

Why is HIV/AIDS referred to as a global/human problem?

In what ways do sociological factors influence health and disease?

How do functionalist, symbolic interactionist, and conflict models differ in their analyses of health?

How does social inequality affect health and health care?

What are some of the consequences of disability?

What is the state of the health-care system in Canada today and how could it be improved?

MAP 11.1 Numbers of HIV-Positive People Around the World, 2000

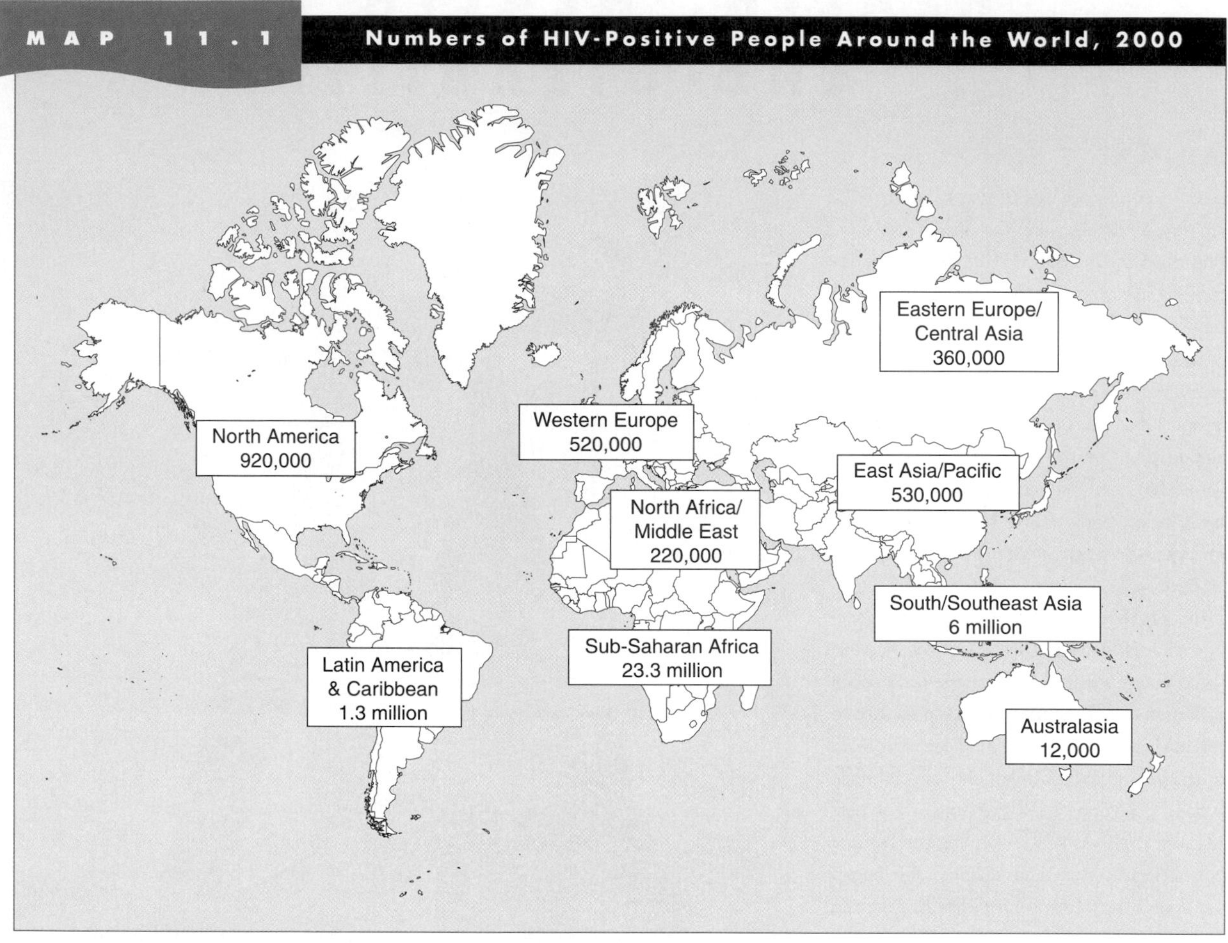

Source: UNAIDS, 2000. Available online at: **www.unaids.org/index.html.** Reprinted by permission.

HEALTH AND MEDICINE

What does the concept of health mean to you? If you were asked whether you are healthy, how would you respond? Although the definition of health may appear to be obvious, consensus on its definition remains elusive. Health was once considered simply the absence of disease. The World Health Organization provides a more inclusive definition of ***health*, calling it a state of complete physical, mental, and social well-being.** Health, as the WHO's definition makes clear, has several dimensions; physical, social, and psychological factors are all important. It does not, therefore, depend solely on the absence of disease or sickness. Health is also socially defined and therefore varies over time and between cultures (Farley, 1992). For example, in our society obesity is viewed as unhealthy, while in other times and places it signalled prosperity and good health.

***Medicine* is an institutionalized system for the scientific diagnosis, treatment, and prevention of illness.** Medicine forms a vital part of the broader concept of ***health care*, which is any activity intended to improve health.** In North American culture, medicine typically is used when there is a failure in health. When people become sick, they seek medical attention to make them healthy again. As the definition of medicine suggests, medicine and health can go hand in hand. Medicine and the larger category of health care have undergone many changes over time. Most recently the field of ***preventive medicine*—medicine that emphasizes a healthy lifestyle in order to prevent poor health before it occurs,** is receiving increasing attention (Appelbaum and Chambliss, 1997).

BOX 11.1 SOCIOLOGY AND EVERYDAY LIFE

How Much Do You Know about HIV/AIDS?

TRUE	FALSE	
T	F	1. Worldwide, most people with AIDS are gay men.
T	F	2. In Canada, it is against the law to knowingly transmit the HIV virus.
T	F	3. HIV, the virus that transmits AIDS, is spreading rapidly among women in some nations.
T	F	4. Nearly 50 percent of people who are HIV-positive worldwide are under the age of 25.
T	F	5. Infants who are born HIV-positive do not live past infancy or early childhood.
T	F	6. People can get AIDS from sharing toilets, toothbrushes, eating utensils, or razors.
T	F	7. People infected with HIV may not show any physical symptoms for ten years or longer and can infect others without realizing it.
T	F	8. Many people with AIDS die of the disease.
T	F	9. In Canada, the majority of new HIV cases occur among homosexual men.
T	F	10. One of the major concerns of AIDS activists is reducing the stigmatization of HIV/AIDS victims.

Answers on page 312.

SOCIOLOGICAL PERSPECTIVES ON HEALTH

Functionalist Perspective on Health: The Sick Role

Functionalists view society as a complex, stable system. Therefore, the normal state of affairs is for people to be healthy and to contribute to their society. Sociologist Talcott Parsons viewed illness as dysfunctional both for the individual who is sick and for the larger society (Parsons, 1951). Sick people may be unable to fulfil their necessary social roles, such as parenting, maintaining a home, or working in the paid labour force. Thus, illness can cause the social system to malfunction. Societies must, therefore, establish boundaries that define who is legitimately sick. Furthermore, those who are sick are expected to get well so they can contribute to the healthy functioning of the social system. According to Parsons, all societies have a ***sick role*—patterns of behaviour defined as appropriate for people who are sick.** He developed a model to describe the characteristics of the sick role:

1. The sick person is exempt from normal social responsibilities. For example, when you are sick you are not expected to go to work or school.
2. The sick person is exempt from responsibility for his or her condition. In other words, the sickness must be the result of an accident or other circumstances beyond the individual's control. Individuals should not be blamed or punished because sickness is not their fault.
3. The sick person must want to get well. The sick role is considered to be a temporary one and the person who does not do everything in his or her power to return to a healthy state is no longer a legitimately sick person and may be considered a hypochondriac, a careless person, or a malingerer.
4. The sick person should seek technically competent help and cooperate with health-care practitioners. An individual who fails to do so gives up any claim to the rights of the sick role.

Critics of Parsons's model, and more generally of the functionalist view of health and illness, argue that it places too much responsibility for illness on the sick people themselves, neglecting the fact that often the actions of other people may be the cause of someone's illness. For example, a child born with fetal alcohol syndrome has this condition because his or her mother consumed alcohol during pregnancy.

BOX 11.1

Answers to the Sociology Quiz on HIV/AIDS

1. **False.** Although AIDS has taken a devastating toll on the gay population in North America, the World Health Organization estimates that about 75 percent of the people with AIDS worldwide were infected through heterosexual intercourse.
2. **False.** No specific law forbids this behaviour. However, in 1995 a Newfoundland man who knowingly infected 19 women was sentenced to 11 years and 3 months in jail after pleading guilty to a charge of criminal negligence causing bodily harm. Also, in 1998 the Supreme Court of Canada ruled that a person could be charged with assault if they did not tell their sexual partners they had HIV/AIDS or other sexually transmitted diseases.
3. **True.** HIV has been spreading rapidly among women. UNAIDS estimated that in 1996, 42 percent of those infected with HIV were women. In Canada women accounted for 19 percent of all diagnosed cases of HIV/AIDS in 1996.
4. **True.** AIDS is found disproportionately among young people, a consequence of the fact that they are more likely either to engage in sexually promiscuous behaviour and/or to be intravenous drug users.
5. **False.** Some children who were born HIV-positive are now reaching their teens. Some of these children have shown no symptoms of AIDS-related illnesses; others have experienced continual medical problems.
6. **False.** AIDS is caused by HIV (human immunodeficiency virus), which is transmitted to men or women through unprotected (vaginal, anal, or oral) sexual intercourse with an infected partner (either male or female), through sharing a contaminated hypodermic needle with someone who is infected, through exposure to contaminated blood or blood products (usually from a transfusion), and through the passing on of the virus by an infected woman to her child during pregnancy, childbirth, or breast-feeding.
7. **True.** Without an HIV antibody test (which indicates whether a person's body has begun making antibodies in response to the virus), it may be impossible for an individual to tell whether he or she has been infected with HIV. And, for those who have taken this test, it can take from three to six months from the time a person is infected for the virus to show up on the test.
8. **False.** People do not actually die of AIDS; they die because HIV makes their bodies so weak they cannot fight off diseases such as pneumonia, tuberculosis, yeast infections, and Kaposi's sarcoma and other forms of cancer. Technically, AIDS is a syndrome, not a disease.
9. **False.** In 1996, 49 percent of victims were injection drug users and 37 percent were men who had sex with men.
10. **True.** Many AIDS victims have suffered hostility and discrimination as a result of their illness. Educational programs and political lobbying by AIDS activists have tried to reduce this stigmatization.

Sources: Based on Weeks, 1992; Gross, 1993; *JAMA*, 1994; Land, 1994; Singer and Deschamps, 1994; Waldram et al., 1995; and Albert and Williams, 1998.

Individuals living in poverty may become sick because of inadequate food and shelter (see Chapter 7, "Social Stratification and Class").

Also, contrary to the functionalist view, individuals may be blamed for their illness, as people who contract HIV or lung cancer often are.

Symbolic Interactionist Theory: The Social Construction of Illness

Symbolic interactionists attempt to understand the specific meanings and causes that we attribute to particular events. In studying health, interactionists focus on the fact that the meaning that social actors give their illness or disease will affect their self-concept and their relationships with others. The interactionist approach is illustrated by society's response to AIDS.

We often try to explain disease by blaming it on those who are ill. This reduces the uncertainty of those of us who fear the disease; nonsmokers who learn that a cancer victim had a two-pack-a-day habit feel comforted that the guilty have been punished and that the same fate is unlikely to befall them. Because of the association of their disease with promiscuous homosexuality and intravenous drug use, victims of AIDS have particularly suffered from blame. How is a person's self-concept affected when he or she is diagnosed with AIDS? How does this diagnosis affect the relationships the person has with others in his or her social world?

In the case of AIDS, the social definition of the illness has had as profound an impact on the AIDS patient as the medical symptoms. According to Giddens (1996:123), AIDS is an example of illness as stigma. As indicated in Chapter 4, a stigma is any physical or social attribute or sign that so devalues a person's social identity that it disqualifies that person from social acceptance. Unlike other illnesses—the ones that provoke sympathy or compassion—an illness that is seen primarily as infectious is perceived as dishonourable or shameful. The result is that sufferers are rejected by the healthy population. Children with AIDS have been driven from their schools; homes of people with AIDS have been burned by those afraid of getting the disease; employees have been fired; and medical professionals have refused treatment to AIDS patients. All of this has happened despite the fact that AIDS cannot be transmitted by casual, everyday contact. However, as the case of AIDS clearly demonstrates, the social definition of an illness may have no basis in medical fact. The incidents of hostility and discrimination directed at individuals with AIDS nevertheless have a profound impact on their self-concept, social relationships, and ability to cope with the illness. The role of the media in shaping the way in which society defines an illness is shown in Box 11.2.

The Social Definition of Health and Illness: The Process of Medicalization Because of their biological characteristics, most of us would agree that conditions such as heart disease, tuberculosis, and cancer are illnesses. You have seen in our discussion of the social construction of illness so far that even in these cases there is also a subjective component to the way illness is defined. This subjective component is very important when we look at conditions that are more ambiguous than cancer or a broken bone. For example: a child who has difficulty learning may be diagnosed as having attention deficit disorder (ADD); a man who occasionally behaves strangely may be called mentally ill; and a woman going through menopause may be defined as having a hormonal deficiency disease. Alternatively, we could view these conditions as part of the range of normal human behaviour. The child might be seen as a poor student, the man as a bit odd, and the woman as a person going through the normal aging process. The way we view these individuals will depend on our cultural perspectives, which can change over time.

The term ***medicalization*** **refers to the process whereby an object or a condition becomes defined and treated by society as a physical or psychological illness.** This process usually entails the application of medical technology in the diagnosis and treatment of the condition (Grant, 1993). Conrad and Schneider (1992) found that medicalization is typically the result of a lengthy promotional campaign conducted by interest groups, often culminating in legislative or other official changes that institutionalize a medical treatment for the new "disease." The interest groups may include scientists acting on the results of their research; those who have the disease, and who may be seeking either a cure or a socially acceptable excuse for their behaviour; and members of the medical industry interested in increasing their profits.

Women's health issues such as those to do with childbirth, menopause, PMS, and contraception have been particularly susceptible to medicalization (Reissman, 1983; Findlay and Miller, 1994), and this process has not necessarily served the interests of women. A 1989 paper by the American Society for Plastic and Reconstructive Surgery provides an extreme example of the subjective nature of disease. This society, the major professional organization representing plastic surgeons, wanted the U.S. government to loosen its restrictions on the use of breast implants. The society based its case on the view that having small breasts constituted a disease. They alleged that this disease resulted in "feelings of

BOX 11.2 SOCIOLOGY AND MEDIA

AIDS IN THE NEWS

At the age of 13, Ryan White learned that he had contracted HIV through blood products used to treat his hemophilia. When school officials told White he could not return to school because of HIV, he fought back and eventually was readmitted. However, White also temporarily became a celebrity.

> We had been in the news so much that reporters were practically part of the family. They came from all over the place, even Japan. I felt like I was growing up with some of them. They followed us into the bathroom to see if we were telling the truth when we said we shared toothpaste and glasses. They stood by the kitchen sink and asked Mom if she was doing dishes by hand so she could use bleach on mine ...
>
> We talked to some reporters more often than we visited with our friends and relatives. (quoted in White and Cunningham, 1992:120–121)

Why did journalists pay so much attention to Ryan White and his plight? Journalists have the ability to transform events—such as White's illness and battle with the school—into news. However, HIV poses unique problems for journalists. Gay men (a stigmatized category) were among the first to be identified with the problem. To report on HIV transmitted by gay men, journalists must refer to blood, semen, sex, and death, all of which are viewed by some media elites as being beyond good taste. Because of these problems, some journalists divided persons with HIV into two categories:

inadequacy, lack of self-confidence, distortion of body image, and a total lack of well-being due to a lack of self-perceived femininity" (cited in Weitz, 1996:123). Of course, the disease could be cured if the victims received expensive, often dangerous breast implants from the plastic surgeons. In Chapter 10, "Sex and Gender," you read about the problem of sexism in our society and about the low self-esteem felt by women that is often the result. Having done so, it will not be difficult to imagine the harm that the plastic surgeons' lobbying effort encouraging women to think of their biologically normal bodies as "diseased" might have on women's self-image.

Just as conditions can be medicalized, so can they be *demedicalized.* For many years, homosexuality was defined as a mental illness, and gays and lesbians were urged to seek psychiatric treatment. Sociologists Peter Conrad and Joseph Schneider (1992) have described the successful fight by gay activists to convince the American Psychiatric Association to remove homosexuality from the association's psychiatric diagnostic manual. At the same time women's groups are trying to demedicalize childbirth and menopause, and redefine them as natural processes rather than as illnesses.

Conflict Theory: Inequalities in Health and Health Care

The conflict approach to health and illness emphasizes the political, economic, and social forces that affect health and the health-care system and the inequities that result from these forces. Among the issues of concern for conflict theorists are the ability of all citizens to obtain health care; the impact of race, class, and gender on health and health care; the relative power of doctors compared with other health workers; the dominance of the medical model of health care; and the role of profit in the health-care system.

BOX 11.2

CONTINUED

"innocent victims" such as Ryan White who acquire the virus through blood transfusions or other means considered beyond their control, and "sources" of the problem, including gay and bisexual men, intravenous drug users, and prostitutes. According to HIV-positive television producer Mary Fisher,

> this way of thinking suggests that we withhold compassion from those whose behaviours may have caused or contributed to their deaths. On these grounds we would never mourn the passing of a heart attack victim who did not exercise, worked under stress, or ate foods high in cholesterol. Persons with lung cancer owing to smoking should be disdained; persons with back injuries from lifting should be despised; the person who sees the ice but nonetheless slips on it should be left in agony where he landed ... This is more than logically ridiculous. It is morally reprehensible. (Fisher, 1993:27–30)

Do you think media coverage of HIV/AIDS divides people into innocent victims and guilty parties? What role should the media play, if any, in disseminating information about HIV/AIDS to the public?

Sources: Based on Molotch and Lester, 1974; Colby and Cook, 1991; White and Cunningham, 1992; Fisher, 1993; and Hernandez, 1994.

While we will consider several of these issues later in this chapter, the role of conflict in the provision of health care is clearly illustrated in the debate over the allocation of money for research and treatment for different diseases. There is competition among those concerned with different diseases; money spent doing research on cancer cannot be spent on heart disease. Conflict also exists among those who take different approaches to research and treatment of a particular disease. Should funds be spent on treatment or prevention? Should nontraditional treatment methods be studied or is the medical model the only legitimate way of responding to disease?

Understandably, groups representing victims of particular types of diseases have lobbied governments and medical groups to give their problem a higher priority and more funding. Thus the priority given to research, prevention, and medical care for particular types of diseases may reflect the power of lobby groups as well as the seriousness of the problem. AIDS activists have been particularly successful in having their concerns reflected in policy. Gay men have been able to work together to form a lobby that has had a powerful impact on securing government support and funding for AIDS research and treatment. As you will learn from reading Box 11.3, AIDS activists have also been very concerned with reducing the stigmatization of HIV/AIDS victims.

Women with breast cancer saw that AIDS research had about ten times the funding of breast cancer research and have also organized. The incidence of breast cancer has risen dramatically; the chances that a Canadian woman will get this type of cancer have risen from 1 in 20 in 1960 to 1 in 8 in the 1990s (Driedger, 1997). However, death rates from the disease are now at their lowest level in four decades, a decline analysts attribute to the increased mammography screening for early detection of the cancer (Statistics Canada, 1997a). However, breast cancer remains a major cause of death for women and little is known about its causes. Women's groups continue to lobby for increased research funding.

BOX 11.3 SOCIOLOGY AND LAW

AIDS AND PUBLIC HEALTH

In 1993, London, Ontario, resident Charles Ssenyonga was charged with criminal negligence causing bodily harm and aggravated sexual assault for knowingly passing AIDS on to several women. At least twenty women had contracted HIV through having unprotected sex with him. Ssenyonga died during his trial, so we don't know what verdict would have been rendered, though in a similar case the Newfoundland Court of Appeal imposed a sentence of eleven years and three months on Raymond Mercer, who had pleaded guilty to criminal negligence causing bodily harm for knowingly infecting women with HIV/AIDS. Canada has no specific law against knowingly infecting others with a sexually transmittable disease, though such laws do exist in several other countries including Australia and in many American states.

Ssenyonga knew in 1985 that he likely had HIV. AIDS was epidemic in his home country of Uganda and one of his former girlfriends there had died of the disease. On several occasions doctors suggested he get tested for HIV. However, he refused and assured his doctors that he was always careful to protect his partners during intercourse. In fact, he was HIV-positive and was having unprotected sex with multiple partners. In early 1989 two of his victims reported him to public health authorities. The Middlesex–London health unit did nothing for a month, then advised Ssenyonga to be tested. In March of 1989 both Ssenyonga and the health department received confirmation of his infection. A restraining order forbidding him to have sex was issued at the request of public health officials. Despite this and despite his assurances to health officials that he would practise only safe sex, he continued to infect more women.

The public health system could not protect Ssenyonga's victims from HIV/AIDS. Doctors who suspected he had the virus could not require him to be tested, and after his diagnosis confirmed that he was HIV-positive his sexual behaviour could not be controlled.

Controlling the spread of HIV has been very controversial. The normal steps taken in dealing with infectious diseases include routine testing for infection, reporting the names of those who have positive tests, tracing contacts to determine who might have been infected, and informing them they have been exposed to the disease. Quarantine has even been used to prevent the spread of disease; in the 1940s and 1950s many Canadians were kept in hospitals so they could not pass on tuberculosis. In Ontario, twelve diseases including syphilis, gonorrhea, and tuberculosis are defined as virulent, and people with these diseases can be forced to stay in a hospital or jail for up to four months for treatment. However, HIV/AIDS is not included in this category. Because it is incurable, health authorities have reasoned, it does not make sense to force

SOCIAL FACTORS IN HEALTH

We often think of health in only physical terms. However, the health of any group is a product of the interaction of a wide range of physiological, psychological, spiritual, historical, sociological, cultural, economic, and environmental factors (Waldram et al., 1995). In this section, we will see how these factors affect the health of people of different ages, genders, and classes in Canada. A basic premise of conflict theory is that groups compete with one another for access to scarce resources. Conflict theorists would predict that because of this competition, the quality of health and health care will vary by age, sex, class, and race. As with other social issues you have studied so far, there are dramatic differences in the health of people in these different social categories.

BOX 11.3

CONTINUED

victims to have treatment. When Dr. Richard Schabas, Ontario's medical officer of health, suggested classifying HIV/AIDS as a virulent disease in order to control rare, irresponsible victims like Ssenyonga who knowingly spread the disease, AIDS activists responded with furious protests. Dr. Schabas was burned in effigy and was given police protection when he received death threats.

Why is HIV/AIDS treated differently from other serious communicable diseases? One reason is the societal reaction to victims of the disease. Homosexual men have had justifiable fears that AIDS testing and reporting would result in discrimination against them. For example, some U.S. school districts wished to use HIV tests to identify and fire gay teachers, and insurance companies were anxious to cancel the policies of victims. Most Canadian provincial human rights codes do not protect homosexuals from discrimination in matters such as housing and employment. To AIDS activists and civil libertarians, Dr. Schabas's suggestion that AIDS victims could be involuntarily detained raised the possibility of homophobic governments locking up large numbers of gay men simply because they were ill. Because of the social consequences of an HIV-positive diagnosis, testing and notification procedures are generally voluntary and almost all testing is done anonymously or with the consent of the person being tested.

Clearly there are weaknesses in our current system of controlling AIDS. However, the argument has been made that actions like mandatory testing and reporting or quarantining some AIDS victims will drive those at risk of AIDS underground, thus increasing the chances of further transmission. If there was a chance that HIV-positive people could be publicly identified, those at risk might choose to avoid the health-care system altogether. In addition, these kinds of coercive control measures would be costly in financial as well as human terms, and would not likely be effective as a general public health measure (Hodgson, 1989).

What are your views on this controversial issue? Should all known partners of HIV victims be informed of their risk? Because medical advances such as AZT treatment for HIV-infected pregnant women and protease inhibitors dramatically reduce HIV levels, should more effort go into identifying those with HIV so that they can be treated? Can societal attitudes be changed so that the consequences of being labelled an HIV/AIDS victim are less severe? Should it be a crime to knowingly spread HIV, or should the problem be dealt with outside the criminal courts?

Sources: Callwood, 1995; Burr, 1997; and Weston and Jeffery, 1994.

Age

Rates of illness and death are highest among the very old and the very young. Mortality rates drop shortly after birth and begin to rise significantly during the middle years. After 65, rates of chronic illness and mortality increase rapidly. This has obvious implications for individuals and their families, but it also has an impact on Canadian society.

Canada is an aging society (see Chapter 15, "Population and Urbanization"). Today, about 12 percent of the population is 65 or over; by 2036 this will double to about 25 percent. Because health-care costs are high for some older people, these costs will begin to rise dramatically after 2010 when the first baby boomers turn 65. This concern with future costs is one of the factors behind the current attempts by provincial and federal governments to

In the summer of 1997, 650 people met in Kingston, Ontario, for the first World Conference on Breast Cancer. The major political goal of the conference was "to do for breast cancer what happened to AIDS in the 1980s—to put breast cancer on the centre stage" (Driedger, 1997).

restructure the operation of health care. For example, the number of cases of one of the most debilitating conditions among the elderly, ***senile dementia*—a term for diseases, such as Alzheimer's, that involve a progressive impairment of judgment and memory**—is forecast to triple by 2031 to nearly 800,000 people (Lipovenko, 1997). Many of these people will require costly institutional care unless changes are made to improve the support available for home care and group homes.

Sex

Prior to this century, women had lower life expectancies than men because of high mortality rates during pregnancy and childbirth. Preventive measures have greatly reduced this cause of female mortality and women now live longer than men. Females born in Canada in 1996 could expect to live about 81 years compared with 76 years for males (Statistics Canada, 2000b). Ingrid Waldron (1994) has identified three factors leading to this sex difference in mortality rates. First, differences in gender roles mean that females are less likely than males to engage in risky behaviour such as drinking alcohol and using drugs, driving dangerously, and engaging in violent activities such as fights. Males are also more likely than females to work in dangerous occupations such as commercial fishing, mining, and construction. Second, females are more likely to make use of the health-care system and so may have problems identified at an earlier, more treatable stage than men, who are more reluctant to consult doctors. Third, it is likely that biological differences contribute, as females have higher survival rates than males at every stage from fetus to old age.

Some health experts have predicted that as the social roles played by females become more like those of males, the mortality gap will narrow. For example, a dramatic rise in lung cancer rates among women has been a consequence of females adopting the same patterns of smoking as males.

Because women live longer than men, many of us assume that women are also healthier. In fact, while men die sooner, women have higher rates of disease and disability. While men at every age have higher rates of fatal diseases, women have higher rates of nonfatal chronic conditions (Waldron, 1994).

Social Class

The poor have worse health and die earlier than the rich. This is also true of poor and rich countries; illness and mortality rates are far higher in less developed countries than in developed nations. Even within the industrialized world, people in countries with the most equal distribution of income (Norway and Sweden) have the best health as measured by life expectancy (Nancarrow Clarke, 1996). In Canada, males living in the highest-income neighbourhoods have a life expectancy almost 6 years longer than males in the lowest-income neighbourhoods. For women the difference is about 2 years (Trovato, 1994). There are similar differences between people in the highest- and lowest-income neighbourhoods for other health indicators. For example, in 1996 the infant mortality rate in Canada's poorest urban neighbourhoods was nearly double that in the richest neighbourhoods (Health Statistics Division, 2000).

While poverty is correlated with poor health, government policy can help reduce its effects.

Alzheimer's disease is a tragedy for the afflicted individuals and for their families. As our population ages, such debilitating conditions will also increasingly place a burden on our health-care system and on the taxpayers who fund it.

Providing the poor with access to medical advice and treatment through universal medicare is one way of doing this. A five-year study comparing cancer survival rates for the poorest one-third of Toronto residents who all had government-funded health care, with their counterparts in Detroit, who typically had little or no health insurance, shows the impact of ensuring the poor have adequate health care (Gorey et al., 1997). Survival rates were higher in Toronto for 12 of the 15 most common types of cancer. For many of these types of cancer, survival rates after five years were 50 percent higher among the poor in Toronto than among those in Detroit. The benefits of government-funded care go particularly to the poor, as this study found no difference among middle- or high-income patients in the two countries.

If access to medical care does improve the health of the poor, why then are Canada's poor still less healthy than its middle and upper classes? The answer is that medical care cannot compensate for the other disadvantages of poverty such as poor housing, hazardous employment, inadequate diet, greater exposure to disease, and the psychological stresses of poverty. The poor are more likely to become injured or sick because of these conditions, so their health is worse despite the availability of care once the medical problem has occurred. The poor may also lack knowledge of preventive strategies and services. For example, college- or university-educated women are twice as likely as women who have not graduated from high school to have mammograms. This means that less-educated women are at a higher risk of dying of breast cancer.

Race, Class, and Health: Canada's Aboriginal People

We have looked at some aspects of the relationship between class and health. The experience of Canada's Aboriginal people clearly illustrates how the disadvantages of race interact with those of class to cause health problems. While the economic disadvantages and the prejudice suffered by Aboriginal people are worse than they are for most other groups of Canadians, the poverty and discrimination that affect Aboriginal people's health also affect the health of other minority groups.

Aboriginal people have a history of serious health problems that begins with their early contact with Europeans. ***Epidemics*—sudden, significant increases in the numbers of people contracting a disease**—of contagious diseases such as tuberculosis, measles, smallpox, and influenza broke out in the early years of this contact. These epidemics were partly due to the fact that Aboriginals had no immunity to these European diseases. They were also caused by new patterns of trade that led to contact with more diverse groups of people than had occurred before European settlement.

While their mortality rates have improved significantly since the middle of this century, Aboriginal people still die earlier than other Canadians. Infant mortality rates among Aboriginal people are twice the Canadian average, and life expectancy is 9 years less than average for Aboriginal men and 7 years less for Aboriginal women, who also have higher than average rates of hospital admission and disease (Wotherspoon, 1994). While infectious diseases among Aboriginals have been brought under control (though their rates remain higher than those of other Canadians), their health problems are now chronic diseases such as heart disease, respiratory problems, and diabetes. HIV/AIDS is also now beginning to affect the Aboriginal community.

What are the reasons for the poorer health of Aboriginal people? A major factor is poverty. Aboriginal people are among the poorest in Canada and suffer from the poor nutrition and other social conditions that go with poverty. Many of the diseases that affect Aboriginal people can also be traced to the inadequate housing, crowding, and poor sanitary conditions common on reserves and in the other communities where they live. The isolation of many Aboriginal communities is also a factor; an illness that could be easily treated in a city hospital can be fatal in a community 500 miles from the nearest doctor.

Aboriginal people also have high rates of violent death and suicide. Rates of homicide for Aboriginal men are 6 times higher than the Canadian average and 4 times higher for women; rates of suicide are 3 times higher for men and twice as high for women than the Canadian averages (Mao et al., 1992). Accidental death rates are also higher: Aboriginal people are three times more likely than other Canadians to die as a result of motor vehicle accidents and twice as likely to die by drowning (Wotherspoon, 1994).

Finally, the legacy of colonialism still affects Aboriginal people's health problems. Anastasia Shkilnyk (1985), who studied the Ojibwa community of Grassy Narrows in northwestern Ontario, attributes the high rates of suicide and violent death and health problems on the reserve to colonial actions such as the destruction of Aboriginal language and religion, the family breakdown caused by enforced attendance at residential schools, and the forced relocation of the community by the Department of Indian Affairs. Environmental destruction by local industries that dumped methyl mercury into the lakes and rivers around the reserve was another contributor. This toxic substance had a direct impact on the health of Grassy Narrows residents and also had an indirect impact by destroying the traditional fishery that was the foundation of the community's way of life.

DISABILITY

What is a disability? There are many different definitions. In business and government, it often is defined in terms of work—for instance, "an inability to engage in gainful employment." Medical professionals tend to define it in terms of organically based impairments—the problem being entirely within the body (Albrecht, 1992). However, not all disabilities are visible to others nor do they necessarily limit people physically. An alternative definition of ***disability*** **as a physical or health condition that stigmatizes or causes discrimination** helps us view disability as residing primarily (although not exclusively) in social attitudes and in social and physical environments (Weitz, 1995). In other words, disability is socially created through everyday experiences that create barriers for individuals with disabilities. According to Blackford (1996), the social system and its planners have failed to provide the universal access that would allow people with disabilities to participate fully in all aspects of life. For example, in an elevator, the buttons may be beyond the reach of persons using a wheelchair. In this context, disability derives from the fact that certain things have been made inaccessible to some people (Weitz, 1995). Michael Oliver (1990) used the term *disability oppression* to describe the barriers that exist for disabled persons in Canadian society. These include economic hardship (from such things as the additional costs of accessibility devices, transportation, and attendant care; or employment discrimination), inadequate government assistance programs, and negative social attitudes toward disabled persons. According to disability rights advocates, disability must be thought of in terms of how society causes or contributes to the problem—not in terms of what is "wrong" with the person with a disability.

Disability in Historical Perspective

Historically, different societies dealt with disabilities on the basis of their culture, values, and technology. For example, in the Neolithic period, some persons with disabling illnesses had a hole drilled in their skull to provide an escape route for the evil spirits that were assumed to be causing the problem (McElroy and Townsend, 1989; Albrecht, 1992). During the Middle

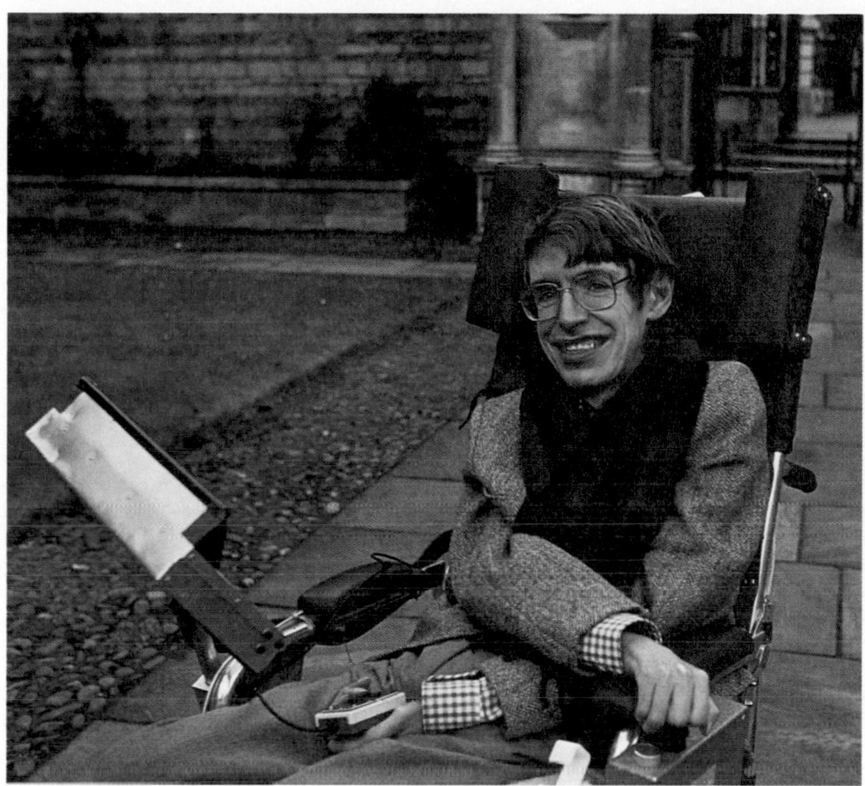

Does life expectancy take on a different meaning for persons with chronic disabilities? While he was still in college, British theoretical physicist Stephen Hawking learned he had Lou Gehrig's disease (amyotrophic lateral sclerosis). Hawking, nevertheless, went on to develop a quantum theory of gravity that forever changed our view of the universe and, as a result, he is considered one of the leading figures in modern cosmology.

Ages, disabilities were seen as an expression of God's displeasure, so the clergy dealt with medical problems.

The mode of subsistence in a society is a major determinant of the social responses to the various types of disabilities. In some hunting and gathering societies, impairments are viewed as punishment for past transgressions, and people with disabilities may be banished or killed; in others, they are fully integrated into the group (Albrecht, 1992). In pastoral societies, the migratory life inherent in continually moving herds of cattle, sheep, or goats to new locations for grazing may have serious consequences for those with an immobilizing disability. By contrast, in horticultural and agrarian societies, in which people settle down to cultivate crops and raise domestic animals, fewer stigmas are associated with disabilities (Albrecht, 1992). At the same time, however, as stable communities are developed, epidemics related to poor sanitation and overcrowding are more likely to occur. For example, during the early stages of industrialization, urban density, lack of adequate sanitation, and poverty all contributed to a rise in the rate of chronic illness and physical disability (Albrecht, 1992).

Disability in Contemporary Society

An estimated 4.2 million people, or 15.5 percent of the population in Canada, have one or more physical or mental disabilities. (For more information on the disabilities of Canadians aged 15 to 65, see Table 11.1.) This number is increasing for several reasons. First, with advances in medical technology, many people who formerly would have died from an accident or illness now survive, although with an impairment. Second, as more people live longer, they are more likely to experience diseases (such as arthritis) that may have disabling consequences (Albrecht, 1992). Third, persons born with serious disabilities are more likely to survive infancy because of medical technology. However, less than 15 percent of persons with a disability today were born with it; accidents and disease account for most of the disabilities in this country.

Although anyone can become disabled, some people are more likely to be or to become disabled than others. Aboriginal people have higher rates of disability than other Canadians, especially more serious disabilities; persons with lower incomes also

TABLE 11.1 DISABLED PERSONS IN CANADA, AGES 15–65, 1990–1991

CHARACTERISTICS	PERCENTAGE
Nature of Disability*	
Mobility	52
Agility	50
Cognitive disability (includes intellectual, mental health, or learning disability)	32
Hearing	25
Vision	9
Speaking	8
*Note: totals do not add up to 100 as disabled persons may have more than one disability.	
Type of Disability	
Severe	14
Moderate	32
Mild	54
Age	
15–34 years	29.4
35–54 years	43.2
55–64 years	27.4
Marital Status	
Never married	24
Married/common law	61
Divorced	7
Separated	4
Widowed	4
Employment Status	
Unemployed	52
Employed	48
Level of Schooling	
University degree	6
High-school diploma	19
Some postsecondary	35

Reproduced by authority of the Minister of Industry, 1996, Statistics Canada, from *Report on Canadian Health and Disability Survey*, Cat. no. 82-555.

have higher rates of disability (Bolaria and Bolaria, 1994).

For persons with chronic illness and disability, life expectancy may take on a different meaning. Knowing that they likely will not live out the full life expectancy for persons in their age cohort, they may come to "treasure each moment," as does James Keller, a baseball coach:

> In December 1992, I found out I have Lou Gehrig's disease—amyotrophic lateral sclerosis, or ALS. I learned that this disease destroys every muscle in the body, that there's no known cure or treatment and that the average life expectancy for people with ALS is two to five years after diagnosis.
>
> Those are hard facts to accept. Even today, nearly two years after my diagnosis, I see myself as a 42-year-old career athlete who has always been blessed with excellent health. Though not an hour goes by in which I don't see or hear in my mind that phrase "two to five years," I still can't quite believe it. Maybe my resistance to those words is exactly what gives me the strength to live with them and the will to make the best of every day in every way. (Keller, 1994)

Environment, lifestyle, and working conditions all may contribute to either temporary or chronic disability. For example, air pollution in automobile-clogged cities leads to a higher incidence of chronic respiratory disease and lung damage, which may result in severe disability in some people. Eating certain types of food and smoking cigarettes increase the risk for coronary and cardiovascular diseases (Albrecht, 1992). In contemporary industrial societies, workers in the second tier of the labour market (primarily recent immigrants, white women, and visible minorities) are at the greatest risk for certain health hazards and disabilities. Employees in data processing and service-oriented jobs also may be affected by work-related disabilities such as arthritis, lower-back pain, and carpal tunnel syndrome.

Nearly one out of six people in Canada have a "chronic health condition which, given the physical, attitudinal, and financial barriers built into the social system, makes it difficult to perform one or more activities generally considered appropriate for persons of their age" (Nessner, 1994). Can a person in a wheelchair have equal access to education, employment, and housing? If public transportation is not accessible to those in wheelchairs, the answer certainly is no. As disability rights activist Mark Johnson put it, "Black people fought for the right to ride in the front of the bus. We're fighting for the right to get on the bus" (quoted in Shapiro, 1993:128).

Living with disabilities is a long-term process. For infants born with certain types of congenital (present at birth) problems, their disability first acquires social significance for their parents and caregivers. In a study of children with disabilities in Israel, sociologist Meira Weiss (1994) challenged the assumption that parents automatically bond with infants, especially those born with visible disabilities. She found that an infant's appearance may determine how parents will view the child. Parents are more likely to be bothered by external, openly visible disabilities than by internal or disguised ones; some of the parents are more willing to consent to or even demand the death of an "appearance-impaired" child (Weiss, 1994). According to Weiss, children born with internal (concealed) disabilities at least initially are more acceptable to parents because they do not violate the parents' perceived body images of their children. Weiss's study provides insight into the social significance people attach to congenital disabilities.

Many disability rights advocates argue that persons with a disability have been kept out of the mainstream of society. They have been denied equal opportunities in education by being consigned to special education classes or special schools. For example, people who grow up deaf often are viewed as disabled. However, many members of the deaf community instead view themselves as a "linguistic minority" that is part of a unique culture (Lane, 1992; Cohen, 1994). They believe they have been restricted from entry into schools and the workforce, not due to their own limitations, but by societal barriers. Why are disabled persons excluded? Susan Wendell offers an explanation:

> In a society which idealizes the body, the physically disabled are often marginalized. People learn to identify with their own strengths (by cultural standards) and to hate, fear, and neglect their own weaknesses. The disabled are not only de-valued for their de-valued bodies; they are constant reminders to the able-bodied of the negative body—of what the able-bodied are trying to avoid, forget, and ignore ... In a culture which loves the idea that the body can be controlled, those who cannot control their bodies are seen (and may see themselves) as failures. (1995:458)

Among persons who acquire disabilities through disease or accidents later in life, the social significance of their disability can be seen in how they initially respond to their symptoms and diagnosis, how they view the immediate situation and their future, and how the illness and disability affect their lives. According to Wendell:

> Disabled people can participate in marginalizing ourselves. We can wish for bodies we do not have, with frustration, shame, self-hatred. We can feel trapped in the negative body; it is our internalized oppression to feel this. Every (visibly or invisibly) disabled person I have talked to has felt this; some never stop feeling it. (1995:458)

When confronted with a disability, most people adopt one of two strategies—avoidance or vigilance. Those who use the avoidance strategy deny their condition so as to maintain hopeful images of the future and elude depression; for example, some individuals refuse to participate in rehabilitation following a traumatic injury because they want to pretend that it does not exist (Weitz, 1995). By contrast, those using the vigilant strategy actively seek knowledge and treatment so that they can respond appropriately to the changes in their bodies (Weitz, 1995).

The combination of a disability and society's reaction to the disability has an impact on the lives of many people. The disabled often suffer from stereotyping; for example, movies are given to depicting villains as individuals with disabilities (think of the *Nightmare on Elm Street* and its sequels and the villains in the Batman movies). Charitable organization fundraising campaigns may contribute to the perception of the disabled as persons who are to be pitied. Prejudice against persons with disabilities may result in either subtle or overt discrimination. It may also be the reason they have difficulty finding employment. While the role of disabled persons in the Canadian labour force has expanded in recent years, compared with nondisabled adults a much smaller proportion of the disabled population is employed. Even when persons with a disability find jobs, they typically earn less than nondisabled persons (H.A.L.S., 1991). Greater inclusion of people with disabilities is a challenge Canadians must accept if we are to achieve our cultural goal of equality for all citizens.

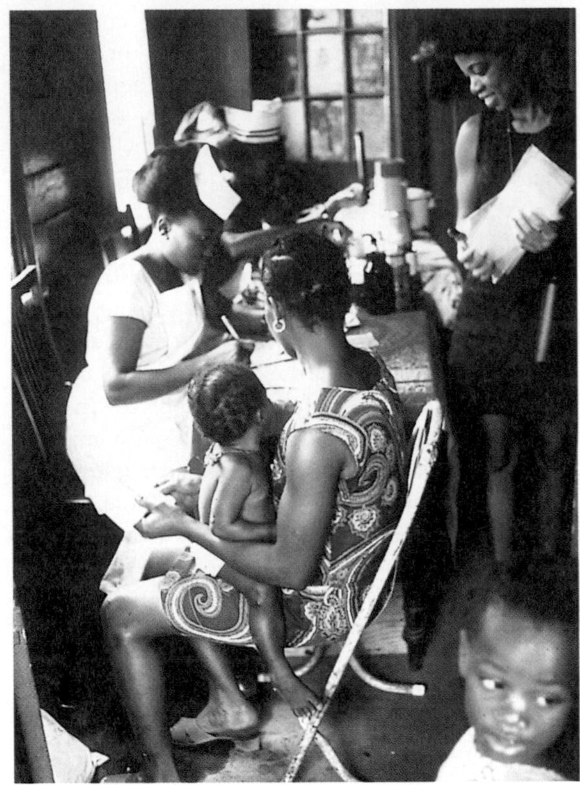

A nurse interviews a mother at a rural health clinic in Sierra Leone. With the support of the World Health Organization, these clinics were established to reduce infant mortality and to improve the health of mothers and their children.

SOCIAL DEVELOPMENT AND HEALTH: A GLOBAL PERSPECTIVE

The difference between rich and poor countries is dramatically reflected in infant mortality rates. While 6 out of every 1000 infants in Canada die before their first birthday, infant mortality rates in the world's poorest countries are far higher. Nigeria, Haiti, and Ethiopia, for instance, have infant mortality rates of 111,109, and 106 per 1000 live births. Life expectancy is correspondingly low; for persons born in Canada in 1996, life expectancy at birth was 79 years, compared with less than 45 years in many poor African nations. Most deaths in less-developed countries are caused by infectious and parasitic diseases that are now rare in the industrialized world.

While statistics paint a grim picture of health in the developing world, a UNICEF report on the health of the world's children puts the situation in even starker terms (1997). Writing of the toll caused by the childhood diseases of measles, diarrhea, malaria, pneumonia, and malnutrition, Monica Sharman and James Tulloch tell us "Children in rich countries do not die from the common, preventable diseases of childhood. Children in poor countries do" (1997:1).

Tremendous progress has nevertheless been made in saving the lives of children over the past fifteen years. Steps such as immunization, oral rehydration therapy for diarrhea, and iodizing salt save as many as five million children each year. Sharman and Tulloch say this progress "must be ranked as one of the great achievements of the second half of the 20th century" (1997:2). However, there continue to be millions of child deaths that could be prevented through simple measures such as improved sanitation, clean water, improved preventive measures such as immunization, and the provision of better local health services.

Government home-care workers march at the Manitoba legislature in April of 1997, protesting the provincial government's plans to contract out their services to private companies. Public opposition to this privatization convinced the government to scale back their plans to a small trial project. Later in the year, the government found that privatization would not save any money and returned all responsibility for home care to government workers.

Of course, not only children in poor countries are dying. Each year 585,000 women—virtually all of them in poor countries—die of complications arising from pregnancy and childbirth. As we have noted, AIDS is becoming an epidemic in developing countries but little has been done to prevent its spread in these countries. (See Box 11.4 for more on the spread of AIDS in Africa, particularly Uganda.) While 90 percent of people currently infected with HIV live in the developing world, only 8 percent of the $18 billion a year spent on treatment, prevention, and research goes to these countries (Piot, 1997). Even worse, the new methods of treatment that have successfully extended the lives of those with AIDS in the developed world are unaffordable in developing countries where average annual incomes are only a fraction of the cost of these treatments.

Health Care in Canada

In 2000 the United Nations once again ranked Canada the best place in the world to live. This prestigious designation is in part based on an assessment of Canada's national health-care system. Unquestionably, this system ranks among the best in the world.

Though cherished by Canadians and envied by many in other countries, some critics feel that Canada's health-care system is in danger of "wasting away" because of budget cuts made by governments in the 1990s (Armstrong and Armstrong, 1996). People in many communities across the country have protested hospital closures and these health-care funding cuts. Public opinion polls demonstrate that there is concern that our health-care system is deteriorating. An international health survey found that in 1988 only 5 percent of Canadians felt their health-care system required major rebuilding. By 1998, 23 percent felt that major changes were needed (Blendon et al., 1998). Other surveys have shown similar declines in satisfaction (*Maclean's*, 1996). The reason for this dissatisfaction is illustrated by the following complaint about an occurrence that is becoming frequent. The complaint was made to Ontario's Patient Care Hotline by a patient who was released from hospital too soon after a serious operation:

> They wanted to discharge me but everything still hurt. I was still weak, weak, weak and there was something very wrong. But never mind, they were telling me I was fine and that it was time for me to go

BOX 11.4 SOCIOLOGY IN GLOBAL PERSPECTIVE

THE AIDS EPIDEMIC IN AFRICA

RAKAI, UGANDA—From the shadows of this mud hut, the gaunt and weary young man stares outside at the pigs playing in the dust under the banana palms. His chest is covered with open sores; skin rashes have left his ebony arms looking as if they are covered in chalk; his army fatigues hang loosely around his waist.

Outside, Charles Lawanga glances toward his ailing second son and lowers his voice. Last year, when the Ugandan army gave him his medical furlough, his son was sick, but at least he could walk, says Lawanga.

Lawanga's brows are furrowed; he has the face of a man who is watching his son die. His eyes sharpen when he hears that an American journalist knows many of the Western doctors working on the disease. The aging man has no intelligence of byzantine scientific intrigues and timorous reporters, or of esoteric distinctions between American political factions. He knows only that the United States is a country of immense wealth, and that the medicine that will save his country and his son will probably come from there. Tears gather in his brown eyes, and he asks, "When will it come? When will there be the cure?" (Shilts, 1988:621).

By the mid-1990s, Uganda had the highest number of recorded HIV cases in Africa—

> home. I was so sick on that day I couldn't hold my head up, couldn't get out of bed or get dressed and I was heaving on and off.

Following release, the patient remained bedridden at home for a month and then was readmitted when a home-care nurse became concerned with the patient's condition:

> They took me to emergency. They found a massive infection ... They operated that evening ... I was in hospital in intensive care for 2 months and on the medical ward for 3 weeks. They told my friend I might pass away. (Armstrong et al., 1997:72)

There is, however, some cause for optimism about the future of our health-care system in that Canadians still highly value their system and are determined to ensure its survival. Public pressure may stop the erosion of health services. Most provinces have begun to put new money into health-care, and the premiers of all provinces have demanded that the federal government place health care funding at the top of the spending priority list. In the 1999 budget, the federal government began restoring some of the money it had cut from health budgets.

Universal Health Care

Canadians have not always had a ***universal health-care system,*** **that is, one in which all citizens receive medical services paid for through taxation revenues.** Prior to the early 1960s Canadians had a "user pay" system, which meant that many people had to pay for health care directly out of their pockets. Individuals who did not have health insurance and who required expensive medical procedures or long-term care, or who developed a chronic illness often suffered severe financial losses. Today under our universal system, if you are sick, you have the right to receive quality medical care regardless of your ability to pay. Individuals do not pay doctor or hospital costs directly, but they are responsible for at least part of the costs of other medical services such as prescription drugs and ambulances.

Health care is a provincial responsibility, and each province has its own medical insurance plan. However, the federal government contributes a significant amount of money to the provinces for health care and enforces basic standards that each province must follow. Provincial plans must meet the following five requirements:

BOX 11.4

CONTINUED

around 1.5 million. AIDS has touched virtually all families in this country, and much of the stigma of this syndrome has diminished because it is now so widespread. Average life expectancy in Uganda is predicted to fall from 59 years to 32 years by 2010.

Will a cause for HIV be found? A vaccine or a cure? What impact will AIDS have on world population size? Currently, it is impossible to assess the demographic impact of AIDS; not enough is known about the patterns of transmission of the current strains of HIV. In Africa (as compared with North America), HIV appears to have been in the population longer, and it infects women and men about equally. Africans are highly vulnerable to AIDS because of malnutrition, rapid population growth, and a continually changing ecological situation.

Should Canada and other developed nations take an active role in trying to limit the AIDS epidemic in sub-Saharan Africa? Why or why not?

Sources: Shilts, 1988; Ehrlich and Ehrlich, 1991; Lorch, 1993; Obbo, 1993; Audubon, 1994; Gibson, 1994; and Weitz, 1996.

1. *Universality*—all Canadians should be covered on uniform terms and conditions;
2. *Comprehensiveness*—all necessary medical services should be guaranteed, without dollar limit, and should be available solely on the basis of medical need;
3. *Accessibility*—reasonable access should be guaranteed to all Canadians;
4. *Portability*—benefits should be transferable from province to province; and
5. *Public administration*—should be operated on a nonprofit basis by a public agency or commission. (Grant, 1993:401)

Although Canada's health-care system continues to rank among the best in the world, it has its critics. One problem they point to is the fact that though drastic cuts in funding have led to reduced resources and services, Canada still spends about 9 percent of its gross domestic product on health care. While this is low in comparison with the U.S. rate (see Table 11.2), it is higher than those of most other industrial countries and it amounts to a sizable expenditure. For example, Canada's 1999 health-care expenditures were $86 billion (Canadian Institute for Health Information, 2000). Of this amount, $60 billion came from government funding, while the remainder came from individuals and medical insurance companies for services not covered by medicare.

Related to the issue of increasing costs and declining resources is the problem of overutilization of health-care services by the Canadian public. Utilization surveys have indicated that Canadians began to use health services more extensively following the introduction of medicare. According to sociologist Karen Grant:

> Canadians have an almost insatiable appetite for medical services, because they do not pay for health services when received, and because they have no knowledge of the actual costs of care, they inappropriately use the system. Frequenting emergency rooms for routine care is perhaps the most common illustration of this problem. (Grant, 1993:401)

While members of the public may not always make the most economical choices, many of the costs of our system are controlled by doctors, who prescribe drugs, admit patients to hospitals, deter-

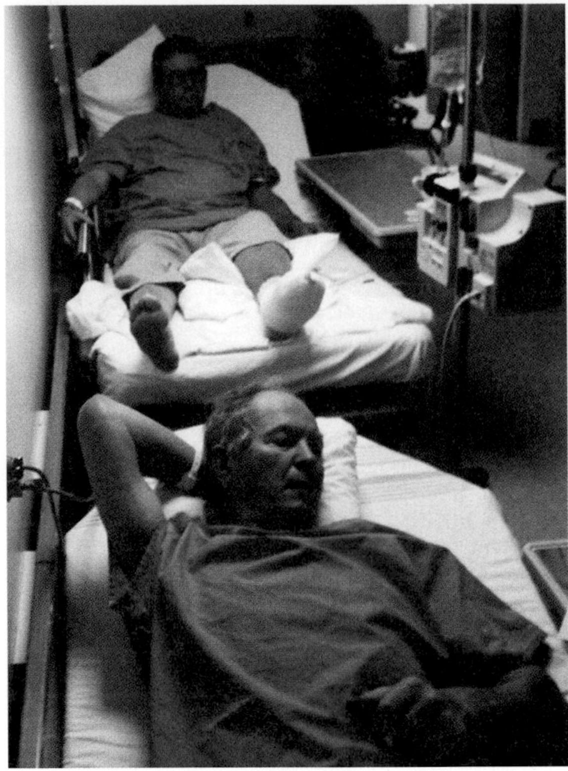

One of the consequences of cutbacks to Canada's health care system has been hospital overcrowding. These patients spent two days in an emergency room hallway because no rooms were available.

mine patients' lengths of stay in hospitals, order tests and examinations, determine the course of treatment that will be used, and recommend follow-up visits. Since patients will do almost anything to ensure their health and since they do not pay directly, they have no incentive to question doctors' recommendations. Reducing the economic control of doctors while ensuring that treatment decisions are made on medical, not economic, grounds is one of the major challenges of taxpayer-funded health-care systems.

A final criticism of the Canadian health-care system is its costly and often wasteful focus on hospitals. Cheaper forms of noninstitutional health care such as home-care services are not subject to national standards, so these services vary widely from province to province and may not be available even when they are the most cost-effective type of care. Thus, people who need minimal care may be housed in expensive acute care hospital beds costing over $1000 per day because community alternatives are not available. The focus on physicians and hospitals can also be costly because it comes at the expense of preventive measures.

While there are difficulties with our system, in many respects it is far better than that of the United States, the only major industrialized country without a health-care system that provides universal coverage to all citizens. While Canada and western European countries treat health care as a basic human right, the United States sees it as a market commodity. Although there is government coverage for seniors, people with disabilities, and some of the poor in the United States, approximately 16 percent of the population—44 million people—have no medical coverage. An even larger number are inadequately covered and face potential ruin if they have a serious illness. In 1999 medical expenses led to 500,000 bankruptcies in the United States and are the leading cause of personal bankruptcy in that country (Wordsworth, 2000). Despite per capita costs in the U.S. system being roughly double those in Canada (see Table 11.2), Canadians are healthier than Americans, have better access to health care, have better treatment outcomes, and are more satisfied with their health-care system than Americans are with theirs (Kendall, Murray, and Linden, 2000).

APPROACHES TO HEALTH CARE

The Medical Model of Illness

The medical model has been the predominant way of thinking about illness in Western industrialized societies for many years. The medical model can best be described by considering its five basic assumptions: that illness is "(1) deviation from normal, (2) specific and universal, (3) caused by unique biological forces, (4) analogous to the breakdown of a machine whose parts can be repaired, and (5) defined and treated through a neutral scientific process" (Weitz, 1996:129). One consequence of this model has been that our society has vested great power in the hands of doctors, who are seen to be

TABLE 11.2 **LIFE EXPECTANCIES AND HEALTH CARE VARIOUS COUNTRIES**

Countries in Order of Life Expectancy	Life Expectancy at Birth, 1996, in Years	Total Expenditure on Health, % of GDP, 1997	Expenditure on Health per Capita, 1997[1]
Japan	80.3	7.3	$1741
Canada	78.5	9.3	2095
Australia	78.2	8.3	1805
France	78.1	9.6	2051
U.K.	76.9	6.7	1347
Germany	76.8	10.4	2339
U.S.	76.1	13.6	4090

[1]Adjusted for cost of living differences.

Reprinted by permission of Gerard Anderson, *Highlights of the 1998 Multinational Comparisons of Health Care*. New York: The Commonwealth Fund, 1998.

the experts in diagnosing and treating illness. While the situation is slowly changing, doctors have gone to great lengths to protect this view and their role at the centre of the health-care system. For example, they have actively resisted those with conflicting views such as midwives, advocates of natural healing methods, and those more concerned with preventing disease than with treating it.

Alternative Approaches

Despite the many successes of modern medicine such as heart pacemakers, arthroscopic surgery, and lung transplants, the medical model of illness is losing some of its dominance. While medical care is an important part of the health-care system, Canadians are recognizing that their health needs cannot be met by medical services alone and that more medical care does not necessarily lead to better health (Grant, 1993). In 1986, the federal government explicitly adopted what is called a health promotion policy, which emphasized prevention of disease and promoted healthy lifestyles and an increase in informal and community-based care (Crichton et al., 1997). The cost crisis in medicare has led the federal government to implement programs that emphasize environment and lifestyle in health promotion. For example, education about the hazards of smoking combined with more effective legislation against the use and advertising of tobacco products can improve public health and save the money now used to treat victims of smoking-related diseases such as emphysema and lung cancer. Responsibility for health-care is shifting away from the government and the health-care system toward the individual and the family.

Issues of cost and benefit to patients have also led to a move toward community-based care in most provinces. Programs such as home care, community health clinics, and alternative care for the elderly have saved costs by reducing the need for more expensive hospital care (Crichton et al., 1997). Many of these community programs also enhance people's quality of life by allowing them to remain in their communities.

The popularity of the holistic health-care movement is a further indication of the move toward a new definition of health. Holism is a philosophical principle, which, translated into everyday language, encompasses the idea of the whole being greater than the sum of its parts. Holism has a long history and reflects the orientations of many ancient therapeutic systems including that of Canadian Aboriginals. Modern scientific medicine has been widely criticized for its focus on diseases and injuries rather than on the prevention of illness and the promotion of overall well-being. Advocates of holistic medicine say the medical model looks at problems in a mechanical fashion without considering their context, while the holistic approach emphasizes the interdependence of body, mind, and environment (Northcott, 1994).

Holism is adaptable to more traditional medical practice and is being adopted by some medical doctors and nurses as well as by practitioners of alternative health care including chiropractors, osteopaths, acupuncturists, and naturopathic doctors. Supporters of the holistic health movement encourage people to take greater individual responsibility for their health and health care, especially with regard to diseases and disabilities that are the products of lifestyle. This approach also urges health-care providers to pay more attention to clients in diagnosing and treating illness, and to develop a greater sensitivity to cultural differences in the ways in which people define and react to illness. It also emphasizes the role of social factors in illness, a view that is now receiving research support (Kendall, Murray, and Linden, 2000).

Alternative approaches will continue to challenge traditional medicine's preoccupation with illness and disease and its focus on treatment by conventional biomedical means. The 1994–95 National Population Health Survey found that many Canadians were making use of alternative medicine. While about 15 percent of those surveyed said they had consulted an alternative practitioner within the previous year, only 2 percent of them said they had relied exclusively on an alternative practitioner within the previous year. Since only 2 percent relied exclusively on alternative medicine, it seems that this form of health care is being used as a complement to traditional medicine rather than replacing it. Of the groups surveyed, college- and university-educated young adults were most likely to use alternative health care. It was also found that women were more likely than men to use alternative health care. Use was much higher in the four western provinces than in the Atlantic region, with rates in Ontario and Quebec falling in the middle.

While its use appears to be growing, some types of alternative medicine are being criticized. Psychologist Barry Beyerstein has recently repeated the most pointed criticism, saying that some of the claims of alternative medical practice have not been empirically verified. He blames the acceptance of such claims on the fact that most people know little about science:

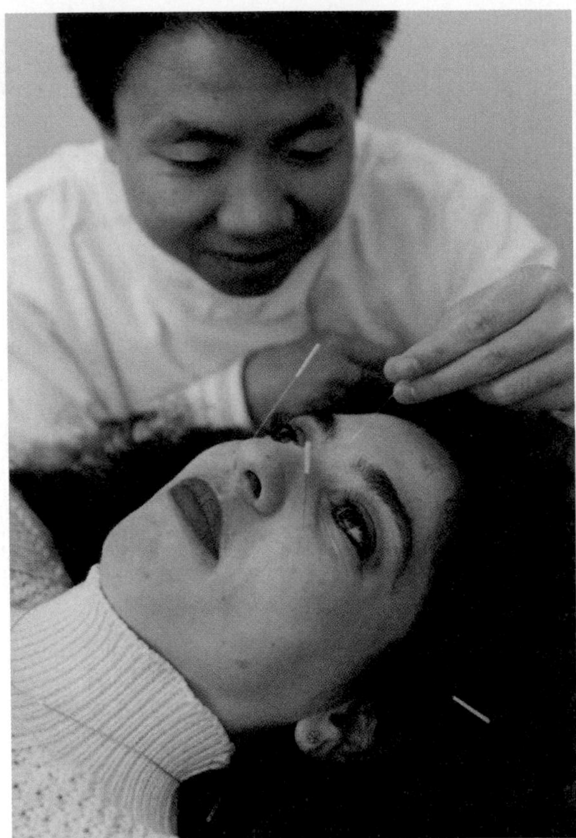

Canadians are increasingly using alternative health-care methods such as acupuncture.

> ... even an elementary understanding of chemistry should raise strong doubts about the legitimacy of homeopathy; a passing familiarity with human anatomy would suggest that "subluxations" of the vertebrae cannot cause all the diseases that chiropractors believe they do; and a quite modest grasp of physiology should make it apparent that a coffee enema is unlikely to cure cancer. But when consumers have not the foggiest idea of how bacteria, viruses, carcinogens, oncogenes, and toxins wreak havoc on bodily tissues, then shark cartilage, healing crystals, and pulverized tiger penis seem no more magical than the latest breakthrough from the biochemistry laboratory. (1997:150)

Beyerstein does, however, see some benefits in alternative medicine. It has, he says, added a comforting human component to a medical world that has become increasingly impersonal and technological. Many alternative healers offer sound advice about prevention and a healthy lifestyle, and some alternative practices do have scientific backing. However, he fears that some alternatives can divert sick people from more effective treatment. Consumers of health care will need to be sufficiently well informed about the variety and nature of the options available to make sound treatment choices in the future. These options will certainly grow in number as alternative therapies become more widely accepted and as some become integrated with conventional medicine.

HEALTH-CARE ISSUES IN THE FUTURE

Health and health care have changed dramatically in this century, and will continue to change in the years to come. Scientific developments such as the mapping of human genes and the new reproductive technologies have already begun to affect our lives. These changes will improve the lives of many but will also create some very difficult social and ethical problems that will continue to be debated for years to come. To give but one example, the ability to determine the sex of our children may lead to an imbalance between males and females. This would have a major impact on courtship and marriage as some in the larger sex group would have no chance to marry, while those in the smaller group would be very much in demand. Can you predict some of the possible consequences this might have on family structure and social relationships?

Unless there is a major shift in the economy, Canadians have likely seen the last of the major cuts to the health-care system. However, the evolution from hospital-based care toward prevention and community care will continue. This change can potentially be a positive one. For example, most of you have many years to live before you reach old age, but think ahead to that time. If you become unable to perform some household tasks such as cooking and cleaning, would you prefer to sell your home and move into institutional care or to receive daily home-care visits that would enable you to continue living independently? The political power of aging baby boomers (see Chapter 15) and the cost of caring for growing numbers of elderly people will force governments to give more serious attention to home-care programs.

However, there is one worry—the shift to community-based health care will not improve matters unless governments put adequate resources into community care. The deinstitutionalization of the mentally ill during the 1970s and 1980s illustrates this danger. Ending the warehousing of mentally ill people in institutions was a good thing. However, rather than providing sufficient funding for community services for the deinstitutionalized patients, governments spent the savings on other things. As a result, many former patients became a burden on their communities and were themselves put at risk because the proper support was not available. If home care is not properly funded, the burden of care will be transferred from the state to relatives who already have busy lives (Armstrong et al., 1997). More than one in eight Canadians are already providing care to people with long-term health problems. Many of these caregivers have reported that providing this help has hurt their jobs, finances, or health (Statistics Canada, 1997b). While many of the caregivers surveyed were willing and able to provide support, government assistance will be necessary for those caregivers who lack the resources to do it alone and for individuals who do not have a network of family and friends to assist them.

While the health of Canadians will likely continue to improve in the future, at the global level there is great cause for concern. You have already read about the impact of AIDS on people living in developing nations and about the precarious health of many of the world's children. Medical authorities now also fear the return of infectious diseases such as cholera, malaria, and tuberculosis that were once controlled by antibiotics and vaccines, and by public health programs like improved sanitation. The reasons for the renewed threat from these diseases include environmental change, the public health consequences of poverty in the developing world, and the fact that global travel has helped bacteria and viruses move easily from one place to another (Taylor, 1997).

The resurgence of diseases such as malaria and tuberculosis and the rapid spread of HIV/AIDS show that health is a social issue as much as it is a medical one. Social factors such as economic inequality, geographic mobility, societal values, human settlement patterns, and the overuse of pesticides and antibiotics all contribute to the spread of disease. Improving the health of the world's population will require social change as well as improved ways of treating the sick.

CHAPTER REVIEW

What is health?
Health is often defined as a state of complete physical, mental, and social well-being.

What is the relationship between health care, medicine, and preventive medicine?
Medicine is an institutionalized system for the scientific diagnosis, treatment, and prevention of illness. Medicine forms a vital part of the broader concept of health care, which is any activity intended to improve health. Preventive medicine is medicine that emphasizes a healthy lifestyle that will prevent poor health before it occurs.

What are the functionalist, conflict, and interactionist perspectives on health and health care?
Functionalists view society as a complex, stable system; therefore, the normal state of affairs is for people to be healthy and to contribute to their society. Illness is seen as dysfunctional for both the individual who is sick and for society. Sickness may result in an inability of the sick person to fulfil his or her necessary social roles. Symbolic interactionists attempt to understand the specific meanings and causes that we attribute to particular events. In studying health, interactionists focus on the fact that the meaning that social actors give their illness or disease will affect their self-concept and their relationships with others. The interactionist approach is illustrated by society's response to AIDS. The conflict approach to health and illness considers the political and social forces that affect health and the health-care system, and the inequities that result from these forces. Among the issues of concern for conflict theorists are the ability of all citizens to obtain health care; the impact of race, class, and gender on health and health care; the relative power of doctors compared with other health-care workers; the dominance of the medical model of health care; and the role of profit in the health-care system.

How do age, sex, and social class affect health?
Rates of illness and death are highest among the old and the very young. Mortality rates drop shortly after birth and begin to rise significantly during the middle years. After 65, rates of chronic illnesses and mortality increase rapidly. While in earlier times women had lower life expectancies than men because of high mortality rates during pregnancy and childbirth, women now live longer than men. Females born in Canada in 1996 could expect to live about 81 years compared with 76 years for males. However, women have higher rates of disease and disability. While men at every age have higher rates of fatal diseases, women have higher rates of nonfatal chronic conditions. The poor have worse health and die earlier than the rich. Illness and mortality rates are far higher for less developed countries than for developed nations. Within the industrialized world, countries with the most equal distribution of income (Norway and Sweden) have the best health as measured by life expectancy.

What is a disability?
A disability is a physical or health condition that stigmatizes or causes discrimination.

What is the difference between a universal health-care system and one in which the user pays for health services?
Canadians have a universal health-care system in which all Canadians receive medical services that are paid for through the tax system. If you are sick, you have the right to receive quality medical care regardless of your ability to pay. Prior to the early 1960s Canadians had a "user pay" system, which meant that many people had to pay for health care directly out of their pockets. Individuals without health insurance who required expensive medical procedures, long-term care, or who developed a chronic illness often suffered severe financial losses. The United States has a user pay system.

Key Terms

disability 320
epidemics 319
health 310
health care 310

medicalization 313
medicine 310
preventive medicine 310
senile dementia 318
sick role 311
universal health-care system 326

Internet Exercises

1. Health Canada is the federal government agency responsible for health matters. Go to the Health Canada Online Web site at **www.hc-sc.gc.ca.** This site discusses current government activities in health promotion. What are the government's priorities? How do you think they have changed over the past decade?
2. Visit the Web page of the American Council on Science and Health (**acsh.org**). What types of health concerns are reflected on this page? The Council says its priority is to distinguish between real and artificial health-care risks. Do any of its views differ from those you have read about in other sources?
3. *The Progress of Nations* is an annual report from UNICEF. Visit its Web site at **unicef.org/pon96**. According to this report, have health conditions been improving around the world? Is there cause for optimism?

Net Links

For more Web links related to the topic of this chapter, see the Nelson sociology Web site: **www.sociologyessentials-2nded.nelson.com.**

Read about a wide variety of diseases including HIV/AIDS at the Web site of the Centers for Disease Control and Prevention:

www.cdc.gov/hiv/pubs/facts.htm

Health Canada has established a comprehensive database on health and health-care issues called the Canadian Health Network; to see it, go to:

www.hc-sc.gc.ca

For recent information about the problems of HIV/AIDS, see the Web site of the Joint United Nations Program on HIV/AIDS at:

www.unaids.org

Learn about the global effort that aims to reduce deaths and illnesses among women and infants, especially in developing countries, at the Safe Motherhood Initiative:

www.safemotherhood.org

For comparative health-care data from a variety of countries, see the International Program in Health Policy section of the Commonwealth Fund Web site:

www.cmwf.org

The article by Gail Fawcett entitled "Canada's Untapped Workplace Resource: People with Disabilities" deals with the issue of barriers to employment faced by disabled persons; to see it, go to:

www.ccsd.ca/perception/per_214a.htm

The Council of Canadians with Disabilities advocates for the right of Canadians with disabilities to be centrally involved in the decision-making processes that affect their lives, and for the removal of barriers to their full participation in matters affecting their lives. The organization has a Web site at:

www.pcs.mb.ca/~ccd

For information about health care in Canada, visit the Canadian Institute for Health Information Web site at:

www.cihi.ca

Questions for Critical Thinking

1. How do you think governments should balance their needs for financial savings and the public need for quality health care? Should everyone receive unlimited health services regardless of cost, or should priorities be set based on provincial and federal budgets?
2. What is the best way for society to control diseases like lung cancer and HIV/AIDS that can be controlled by changing people's behaviour?
3. What is the role of alternative therapies in health care? Have you or your friends and relatives made use of alternative treatments?
4. In your view, what constitutes a disability? Do you think disabled persons can participate more fully in society?

Suggested Readings

Terry Albert and Gregory Williams. *The Economic Burden of HIV/AIDS in Canada*. Ottawa: Canadian Policy Research Networks, 1998.

Gary L. Albrecht. *The Disability Business: Rehabilitation in America*. Newbury Park: Sage, 1992.

Pat Armstrong and Hugh Armstrong. *Wasting Away: The Undermining of the Canadian Health Care System*. Toronto: Oxford University Press, 1996.

Juanne Nancarrow Clarke. *Health, Illness and Medicine in Canada*. Toronto: McClelland and Stewart, 1990.

James B. Waldram, D. Ann Herring, and T. Kue Young. *Aboriginal Health in Canada: Historical, Cultural, and Epidemiological Perspectives*. Toronto: University of Toronto Press, 1995.

Rose Weitz. *The Sociology of Health, Illness, and Health Care: A Critical Approach*. Belmont: Wadsworth, 1995.

World Health Organization. *Fifty Facts from the World Health Report 1998*. Available: **www.who.int/whr/1998/factse.htm**

INFOTRAC® COLLEGE EDITION

Either from the *Sociology In Our Times: The Essentials* Web site (**www.sociologyessentials-2nded.nelson.com**) or directly from your Web browser, you may access InfoTrac® College Edition, an online university library that includes over 600 popular and scholarly journals in which you can find articles related to the topics in this chapter.

CHAPTER 12

From early experiences with colonial masters in Britain and France to its current relationship with the United States, Canada has always lived in the political and economic shadow of stronger countries. Our country's political and economic status has affected our internal development and our social structure, and has led to a concern over our national identity. This concern was the basis for some very passionate opposition to the Canada-U.S. Free Trade Agreement:

"Canada is not a commodity to be bargained away to the highest bidder in the marketplace. This is essentially why I object to the agreement before us.... This is my country. This is your country. It is all we have. I give no one the right to sell it. I give no one the responsibility to weaken it.... [Canadians] cleared the land, conquered the wilderness, filled the space, harnessed the rivers, and built our cities, our villages, and our community life. In the process we became a distinct people with our own ways of looking at and doing things, with a cultural identity that speaks of us, and with a profound sense of belonging to the land and to the planet Earth. I want this to continue.... Our people have always known in their hearts that there was a price to be paid to be Canadian. Often the lure of the south has been powerful. It would be so much easier to give in; but we would lose ourselves in the shuffle. We have always felt that and that is why we have resisted the continental pull. We must do it again." (Laurier LaPierre, 1987:242–43)

This fear of being absorbed by the United States is nothing new. Consider Pierre Berton's description of the way in which Sir John A. Macdonald, our first prime minister, promoted his vision of a national railway linking eastern and western Canada:

> See him now, on that memorable December day in 1880. He is old and tired, his face veined from too much gin and too much port, but pale now from a crippling stomach ailment that makes it all but impossible for him to stand. Yet stand he does for more than three hours, delivering the finest speech of his career, hammering home the adverbs as he cries out that the railway will be built, 'vigorously, continuously, systematically and successfully!' It will be an all-Canadian line "which will give us a great and united, rich and improving, developing

POLITICS AND THE ECONOMY

> Canada, instead of making us tributary to American bondage, to American tolls, to American freights, to all the little tricks and big tricks that the American railways are addicted to for the purpose of destroying our road." This is vintage Macdonald, the bold rhetoric that turned him into a Canadian icon. (Berton, 1987:25)

Both free trade and the development of the railroad show the close linkage between these economic and political factors. Both LaPierre and Macdonald were very concerned that closer economic ties with the United States would lead to a loss of political sovereignty.

Politics and the economy are so intertwined that many social scientists speak of the two as a single entity, the *political economy*. Sociologists have studied Canadian society using the political economy framework, which "investigates the relationship between economy and politics as they affect the social and cultural life of societies" (Clement and Williams, 1989:6).

Wallace Clement and Daniel Drache have outlined some of the issues that Canadian sociologists and economists have addressed using the political economy perspective:

1. The implications of external relations for internal development, especially early colonial ties with France and the United Kingdom and the current dependence on the United States in many economic, political, and military activities.
2. The origin of Canadian capitalism in a staple economy, its movement into commercial and financial specialization and its continued reliance on resource extraction.
3. The dependence on external markets, both as outlets for raw materials (making Canada vulnerable to world conditions) and as capital sources (which ultimately act as a drain on investment capital).
4. The effect of technology and the ownership of that technology, especially patent rights, in shaping the economy and labour force.
5. The continued survival of two nations within a single state—the conquered French and the conquering English—and the demise of the native people, along with the reactions of these repressed minorities (1978: iv–v).

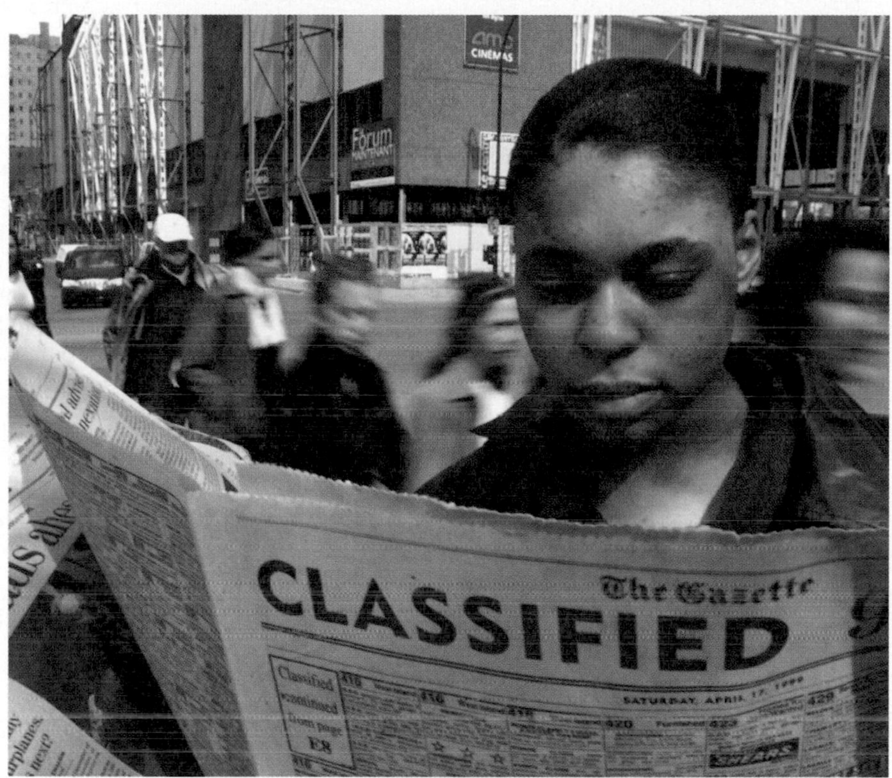

Each of these issues highlights the interdependence of economic and political factors. The way in which a society is organized to produce goods and services and the political structure of that society have an impact on all of our social institutions. In this chapter, you will learn about different ways of governing including monarchies, authoritarian and totalitarian governments, and democracies as well as different types of economic structures including capitalist, socialist, and mixed economies. Before reading on, test your knowledge about economic and political life in Canada by taking the quiz in Box 12.1.

QUESTIONS AND ISSUES

CHAPTER FOCUS QUESTION: What effect does the linkage of politics and the economy have on Canadian society?

What is the relationship between power and authority? Why do people accept authority?

What are the major political systems in the world?

Whose interests are reflected in political decisions?

How is work in Canada affected by changes in the economy?

What are the key assumptions of capitalism and socialism? How do these economic systems affect our political and social lives?

How will the nature of work change in the future?

POLITICS, POWER, AND AUTHORITY

According to political analyst Michael Parenti (1998:7–8), many people underrate the significance of politics in daily life:

> Politics is something more than what politicians do when they run for office. Politics is concerned with the struggles that shape social relations within societies and affairs between nations. The taxes and prices we pay and the jobs available to us, the chances that we will live in peace or perish in war, the costs of education and the availability of scholarships, the safety of the airliner or highway we travel on, the quality of the food we eat and the air we breathe, the availability of affordable housing and medical care, the legal protections against racial and sexual discrimination—all the things that directly affect the quality of our lives are influenced in some measure by politics ... To say you are not interested in politics, then, is like saying you are not interested in your own well-being. (Michael Parenti, 1994:7–8)

***Politics* is the social institution through which power is acquired and exercised by some people and groups.** In contemporary societies, the government is the primary political system. ***Government* is the formal organization that has the legal and political authority to regulate the relationships among members of a society and between the society and those outside its borders.** Some social scientists refer to government as the ***state*—the political entity that possesses a legitimate monopoly over the use of force within its territory to achieve its goals.**

***Power* is the ability of persons or groups to carry out their will even when opposed by others** (Weber, 1968/1922). Through the use of persuasion, authority, or force, some people are able to get others to acquiesce to their demands. Consequently, power is a *social relationship* that involves both leaders and followers. Power also is a dimension in the structure of social stratification. Persons in positions of power control valuable resources of society—including wealth, status, comfort, and safety—and are able to influence the actions of others by awarding or withholding those resources (Dye and Zeigler, 1993).

The most basic form of power is force or military might. Initially, force may be used to seize and hold power. Max Weber suggested, however, that force is not the most effective long-term means of gaining compliance, because those who are being ruled do not accept as legitimate those who are doing the ruling. Consequently, most leaders do not want to base their power on force alone; they seek to legitimize their power by turning it into authority.

***Authority* is power that people accept as legitimate rather than coercive.** People have a greater tendency to accept authority as legitimate if they are economically or politically dependent on those who hold power. They also may accept authority more readily if it reflects their own beliefs and values (Turner, Beeghley, and Powers, 1995). *Legitimation* refers to the process by which power is institutionalized and given a moral foundation to justify its existence. Weber outlined three *ideal types* of authority—charismatic, traditional, and rational-legal—each of which has a different basis of legitimacy and a different means of administration.

Charismatic Authority

According to Weber, ***charismatic authority* is power legitimized on the basis of a leader's exceptional personal qualities** or the demonstration of extraordinary insight and accomplishment, which inspire loyalty and obedience from followers. Charismatic leaders may be politicians, soldiers, and entertainers, among others (Shils, 1965; Bendix, 1971).

From Weber's perspective, a charismatic leader may be either a tyrant or a hero. Thus, charismatic authority has been attributed to such diverse historical figures as Jesus Christ, Napoleon, Julius Caesar, Adolf Hitler, Winston Churchill, and Martin Luther King, Jr. Among the most charismatic leaders in Canadian politics have been Pierre Trudeau and Lucien Bouchard. Bouchard's personal appeal almost led to a separatist victory in the 1995 referendum, which, under the distinctly uncharismatic Jacques Parizeau, looked to be heading for certain defeat.

Charismatic authority generally tends to be temporary and unstable; it derives primarily from individual leaders (who may change their minds, leave, or die) and from an administrative structure usually limited to a small number of faithful followers. For this reason, charismatic authority often becomes rou-

BOX 12.1 SOCIOLOGY AND EVERYDAY LIFE

How Much Do You Know About Canada's Political Economy?

TRUE	FALSE	
T	F	1. Canada's Aboriginal peoples have been able to vote in federal elections since 1867, the year of Confederation.
T	F	2. Governments tend to make their decisions based on a broadly representative sampling of the opinions of all citizens.
T	F	3. Under most proposals for Aboriginal self-government, Aboriginal groups in Canada would have total control over their territory and would be considered sovereign nations.
T	F	4. Many of the new jobs being created in the service sector pay poorly and offer little job security.
T	F	5. Women are more likely than men to hold part-time jobs.
T	F	6. It is possible for a person to start with no money and to build a personal fortune worth $100 billion in just over 20 years.
T	F	7. New office technology has made it possible for clerical workers to function with little or no supervision.
T	F	8. Unions were established in Canada with the full cooperation of industry and government, whose leaders recognized the need to protect the interests of workers.
T	F	9. Governments around the world are losing their ability to set national policy because of global market forces.

Answers on page 340.

Two solitudes: Quebec Premier Lucien Bouchard and Prime Minister Jean Chrétien are the two people responsible for Canada's future as a nation. Does the body language in this photo suggest that cooperation is likely?

BOX 12.1

Answers to the Sociology Quiz on Canada's Political Economy

1. **False.** Aboriginal people did not have voting rights in federal elections until 1960.
2. **False.** Special interest groups and various elites in society have far more influence on government policy than do average citizens.
3. **False.** Some Aboriginal groups, including some Quebec Mohawks, argue that they have the status of sovereign nations, but most Aboriginal people have a more limited view of self-government.
4. **True.** Many of the new jobs being created in the service sector, such as nurse's aide, child-care worker, hotel maid, and fast-food server, offer little job security and low pay.
5. **True.** Women account for nearly 70 percent of part-time workers.
6. **True.** Bill Gates, founder of Microsoft, dropped out of college and turned his idea for a computer operating system into a fortune that in 2000 was worth $100 billion.
7. **False.** Clerical workers still work under supervision; however, they may not even know when they are being observed because of new technology. For example, a supervisor may examine a clerk's work on a computer network without the employee knowing about it, and an airline reservationist's supervisor may listen in on selected conversations with customers.
8. **False.** The struggle to unionize in Canada was always difficult and often bloody. Governments often worked with employers to make union organizing difficult.
9. **True.** Trade agreements such as the North American Free Trade Agreement and the power of huge multinational corporations have reduced the sovereignty of national governments. The impact of globalization has been particularly acute in countries that lack the resources to provide a basic manufacturing infrastructure and a minimally trained labour force.

Sources: Based on Boldt, 1993; Dyck, 1996; Garson, 1989; Zuboff, 1988; Hodson and Sullivan, 1990; Feagin and Feagin, 1996; and Rifkin, 1995.

tinized. The ***routinization of charisma*** **occurs when charismatic authority is succeeded by a bureaucracy controlled by a rationally established authority or by a combination of traditional and bureaucratic authority** (Turner, Beeghley, and Powers, 1995). According to Weber (1968/1922:1148), "It is the fate of charisma to recede … after it has entered the permanent structures of social action." However, charisma cannot always be successfully transferred to organizations. Many organizations, particularly religious ones, fail when the leader departs.

Traditional Authority

In contrast to charismatic authority, ***traditional authority*** **is power that is legitimized by respect for long-standing custom.** In preindustrial societies, the authority of traditional leaders, such as kings, queens, pharaohs, emperors, and religious dignitaries, usually is grounded in religious beliefs and established practices. For example, British kings and queens historically have claimed that their authority came from God. Members of subordinate classes obey a traditional leader's edicts out of economic and political dependency and sometimes personal loyalty. However, custom and religious beliefs are sufficient to maintain traditional authority for extended periods of time only as long as people share similar backgrounds and accept this type of authority as legitimate.

As societies industrialize, traditional authority is challenged by a more complex division of labour and by the wider diversity of people who now inhabit the area as a result of migration. In industrialized societies, people do not share the same viewpoint on many issues and tend to openly question traditional authority. As the division of labour becomes more complex, political and economic institutions become increasingly interdependent (Durkheim, 1933/1893).

Weber predicted that traditional authority would inhibit the development of capitalism. He stressed that capitalism cannot fully develop when rules are not logically established, when officials follow rules

CONCEPT TABLE 12.A

WEBER'S THREE TYPES OF AUTHORITY

Max Weber's three types of authority are shown here in global perspective. Charismatic authority is exemplified by former prime minister Indira Gandhi of India. Sultan Ali Mirah, leader of Ethiopia's Afar Liberation Front, is an example of traditional authority sanctioned by custom. Australian Supreme Court justices (shown here at the opening of Parliament in Perth, Australia) represent rational-legal authority, which depends on established rules and procedures.

	Description	Examples	
Charismatic	Based on leaders' personal qualities Temporary and unstable	Napoleon Adolf Hitler Indira Gandhi	
Traditional	Legitimized by long-standing custom Subject to erosion as traditions weaken	Patrimony (authority resides in traditional leader supported by larger social structures, as in old British monarchy) Patriarchy (rule by men occupying traditional positions of authority, as in the family)	
Rational-legal	Legitimized by rationally established rules and procedures Authority resides in the office, not the person	Modern British Parliament Canadian prime minister, Parliament, federal bureaucracy	

arbitrarily, and when leaders are not technically trained (Weber, 1968/1922; Turner, Beeghley, and Powers, 1995). Weber believed that capitalism worked best in systems of rational-legal authority.

Rational-Legal Authority

According to Weber, ***rational-legal authority*** is **power legitimized by law or by written rules and**

regulations. Rational-legal authority is also called *bureaucratic authority*. As you will recall from Chapter 5, bureaucracies are characterized by a clear-cut division of labour, hierarchy of authority, formal rules, impersonal enforcement of rules, and job security based on a person's technical qualifications. In rational-legal authority, power is legitimized by procedures; if leaders obtain their positions in a procedurally correct manner (such as by election or appointment), they have the right to act.

Canada's political system gives rational-legal authority to the office of the prime minister, for example, by specifying the procedures by which persons hold the office as well as its duties and limitations. Rational-legal authority also is held by other elected or appointed government officials and by officers in a formal organization. However, authority is invested in the *office*, not in the *person* who holds the office. For example, when the Conservatives lost the 1993 federal election, Kim Campbell passed on the power of the office of prime minister to Jean Chrétien and no longer had any involvement in government.

In a rational-legal system, bureaucracy is the apparatus responsible for creating and enforcing rules in the public interest. Weber believed that rational-legal authority was the only means to attain "efficient, flexible, and competent regulation under a rule of law" (Turner, Beeghley, and Powers, 1995:218). Weber's three types of authority are summarized in Concept Table 12.A.

GLOBAL POLITICAL SYSTEMS

Political systems as we know them today have evolved slowly. In the earliest societies, politics was not an entity separate from other aspects of life. As we will see, however, all groups have some means of legitimizing power.

Hunting and gathering societies do not have political institutions as such because they have very little division of labour or social inequality. Leadership and authority are centred in the family and clan. Individuals acquire leadership roles due to personal attributes such as great physical strength, exceptional skills, or charisma (Lenski, Lenski, and Nolan, 1991).

Political institutions first emerged in agrarian societies as they acquired surpluses and developed greater social inequality. Elites took control of politics and used custom or traditional authority to justify their position. When cities developed circa 3500–3000 B.C.E., the *city-state*—a city whose power extended to adjacent areas—became the centre of political power.

Nation-states, as we know them, began to develop in Spain, France, and England between the twelfth and fifteenth centuries (see Tilly, 1975). A *nation-state* is a unit of political organization that has recognizable national boundaries and whose citizens possess specific legal rights and obligations. Nation-states emerge as countries develop specific geographic territories and acquire greater ability to defend their borders. Improvements in communication and transportation make it possible for people in a larger geographic area to share a common language and culture. As charismatic and traditional authority are superseded by rational-legal authority, legal standards come to prevail in all areas of life, and the nation-state claims a monopoly over the legitimate use of force (P. Kennedy, 1993).

Approximately 190 nation-states currently exist throughout the world. Four main types of political systems are found in them: monarchies, authoritarian systems, totalitarian systems, and democracies.

Monarchies

A ***monarchy* is a political system in which power resides in one person or family and is passed from generation to generation through lines of inheritance.** Monarchies are most common in agrarian societies and are associated with traditional authority patterns. However, the relative power of monarchs has varied across nations, depending on religious, political, and economic conditions. *Absolute monarchs* claim a hereditary right to rule (based on membership in a noble family) or a divine right to rule (in other words, a God-given right to rule that legitimizes the exercise of power). In *limited monarchies*, rulers depend on powerful members of the nobility to retain their thrones. Unlike absolute monarchs, limited monarchs are not considered to be above the law. In *constitutional monarchies*, the royalty serve as symbolic rulers or heads of state while actual authority is held by elected officials in the national parliaments. In such present-day monarchies as the United Kingdom,

President Saddam Hussein's totalitarian government retains an iron grip on the people of Iraq.

Sweden, Japan, and the Netherlands, members of royal families primarily perform ceremonial functions.

Authoritarian Systems

An ***authoritarian political system* is one controlled by rulers who deny popular participation in government.** A few authoritarian regimes have been absolute monarchies in which rulers claimed a hereditary right to their position. Today, Saudi Arabia and Kuwait are examples of authoritarian absolute monarchies. *Dictatorships*, in which power is gained and held by a single individual, also are authoritarian in nature. Pure dictatorships are rare: all rulers need the support of the military and the backing of business elites to maintain their position. *Military juntas* result when military officers seize power from the government, as has happened in recent years in Nigeria, Chile, and Haiti.

Totalitarian Systems

A ***totalitarian political system* is one in which the state seeks to regulate all aspects of people's public and private lives.** Such systems rely on modern technology to monitor and control people; mass propaganda and electronic surveillance are widely used to influence people's thinking and control their actions. One example of a totalitarian regime was that of the National Socialist (Nazi) party in Germany during World War II, where military leaders sought to control all aspects of national life, not just government operations. Other examples include the former Soviet Union and contemporary Iraq under Saddam Hussein's regime.

To keep people from rebelling, totalitarian governments enforce conformity: people are denied the right to assemble for political purposes; access to information is strictly controlled; and secret police enforce compliance, creating an environment of constant fear and suspicion.

Democracies

A ***democracy* is a political system in which the people hold the ruling power either directly or through elected representatives.** In an ideal-type democracy, people would actively and directly rule themselves. *Direct participatory democracy* requires that citizens be able to meet regularly to debate and decide the issues of the day. Historical examples of direct democracy might include ancient Athens or a town meeting in colonial New England. However, the extent to which such meetings actually reflected the wishes of most people has been the subject of scholarly debate. Moreover, the impracticality of involving an entire citizenry in direct decision making becomes evident in nations containing millions of adults.

In most democratic countries, including Canada, people have a voice in the government through *representative democracy*, whereby citizens elect representatives to serve as bridges between themselves and the government. In a representative democracy, elected representatives are supposed to convey the concerns and interests of those they represent, and the government is expected to be responsive to the wishes of the people. Elected officials are held accountable to the people through elections.

However, representative democracy is not always equally accessible to all people in a nation. Throughout Canada's history, for example, members of subordinate groups have been denied full participation in the democratic process. Aboriginals, women, Asians, and South and East Asians have in the past been prohibited from voting. Today, the Charter of Rights and Freedoms guarantees that all Canadians have the right to democratic participation.

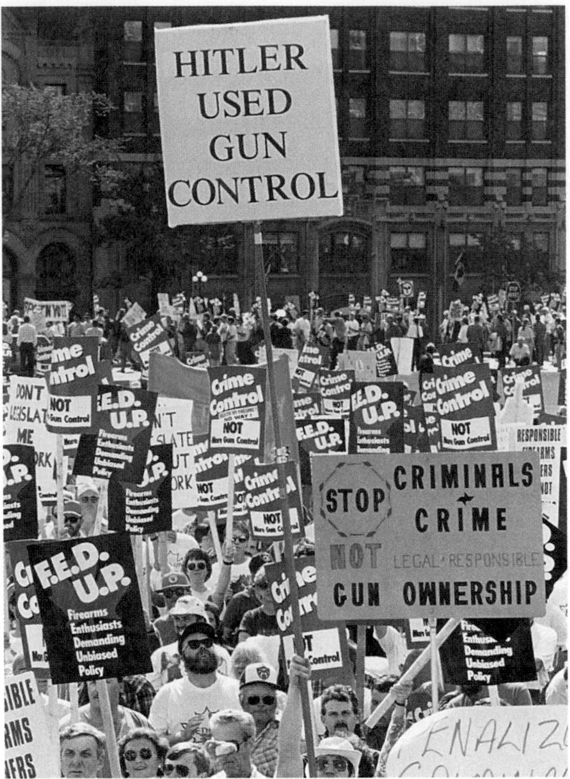

In addition to direct contact with legislators, special interest groups like the "gun lobbiests" try to influence policy making by mobilizing constituents and stirring up public opinion. Recent years have seen a proliferation of single-issue groups like those on both sides of the gun control issue. The strong feelings of gun owners are shown in this Ottawa rally.

PERSPECTIVES ON POWER AND POLITICAL SYSTEMS

Is political power in Canada concentrated in the hands of the few or distributed among the many? Sociologists and political scientists have suggested many different answers to this question; however, two prevalent models of power have emerged: pluralist and elite.

Functionalist Perspectives: The Pluralist Model

The pluralist model is rooted in a functionalist perspective, which assumes that people share a consensus on central concerns, such as freedom and protection from harm, and that the government serves important functions in society that no other institution can fulfil. According to Emile Durkheim (1933/1893), the purpose of government is to socialize people to become good citizens, to regulate the economy so that it operates effectively, and to provide the necessary services for citizens. Contemporary functionalists state the four main functions of government as follows: (1) maintaining law and order, (2) planning and directing society, (3) meeting social needs, and (4) handling international relations, including warfare.

If government at national, provincial, and local levels is responsible for these functions, what role do people play in the political system? What keeps the government from becoming all-powerful? What happens when people do not agree on specific issues or concerns? Functionalists suggest that divergent viewpoints lead to a system of political pluralism in which the government functions as an arbiter between competing interests and viewpoints. According to the ***pluralist model,*** **power in political systems is widely dispersed throughout many competing interest groups** (Dahl, 1961). Many of these are ***special interest groups*****—political coalitions made up of individuals or groups that share a specific interest they wish to protect or advance with the help of the political system** (Greenberg and Page, 1993). Examples of special interest groups are the Business Council on National Issues, the Canadian Labour Congress, the National Action Committee on the Status of Women, and the Assembly of First Nations.

From a pluralist perspective, representative democracy (coupled with the checks and balances provided by our legal system, and the division of governmental powers between a central government and smaller units such as provinces and municipalities) ensures that no one group can overpower the others and that individual rights are protected.

Conflict Perspectives: Elite Models

Although conflict theorists acknowledge that the government serves a number of important purposes

FIGURE 12.1 Pluralist and Elite Models

PLURALIST MODEL

- Decisions are made on behalf of the people by leaders who engage in bargaining, accommodation, and compromise.
- Competition among leadership groups makes abuse of power by any one group difficult.
- Power is widely dispersed and people can influence public policy by voting.
- Public policy reflects a balance among competing interest groups.

ELITE MODEL

- Decisions are made by a small group of elite people.
- Consensus exists among the elite on the basic values and goals of society.
- Power is highly concentrated at the top of a pyramid-shaped social hierarchy.
- Public policy reflects the values and preferences of the elite.

in society, they assert that government exists for the benefit of wealthy or politically powerful elites who use the government to impose their will on the masses. According to the ***elite model,* power in political systems is concentrated in the hands of a small group of elites and the masses are relatively powerless.** The pluralist and elite models are compared in Figure 12.1.

Early Italian sociologists Vilfredo Pareto (1848–1923) and Gaetano Mosca (1858–1941) were among the first to show that concentration of power may be inevitable within societies. Pareto first used the term *elite* to refer to "the few who rule the many" (G. Marshall, 1994). Similarly, Karl Marx claimed that under capitalism, the government serves the interests of the ruling (or capitalist) class that controls the means of production.

From this perspective, a few of the "best and brightest" among the masses may rise to elite positions by acquiring the requisite education, experience, leadership skills, and other attributes of the elite (Dye and Zeigler, 1993). However, those who do not share the attitudes, political philosophy, gender, or race of the elites will not succeed in this way.

C. WRIGHT MILLS AND THE POWER ELITE Sociologist C. Wright Mills (1959) examined the power structure of the United States and concluded that a power elite occupied the upper echelon of the power pyramid. The ***power elite* is composed of leaders at the top of business, the executive branch of the federal government, and the military.** Of these three, Mills speculated that the "corporate rich" (the highest-paid officers of the biggest corporations) were the most powerful because of their unique ability to parlay the vast economic resources at their disposal into political power. At the middle level of the pyramid, Mills placed the legislative branch of government, special interest groups, and local opinion leaders. The bottom (and widest layer) of the pyramid is occupied by the unorganized masses who are relatively powerless and vulnerable to economic and political exploitation.

Mills emphasized that individuals who make up the power elite have similar class backgrounds and interests; many of them also interact on a regular basis. Members of the power elite are able to influence many important decisions.

G. William Domhoff and the Ruling Class According to sociologist G. William Domhoff (1978), the *ruling class* is made up of the corporate rich, who make up less than 1 percent of the population. Domhoff uses the term *ruling class* to signify a relatively fixed group of privileged people who wield sufficient power to constrain political processes and serve underlying capitalist interests.

Like Mills, Domhoff asserted that individuals in the upper echelon are members of a business class that owns and controls large corporations. The intertwining of the upper class and the corporate community produces economic and social cohesion. Members of the ruling class also are socially and economically linked with one another. They attend the same schools, belong to the same clubs, frequently socialize together and belong to the same corporate boards. Consider the example of Paul Demarais and Power Corporation. Desmarais, who controls this company, is also a close friend of former prime ministers Pierre Trudeau and Brian Mulroney, and of Prime Minister Jean Chrétien—in fact, Desmarais's son is married to Chrétien's daughter. A wide variety of senior politicians and government bureaucrats move back and forth between senior Power Corporation positions and government service. With these contacts, Desmarais certainly has no difficulty in having his views heard by those responsible for Canada's governmental policy.

According to Domhoff (1983), the corporate rich influence the political process in three ways. First, they affect the candidate selection process by helping to finance campaigns and providing favours to political candidates. Second, through participation in the special interest process, the corporate rich are able to obtain favours, tax breaks, and favourable regulatory rulings. Finally, the corporate rich in Canada may gain access to the policy-making process through their appointments to governmental bodies such as the Senate.

POLITICS AND GOVERNMENT IN CANADA

The Canadian political process consists of formal elements, such as the duties of the prime minister and the legislative process, and informal elements, such as the role of political parties in the election process. We now turn to an examination of these informal elements, including political parties, political socialization, and political attitudes.

Political Parties

A *political party* is an organization whose purpose is to gain and hold legitimate control of government; it usually is composed of people with similar attitudes, interests, and socioeconomic status. A political party (1) develops and articulates policy positions, (2) educates voters about issues and simplifies the choices for them, and (3) recruits candidates who agree with those policies, helps those candidates win office, and holds the candidates responsible for implementing the party's policy positions.

Ideal Type Versus Reality Ideally, political parties will offer clear alternatives to the electorate—alternatives that reflect the aspirations, concerns, and viewpoints of the population. For two reasons, this is usually not the case. First, major political parties rarely offer voters clear policy alternatives. Most voters view themselves as being close to the centre of the political spectrum (extremely liberal being the far left of that spectrum and extremely conservative being the far right). Although the definitions of liberal and conservative vary over time, *liberals* tend to focus on equality of opportunity and the need for government regulation and social safety nets. By contrast, *conservatives* are more likely to emphasize economic liberty and freedom from government interference (Greenberg and Page, 1993). However, because most voters con-

When people move from one country to another, they learn new political attitudes, values, and behaviour. This citizenship ceremony was held in Quebec City during National Citizenship Week. What role do you think these new Canadians will play in Quebec politics?

sider themselves moderates, neither the Progressive Conservatives nor the Liberals (the two parties that have governed Canada since Confederation) moved very far from the middle. Parties like the NDP and the Canadian Alliance, which choose to maintain some ideological purity, run the risk of being marginalized and are very unlikely to win a national election. While these parties have not won electoral power, they have been successful in having their ideas implemented. During the 1960s and 1970s, many of the social policies advocated by the NDP were implemented by Liberal and Progressive Conservative governments. During the 1990s the Reform Party (the predecessor of the Canadian Alliance) was much more successful in having its deficit-cutting agenda implemented by federal and provincial governments than it was in convincing Canadians it should be given the power to run the country.

The second reason the major political parties rarely offer clear alternatives that reflect the viewpoints of the population is that they, like most political parties, are dominated by active elites who are not representative of the general population. Many represent special interests and tend to come from the upper echelons of society. Thus the poor, women, and racial minorities have not been included in drafting party policy or in selecting party leaders. Many people involved in politics today tend to work outside the traditional party structure, often in single-issue interest groups. Organizations like the National Action Committee for the Status of Women, Greenpeace, and various Aboriginal groups have been very effective in advancing their agendas and in getting grassroots involvement without attaching themselves to a particular political party.

Politics and the People

Why do some people vote while others do not? How do people come to think of themselves as being conservative, moderate, or liberal? Key factors include individuals' political socialization, attitudes, and participation.

POLITICAL SOCIALIZATION ***Political socialization*** **is the process by which people learn political attitudes, values, and behaviour.** For young children, the family is the primary agent of political socialization, and children tend to learn and hold many of the same opinions as their parents. By the time children reach school age, they typically identify with the political party (if any) of their parents (Burnham, 1983). As they grow older, other agents of socialization, including peers, teachers, and the media, begin to affect children's political beliefs. Over time, these other agents may cause people's political attitudes and values to change, and they may cease to identify with the political party of their parents. Even for adults, political socialization continues through the media, friends, neighbours, and colleagues in the workplace.

The swearing in of the new cabinet after the 1997 election. In our system of parliamentary democracy, power rests in the hands of the prime minister and the cabinet. Individual members of Parliament have little influence on government policy.

Political Attitudes In addition to the socialization process, people's socioeconomic status affects their political attitudes, values, beliefs, and behaviour. For example, individuals who are very poor or who are unable to find employment tend to believe that society has failed them, and therefore they also tend to be indifferent toward the political system (Zipp, 1985; Pinderhughes, 1986). Believing that casting a ballot would make no difference to their own circumstances, they are unlikely to vote.

In general, voters tend to select candidates and political parties based on social and economic issues they consider important to their lives. *Social issues* are those relating to moral judgments or civil rights, ranging from abortion rights to equal rights for homosexuals.

Economic issues fall into two broad categories: (1) the amount that should be spent on government programs, and (2) the extent to which these programs should encourage a redistribution of income and assets. Those holding liberal political views believe that without government intervention, income and assets would become concentrated in the hands of even fewer people and that the government must act to redistribute wealth, thus ensuring that everyone gets a "fair slice" of the economic "pie." In order to accomplish this, they envision that larger sums of money must be raised and spent by the government on such programs. Conservatives contend that such programs are not only unnecessary but also counterproductive. That is, programs financed by tax increases decrease people's incentive to work and to be innovative, and make people dependent upon the government.

Social class is correlated with political attitudes. People in the upper classes tend to be more conservative on economic issues and more liberal on social issues. Upper-class conservatives generally favour equality of opportunity but do not want their own income and assets taxed heavily to abolish poverty or societal problems that they believe some people bring upon themselves. Most of Canada's social programs faced opposition from corporate and upper-class interests, and some of these groups led the call for cuts to these programs in the 1990s. By contrast, people in the lower classes tend to be conservative on social issues, such as capital punishment or abortion rights, but liberal on economic issues, such as increasing the minimum wage and expanding social programs.

Despite these tendencies, there is probably less of a connection between voting behaviour and social class in Canada than in many other industrialized countries. The Liberal Party has typically attracted voters from all classes, while the NDP gets a high proportion of its support from skilled and unskilled labour. Even so, more voters from the skilled and unskilled labour classes vote for parties other than the NDP. Canadian voters, moreover, tend to be fickle at the polls and frequently switch parties. For example, looking at the results of the 1988 and 1993 federal elections, one sees that more voters switched parties in 1993 than voted for the one they had chosen in 1988 (Pammett, 1993). This is the reason the Progressive Conservatives, who had won the majority of the seats in the 1988 election, kept only two of them after the 1993 election.

MAJOR POLITICAL ISSUES IN CANADA: QUEBEC SEPARATISM AND ABORIGINAL SELF-GOVERNMENT

The Quiet Revolution and Quebec Nationalism

Because of our former colonial status and the dissatisfaction of many Quebec nationalists with the current political structure, constitutional matters have been much more prominent in Canada than in most other countries. The following review of events from the early 1960s onwards provides a background for the very close results of the 1995 referendum on separation. They are events that even after the referendum continue to play a major role in the political, economic, and social life of Canada.

The constitutional crises of recent years were set in motion by the Quiet Revolution, which began in Quebec in the 1960s. The term of Premier Jean Lesage (1960–1966) saw a dramatic change. Prior to 1960, Quebec had been a very traditional society. The Catholic Church and the family were at the core of French-Canadian society, and economic power was in the hands of English Canadians. In a very short time Quebec underwent a dramatic transformation into a secular, urban society with a modern educational system, public health and welfare programs, and a provincially controlled electric power system. A new sense of nationalism was used as a core ideology to justify the expanded role of the state. This nationalism was clearly expressed in the 1962 Liberal campaign slogan *maîtres chez nous* ("masters in our own house"). Economic and social reform would strengthen French culture. The state would replace the church at the heart of Quebec society. To pursue its agenda of renewal, the Quebec government began demanding, and receiving, more control over matters traditionally managed by the federal government.

As Quebec became more like the rest of North America in most other respects, language came to be its major distinguishing feature, assuming both a real and a symbolic role in the province's political future. English was the language of business in the province, and French-Canadian owners and managers were rare. In a series of legislative steps beginning in the 1960s, the provincial government moved to ensure that French became the language of business.

By any measure, the Quiet Revolution has been a success. A large body of legislation now protects the French language in Quebec. Regulations requiring immigrant children to attend French-language schools and restrictions on the use of English on commercial signs have reinforced the dominant role of the French language in Quebec. Quebeckers have gained control over their province's economy and over its other major social institutions including culture, politics, and government.

While the transformation of Quebec was remarkably rapid, it was not rapid enough for some. Nationalist groups, which began to emerge in the 1960s, saw independence as the only means by which Quebec could fulfil its destiny. At the same time, another vision was offered by Quebeckers like Pierre Trudeau who felt that Quebec's aspirations could best be fulfilled within Canada. For Trudeau, cultural survival did not depend on political sovereignty; a strong federal government, which actively promoted bilingualism, was the best guarantee that French would survive in a predominantly English North America. As prime minister, Trudeau brought in the Official Languages Act in 1969, which made the federal public service bilingual. This provided opportunities for francophones and helped to ensure that Canadians in all parts of the country could receive services in either language. The government also began to encourage French immersion programs in schools in English Canada.

These changes met with vociferous resistance from some English Canadians. Consider matters from

Aboriginal leaders have played a prominent role in Canadian politics during the past decade. As questions of self-government, Aboriginal rights, and land claims have been considered, two of the most important leaders have been Phil Fontaine, former grand chief of the Assembly of First Nations, and Elijah Harper, a former member of the Manitoba legislature and of the federal parliament.

the perspective of those opposed to bilingualism. As Quebec was becoming more autonomous and less bilingual, the need for bilingualism was being promoted throughout the rest of the country (Dyck, 1996). Unilingual anglophone civil servants had to learn French if they wished to be promoted and bilingualism was clearly a major part of the federal political agenda. Many felt that Quebec was blackmailing the federal government at the expense of the other provinces. With extreme Quebec nationalists on one side and those in the rest of Canada who were tired of "having French forced down their throats" on the other, the stage was set for the decades of constitutional debate that continues today.

Aboriginal Self-Government

Canada's constitutional debate has focused on the role of our "two founding peoples"—the English and the French. Aboriginal peoples have strongly objected to this view of Canadian history. Anthropologist Olive Dickason, a Métis, has pointed out that when the Europeans first came to North America, fifty-five Aboriginal First Nations were on the continent. Each of these nations had its own government, territory, culture, and language. Aboriginal objections to the notion of two founding peoples also focus on the issue of which groups will have political power in the future. Quebec claims a special status that entitles it to certain powers to govern its own people, and also certain rights within the federation such as having three Quebec members of the Supreme Court. Aboriginal peoples also claim a unique status based on their position as Canada's First Nations and have, because of that position, pursued their right to self-government.

While the issue of self-government is extremely complex, some background will help in understanding the broad issues involved. In 1763, the British government issued a royal proclamation that formed the basis for the negotiation of treaties with Aboriginal groups. Without a background in European law, Aboriginal peoples did not realize that title to the land had passed to the Crown. They were, however, still entitled to the use and benefit of that land through their "Aboriginal title" (Boldt, 1993). Following Confederation, Aboriginal peoples came under the control of the government. The mechanism for this control, the Indian Act, was passed in 1876 and gave government bureaucrats almost total control over Native peoples. The Act even went so far as to define a "person" as "an individual other than an Indian" (Hamilton and Sinclair, 1991).

The consequences of the Indian Act were profound. For example, Aboriginal children were forced to attend residential schools (which meant that generations of children were not raised with their families); traditional religious practices were restricted; Aboriginal people did not fully control their own land and could not sell agricultural products off the reserve; and the government imposed a "pass system," which restricted the right of Aboriginal peoples to travel off their reserves. Aboriginal peoples did not have full voting rights in federal elections until 1960. As sociologist Menno Boldt has observed, contemporary "Indian powerlessness has its roots in Canada's Indian policies" (1993:xvii).

In the 1960s, the federal government began to review its policies concerning Aboriginal peoples. A White Paper, tabled in 1969, proposed assimilation of Aboriginal peoples. Treaties were to be dropped, reserves were to become like neighbouring non-Aboriginal communities, and Aboriginal rights and Aboriginal land titles were to be discarded. The "Aboriginal problem" would disappear, it was thought, if Aboriginal people became, in Pierre Trudeau's words, "Canadians as all other Canadians" (Boldt, 1993). Reaction to this paper marked a watershed in Aboriginal politics. A national campaign, which ultimately forced the government to drop its proposals, became a countrywide movement and led to the formation of several pan-Indian organizations, including the Assembly of First Nations (Hamilton and Sinclair, 1991). Rather than accepting the federal government's assimilationist model, Aboriginal leaders embraced nationalism. Self-government, Aboriginal rights, and land claims became the rallying points of the movement.

Aboriginal people feel their status as Canada's first people, who were never conquered and who signed voluntary treaties with the Crown, entitles them to the right of self-determination and to protection of their culture and customs. They believe these rights are not *granted* by the Canadian government, but are inherently theirs. On the other hand, the positions of the federal and the provincial governments have been that the right to self-determination could only be extended as powers delegated to Aboriginal people by government through legislation or constitutional change. Further, the powers that would be granted by government would extend only to powers now held by municipal governments rather than the much broader powers sought by Aboriginal peoples. It is difficult to predict where the current process of ending the colonial rule of Aboriginals will lead. One major change occurred in 1999, when Inuit took over government of the newly created Nunavut Territory, encompassing over 350,000 square kilometres of land in the Northern and Eastern Arctic. While the federal government accepted the inherent nature of Aboriginals' right to self-government in 1995 and is committed to dismantling the Department of Indian Affairs and Northern Development, the future form of that government is not at all clear—not even among Aboriginal people themselves. Also, many problems must be solved along the way, including decisions about how the growing number of urban Aboriginals will be included, the applicability of the Canadian Charter of Rights and Freedoms to Aboriginal communities, and sources of funding for this new order of government. The possible separation of Quebec also creates some interesting issues. While separatists argue strongly for their right to self-determination and for their recognition as a "people," they do not accept that Aboriginals in the resource-rich northern part of Quebec have the same right.

THE ECONOMY

The ***economy* is the social institution that ensures the maintenance of society through the production, distribution, and consumption of goods and services.** *Goods* are tangible objects that are necessary (such as food, clothing, and shelter) or desired (such as VCRs and electric toothbrushes). *Services* are intangible activities for which people are willing to pay (such as dry cleaning, a movie, or medical care). While some services are produced by human labour (the plumber who unstops your sink, for example), others primarily are produced by capital (such as communication services provided by a telephone company). *Labour* consists of the physical and intellectual services, including training, education, and individual abilities, that people contribute to the production process (Boyes and Melvin, 1994). *Capital* is wealth (money or property) owned or used in business by a person or corporation.

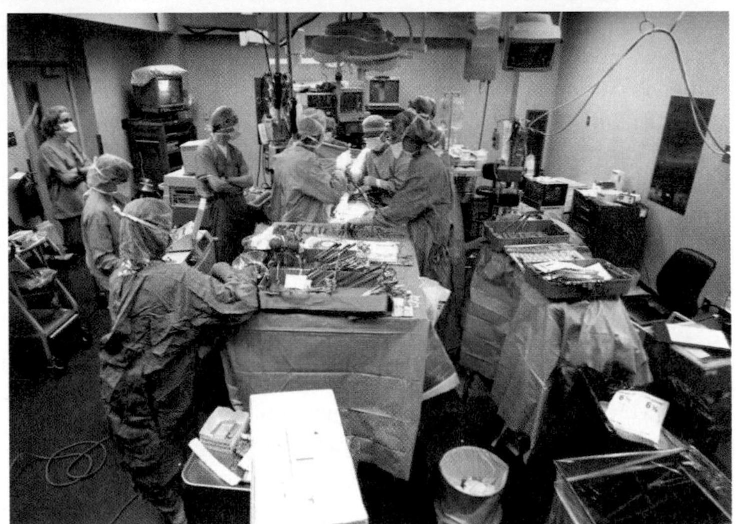

The nature of work is markedly different in the three main types of economies. In preindustrial economies, most workers are directly involved in extracting raw materials and natural resources from the environment. The development of a surplus leads to bartering and the use of money as a medium of exchange. In industrial economies, production and distribution of goods are much more complex and work tends to become specialized and repetitive. In postindustrial economies, workers increasingly are involved in providing services such as health care rather than in manufacturing goods.

Preindustrial, Industrial, and Postindustrial Economies

In all societies, the specific method of producing goods is related to the technoeconomic base of the society. In each society, people develop an economic system, ranging from simple to very complex, for the sake of survival.

Preindustrial Economies Hunting and gathering, horticultural and pastoral, and agrarian societies all have preindustrial economic structures (previously discussed in Chapter 7, "Social Stratification and Class"). Most workers engage in ***primary sector production*****—the extraction of raw materials and natural resources from the environment.** These materials and resources typically are consumed or used without much processing.

The *production* units in hunting and gathering societies are small; most goods are produced by family members. The division of labour is by age and gender. The potential for producing surplus goods increases as people learn to domesticate animals and grow their own food. In horticultural and pastoral societies, the economy becomes distinct from family life. The distribution process becomes more complex with the accumulation of a *surplus* that allows some people to engage in activities other than food production. In agrarian societies, production is related primarily to producing food. However, workers have a greater variety of specialized tasks, such as warlord or priest; for example, warriors are necessary to protect the surplus goods from plunder by outsiders (Hodson and Sullivan, 1990).

INDUSTRIAL ECONOMIES Industrialization brings sweeping changes to the system of production and distribution of goods and services. Drawing on new forms of energy (such as steam, gasoline, and electricity) and technology, factories become the primary means of producing goods. Wage labour is the dominant form of employment relationship; workers sell their labour to others rather than working for themselves or with other members of their family. In a capitalist system, this means that the product belongs to the factory owner and not to those whose labour creates that product.

Most workers engage in ***secondary sector production*****—the processing of raw materials (from the primary sector) into finished goods.** For example, steel workers process metal ore; auto workers then convert the ore into automobiles, trucks, and buses. In industrial economies, work becomes specialized and repetitive, activities become bureaucratically organized, and workers primarily work with machines instead of with one another. Mass production results in larger surpluses that benefit some people and organizations but not others.

POSTINDUSTRIAL ECONOMIES A ***postindustrial economy*** **is based on the provision of services rather than goods**—as the primary source of livelihood for workers and of profit for owners and corporate shareholders. The service sector includes a wide range of activities, such as fast-food service, transportation, communication, education, real estate, advertising, sports, and entertainment. In 1996, 74 percent of Canadian workers were employed in service industries compared with 20 percent in manufacturing and only 5 percent in primary industries (Krahn and Lowe, 1998).

A number of factors created the service economy. Mechanization and technological innovation have allowed fewer workers to produce far more in both the manufacturing and primary sectors. Robots have replaced assembly line workers, and tractors and factory ships have enabled farmers and fishers to produce more than their predecessors. The expansion of our economy and the increased leisure time available have increased the demand for a wide variety of services. Finally, much of the low-skilled production is now done offshore, where wages are much lower, leaving components such as design, sales, and marketing in North America, Europe, and Japan.

Highly skilled "knowledge workers" in the service economy have benefited from the postindustrial economy. However, these benefits have not been felt by those who do routine production work, such as manufacturing and data entry workers, and personal services providers, including restaurant workers and sales clerks. The positions filled by these service-sector workers form a second tier where labour is typically unskilled and poorly paid.

GLOBAL ECONOMIC SYSTEMS

Capitalism and socialism have been the principal economic models in industrialized countries over the past hundred years. Sociologists often use two criteria—property ownership and market control—to distinguish between types of economies. Keep in mind, however, that no society has a purely capitalist or socialist economy.

Capitalism

Capitalism **is an economic system characterized by private ownership of the means of production, from which personal profits can be derived through market competition and without government intervention.** Most of us think of ourselves as "owners" of private property because we own a car, a stereo, or other possessions. However, most of us are not capitalists; we *spend money* on the things we own, rather than *making money* from them. Capitalism is not simply the accumulation of wealth, but also the "use of wealth ... as a means for gathering more wealth" (Heilbroner, 1985:35). Relatively few people own the means of production and the rest of the workers in the private sector are paid to work for these "capitalists." "Ideal" capitalism has four distinctive features: (1) private ownership of the means of production, (2) pursuit of personal profit, (3) competition, and (4) lack of government intervention.

PRIVATE OWNERSHIP OF THE MEANS OF PRODUCTION Capitalist economies are based on the right of individuals to own income-producing property, such as land, water, mines, and factories and to "buy" people's labour.

The early Canadian economy was based on the sale of *staples*—goods associated with primary industries including lumber, wheat, and minerals. Economist Harold Innis (1984/1930) showed how the early Canadian economy was driven by the demands for raw materials by the colonial powers of France and Britain. This began early in Canada's history; in 1670 a British royal charter gave the privately held Hudson's Bay Company exclusive control over much of what is now western Canada, which was the source of the very lucrative fur trade.

In the early stages of industrial capitalism (1850–1890), virtually all of the capital for investment was individually owned, and a few individuals and families controlled all the major trade and financial organizations in Canada. Under early monopoly capitalism (1890–1940), most ownership rapidly shifted from individuals to huge ***corporations*—large-scale organizations that have legal powers, such as the ability to enter into contracts and buy and sell property, separate from their individual owners.** During this period, major industries came under the control of a few corporations owned by shareholders. For example, the automobile industry in North America came to be dominated by the "Big Three"—General Motors, Ford, and Chrysler. Industrial development in Canada lagged behind that of many other countries as business focused on exporting raw materials and importing finished products. Many of the industries that did establish themselves in Canada were branch plants of large American and British corporations whose profits flowed back to their home countries. Economist Kari Levitt (1970) was among the first to show that this foreign private investment posed a threat to Canadian sovereignty as fundamental economic decisions were made outside the country.

Today, ***multinational corporations*—large companies that are headquartered in one country and have subsidiaries or branches in other countries**—play a major role in the economies and governments of many nations. Multinational corporations also are referred to as *transnational corporations* because they sell and produce goods abroad. These corporations are not dependent on the labour, capital, or technology of any one country and may move their operations to countries where wages and taxes are lower and potential profits are higher.

PURSUIT OF PERSONAL PROFIT A tenet of capitalism is the belief that people are free to maximize their individual gain through personal profit; in the process, the entire society will benefit from their activities (Smith, 1976/1776). Economic development is assumed to benefit both capitalists and workers, and the general public also benefits from public expenditures (such as for roads, schools, and parks) made possible through an increase in business tax revenues.

During the period of industrial capitalism, however, specific individuals and families (not the general public) were the primary recipients of profits. For many generations, descendants of some of the early industrial capitalists have benefited from the economic deeds (and misdeeds) of their ancestors. For example, the Seagram company fortune (controlled by the Bronfman family) was based on the profits made from bootlegging during Prohibition. In early monopoly capitalism, some stockholders derived massive profits from companies that held near-monopolies on specific goods and services. In advanced (late) monopoly capitalism, profits have become even more concentrated as a few large corporations control more of the market through expansion and the acquisition of competitors. Ownership of these companies is more broadly held among Canadians through pension plans and mutual funds but these shareholders do not *control* the companies.

COMPETITION In theory, competition acts as a balance to excessive profits. When producers vie with one another for customers, they must be able to offer innovative goods and services at competitive prices. However, from the time of early industrial capitalism, the trend has been toward less, rather than more, competition among companies; profits are higher when there is less competition. For example, the highly profitable Microsoft Corp. so dominates certain areas of the computer software industry that it has virtually no competitors in those areas. In 2000, the U.S. government successfully prosecuted Microsoft for unlawfully trying to monopolize the Internet browser market.

How do large companies restrict competition? One way is by temporarily setting prices so low that weaker competitors are forced out of business. Ultramar, which owns 1400 gasoline stations in Quebec and Atlantic Canada, started a gasoline price war that saw gas prices in Quebec fall from 63 to 19.9 cents per litre in 1996. One Nova Scotia independent station owner complained that

Gasoline price wars benefit consumers. However, they may also be part of a strategy in which major companies put smaller competitors out of business.

Ultramar was charging him 50 cents a litre for wholesale gasoline, while it was retailing its own gasoline at a nearby station for 42.9 cents per litre. While this provides a temporary benefit to consumers, it reduces competition by forcing small retailers out of the market. The large companies recoup their losses when the competition has disappeared.

What appears to be competition among producers *within* an industry actually may be "competition" among products, all of which are produced and distributed by relatively few corporations. An ***oligopoly*** **exists when several companies overwhelmingly control an entire industry.** An example is the music industry, in which a few giant companies are behind many of the labels and artists known to consumers.

Corporations with control both within and across industries often are formed by a series of mergers and acquisitions across industries. These corporations are referred to as ***conglomerates*****—combinations of businesses in different commercial areas, all of which are owned by one holding company.** Media ownership is a case in point: companies such as Time Warner have extensive holdings in radio and television stations, cable television companies, book publishing firms, and film production and distribution companies, to name only a few. Similarly, a small number of companies control most of Canada's newspapers.

LACK OF GOVERNMENT INTERVENTION Proponents of capitalism say that ideally capitalism works best without government intervention in the marketplace. This policy of laissez-faire was advocated by economist Adam Smith in his 1776 treatise *An Inquiry into the Nature and Causes of the Wealth of Nations*. Smith argued that when people pursue their own selfish interests, they are guided "as if by an invisible hand" to promote the best interests of society (see Smith, 1976/1776). Today, terms such as *market economy* and *free enterprise* often are used, but the underlying assumption is the same: that free market competition, not the government, should regulate prices and wages.

However, the "ideal" of unregulated markets benefiting all citizens has seldom been realized. Individuals and companies in pursuit of higher profits have run roughshod over weaker competitors, and small businesses have grown into large monopolistic corporations. Accordingly, government regulations were implemented in an effort to curb the excesses of the marketplace brought about by laissez-faire policies. While its effectiveness can be debated, Canada does have a Competitions Bureau with the mandate of ensuring that corporations compete fairly.

Ironically, much of what is referred to as government intervention has been in the form of aid to business. Canadian governments have always been intimately involved with business. To encourage settlement of the West, the government gave subsidies and huge tracts of land to the Canadian Pacific Railway to encourage the construction of a national railway. Many corporations receive government assistance in the form of public subsidies and protection from competition by tariffs, patents, and trademarks. Government intervention has included billions of dollars in tax credits for corporations, large subsidies or loan guarantees to manufacturers, and subsidies and tariff protection for farmers. Overall, most corporations have gained much more than they have lost as a result of government involvement in the economy.

Socialism

***Socialism* is an economic system characterized by public ownership of the means of production, the pursuit of collective goals, and centralized decision making.** Like "pure" capitalism, "pure" socialism does not exist. Karl Marx described socialism as a temporary stage en route to an ideal communist society. Although the terms *socialism* and *communism* are associated with Marx and often are used interchangeably, they are not identical. Marx defined communism as an economic system characterized by common ownership of all economic resources (G. Marshall, 1994). In *The Communist Manifesto* and *Das Kapital*, he predicted that the working class would become increasingly impoverished and alienated under capitalism. As a result, the workers would become aware of their own class interests, revolt against the capitalists, and overthrow the entire system. After the revolution, private property would be abolished and capital would be controlled by collectives of workers who would own the means of production. The government (previously used to further the interests of the capitalists) no longer would be necessary. People would contribute according to their abilities and receive according to their needs (Marx and Engels, 1967/1848; Marx, 1967/1867). Over the years, state control was added as an organizing principle for communist societies. "Ideal" socialism has three distinctive features: (1) public ownership of the means of production, (2) pursuit of collective goals, and (3) centralized decision making.

Public Ownership of the Means of Production In a truly socialist economy, the means of production are owned and controlled by a collectivity or by the state, not by private individuals or corporations. Prior to the early 1990s, the state owned all the natural resources and almost all the capital in the Soviet Union. In the 1980s, for example, state-owned enterprises produced more than 88 percent of agricultural output and 98 percent of retail trade, and owned 75 percent of the urban housing space (Boyes and Melvin, 1994). At least in theory, goods were produced to meet the needs of people. Access to housing and medical care were considered a right.

Leaders of the former Soviet Union and some Eastern European nations decided to abandon government ownership and control of the means of production because the system was unresponsive to the needs of the marketplace and offered no incentive for increased efficiency (Boyes and Melvin, 1994). Shortages and widespread unrest led to the reform movement headed by former president Mikhail Gorbachev in the late 1980s.

In the 1990s, Russia and other states in the former Soviet Union attempted to privatize the ownership of production. In *privatization*, resources are converted from state ownership to private ownership; the government takes an active role in developing, recognizing, and protecting private property rights (Boyes and Melvin, 1994).

Pursuit of Collective Goals Ideal socialism is based on the pursuit of collective goals, rather than on personal profits. Equality in decision making replaces hierarchical relationships (such as between owners and workers or political leaders and citizens). Everyone shares in the goods and services of society, especially necessities such as food, clothing, shelter, and medical care based on need, not on ability to pay. In reality, however, few societies can or do pursue purely collective goals.

Centralized Decision Making Another tenet of socialism is centralized decision making. In theory, economic decisions are based on the needs of society; the government is responsible for facilitating the production and distribution of goods and services. Central planners set wages and prices to ensure that the production process works. When problems such as shortages and unemployment arise, they can be dealt with quickly and effectively by the central government (Boyes and Melvin, 1994).

The collapse of state socialism in the former Soviet Union was due partly to the declining ability of the Communist Party to act as an effective agent of society and partly to the growing incompatibility of central planning with the requirements of a modern economy (see Misztal, 1993).

THE SOCIAL ORGANIZATION OF WORK

Work in industrialized countries such as Canada is highly differentiated and often fragmented because people have many kinds of occupations. Some occupations are referred to as professions.

Occupations

***Occupations* are categories of jobs that involve similar activities at different work sites** (Reskin and Padavic, 1994). There are hundreds of different types of occupations. Historically, occupations have been classified as blue collar and white collar. Blue-collar workers primarily were factory and craftworkers who did manual labour; white-collar workers were office workers and professionals. However, contemporary workers in the service sector do not easily fit into either of these categories; neither do the so-called pink-collar workers, who are primarily women and who are employed in occupations such as preschool teacher, dental assistant, secretary, and clerk (Hodson and Sullivan, 1990).

Professions

What occupations are professions? Athletes who are paid for playing sports are referred to as "professional athletes." Dog groomers, pest exterminators, automobile mechanics, and nail technicians (manicurists) also refer to themselves as professionals. Although sociologists do not always agree on exactly which occupations are professions, most do agree that the term *professional* includes most doctors, natural scientists, engineers, computer scientists, accountants, economists, social scientists, psychotherapists, lawyers, policy experts of various sorts, professors, at least some journalists and editors, some clergy, and some artists and writers.

CHARACTERISTICS OF PROFESSIONS ***Professions* are high-status, knowledge-based occupations.** Sociologists use five criteria to determine which occupations are professions (Freidson, 1970, 1986; Larson, 1977):

1. *Abstract, specialized knowledge*. Professionals have abstract, specialized knowledge of their field, based on formal education and interaction with colleagues.
2. *Autonomy*. Professionals are autonomous in that they can rely on their own judgment in selecting the relevant knowledge or the appropriate technique for dealing with a problem. They expect patients, clients, or students to respect that autonomy.
3. *Self-regulation*. In exchange for autonomy, professionals theoretically are self-regulating. All professions have licensing, accreditation, and regulatory associations that set professional standards and that require members to adhere to a code of ethics as a form of public accountability.
4. *Authority*. Because of their authority, professionals expect compliance with their directions and advice.
5. *Altruism*. Ideally, professionals have concern for others. The term ***altruism* implies some degree of self-sacrifice whereby professionals go beyond self-interest or personal comfort so that they can help a patient or client** (Hodson and Sullivan, 1990).

In the past, job satisfaction among professionals generally has been very high because of relatively high levels of income, autonomy, and authority. In the future, some professionals may become the backbone of a postindustrial society while others may suffer from "intellectual obsolescence" if they cannot keep up with the knowledge explosion (Leventman, 1981).

Women have made significant gains in the professions. Katherine Marshall found that the number of women employed in traditionally male-dominated professions in Canada rose by 42 percent between 1981 and 1986, compared with a 9 percent increase for men (Marshall, 1990). This increase continued throughout the next decade. From 1981 to 1996 women's share of employment rose from 17 percent to 36 percent among doctors, from 8 percent to 22 percent among dentists, and from 16 percent to 42 percent among lawyers (Marshall, 1990;

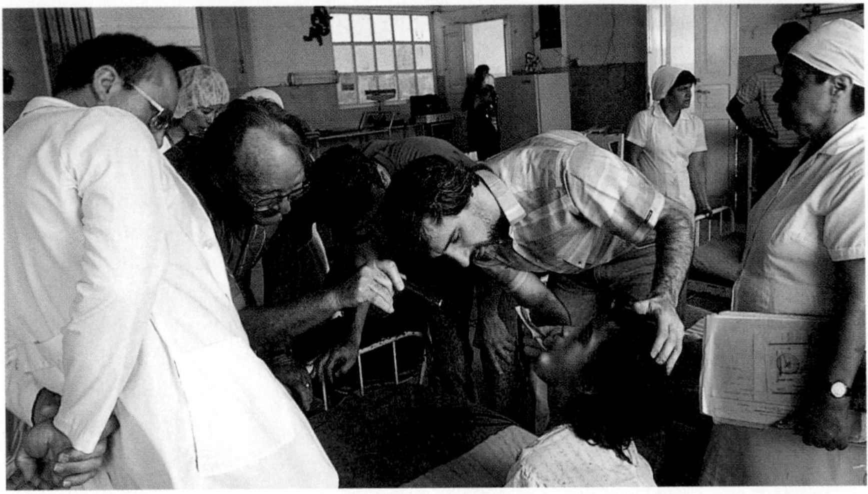

Professionals are expected to share their knowledge and display concern for others. These surgeons have volunteered their services to people in Ecuador.

Human Resources Development Canada, 1999). These percentages will continue to grow, as women now make up over half of the students in many professional schools.

Upper-Tier Jobs: Managers and Supervisors

A wide variety of occupations are classified as "management" positions. The generic term *manager* often is used to refer to executives, managers, and administrators (Hodson and Sullivan, 1990). At the upper level of a workplace bureaucracy are *executives*, who control the operation of their organizations. *Administrators* often work for governmental bureaucracies or organizations dealing with health, education, or welfare (such as hospitals, colleges and universities, and nursing homes) and usually are appointed. *Managers* typically have responsibility for workers, physical plants, equipment, and the financial aspects of a bureaucratic organization. Women have increasingly gained access to management positions at this level, especially middle management positions. In 1993, 42 percent of those working in management and administrative positions in Canada were women, up from 29 percent in 1982 and 6 percent in 1971 (Statistics Canada, 1994a).

Lower-Tier and Marginal Jobs

Positions in the lower tier of the service sector are characterized by low wages, little job security, few chances for advancement, and higher unemployment rates. Typical lower-tier positions include janitor, waitress, messenger, sales clerk, typist, file clerk, farm labourer, and textile worker. Large numbers of young people, recent immigrants, and women are employed in this sector.

According to the employment norms of this country, a job should (1) be legal, (2) be covered by government work regulations, such as minimum standards of pay, working conditions, and safety standards, (3) be relatively permanent, and (4) provide adequate pay with sufficient hours of work each week to make a living (Hodson and Sullivan, 1990). However, many lower-tier service sector jobs do not meet these norms and therefore are marginal. ***Marginal jobs* differ from the employment norms of the society in which they are located;** examples in the Canadian labour market are personal service and household workers.

Some manufacturing jobs also may be marginalized especially in peripheral industries such as garment or microelectronics manufacturing that operate in markets where prices are subject to sudden, intense fluctuations and where labour is a significant part of the cost of the goods sold (Hodson and Sullivan, 1990). Although "high-tech" occupations (such as those in engineering and computer technology) are viewed by some as the wave of the future, many jobs in this field are marginal. Assembly-line jobs in high-tech industries often are boring, low-paying, and hazardous. These industries also are more likely to export jobs to other regions of

Robots at this Honda factory exemplify the deskilling of jobs through automation. What are managers' responsibilities in workplaces such as this?

the country or to developing nations, where labour costs are lower. The term *global assembly line* is used to describe situations in which corporations hire workers, usually girls and young women, in developing nations at very low wages to work under hazardous conditions. Despite the grim work environment, such jobs represent a temporary respite from grinding poverty for many workers (Ehrenreich and Fuentes, 1981; Women Working Worldwide, 1991).

Contingent Work

Contingent work **is part-time or temporary work** that offers advantages to employers but that can be detrimental to the welfare of workers. Contingent work is found in every segment of the workforce, including colleges and universities, where tenure-track positions are fewer in number than in the past and a series of one-year, non-tenure-track appointments at the lecturer or instructor level has become a means of livelihood for many instructors. The federal government is part of this trend, as is private enterprise. For example, the health-care field continues to undergo significant change, as governments try to cut health costs. Nurses, personal care homeworkers, and others in this field increasingly are employed through temporary agencies as their jobs are contracted out.

Employers benefit by hiring workers on a part-time or temporary basis. They are able to cut costs, maximize profits, and have workers available only when they need them. As some companies have cut their workforce, or downsized, they have replaced regular employees who had higher salaries and full benefit packages with part-time and hourly wage employees who receive lower wages and no benefits. Although some people voluntarily work part-time (such as through job sharing and work sharing), many people are forced to do so because they lack opportunities for full-time employment. Sociologist Harvey Krahn (1995a) found that between 1976 and 1994, the number of part-time jobs increased at an average rate of 6.9 percent annually, whereas the rate was 1.5 percent for full-time jobs. By 2000 about 18 percent of the labour force worked part time.

While employers find it easier to cope with changes in the economy using part-time and temporary employees, these workers have no economic security and can find themselves quickly unemployed during economic hard times.

Unemployment

The ***unemployment rate*** **is the percentage of unemployed persons in the labour force actively seeking jobs.** The unemployment rate is not a complete measure of unemployment because it does not include those who have become discouraged and have stopped looking for work, nor does it count students, even if they are looking for employment. Unemployment rates vary by year, region, gender, race, age, and with the presence of a disability.

- *Yearly variations.* The Canadian unemployment rate reached a post–World War II high in the early 1980s, when it climbed above 11 percent. For most of the 1990s it was above 10 percent. In August 2000, 7.1 percent of the workforce was unemployed.
- *Regional differences*. Canada's regions have widely different rates of unemployment. Newfoundland,

BOX 12.2 CRITICAL THINKING

THE END OF WORK?

Political economists have studied the impact of technology and the ownership of that technology on the economy and the labour force. In recent years, globalization of trade has put pressure on companies to reduce costs and many have tried to do this by developing technology that allows them to reduce their work forces. Economist and futurist Jeremy Rifkin (1995) thinks that work as we know it is coming to an end. Rifkin feels that we are moving into a postindustrial, information-based economy in which factory work, clerical work, middle management, and many other traditional jobs will soon fall victim to technology. Bank machines and Internet banking will replace tellers, robots will replace factory workers, and electronic scanners will replace cashiers. When agriculture mechanized, displaced workers found jobs in industry; when industry turned to computers, service jobs became available. However, the information age does not hold the same potential for jobs. According to Rifkin some *knowledge workers*—the engineers, technicians, and scientists who are leading us into the information age—will gain, but there will be little work for the rest of us. We will have an elite workforce, not a mass workforce. The elites will be well paid; Microsoft's Bill Gates made a $100-billion fortune in about twenty years. However, the majority have not received the benefits of the postindustrial society. Many people do not have jobs and many of those with jobs have seen declines in their purchasing power. Nathan Gardels fears that the unemployed face economic irrelevance: "we don't need what they have and they can't buy what we sell" (quoted in Rifkin, 1995:215).

Two questions arise from Rifkin's analysis. First, what does society do with the millions of people who may not be needed by employers? Second, how do we persuade the top 20 percent, who are receiving the benefits of productivity gains, to share them with the bottom 80 percent who are bearing the burden of change? One answer is to gradually shorten the work week to 30 hours for the same pay using productivity gains to pay the bill. Earlier technological revolutions resulted in reduced hours of work which is evident in the decrease from eighty hours per week in the nineteenth century to the current level of forty hours per week. Leisure, rather than formal work, would become the focus of people's lives. France has moved in this direction by legislating a 35-hour work week to create more jobs. The second is to redefine what we now define as work. Rifkin

with rates frequently above 20 percent, has traditionally had the highest. Rates in the other Atlantic provinces and in Quebec are also usually higher than the Canadian average.

- *Gender*. Male and female unemployment rates have been very similar for the past two decades. While women formerly had higher rates of unemployment than men, their rates have recently been slightly lower than those of male workers (Statistics Canada, 2000a).
- *Race*. Data from the 1986 census showed that visible minorities (a category that does not include Aboriginals) had an unemployment rate that was only slightly higher than the national average. However, despite higher levels of education, their average employment income was lower than for Canadians overall. Aboriginal Canadians had rates of unemployment that were more than double the national average (Moreau, 1994).

BOX 12.2

CONTINUED

suggests countries turn to the nonprofit *civil sector*—community service activities now largely carried out by volunteers—as a source of jobs. The civil sector includes activities such as social services, health care, education, the arts, and assisting the disadvantaged. Not only would this create jobs, but it would also strengthen our communities.

What incentives exist to encourage change? The after-tax purchasing power of Canadians has declined during the past decade and the lack of jobs means that the number of potential customers may decline. Decades ago, Henry Ford recognized that only well-paid workers could buy his cars. Many economists blame the depression of the 1930s on the failure of business leaders to recognize that they had to share the benefits of increased productivity with their workers (Rifkin, 1995). The same threat may exist now: if people do not have adequate incomes, they will be unable to purchase the goods and services created by the new technology.

Increased inequality also destabilizes society. The United States, which has the greatest disparity between rich and poor in the industrialized world, now incarcerates about 2 percent of its adult male population and has a much higher crime rate than most other countries. Riots in the 1990s in Jakarta, Indonesia, were partly caused by young people who were angry at the growing gap between rich and poor and at their own lack of opportunity (Stackhouse, 1996). Rifkin argues that the rich can either use some of their gains to create a fortress economy or they can use the same money to prevent it. Also, the public, unions, and some politicians have already begun to protest the growing trend toward paying executives enormous salaries while their workers are being laid off or having their wages cut.

Rifkin's view of the future may be wrong. His critics argue that while the nature of work has changed in our postindustrial society, there are now more jobs, not fewer. In North America millions of new jobs have been created over the past decade and some futurists believe that this technology-led growth will continue. However, Rifkin's scenario is a plausible one and his work points out the way in which fundamental changes in our economy can affect all of us.

Sources: Rifkin, 1995; and Stackhouse, 1996.

- *Age.* Youth have higher rates of unemployment than older persons. Unemployment rates for people aged 15 to 24 are as much as 50 percent higher than the overall unemployment rate.
- *Presence of a disability.* People with disabilities were much less likely to be employed than other Canadians. According to a 1990 study by David Gower (1990), while 640,000 disabled persons aged 15 to 64 were employed, their employment rate was only about two-thirds that of the nondisabled population. Even those with jobs were often underemployed in jobs below their qualifications.

Canada's unemployment rates have historically been higher than those of most other industrial countries. They declined substantially at the end of the last decade, but still remain much higher than those of the United States and Japan. However, unemployment has risen to unusually high levels in many European countries in recent years, and Canada's rates are low compared with the rates in some of these countries.

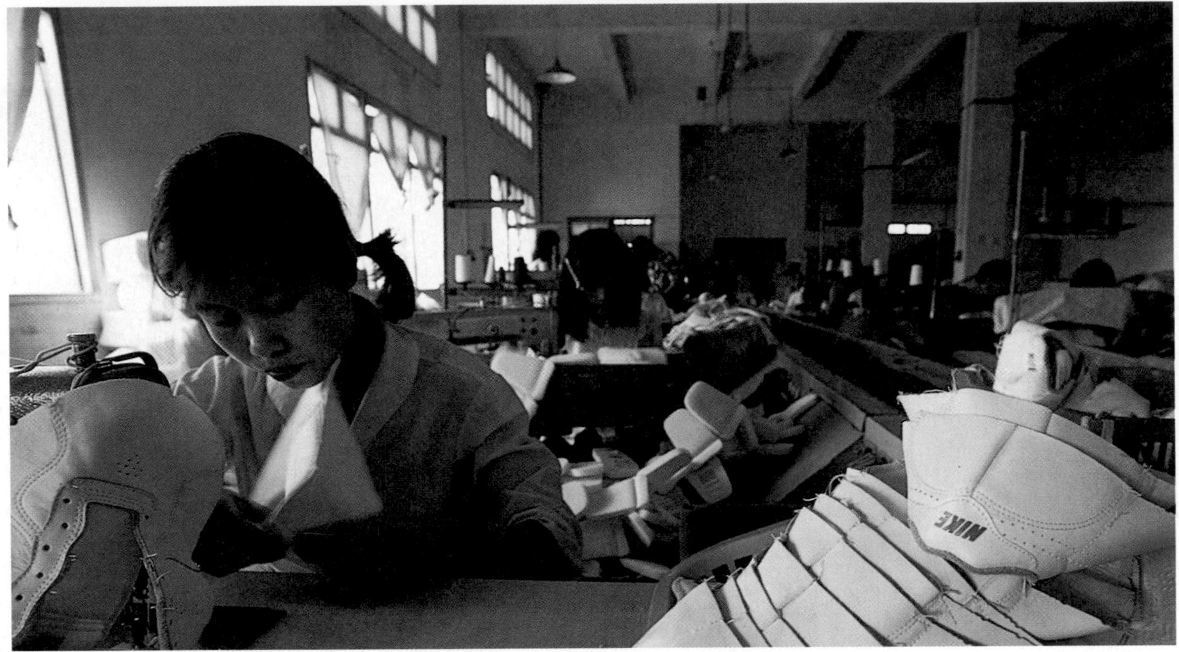

Workers in developing nations—often women or young girls—make or assemble a number of products sold in North America and other developed nations. Workers in China make many Nike products; in the United States, Nike employees are primarily involved in nonmanufacturing work, including research, design, and retailing.

LABOUR UNIONS

In their individual and collective struggles to improve their work environment and gain some measure of control over their own work-related activities, workers have used a number of methods. Many have joined labour unions to gain strength through collective actions.

Tired of toiling for the benefit of capitalists instead of for themselves, some workers banded together to form labour unions in the middle of the nineteenth century. Craftspeople such as printers, tailors, and blacksmiths were the first to organize, and their efforts led to the passage of the Trade Unions Act in 1872, which legalized union activity in Canada. A ***labour union* is a group of employees who join together to bargain with an employer or a group of employers over wages, benefits, and working conditions.**

During the period of monopoly capitalism, as industries such as automobile and steel manufacturing shifted to mass production, workers realized that they needed more power to improve poor working conditions. The suppression of the Winnipeg General Strike in 1919 and the employment crisis during the Depression of the 1930s had devastated unions. Those that remained were largely based in the United States and usually organized to benefit specific trades such as bricklayers and carpenters.

Industrial unions faced a long struggle to organize. Relations between workers and managers were difficult and violence against workers was often used to fight unionization. Ultimately, organizers were successful, and unions have been credited with gaining an eight-hour workday and a five-day work week, health and retirement benefits, sick leave and unemployment insurance, and workplace health and safety standards for many employees.

Union membership grew dramatically throughout much of this century, particularly during the two world wars, when labour shortages and economic growth made union expansion easy, and in the 1970s when governments allowed public servants to

Unions have often been negatively portrayed in the media. This stereotyping can make it more difficult for unions to obtain support from the public.

unionize (Krahn and Lowe, 1993). In 1990, over 36 percent of the nonagricultural paid workforce belonged to unions. However, union membership declined overall during the 1980s and 1990s as economic recessions and massive layoffs in government and industry reduced the numbers of unionized workers and severely weakened the bargaining power of unions. You have seen that jobs have shifted from manufacturing and manual work to the service sector where employees have been less able to unionize. While white-collar workers in the public sector such as teachers and civil servants have successfully organized, white-collar workers in the private sector remain largely unorganized. For example, only 4 percent of workers in banks and other financial services belong to unions. Women now make up nearly half of all union membership and have accounted for most of the growth in membership over the past decade. In 1999, 29 percent of all female paid workers were unionized, compared with 31 percent of male paid workers (Statistics Canada, 1999).

The rate of union membership among workers in Canada is higher than in Japan and the United States, but far lower than in most Western European countries. Thirty years ago, the union membership rate in the United States was the same as in Canada, but it is now less than half. American industry has been very anti-union, and state and federal laws have not protected the rights of workers to unionize.

In most industrialized countries, collective bargaining by unions has been dominated by men. However, in many countries, including Sweden, Germany, Austria, and Great Britain, women workers have made important gains as a result of labour union participation, as discussed in Box 12.3.

Difficult times may lie ahead for unions. The growing diversity of the workforce, the increase in temporary and part-time work, the threat of global competition, the ease with which jobs can be moved from one country to another, and the replacement of jobs by technology are just a few of the challenges that lie ahead. The next decade will be a critical time in the future of the labour movement. How do you think union leaders can change their organizations to meet the new realities of the world of work?

POLITICAL AND ECONOMIC ISSUES FOR THE FUTURE

What impact will the changing global economy have on the future of government in Canada and how will government decisions affect the economy? These questions will have a major impact on our lives in the future.

Some observers have asked if governments of modern nation-states will simply become obsolete in the twenty-first century. Through the 1990s there was some erosion of the powers of national governments throughout the world and a corresponding increase in the importance of transnational bodies and global corporations. Many of Europe's major nations have given up some of their powers to the European Community and will soon have a common currency. In North America, economic disputes between the members of the North American Free Trade Agreement are decided by independent panels rather than by governments; and globally the General Agreement on Trades and Tariffs brings together 124 nations in the World

BOX 12.3 SOCIOLOGY IN GLOBAL PERSPECTIVE

WOMEN AND LABOUR ACTIVISM

Women workers in industrialized nations currently fare much better than their counterparts in other parts of the global economy. In many situations, workers have been denied the right to organize and unionize in free trade zones and home-based production industries. Some nations have no labour laws dealing with minimum wages, maternity benefits, equal pay, and leave; others have not enforced existing laws. In the global economy, many working women (along with men) lack not only union representation but also basic human rights.

Even among the most industrialized nations in the world—such as Sweden, Great Britain, the United States, Germany, and Canada—almost all union negotiators are men. The issues most often brought forward by these negotiators are those affecting "all" workers, often to the exclusion of issues that primarily affect women. Take, for example, the issue of the shorter workweek. Most women who do not have child-rearing responsibilities, as well as most men, want a shorter *workweek*, while most women who have child-rearing responsibilities prefer a shorter *workday* so that they can share child-care duties with other persons.

In recent years, however, some women union members in industrialized countries have become much more savvy at "using the system." For example, through labour-management negotiations, workers have bargained for higher safety standards than those required by law. However, struggles over what were perceived to be "women's issues" often produced

Trade Organization, which is empowered to rule on trade matters. While these agreements facilitate world trade, they also reduce the sovereignty of participating countries whose laws must be consistent with broader regulations.

Do such agreements signal the end of individual governments? Despite trade alliances, many analysts believe that nation-states remain of great significance. According to scholar Paul Kennedy (1993: 134), individual nations will remain the primary locus of identity for most people. Regardless of who their employer is and what they do for a living, individuals pay taxes to the state, are subject to its laws, serve (if need be) in its armed forces, and can travel abroad only by having its passport. Therefore, as new challenges arise, most people in democracies will turn to their own governments and demand solutions.

What is the future of democracy? Today, millions of people around the globe remain committed to what they believe are the "ideals of democracy." Similarly, millions of people in Eastern Europe, the former Soviet Union, Latin America, and China have put their lives on the line for democracy, with varying degrees of success. The number of countries with democratic governments has been increasing and globalization is moving others in that direction.

Borderless markets and industries defy political boundaries. For example, Japanese cars are produced in Canada and the United States using components that can be made virtually anywhere in the world. Capital and jobs can move very rapidly, so governments have much less power to intervene in markets.

Most futurists predict that transnational corporations will become even more significant in the global economy of tomorrow. As they continue to compete for world market shares, these corporations will become even less aligned with the values of any one nation. However, those who advocate increased globalization typically focus on its potential impact on industrialized nations, not the effect it may have on the 80 percent of the world's population that resides in lower-income nations. Persons in less industrialized nations may become increasingly baffled and resentful when they are bombarded with media images of affluence and consumption that are not attainable for them (P. Kennedy, 1993).

BOX 12.3

CONTINUED

conflict among union leaders. Many male union leaders typically saw certain issues as just that—"women's issues." Ironically, some of their perceptions began to change as they became more aware that some of the health and safety problems in many factories, mines, and other work settings also affected men.

European unions have made many advances in dealing with some of these problem areas. For example, German and Austrian unions have been instrumental in instituting inspection systems to identify work hazards. In Germany and Sweden, unions have bargained for relief from "repetitive motion" injuries such as carpal tunnel syndrome (a hand and wrist disorder associated with excessive use of computer keyboards and typewriters) for thousands of women computer operators. Men in the manufacturing sector also benefited from the negotiations because their work is repetitive and may lead to back, leg, hand, and eye injuries.

In European countries and in Canada, the number of women in unions is increasing at a faster rate than for men. Canadian women have had some success in attaining leadership roles and serving on the national boards of unions. As a result, issues important to women, including pay equity and maternity leave, have recently been addressed in collective bargaining.

Sources: Based on Cook, Lorwin, and Daniels, 1992; National Safety Council, 1992; Suss, 1986; and Tomasevski, 1993.

The chasm between rich and poor nations will probably widen in the future as industrialized nations purchase fewer raw materials from industrializing countries and more products and services from one another. This change will take place because raw materials of all sorts are no longer as important to manufacturers in industrialized nations. For example, oil may become less important as a power source with the development of solar power and other forms of energy.

What effect will global political and economic changes have on the average worker? In recent years, the average worker in Canada and other developed countries has benefited more than have workers in less developed and developing countries from global economic growth. The average citizen of Switzerland, for example, has an income several hundred times that of a resident of Ethiopia. More than a billion of the world's people live in abject poverty; for many, this means attempting to survive on less than $370 a year (P. Kennedy, 1993). According to a recent United Nations Report, the total wealth of the world's 358 billionaires equals the combined incomes of the poorest 45 percent of the world's population—2.3 billion people (United Nations Development Program, 1996). While some countries, including many in Southeast Asia and Latin America, will begin to enter the developed world, others, particularly in Africa, will continue to fall further behind the rest of the world.

Regardless of the impact of globalization on individual countries, the process will almost inevitably continue. A global workplace is emerging in which telecommunications networks will link workers in distant locations. In the developed world, the skills of some professionals will transcend the borders of their own countries. For example, there is a demand for the services of international law specialists, engineers, and software designers across countries. Even as nations become more dependent on one another, they also will become more competitive in the economic sphere. While the prospects for greater economic equality do not appear to be bright, perhaps we should not be too pessimistic. According to sociologist G. William Domhoff (1990:285), "If history teaches us anything, it is that no one can predict the future."

CHAPTER REVIEW

What is power?
Power is the ability of persons or groups to carry out their will even when opposed by others.

What are the three types of authority?
Max Weber identified three types of authority. Charismatic authority is based on a leader's exceptional personal qualities. Traditional authority is based on respect for custom. Rational-legal authority is based on law or written rules and regulations.

What are the main types of political systems?
There are four main types of contemporary political systems. In a monarchy, one person is the ruler of the nation. In authoritarian systems, rulers tolerate little or no public opposition and generally cannot be removed from office by legal means. In totalitarian systems, the state seeks to regulate all aspects of society and to monopolize all societal resources in order to control completely both public and private life. In a democratic system, the powers of the government are derived from the consent of all the people.

What are the pluralist and elite perspectives on power?
According to the pluralist (functionalist) model, power is widely dispersed throughout many competing interest groups. People influence policy by voting, joining special interest groups and political campaigns, and forming new groups. According to the elite (conflict) model, power is concentrated in a small group of elites, while the masses are relatively powerless.

What is the primary function of the economy?
The economy is the social institution that ensures the maintenance of society through the production, distribution, and consumption of goods and services.

How do the three major contemporary economic systems differ?
Over the past hundred years, capitalism, socialism, and mixed economies have been the main economic systems in industrialized countries. Capitalism is characterized by ownership of the means of production, pursuit of personal profit, competition, and limited government intervention. Socialism is characterized by public ownership of the means of production, the pursuit of collective goals, and centralized decision making. In mixed economies, elements of a capitalist, market economy are combined with elements of a command, socialist economy.

What are the functionalist, conflict, and interactionist perspectives on the economy and work?
According to functionalists, the economy is a vital social institution because it is the means by which needed goods and services are produced and distributed. Business cycles represent the necessary rise and fall of economic activity relative to long-term economic growth. Conflict theorists view business cycles as the result of capitalist greed. In order to maximize profits, capitalists suppress the wages of workers who, in turn, cannot purchase products, making it necessary for capitalists to reduce production, close factories, lay off workers, and adopt other remedies that are detrimental to workers and society. Interactionists focus on the microlevel of the economic system, particularly on the social organization of work and its effects on workers' attitudes and behaviour.

What is a labour union?
A labour union is a group of employees who join together to bargain with an employer or a group of employers over wages, benefits, and working conditions.

Key Terms

power elite 345
primary sector production 352
professions 357
rational-legal authority 341
routinization of charisma 340
secondary sector production 353
socialism 356
special interest groups 344
state 338
totalitarian political system 343
traditional authority 340
unemployment rate 359

Internet Exercises

1. Visit the Adam Smith Institute (**www.adamsmith.org.uk**). Read through some of Adam Smith's writings. How do his ideas about capitalism compare with the way you see capitalism operating today?
2. Use Google (**www.google.com**) to search for *labour unions Canada*. What union seems to be the most well represented on the Internet? Visit the Labornet page (**www.labornet.org**). Do you think that the Internet can bring labour unions from around the world together? What effect would a global union have on the world economy, and on the way in which business operates?
3. There are many political parties in Canada, and most use the Internet to convey their message. Visit the sites of the most prominent parties on following pages:

   The Liberal Page (**www.liberal.ca**)
   The NDP Page (**www.ndp.ca**)
   The Progressive Conservative Page (**www.pcparty.ca**)
   The Bloc Québécois Page (**www.blocquebecois.org**)
   The Canadian Alliance Page (**www.canadianalliance.ca**)
   The Communist Party of Canada Page (**www.communist-party.ca**)
   The Green Party (**www.green.ca**)

   How do the popularity and funding of a party affect the type of page design a party uses for its Web site? How do the different pages reflect the interests of the parties? Do some of the parties reflect regional interests, or do they all attempt to reflect Canadian interests as a whole?

Net Links

For more Web links related to the topic of this chapter, see the Nelson sociology Web site: **www.sociologyessentials-2nded.nelson.com**.

Two very important developments on the road to self-government are the Royal Commission on Aboriginal Peoples at:

www.inac.gc.ca/rcap/index-e.html

and the Nisga'a Land Agreement at:

www.aaf.gov.bc.ca/aaf/treaty/nisgaa/nisgaa.htm

The Web site of the Department of Indian and Northern Affairs, including the government's response to the Royal Commission on Aboriginal People, is available at:

www.inac.gc.ca/index_e.html

Toronto lawyer Bill Henderson maintains an exceptionally useful Web site with links to a wide variety of sites dealing with Aboriginal people and issues at:

www.bloorstreet.com/300block/aborl.htm

The International Institute for Democracy and Electoral Assistance has a Web site that discusses women in politics. It has some interesting material on the representation of women in parliaments; to see it, go to:

www.idea.int/women

For a large collection of Canadian government information on the Internet, go to:

http://dsp-psd.pwgsc.gc.ca/dsp-psd/Reference/cgii_index-e.html

For a left-wing perspective on economic and labour issues, go to the Canadian Centre for Policy Alternatives at:

www.policyalternatives.ca

For a right-wing perspective on economic and labour issues, go to the Fraser Institute at:

www.fraserinstitute.ca

For a look at the changing nature of work in Canada, read the Government of Canada's Collective Reflection on the Changing Workplace at:

www.reflection.gc.ca

LabourNet uses computer communications as a means of building an international labour movement; see:

www.labournet.ca

For a wide range of information on labour and the labour force in Canada, go to the Web site of Human Resources Development Canada (the government department responsible for employment matters) at:

www.hrdc-drhc.gc.ca

Questions for Critical Thinking

1. If you were the manager of the computer software division of a company, how might you encourage innovation among your technical employees? How might you encourage efficiency? If you were the manager of a fast-food restaurant, how might you increase job satisfaction and decrease job alienation among your employees?
2. Using Chapter 1 as a guide, design a study to determine the degree of altruism in certain professions. What might be your hypothesis? What variables would you study? What research methods would provide the best data for analysis?
3. Many occupations will change or disappear in the future. Think of a specific occupation or profession and consider its future. For example, what will be the role of the librarian when books, journals, and abstracts are all instantly accessible on the Internet?
4. Who is ultimately responsible for decisions and policies that are made in a democracy such as Canada: the people or their elected representatives?
5. How does your school (or workplace) reflect a pluralist or elite model of power and decision making?

Suggested Readings

These books examine politics from a sociological perspective:

G. William Domhoff. *The Power Elite and the State: How Policy Is Made in America*. New York: Aldine de Gruyter, 1990.

Anthony M. Orum. *Introduction to Political Sociology: The Social Anatomy of the Body Politic* (3rd ed.). Englewood Cliffs, N.J.: Prentice-Hall, 1988.

In-depth information about politics and government is provided in this political science text:

Rand Dyck. *Canadian Politics: Critical Approaches* (2nd ed.). Toronto: Nelson Canada, 1996.

Two books that are helpful in understanding Aboriginal political issues are:

Menno Boldt. *Surviving as Indians: The Challenge of Self-Government*. Toronto: University of Toronto Press, 1993.

Olive Dickason. *Canada's First Nations*. Toronto: McClelland and Stewart, 1992.

For a good overview of Quebec separatism and related issues, you can read:

Ramsay Cook. *Canada, Quebec and the Uses of Nationalism* (2nd ed.). Toronto: McClelland and Stewart, 1995.

Marcel Rioux. *Quebec in Question*. Toronto: James Lorimer and Company, 1971.

A very good general book on the sociology of work is:

Harvey J. Krahn and Graham S. Lowe. *Work, Industry, and Canadian Society*. Scarborough, Ont.: Nelson Canada, 1993.

These books provide more information about capitalism:

Peter L. Berger. *The Capitalist Revolution: Fifty Propositions About Prosperity, Equality, and Liberty*. New York: Basic Books, 1986.

Harry Braverman. *Labour and Monopoly Capital: The Degradation of Work in the Twentieth Century*. New York: Monthly Review Press, 1974.

Karl Marx. *Selected Writings in Sociology and Social Philosophy*. Thomas B. Bottomore and Maximilian Rubel (eds.). New York: McGraw-Hill, 1964.

Books that provide interesting insights on the sociology of work include:

Patrick Burman. *Killing Time, Losing Ground: Experiences of Unemployment*. Toronto: Wall and Thompson, 1988.

Barbara Garson. *The Electronic Sweatshop: How Computers Are Transforming the Office of the Future into the Factory of the Past*. New York: Penguin Books, 1989.

Ben Hamper. *Rivethead: Tales from the Assembly Line*. New York: Time Warner, 1992.

Jeremy Rifkin. *The End of Work*. New York: G.P. Putnam's Sons, 1995.

Studs Terkel. *Working: People Talk About What They Do All Day and How They Feel About What They Do*. New York: Ballantine Books, 1985.

Scholarly works on labour unions include:

Irving Abella. *On Strike: Six Key Labour Struggles in Canada 1919–1949*. Toronto: James Lewis and Samuel, 1974.

Berch Berberoglu (ed.). *The Labor Process and the Control of Labor: The Changing Nature of Work Relations in the Late Twentieth Century*. Westport, Conn.: Praeger, 1993.

INFOTRAC® COLLEGE EDITION

Either from the *Sociology In Our Times: The Essentials* Web site (**www.sociologyessentials-2nded.nelson.com**) or directly from your Web browser, you may access InfoTrac® College Edition, an online university library that includes over 600 popular and scholarly journals in which you can find articles related to the topics in this chapter.

CHAPTER 13

Families in Global Perspective
- Defining *Family*
- Family Structure
- Marriage Patterns
- Descent and Inheritance
- Power and Authority in Families

Perspectives on Families
- Functionalist Perspectives
- Conflict Perspectives
- Feminist Perspectives
- Interactionist Perspectives

Developing Intimate Relationships and Establishing Families
- Love and Intimacy
- Cohabitation
- Marriage
- Housework

Child-Related Family Issues and Parenting
- Deciding to Have Children
- Adoption
- New Reproductive Technologies
- Single Parenting

Transitions and Problems in Families
- Violence in Families: Wife and Child Abuse
- Divorce
- Remarriage

Family Diversity
- Gay and Lesbian Families
- Singlehood
- Aboriginal Families

Family Issues in the Future

Author Robert Mason Lee's discussion of his family exemplifies the increasing complexity of modern-day family life:

"I'll be travelling at Christmas, as many men travel, to be with the girl of my dreams. She is as excited about this as I am: when I sent her the E-mail informing her of my flight plans, she replied, 'Yippee!' But she didn't linger over the mushy stuff. 'It's lunch time, Gotta go, XOX-OXOXO.'

"My girl has to run when it's lunch time, because she is still only nine years old. As her father, I find myself surprised that hers has become the most constant relationship of my adult life. It wasn't supposed to be that way. The plan was to marry, start a family, and become a constant for my children. Instead, I started a family, obtained a divorce, and now find that my child has become a constant for me. Christmas is the time of year that reveals the anchors in our lives, and I no longer go home to my parents for Christmas. Yet, as an adult, my child doesn't come home to me. Instead, I go home to my child.

"Jacqueline loves nothing more than a party, and there will be a party on Christmas Eve, where the lines of marriage, remarriage, blood and love will weave a pattern of Celtic complexity. I know, for example, that my present girlfriend will have a high old time with my daughter's younger sister by my first wife's second marriage, because they are both so naughty … It is the one time of the year when everyone gets together like this, and it is all on account of the children.

"When the party winds down, I'll be putting my daughter to bed with visions of sugarplums; on Christmas morn, I'll be there to open gifts. I've done neither of these since she was an infant … Until now ours has been the typically divided Christmas of the typically divided home—I got Jacqueline either just before, or just after, the big day. We adapted our own traditions to make all of this seem normal.

"Although she had never previously heard of such a thing, she jumped on my worldly knowledge that Santa could be recalled for a 'post-Christmas' delivery. In fact, it made sense that Santa would do such a thing, with so many kids of divorce around." (Mason Lee, 1998:A14)

FAMILIES AND INTIMATE RELATIONSHIPS

Fifty years ago, the majority of Canadian families consisted of two adults in a permanent union that produced three to five children. Other kinds of families were the exception. Today when we think of families, we think of diversity and change, and exceptions are the rule (Vanier Institute of the Family, 1998). The experiences of the family in the above narrative certainly are not unique. Children are experiencing the separation of their parents at increasingly earlier ages. Separation and divorce, remarriage, and blended or reconstituted families are a reality for many Canadians. Despite these changes, family life continues to be a source of great personal satisfaction and happiness. A recent opinion poll indicated that over 85 percent of respondents felt family life was very important (Bibby, 1995).

In this chapter, we examine the diversity and complexity of families and intimate relationships. In the process, we will focus on issues such as changing patterns of marriage and divorce, work versus parenting demands, and other problems facing contemporary families. Before reading on, test your knowledge about the changing family by taking the quiz in Box 13.1.

Questions and Issues

CHAPTER FOCUS QUESTION: How is social change affecting the Canadian family?

Why is it difficult to define family*?*

How do marriage patterns vary across cultures?

What are the key assumptions of functionalist, conflict, feminist, and interactionist perspectives on families?

What significant trends affect many Canadian families today?

Why do some analysts argue that the family as we know it will become extinct in the twenty-first century?

Despite the idealized image of "the family," North American families have undergone many changes in the past century as exemplified by the case of Carol Hoard and newborn K.C., who was conceived after his father, Ron, died from a heart attack. The new reproductive technologies available today raise many questions about how we define *family*.

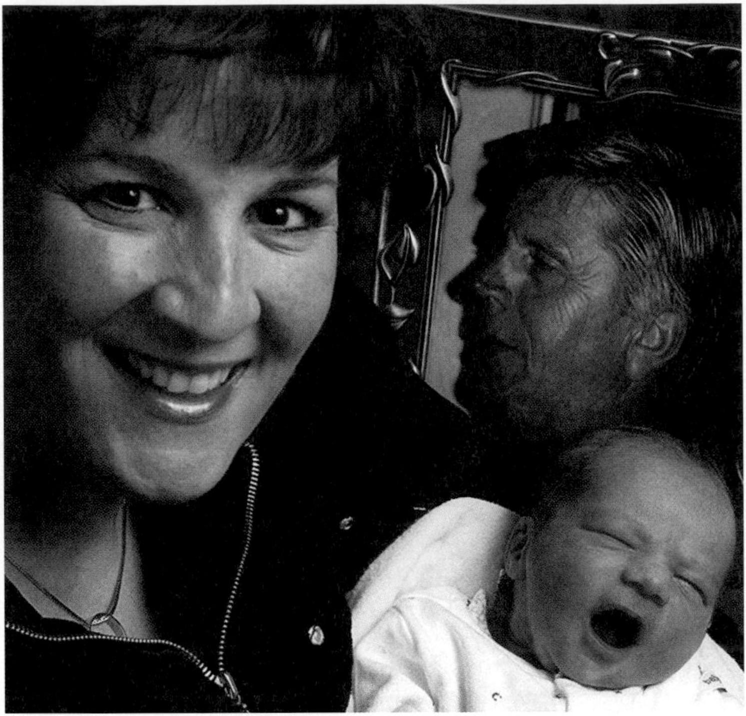

FAMILIES IN GLOBAL PERSPECTIVE

Defining *Family*

What is a family? Although we all have a family of some form or another, and we all understand the concept of family, it is not an easy concept to define. More than ever, this term means different things to different people. For example, Hutterite families in Canada live in communal situations, in which children from about the age of three spend most of their days in school. The children also eat their meals in a communal dining hall, away from their parents. In this case, the community is the family as opposed to a traditional nuclear family.

Aboriginal peoples in Canada also tend to have a much broader idea of family membership. Children are often cared for by relatives in the extended family. A social worker may define a family as consisting of parents and children only. Some Aboriginal parents may be perceived as neglecting their children, when the parents feel the children are safe and well cared for by "their family"—that is, by uncles, grandparents, or other relatives (Ward, 1998).

Similarly, gay men and lesbians often form unique family forms. Many gay men and lesbians have ***families we choose*****—social arrangements that include intimate relationships between couples and close familial relationships with other couples and with other adults and children** (Kirby and Robinson, 1998). According to sociologist Judy Root Aulette (1994), "families we choose" include both blood and legal ties, but they also include *fictive kin*—persons who are not actually related by blood but are accepted as family members. For example, fictive kin are included in this woman's plans for procreation:

> When I go to have a kid, I'm not gonna have my sisters as godparents. I'm gonna have people around me, that are gay. No, I call on my inner family—my community, or whatever—to help me with my life. So there's definitely a family. (quoted in Weston, 1991:108)

In a society as diverse as Canada, talking about "a family" as though a single type of family exists or ever did exist is inaccurate. In reality, different

BOX 13.1 SOCIOLOGY AND EVERYDAY LIFE

How Much Do You Know about the Changing Family in Canada?

True	False	
T	F	1. The number of common-law relationships has increased dramatically over the past fifteen years.
T	F	2. Men are as likely as women to be single parents.
T	F	3. One out of every two marriages ends in divorce.
T	F	4. Polygamy, being married to more than one person at the same time, is against the law in Canada.
T	F	5. The incidence of reported spousal assault has increased dramatically over the past fifteen years.
T	F	6. People marry at a much later age now than they did several decades ago.
T	F	7. Nearly 25 percent of all marriages are dual-earner marriages.
T	F	8. Test-tube babies are grown entirely outside the mother's womb.
T	F	9. People who marry young are more likely to divorce than those who marry later in life.
T	F	10. Most people who divorce marry again.

Answers on page 374.

groups will define their family lives in unique ways, depending on a number of factors such as their socioeconomic background, immigrant status, religious beliefs, or cultural practices and traditions (Baker, 1996).

For many years, a standard sociological definition of *family* has been a group of people who are related to one another by bonds of blood, marriage, or adoption and who live together, form an economic unit, and bear and raise children (Benokraitis, 1997). Many people believe that this definition should not be expanded—that social approval should not be extended to other relationships simply because the persons in those relationships wish to consider themselves a family. However, others challenge this definition because it simply does not match the reality of family life in contemporary society (Eichler, 1981; Lynn, 1996; Vanier Institute of the Family, 1998). Today's families include many types of living arrangements and relationships, including single-parent households, unmarried couples, lesbian and gay couples, and multiple-generation families that include grandparents, parents, and children, for example. To accurately reflect the reality of family life, we need an encompassing definition of what constitutes a family. Accordingly, we will define ***families* as relationships in which people live together with commitment, form an economic unit, care for any young, and consider their identity to be significantly attached to the group.** Sexual expression and parent–children relationships are a part of most, but not all, family relationships (based on Benokraitis, 1997; Lamanna and Riedmann, 1997).

In our study of families, we will use our sociological imagination to see how our personal experiences are related to the larger happenings in our society. At the microlevel, each of us has our own "biography," based on our experience within a family; at the macrolevel, our families are embedded in a specific social context that has a major impact on them (Aulette, 1994). We will examine the institution of the family at both of these levels, starting with family structure and characteristics.

Family Structure

EXTENDED AND NUCLEAR FAMILIES Sociologists distinguish between extended and nuclear families based on the number of generations that live within a household. An ***extended family* is a family unit composed of relatives in addition to parents and children who live in the same household.** These families often include grandparents, uncles, aunts, or other relatives who live

BOX 13.1

Answers to the Sociology Quiz on the Changing Family in Canada

1. **True.** Between 1981 and 1995, the number of common-law families almost tripled. Common-law families now represent almost 12 percent of Canadian families.
2. **False.** Eighty-two percent of single-parent families in Canada are headed by a mother.
3. **False.** Current estimates are that about one-third of marriages will end in divorce.
4. **True.** Monogamy is the only legally sanctioned form of marriage in Canada.
5. **True.** This trend is in part the result of the implementation of "zero tolerance" policies, which direct that charges be laid in all domestic violence cases.
6. **True.** In 1997 the average marrying age was 27 for women and 29 for men. In 1971 it was 22 for women and 25 for men.
7. **False.** Approximately 62 percent of all marriages in Canada are dual-earner marriages—marriages in which both spouses are in the labour force.
8. **False.** Test-tube babies are babies conceived by fertilizing an egg removed from a woman with a sperm in a laboratory, and then implanting the fertilized egg (embryo) into the woman.
9. **True.** Those who marry at an early age have a higher rate of divorce.
10. **True.** An estimated 76 percent of divorced men and 64 percent of divorced women remarry and the majority do so within three years of their divorce.

Sources: Balakrishnan et al., 1987; Statistics Canada, 1995b; Gorlick, 1995; Oderkirk and Lochhead, 1995; Richardson, 1996; Statistics Canada, 1996a; Statistics Canada, 1999c; and Statistics Canada, 1999d.

in close proximity to the parents and children, making it possible for family members to share resources. In horticultural and agricultural societies, extended families are extremely important; having a large number of family members participate in food production may be essential for survival. Today, extended family patterns are found in Latin America, Africa, Asia, and some parts of Eastern and Southern Europe (Busch, 1990).

A ***nuclear family* is a family composed of one or two parents and their dependent children, all of whom live apart from other relatives.** A traditional definition specifies that a nuclear family is made up of a "couple" and their dependent children; however, this definition is becoming increasingly outdated as significant changes occur in the structure of families. As shown in Figure 13.1, in 1996, just over 50 percent of all households were composed of married couples with children under the age of 18, as compared to 57 percent in 1981. The second-largest family type, at almost 30 percent, were married couples without children living at home. This group consisted of childless couples and couples whose children no longer lived at home (empty-nesters) (Statistics Canada, 1997c).

THE FAR SIDE
By GARY LARSON
©1988 Universal Press Syndicate
Larson
3-14
"Bob and Ruth! Come on in .... Have you met Russell and Bill, our 1.5 children?"

The Far Side © 1988; Distributed by Universal Press Syndicate. Reprinted with permission.

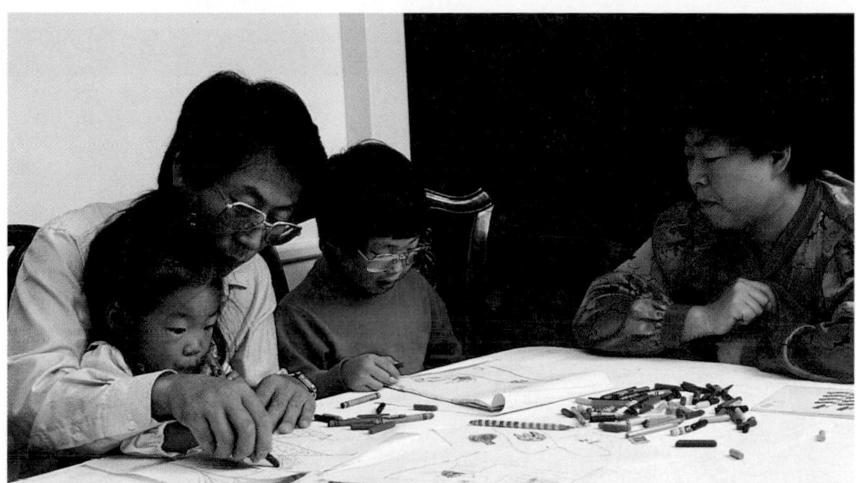

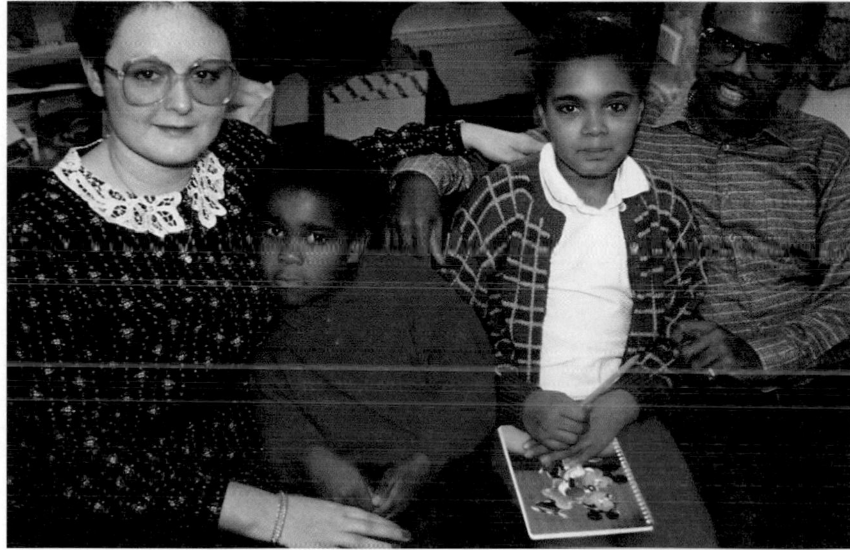

While the relationship between a husband and wife is based on legal ties, relationships between parents and children may be established either by blood ties or by legal ties.

Nuclear families are smaller than they were twenty years ago; whereas the average family size in 1971 was 3.7 persons, in 1996 it was 3.1 persons (Statistics Canada, 1997c). This decrease has been attributed to declining fertility rates, economic factors (i.e., the cost of having children, an indicator of which is the increased number of households in which both husband and wife work outside of the home), and delayed childbearing.

Marriage Patterns

Across cultures, families are characterized by different forms of marriage. ***Marriage* is a legally recognized and/or socially approved arrangement between two or more individuals that carries certain rights and obligations and usually involves sexual activity.** In most societies, marriage involves a mutual commitment by each partner, and linkages between two individuals and families are publicly demonstrated.

In Canada, the only legally sanctioned form of marriage is ***monogamy*—a marriage between two partners of the opposite sex.** For some people, marriage is a lifelong commitment that ends only with the death of a partner. For others, marriage is a commitment of indefinite duration. Through a pattern of marriage, divorce, and remarriage, some people practise *serial monogamy*—a succession of marriages in which a person has several spouses over

FIGURE 13.1 Family Structure

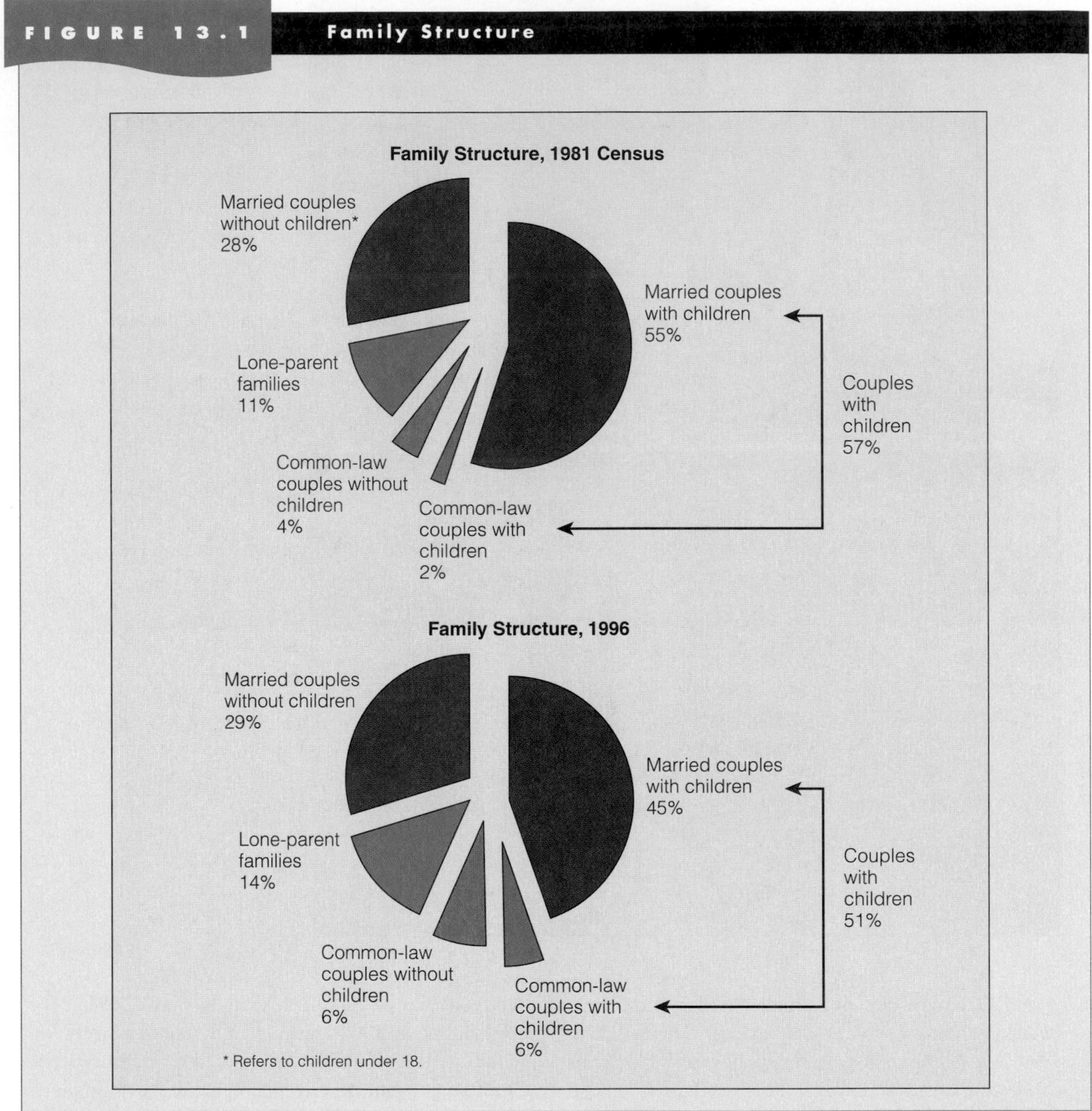

Adapted with permission from Statistics Canada, "Canadian Families: Diversity and Change," Cat. no. 12F0061XFE.

a lifetime but is legally married to only one person at a time.

***Polygamy* is the concurrent marriage of a person of one sex with two or more members of the opposite sex** (G. Marshall, 1994). The most prevalent form of polygamy is ***polygyny*—the concurrent marriage of one man with two or more women.** Polygyny has been practised in a number of societies, including by some in parts of Europe until the Middle Ages. More recently, some marriages in Islamic societies in Africa and Asia have been polygynous; however, the cost of providing for multiple wives and numerous children makes the practice impossible for all but the wealthiest men.

The second type of polygamy is ***polyandry*—marriage of one woman with two or more men.** Polyandry is very rare; when it does occur it usually takes place in societies in which men greatly outnumber women because of high rates of female infanticide.

To this point, we have examined a variety of marriage and family patterns found around the world. Regardless of the exact patterns followed by families, virtually all share certain common purposes and may have somewhat similar consequences for individual members.

Descent and Inheritance

Even though a variety of marital patterns exist across cultures, virtually all forms of marriage establish a system of descent so that kinship can be determined and inheritance rights established. In preindustrial societies, kinship is usually traced through one parent (unilineally). The most common pattern of unilineal descent is ***patrilineal descent*—a system of tracing descent through the father's side of the family.** Patrilineal systems are set up in such a manner that a legitimate son inherits his father's property and sometimes his position upon the father's death. In nations such as India, where boys are seen as permanent patrilineal family members while girls are seen as only temporary family members, girls tend to be considered more expendable than boys (O'Connell, 1994). Even with the less common pattern of ***matrilineal descent*—a system of tracing descent through the mother's side of the family**—women may not control property. However, inheritance of property and position usually is traced from the maternal uncle (mother's brother) to his nephew (mother's son). In some cases, mothers may pass on their property to daughters.

In contrast, in industrial societies, kinship usually is traced through both parents (bilineally). The most common form is ***bilateral descent*—a system of tracing descent through both the mother's and father's sides of the family.** This pattern is used in Canada for the purpose of determining kinship and inheritance rights; however, children typically take the father's last name.

Power and Authority in Families

Descent and inheritance rights are intricately linked with patterns of power and authority in families. The most prevalent forms of familial power and authority are patriarchy, matriarchy, and egalitarianism. A ***patriarchal family* is a family structure in which authority is held by the eldest male (usually the father).** The male authority figure acts as head of the household and holds power and authority over the women and children as well as over other males. A ***matriarchal family* is a family structure in which authority is held by the eldest female (usually the mother).** In this case, the female authority figure acts as head of the household. Although there has been a great deal of discussion about matriarchal families, scholars have found no historical evidence to indicate that true matriarchies ever existed.

The most prevalent pattern of power and authority in families is patriarchy. Across cultures, men are the primary (and often sole) decision makers regarding domestic, economic, and social concerns facing the family.

An ***egalitarian family* is a family structure in which both partners share power and authority equally.** Recently, a trend toward more egalitarian relationships has been evident in a number of countries as women have sought changes in their legal status and increased educational and employment opportunities. Some degree of economic independence makes it possible for women to delay marriage or to terminate a problematic marriage (Ward, 1998). Among gay and lesbian couples, power and authority issues also are important. While some analysts suggest that legalizing marriage among gay couples would reproduce more egalitarian relationships, others argue that such marriages would reproduce inequalities in power and authority found in conventional heterosexual relationships (Kirby and Robinson, 1998).

PERSPECTIVES ON FAMILIES

The ***sociology of family* is the subdiscipline of sociology that attempts to describe and explain patterns of family life and variations in family structure.** Functionalist perspectives emphasize the functions that families perform at the macrolevel of society, while conflict and feminist perspectives focus on families as a primary source of social inequality. By contrast, interactionists examine microlevel interactions that are integral to the roles of different family members.

Functionalist Perspectives

Functionalists emphasize the importance of the family in maintaining the stability of society and the well-being of individuals. According to Emile Durkheim, marriage is a microcosmic replica of the larger society; both marriage and society involve a mental and moral fusion of physically distinct individuals (Lehmann, 1994). Durkheim also believed that a division of labour contributed to greater efficiency in all areas of life—including marriages and families—even though he acknowledged that this division imposed significant limitations on some people.

Talcott Parsons was a key figure in developing a functionalist model of the family. According to Parsons (1955), the husband/father fulfils the *instrumental role* (meeting the family's economic needs, making important decisions, and providing leadership) while the wife/mother fulfils the *expressive role* (running the household, caring for children, and meeting the emotional needs of family members).

Contemporary functionalist perspectives on families derive their foundation from Durkheim and Parsons. Division of labour makes it possible for families to fulfil a number of functions that no other institution can perform as effectively. In advanced industrial societies, families serve four key functions:

1. *Sexual regulation*. Families are expected to regulate the sexual activity of their members and thus control reproduction so that it occurs within specific boundaries. At the macrolevel, incest taboos prohibit sexual contact or marriage between certain relatives. For example, virtually all societies prohibit sexual relations between parents and their children and between brothers and sisters. Sexual regulation of family members by the family is supposed to protect the principle of legitimacy—the belief that all children should have a socially and legally recognized father (Malinowski, 1964/1929).
2. *Socialization*. Parents and other relatives are responsible for teaching children the necessary knowledge and skills to survive. The smallness and intimacy of families make them best suited for providing children with the initial learning experiences they need.
3. *Economic and psychological support*. Families are responsible for providing economic and psychological support for members. In preindustrial societies, families are economic production units; in industrial societies, the economic security of families is tied to the workplace and to macrolevel economic systems. In recent years, psychological support and emotional security have been increasingly important functions of the family (Chafetz, 1989).
4. *Provision of social status*. Families confer social status and reputation on their members. These statuses include the ascribed statuses with which individuals are born, such as race/ethnicity, nationality, social class, and sometimes religious affiliation. One of the most significant and compelling forms of social placement is the family's class position and the opportunities (or lack thereof) resulting from that position. Examples of class-related opportunities include access to quality health care, higher education, and a safe place to live. Media depictions of how members of working-class families may attempt to deal with the frustrations of everyday life are discussed in Box 13.2.

Conflict Perspectives

Both conflict and feminist analysts view functionalist perspectives on the role of the family in society as idealized and inadequate. Rather than operating harmoniously and for the benefit of all members, families are sources of social inequality and conflict over values, goals, and access to resources and power (Benokraitis, 1997).

The foundation of conflict views of the family appeared in the works of Friedrich Engels, a friend and colleague of Karl Marx. In his classic work *The Origin of the Family, Private Property and the State* (1972), which was first published in 1884, Engels argued that the family in a capitalist society is an exploitive social institution that is primarily responsible for the oppression of women. Conflict theorists view the relationship between husbands and wives as similar to the relationship between capitalists and their workers. Women are dominated by men in the home in the same manner that workers are dominated by capitalists and managers in factories. Just as workers exchange their labour for a wage, so do wives exchange their domestic labour for the economic support of their husbands. While childbearing and care for family members in the home contribute to capitalism, these activities also rein-

BOX 13.2 SOCIOLOGY AND MEDIA

THE SIMPSONS: MIDDLE-CLASS FAMILY LIFE

In one episode of *The Simpsons*, the popular animated television series, Marge Simpson (the wife and mother) reads a "checklist for family problems" to Homer (the husband and father):

MARGE: Do you need a beer to fall asleep?
HOMER: Thank you, that'd be nice.
MARGE: Do you ever hide beer around the house?

[Homer removes a beer from the top of the commode in the bathroom.]

MARGE: Do you ever fantasize that you are someone else?

[Homer looks in the mirror, humming the tune "Can-Can."]

MARGE: Homie, I'd like you to do something for me. I want you to give up beer for a month.
HOMER: You got it! No deer for a month.
MARGE: Did you say "beer" or "deer"?
HOMER: Deer.

In this exchange, Marge represents the dutiful working-class wife who hopes to get her husband to drink less. Homer blissfully ignores her hints and suggestions because he finds that beer relaxes him after a stressful day at work. On another occasion, Homer talks with Bart (the son) about his drinking:

HOMER: ... Daddy has to go to a beer-drinking contest today.
BART: Think you'll win?
HOMER: Son, when you participate in sporting events, it's not whether you win or lose, it's how drunk you get.
BART: Gotcha. ...

The fictional Simpson family is one of the most popular working-class families of all time; however, several decades ago, *The Simpsons* could never have been shown on television. The earliest family comedies (such as *Father Knows Best, The Adventures of Ozzie and Harriet,* and *Leave It to Beaver*) idealized the white middle-class nuclear family and depicted the father as a *superdad*. The children were respectful, unlike Bart, who says exactly what is on his mind. The early shows offered endless images of "adoring and endearing couples who were blessed with squeaky-clean kids" (Medved, 1992:129); they created a powerful and lasting vision of how the nuclear family is *supposed to be*. Unlike Homer Simpson, the male characters in 1950s and 1960s family shows never consumed alcoholic beverages.

Beginning in the late 1960s and early 1970s, some situation comedies based on working-class families depicted fathers quite differently from the superdads of the middle class. Working-class fathers were more likely to have a few beers or to talk about being "hung over" from their "night out with the boys." Working-class fathers routinely were depicted as inept or made the butt of jokes. As for Homer Simpson, his bumbling but well-intentioned behaviour has endeared him to many viewers, who feel that his character captures the essence of many men's existences. Similarly, many women identify with the overworked and underappreciated Marge Simpson who, even as a cartoon character, realistically shows that raising a family can be a tough but rewarding experience. *The Simpsons* reflects a working-class, "we-stick-together-and-survive-on-our-own" ethic.

Sources: Based on Cantor and Cantor, 1992; Coontz, 1992; Duffy, 1992; and Medved, 1992.

force the subordination of women through unpaid (and often devalued) labour. As a result, husbands—like capitalists—enjoy more power and privilege within the family. Engels predicted that the oppression of women would end when women moved out of the private sphere of the home and into the paid workforce. As discussed in Chapter 10 ("Sex and Gender"), women's oppression has not disappeared as a result of the dramatic increases in the number of women in the paid workforce. In many ways, it has become more prevalent as women struggle with issues of gender inequality in pay and benefits, job advancement, and balancing career and home responsibilities. Other conflict analysts are concerned with the effect that class conflict has on the family. The exploitation of the lower classes by the upper classes contributes to family problems such as high rates of divorce and overall family instability.

Feminist Perspectives

Feminist theory has contributed to radical changes in the sociological study of families. Feminist theorists have been primarily responsible for redefining the concept of "the family," focusing on the diversity of family arrangements. Some feminist scholars reject the "monolithic model of the family" (Eichler, 1981:368), which idealizes one family form: the family with a male breadwinner and stay-at-home wife and children. Feminist theorists argue that limiting our concept of family to this traditional form means ignoring or denigrating diverse family forms, such as single-parent families, childless families, gay or lesbian families, and stepfamilies (Mackie, 1995:50). Roles within the family are viewed by feminist theorists as primarily socially constructed rather than biologically determined. Feminist scholars have challenged a number of common assumptions about family life and the roles we fulfil within families (Hamilton, 1988). For example, they question whether all "real" women want to be mothers, or whether the inequality between traditional husbands and wives is "natural" (Duffy, 1988:111).

In contrast to conflict theory, which focuses on class and property arrangements as the source of inequality within the family, feminist perspectives on inequality focus on ***patriarchy*—a hierarchical system of social organization in which cultural, political, and economic structures are controlled by men.** From this viewpoint, men's domination over women existed long before private ownership of property and capitalism (Mann, 1994). Women's subordination is rooted in patriarchy and men's control over women's labour power (Hartmann, 1981). Although the division of labour may appear to be an equal pooling of contributions within the family unit, feminist scholars view women as giving much but receiving less in return. According to sociologist Patricia Mann, "Male power in our society is expressed in economic terms even if it does not originate in property relations; women's activities in the home have been undervalued at the same time as their labor has been controlled by men" (Mann, 1994:42). The power discrepancy and economic dependency created in a patriarchal family system was demonstrated in sociologist Meg Luxton's study of families in Flin Flon, Manitoba. Consider this husband's comments: "You'd never work like I do. That's hard work, real work that earns money. And that money keeps you alive. Don't you forget it" (Luxton, 1980:164). As these comments reveal, men may feel that they have earned special privileges as a result of their breadwinner status. On the other hand, a woman's economic dependence means that her needs become secondary in the family (Luxton, 1980).

Feminist perspectives on families primarily focus on the problems of dominance and subordination inherent in relationships. Specifically, feminist theorists have acknowledged what has been described as the "dark side of the family," focusing on research efforts on issues such as child abuse, wife abuse, and violence against the elderly (Johnson, 1996b). Feminist explanations take into account the unequal political relationship between women and men in families and outside of families (Comack, 1996b; Smith, 1985; Hamilton, 1988). Some feminist analysts explain wife abuse as a conscious strategy used by men to control women and perpetuate gender inequality (Harris, 1991; Smith, 1996).

To remedy problems such as wife battering, the subordination of women in all areas of society would have to be eliminated. A starting point might be the elimination of factors fostering violence, such as media images that "convey strong messages that men are sexual predators and sexually dominant in their relationships with women" (Johnson, 1996b:7). These messages serve to "glorify and romanticize assaults and other violent behavior" (Aulette, 1994:329).

CONCEPT TABLE 13.A

THEORETICAL PERSPECTIVES ON FAMILIES

	Focus	Key Points	Perspective on Family Problems
Functionalist	Role of families in maintaining stability of society and individuals' well-being	In modern societies, families serve the functions of sexual regulation, socialization, economic and psychological support, and provision of social status.	Family problems are related to changes in social institutions such as the economy, religion, education, and law/government.
Conflict	Families as sources of conflict and social inequality	Families both mirror and help to perpetuate social inequalities based on class and gender.	Family problems reflect social patterns of dominance and subordination.
Feminist	Families as patriarchal institutions	Women's subordination is rooted in patriarchy and men's control over women's labour power.	Family problems such as child abuse, wife abuse, and elder abuse are the result of attempts to control women and perpetuate gender inequality.
Interactionist	Family dynamics, including communication patterns and the subjective meanings people assign to events	Interactions within families create a shared reality.	How family problems are perceived and defined depends on patterns of communication, the meanings people give to roles and events, and individuals' interpretations of family interactions.

A feminist analysis of families provides not only a theoretical perspective, but also a broad movement for social change. Supported by a variety of advocacy groups and networks, feminists have brought women's private problems such as wife abuse, and the financial difficulties of economically dependent wives, into the public arena (Cheal, 1991; Nelson and Robinson, 1999).

Interactionist Perspectives

Early interactionists viewed the communication process in families as integral to the roles that different family members play. Interactionists examine the roles of husbands, wives, and children as they act out their own parts and react to the actions of others. From this perspective, what people think, as well as what they say and do, is very important in understanding family dynamics.

According to sociologists Peter Berger and Hansfried Kellner (1964), interaction between marital partners contributes to a shared reality. Although newlyweds bring separate identities to a marriage, over time they construct a shared reality as a couple. In the process, the partners redefine their past identities to be consistent with new realities. Development of a shared reality is a continuous process, taking place not only in the family but also in any group in which the couple participates. Divorce is the reverse of this process; couples may start with a shared reality and, in the process of uncoupling, gradually develop separate realities (Vaughan, 1985).

Interactionists explain family relationships in terms of the subjective meanings and everyday interpretations people give to their lives. As sociologist Jessie Bernard (1982/1973) pointed out, women and men experience marriage differently, and a marriage, in effect, contains two marriages: "his marriage" and "her marriage." While a husband may see his marriage very positively, his wife may feel less positive about her marriage, and vice versa. Researchers have found that husbands and wives may give very different accounts of the same event, and their "two realities" frequently do not coincide (Safilios-Rothschild, 1969).

How do interactionists view problems within the family? Some focus on the terminology used to describe these problems, examining the extent to which words convey assumptions or "realities" about the nature of the problem. For example, violence between men and women in the home often is referred to as *spouse abuse* or *domestic violence*. However, these terms imply that women and men play equal roles in the perpetration of violence in families, overlooking the more active part men usually play in such aggression.

Analysts using a social constructionist approach note that definitions concerning family violence are not only socially constructed but also have an effect on how people are treated. In one study of a shelter for battered women, analysts found that workers made decisions about whom to assist and how to assist them based on their own understanding of what constitutes a "real" battered woman (Loseke, 1992).

Concept Table 13.A summarizes these sociological perspectives on the family. Taken together, these perspectives on the social institution of families help us understand both the good and bad sides of familial relationships. Now we shift our focus to love, marriage, intimate relationships, and family issues in Canada.

DEVELOPING INTIMATE RELATIONSHIPS AND ESTABLISHING FAMILIES

It has been said that we are "in love with love." Why is this so? Perhaps the answer lies in the fact that our ideal culture emphasizes "*romantic* love," which refers to a deep emotion, the satisfaction of significant needs, a caring for and acceptance of the person we love, and involvement in an intimate relationship (Lamanna and Riedmann, 1997).

Love and Intimacy

How have Canadians viewed love and intimacy in the past? During the Industrial Revolution in the late nineteenth century, people came to view work and home as separate spheres in which different feelings and emotions were appropriate (Coontz, 1992). The public sphere of work—men's sphere—emphasized self-reliance and independence. In contrast, the private sphere of the home—women's sphere—emphasized the giving of services, the exchange of gifts, and love. Accordingly, love and emotions became the domain of women, and work and rationality the domain of men (Lamanna and Riedmann, 1997).

Although the roles of women and men have changed dramatically since the Industrial Revolution, men and women still do not always share the same perspectives about romantic love. Moreover, they typically do not express their feelings in the same manner. According to sociologist Francesca Cancian (1990), women tend to express their feelings verbally, whereas men tend to express their love through nonverbal actions, such as running an errand for someone or repairing a child's broken toy. Women may not always interpret men's routine actions as signs of love—a fact that deeply frustrates many men, as one noted when he was asked how he showed his love for his wife.

> What does she want? Proof? She's got it, hasn't she? Would I be knocking myself out to get things for her—like to keep up this house—if I didn't love her? Why does a man do things like that if not because he

What is love? In Western society, an idealized picture of romantic love can be found as early as the Middle Ages. Do you think that people today have a different perspective on love?

> loves his wife and kids? I swear, I can't figure out what she wants. (quoted in Rubin, 1976:146)

Told of his response, his wife said, "It's not enough that he supports us and takes care of us. I appreciate that, but I want him to share things with me. I need him to tell me his feelings" (quoted in Rubin, 1976:146).

Love, intimacy, and sexuality are closely intertwined. Intimacy may be psychic ("the sharing of minds") or sexual, or both. Although sexuality is an integral part of many intimate relationships, perceptions about sexual activities vary from one culture to the next and from one era to another. For example, kissing is found primarily in Western cultures; many African and Asian cultures view kissing negatively (Reinisch, 1990).

For over forty years, the work of biologist Alfred C. Kinsey was considered the definitive research on human sexuality, even though some of his methodology had serious limitations. More recently, the National Opinion Research Center at the University of Chicago conducted the National Health and Social Life Survey (see Laumann et al., 1994; Michael et al., 1994). Based on interviews with more than 3400 men and women aged 18 to 59, this random survey tended to reaffirm the significance of the dominant sexual ideologies. Most respondents reported that they engaged in heterosexual relationships, although 9 percent of the men said they had had at least one homosexual encounter resulting in orgasm. While 6.2 percent of men and 4.4 percent of women said that they were at least somewhat attracted to others of the same gender, only 2.8 percent of men and 1.4 percent of women identified themselves as gay or lesbian. According to the study, persons who engaged in extramarital sex found their activities to be more thrilling than those with their marital partner, but they also felt guilty. Persons in sustained relationships such as marriage or cohabitation found sexual activity to be the most satisfying emotionally and physically.

Cohabitation

***Cohabitation* refers to a couple's living together without being legally married.** Many couples choose to live together before marrying or as an alternative to marriage. Although cohabitation or living together is a relatively new alternative to traditional marriage in Canada, in some parts of the world, especially Africa, Latin America, and Sweden, it has been practised for hundreds of years (Cunningham and Antill, 1995).

FIGURE 13.2 Couples Living Common Law by Province, 1981 and 1996

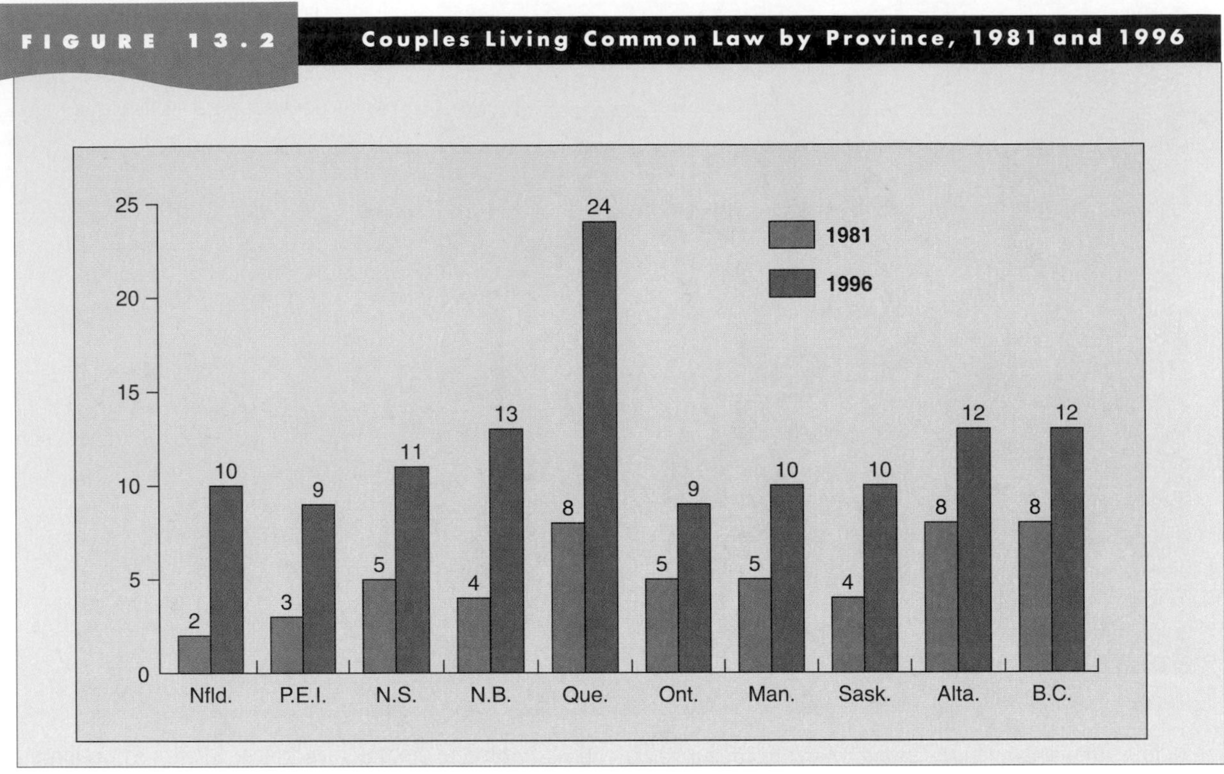

Adapted with permission from Statistics Canada, "Families: Number, Type, and Structure," Cat. no. 93-312; and "Families: Social and Economic Characteristics," Cat. no. 93-320.

Attitudes about cohabitation have changed in the past two decades. In Canada, it has become increasingly popular. The census defines *common-law* partners as two persons of the opposite sex who are not legally married, but live together as husband and wife. The growth of common-law families is the strongest of all family structures (Statistics Canada, 1997c). Almost half of common-law-couple families include children, whether born to the current union or brought to the family from previous unions. The proportion of people in common-law unions varies considerably by province (see Figure 13.2). In Quebec, one in four couples lives common-law, making it the province with the highest rate of common-law families.

Those most likely to cohabit are young adults between the ages of 15 and 24. In 1990, nearly 82 percent of all 15- to 19-year-olds in a couple union were living common-law. Cohabitation is also common among Canadian university and college students, an estimated 25 percent of whom report having cohabited at some time. While "living together" or living common-law is often a prelude to marriage for young adults, common-law unions are also becoming a popular alternative both to marriage and to remarriage following divorce or separation (Stout, 1994; Dumas, 1997).

Today, some people view cohabitation as a form of "trial marriage." For others, however, cohabitation is not a first step toward marriage. Studies have found that cohabiting partners are often not as committed to their relationship as married couples are. Couples who cohabit do not face the same legal difficulties as divorcing couples. Furthermore, their relationship is regarded socially as less permanent than marriage. Studies have shown that fewer than half of such relationships culminate in marriage (McDaniel, 1994; Statistics Canada, 2000d). However, if the cohabiting couple has children they are less likely to separate (Wu, 1995).

Does cohabitation contribute to marital success? Some studies have found that cohabitation has little or no effect on marital adjustment, emotional closeness, satisfaction, and intimacy (White, 1987). However, other evidence suggests that couples who cohabit report poorer-quality relationships than married couples (Ward, 1998). In a study that examined the relationship between cohabiting before marriage and the likelihood of divorce, researchers concluded that those who had cohabited were both less satisfied with their marriage and less committed to the institution of marriage than those who married without having first cohabited (Baker, 1996). The researchers theorized that cohabitation may contribute to people's individualistic attitudes and values while making them more aware that alternatives to marriage exist (Axinn and Thornton, 1992; Thomson and Colella, 1992).

Marriage

Why do people get married? Couples get married for a variety of reasons. Some do so because they are "in love," desire companionship and sex, want to have children, feel social pressure, are attempting to escape from a bad situation in their parents' home, or believe that they will have more money or other resources if they get married. These factors notwithstanding, the selection of a marital partner actually is fairly predictable. As previously discussed, most people in Canada tend to choose marriage partners who are similar to themselves. ***Homogamy*** **refers to the pattern of individuals marrying those who have similar characteristics, such as race/ethnicity, religious background, age, education, or social class.** However, homogamy provides only the general framework within which people select their partners; people are also influenced by other factors. For example, some researchers claim that people want partners whose personalities match their own in significant ways. Thus, people who are outgoing and friendly may be attracted to people with those same traits. However, other researchers claim that people look for partners whose personality traits differ from but complement their own.

Regardless of the individual traits of marriage partners, research indicates that communication and emotional support are crucial to the success of marriages. Common marital problems include lack of emotional intimacy, poor communication, and lack of companionship. One study concluded that for many middle- and upper-income couples, women's paid work was critical to the success of the marriages. People who have a strong commitment to their work have two distinct sources of pleasure—work and family. For members of the working class, however, work may not be a source of pleasure. For all women and men, balancing work and family life is a challenge (Baker and Lero, 1996).

Housework

Thirty years ago, most Canadian families relied on one wage earner. Today over 60 percent of all families in Canada are ***dual-earner families*****—families in which both partners are in the labour force** (see Figure 13.3). Most employed women hold full-time, year-round jobs. Even when their children are very young, most working mothers are employed full-time.

Moreover, as discussed in Chapter 10, many married women leave their paid employment at the end of the day and go home to perform hours of housework and child care. Sociologist Arlie Hochschild (1989) refers to this as the ***second shift*****—the domestic work that employed women perform at home after they complete their workday on the job.** Thus, many married women today contribute to the economic well being of their families and also meet many, if not all, of the domestic needs of family members by cooking, cleaning, shopping, taking care of children, and managing household routines. According to Hochschild, the unpaid housework women do on the second shift amounts to an extra month of work each year. This pattern is consistent regardless of whether the woman is employed full-time or part-time (Marshall, 1995). Across race, class, and culture, numerous studies have confirmed that domestic work remains primarily women's work (Canadian Council on Social Development, 1996). (See Box 13.3 for a discussion of family life in Japan.)

In recent years, more husbands have attempted to share some of the household and child-care responsibilities, especially in families in which the wife's earnings are essential to family finances (Ward, 1998). In contrast, husbands who see themselves as the primary breadwinners are less likely to share housework with their wives. Even when husbands share some of the household responsibilities, however, they typically spend much less time on these activities than do their wives (Canadian Council on Social Development, 1996). Women and men perform different household tasks, and the deadlines for their work vary widely. Recurring tasks that have

BOX 13.3 SOCIOLOGY IN GLOBAL PERSPECTIVE

FAMILY LIFE IN JAPAN

Traditionally, Japanese women have been socialized to fulfil the "good wife/wise mother" role and find satisfaction primarily in marriage and motherhood. Although Japan is experiencing many social changes, traditional values still dictate that a Japanese girl is not a woman until she marries. Popular culture supports this ideal as well. For example, smiling newlyweds and wistful brides routinely are featured in magazine ads for wedding halls.

Japanese women who currently are in the 40–50 age cohort were taught *amae*—the belief that a very strong bond should exist between a mother and her children because the dependence a child learns from the mother can be transferred to the group as the child grows older. As a result, many of these women, as mothers, gave almost twenty-four-hour-a-day care and attention to their children, including picking them up immediately when they cried and always being there for them.

However, the practice of *amae* is now being questioned. After the children leave home, many Japanese mothers feel that they have lost their sense of purpose *(ikigai)* and begin to search for something else to occupy their time. After years of diapering babies, overseeing homework, and meeting all of the needs of their children, many women lack self-confidence and marketable skills. Consequently, middle age becomes a time of crisis. While some take classes to widen their horizons, others may turn to drinking, out of fear of rejection or feelings of depression and boredom. At this time, some husbands are at the height of their careers and are working long hours or entertaining clients.

Today, many younger women in Japan are employed. Like women in Canada, however, they often have a second shift of housework averaging three hours a day as compared with their husbands' eight minutes a day. However, traditional roles increasingly are being challenged by women (and some men) in Japan. Many more children now are entrusted to child-care centres, whereas in the past it was unthinkable to have strangers take care of one's children. As is true with many changes in Japanese society today, the long-term effects of this change are as yet unknown.

Although Japanese women have been socialized to fulfil the "good wife/wise mother" role, many of them currently are employed and face the same "double shift" as many Canadian women.

Sources: Based on Kitano and Chi, 1986–87; Shorto, 1991; Kitano et al., 1992; Benokraitis, 1997; and Jung, 1994.

FIGURE 13.3 Dual-Earner Families, 1967–1996

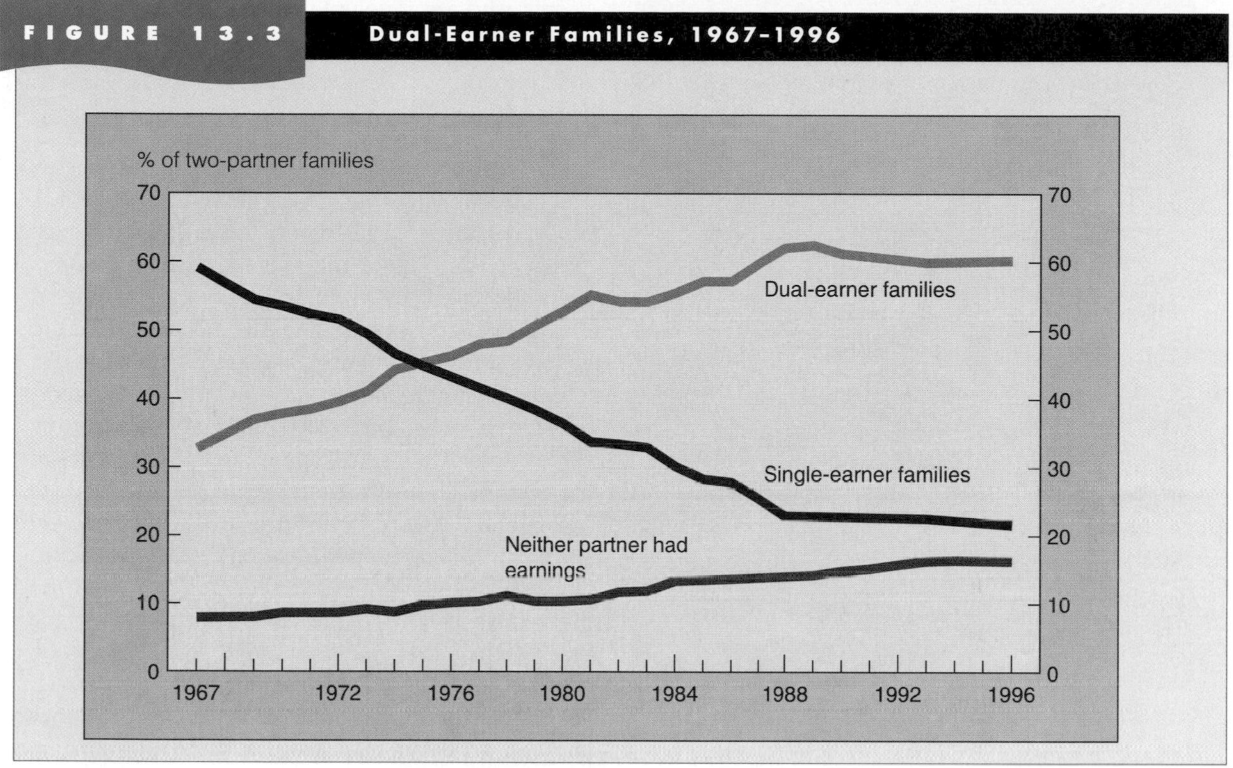

Adapted with permission from Statistics Canada, *The Daily*, 23 October 1998. Cat. no. 11-001.

specific times for completion (such as bathing a child or cooking a meal) tend to be the women's responsibility, whereas men are more likely to do the periodic tasks that have no highly structured schedule (such as mowing the lawn or changing the oil in the car) (Hochschild, 1989; Marshall, 1994). Many men also are more reluctant to perform undesirable tasks such as scrubbing the toilet or diapering a baby, or to give up leisure pursuits.

Couples with more egalitarian ideas about women's and men's roles tend to share more equally in food preparation, housework, and child care (Wright et al., 1992). For some men, the shift to a more egalitarian household occurs gradually, as Wesley, whose wife works full-time, explains:

> It was me taking the initiative, and also Connie pushing, saying "Gee, there's so much that has to be done." At first I said, "But I'm supposed to be the breadwinner," not realizing she's also the breadwinner. I was being a little blind to what was going on, but I got tired of waiting for my wife to come home to start cooking, so one day I surprised the hell out [of] her and myself and the kids, and I had supper waiting on the table for her. (quoted in Gerson, 1993:170)

Women employed full-time who are single parents probably have the greatest burden of all; they have complete responsibility for the children and the household, often with little or no help from ex-husbands or relatives.

CHILD-RELATED FAMILY ISSUES AND PARENTING

Deciding to Have Children

Not all couples become parents. Those who decide not to have children often consider themselves to be "child-free," while those who want to have children but cannot do so may consider themselves "childless." Research on voluntary childlessness in Canada reveals that one-third of childless couples decide before marriage that they do not want children

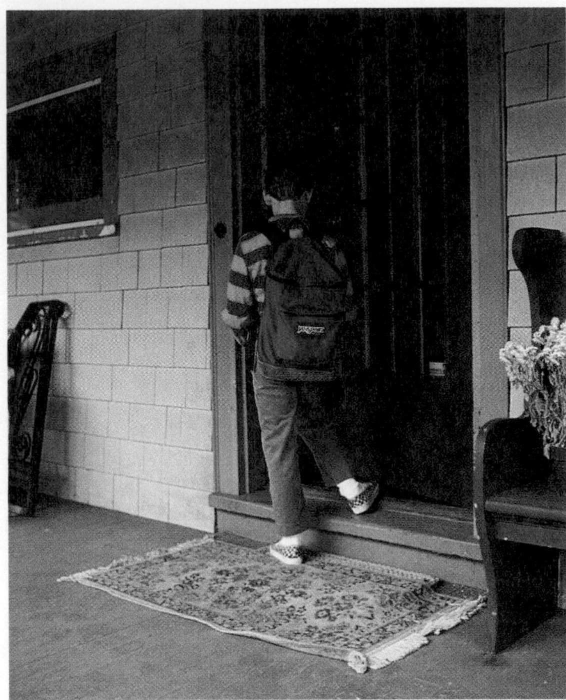

Dual-earner marriages are a challenge for many children as well as their parents. While parents are at work, latchkey children often are at home alone.

(Veevers, 1980 and 1991). Couples remain childless for a number of reasons including the view that pregnancy is a form of illness, or a condition that reduces one's sexual appeal; the association of motherhood with dependency or incompetence; and the interference of children with career advancement, travelling, and marital stability. Do couples need to have children to be happy? According to the research, the answer is no. Studies have found that child-free couples report greater marital satisfaction than do couples with children (Ramu, 1984). However, despite this fact, childless couples experience higher rates of divorce. Although only about 20 percent of couples are childless, between 50 to 70 percent of divorces in Canada are obtained by childless couples (Adams, 1990).

According to sociologist Charlene Miall (1986), women who are involuntarily childless engage in "information management" to combat the social stigma associated with childlessness. Their tactics range from avoiding people who make them uncomfortable to revealing their infertility so that others will not think of them as "selfish" for being childless. People who are involuntarily childless may choose to become parents by adopting a child.

Adoption

Adoption is a legal process through which the rights and duties of parenting are transferred from a child's biological and/or legal parents to new legal parents. This procedure gives the adopted child all of the rights of a biological child. In most adoptions, a new birth certificate is issued, and the child has no future contact with the biological parents. In Canada, adoption is regulated provincially. Therefore, adopted persons' access to information regarding their "biological parents" varies, as does their desire to access this information (Jackson, 1993).

Matching children who are available for adoption with prospective adoptive parents can be difficult. The available children have specific needs, and the prospective parents often set specifications on the type of child they want to adopt. Ironically, while thousands of children are available for adoption each year in North America, prospective parents seek out children in developing nations such as Romania, South Korea, and India. The primary reason is that the available children in Canada are thought to be "unsuitable." They may have disabilities or illnesses, or their undesirability may be due to their being nonwhite (most prospective parents are white) or too old (Zelizer, 1985). In addition, fewer infants are available for adoption today than in the past because better means of contraception exist, abortion is more readily available, and more single parents decide to keep their babies. Consequently, the demand for adoptive children is growing, while the supply of children available for adoption is shrinking. In Canada, there are three applicants for each public adoption and almost as many for private adoptions. In addition, in 1990, an estimated 2000 to 5000 Canadians were actively pursuing international adoptions.

New Reproductive Technologies

The availability of a variety of reproductive technologies is having a dramatic impact on traditional concepts of the family and parenthood. Since the first "test tube" baby was born in 1985, there has been an explosion of research, clinical practice, and experimentation in the area of reproductive technology. Procedures used in the creation of new life, such as artificial insemination and in vitro fertilization, are referred to as methods of assisted reproduction (Achilles, 1996). These procedures have raised some controversial ethical issues in terms of what role medical science should play in the creation of human life (Eichler, 1996).

Artificial insemination is the oldest, simplest, and most common type of assisted reproduction. It has been suggested that the word "artificial" is misleading and that a more accurate term for this procedure would be "alternative insemination" (Achilles, 1996:349). (See also Box 13.4.)

There are several complex issues concerning the moral, legal, and social implications of artificial insemination. In most cases the woman is given no information about the donor and the donor is not told if a pregnancy has occurred. The result of this anonymity is that neither mother nor the individuals conceived through donor insemination will have access to information regarding the biological father. With the exception of Quebec and Yukon, the law does not provide protection for the participants in this procedure. In Quebec, a child born through artificial means is legally considered to be the child of the *social* father, that is, the father who rears the child. In Yukon, donors are protected from possible legal action by offspring or donor sperm recipients (Achilles, 1996).

The term *test-tube baby* is often used incorrectly to describe babies conceived through *in vitro* fertilization. An actual test-tube baby would require conception, gestation, and birth to occur outside of a woman's body. To date, this technology has not been developed (Achilles, 1996). In vitro (Latin for "in glass") fertilization involves removing an egg from a woman, fertilizing the egg with the sperm in a petri dish, and then implanting the fertilized egg (embryo) into the woman. Critics of this procedure have suggested that the success rate is no better than the probability of an infertile couple's having a child without medical intervention.

Another alternative available to couples with fertility problems is the use of a surrogate, or substitute, mother to carry a child for them. There are two types of surrogacy. In *traditional surrogacy* the surrogate is artificially inseminated with the father's sperm. The child is biologically related to the surrogate and the father. In the second type of surrogacy, *gestational surrogacy*, the sperm and the eggs from the infertile couple are transferred to the surrogate using an assisted reproductive technology (such as in vitro fertilization). With gestational surrogacy the surrogate carries the child but is not biologically or genetically related to it.

All of this may be very confusing. One of the many reasons we have so much difficulty with these new reproductive technologies is because they are just that—new. They are new to our society and also new to our concept of the family. In fact, we have yet to develop accurate terminology to incorporate all of these new alternatives.

In light of all the assisted reproductive technologies available, what does the term "parent" mean? How many "parents" does the child have? Is "mother" an accurate term for the gestational surrogate mother? The practice of surrogate motherhood also raises important questions about the position of women in society and about women's relationships to men and to their offspring (Overall, 1991).

Single Parenting

Single parenting is not a new phenomenon in Canada. However, one of the most significant changes in Canadian families is the dramatic increase in single-parent families. Today, there are over a million single-parent families. In the past, most single-parent families were created when one parent died. Today, the major causes of single parenthood are separation and divorce (Canadian Council on Social Development, 1996). Recent estimates suggest that up to one-third of all Canadian mothers will be single parents at some stage in their lives (Marcil-Gratton, 1993).

Even for a person with a stable income and a network of friends and family to help with child care, raising a child alone can be an emotional and financial burden. Eighty-two percent of lone-parent families are headed by a mother (Oderkirk and Lochhead, 1995). According to sociologists Sara McLanahan and Karen Booth (1991), children in mother-only families are more likely than children in two-parent families to exhibit poor academic achievement, higher school absentee and dropout rates, higher early marriage and early parenthood rates, and higher divorce rates, and to be more likely to abuse drugs and alcohol. Does living in a one-parent family cause all of this? Certainly not! Many other factors—including discrimination, unsafe neighbourhoods, and high crime rates—contribute to these problems.

BOX 13.4 CRITICAL THINKING

Reproductive Technology and the Future of the Family: A Feminist Critique

Reproductive technology is burgeoning, and so is discussion about it by sociologists, legal experts, feminists, and philosophers. Many—but especially doctors, lawyers, and scientists—are willing to sing the praises of reproductive technology, yet they seldom stop to consider its implications for our future. The general rules appear to be: (1) what can be done should be done, and (2) if it is possible to manipulate human reproduction, then human reproduction should be manipulated.

What are some of the potential effects of reproductive technologies on human relationships? Sociologist Christine Overall considers this question in the context of the different assisted reproductive technologies available.

Fetal Sex Preselection: This term refers to various means that have been proposed for the purpose of determining, at the time of conception, the sex of the fetus. Many questions are raised with respect to fetal sex preselection: Are individuals ever justified in making use of these techniques to determine the sex of their child? If so, when and why are they justified, and if not, why are they not justified? Also, would widespread use of sex preselection techniques result in a change in the sex ratio: that is, if people could choose, would far more males than females be born? Would the use of these procedures produce a decrease in population, since people would, from the start, get exactly the number and kind of children they want? Parents would no longer need to have "just one more child" to obtain a child of the desired sex.

The use of fetal sex preselection appears to imply that children are wanted, not for their own sake—that is, for their individual characters and abilities—but rather for the sake of the gender they represent.

Prenatal Diagnosis: This term refers to the use of such techniques as ultrasound tests, chorionic villi sampling, and amniocentesis. These procedures provide information about possible birth defects in the fetus, as well as its sex. The issue with these technologies is, will a fetus found to be defective be aborted? Can a woman freely choose to continue the pregnancy if she so desires, or is pressure exerted on her to have an abortion? A consequence of using these procedures may be that the autonomy of the woman is not increased but decreased.

Although there can be no doubt that these procedures will permit the birth of more and more healthy babies, some fear that the widespread use of prenatal diagnosis and fetal surgery will mean that in the future many children born with handicaps will tend to be regarded as unfortunate mistakes who should have been eliminated before birth.

Lesbian mothers and gay fathers are counted in some studies as single parents; however, they often share parenting responsibilities with same-sex partners. Due to ***homophobia* (hatred and fear of homosexuals and lesbians)**, lesbian mothers and gay fathers are more likely to lose custody to a heterosexual parent in divorce cases (Arnup, 1995; R. Epstein, 1996; Robinson et al., 1998).

Single fathers who do not have custody of their children may play a relatively limited role in the lives of those children. While some remain actively involved in their children's lives, others may become "Disneyland daddies" who spend time with their children in recreational activities and buy them presents for special occasions but have a very small part in the children's day-to-day lives. Sometimes, this

BOX 13.4

CONTINUED

Surrogate Motherhood: In cases where a woman for a variety of reasons is unable to sustain a pregnancy, she may choose to hire a woman—referred to as a surrogate—to carry her child. Once again many complex questions arise when considering this procedure. What happens if the baby is born with a defect or is not the sex the couple wanted? Does the commissioning couple have to accept "damaged goods"? What is the fate of a child for whom no one wants to take responsibility? What if the surrogate mother produces not one baby but two? While the commissioning couple seem to be getting double for their money, what if they only want one? Are they entitled to both children?

One of the most serious legal complications that has so far arisen with some frequency in surrogate arrangements is that some mothers are unwilling to surrender the child after it is born. The other side of the coin is that some couples have been known to change their minds about taking the baby they have ordered, if their circumstances change. If the surrogate mother also does not want the baby, it is an unwanted child.

Women who seek work as surrogate mothers are often poor and uneducated. For them, surrogacy may appear to be a sort of last resort. In becoming surrogates, they take on work that denies their individuality, that values them only to the extent that they are successful and healthy reproductive machines. Although the practice of surrogate motherhood appears to increase our reproductive freedom by allowing some infertile women and men (at least those who are wealthy) to acquire a baby, in fact, because of its highly commercialized form, it diminishes at least some women's reproductive freedom and control. For, as the popular press has so aptly suggested, surrogacy amounts to no more than a depersonalized rent-a-womb arrangement.

New reproductive technology generates many conflicts and contradictions. It has the potential to be both an asset and a liability for the future of human relationships. Perhaps the main source of this ambiguity is the question of power that it raises. If women and men, both as individuals and collectively, share control over reproductive technology, it may be put to uses that benefit us all. But if, as now seems to be the case, most people are able to exert very little control over research into the development and applications of reproductive technology, it may be a real threat to our hopes for a humane future.

Adapted with permission from Overall, 1991.

limited role is by choice, but more often, it is caused by workplace demands on time and energy, the location of the ex-wife's residence, and the limitations placed on the visitation arrangements.

Currently, men head close to one-fifth of lone-parent families; among many of these men, a pattern of "involved fatherhood" has emerged (Gerson, 1993). For example, in a study of men who became single fathers because of their wives' deaths, desertion, or relinquishment of custody, sociologist Barbara Risman (1987) found that the men had very strong relationships with their children.

TRANSITIONS AND PROBLEMS IN FAMILIES

Families go through many transitions and experience a wide variety of problems, ranging from separation and divorce, to unplanned pregnancy, to family violence. These all-too-common experiences highlight two important facts about families: (1) for good or ill, families are central to our existence, and (2) the reality of family life is far more complicated than the idealized image found in the media and in many political discussions. Whereas some families provide their members with love, warmth, and satisfying emotional experiences, other families may be hazardous to the individual's physical and mental well-being. Because of this dichotomy in family life, sociologists have described families as both a "haven in a heartless world" (Lasch, 1977) and a "cradle of violence" (Gelles and Straus, 1988).

Violence in Families: Wife and Child Abuse

Violence between men and women in the home is often referred to as spouse abuse or domestic violence. *Spouse abuse* refers to any intentional act or series of acts—whether physical, emotional, or sexual—that causes injury to a female or male spouse (Wallace, 1996). According to sociologists, spouse abuse refers not only to people who are married but also to those who are cohabiting or involved in a serious relationship, as well as those individuals who are separated or living apart from their former spouse (Wallace, 1996). As discussed in Chapter 4, *child abuse* refers to physical or sexual abuse and/or neglect by a parent or caregiver.

How much do we know about violence in families? Violence against spouses and children is clearly an extreme form of family dysfunction. However, sociologists have difficulty studying family violence because it is often hidden from outsiders and not reported to law enforcement authorities. This is particularly true in cases of child abuse because the powerlessness of children in the family assures that most incidents remain hidden (Rodgers and Kong, 1996). Statistics on the incidence of familial child abuse capture only those cases that come to the attention of official agencies. Data on the extent of wife assault in Canada is more extensive and is based on police reports and findings from self-report studies such as the 1993 Violence Against Women (VAW) survey. Reports from these sources of information indicate that 3 in 10 women have experienced physical or sexual abuse at the hands of a marital partner.

Children who are raised in an environment of violence suffer profoundly, even if they are not the direct targets. Their own physical and emotional needs are often neglected and they may learn by example to deal with conflict through violence (Canadian Council on Social Development, 1996).

Only within the last few decades have various forms of domestic violence been defined as intolerable criminal offences. Historically, domestic abuse was seen as a private family matter.

Why has our society been slow to respond to the problem of domestic violence, whether in the form of child or spouse abuse? Until recently, individuals and law enforcement officials have followed a policy of *nonintervention*, which was based on a strong reluctance to interfere in other people's family matters. Police reacted to calls for assistance with frustration or apathy, viewing responses to "domestic" calls as a waste of valuable time and resources. The general perception was that battered women could simply leave an abusive relationship if they wanted to.

The women's movement was largely responsible for bringing the issue of wife abuse into the public and political arenas in the 1970s. During the same period, child sexual abuse was "discovered" and found to be much more extensive than ever imagined (Rodgers and Kong, 1996:116). This growing awareness led to the organization of shelters for victims of family violence and to changes in the criminal justice system's response to spousal assault and child abuse. The first step in providing protection against domestic violence occurred in the early 1980s, when police forces across Canada were given directives making it mandatory for them to lay charges where there are reasonable grounds to believe an assault has occurred. Before these policies were implemented, the onus was on the abused spouse to lay charges. Many victims of spousal abuse refused to have their spouses charged because they feared provoking them to further violence. In 1983, the sexual assault laws were changed so that men could be charged with sexually assaulting their wives. At the same time the Canada Evidence Act

FIGURE 13.4 Divorces in Canada, 1950–1996

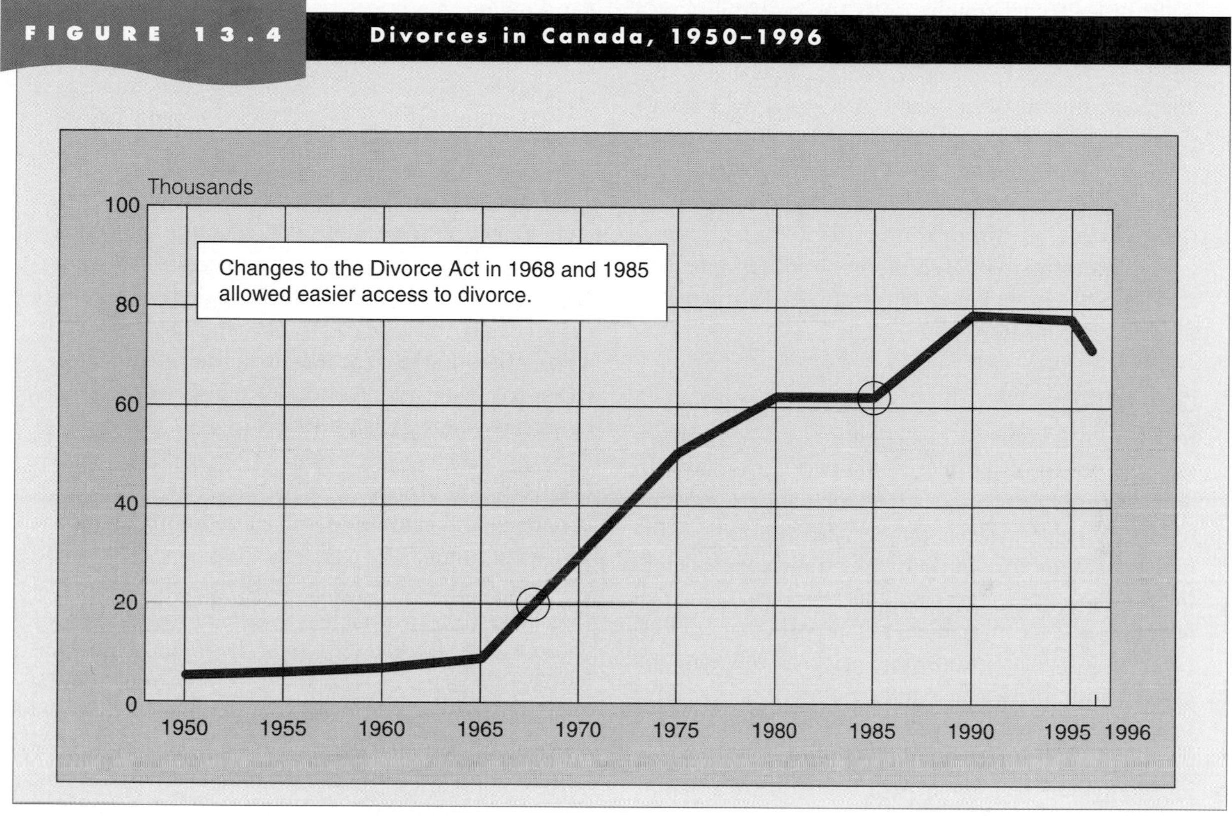

Reprinted with permission from Statistics Canada, *The Daily*, October 14, 1997.

was revised to permit wives to testify against their husbands (Johnson, 1996a). Finally, in order to provide better protection to children, legislation was enacted that encompassed a range of sexual offences against children (Rodgers and Kong, 1996). Despite these legislative changes and efforts to change attitudes, violence continues to be a much too common occurrence in families.

Divorce

Divorce is the legal process of dissolving a marriage that allows former spouses to remarry if they so choose. Prior to 1968 it was difficult to obtain a divorce in Canada. A divorce was granted only on the grounds of adultery. In 1968 the grounds for divorce were expanded to include marital breakdown (i.e., desertion, imprisonment, or separation of three or more years) and marital offences (physical or mental cruelty). In 1985 the Divorce Act introduced "no fault" provisions that made marital breakdown the sole ground for divorce. Under no-fault divorce laws, proof of "blameworthiness" is no longer necessary. However, when children are involved, the issue of "blame" may assume greater importance in the determination of parental custody.

Have you heard statements such as "One out of every two marriages ends in divorce"? Statistics might initially appear to bear out this statement. In 1997, for example, 159,350 Canadian couples married and 67,408 divorces were granted (Statistics Canada, 1998d). However, comparing the number of marriages with the number of divorces from year to year can be misleading. The couples who divorce in a given year are very unlikely to come from the group that married that year. In addition, in years when the economy is in a recession people may delay getting married but not divorced (McVey and Kalbach, 1995). Some people also may go through several marriages and divorces, thus skewing the divorce rate. The likelihood of divorce goes up with each subsequent marriage in the serial monogamy pattern.

In order to accurately assess the probability of a marriage ending in divorce, it is necessary to use what is referred to as a *cohort approach*. This approach establishes probabilities based on assumptions about how the various age groups (cohorts) in society might behave, given their marriage rate, their age at first marriage, and their responses to various social, cultural, and economic changes. Canadian estimates based on a cohort approach are that 30 to 40 percent of marriages will end in divorce (Richardson, 1996).

CAUSES OF DIVORCE Why do divorces occur? As you will recall from Chapter 1, sociologists look for correlations (relationships between two variables) in attempting to answer questions such as this. Existing research has identified a number of factors at both the macro- and microlevel that make some couples more or less likely to divorce. At the macrolevel, societal factors contributing to higher rates of divorce include changes in social institutions, such as religion, the family, and the legal system. Some religions have taken a more lenient attitude toward divorce, and the social stigma associated with divorce has lessened. Further, as we have seen in this chapter, the family institution has undergone a major change that has resulted in less economic and emotional dependency among family members—and thus reduced a barrier to divorce. And, as Figure 13.4 demonstrates, the liberalization of divorce laws in Canada has had a dramatic impact on the divorce rate.

At the microlevel, a number of factors contribute to a couple's "statistical" likelihood of becoming divorced. Some of the primary social characteristics of those most likely to get divorced include:

- Marriage at an early age (15–19) (Balarkishnan et al., 1987)
- A short acquaintanceship before marriage (Grover et al., 1985)
- Disapproval of the marriage by relatives and friends (Goode, 1976)
- Limited economic resources and low wages (Nett, 1993)
- A high school education or less (although deferring marriage to attend college may be more of a factor than education per se) (Burch and Madan, 1987)
- Previous marriages (Richardson, 1996)
- The presence of children (depending on their gender and age at the beginning of the marriage) (Rankin and Maneker, 1985; Morgan, Lye, and Condran, 1988; Martin and Bumpass, 1989)

The interrelationships of these and other factors is complicated. For example, the effect of age is intertwined with economic resources: persons from families at the low end of the income scale tend to marry earlier than those at more affluent income levels. Thus, the question becomes whether age itself is a factor or whether economic resources are more closely associated with divorce.

CONSEQUENCES OF DIVORCE Divorce may have a dramatic economic and emotional impact on family members. The exact number of children affected by divorce in Canada is difficult to determine because no official information is available on out-of-court custody decisions. In 1996, approximately 60,000 Canadian children were involved in divorce cases in which the courts made custody decisions. In seven out of ten of these cases, the mother was awarded custody (Doyle Driedger, 1998; Robinson, 1998). Parental joint custody is also an option for some divorcing couples. When joint custody is a voluntary arrangement and when there is motivation to make it work, it has benefits for both children and parents (Richardson, 1996). Joint custody allows the children to maintain regular contact with both parents, which can ease the adjustment to the marriage breakup, and give parents more time to adjust to their new lives. However, this arrangement may also create unique problems for children, who must adjust to living in two homes and to the fact that their parents no longer live together.

Divorce not only changes relationships for the couple involved and their children but also for other relatives. In some divorces, grandparents feel that they are the big losers. To see their grandchildren, the grandparents have to keep in touch with the parent who has custody. In-laws are less likely to be welcome and may be seen as being on the "other side" simply because they are the parents of the ex-spouse. Recently, some grandparents have sued for custody of minor grandchildren. They generally have not been successful except in cases where questions existed about the emotional stability of the biological parents or the suitability of a foster care arrangement.

The consequences of divorce are not entirely negative. For some people, divorce may be an opportunity to terminate destructive relationships. For others, it may represent a means to achieve personal growth by enabling them to manage their lives and social relationships and establish their own identity.

Remarriage

Remarriage has been described as "the triumph of hope over experience" (Spencer, 1993:223). Most people who divorce get remarried (McVey and Kalbach, 1995), and most divorced people remarry others who have been divorced. For example, approximately one in five men and women who were legally married during the early 1990s had been married before (Statistics Canada, 1997c). Remarriage rates, however, vary by gender. At all ages, a greater proportion of men than women remarry (an estimated 76 percent of men and 64 percent of women), but both often do so relatively soon after their divorce (Gorlick, 1995). Remarriage is also affected by age level and level of education. Among women, the older a woman is at the time of divorce, the lower the likelihood of her remarrying. Women who have not graduated from high school and have young children tend to remarry relatively quickly; by contrast, women with a university degree and without children are less likely to remarry (Nett, 1993). Some of these remarriages involve children from a previous relationship, thus creating stepfamilies or *blended families*, which consist of a husband and wife, children from previous marriages, and children (if any) from the new marriage. In Canada, an estimated 7 percent of children under the age of 12 live in stepfamilies (Cheal, 1996).

FAMILY DIVERSITY

Gay and Lesbian Families

Lesbians and gay men grow up in families, establish long-lasting, committed, emotional relationships, and sometimes become parents. Nevertheless, until recently, discussions of gay and lesbian relationships and families have been excluded from discussions of the family. In fact, these relationships were considered by many as threatening to notions of the traditional family. Notions of the family that are limited to unions between members of the opposite sex are examples of ***heterosexism*****—an attitude in which heterosexuality is considered the only valid form of sexual behaviour, and gay men, lesbians, and bisexuals are inferior to heterosexual people.**

In Canada, gay and lesbian couples have been prohibited from legally marrying, sponsoring their partner's immigration to Canada, obtaining custody of their children, jointly adopting children, or receiving spousal benefits and survivor's pensions. This lack of recognition has had emotional, legal, and economic consequences for same-sex families (O'Brien and Weir, 1995).

Since the advent of the gay liberation movement in the 1970s, there has been a growing recognition and acceptance of homosexual relationships as family relationships (Eichler, 1997). Recently, some gay and lesbian activists have sought recognition of ***domestic partnerships*****—household partnerships in which an unmarried couple lives together in a committed, sexually intimate relationship and is granted the same rights and benefits as those accorded married heterosexual couples** (Gerstel and Gross, 1995).

Despite the failure of the law to recognize gay marriages, many lesbian and gay couples consider themselves married and living in lifelong commitments.

In contrast to stereotypes of same-sex relationships as short-term, promiscuous, and noncommittal, research on homosexual relationships indicates that partnerships lasting twenty years or more are not uncommon (Peplau, 1991). In fact, the breakup rates of married or cohabiting heterosexual couples and lesbian and gay couples have been found to be approximately equal (O'Brien and Weir, 1995). However, studies have found that lesbian and gay relationships are more egalitarian than heterosexual relationships. This finding is in part attributable to the fact that in virtually all lesbian and gay relationships both partners are wage earners (Eldridge and Gilbert, 1990; Sum Quod Sum Foundation, 1997).

An increasing number of lesbian and gay males form families with children. This may occur in a variety of ways. In many cases, lesbian mothers and gay fathers may have children from a previous marriage or relationship. However, not all children in same-sex families are products of previous heterosexual

Adoption is a complex legal process for most parents; it can be even more complicated for gay and lesbian couples.

relationships. Lesbian women may become pregnant through artificial insemination. Lesbian mothers and gay fathers may also form families through fostering or adoption. Unlike many heterosexual families in which both mother and father have genetic links to their children, gay and lesbian families always have a nonbiological parent. These nonbiological parents are often not regarded as parents either socially or legally. For example, nonbiological parents may not be granted admission to parent–teacher interviews, or may be denied permission to make important medical decisions for their children if the biological parent is unavailable. Anne, a lesbian mother, describes one of her encounters with the medical profession:

> You can tell the doctor three times, "Talk to me like I'm his mother; so is she," and they don't get it. Sometimes they really say, "I don't know what you're talking about." [And we'll answer,] "We're two lesbians, we're both the mother." "Huh. No, I'll talk to the one with the dress, that's safe." (quoted in Epstein, 1996:123)

Recently, several high-profile court challenges have pushed the public debate toward considering gay and lesbian spouses and families as such (Eichler, 1997). For example, in 1992 the Ontario Human Rights Commission agreed that spousal benefits should be granted to the same-sex partner of a civil servant. In 1995 gay and lesbian couples in Ontario won the right to adopt the biological children of their partners. In 1998 B.C. courts ruled that both biological and nonbiological parents in same-sex families have the same legal rights regarding their children. Most recently, the Supreme Court of Canada declared Ontario's Family Support Act unconstitutional because its definition of a spouse excludes men and women involved in same-sex relationships. This landmark decision is expected to place an estimated 1000 laws across the country into question (Gatehouse, 1999). Slowly, the laws are being challenged and much will likely change over the next decade.

Singlehood

While marriage at increasingly younger ages was the trend in Canada during the first half of the twentieth century, by the 1960s the trend had reversed itself, and many more adults were remaining single. In 1971, close to half of Canadians aged 20 to 24 were already married. In 1996, almost 90 percent of Canadians in the same age group were single (Statistics Canada, 1997c). Currently, approximately 25 percent of households in Canada are one- or single-person households. However, this estimate includes people who are divorced, widowed, and those who have never married. Given the fact that nine out of ten Canadians marry at some time in their lives, single status is often temporary. Only an estimated 10 percent of the population will remain single throughout their lives (Nett, 1993).

Some never-married singles remain single by choice. Reasons include more opportunity for a career (especially for women), the availability of sexual partners without marriage, the belief that the single lifestyle is full of excitement, and the desire for self-sufficiency and freedom to change and experiment (Stein, 1976, 1981). Some scholars have concluded that individuals who prefer to remain single hold more individualistic values and are less family-oriented than those who choose to marry. Friends and personal growth tend to be valued more highly than marriage and children (Alwin, Converse, and Martin, 1985; Nett, 1993). Other never-married singles remain single out of necessity. Being single is an economic necessity for those who cannot afford to marry and set up their own household (Boyd and Norris, 1999).

Aboriginal Families

It is difficult to discuss Native families given the fact that Aboriginal peoples in Canada are by no means a homogeneous group. Native peoples are composed of many distinct nations with different histories, cultures, economic bases, and languages (Das Gupta, 1995). However, in all Aboriginal families, the extended family was seen as central to both the individual and the community. The concept of family was defined very broadly. For example, to the Ojibwa, *family* referred to individuals who worked as a unit and were bound together by responsibility and friendship as well as kinship ties. Family size averaged between 20 and 25 persons (Shkilnyk, 1985). A band member describes the economic cooperation and sharing that once existed within the Ojibwa family:

> Trapping kept the family together because everyone in the family had something to do; the man had to lay traps and check them; the woman skinned the animals, cooked, and looked after the kids. The grandparents helped with the kids; they taught them manners, how to behave, and told them stories about our people. The kids, if they were old enough, had work to do. (Shkilnyk, 1985:81)

Under this extended and cooperative family system, Native families were extremely successful in ensuring the survival and well-being of their members. Four hundred years after contact with the European settlers, the current state of family disruption is evident when you consider the following data. The proportion of Aboriginal children who are removed from their homes as a result of parental abuse or neglect is ten times that of non-Aboriginal children; the proportion of Aboriginal children who commit suicide is seven times the rate for non-Aboriginal children; wife abuse among Aboriginal peoples is said to be at least seven times the national average; and mass disclosures of previously hidden sexual and physical abuse of Aboriginal children are being made (Timpson, 1995:9).

How did this happen? Sociologist Tania Das Gupta (1995) explains that the destruction of the traditional Aboriginal family was the result of interventionist strategies employed by the Canadian church and state. Families were displaced from their traditional lands, moved to reserves, and denied access to the resources that were central to the economic survival of the extended family unit. Aboriginal children were removed from their families and placed in residential schools (where they were often sexually and physically abused) or adopted by non-Aboriginal families. Generations of Aboriginal children were separated from their families and their communities, and this separation also served to sever links with Aboriginal culture and languages.

After generations of cultural and spiritual destruction, Aboriginal peoples are now reclaiming their culture. They have also united behind the goal of self-government, especially in the areas of social services and child welfare (Das Gupta, 1995). Aboriginal peoples believe in maintaining the ties between children and their natural parents, as well as caring for children within their Aboriginal communities. This they see as essential to the rebuilding of Aboriginal families in Canada. Many Aboriginal communities are striving to return to the practices and values that traditionally nourished Aboriginal family life: respect for women and children, mutual responsibility, and, above all, the general creed of sharing and caring (Royal Commission of Aboriginal Peoples, 1995:81).

FAMILY ISSUES IN THE FUTURE

As we have seen, families and intimate relationships have changed dramatically over the past hundred years. Some people believe that family as we know it is doomed. Others believe that a return to traditional values will save this important social institution and create greater stability in society. Family diversity is perceived as an indication that Canadian families are in "decline" or "crisis." However, as sociologist Ellen Gee reminds us, "Family diversity is the norm in Canadian society, past and present. Only for a short period in history ... did Canadian families approach uniformity, centered around near-universal marriage and parenthood, family 'intactness' and highly differentiated gender roles" (1995:80). The diversity in Canadian families has simply taken on new forms, with increases in common-law unions, gay and lesbian families, and single-parent and blended families.

One of the most notable changes in the past fifty years has been the increase in dual-wage earner families. The labour force participation rate of women, particularly married women, has increased dramatically. However, regardless of women's labour force participation, women are still primarily responsible for child care and domestic chores (Canadian Council on Social Development, 1996). The absence of adequate, affordable child care, inflexible work hours, and parental leave policies means that work is structured in ways that are not "user friendly" for family life (Gee, 1995:102). A challenge for families in the next century is to find ways to reconcile family and work contradictions. As gender roles continue to change, we can expect to see a greater degree of egalitarianism within the family.

One of the most disturbing issues and one that will continue to affect the quality and stability of family relationships in the future is family violence. The latter part of this century has been marked by the "discovery" of the dark side of the family—child abuse (including physical, sexual, and emotional abuse), wife abuse, and elder abuse. As Elizabeth Comack notes:

> The ideal of the family as a "private domain" and a "resting place" or "sanctuary" has been shattered by the finding that violence in the home is a frequent occurrence in contemporary society, and that violence between adults is systematically and disproportionately directed against women. (Comack, 1996a:155)

Armed with the knowledge that the family is not immune to this violence, the challenge of the twenty-first century is to find effective strategies to reduce the incidence of family violence.

A final issue to consider in this new century is the impact of new reproductive technologies on families. As Margrit Eichler says of these technologies, "There is probably no other recent social development which has a potentially more far-reaching impact on the very nature of the family, on our understandings as to what it means to be a parent, and on the rights and obligations attached to this status" (1988a:280). New reproductive technologies have the capacity to revolutionize family life. Whether or not people will choose to take advantage of the possibilities, and whether or not governments will allow certain services to be delivered, remain to be seen (Baker, 1996).

Regardless of problems facing families in the future, the family remains the central institution in the lives of most Canadians. A recent national opinion poll found that over three-quarters of Canadians regard the family as the most important thing in their lives, more important than their career or religion. Ninety-two percent of the respondents with young children at home indicated that the family is becoming more important to them. Finally, an overwhelming majority demonstrated their faith in the family by indicating that they want to marry and have children (although fewer children) (Vanier Institute of the Family, 1998). Individuals in families are now freer to establish the kinds of family arrangements that best suit them.

CHAPTER REVIEW

What is a family?

Families may be defined as relationships in which people live together with commitment, form an economic unit and care for any young, and consider their identity to be significantly attached to the group.

What is the difference between extended families and nuclear families?
An extended family is a family unit composed of relatives in addition to parents and children who live in the same household. A nuclear family is a family composed of one or two parents and their dependent children, all of whom live apart from other relatives.

What pattern of marriage is legally sanctioned in Canada?
Monogamy, marriage to one person at a time, is the only form of marriage sanctioned by law in Canada.

What are the functionalist, conflict, feminist, and interactionist perspectives on families?
Functionalists emphasize the importance of the family in maintaining the stability of society and the well-being of its individuals. Functions of the family include sexual regulation, socialization, economic and psychological support, and provision of social status. Both conflict and feminist perspectives view the family as a source of social inequality and as an arena for conflict over values, goals, and access to resources and power. Conflict theorists view the family in a capitalist society as an exploitive institution that is primarily responsible for women's oppression. Feminist scholars focus on patriarchy as the source of inequality between men and women. Interactionists explain family relationships in terms of the subjective meanings and everyday interpretations people give to their lives.

How are Canadian families changing?
Cohabitation has increased significantly in the past two decades. With the rise in dual-earner marriages, women increasingly have been burdened by the second shift—the domestic work that employed women perform at home after they complete their paid workday. The number of single-parent families has also increased dramatically.

What are some of the diverse family forms in Canada today?
Although all families share certain characteristics, each family is unique. An increasing number of Canadians are choosing to remain single—currently approximately 25 percent of households are single households. Lesbians and gay men establish long-lasting committed relationships and sometimes become parents. These families have received increasing recognition and acceptance both legally and socially in recent decades. Aboriginal families, although diverse, view the extended family as central to both the individual and the community. Aboriginal peoples believe that maintaining the ties between children and their natural parents and caring for children within their Aboriginal communities are essential to rebuilding Aboriginal families in Canada.

Key Terms

bilateral descent 377
cohabitation 383
domestic partnerships 395
dual-earner families 385
egalitarian family 377
extended family 373
families 373
families we choose 372
heterosexism 395
homogamy 385
marriage 375
matriarchal family 377
matrilineal descent 377
monogamy 375
nuclear family 374
patriarchal family 377
patriarchy 380
patrilineal descent 377
polyandry 377
polygamy 376
polygyny 376
second shift 385
sociology of family 377

Internet Exercises

1. The Internet is a good place for grassroots activism because it allows people from all over the world with similar concerns to interact with one another. Domestic violence is a concern all over the world. Using Alta Vista (**www.altavista.com**), do a search on the term *domestic violence*. Two of the sites that should come up are the Domestic Violence Hotlines site and the Domestic Violence: Shelters, Hotlines, and Related Services site. Visit these sites and follow some of the links to others. How can these sites help victims of violence? How can they help other centres set up aid for victims?
2. Something that has become very popular on the Internet in recent years is genealogy. Use any search engine to do a search on your last name. How many

other people's names come up? To the best of your knowledge, are any of them related to you?

3. Visit the Child & Family Canada page (**www.cfc-edc.ca/**). Find the discussion of the influence of media on children. What conclusion can you draw from this material?

Net Links

For more Web links related to the topic of this chapter, see the Nelson sociology Web site: **www.sociologyessentials-2nded.nelson.com**.

The Vanier Institute of the Family provides the most comprehensive information on Canadian families on its Child and Family Web site; to see it, go to:

www.cfc-efc.ca/docs/00000001.htm

PFLAG (Parents and Friends of Lesbians and Gays) is a national organization promoting the health and well-being of gay, lesbian, and bisexual persons and their families and friends; its Web site is at:

www.pflag.ca

Vis-à-vis, Canada's national newsletter on family violence, discussed important information on programs and initiatives aimed at reducing violence in the family. The final issue was published in the summer of 1996. Back issues are available at:

www.ccsd.ca/visavis.html

The executive summary of the Royal Commission on New Reproductive Technologies entitled "Proceed with Care" includes a detailed examination and recommendations of how new reproductive technologies should be handled in Canada; to read it, go to:

www.ualberta.ca/~ethics/bb-nrtex.htm

Questions for Critical Thinking

1. In your own thinking, what constitutes an ideal family?
2. Could the following be considered families?
   - man, woman, no children; married but living apart
   - woman, woman, child of one woman; living together. Women are a same-sex couple.
   - man, his biological child and woman (not his wife) with whom he has a sexual relationship; living together
   - four adults; sharing a household for many years. None are a same-sex couple.
3. Suppose you wanted to find out about women's and men's perceptions about love and marriage. What specific issues might you examine? What would be the best way to conduct your research?
4. Discuss the changes Canadian families are experiencing today. Are these changes an indication that the family as we know it is about to become extinct?

Suggested Readings

These comprehensive textbooks offer in-depth information on families and intimate relationships:

Nijole V. Benokraitis. *Marriage and Families: Changes, Choices, and Constraints*. Englewood Cliffs, N.J.: Prentice-Hall, 1997.

Margrit Eichler. *Family Shifts: Families, Policies, and Gender Equality*. Don Mills, Ont.: Oxford University Press, 1997.

G.N. Ramu. *Marriage and the Family in Canada Today*. Scarborough, Ont.: Prentice Hall, 1993.

These books provide new insights on the diversity of family life:

K. Ishwaran. *Family and Marriage: Cross-Cultural Perspectives*. Toronto: Thompson Educational Publishing, 1992.

Marion Lynn. *Voices: Essays on Canadian Families*. Scarborough Ont.: Nelson, 1996.

Nancy Mandell and Ann Duffy. *Canadian Families Diversity, Conflict, and Change*. Scarborough, Ont.: ITP Nelson, 1995.

A historical perspective on Canadian families may be found in:

Jane Ursel. *Private Lives, Public Policy: 100 Years of State Intervention in the Family*. Toronto: Women's Press, 1992.

For additional information about family problems, see:

Arlie Russell Hochschild. *The Second Shift: Working Parents and the Revolution at Home*. New York: Viking/Penguin, 1989.

INFOTRAC® COLLEGE EDITION

Either from the *Sociology In Our Times: The Essentials* Web site (**www.sociologyessentials-2nded.nelson.com**) or directly from your Web browser, you may access InfoTrac® College Edition, an online university library that includes over 600 popular and scholarly journals in which you can find articles related to the topics in this chapter.

CHAPTER 14

For most of Canada's history, religion played a major role in the development and maintenance of educational institutions. Religious instruction was considered an essential component of "becoming educated." Which religion was to be taught was relatively simple—it was Christianity in either its Catholic or Protestant form. Today, things are not that simple—while the majority of Canadians are Christians, with Catholics making up 46 percent and Protestants 33 percent, other religions such as Hinduism, Islam, Buddhism, Confucianism, Sikhism, and others too numerous to mention are now part of our Canadian mosaic (Statistics Canada, 1996a). Currently, there is no consensus among Canadians regarding what role religion should play in education.

Should students receive religious instruction in the classroom? If so, which religions should be included? Should prayer be offered in schools? Should participation in prayer be voluntary or compulsory? In our multiethnic society, these questions are becoming increasingly difficult to answer. Some parents feel that religious instruction is necessary, suggesting that secularization in the public school system is contributing to a declining morality.

Albertans Dick and Joanne Barendregt teach their children at home. While home-schooling is relatively common in Canada, the Barendregts are part of a growing network of parents who do not register their children or allow provincial officials to monitor their children's education because they feel this would interfere with their religious freedom. The couple decided to educate their children at home after they found that one of their children's textbooks had a section on evolution that conflicted with their religious views.

Joanne Barendregt feels that "in two or three years, they're going to regulate what we feed our children ... and after that it will be our reproductive systems." She goes on to say that "we feel the highest calling a girl can have is to be a wife and mother first. We teach that that is their purpose ... We are not changing. You [society] have changed. You're trying to destroy our [religious] heritage." Her husband says they will not register with the government because "we will not have a partnership with a government that promotes and allows homosexuality to continue, and abortion." (Mitchell, 1999:A7)

EDUCATION AND RELIGION

The Barendregts feel that religious instruction is a vital part of education. However, others feel that the educational system must be separate from religion and that the curriculum should be based on secular concerns.

Proponents of this point of view suggest that in our multicultural society no religion should be espoused or endorsed. How can schools teach religious values that might conflict with the values and customs of a significant number of students? How might students and teachers who come from diverse religious and cultural backgrounds feel about instruction or organized prayer in public schools? Rick Nelson, a teacher in the public school system, explains his concern about the potential impact of religion in his classroom:

"I think it really trivializes religion when you try to take such a serious topic with so many different viewpoints and cover it in the public schools. At my school we have teachers and students who are Hindu. They are really devout, but they are not monotheistic. I am not opposed to individual prayer by students. But when there is a group prayer, who's going to lead the group?" (CNN, 1994)

This argument is only one in a lengthy history of debates about the appropriate relationship between public education and religion in Canada. For many years, controversies have arisen periodically over topics such as moral education, anti-Semitism, sex education, evolutionary theory, school prayer, and the subject matter of textbooks and library books.

Who is to decide what should be taught in public schools? What is the purpose of education? Of religion? In this chapter, we examine education and religion, two social institutions that have certain commonalities both as institutions and as objects of sociological inquiry. Before reading on, test your knowledge about the impact religion has on education in Canada by taking the quiz in Box 14.1.

Questions and Issues

CHAPTER FOCUS QUESTION: Why are education and religion powerful and influential forces in contemporary societies?

What impact does education have on the lives of Canadians?

What unique functions might religion serve that no other institution can fulfil?

How do religious groups differ in organizational structure?

What actions could be taken to resolve debates over religious values and public education?

Debates about what children should be taught in schools have taken place throughout the history of Canadian public education. The issue of teaching creationism versus evolution in science classrooms is only one example of the intersection of religion and education.

AN OVERVIEW OF EDUCATION AND RELIGION

Education and religion are powerful and influential forces in contemporary societies. Both institutions impart values, beliefs, and knowledge considered essential to the social reproduction of individual personalities and entire cultures (Bourdieu and Passeron, 1990). Education and religion both grapple with issues of societal stability and social change, reflecting society even as they attempt to shape it. Education and religion also share certain commonalities as objects of sociological study; for example, both are socializing institutions. While early socialization primarily is informal and takes place within our families and friendship networks, as we grow older, socialization passes to the more formalized organizations created for the specific purposes of education and religion.

Areas of sociological inquiry that specifically focus on these institutions are (1) the *sociology of education*, which primarily examines formal education or schooling in industrial societies, and (2) the *sociology of religion*, which focuses on religious groups and organizations, on the behaviour of individuals within these groups, and on ways in which religion is intertwined with other social institutions (K. Roberts, 1995). Let's start our examination by looking at sociological perspectives on education.

SOCIOLOGICAL PERSPECTIVES ON EDUCATION

Education **is the social institution responsible for the systematic transmission of knowledge, skills, and cultural values within a formally organized structure.** In all societies, people must acquire certain knowledge and skills in order to survive. In less developed societies, these skills might include hunting, gathering, fishing, farming, and self-preservation. In contemporary, developed societies, knowledge and skills often are related to the requirements of a highly competitive job market. As a result, developed societies have adopted the policy of universal education, according to which everyone receives at least some level of formal education.

Sociologists have divergent perspectives on the purpose of education in contemporary society. Functionalists suggest that education contributes to the maintenance of society and provides people with an opportunity for self-enhancement and upward social mobility. Conflict theorists argue that education perpetuates social inequality and benefits the dominant class at the expense of all others. Interactionists focus on classroom dynamics and the effect of self-concept on grades and aspirations.

BOX 14.1 SOCIOLOGY AND EVERYDAY LIFE

How Much Do You Know about the Impact of Religion on Education in Canada?

TRUE	FALSE	
T	F	1. Provincial governments in Canada do not fund separate religious schools.
T	F	2. Virtually all contemporary sociologists have advocated the separation of moral teaching from academic subject matter.
T	F	3. The federal government has limited control over how funds are spent by school districts because most of the money comes from the provinces.
T	F	4. Enrolment in parochial schools has decreased in Canada as interest in religion has waned.
T	F	5. Canadian courts have insisted that schools close on the holy days of all major religions.
T	F	6. The number of children from religious backgrounds other than Christian has grown steadily in public schools over the past three decades.
T	F	7. Debates over textbook content focus only on elementary education because of the vulnerability of young children.
T	F	8. Increasing numbers of parents are instructing their own children through home-schooling because of their concerns about what public schools are (or are not) teaching their children.
T	F	9. Most members of the baby boom generation have no religious affiliation today because they received no religious instruction in school.
T	F	10. Prayer in public schools in Canada may be offered on a voluntary basis.

Answers on page 406.

Functionalist Perspectives on Education

Functionalists view education as one of the most important components of society. According to Durkheim, education is crucial for promoting social solidarity and stability in society: it is the "influence exercised by adult generations on those that are not yet ready for social life" (Durkheim, 1956:28). Durkheim also asserted that moral values are the foundation of a cohesive social order and that schools have the responsibility of teaching a commitment to the common morality. Although his work on this topic, entitled *Moral Education*, was unfinished at the time of his death, contemporary sociologists Jonathan H. Turner, Leonard Beeghley, and Charles H. Powers (1995:46) have summarized some of Durkheim's ideas on the functions of education in this way:

> The commitment to the common morality must be learned in schools, where the teacher operates as the functional equivalent of the priest. The teacher gives young students an understanding of and a reverence for the nature of the society and the need to have a morality that regulates passions and provides attachments to groupings organized to pursue societal goals. Such educational socialization must assure that the common morality is a part of the students' motivational needs ... their cognitive orientations ... and their self-control processes.

From this perspective, teachers are the functional equivalent of priests in teaching students about morality. Students must be taught to put the group's needs ahead of their individual desires and aspirations. Like Durkheim, contemporary functionalists suggest that education has specific functions in society, both manifest and latent.

BOX 14.1

Answers to the Sociology Quiz on the Impact of Religion on Education in Canada

1. **False.** Schools operated by the Catholic Church are provincially funded in several provinces.
2. **False.** Obviously, contemporary sociologists hold strong beliefs and opinions on many subjects; however, most of them do not think it is their role to advocate specific stances on a topic. Early sociologists were less inclined to believe that education had to be "value-free." For example, Durkheim strongly advocated that education have a moral component and that schools had a responsibility to perpetuate society by teaching a commitment to the common morality.
3. **True.** Under the terms of the British North America Act, education is a provincial responsibility. Public school revenue comes from local funding through property taxes and provincial funding from a variety of sources. The federal government is responsible for maintaining schools for Aboriginal people, running a military college, funding adult education programs, and overseeing educational programs in federal penitentiaries.
4. **False.** In recent years, just the opposite has happened. As parents have begun feeling that their children were not receiving the type of education the parents desired for them in public schools, parochial schools have flourished. Most religions have established their own parochial schools.
5. **False.** The courts have upheld the right of school boards to allow holidays only for the major Christian holy days of Christmas and Good Friday (see Box 14.2, "A Legal Challenge to Religious Holidays in Schools").
6. **True.** Although about 83 percent of Canadians aged 18 and over describe their religion as one of the forms, or denominations, of Christianity, the number of those who either adhere to no religion or who are Jewish, Muslim/Islamic, Sikh, Buddhist, or Hindu has increased significantly.
7. **False.** Attempts to remove textbooks occur at all levels of schooling. A recent case involved the removal of Chaucer's "The Miller's Tale" and Aristophanes' *Lysistrata* from a high school curriculum.
8. **True.** Some parents choose home-schooling for religious reasons. Others embrace it for secular reasons, including fear for their children's safety and concerns about the quality of public schools.
9. **False.** Most baby boomers did receive religious instruction, either in private schools or in public schools where prayer and Bible reading took place.
10. **True.** Parents must sign consent forms for their children to participate in prayers in public schools.

Sources: Based on Johnson, 1994; Ballantine, 1993; Greenberg and Page, 1993; Kosmin and Lachman, 1993; Roof, 1993; Sullivan, 1993; and Gibbs, 1994.

MANIFEST FUNCTIONS OF EDUCATION Some purposes of education are ***manifest functions*—open, stated, and intended goals or consequences of activities within an organization or institution.** An example of a manifest function in education is the teaching of specific subjects, such as science, mathematics, reading, history, and English. Education serves five major manifest functions in society:

1. *Socialization.* From kindergarten through university, schools teach students the student role, specific academic subjects, and political socialization. In kindergarten, children learn the appropriate attitudes and behaviour for the student role (Ballantine, 1997). In primary and secondary schools, students are taught specific subject matter appropriate to their age, skill level, and previous educational experience.
2. *Transmission of culture.* Schools transmit cultural norms and values to each new generation and play an active part in the process of assimilation,

BOX 14.2 CRITICAL THINKING

A Legal Challenge to Religious Holidays in Schools

Like millions of other young Canadians, 14-year-old Aysha Bassuny returned to school in September of 1994. But the Ottawa Board of Education delayed the start of her school year for two days so that Jewish students could observe the Jewish New Year—Rosh Hashanah. "It's not fair," said Bassuny, a Grade 10 student at suburban Brookfield High School, who wears the traditional Islamic head scarf, the hijab. "I have to miss school for my holy days and the Jewish kids don't. You cannot have it for one group and not the other."

In July 1995, the Islamic Schools Federation of Ontario, which represents independent Muslim schools, launched a lawsuit against the Ottawa Board of Education alleging that the rights of Muslims to freedom of conscience and religion under the Charter of Rights were undermined by the board's actions. The lawsuit argued that schools with significant numbers of Muslim students should be required to observe two important Islamic holidays. The Islamic Federation chose Ottawa as a test case, believing that a victory there would set a precedent across the country.

This dispute began in April 1994, when the Ottawa board agreed to what seemed at the time to be a modest request from Ottawa's Jewish community—to delay the start of the school year so that Jewish students could observe Rosh Hashanah without missing the crucial first two days of school. According to Jewish community leader Ron Singer, the request was entirely reasonable, because it did not mean a permanent change in the school year: the Jewish calendar is based on the cycles of the moon, and Rosh Hashanah coincides with the opening of school only once every forty years.

On the other side of the issue, the lawyer for the Islamic Schools Federation of Ontario said that the problem was one of equity: "The issue is the recognition of two religions, Christian and Jewish, and the rejection of another, Muslim."

Those involved in the dispute said they recognized that, if taken to its logical extreme, the rapid growth of Canada's Muslim, Buddhist, Hindu, and Sikh communities could lead to a school year with as many as 15 religious holidays. One school board member conceded that it is "a tough problem." It is also one that an increasingly multicultural society will be unable to avoid.

The lawsuit was rejected by the Ontario Divisional Court and in July 1997 the Ontario Appeal Court refused to hear the appeal of the Islamic Schools Federation, so at least for now Ontario schools are not required to recognize the holidays of minority religious groups. Do you think it is fair that Christian holidays are recognized while the holidays of other religions are not?

Source: Adapted from Fisher, 1994.

whereby recent immigrants learn the dominant cultural values, attitudes, and behaviour.

3. *Social control*. Schools are responsible for teaching values such as discipline, respect, obedience, punctuality, and perseverance. Schools teach conformity by encouraging young people to be good students, conscientious future workers, and law-abiding citizens.
4. *Social placement*. Schools are responsible for identifying the most qualified people to fill available positions in society. As a result, students are channelled into programs based on

Although schools may contribute to social control in society, today's school officials find control increasingly difficult to maintain. This Toronto school has implemented a cooperative program operated by staff and students.

individual ability and academic achievement. Graduates receive the appropriate credentials for entry into the paid labour force.

5. *Change and innovation*. Schools are a source of change and innovation. As student populations change over time, new programs are introduced to meet societal needs; for example, sex education, drug education, and multicultural studies have been implemented in some schools to help students learn about pressing social issues. Innovation in the form of new knowledge is required of colleges and universities. Faculty members are encouraged, and sometimes required, to engage in research and to share the results with students, colleagues, and others.

LATENT FUNCTIONS OF EDUCATION In addition to manifest functions, all social institutions, including schools, have some ***latent functions*—hidden, unstated and sometimes unintended consequences of activities within an organization or institution.** Education serves at least three latent functions:

1. *Restricting some activities*. Early in the twentieth century, all provinces passed mandatory education laws that are still in effect today and that require children to attend school until they reach a specified age (usually 16) or until they complete a minimum level of formal education (generally, completion of Grade 8). The assumption was that an educated citizenry and workforce are necessary for the smooth functioning of democracy and capitalism. Out of these laws grew one latent function of education: to keep students off the street and out of the full-time job market for a number of years, thus helping keep unemployment within reasonable bounds (Braverman, 1974).
2. *Matchmaking and production of social networks*. Because schools bring together people of similar ages, social class, and race/ethnicity, young people often meet future marriage partners and develop social networks there that may last for many years.
3. *Creation of a generation gap*. Students may learn information in school that contradicts beliefs held by their parents or their religion. Debates over the content of textbooks and library books typically centre on information that parents deem unacceptable for their children. When education conflicts with parental attitudes and beliefs, a generation gap is created if students embrace the newly acquired perspective.

Conflict Perspectives on Education

In contrast to the functionalist perspective, conflict theorists argue that schools perpetuate class, racial-ethnic, and gender inequalities in society, as some groups seek to maintain their privileged position at the expense of others (Guppy, 1984; Ballantine, 1993).

REPRODUCTION OF CLASS Conflict theorists argue that education is a vehicle for reproducing existing class relationships. According to French sociologist Pierre Bourdieu, students have differing amounts of ***cultural capital*—social assets that include values, beliefs, attitudes, and competencies in language and culture** (Bourdieu and Passeron, 1990). Cultural capital involves "proper" attitudes toward education, socially approved dress and manners, and knowledge about books, art, music, and other forms of high and popular culture. Middle- and upper-income parents endow their children with more cul-

"Rich" schools and "poor" schools are readily identifiable by their buildings, equipment, and size of classes. What are the social consequences of unequal funding for schools?

tural capital than do working-class and poverty-level parents. Because cultural capital is essential for acquiring an education, children with less cultural capital have fewer opportunities to succeed in school. For example, standardized tests, which are used for grouping students by ability and for assigning students to classes, often measure students' cultural capital rather than their "natural" intelligence or aptitude. Thus, a circular effect occurs: students with dominant cultural values are more highly rewarded by the educational system; in turn, the educational system teaches and reinforces those values that sustain the elite's position in society.

Many Canadian schools practise "streaming" or ***tracking*—the categorical assignment of students based on test scores, previous grades, or both, to different types of educational programs.** The educational justification for streaming is that it is easier to teach students with similar abilities. However, research has shown that tracking may have a bad effect on students' subsequent academic achievements and career choices (Oakes, 1985). Instead of enhancing school performance, tracking systems may result in students dropping out of school or ending up in dead-end situations because they have not taken the courses required for university.

THE HIDDEN CURRICULUM According to conflict theorists, the ***hidden curriculum* is the transmission of cultural values and attitudes, such as conformity and obedience to authority, through implied demands found in rules, routines, and regulations of schools** (Snyder, 1971). Although students from all social classes are subjected to the hidden curriculum, working-class and poverty-level students may be affected the most adversely (Cookson and Hodges Persell, 1985; Polakow, 1993; Ballantine, 1997). In a study of five elementary schools located in different communities, significant differences were found in the manner in which knowledge was transmitted to students even though the curriculum was organized similarly (Anyon, 1980). Schools for working-class students emphasize procedures and rote memorization without much decision making, choice, and explanation of why something is done a particular way. Schools for middle-class students stress the processes (such as figuring and decision making) involved in getting the right answer. Schools for affluent students focus on creative activities in which students express their own ideas and apply them to the subject under consideration. Schools for students from elite families work to develop students' analytical powers and critical thinking skills, and teach them how to apply abstract principles to problem solving.

Through the hidden curriculum, schools make working-class and poverty-level students aware that they will be expected to take orders from others, arrive at work on time, follow bureaucratic rules, and experience high levels of boredom without complaining (Richer, 1988). Over time, these students may be disqualified from higher education and barred from obtaining the credentials necessary for well-paid occupations and professions (Bowles and Gintis, 1976). Educational credentials are extremely important in societies that emphasize ***credentialism*—a process of social selection in which class advantage and social status are linked to the possession of academic qualifications** (Collins, 1979; G. Marshall, 1994). Conflict theorists point out that the credentials required for a job often bear little resemblance to the actual skills and responsibilities of the job. Why then are degrees so important? The answer is that without them access to prestigious, high-paying jobs is limited. In other words, credentials serve a gatekeeping function, allowing professional groups such as doctors, lawyers, and accountants to exclude anyone without the proper education, thus keeping wages high and regulating the labour market (Collins, 1979). The result is a process of social selection in which class advantage and social status are linked to the possession of academic credentials (Collins, 1979; Marshall, 1994). According to conflict theorists, credentialism is not driven by an actual need for increased knowledge, but rather by the desire on the part of the members of professional groups to protect their own vested interests, namely income, prestige, autonomy, and power.

SOCIAL CLASS IN HIGHER EDUCATION Even for students who complete high school, access to colleges and universities is determined not only by prior academic record but also by the ability to pay. Although public institutions such as community colleges and universities are funded primarily by tax dollars, the cost of attending such institutions has increased dramatically over the past decade. Even with the lower cost of attending community colleges, the enrolment of low-income students at these institutions has dropped since the 1980s as a result of declining scholarship funds and the necessity for many students to work full- or part-time to finance their education. In contrast, not only do students from affluent families have no trouble funding their education at Canadian institutions, but they are also more likely to attend prestigious private colleges or universities outside of Canada where tuition fees alone may be more than $20,000 per year (Fennell, 1993).

Thus, the ability to pay for a university education reproduces the class system. Some students lack access to higher education because of a lack of money; those who do attend university are stratified according to their ability to pay. In addition, a study of Ontario high school students by Porter, Porter, and Blishen (1982) showed a strong relationship between family occupational status and the likelihood of university attendance. Seventy-eight percent of the higher-class students were in university-track programs, compared with only 40 percent of the lower-class students. These patterns of inequality repeat themselves, as is seen in Figure 14.1, which shows that average earnings are much higher for Canadians with university degrees than for those without them. In sum, to conflict theorists, education reproduces social inequalities that create a stratified class structure in Canadian society.

Interactionist Perspectives on Education

Unlike functionalist analysts, who focus on the functions and dysfunctions of education, and conflict theorists, who focus on the relationship between education and inequality, interactionists focus on classroom communication patterns and educational practices, such as labelling, that affect students' self-concept and aspirations.

EDUCATION AND THE SELF-FULFILLING PROPHECY For some students, schooling may become a self-fulfilling prophecy. According to sociologist Robert Merton (1968), a ***self-fulfilling prophecy* is an unsubstantiated belief or prediction resulting in behaviour that makes the originally false belief come true.** For example, if a teacher (as a result of stereotypes based on the relationship between IQ and race) believes that some students of colour are less capable of learning, that teacher (sometimes without even realizing it) may treat them as if they were incapable of learning.

What is the effect of teacher expectations on students? Does the practice of tracking or streaming students lead to self-fulfilling prophecies for individual students? Social psychologist Robert Rosenthal (1969) designed an experiment to answer these questions. Rosenthal told teachers at an elementary school that he had developed a new test that would identify those children who were likely to "spurt ahead" during the next year. The children were then tested and the teachers were provided with a list of the names of the "spurters" and were instructed to watch their progress without revealing their expectations to the students or the students'

FIGURE 14.1 Average Earnings by Education, 1995

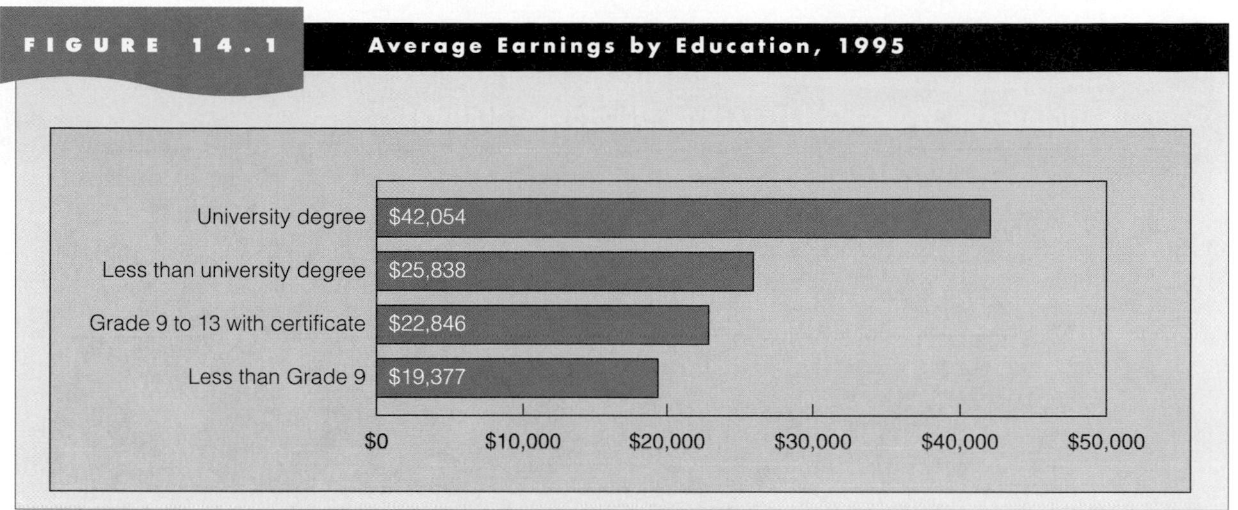

Reprinted by permission from Statistics Canada, 1998. "1996 Census: Sources of Income, Earnings and Total Income, and Family Income." *The Daily*, May 12.

parents in any way. In fact, the test had no predictive value, and the names that Rosenthal provided had been selected at random. The only characteristic that distinguished these children from their classmates was the teachers' expectations of their success. A year later, Rosenthal found marked academic gains among the "spurters." He concluded that the teachers had changed their attitudes toward these children in subtle ways and had influenced their progress as a result. In other words, the teachers' expectations had created a self-fulfilling prophecy. Rosenthal's findings, however, became controversial because attempts to replicate his experiment produced mixed results. But a good deal of research confirms that positive teacher expectations generally contribute to more success from students (Snyder, 1971).

EDUCATION AND LABELLING In the past, IQ testing has resulted in labelling of students. For example, studies in the United States found that many African American and Mexican American children were placed in special education classes on the basis of IQ scores even when they simply could not understand the tests. Similar research in Canada indicates that in elementary schools, special education classes are filled with children from visible minority groups, and in high schools visible minority students are overrepresented in the technical and vocational streams (Curtis, Livingston, and Smaller, 1992). According to labelling theory, terms such as *learning disabled* are social constructions that lead to stigmatization and may be incorporated into the everyday interactions of teachers, students, and parents (Carrier, 1986; Coles, 1987). Labels placed on students by educators may indeed become a self-fulfilling prophecy if students become convinced that they are less intelligent and thus less capable than others. However, some programs have been shown to have a positive effect on students who scored lower on IQ tests. For example, a study in Ypsilanti, Michigan, found that an intensive program for high-risk children involving preschool education and home visits had a lasting impact on high-risk children, who were less likely to be absent from school or be classified as intellectually disabled and more likely to graduate from high school and become employed (Passell, 1994).

A self-fulfilling prophecy also can result from labelling students as "gifted." Gifted students are considered to be those with above-average intellectual ability, academic aptitude, creative or productive thinking, or leadership skills (Ballantine, 1993). When some students are labelled as better than others, they may achieve at a higher level because of the label.

Ironically, such labelling may also result in discrimination against these students Studies of girls labelled as "gifted" have found that many routinely deny their intelligence because they feel that academic achievement might keep them from being popular with others (see Eder, 1985; Eder and

BOX 14.3 SOCIOLOGY IN GLOBAL PERSPECTIVE

RELIGION AND WOMEN'S LITERACY IN DEVELOPING NATIONS

> Education is a powerful agent of progress. Literacy is the most basic and necessary of learning skills.—Maria Luisa Jauregui de Gainza, Literacy Specialist, UNESCO

Women's literacy has been referred to as the "challenge of the decade." Organizations such as the United Nations believe that the education of women in developing nations is a high priority not only for national development but also for the well-being of children and families.

An estimated 95 percent of all illiterate people are concentrated in the developing nations of Southeast Asia and sub-Saharan Africa. There, one-third of all women are illiterate, compared with one-fifth of the men. In the least-developed nations, 79 percent of adult women are illiterate. Even with organizations such as the United Nations Educational, Scientific and Cultural Organization (UNESCO) attempting to eradicate illiteracy, the problem remains.

Many factors stand in the way of women's literacy, including religious beliefs that subordinate women and emphasize a traditional gendered division of labour, such as "care of children, maintenance of the household, care of older family members and the ill, servicing their husband and his relevant kin, maintenance of the network of familial ties, and servicing of the community" (Ballara, 1992:x). Religions that confine women's activities to domestic tasks and stress their role as wives and mothers often limit their access to education and produce feelings of low self-esteem and isolation.

Parker, 1987). Ashley Reiter, a first-place winner in a national mathematics competition, described her middle school years as a "smart girl's torture chamber":

> No one would speak to me. I wouldn't even go into the cafeteria for lunch. Long tables stretched the length of the whole room, but wherever I sat, people acted as if I wasn't in the right place. So I would go to the library. It was definitely not cool to be smart in seventh and eighth grade, especially for a girl. Some kids thought they would lose their reputation just by speaking to someone smart. (quoted in Sadker and Sadker, 1994:93)

Some analysts suggest that girls receive subtle cues from adults that lead them to attribute success to *effort* while boys learn to attribute success to their *intelligence* and *ability*. Conversely, girls attribute their failure to lack of ability while boys attribute failure to lack of effort (Sadker and Sadker, 1994).

Current Issues in Canadian Education

Across Canada, thousands of alarmed parents are voicing their concerns regarding their provincial public education systems which, they maintain, are doing a poor job of teaching their children (Fennell, 1993). Although parents may have always been difficult to please, Table 14.1 shows that since 1973 more and more parents have become dissatisfied with the quality of their children's education. Most of the criticism has been directed at inadequate educational standards and at high dropout rates.

INADEQUATE STANDARDS A Decima poll conducted in 1993 surveyed 500 university students and found that only 52 percent felt that high school had prepared them properly for university. What is missing? According to a University of Toronto engineering student, not enough emphasis is placed on reading and writing. "Grammar might be worth only five

BOX 14.3

CONTINUED

Ultimately, the main reason most women (and men) are illiterate is poverty. Because of poverty daily survival becomes far more important than learning how to read or compute math problems. Some analysts have found that schools in the poorest developing nations are becoming even more impoverished.

Is there hope for the future? Media campaigns and numerous projects are actively promoting literacy. Perhaps a greater awareness of the problem is the first step toward its eradication. Are the problems of women in developing nations in any way related to your life? Using your sociological imagination, can you think of ways in which their "fate" might be intertwined with yours?

Women throughout the world experience a lack of educational opportunities. In hopes of increasing women's literacy in Nepal, Save the Children Foundation provides adult education classes.

Sources: Based on Ballara, 1992; and Ballantine, 1997.

TABLE 14.1 PARENTS' DISSATISFACTION WITH CHILDREN'S EDUCATION, 1973, 1978, 1992

Question: Are you satisfied or dissatisfied with the education children are getting today?

CANADA	SATISFIED	DISSATISFIED	DON'T KNOW
1992	35%	56%	9%
1978	34	53	13
1973	51	41	8
REGIONAL BREAKDOWN, 1992			
Atlantic	41	54	6
Quebec	37	55	8
Ontario	30	61	10
Prairies	49	45	6
B.C.	25	63	12

Note: Percentages may not add up to 100, due to rounding. Reprinted with permission—The Toronto Star Syndicate.

BOX 14.4 SOCIOLOGY AND TECHNOLOGY

THE TECHNOLOGY REVOLUTION IN THE CLASSROOM: EQUALIZING OPPORTUNITY

Technology itself is not new, but its importance as an educational issue has exploded in the past few years as computers have moved into classrooms and workplaces. No longer simply an object of study for those who wish to pursue "technical" careers, technology—particularly computer technology—has become an essential educational tool. Like reading or writing, it is now recognized as a prerequisite for student success. Word processing, simulations, and computerized data analysis have become as standard in schools as typewriters and adding machines a generation ago. In fact, the technological revolution is moving at such a rapid pace that any review of "current" activities is certain to be obsolete by the time it is read.

Canada was one of the first countries in the world to link its entire student body to the information highway. In 1995 Newfoundland became the first province with full Internet access, linking all schools to the World Wide Web and the Internet; by 1997, virtually all schools in the country had access to the Internet via the SchoolNet national electronic network. Despite overall reductions in education budgets, most provinces have introduced systematic plans to expand the role of technology in the curriculum, primarily through the acquisition of computer hardware and software for classroom use.

A number of provinces have set specific targets for classroom computer acquisition. For example, British Columbia announced a five-year plan in 1995 to have one computer in place for every three secondary students and every six elementary students, and Nova Scotia has set a goal of one computer for every ten students by the year 2000. To help the provinces meet these objectives, Industry Canada's "Computers in the Schools" program has moved thousands of used computers, software, and other technologies from industry into Canadian classrooms. In co-operation with

marks on a paper ... If you want help you really have to motivate yourself" (Fennell, 1993:24). Much of the blame for inadequate standards is directed at *child-centred education*—a system that encourages students to progress at their own rate. Critics of child-centred education argue that because this system does not impose clear standards, it has become unaccountable and is producing children who cannot read and write. However, according to education specialists such as Patricia Holborn, a teaching consultant at Simon Fraser University:

> The child-centered system prepares children to be more than just good readers and writers. Unlike more traditional approaches where children learn by memorization, child-centered programs teach children to think and learn independently or co-operatively. (quoted in Fennell, 1993:24)

DROPPING OUT Although the overall school dropout (or school leaver) rate has significantly decreased in recent decades, about 15 percent of people under the age of 24 still leave school before earning a high school diploma. Ethnic and class differences are important factors in the data on dropout rates. For example, Aboriginal students have a dropout rate of over 40 percent. Recent immigrants to Canada were much less likely to drop out before they had completed high school. The dropout rate also varies by region—Prince Edward Island had the highest proportion of school dropouts in 1995 at 21 percent, while Saskatchewan and Alberta had the lowest at 11 percent (Clark, 1997).

Why do students drop out? According to a survey on school leavers by S.N. Gilbert and B. Orok (1993), male school leavers identified a preference for work over school, boredom, financial pressures,

BOX 14.4

CONTINUED

provincial and territorial governments and the private sector, the program had placed more than 20,000 computers and 40,000 pieces of software in schools and libraries by 1997.

Once in place, computers are being used to train teachers as well as students, and to offer computer training and Internet access to the community. Human Resources Development Canada has set up the Office of Learning Technologies (OLT) expressly to provide funding support to innovative learning opportunities using new technologies.

Proponents of computers in schools see them as a powerful tool for levelling the playing field in Canadian classrooms. Their capacity to retrieve information is nearly limitless, and equally available in urban, rural and remote locations; they can be equipped with features that allow many children with disabilities to work alongside their classmates; and they increase understanding within Canada and internationally by allowing students to connect with individuals and classrooms across the country and around the world.

Nevertheless, there are those who have reservations about the expanding role of computer technology in schools. Some parents and teachers continue to fear that, in the face of reduced school budgets, students may find themselves facing machines more frequently than teachers. They also express concern about the quality and suitability of information available on the Internet. Educators stress the importance of teaching students the skills to evaluate that information, since, at this point, the Internet does not impose standards equivalent to those of the publishing industry, or exercise the judgement of a school librarian.

Excerpted with permission from *Education in Canada: An Overview* by Paula Dunning (Toronto: Canadian Education Association, 1997).

and problems with teachers as the most important reasons for quitting school. Female school leavers also identified boredom and a preference for work as important reasons for leaving school. However, they also cited problems with school work and pregnancy/marriage as factors involved in their decision to quit school. Although critics of the public education system point to high dropout rates as proof of the public education system's failure, dropout rates in Canada have actually declined since the 1950s when approximately 70 percent of students were not completing high school (Fennell, 1993).

EDUCATIONAL REFORM Efforts to address the problems in the public school system have met with varying results. At the same time, more and more parents who have the financial resources to do so are choosing to put their children in private schools. Other dissatisfied parents have joined lobby groups that seek to promote a return to a more traditional education system with an emphasis on the three R's. Provincial strategies to improve the quality of education and reduce the number of dropouts do, in some cases, support this back-to-basics philosophy. For example, in Alberta, Manitoba, Ontario, Nova Scotia, and New Brunswick, education officials are moving toward programs that place more emphasis on standardized testing and instruction in the core subjects—such as reading and writing. The educational system is changing in many other ways. One of the potentially most significant changes is the increased use of technology in the classroom (see Box 14.4, "The Technology Revolution in the Classroom").

Throughout the world, people seek the meaning of life through traditional and nontraditional forms of religion. These Italian spiritual seekers are meeting together at a Mayan ruin in quest of harmonic convergence.

RELIGION IN HISTORICAL PERSPECTIVE

***Religion* is a system of beliefs, symbols, and rituals, based on some sacred or supernatural realm, that guides human behaviour, gives meaning to life, and unites believers into a community** (Durkheim, 1947/1912). For many people, religious beliefs provide the answers for the difficult questions about the meaning of life and death.

Religion and the Meaning of Life

Religion seeks to answer important questions such as why we exist, why people suffer and die, and what happens when we die. Whereas science and medicine typically rely on existing scientific evidence to respond to these questions, religion seeks to explain suffering, death, and injustice according to the realm of the sacred. According to Emile Durkheim, the term ***sacred* refers to those aspects of life that are extraordinary or supernatural**—in other words, those things that are set apart as "holy." People feel a sense of awe, reverence, deep respect, or fear for that which is considered sacred. Across cultures and in different eras, many things have been considered sacred, including invisible gods, spirits, specific animals or trees, altars, crosses, holy books, and special words or songs that only the initiated could speak or sing (Collins, 1982). Those things that people do not set apart as sacred are referred to as ***profane*—the everyday, worldly aspects of life** (Collins, 1982). Sacred beliefs are rooted in the holy or supernatural, whereas secular beliefs have their foundation in scientific knowledge or in everyday explanations. For example, in the educational debate between creationists and evolutionists, advocates of creationism view it as a belief founded in sacred (Biblical) teachings, while advocates of evolutionism assert that their beliefs are based on provable scientific facts.

In addition to beliefs, religion is also composed of symbols and rituals. According to anthropologist Clifford Geertz (1966), religion is a set of cultural symbols that establish powerful and pervasive moods and motivations to help people interpret the meaning of life and establish a direction for their behaviour. People often act out their religious beliefs in the form of ***rituals*—regularly repeated and carefully prescribed forms of behaviour that symbolize a cherished value or belief** (Kurtz, 1995). Rituals range from songs and prayers to offerings and sacrifices that worship or praise a supernatural being, an ideal, or a set of supernatural principles. Rituals differ from everyday actions in that they have very strictly determined behaviour. According to sociologist Randall Collins (1982:34), "In rituals, it is the forms that count. Saying prayers, singing a hymn, performing a primitive sacrifice or a dance, marching in a procession, kneeling before an idol or making the sign of the cross—in these, the action must be done the right way."

SOCIOLOGICAL PERSPECTIVES ON RELIGION

Whereas school attendance is compulsory up to a certain grade level, people can choose whether they want to participate in organized religion in Canada. Nevertheless, according to sociologist Meredith B. McGuire (1992:3), religion as a social institution is a powerful, deeply felt, and influential force in human society. Sociologists study the social institution of religion because of the importance religion holds for many people, and because they want to know more about the influence of religion on society, and vice versa (McGuire, 1992).

The major sociological perspectives have different outlooks on the relationship between religion and society. Functionalists typically emphasize the ways in which religious beliefs and rituals can bind people together. Conflict explanations suggest that religion can be a source of false consciousness in society. Interactionists focus on the meanings that people give to religion in their everyday life.

The Functionalist Perspective on Religion

Emile Durkheim was one of the first sociologists to emphasize that religion is essential to the maintenance of society. He suggested that religion was a cultural universal found in all societies because it met basic human needs and served important societal functions.

For Durkheim, the central feature of all religions is the presence of sacred beliefs and rituals that bind people together in a collectivity. In his studies of the religion of the Australian Aborigines, for example, Durkheim found that each clan had established its own sacred totem, which included kangaroos, trees, rivers, rock formations, and other animals or natural creations. To clan members, their totem was sacred; it symbolized some unique quality of their clan. People developed a feeling of unity by performing ritual dances around their totem, which caused them to abandon individual self-interest. Durkheim suggested that the correct performance of the ritual gives rise to religious conviction. Religious beliefs and rituals are *collective representations*—group-held meanings that express something important about the group itself (McGuire, 1992:177). Because of the intertwining of group consciousness and society, functionalists suggest that religion has three important functions in any society:

1. *Meaning and purpose.* Religion offers meaning for human experience. Some events create a profound sense of loss on both an individual basis (such as injustice, suffering, and the death of a loved one) and a group basis (such as famine, earthquake, economic depression, or subjugation by an enemy). Inequality may cause people to wonder why their own personal situation is no better than it is. Most religions offer explanations for these concerns. Explanations may differ from one religion to another, yet each tells the individual or group that life is part of a larger system of order in the universe (McGuire, 1992). Some (but not all) religions even offer hope of an afterlife for persons who follow the religion's tenets of morality in this life. Such beliefs help make injustices in this life easier to endure.
2. *Social cohesion and a sense of belonging.* By emphasizing shared symbolism, religious teachings and practices help promote social cohesion. An example is the Christian ritual of communion, which not only commemorates a

TABLE 14.2 MAJOR WORLD RELIGIONS

RELIGION	CURRENT FOLLOWERS	FOUNDER/ DATE	BELIEFS
Christianity	1.7 billion	Jesus Christ; 1st century C.E.	Monotheistic. Jesus is the Son of God. Through good moral and religious behaviour (and/or God's grace), people achieve eternal life with God.
Islam	950 million	Muhammad; ca. 610 C.E.	Monotheistic. Muhammad received the Qu'ran (scriptures) from God. On Judgment Day, believers who have submitted to God's will, as revealed in the Qu'ran, will go to an eternal Garden of Eden.
Hinduism	719 million	No specific founder; ca. 1500 B.C.E.	Polytheistic. Brahma (creator), Vishnu (preserver), and Shiva (destroyer) are divine. Union with ultimate reality and escape from eternal reincarnation are achieved through yoga, adherence to scripture, and devotion.
Buddhism	309 million	Siddhartha Gautama; 6th to 5th centuries B.C.E.	Nontheistic. Through meditation and adherence to the Eightfold Path (correct thought and behaviour), people can free themselves from desire and suffering, escape the cycle of eternal rebirth, and achieve nirvana (enlightenment).
Judaism	18 million	Abraham, Isaac, and Jacob; ca. 2000 B.C.E.	Monotheistic. God's nature and will are revealed in the Torah (Hebrew scripture) and in His intervention in history. God has established a covenant with the people of Israel, who are called to a life of holiness, justice, mercy, and fidelity to God's law.
Confucianism	5.9 million	K'ung Fu-Tzu (Confucius); 6th to 5th centuries B.C.E.	Neither polytheistic nor monotheistic. The sayings of Confucius (collected in the *Analects*) stress the role of virtue and order in the relationships between individuals, their families, and society.

Source: National Opinion Research Centre, *General Social Survey* (1989):156–159. Reprinted by permission.

The shared experiences and beliefs associated with religion have helped many groups maintain a sense of social cohesion and a feeling of belonging in the face of prejudice and discrimination.

historical event but also allows followers to participate in their union ("communion") with other believers (McGuire, 1992). All religions have some forms of shared experience that rekindle the group's consciousness of its own unity.

3. *Social control and support for the government.* All societies attempt to maintain social control through systems of rewards and punishments. Sacred symbols and beliefs establish powerful, pervasive, long-lasting motivations based on the concept of a general order of existence (Geertz, 1966). In other words, if individuals consider themselves to be part of a larger order that holds the ultimate meaning in life, they will feel bound to one another (and past and future generations) in a way that otherwise might not be possible (McGuire, 1997).

Religion also helps maintain social control in society by conferring supernatural legitimacy on the norms and laws in society. In some societies, social control occurs as a result of direct collusion between the dominant classes and the dominant religious organizations. For example, as discussed in Chapter 12, absolute monarchs often have claimed a divine right to rule.

The Conflict Perspective on Religion

While many functionalists view religion as serving positive functions in society, some conflict theorists view religion negatively.

KARL MARX ON RELIGION For Marx, *ideologies*—"systematic views of the way the world ought to be"—are embodied in religious doctrines and political values (Turner, Beeghley, and Powers, 1995:135). These ideologies also serve to justify the status quo and to retard social change. The capitalist class uses religious ideology as a tool of domination to mislead the workers about their true interests. For this reason, Marx wrote his now famous statement that religion is the "opiate of the masses." People become complacent because they have been taught to believe in an afterlife in which they will be rewarded for their suffering and misery in this life. Although these religious teachings soothe the masses' distress, any relief is illusory. Religion unites people under a "false consciousness," according to which they believe they have common interests with members of the dominant class (K. Roberts, 1995).

MAX WEBER ON RELIGION Whereas Marx believed that religion retarded social change, Weber argued just the opposite. For Weber, religion could be a catalyst to produce social change. In *The Protestant Ethic and the Spirit of Capitalism* (1976/1904–1905), Weber asserted that the religious teachings of John Calvin were directly related to the rise of capitalism. Calvin emphasized the doctrine of *predestination*—the belief that, even before they are born, all people are divided into two groups, the saved and the damned, and only God knows who will go to heaven (the elect) and who will go to hell. Because people cannot know whether they will be saved, they tend

According to Marx and Weber, religion serves to reinforce social stratification in a society. For example, according to Hindu belief, a person's social position in his or her current life is a result of behaviour in a former life.

to look for earthly signs that they are among the elect. According to the Protestant ethic, those who have faith, perform good works, and achieve economic success are more likely to be among the chosen of God. As a result, people work hard, save their money, and do not spend it on worldly frivolity; instead, they reinvest it in their land, equipment, and labour (Chalfant, Beckley, and Palmer, 1994).

The spirit of capitalism grew in the fertile soil of the Protestant ethic. As people worked ever harder to prove their religious piety, structural conditions in Europe led to the Industrial Revolution, free markets, and the commercialization of the economy—developments that worked hand in hand with Calvinist religious teachings. From this viewpoint, wealth was an unintended consequence of religious piety and hard work.

Like Marx, Weber was acutely aware that religion could reinforce existing social arrangements, especially the stratification system. The wealthy can use religion to justify their power and privilege: it is a sign of God's approval of their hard work and morality (McGuire, 1997). As for the poor, if they work hard and live a moral life, they will be richly rewarded in another life.

From a conflict perspective, religion tends to promote conflict between groups and societies. According to conflict theorists, conflict may be *between* religious groups (for example, anti-Semitism), *within* a religious group (for example, when a splinter group leaves an existing denomination), or *between a religious group and the larger society* (for example, the conflict over religion in the classroom). Conflict theorists assert that, in attempting to provide meaning and purpose in life while at the same time promoting the status quo, religion is used by the dominant classes to impose their own control over society and its resources (McGuire, 1992). Many feminists object to the patriarchal nature of most religions; some advocate a break from traditional religions, while others seek to reform religious language, symbols, and rituals to eliminate the elements of patriarchy (Renzetti and Curran, 1992).

The Interactionist Perspective on Religion

Thus far, we have been looking at religion primarily from a macrolevel perspective. Interactionists focus their attention on a microlevel analysis that examines the meanings that people give to religion in their everyday life.

RELIGION AS A REFERENCE GROUP For many people, religion serves as a reference group to help them define themselves. Religious symbols, for example, have meaning for large bodies of people. The Star of David holds special significance for Jews, just as the crescent moon and star do for Muslims and the cross does for Christians. It has been said that the symbolism of religion is so very powerful because it "expresses the essential facts of our human existence" (Collins, 1982:37).

His Religion and Her Religion Not all people interpret religion in the same way. In virtually all religions, women have much less influence in establishing social definitions of appropriate gender roles both within the religious community and in the larger community (McGuire, 1997). Therefore, women and men may belong to the same religious group, but their individual religion will not necessarily be a carbon copy of the group's entire system of beliefs. In fact, according to McGuire (1997), women's versions of particular religions probably differ markedly from men's versions. For example, whereas an Orthodox Jewish man may focus on his public ritual roles and his discussion of sacred texts, Orthodox Jewish women have few ritual duties and are more likely to focus on their responsibilities in the home. Consequently, the meaning of being Jewish may be different for women than for men.

Religious symbolism and language typically create a social definition of the roles of men and women. For example, religious symbolism may depict the higher deities as male and the lower deities as female. Sometimes, females are depicted as negative, or evil, spiritual forces. For example, the Hindu goddess Kali represents men's eternal battle against the evils of materialism (Daly, 1973). Historically, language has defined women as being nonexistent in the world's major religions. Phrases such as "for all men" in Catholic and Episcopal services gradually have been changed to "for all," but some churches retain the traditional liturgy. Although there has been resistance, especially by women, to some of the male-centred terms, overall inclusive language is less common than older male terms for God (Briggs, 1987).

Many women resist the subordination they have experienced in organized religion. They have worked to change the existing rules that have excluded them or placed them in a clearly subordinate position.

TYPES OF RELIGIOUS ORGANIZATIONS

Religious groups vary widely in their organizational structure. While some groups are large and somewhat bureaucratically organized, others are small and have a relatively informal authority structure. Some require total commitment from their members; others expect only partial commitment. Sociologists have developed typologies or ideal types of religious organization to enable them to study a wide variety of religious groups. The most common categorization sets forth four types: ecclesia, church, sect, and cult.

Ecclesia

Some countries have an official or state religion known as the ***ecclesia*—a religious organization that is so integrated with the dominant culture that it claims as its membership all members of a society.** Membership in the ecclesia occurs as a result of being born into the society, rather than by any conscious decision on the part of individual members. The linkages between the social institutions of religion and government often are very strong in such societies. Although no true ecclesia exists in the contemporary world, the Anglican Church (the official church of England), the Lutheran Church in Sweden and Denmark, the Catholic Church in Spain, and Islam in Iran and Pakistan come fairly close.

The Church-Sect Typology

To help explain the different types of religious organizations found in societies, Ernst Troeltsch (1960/1931) and his teacher, Max Weber (1963/1922), developed a typology that distinguishes between the characteristics of churches and sects (see Table 14.3). Unlike an ecclesia, a church is not considered to be a state religion; however, it may still have a powerful influence on political and economic arrangements in society. A ***church* is a large, bureaucratically organized religious organization that tends to seek accommodation with the larger society in order to maintain some degree of control over it.** Church membership is largely based on birth; children of church members typically are baptized as infants and become lifelong members of the church. Older children and adults may choose to join the church, but they are required to go through an extensive training program that culminates in a ceremony similar to the one that infants go through. Leadership is hierarchically arranged, and clergy generally have many years of formal education. Churches have very restrained services that appeal

TABLE 14.3 CHARACTERISTICS OF CHURCHES AND SECTS

CHARACTERISTIC	CHURCH	SECT
Organization	Large, bureaucratic organization, led by a professional clergy	Small, faithful group, with high degree of lay participation
Membership	Open to all; members usually from upper and middle classes	Closely guarded membership, usually from lower classes
Type of Worship	Formal, orderly	Informal, spontaneous
Salvation	Granted by God, as administered by the church	Achieved by moral purity
Attitude toward Other Institutions and Religions	Tolerant	Intolerant

to the intellect rather than the emotions (Stark, 1992). Religious services are highly ritualized; they are led by clergy who wear robes, enter and exit in a formal processional, administer sacraments, and read services from a prayer book or other standardized liturgical format.

Midway between the church and the sect is a ***denomination*—a large, organized religious body characterized by accommodation to society but frequently lacking the ability or intention to dominate society** (Niebuhr, 1929). Denominations have a trained ministry, and while involvement by lay members is encouraged more than in the church, their participation usually is limited to particular activities, such as readings or prayers. Denominations tend to be more tolerant and less likely than churches to expel or excommunicate members. This form of organization is most likely to thrive in societies characterized by *religious pluralism*—a situation in which many religious groups exist because they have a special appeal to specific segments of the population. Perhaps because of its diversity, Canada has more denominations than most other countries.

A ***sect* is a relatively small religious group that has broken away from another religious organization to renew what it views as the original version of the faith.** Unlike churches, sects offer members a more personal religion and an intimate relationship with a supreme being, who is depicted as taking an active interest in the individual's everyday life. Whereas churches use formalized prayers, often from a prayer book, sects have informal prayers composed at the time they are given. Whereas churches typically appeal to members of the upper classes, and denominations to members of the middle and upper classes, sects seek to meet the needs of people who are low in the stratification system—that is, the masses (Stark, 1992).

Cults

A ***cult* is a religious group with practices and teachings outside the dominant cultural and religious traditions of a society.** Although many people view cults negatively, all major religions (including Judaism, Islam, and Christianity) and some denominations (such as the Mormons) started as cults. Cult leadership is based on charismatic characteristics of the individual, including an unusual ability to form attachments with others (Stark, 1992:417). An example is the religious movement started by Reverend Sun Myung Moon, a Korean electrical engineer who believed that God had revealed to him that Judgment Day was rapidly approaching. Out of this movement, the Unification Church, or "Moonies," grew and flourished, with new members recruited through their personal attachment to present members (Stark, 1992).

TRENDS IN RELIGION IN CANADA

Canada's Religious Mosaic

Until the end of the nineteenth century, Canada was a country whose population was almost entirely Protestant and Catholic. Changes in the number of members of the major religious groups in Canada since then are shown in Figure 14.2. Today, Catholics, at 46 percent of the population, are the largest religious group in Canada.

In 1995, 5 percent of Canadians were affiliated with "other" religions, including Eastern Orthodox, Judaism, and Eastern non-Christian religions such as Islam, Buddhism, Hinduism, Sikhism, and parareligious groups. The number of those who fall under the category "no religion" has grown rapidly going from 56,679 in 1951 to almost 3.4 million in 1991 (McVey and Kalbach, 1995) and over 4 million in 1996. Does this mean that Canadians are rejecting religion? An answer to this question can be found in examining other recent trends in religion in Canada.

Religious Belief and Church Attendance

Religion in Canada is very diverse. Pluralism and religious freedom are among the cultural values most widely espoused. However, is Canada a religious society? The answer depends on how you look at things. Nationally church attendance, public confidence in church leadership, and church influence have all gradually declined since the late 1940s (Bibby, 1987, 1996).

Religious affiliation has been tracked through the census, the annual General Social Survey (GSS), and opinion polls. Over the past fifty years, attendance at religious services has declined precipitously (Clark, 1998). A 1946 Gallup poll reported that 67 percent of Canadian adults had attended religious services during the previous week. By 1996, the General Social Survey found that attendance at weekly religious services had declined to only 20 percent. A generation ago, most Canadians attended religious services; today only a small minority attend.

In recent years different denominations have seen different rates of decline (Clark, 1998). The 1996 GSS found that 24 percent of Roman Catholics attended weekly services, a marked drop from 37 percent attendance in 1986. Nearly one in three Roman Catholics did not attend church at all in 1996 compared with one in seven in 1986. During the same period attendance in the mainline Protestant churches (United, Anglican, Presbyterian, and Lutheran) dropped from 17 percent to 14 percent. However, members of conservative Protestant denominations (Baptist, Pentecostal) have maintained 50 percent to 60 percent attendance rates. While 30 percent of Canadians claim affiliation with the mainline Protestant denominations compared with 8 percent for the conservative denominations, the latter now have more people who are regular participants than do the mainline churches (Posterski and Barker, 1993). Most other religions (including Judaism, Hinduism, Buddhism, and Sikhism) have also seen serious declines in the percentages of people attending services, although some have seen a stabilization or even an increase in the number of members because of immigration.

While attendance rates have declined for all age groups, the drop has been particularly large for younger people. Thirty-four percent of those 65 years of age and over are regular church attenders, compared with only 12 percent of 15- to 24-year-olds. This loss of young members does not bode well for the future of Canadian churches, as the vast majority of regular adult church attendees had also been regular attenders in childhood. This means that as older members die, there will likely be fewer and fewer people taking their places in the pews.

On the other hand, despite the decline in involvement with the institutional church, the vast majority of Canadians still report a religious affiliation and affirm that they believe in God. However, both of these measures have also declined in recent years. In 1961, only 1 percent of Canadians reported no religious affiliation; by 1996, this had increased to 13 percent (Clark, 1998). In 1975, 89 percent of Canadians reported that they believed in God compared with 81 percent in 1995 (Bibby, 1995). Despite these declines, the vast majority of Canadians still have religious affiliations and beliefs. This view is further supported by a 1993 poll that found that 75 percent of Canadians expressed a belief in the death and the resurrection of Jesus, the basic tenet of Christianity. Almost one-third of the adult population claimed to pray daily and more than half reported reading the Bible or other religious literature at least occasionally (Nemeth et al., 1993).

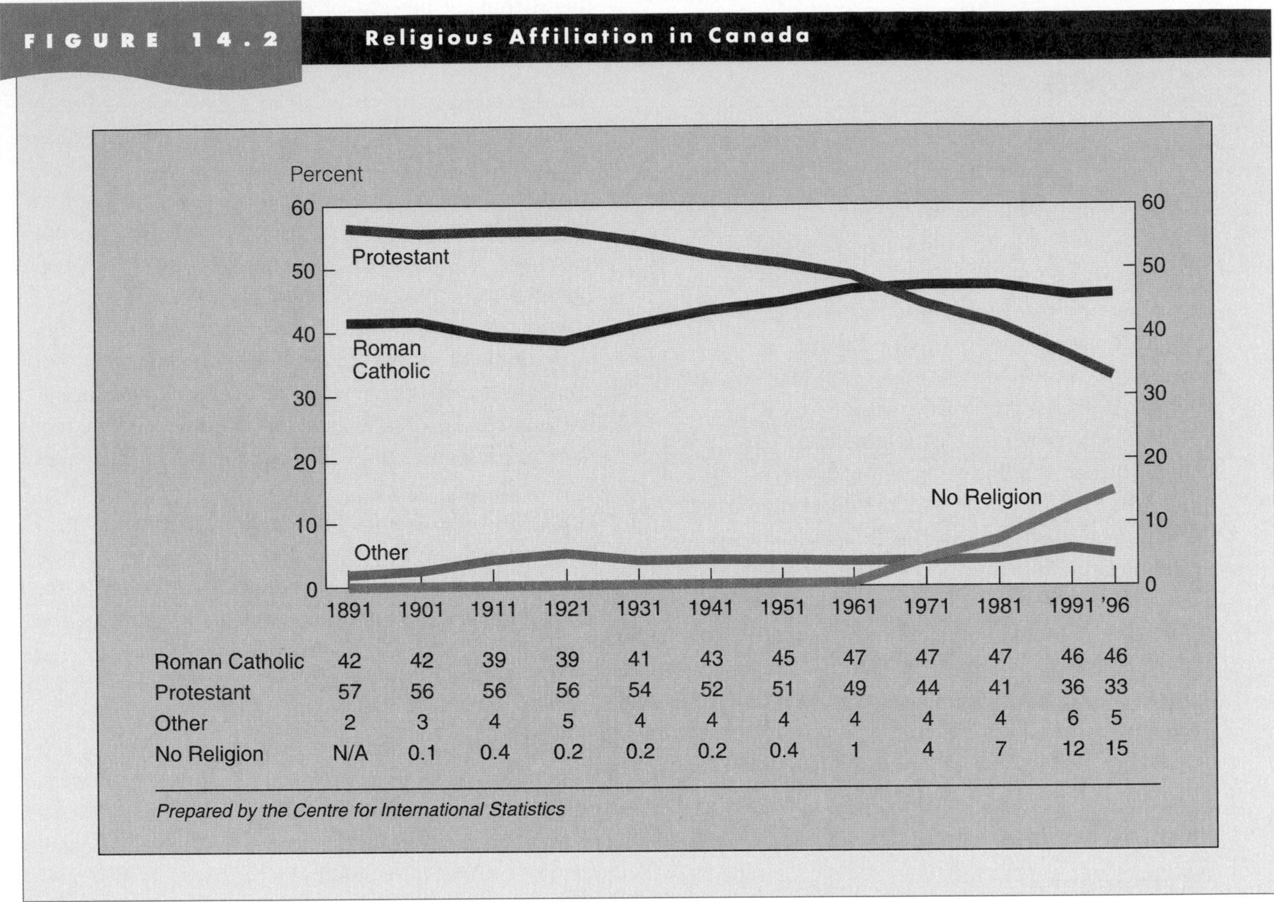

	1891	1901	1911	1921	1931	1941	1951	1961	1971	1981	1991	'96
Roman Catholic	42	42	39	39	41	43	45	47	47	47	46	46
Protestant	57	56	56	56	54	52	51	49	44	41	36	33
Other	2	3	4	5	4	4	4	4	4	4	6	5
No Religion	N/A	0.1	0.4	0.2	0.2	0.2	0.4	1	4	7	12	15

FIGURE 14.2 Religious Affiliation in Canada

Sources: Vanier Institute of the Family, 1994. Reprinted by permission. 1996 figures from Statistics Canada, *General Social Survey*, Cat. no. 11-612. Used by permission.

In addition to their religious beliefs, Canadians also show an interest in other aspects of spirituality. Table 14.4 shows that most Canadians believe that some people have psychic powers; that supernatural and evil forces exist; that there is life after death; and that some people have extrasensory perception. A significant minority believe that astrology has some merit; that it is possible to make contact with the spirit world; that they have experienced God; and that they will be reincarnated after death.

The results of these surveys lead us to an interesting paradox. Church attendance has dramatically declined despite the fact that most Canadians report some religious affiliation, express a belief in God, and believe in other spiritual aspects of life. It should be noted that people have not rejected the churches completely. Most still rely on the organized church for services such as baptisms, weddings, and funerals. However, they are not regular participants in religious activities, choosing instead to adopt what researcher Reginald Bibby calls "religious fragments"—isolated beliefs, isolated practices, and isolated services (1987). They receive spiritual sustenance from their religions, but they also draw on alternatives such as astrology, extrasensory perception, and New Age practices such as healing with crystals that serve as adjuncts to traditional religious practice. Theologian Tom Harper sums up this approach to religion:

> There is a huge spiritual quest going on. There's a lot of attempts at quick fixes and spiritual junk food as well. But even the silly fringe is part of it ... People seem intuitively aware that something is missing in their lives, and there's a reaction against traditional religion. (quoted in McDonald, 1994:42)

TABLE 14.4 SPIRITUAL BELIEFS OF CANADIANS

	PERCENTAGE AGREEING	
	TEENS	ADULTS
God exists	81	83
Divinity of Jesus	80	75
Some people have psychic powers	69	59
Supernatural forces exist	66	*
Life after death	64	68
Evil forces exist	64	*
Astrology	53	34
Extrasensory perception	52	59
Contact within the spirit world	44	39
I have experienced God	34	46
I will be reincarnated	32	27

*Figures unavailable.
Reprinted by permission of Donald Posterski, *Where's a Good Church?* Winfield, B.C.: Wood Lake Books, Inc. 1993.

Fundamentalism

The rise of a new fundamentalism has occurred at the same time as a number of mainline denominations have been losing membership. The term *religious fundamentalism* refers to a conservative religious doctrine that opposes intellectualism and worldly accommodation in favour of restoring a traditional otherworldly focus. In Canada, fundamentalism has been gaining popularity, primarily among Protestants, but also among Roman Catholics and Jews. Whereas "old" fundamentalism usually appealed to people from lower-income, rural backgrounds, the "new" fundamentalism appears to have a much wider following among persons from all socioeconomic levels, geographical areas, and occupations. "New-right" fundamentalists have been especially critical of *secular humanism*—a belief in the perfectibility of human beings through their own efforts rather than through a belief in God and religious conversion. According to fundamentalists, "creeping" secular humanism has been most visible in the public schools, which, instead of offering children a fair and balanced picture, are teaching things that seem to children to prove their parents' lifestyle and religion are inferior and perhaps irrational (Carter, 1994:52). The new-right fundamentalists claim that banning the teaching of Christian beliefs in the classroom while teaching things that are contrary to their faith is an infringement on their freedom of religion (Jenkinson, 1979). As we have seen in this chapter, the debate continues over what should be taught and what practices (such as Bible reading and prayer) should be permitted in public schools. The selection of textbooks and library materials is an especially controversial issue. Starting in the 1960s, books considered to have racist and sexist biases were attacked by civil rights activists and feminists. Soon thereafter, challenges were brought by extremely conservative groups to protest the use of books that they alleged had "factual inaccuracies" (such as a criticism of the free enterprise system) or morally objectionable subject matter or language (see Shor, 1986; Wong, 1991; Bates, 1994). For example, a small group of parents recently convinced the Durham, Ontario, Regional School Board to restrict the classroom reading of Harry Potter books because the novels contain references to witchcraft and magic. This debate, along with the message of fundamentalism, has been transformed into an international issue because of the growth of the electronic church and the Internet, as discussed in Box 14.5.

EDUCATION AND RELIGION IN THE FUTURE

This chapter ends as it began by noting that education and religion remain important social institutions in the twenty-first century. Also remaining, however, will be the controversies that we have discussed—controversies that your generation must attempt to resolve.

With regard to education, questions will remain about what should be taught, not only in terms of preparing your children for their adult lives and the world of work but also in regard to the values to which you want your child exposed. Unlike many other countries, no central authority in Canada decides the curriculum to be taught to all students nationwide. Rather, each province enacts its own laws and regulations, with local school boards frequently making the final determination. Accordingly, no general standards exist regarding what is to be *taught* to students or how, although many provinces now have adopted levels regarding what (as a minimum) must be *learned* in order to graduate from high school.

BOX 14.5 SOCIOLOGY AND TECHNOLOGY

IN THE MEDIA AGE: THE ELECTRONIC CHURCH AND THE INTERNET

In a single telecast, I preach to millions more than Christ did in His entire lifetime.—Billy Graham (quoted in K. Roberts, 1995:360)

Television and the Internet are transforming both religion and education in the United States and Canada. Although television has been used as a medium of communication by ministers since the 1950s, the electronic church has far surpassed most people's wildest estimates by becoming a multimillion-dollar industry with audiences ranging in size from 10 million to 130 million in the United States.

When religious services were first televised, many were church services conducted by a local congregation and carried by a regional television station primarily for the benefit of shut-ins and those who had no "church home" in the community. In the 1950s and early 1960s, the few nationally televised religious programs featured people like the Rev. Bishop Fulton J. Sheen, an established spokesperson for the Roman Catholic Church, or evangelists such as Billy Graham who were televised while conducting a revival or "crusade" in some remote part of the world.

By comparison, most contemporary televangelists are entrepreneurs whose success hinges on presenting a message that "sells well" and generates the extremely large sums of money needed to keep the "television ministry" profitable.

Though some televangelists have been discredited because of sexual or financial misconduct, others have taken their place not only to proclaim the "gospel" but also to become spokespersons for a conservative political agenda.

While televangelists have a great deal of impact in the United States, they have not been as successful in Canada. According to Reginald Bibby (1998), fewer than 5 percent of Canadians regularly watch religious services on television, which is quite a fall from the 29 percent who watched or listened to services on tele-

The debate over what should be taught obviously is not limited to just religious and moral issues; rather, it includes the entire curriculum. If, as critics assert, academic achievement in Canada compares unfavourably with the level of achievement by students in many other countries, what can be done to change it? Some policy initiatives have been introduced in the public school system that should result in an improvement in the quality of education. For example, *compensatory education programs*, including preschool, remedial, or extra education programs, which provide additional learning assistance to disadvantaged children, have been designed to offset the effects of poverty, deprivation, and disadvantage on school performance (Guppy, 1995).

School enrolments will continue to grow and diversify as baby boomers continue to have children and immigration to Canada creates an increasingly ethnically diverse population of students. The challenge in the twenty-first century lies in finding ways to facilitate learning in a pluralistic school system—meeting the needs of students in terms of their distinct cultural, linguistic, and religious traditions.

Religion faces similar challenges in the twenty-first century. Religious organizations will continue to be important in the lives of many people; however, the influence of religious beliefs and values will be felt even by those who claim no religious beliefs of their own. In many nations the rise of religious nationalism has led to the blending of strongly held religious and political beliefs. Although the rise of religious nationalism is occurring throughout the world, it is especially strong in the Middle East, where Islamic nationalism has spread rapidly.

In Canada, the influence of religion will be evident in ongoing battles over religion in the schools, abor-

BOX 14.5

CONTINUED

vision and radio in 1958. Further, most of those who did watch religious programs on television also attended church services regularly. This means that television has not become an electronic church replacing more traditional forms of worship. Only a few televangelists such as David Mainse have become nationally known in Canada, and none have any political influence.

By comparison, the Internet is just beginning to have an impact on religion. Some religious groups now have begun to use it to spread their message. For example, the Catholic Information Center on the Internet (**www.catholic.net**) was established to provide a wide range of services including a review of recent Church-related news stories; discussions of Church teachings; and a solicitation to inactive Catholics to become reinvolved with the Church. While the Internet is a good way for mainline churches to get their message out, it also provides a means for newer spiritual groups to try to attract new followers. For example, the Fishgoat's Leaves of Wonder site (**www.gatewest.net/~dem/low/lowtoc.html**) provides information about Wicca and Magick for those who might have an interest in paganism.

While the Internet may be a useful tool for religious groups, it raises questions and concerns because controlling what young people read on the Internet is almost impossible. Some religious groups have begun pressing for limits to the type of information available on this network, or at least to limits on young people's access to certain types of information. How do you think religious organizations should respond to this problem? Is censorship of the Internet either possible or desirable?

Sources: Based on Hadden and Swann, 1981; Frankl, 1987; Hadden and Shupe, 1988; McGuire, 1997; Kosmin and Lachman, 1993; Tidwell, 1993; Bates, 1994; Bibby, 1998; and K. Roberts, 1995.

tion, gay rights, and women's issues, among others. On some fronts, religion may unify people; on others, it may contribute to confrontations among individuals and groups. For Canada, however, one of our most cherished freedoms is religious freedom. Maintaining an appropriate balance between the social institutions of education and religion will be an important challenge in this country in the twenty-first century.

CHAPTER REVIEW

How are the social institutions of education and religion similar?

Education and religion are powerful and influential forces in society. Both institutions impart values, beliefs, and knowledge considered essential to the social reproduction of individual personalities and entire cultures.

What is the primary function of education?

Education is the social institution responsible for the systematic transmission of knowledge, skills, and cultural values within a formally organized structure.

What are the functionalist, conflict, and interactionist views of education?

According to functionalists, education has both manifest functions (socialization, transmission of culture, social control, social placement, and change and innovation) and latent functions (keeping young people off the streets and out of the job market, matchmaking and producing social networks, and creating a generation gap). From a conflict perspective, education is used to perpetuate class, racial-ethnic, and gender inequalities through ability grouping and a hidden curriculum that teaches subordinate groups conformity and obedience. According to interactionists, education may be a self-fulfilling prophecy for some students, such that these students come to perform up—or down—to the expectations held for them by teachers.

What is religion?
Religion is a system of beliefs, symbols, and rituals, based on some sacred or supernatural realm, that guides human behaviour, gives meaning to life, and unites believers into a community.

What are the functionalist, conflict, and interactionist views of religion?
According to functionalists, religion has three important functions in any society: (1) providing meaning and purpose to life, (2) promoting social cohesion and a sense of belonging, and (3) providing social control and support for the government. From a conflict perspective, religion can have negative consequences in that the capitalist class uses religion as a tool of domination to mislead workers about their true interests. However, Max Weber believed that religion could be a catalyst for social change. Interactionists examine the meanings that people give to religion and the meanings they attach to religious symbols in their everyday life.

What are the different types of religious organizations?
Religious organizations can be categorized as ecclesia, churches, denominations, sects, and cults. Some of the world's major religions started off as cults built around a charismatic leader.

Key Terms

church 421
credentialism 410
cult 422
cultural capital 408
denomination 422
ecclesia 421
education 404
hidden curriculum 409
latent functions 408
manifest functions 406
profane 416
religion 416
rituals 417
sacred 416
sect 422
self-fulfilling prophecy 410
tracking 409

Internet Exercises

1. The Canadian Education Association has a Web site at:

   www.acea.ca

   What information can you find on recent trends in education in Canada?

2. Canada's SchoolNet is designed to promote the effective use of information technology among Canadians by helping schools and public libraries connect to the Internet. Visit SchoolNet's home page at:

   www.schoolnet.ca

   and explore what subject areas are available under Learning Resources. What sociology Web sites can you locate in Learning Resources?

3. Go to the Yahoo Canada Web site at:

   www.ca.yahoo.com

   In the Society and Culture section of the home page, go to Religion. Then go to Canada Only, then to Faiths and Practices. Find two nontraditional faiths or beliefs that you are not familiar with and go to their Web sites. What are some of the fundamental principles of these faiths?

4. Go to the Virtual Religion Index at:

   religion.rutgers.edu/vri

   What Web sites can you find referenced at this site that will tell you about the religious practices of North America's Aboriginal peoples?

Net Links

For more Web links related to the topic of this chapter, see the Nelson sociology Web site: **www.sociologyessentials-2nded.nelson.com**.

The Canadian Federation of Students represents about half a million students at over 60 universities, colleges, and technical institutes across Canada. Its Web site has been established to offer students, the general public, media, and government officials information on the issues facing college and university students today; to see it go to:

www.cfs-fcee.ca

The United Nations Educational, Scientific, and Cultural Organization's (UNESCO) Education Information Service provides global educational news, statistics, updates on programs and activities, and current publications on education; its address is:

www.unesco.org/education

To see the Web site of the World Council of Churches, go to:

www.wcc-coe.org/wcc/english.html

Much of civilization's greatest art was commissioned by religious organizations. Visit the Vatican's Sistine Chapel with its ceiling painted by Michelangelo at:

www.kfki.hu/~arthp/tours/sistina/index.html
www.science.wayne.edu/~mcogan/Humanities/Sistine/index.html

Questions for Critical Thinking

1. What are the major functions of religion and education for individuals and for societies? Why do these functions overlap in Canada? How would you design a research project to study the everyday effects of fundamentalist religion on everyday life? What kinds of data would be most accessible?
2. Why do some theorists believe that education is a vehicle for decreasing social inequality whereas others believe that education reproduces existing class relationships?
3. Why does so much controversy exist over what should be taught in Canadian public schools?
4. If Durkheim, Marx, and Weber were engaged in a discussion about religion, on what topics might they agree? On what topics would they disagree?

Suggested Readings

This book provides more information about the sociology of education:

Jeanne H. Ballantine. *The Sociology of Education: A Systematic Analysis* (4th ed.). Englewood Cliffs, N.J.: Prentice-Hall, 1997.

Comprehensive discussions on problems in today's schools may be found in the following studies:

Maude Barlow and Heather-Jane Robertson. *Class Warfare: The Assault on Canada's Schools*. Toronto: Key Porter Books, 1994.

Neil Guppy and Scott Davies. *Education in Canada: Recent Trends and Future Challenges*. Ottawa: Statistics Canada, 1998.

These books provide more information on religion in Canada:

Reginald Bibby. *Fragmented Gods: The Poverty and Potential of Religion in Canada*. Toronto: Irwin, 1996.

W.E. Hewitt (ed.). *The Sociology of Religion: A Canadian Focus*. Toronto: Butterworths, 1993.

Useful books on the world's religions include the following:

Lester Kurtz. *Gods in the Global Village: The World's Religions in Sociological Perspective*. Thousand Oaks, Cal.: Pine Forge, 1995.

Warren Matthews. *World Religions*. St. Paul, Minn.: West, 1995.

INFOTRAC® COLLEGE EDITION

Either from the *Sociology In Our Times: The Essentials* Web site (**www.sociologyessentials-2nded.nelson.com**) or directly from your Web browser, you may access InfoTrac® College Edition, an online university library that includes over 600 popular and scholarly journals in which you can find articles related to the topics in this chapter.

CHAPTER 15

Moving to a new country and getting used to a new culture can be difficult, but the transition is easier for those who have support from others who share the same experience. Consider the contrast between the lives of the two women—one described and one quoted—below. The following excerpt is from an interview with the child of a Sikh woman:

"My mother had it hard when I was growing up. We had a small rented farm in the Okanagan Valley, where there were then very few Sikhs. I made friends with Canadians at school. Since I knew English fluently I often talked with the neighbours, as did my father. Mother wasn't so lucky. She never learned English well enough to communicate easily, so never really had any good Canadian friends. There were so few other Sikh families around that she had little contact with them either. For her, the family was everything." (Buchignani, Indra, and Srivastiva, 1985:76)

In the next excerpt a woman who moved from Hong Kong to a Canadian city with a large middle-class Chinese community talks about her Chinese friends in Canada:

"I feel we have more in common with each other. We often get together and reminisce about our lives in Hong Kong. We also laugh about our ignorance of Canadian culture and the little faux pas that we get ourselves into. Other times, we exchange information about schools, dentists, and other practical knowledge. Or we marvel at the high price we now pay for little things such as cooking wares and stockings. I have a feeling of solidarity when I talk to these people. They understand where I'm coming from." (Man, 1996:290)

POPULATION AND URBANIZATION

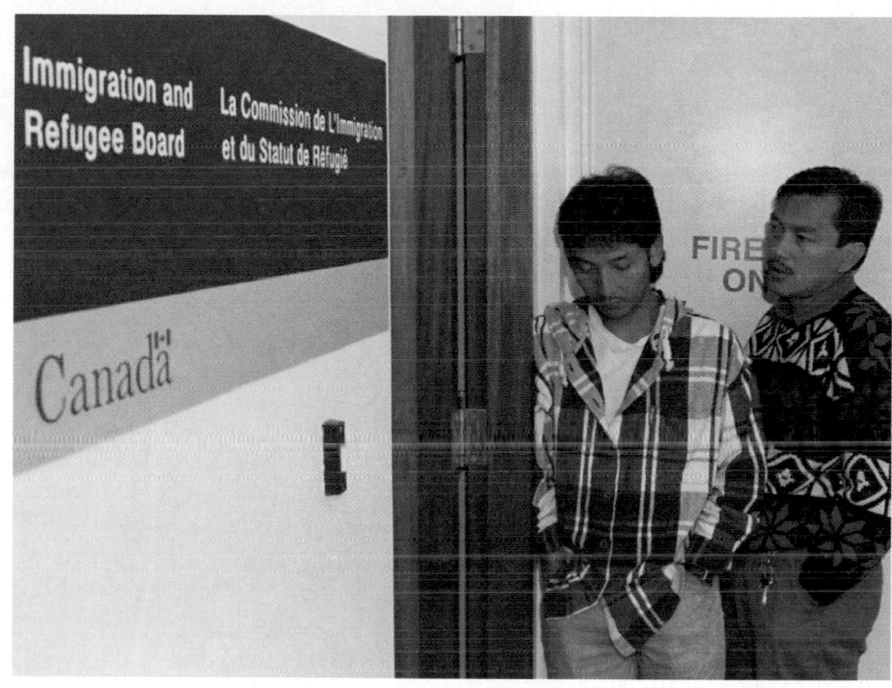

The presence of others from one's former home plays a large role in determining where new immigrants settle in Canada. This has meant that cities such as Toronto and Vancouver have very high proportions of recent immigrants, while other communities have almost none. Immigration is just one of the demographic factors changing Canada and the rest of the world. The phenomena of births, deaths, and the movement of people interact to affect us all in very complex ways.

In this chapter, we will explore the dynamics of population growth and urban change. In the process we will periodically focus on immigration and its importance to Canadian society. Before reading on, test your knowledge about the causes and consequences of immigration by taking the quiz in Box 15.1.

Questions and Issues

CHAPTER FOCUS QUESTION: What are the major social processes affecting Canada's population?

What causes global population growth?

How are people affected by population changes?

What impact has the baby boom had on Canada's population?

How do ecological/functionalist and political economy/conflict models differ in their explanations of urban growth?

What is meant by the experience of urban life, and how do sociologists seek to explain this experience?

What are the best- and worst-case scenarios regarding population and urban growth in the twenty-first century, and how might some of the worst-case scenarios be averted?

Canada has a long history of immigration. In this photo, the Netherlands' ambassador welcomes a shipload of Dutch immigrants to Canada in 1947.

DEMOGRAPHY: THE STUDY OF POPULATION

Although population growth has slowed in Canada, the world's population of almost 6 billion in 1999 is increasing by 78 million people per year (United Nations, 1998). By 2050 there will be an estimated 9 billion people in the world (United Nations, 1998). Virtually all of this growth will come in the less developed nations of the world. The population in many of the developed nations may actually decrease over this period. This means that people in different parts of the world face dramatically different futures. While many people in developing countries face starvation because of rapidly increasing populations, Canadians have a much different problem. Because of very low birth rates, our population is aging and there are concerns about how a relatively small number of young workers will support large numbers of elderly people.

Why does the population grow rapidly in some nations? What are the consequences of low birth rates in industrialized countries? What impact does immigration have on the immigrants and on the country of destination? What effect might a widespread AIDS crisis have on world population? How large will our cities be in twenty years? These questions are of interest to scholars who specialize in the study of ***demography*—the subfield of sociology that examines population size, composition, and distribution.** Many sociological studies use demographic analysis as a component in the research design.

Increases or decreases in population can have a powerful impact on the social, economic, and political structures of societies. Demographers define ***population* as a group of people who live in a specified geographic area**. Only three variables can change a population: *fertility* (births), *mortality* (deaths), and *migration* (movement from one place to another).

Fertility

***Fertility* is the actual level of childbearing for an individual or a population.** The level of fertility in a society is based on biological and social factors, the primary biological factor being the number of women of childbearing age (usually between ages 15 and 45). Other biological factors affecting fertility include the general health and level of nutrition of women of childbearing age. Social factors influencing the level of fertility include the roles available to women in a society and prevalent viewpoints regarding what constitutes the "ideal" family size.

Based on biological capability alone, most women could produce twenty or more children during their childbearing years. *Fecundity* is the potential number of children that could be born if every woman reproduced at her maximum biological capacity. Fertility rates are not as high as fecundity rates because

BOX 15.1 SOCIOLOGY AND EVERYDAY LIFE

How Much Do You Know about Immigration to Canada?

TRUE	FALSE	
T	F	1. Immigrants usually become a drain on the taxpayer because they have high rates of welfare use.
T	F	2. Immigrants are not evenly distributed across the country, because many prefer to settle in large cities.
T	F	3. Most immigrants to Canada are refugees.
T	F	4. Canada has had rates of immigration in the past that were higher than current rates.
T	F	5. There is no limit to the number of family-sponsored immigrants who are allowed into Canada.
T	F	6. Immigrants have lower rates of crime than other Canadians.
T	F	7. If we do not maintain rates of immigration that are high by world standards, our population will eventually decline.
T	F	8. About 3 percent of Canada's population was not born in Canada.
T	F	9. Canada welcomed hundreds of thousands of Jewish refugees fleeing Nazi persecution during World War II.
T	F	10. Most countries of the world have open immigration and citizenship policies like those of Canada.

Answers on page 434.

people's biological capabilities are limited by social factors such as practising voluntary abstinence and refraining from sexual intercourse until an older age, as well as by contraception, voluntary sterilization, abortion, and infanticide (Davis and Blake, 1956). Government policies, such as China's one-child policy, also may have an effect on fertility.

The most basic measure of fertility is the ***crude birth rate*—the number of live births per 1000 people in a population in a given year.** In 1996, the crude birth rate in Canada was less than 13 per 1000, compared with a post–World War II high rate of 28 per 1000 in 1956 and around 40 per 1000 at the time of Confederation. This measure is referred to as a "crude" birth rate because it is based on the entire population and is not "refined" to incorporate significant variables affecting fertility, such as age, marital status, religion, or race/ethnicity.

In most of the industrialized world, women are having fewer children. Crude birth rates in Japan, Italy, and Spain are just over 9 per 1000; in the United Kingdom and France they are 13 per 1000 (about the same as in Canada), and in the United States they are 15 per 1000. However, families are much larger in underdeveloped, agricultural regions of the world where children's labour is essential to a family's economic survival and child mortality rates are still very high. Countries with high crude birth rates (more than 40 per 1000) include Nigeria, Somalia, and Ethiopia (Central Intelligence Agency, 1998).

Mortality

The primary cause of world population growth in recent years has been a decline in ***mortality*—the incidence of death in a population.** The simplest measure of mortality is the ***crude death rate*—the number of deaths per 1000 people in a population in a given year.** Mortality rates have declined dra-

BOX 15.1

Answers to the Sociology Quiz on Immigration to Canada

1. **False.** Immigrants are less likely to be on welfare than people born in Canada. A study by the Economic Council of Canada using the 1986 census found that the proportion of welfare recipients among recent immigrants (12.5 percent) was smaller than among people born in Canada (13.8 percent). Immigrants are more highly educated and more likely to be working than native-born Canadians.
2. **True.** Immigrants are more likely to settle in large cities. A high proportion of immigrants live in Toronto, Vancouver, and Montreal.
3. **False.** This figure varies from year to year, but, for example, in 1998, only 12 percent of immigrants to Canada were refugees.
4. **True.** Immigration rates fluctuate widely and at times in the past they have been much higher than they are today.
5. **False.** Each year the government determines the number of family-sponsored immigrants who will be admitted. In 1998 about 28 percent of immigrants were family class.
6. **True.** Immigrants were significantly underrepresented in the population of those incarcerated in the federal correctional system in 1989 and 1991.
7. **True.** Birth rates in Canada are currently below replacement level. When the baby boom generation begins to die (after 2025), Canada will lose population unless we give entry to about 250,000 immigrants each year.
8. **False.** About 17 percent of Canadian residents were born in other countries.
9. **False.** While most Canadians are proud of this country's record in accepting refugees, our policies were not always as liberal as they are today. Very few Jewish refugees were admitted to Canada during the Holocaust.
10. **False.** Canada has one of the highest rates of legal immigration in the world. Most countries discourage immigration and many will not give citizenship to anyone not born to parents who themselves are citizens of that country.

Sources: Based on Abella and Troper, 1982; Beaujot, 1991; Economic Council of Canada, 1991; Gordon and Nelson, 1993; Matas, 1995; McVey and Kalbach, 1995; Statistics Canada, 1998; and Citizenship and Immigration, 1999.

matically in the last two hundred years. In 1867, the crude death rate in Canada was 21 deaths per 1000—half of what it had been one hundred years earlier. By 1995 the death rate had dropped to 7 per 1000. This decline has been due to the fact that infectious diseases such as malaria, polio, cholera, tetanus, typhoid, and measles have been virtually eliminated by improved nutrition, sanitation, and personal hygiene and by vaccination. As the burden of communicable diseases has steadily declined, the major causes of death in the developed world are now chronic and degenerative diseases such as heart disease and cancer. Table 15.1 illustrates how this trend has affected Canada.

While mortality rates have dropped significantly in the less developed and developing nations, they are still 2 to 3 times higher than those of developed countries. In many countries, infectious diseases remain the leading cause of death; in some areas, mortality rates are increasing rapidly as a result of HIV/AIDS and a resurgence of tuberculosis. (See Chapter 11, "Health, Health Care, and Disability.")

In addition to the crude death rate, demographers often measure the ***infant mortality rate*—the number of deaths of infants under 1 year of age per 1000 live births in a given year.** The infant mortality rate is an important reflection of a society's level of preventive (prenatal) medical care, maternal nutrition, childbirth procedures, and neonatal care for infants, and it is often used by sociologists as a measure of a country's social development. The impact of modernization on infant

Women in agricultural regions of the world, such as that of Kenya, tend to have more children. Children's labour in these regions is essential to the family's economic survival and child mortality rates are very high.

TABLE 15.1 LEADING CAUSES OF DEATH, CANADA, 1880–81 AND 1996

RANK	1880–81*	RANK	1996
1	Consumption (Tuberculosis)	1	Cancer
2	Diphtheria	2	Heart disease
3	Lung disease	3	Stroke
4	Old age	4	Obstructive lung disease
5	Brain disease	5	Accidental injury
6	Heart & blood disease	6	Pneumonia/Flu
7	Scarlet fever	7	Suicide
8	Croup	8	Diabetes
9	Bowel disease	9	Arterial disease
10	Debility	10	Central nervous system disease

*Includes P.E.I., N.B., N.S., Que., Ont., Man., B.C., and the Territories.

1880 data: Reprinted by permission of Statistics Canada, adapted from *Mortality—Summary List of Cases, 1991b*, Cat. no. 84-209; 1996 data: Reprinted by permission from Mark Nicols, "Men's Health," *Maclean's*, February 22, 1999.

We live in a time when the death of children is no longer a common event.

mortality rates has been dramatic. In 1921 the infant mortality rate in Canada was 102 deaths per 1000 live births; by 1996 it had declined to 5.6 per 1000 live births (Statistics Canada, 1998). This can be compared with present rates of 7 per 1000 in the United States, 6 in the United Kingdom, and 4 in Japan.

Underdeveloped countries with high birth rates also have high infant mortality rates. For example, the infant mortality rates for Afghanistan, Ethiopia, and Haiti are (respectively) 143, 125, and 99 per 1000 live births (Central Intelligence Agency, 1998).

Infant mortality rates and crude death rates are high among Canada's Aboriginal population, whose members suffer severe social disadvantages compared with the rest of the population and often lack access to health care services. The infant mortality rate is nearly double the rate for the Canadian population as a whole (Beaujot, 1991).

Our declining mortality rates have led to substantial increases in ***life expectancy,* which is an estimate of the average lifetime in years of people born in a specific year.** For persons born in Canada in 1996, for example, life expectancy at birth was about 79 years. Within Canada, life expectancy is lower for Aboriginal people. On average, Aboriginal people live about 7 years less than do members of the non-Aboriginal population, though this difference has been reduced in the past decade. Life expectancy also varies by sex; for example, females born in Canada in 1996 could expect to live about 81 years compared with 76 years for males (Statistics Canada, 2000).

Migration

***Migration* is the movement of people from one geographic area to another for the purpose of changing residency.** Migration involves two types of movement: immigration and emigration. ***Immigration* is the movement of people into a geographic area to take up residency,** while ***emigration* is the movement of people out of a geographic area to take up residency elsewhere.** Migration affects the size and distribution of population in a given area. In Canada, people are not evenly distributed throughout the country; most Canadians live in densely populated areas while much of the country is sparsely populated. *Density* is the number of people living in a specific geographic area. Density may be measured by the number of people who live per room, per block, or per square kilometre.

Migration may be either international (movement between two nations) or internal (movement within national boundaries). When people migrate internationally, demographers refer to the country they leave as their *country of origin*; the country they enter is known as their *country of destination.*

INTERNAL MIGRATION Internal migration has occurred throughout Canada's history and has significantly changed the distribution of our population over time. In the late nineteenth and early twentieth centuries, a major population shift occurred as Canada was transformed from a rural to an urban nation. At the time of Confederation, about 80 percent of the population resided in rural areas; today, almost 80 percent are urban. While Canada is now an urban country, the degree of urbanization among the

Political unrest, violence, and war are "push" factors that encourage people to leave their country of origin. Shown here are a shipload of Liberian refugees awaiting political asylum in Ghana (left) and Bosnian refugees fleeing Serb-held parts of Sarajevo (right). Civil wars cause massive population movement.

provinces varies, ranging from 82 percent of the population of Ontario to only 40 percent of Prince Edward Island residents (McVey and Kalbach, 1995).

People also move from one province to another. Over the past two decades, British Columbia, Ontario, and Alberta have attracted the most internal migrants. Can you think of reasons for this internal population shift?

International Migration People migrate either voluntarily or involuntarily. *Pull* factors such as a democratic government, religious freedom, employment opportunities, or a more temperate climate may draw voluntary immigrants to a nation. *Push* factors such as political unrest, violence, war, famine, plagues, and natural disasters may encourage people to leave one area and relocate elsewhere. Involuntary, or forced, migration usually occurs as a result of political oppression, such as when Jews fled Nazi Germany in the 1930s or when Haitians left their country to escape the Cedras regime in the 1990s. Slavery is the most striking example of involuntary migration; the ten to twenty million Africans transported forcibly to the Western Hemisphere prior to 1800 did not come by choice.

Most of Canada's thirty million people are immigrants or the descendants of immigrants. Thus, immigration has been a critical factor in the country's growth and development. Our immigration policy is one of the most open in the world, and we have much higher rates of legal immigration than almost any other country. Immigrants make up over 17 percent of Canada's population (Statistics Canada, 1998).

Figure 15.1 shows that immigration levels over the past 140 years or so have fluctuated a great deal. Economic conditions, wars, pressures from refugees, and changes in government policies have all contributed to these shifts. Following the end of the economic depression in 1896, the government began to promote immigration to encourage settlement of the West. In the years just before World War I as many as 400,000 people per year immigrated to Canada, a number that has never been exceeded. Most of these immigrants were European and many of them settled the farms, towns, and cities of the Prairie provinces. The beginning of World War I caused a precipitous decline in immigration. While numbers increased again after the war, the Great Depression and World War II meant very low levels of immigration for almost twenty years. During this period more people left Canada than arrived here. Immediately after World War II, immigration rates again climbed. Canada built a large industrial capacity during the war, and the postwar economy was very strong. Skilled foreign workers were needed to help with the expansion. Political instability and economic difficulty in Europe meant that many people were willing to leave to find a better life elsewhere. The postwar immigration peak in 1956–57 was a result both of Canada's acceptance of great numbers of refugees who were escaping the unsuccessful Hungarian Revolution and of its providing a home for British subjects leaving Egypt following the Suez crisis.

Until 1962 Canada's immigration regulations permitted discrimination on the basis of racial and ethnic

FIGURE 15.1 Annual Levels of Canadian Immigration, 1860–1998

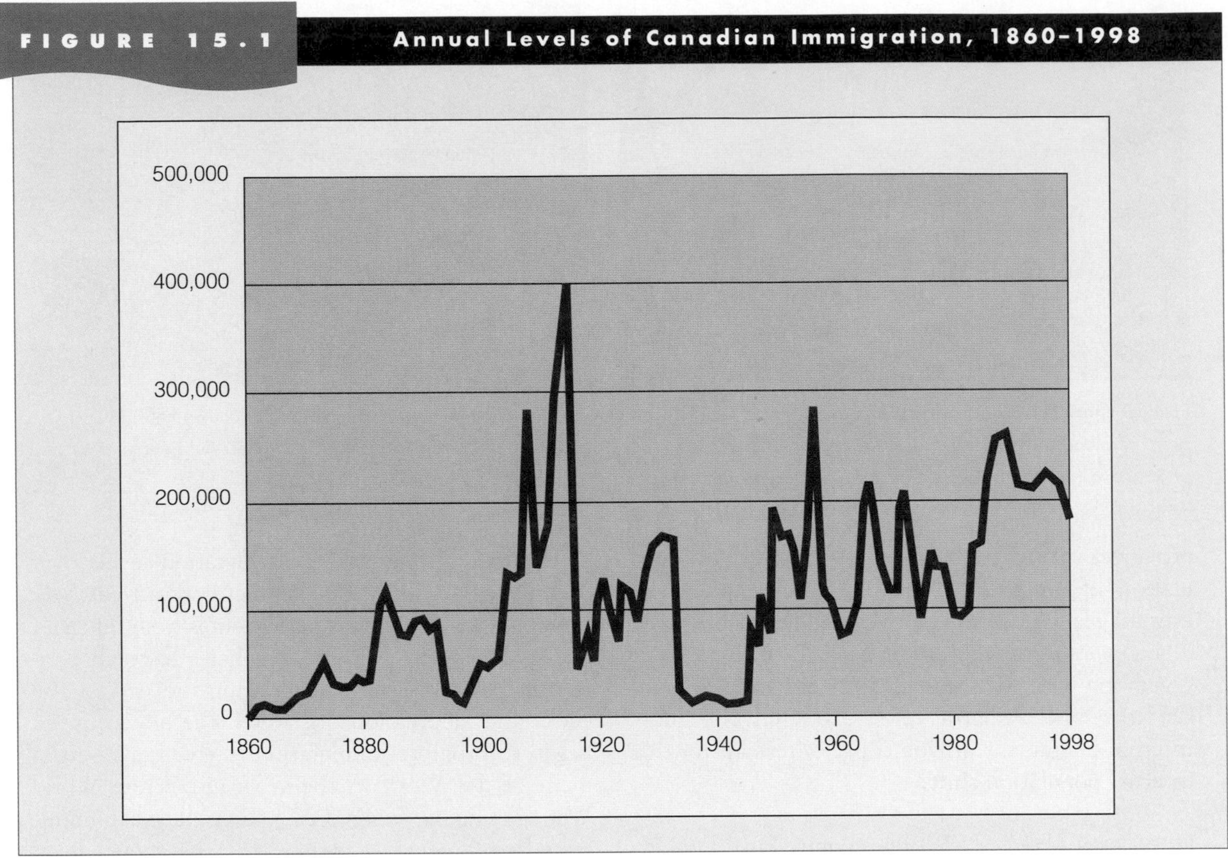

Source: *Facts and Figures, 1998: Immigration Overview.* Ottawa: Citizenship and Immigration Canada. C&I-291-06-99E, 1999.

origin (see Box 15.2). At various times, Chinese, Japanese, and South Asians were prohibited from immigrating to Canada, and the 1953 Immigration Act allowed the government to bar entry on the grounds of race, ethnicity, or even "peculiar customs, habits, modes of life or methods of holding property" (Beaujot, 1991:109). Preference was given to whites, particularly those of British origin. These discriminatory restrictions were lifted in 1962, and from then on the face of immigration changed dramatically. Compare the top ten source countries of immigrants arriving in 1957 with those of immigrants who came in 1998, as shown in Table 15.2. Whereas, in 1957, the vast majority of immigrants were whites from northern Europe, in 1998 immigrants to Canada came from all over the world and represented many different ethnic groups and cultures. While this diversity would not have been possible under the old rules, the factors "pushing" immigrants have also changed. For the past thirty years, most western European countries have had very strong economies, low unemployment rates, and stable governments. Living under these conditions, people have had little reason to emigrate. On the other hand, conditions in many other parts of the world have been less favourable, so emigration to Canada has been seen positively. Most of the leading countries from which we drew immigrants in 1998 had some combination of political turmoil, war, or poverty.

For most of the 1990s the number of immigrants coming to Canada annually remained at between 200,000 and 250,000 persons. This is the result of government policy aimed at achieving a stable population in the future in the face of declining birth rates and an aging population.

Population Composition

Changes in fertility, mortality, and migration affect the ***population composition*****—the biological and social characteristics of a population,** including

TABLE 15.2 CANADIAN IMMIGRANTS' TOP TEN COUNTRIES OF ORIGIN, 1957 AND 1998

1957				1998			
RANK	COUNTRY	NUMBER OF PEOPLE	% OF TOTAL IMMIGRATION	RANK	COUNTRY	NUMBER OF PEOPLE	% OF TOTAL IMMIGRATION
1	U.K.	108,989	38.6	1	China	19,749	11.34
2	Hungary	31,643	11.2	2	India	15,327	8.80
3	Germany	28,430	10.0	3	Philippines	8,172	4.69
4	Italy	27,740	9.8	4	Hong Kong	8,083	4.64
5	Netherlands	11,934	4.2	5	Pakistan	8,081	4.64
6	U.S.	11,008	3.9	6	Taiwan	7,164	4.11
7	Denmark	7,683	2.7	7	Iran	6,772	3.89
8	France	5,869	2.0	8	Korea	4,910	2.82
9	Austria	5,714	2.0	9	U.S.	4,764	2.74
10	Greece	5,460	1.9	10	Russia	4,299	2.47

Source: *Facts and Figures, 1998: Immigration Overview*. Ottawa: Citizenship and Immigration Canada. C&I-291-06-99E, 1999.

age, sex, ethnic origin, marital status, education, occupation, income, and size of household.

For demographers, sex and age are significant population characteristics; they are key predictors of fertility and mortality rates. The age distribution of a population has a direct bearing on the demand for schooling, health, employment, housing, and pensions. The distribution of a population can be depicted in a ***population pyramid*****—a graphic representation of the distribution of a population by sex and age.** Population pyramids are a series of bar graphs divided into five-year age cohorts; the left side of the pyramid shows the number or percentage of males in each age bracket; the right side provides the same information for females.

The age/sex distribution in developed nations no longer has the appearance of a pyramid, but rather is more rectangular or barrel-shaped (see France in Figure 15.2) or diamond-shaped (see Canada in Figure 15.4). Developed nations have low birth rates and an increasing number of older people. You can see in Figure 15.2 that a developing nation such as Iran has a population distribution that fits the classic population pyramid. Iran has high fertility and mortality rates, which means a large number of children and few older people. The population pyramid for Russia has some unusual features that have been caused by catastrophic events such as the two World Wars, the Civil War of 1917–1922, famine in the 1920s and 1930s, and the recent dramatic decline in birth rates. For example, the large number of males killed during World War II gave Russia the lowest male-to-female ratio in the world. The irregularities in Russia's population pyramid will affect patterns of population growth and aging for decades to come (Institut National d'Etudes Demographiques, 1997). (Population pyramids for Canada are shown later in this chapter in Figure 15.4.)

The Baby Boom and the Baby Bust

One very simple fact will help you to understand many things about Canadian society: every year you get one year older, and, more importantly, so does everyone else. Until recently, the age structure of the population was something of a hidden factor.

BOX 15.2 SOCIOLOGY AND LAW

IMMIGRATION AND THE LAW IN CANADA

Canadians can be proud of having welcomed immigrants from around the globe. However, the record has not been consistently good; at times in the past our immigration policy has been exclusionary and racist.

Shortly after the turn of the century, some Canadians began to express concerns about immigration from East Asia and South Asia. The first Chinese immigrated to Canada in the 1850s; many were recruited to work as labourers on the construction of the Canadian Pacific Railway. South Asians began to immigrate to Canada in 1903. While the numbers of both groups were small, these immigrants were treated very poorly and subjected to discrimination. British Columbia, where the two groups were largely concentrated, passed a number of laws restricting the rights of Chinese and Japanese. For example, the Chinese and Japanese were denied the right to vote in 1872 and 1895, respectively, and many restrictions were imposed on their right to work. The federal government levied a head tax on the Chinese in 1885 to restrict their immigration and in 1923 passed the Chinese Immigration Act, which virtually disallowed new immigration from East Asia.

While these regulations now seem appalling, Canadians were no worse than most other Western countries, which also had very restrictive immigration policies. The view that Anglo-Saxons were biologically superior

While age differences among individuals were obvious, researchers and planners often failed to recognize the impact of changes in the *age structure* of the population.

One of the most significant demographic changes in Canadian history was the *baby boom*—the dramatic increase in births that occurred between 1946 and 1966. The boom was caused by young couples who married and began having families in the years immediately following the war. The high birth rates of the baby boom were followed by the *baby bust*, which saw birth rates fall to the very low levels where they remain today. While many demographic changes are subtle and take place over a long period of time, the baby boom was a rapid reversal of a long-term downward trend in birth rates. This increase is shown in Figure 15.3. By the end of the boom in 1966, one-third of all the people in Canada had been born in the preceding fifteen years.

The baby boom and baby bust have had a dramatic impact on Canada's age structure, which can be seen in the series of population pyramids in Figure 15.4. The 1961 pyramid shows the population of Canada toward the end of the baby boom. There are large numbers of young people because of the boom. The relatively small number of people aged 15 to 24 is the result of low birth rates during the Depression and World War II. In the 1981 pyramid, we can see the consequences of the baby boom and the drop in fertility rates (baby bust) that followed. The pyramid for 2006 shows an increased number of older people as the oldest baby boomers approach 60. Finally, in the 2031 pyramid, mortality has begun to affect the baby boomers, and the survivors are now 65 to 85 years of age.

To help understand the impact of the baby boom, think of it as a twenty-year bulge in the population pyramid. Each year, this bulge moves one year up the pyramid as the baby boom cohort ages. You can easily track this bulge in the population pyramids in Figure 15.4. Some demographers have used the analogy of a pig that has been swallowed by a python to describe the way in which the baby boom generation has moved up the population pyramid. It is interesting to compare Canada's demographic structure with those of other countries. For example, you can see from Figure 15.2 that Iran, which is a developing society, has a constant baby boom—it is con-

BOX 15.2

CONTINUED

was backed by many leading scientists of the day, and the admission of other races was seen as a danger to white democracies.

Many Canadians are also unaware that for many years our immigration policy restricted the admission of Jews. This was because of anti-Jewish sentiment and because Jews settled in urban areas and rejected the rural settlement preferred by the government. Even during World War II, when millions of Jews were being exterminated in Europe, Canada would not open its doors to Jewish refugees. No country made the immigration of Jews a priority during the Holocaust, but Canada's record was particularly poor. Between 1933 and 1945 Canada admitted fewer than 5000 Jews, whereas during the same period 200,000 were allowed into the United States and 70,000 into the United Kingdom. Despite significant and vocal support among Canadians for taking action to save Jewish refugees, then prime minister Mackenzie King and his cabinet refused. The attitude of the government is summed up in the words of a senior Canadian official who, when asked by journalists in early 1945 how many Jews would be admitted to Canada following the war, replied "None is too many" (Abella and Troper, 1982:xxi).

Sources: Based on Abella and Troper, 1982; Ghosh and Kanungo, 1992, and Statutes of Canada, 1910 C.27.

tinually adding young people to its population as its population rapidly expands. On the other hand, France did not have a baby boom after the war, so its age structure is quite different from Canada's. The age structure of many European countries is much like that of France. Besides Canada, the only other countries that had a baby boom were Australia and the United States.

The baby boom has transformed society in many different ways. Because it has always been the largest age group, the baby boom generation has had a tremendous impact. Beginning in the late 1940s, many businesses saw their markets expand. Manufacturers of baby food, diapers, and children's toys flourished and obstetricians were in great demand. As the cohort aged, school construction increased dramatically and teaching jobs were plentiful. By the mid-1960s university enrolments began to climb and many new universities opened to meet the demand. You will recall from Chapter 6 ("Deviance and Crime") that crime rates also began to increase at this time. The explanation is that the baby boomers had entered the 15 to 24 age group during which criminal behaviour is most common. In the mid-1970s house prices rose quickly in most Canadian cities, as the baby boomers began to settle down and raise families.

Because of the baby bust, many of these changes reversed themselves in the 1980s. Schools that had been built to house the soaring numbers of children in the 1960s were forced to close twenty years later and school boards had to deal with an oversupply of teachers. By the 1990s both university enrolments and crime rates had begun to decline. Corporations that had targeted youthful consumers began to reorient their products and their advertising to appeal to an older market.

What of the future? The baby boom cohort is now entering middle age and the first of its members will reach 65 in the year 2011. Our society will soon begin to have a much higher proportion of older persons than it does today. In 1971, about 8 percent of Canadians were 65 and over; by 2011 the percentage will be 16 percent; and by 2036 it will likely stabilize at almost 25 percent. There will be about 9 million Canadians over 65, compared with 3.7 million now.

FIGURE 15.2 Population Pyramids for Russia, Iran, and France

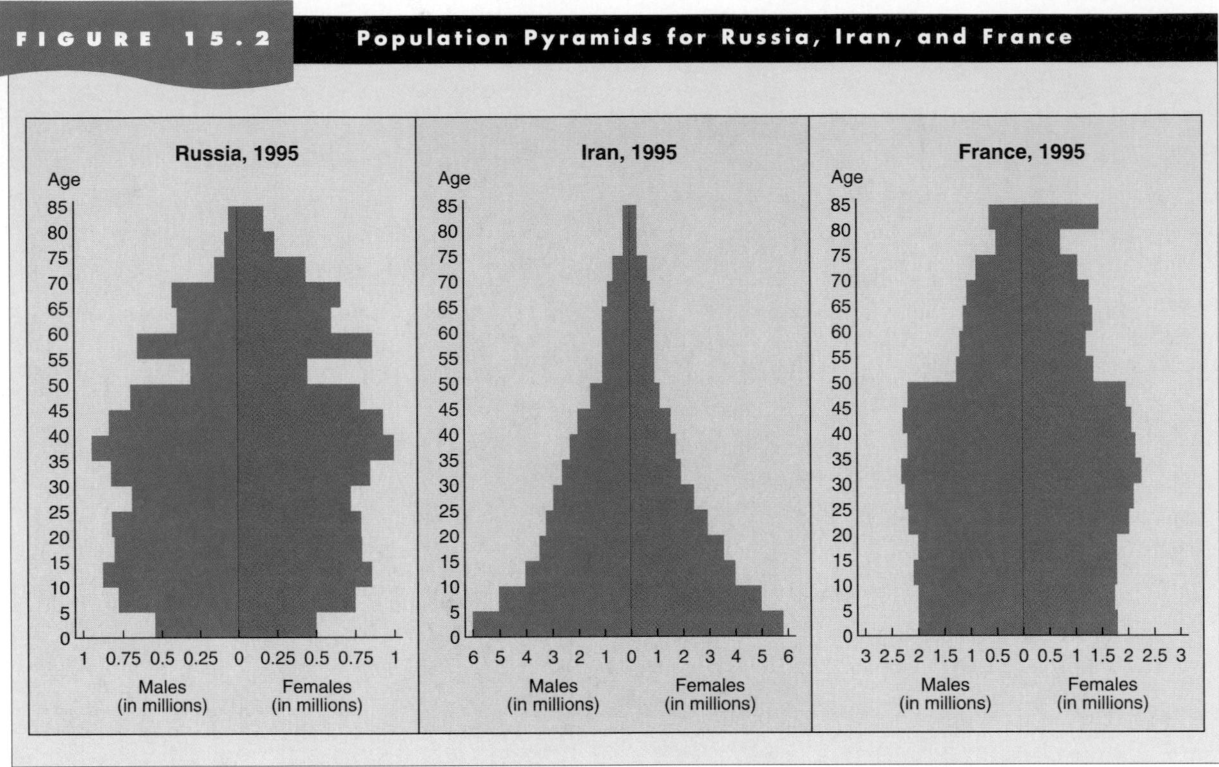

From *Population: An Introduction to Concepts and Issues,* 6th ed., by J.R. Weeks. © 1996. Reprinted by permission of Wadsworth Publishing, a division of International Thomson Publishing. Fax 800-730-2215.

The aging of our population is causing concern in a number of areas. Since the elderly are the biggest users of health care, governments are trying to get health costs under control before the baby boomers begin to reach the age where they start to have serious health concerns. Those responsible for the Canada Pension Plan have increased contribution rates so that the Plan can stay in operation.

One final trend worth noting is the *baby boom echo*—the children of the baby boomers. You can see this echo in Figure 15.4, which shows a relatively large cohort following about twenty years behind the baby boom. Even though the baby boomers had far fewer children than their parents (about 1.66 children per family compared with the more than 3 children their parents had), there were so many of them that their children are having a significant impact. The leading edge of the echo generation were about 19 years old in 2000, so they will have an impact on such things as high school and university enrolments and crime rates over the next two decades.

THE BABY BOOM AND IMMIGRATION POLICY One consequence of our current low birth rate is possible depopulation. Fertility of 2.1 children per woman is needed to ensure the replacement of a population. Two children will replace the parents, and the additional 0.1 compensates for deaths that occur before potential parents reach reproductive age. This level of fertility will eventually lead to a stable population with zero population growth except for that caused by migration. In Canada, our fertility is now less than 1.7 children per woman, which will not provide replacement of our population. If this level of fertility remains constant for the next several decades, Canada will begin losing population when the baby boomers begin to die. You can see this in the 2031 population pyramid in Figure 15.4. At present, besides losing population through death, we also lose about 60,000 people each year to emigration.

As Figure 15.1 shows, during most of the 1990s Canada admitted between 200,000 and 250,000 immigrants annually. This number was chosen because demographers have calculated that to stabi-

FIGURE 15.3 Canadian Period Total Fertility Rates, 1871–1989

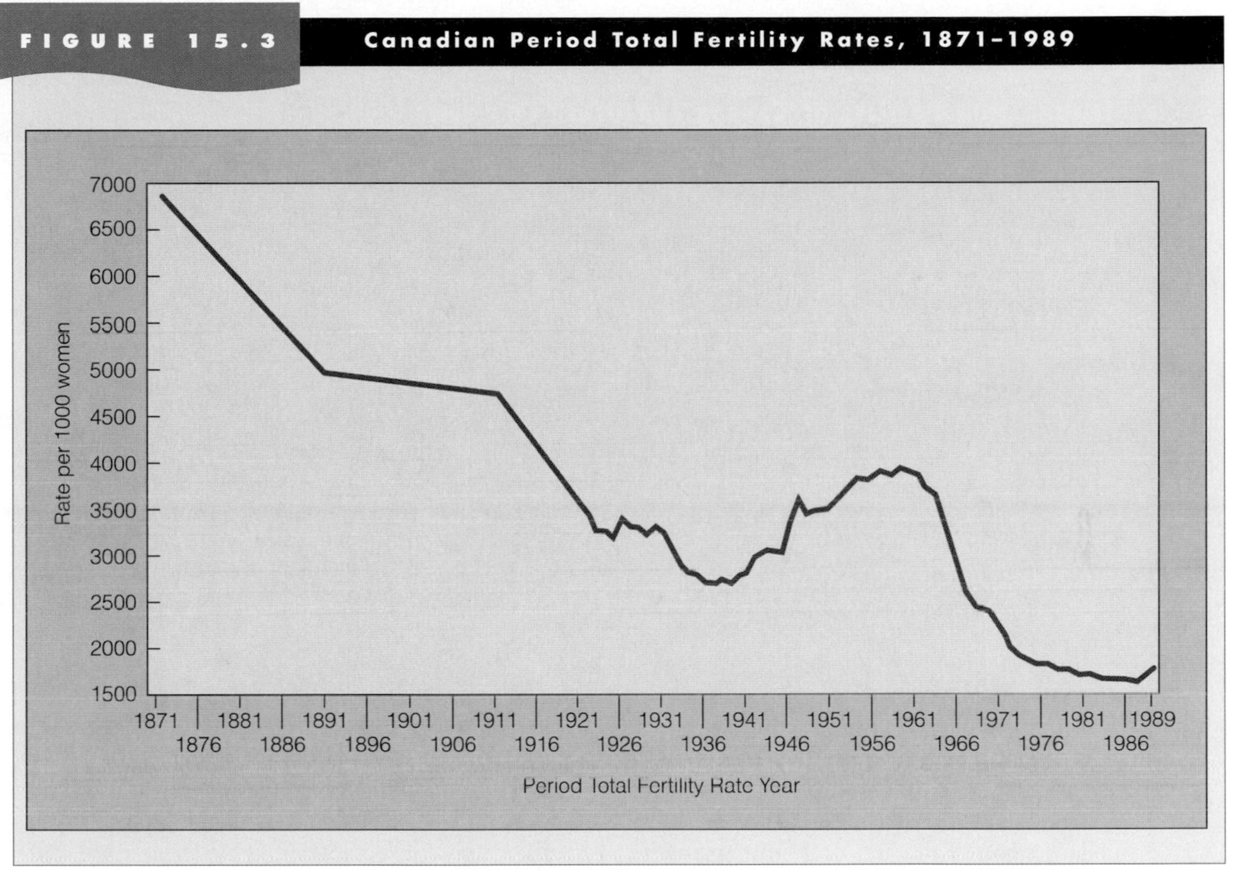

Sources: Romaniuc, 1994:121–22; Beaujot and McQuillan, 1982:54; and Dumas, 1990:18.

lize the population we need about 250,000 immigrants a year. Thus, the baby bust has had an important impact on our immigration policies.

POPULATION GROWTH IN A GLOBAL CONTEXT

What are the consequences of global population growth? Scholars do not agree on the answer to this question. Some biologists have warned that Earth is a finite ecosystem that cannot support the 9 billion people predicted to be living on the planet by 2050; however, some economists have predicted that free-market capitalism is capable of developing innovative ways to solve such problems, and religious opponents of birth control assure us that God will provide. This debate is not a new one; for several centuries, strong opinions have been voiced about the effects of population growth on human welfare.

The Malthusian Perspective

English clergyman and economist Thomas Robert Malthus (1766–1834) was one of the first scholars to systematically study the effects of population.

According to Malthus, the population, if left unchecked, would exceed the available food supply. He argued that the population would increase in a geometric (exponential) progression (2, 4, 8, 16 ...), while the food supply would increase only by an arithmetic progression (1, 2, 3, 4 ...). In other words, a *doubling effect* occurs: two parents can have four children, sixteen grandchildren, and so on, but food production increases by only one hectare at a time. Thus, population growth inevitably surpasses the food supply, and the lack of food ultimately ends population growth and perhaps eliminates the

BOX 15.3 SOCIOLOGY IN GLOBAL PERSPECTIVE

IMMIGRATION POLICIES OF CANADA AND OTHER COUNTRIES

Canadian immigration laws and policies are among the most open in the world. Each year Canada accepts as immigrants just under 1 percent of our population, and all of them have the right to obtain citizenship. Israel takes in about 2 percent of its population annually, while the other two leading destination countries for immigrants, Australia and the United States, each accept less than one-half of a percent of their populations. Most of the world's countries accept few or no immigrants, though many do accept refugees, at least on a temporary basis. Receiving countries react to immigration in three different ways.

The first is *differential exclusion*, according to which immigrants are allowed in certain areas of society, chiefly the labour market, but denied access to other areas such as health care, education, and social benefits. The result of this is the permanent marginalization of people who are essentially permanent residents but who cannot become citizens.

existing population (Weeks, 1992). Even in a best-case scenario, overpopulation results in poverty.

However, Malthus suggested that this disaster might be averted by either positive or preventive checks on population. *Positive checks* are mortality risks such as famine, disease, and war; *preventive checks* are limits to fertility. For Malthus, the only acceptable preventive check was *moral restraint*; people should practise sexual abstinence before marriage and postpone marriage as long as possible in order to have only a few children.

The Marxist Perspective

According to Karl Marx and Friedrich Engels, the food supply is not threatened by overpopulation; technologically, it is possible to produce the food and other goods needed to meet the demands of a growing population. Marx and Engels viewed poverty as a consequence of the exploitation of workers by the owners of the means of production.

From this perspective, overpopulation occurs because capitalists want to have a surplus of workers (an industrial reserve army) so as to suppress wages and force workers concerned about losing their livelihoods to be more productive. Marx believed that overpopulation would contribute to the eventual destruction of capitalism: unemployment would make the workers dissatisfied, resulting in a class consciousness based on their shared oppression and in the eventual overthrow of the system. In a socialist regime, enough food and other resources would be created to accommodate population growth.

Marx and Engels made a significant contribution to the study of demography by suggesting that poverty, not overpopulation, is the most important issue with regard to the food supply in a capitalist economy. Although Marx and Engels offer an interesting counterpoint to Malthus, some scholars argue that the Marxist perspective is self-limiting because it attributes the population problem solely to capitalism. In actuality, nations with socialist economies have demographic trends similar to those in capitalist societies.

The Neo-Malthusian Perspective

More recently, *neo-Malthusians* (or "new Malthusians") have re-emphasized the dangers of overpopulation. To neo-Malthusians, Earth is "a dying planet" with too many people, too little food, and environmental degradation (Ehrlich, 1971). Overpopulation and rapid population growth result in global environmental problems, ranging from global warming and rain forest destruction to famine and vulnerability to epidemics such as AIDS (Ehrlich, Ehrlich and Daily, 1995). Environmental problems worsen as countries such as India and China, with their large popula-

BOX 15.3

CONTINUED

The second immigration model is *assimilationist*, whereby immigrants are incorporated into the host society through a one-sided process of change. Immigrants are expected to become the same as the majority. This is sometimes referred to as the "melting pot approach."

The third model is *pluralism*, according to which immigrants are encouraged to form ethnic communities that can have equal rights while retaining their diversity in language, culture, and other matters. Citizenship is readily given to legal immigrants, and even to children of illegal immigrants. Canada has a multicultural policy that actively supports the rights of ethnic communities.

Source: Castles, 1995.

tions, modernize and begin to use resources at a rate closer to that of industrialized countries.

Throughout history, population growth and epidemic diseases have interacted to shape human destiny. People are extremely vulnerable to disease if they already are debilitated from inadequate nutrition, unclean water supplies, poor medical care, and lack of sanitation.

Are the neo-Malthusians correct? Will population increases leave many populations vulnerable to mass death through starvation and disease? Some possible outcomes are found in the work of Thomas Homer-Dixon, a University of Toronto political scientist who is often placed in the neo-Malthusian camp. Homer-Dixon feels that increases in population and resource consumption will lead to significant environmental changes including scarcities of soil, water, and climatic instability (1993). The strains caused by these scarcities may lead to unrest, including war, revolution, ethnic violence, and riots. The gloominess of this scenario is tempered by the fact that Homer-Dixon does not feel that population disaster is inevitable. Human social and technical ingenuity can overcome or at least delay the consequences of population increase. For example, despite decades of predictions that China will be unable to support its population, the average caloric intake in China has been rising as the country has massively increased its production of food. Unfortunately, there is no guarantee that solutions to the predicted problems will be found. Ingenuity is itself a function of a country's social institutions, and in many countries these institutions are too fragmented or too lacking in human and physical resources to solve their problems. In addition, political turmoil has been an obstacle; unrest has kept many countries, for example, those in sub-Saharan Africa, from progressing and, without major reform, their future is gloomy. Ultimately, the future of humanity will depend on both national and international action to solve the problems created by population growth and environmental damage.

Demographic Transition Theory

Some scholars who disagree with the neo-Malthusian viewpoint suggest that the theory of demographic transition offers a more accurate picture of future population growth. ***Demographic transition* is the process by which some societies have moved from high birth and death rates to relatively low birth and death rates as a result of technological development.** Although demographic transition theory initially was applied to population changes brought about by the Industrial Revolution in western Europe and North America, it recently has emerged as a dominant perspective in contemporary demography (Weeks, 1992). Demographic

FIGURE 15.4 Population by Age and Sex, Canada, 1961 and 1981 (Census), 2006 and 2031

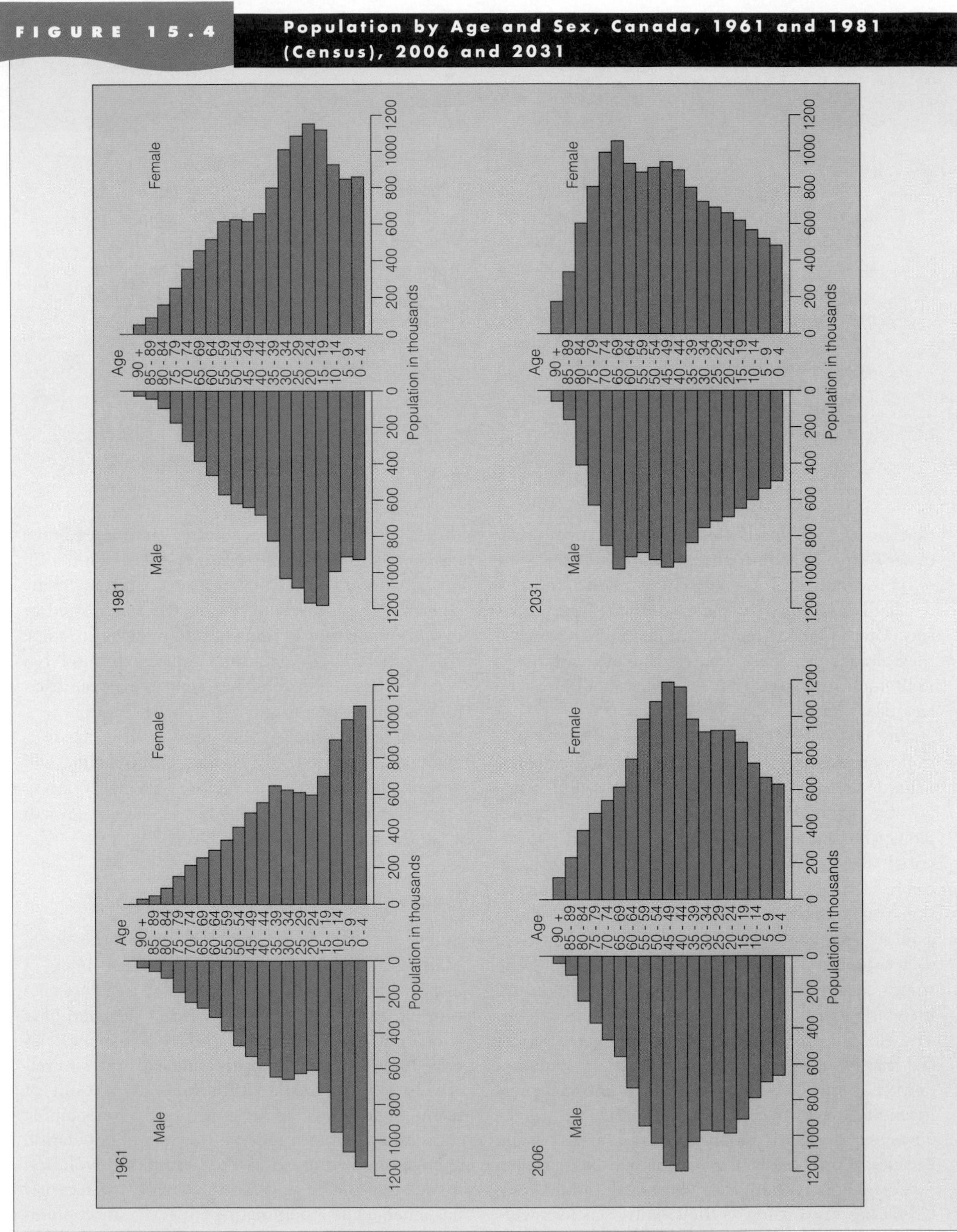

Reprinted by permission of Statistics Canada, adapted from *Population Projections for Canada, Provinces and Territories 1984–2006*, Cat no. 91-520; and from *1961 Census Bulletin* 1.2-2.

FIGURE 15.5 The Demographic Transition

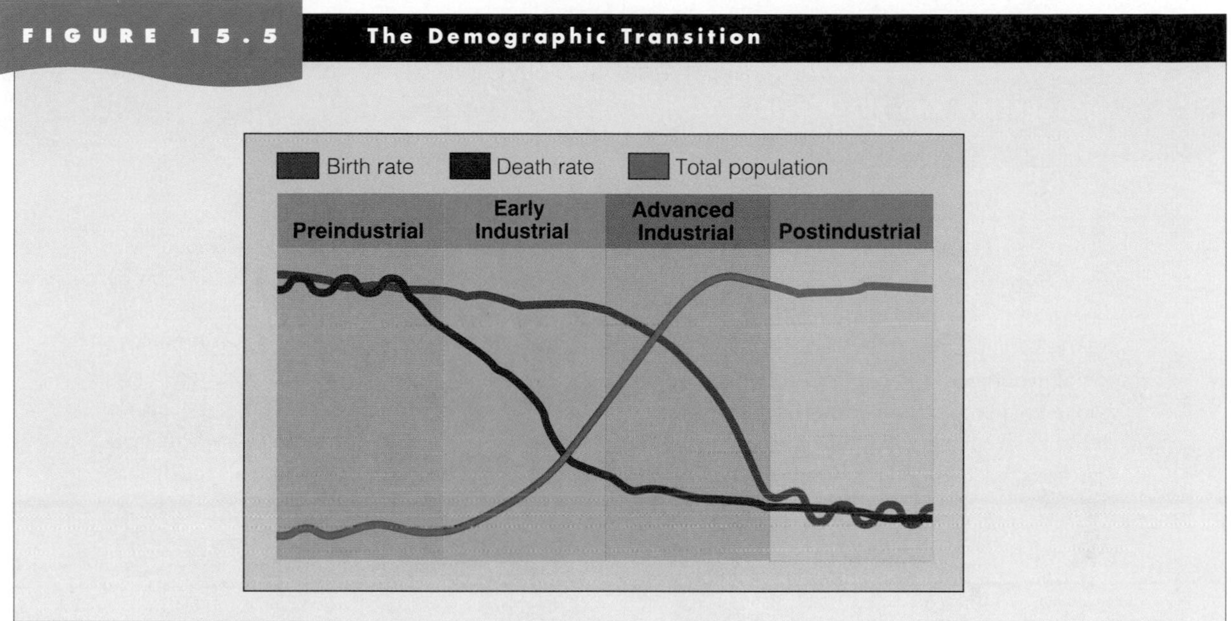

transition is linked to four stages of economic development (see Figure 15.5):

- *Stage 1: Preindustrial societies*. Little population growth occurs because high birth rates are offset by high death rates. Children are viewed as an economic asset because of their ability to work, but infant and child mortality rates are high due to lack of sanitation and poor nutrition. Life expectancy is around 30 years.

- *Stage 2: Early industrialization*. Significant population growth occurs because birth rates remain relatively high while death rates decline. Improvements in health, sanitation, and nutrition produce a substantial decline in infant mortality rates. Overpopulation is likely to occur because more people are alive than the society has the ability to support. However, social institutions continue to promote high fertility. This stage occurred over a century ago in Europe, but many developing nations—especially in Africa, Asia, and Latin America—currently are in this stage.

- *Stage 3: Advanced industrialization and urbanization*. Very little population growth occurs because both birth rates and death rates are low. The birth rate declines as couples control their fertility through contraception and become less likely to adhere to religious directives against its use. Children are not viewed as an economic asset; they consume income rather than produce it. Societies in this stage attain zero population growth—the point at which no population increase occurs from year to year.

- *Stage 4: Postindustrialization*. Birth rates continue to decline as more women gain full-time employment and the cost of raising children continues to increase. The population grows very slowly, if at all, because the decrease in birth rates is coupled with a stable death rate.

Debate continues over whether this evolutionary model accurately explains the stages of population growth in all societies. Advocates note that demographic transition theory highlights the correlation between technological development and a slowing of population growth—a relationship that makes Malthus's predictions obsolete. Scholars also point out that demographic transitions occur at a faster rate in industrializing nations than they previously did in the nations that already are industrialized. Critics suggest that demographic transition theory best explains development in Western societies. Many regions of the Third World may never achieve a steady growth in social and economic wealth unless fertility levels first decline, so other routes to population control must be found.

BOX 15.4 SOCIOLOGY AND MEDIA

IMMIGRATION AND THE MEDIA

Just after the turn of the twentieth century, a great deal of hostility was directed at nonwhite immigrants. The media actively promoted this racism by publishing inflammatory articles about racial minorities. These articles not only affected public opinion, but were also used by legislators to justify laws that targeted minority immigrants. The work of Judge Emily Murphy of Edmonton, the first woman judge in the British Empire, was particularly influential. A series of five articles by Murphy, which were published in *Maclean's* magazine, shaped Canada's drug laws throughout the 1920s; their effects live on in our present narcotics legislation. These articles also shaped the attitudes of Canadians toward nonwhite immigrants by attributing the drug problem to Chinese

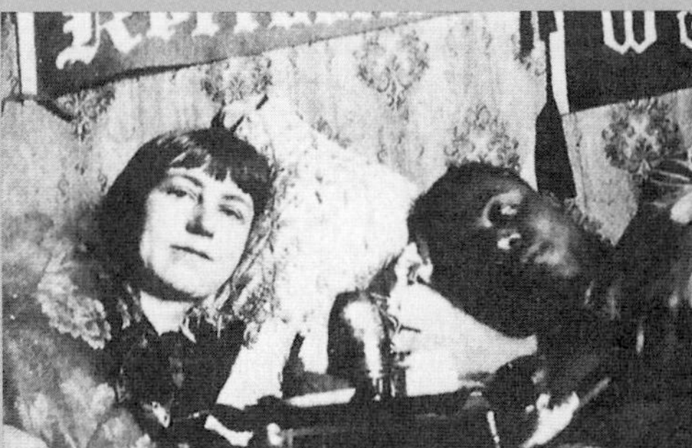

Opium addicts

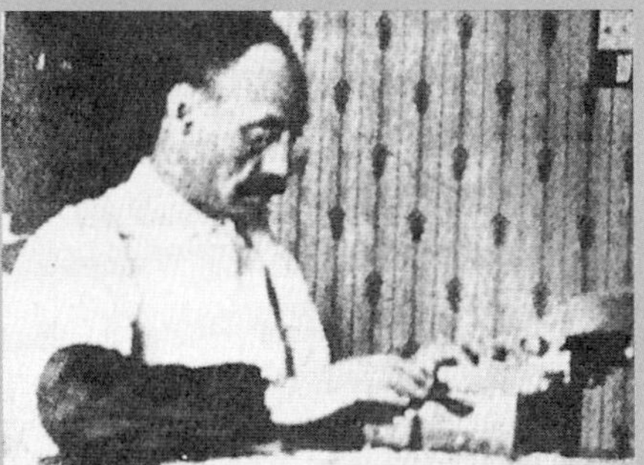

The keeper of an opium den

These photographs appeared in Judge Murphy's book *The Black Candle* (Murphy, 1922), which, like her articles published in *Maclean's* in the 1920s, were used by legislators to justify laws that targeted minority immigrants.

URBANIZATION AND THE GROWTH OF CITIES

***Urban sociology* is a subfield of sociology that examines social relationships and political and economic structures in the city.** According to urban sociologists, a *city* is a relatively dense and permanent settlement of people who secure their livelihood primarily through nonagricultural activities.

Although cities have existed for thousands of years, only about 3 percent of the world's population lived in cities two hundred years ago, as compared with almost 50 percent today. In Canada, the population is even more concentrated: almost 80 percent of us live in areas defined as urban and about 30 percent live in the three major metropolitan areas of Toronto, Montreal, and Vancouver. To understand the process by which increasing numbers of people have become urban residents, we first need to examine how cities began.

Emergence and Evolution of the City

Cities are a relatively recent innovation. The earliest humans are believed to have emerged anywhere from 40,000 to one million years ago, and permanent human settlements are believed to have first begun about 8000 B.C.E. However, some scholars date the development of the first city between 3500 and 3100 B.C.E., depending largely on whether a

BOX 15.4

CONTINUED

and black "villains" who, according to Judge Murphy, were trying to spread the drug habit in order to seduce white women and to destroy the Anglo-Saxon way of life.

Judge Murphy felt that nonwhite immigrants were a threat to the Canadian way of life. In *Maclean's*, she wrote of a detective who had a special talent for smelling cooked opium. Two of the detective's cases involved a "Chinaman" and a beautiful young girl he found smoking opium under a piano case, and a "negro" smoking opium in a wardrobe with a "white woman on either side of him." Her articles were illustrated with photographs of opium smokers (almost all of whom were women and/or nonwhite men) and cartoons (which were also racially demeaning). Each article featured a caricature of a Chinese opium smoker with smoke coming out of each ear. She saw the Chinese drug pedlar as one who was perhaps unknowingly carrying out the wishes of his superiors who were trying to bring about the "downfall of the white race." The "Negroes coming into Canada," she wrote, "have similar ideas."

The same conspiratorial view was advanced by other media. For example, in 1911, the *Montreal Herald* responded to the immigration of 58 black women domestics from Guadeloupe by reporting that the "dark-skinned domestics were the advanced guard for others to follow."

That these views were so freely expressed in the media certainly made it easy for politicians and members of the public to follow the same racist line. The views, moreover, help to explain why Canada had racially based immigration policies for much of this century.

Sources: Based on Calliste, 1993/94; Murphy, 1922; and Cook, 1969.

formal writing system is considered a requisite for city life (Sjoberg, 1965; Weeks, 1992; Flanagan, 1995).

According to sociologist Gideon Sjoberg (1965), three preconditions must be present in order for a city to develop:

1. A *favourable physical environment*, including climate and soil favourable to the development of plant and animal life and an adequate water supply to sustain both
2. *An advanced technology* (for that era) that could produce a social surplus in both agricultural and nonagricultural goods
3. A *well-developed social organization*, including a power structure, in order to provide social stability to the economic system

Based on these prerequisites, Sjoberg places the first cities in the Middle Eastern region of Mesopotamia or in areas immediately adjacent to it at about 3500 B.C.E. However, not all scholars concur; some place the earliest city in Jericho (located in present-day Jordan) at about 8000 B.C.E., with a population of about six hundred people (see Kenyon, 1957). As Sjoberg points out, however, Jericho had no known formal writing system; therefore, a political structure and an economy (both essential to the establishment of a city) would not have been able to function effectively.

The earliest cities were not large by today's standards. The population of the larger Mesopotamian centres was between five and ten thousand (Sjoberg, 1965). The population of ancient Babylon (probably

Toronto's Highway 401 at rush hour illustrates the development of postindustrial cities in which people commonly commute long distances to work.

founded around 2200 B.C.E.) may have grown as large as 50,000 people; Athens may have held 80,000 people (Weeks, 1992). Four to five thousand years ago, cities with at least 50,000 people existed in the Middle East (in what today is Iraq and Egypt) and Asia (in what today is Pakistan and China), as well as in Europe. About 3500 years ago, cities began to reach this size in Central and South America.

Preindustrial Cities

The largest preindustrial city was Rome; by 100 C.E. it may have had a population of 650,000 (Chandler and Fox, 1974). With the fall of the Roman Empire in 476 C.E., the nature of European cities changed. Seeking protection and survival, those persons who lived in urban settings typically did so in walled cities containing no more than 25,000 people. For the next six hundred years the urban population continued to live in walled enclaves, as competing warlords battled for power and territory during the "dark ages." Slowly, as trade increased, cities began to tear down their walls. Some walled cities still exist; Quebec City is the only walled city on this continent.

Preindustrial cities were limited in size by a number of factors. For one thing, crowded conditions and a lack of adequate sewage facilities increased the hazards from plagues and fires, and death rates were high. For another, food supplies were limited. In order to generate food for each city resident, at least fifty farmers had to work in the fields (Davis, 1949), and animal power was the only means of bringing food to the city. Once foodstuffs arrived in the city, there was no effective way to preserve them.

Canadian communities arose as settlement extended to new parts of this large country. Until the building of the Canadian Pacific Railway, much of Canada was accessible only by water, so most of our settlements, including those that have grown into large cities, were in areas with access to waterways. Transportation routes were particularly important for a colony whose main function was sending large quantities of raw materials such as timber, wheat, and beaver pelts overseas to European markets. Virtually all of our large cities are located on oceans, lakes, or large rivers.

Industrial Cities

The Industrial Revolution changed the nature of the city. Factories sprang up rapidly as production shifted from the primary, agricultural sector to the secondary, manufacturing sector. With the advent of factories came many new employment opportunities not available to people in rural areas. Factories required a concentration of population to act as a labour force. Emergent technology, including new forms of transportation and agricultural production, made it easier for people to leave the countryside and move to the city. Between 1700 and 1900, the population of many European cities mushroomed. Although the Industrial Revolution did not start in North America until the mid-nineteenth century, the effect was similar. Between 1871 and 1911 the population of Toronto grew by 700 percent and that of Montreal by 450 percent (Nader, 1976). By 1911 both cities had roughly 500,000 people and were on their way to becoming major metropolises. A ***metropolis* is one or more central cities and their surrounding suburbs that dominate the economic and cultural life of a region.** A ***central city* is the densely populated centre of a metropolis.**

The growth of cities during the industrial period was something of a mixed blessing. As cities grew in size and density, overcrowding, poor sanitation, and lack of a clean water supply often led to the spread of epidemic diseases and contributed to a high death rate. In Europe, mortality rates were higher in cities than in rural areas until the nineteenth century, and this remains the case in many cities in the developing world today.

Postindustrial Cities

Since the 1950s, postindustrial cities have emerged in technologically advanced countries, the economies of which have gradually shifted from secondary (manufacturing) production to tertiary (service and information-processing) production. As more traditional industries such as textile manufacturing, steel producing, and many different types of light manufacturing have become obsolete or have been moved to other, lower-wage countries, cities have had to either change or face decline. For example, cities in New Brunswick have been economically devastated by the loss of many jobs in traditional industries such as shipbuilding and railroad maintenance, as well as in resource industries associated with the fishing industry. The province has tried to counteract these losses by moving into the technologically based field of telephone call centres, in which workers perform tasks such as telephone marketing and airline-reservation handling.

Postindustrial cities are dominated by "light" industry, such as computer software manufacturing; information-processing services, such as airline and hotel reservation services; educational complexes; medical centres; convention and entertainment centres; and retail trade centres and shopping malls. Most families do not live close to a central business district. Technological advances in communication and transportation make it possible for middle- and upper-income individuals and families to have more work options and to live greater distances from the workplace. Some futurists feel that communications technology, along with the retirement plans of the baby boomers, may soon lead to a degree of de-urbanization. People who do not have to be physically present in the city centre each day may find a rural or semirural lifestyle an attractive alternative to the commuting and high housing prices that are a part of life in a large city.

PERSPECTIVES ON URBANIZATION AND THE GROWTH OF CITIES

Functionalist Perspectives: Ecological Models

Functionalists examine the interrelations among the parts that make up the whole. Therefore, in studying the growth of cities, they emphasize the life cycle of urban growth. Like the social philosophers and sociologists before him, University of Chicago sociologist Robert Park (1915) based his analysis of the city on *human ecology*—the study of the relationship between people and their physical environment. According to Park (1936), economic competition produces certain regularities in land use patterns and population distributions. Applying Park's idea to the study of urban land use patterns, sociologist Ernest W. Burgess (1925) developed the concentric zone model to explain why some cities expand radially from a central business core.

CONCENTRIC ZONE MODEL Burgess's *concentric zone model* is a description of the process of urban growth that views the city as a series of circular areas or zones, each characterized by a different type of land use, that developed from a central core (see Figure 15.6a). *Zone 1* is the central business district and cultural centre (retail stores, financial institutions, hotels, and theatres, for example), in which high land prices cause vertical growth in the form of

FIGURE 15.6 Three Models of the City

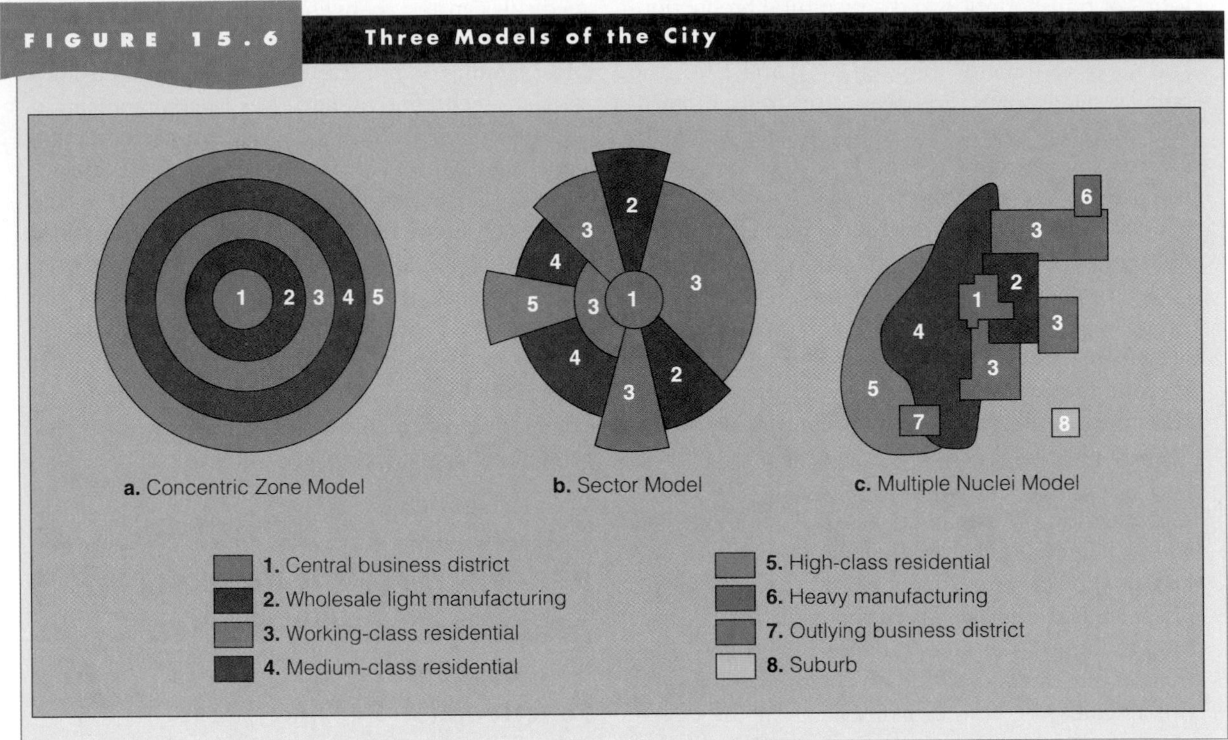

Adapted from Harris and Ullman, 1945.

skyscrapers. *Zone 2* is the zone of transition. As the city expanded, houses formerly occupied by wealthy families were divided into rooms that now are rented to recent immigrants and poor persons; this zone also contains wholesale light manufacturing and marginal businesses (such as secondhand stores, pawnshops, and taverns). *Zone 3* contains working-class residences and shops and ethnic enclaves, such as Little Italy. *Zone 4* is composed of homes for affluent families, single-family residences of white-collar workers, and shopping centres. *Zone 5* is a ring of small cities and towns populated by wealthy persons who commute to the city to work and by wealthy people living on estates.

Two important ecological processes are involved in the concentric zone theory: invasion and succession. ***Invasion* is the process by which a new category of people or type of land use arrives in an area previously occupied by another group or land use** (McKenzie, 1925). For example, Burgess noted that recent immigrants and low-income individuals "invaded" Zone 2, which had formerly been occupied by wealthy families. ***Succession* is the process by which a new category of people or type of land use gradually predominates in an area formerly dominated by another group or activity** (McKenzie, 1925). In Zone 2, for example, when some of the single-family residences were sold and subsequently divided into multiple housing units, the remaining single-family owners moved out because the "old" neighbourhood had changed. As a result of their move, the process of invasion was complete and succession had occurred.

Invasion and succession typically operate in an outward movement: those who are unable to "move out" of the inner rings are those without upward social mobility, so the central zone ends up being primarily occupied by the poorest residents.

The concentric zone model demonstrates how economic and political forces play an important part in the location of groups and activities, and it shows how a large urban area can have internal differentiation (Gottdiener, 1985). However, the model is most applicable to older cities that experienced high

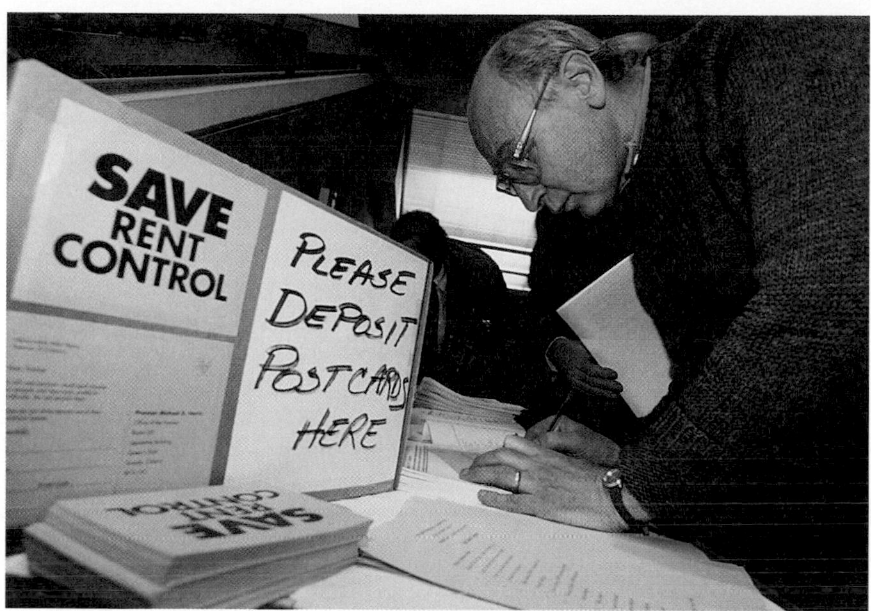

According to conflict theorists, members of the capitalist class make decisions that limit the choices of ordinary citizens, such as how affordable or unaffordable their housing will be. However, scenes like this show that tenants may become active participants in class conflict over the usage of urban space.

levels of immigration early in the twentieth century (Queen and Carpenter, 1953). No city, including Chicago (on which the model is based), entirely conforms to this model.

The Sector Model In an attempt to examine a wider range of settings, urban ecologist Homer Hoyt (1939) studied the configuration of 142 cities. Hoyt's *sector model* emphasizes the significance of terrain and the importance of transportation routes in the layout of cities. According to Hoyt, residences of a particular type and value tend to grow outward from the centre of the city in wedge-shaped sectors, with the more expensive residential neighbourhoods located along the higher ground near lakes and rivers or along certain streets that stretch in one direction or another from the downtown area (see Figure 15.6b). By contrast, industrial areas tend to be located along river valleys and railroad lines. Middle-class residential zones exist on either side of the wealthier neighbourhoods. Finally, lower-class residential areas occupy the remaining space, bordering the central business area and the industrial areas.

The Multiple Nuclei Model According to the *multiple nuclei model* developed by urban ecologists Chauncey Harris and Edward Ullman (1945), cities do not have one centre from which all growth radiates, but rather they have numerous centres of development based on specific urban needs or activities (see Figure 15.6c). As cities began to grow rapidly, they annexed formerly outlying and independent townships that had been communities in their own right. In addition to the central business district, other nuclei developed around activities such as an educational institution, a medical complex, or a government centre. Residential neighbourhoods may exist close to or far away from these nuclei.

Differences Between Canadian and U.S. Cities The models of urban growth discussed above were developed to explain the growth of U.S. cities. They do not fit preindustrial cities (most of which have their slums on the outskirts of the city rather than in the central core) nor do they fit cities such as those in Europe that were relatively large before they industrialized. Because they developed on the same continent and at about the same time, there are many similarities between Canadian and American cities, but the models probably do not apply as well to Canadian cities, which differ from U.S. cities in the following important ways (Gillis, 1995; Wolfe, 1992):

1. Canadian cities are higher in density, which means they have less urban sprawl. It is cheaper to provide services in compact cities, and commuting to work is far easier.

2. The core areas of Canadian cities are much healthier than those in the United States. In many U.S. cities, residents have moved to the suburbs to avoid crime, high taxes, and other inner-city problems. This has created what some observers refer to as "doughnut cities," with poor central core areas that have no industry, no job opportunities, poor schools, deteriorated housing, and no tax base to help improve things. The strength of our urban core areas is a major reason Canadian cities have much lower crime rates than American cities.
3. Urban Canadians rely on public transit more than do Americans, though both countries are far behind European cities in public transit use. Because of this, our cities are less divided by freeways than American urban areas.
4. Racial tension has been far less pronounced in Canada than in the United States, where it has led to many problems including urban riots and "white flight" to the suburbs.
5. Canadian and U.S. public housing policies have been very different. With a few exceptions, such as Toronto's Regent Park and Montreal's Jeanne Mance, governments in Canada have not built large-scale high-rise developments. Public housing in Canada has taken the form of small, infill projects in established neighbourhoods. Thus we have not faced the problem of large numbers of economically disadvantaged people crowded into areas that can easily be neglected by the rest of society.

Conflict Perspectives: Political Economy Models

Conflict theorists argue that cities do not grow or decline by chance. Rather, they are the product of specific decisions made by members of the capitalist class and political elites. These far-reaching decisions regarding land use and urban development benefit the members of some groups at the expense of others (see Castells, 1977/1972). Karl Marx suggested that cities are the arenas in which the intertwined processes of class conflict and capital accumulation take place; class consciousness and worker revolt were more likely to develop when workers were concentrated in urban areas (Flanagan, 1995).

Capitalism and Urban Growth According to political economy models, urban growth is influenced by capital investment decisions, power and resource inequality, class and class conflict, and government subsidy programs. Members of the capitalist class choose corporate locations, decide on sites for shopping centres and factories, and spread the population that can afford to purchase homes into sprawling suburbs located where the capitalists think they should be located (Feagin and Parker, 1990).

Business involvement in urban development is nothing new. Winnipeg became a major transportation centre because of its location at the junction of the Red and Assiniboine Rivers. However, because of Winnipeg's flooding problems, the small community of Selkirk was originally chosen for the route of the Canadian Pacific Railway (CPR). After several years of intensive lobbying by Winnipeg's political and business leaders, along with promises of subsidies to the CPR, the line was built through Winnipeg in 1881. According to Ruben Bellan (1978), Sir Donald Smith, the man who drove the last spike to finish the transcontinental railway, was instrumental in having the route shifted to Winnipeg. A key figure in building the CPR, Smith was also the largest shareholder in the Hudson's Bay Company, which owned a large block of land in the centre of Winnipeg. During the land boom that followed the announcement of the railway's new route, the Hudson's Bay Company made millions of dollars selling this land.

Today, a small number of financial institutions and developers finance and construct most of Canada's major and many of its smaller urban development projects, including skyscrapers, shopping malls, and suburban housing projects, across the country. These decision makers set limits on the individual choices of the ordinary citizen with regard to real estate, just as they do with regard to other choices (Feagin and Parker, 1990). They can make housing more affordable or totally unaffordable for many people. Ultimately their motivation rests not in benefiting the community, but in making a profit. The cities they produce reflect this mindset.

One of the major results of these urban development practices is *uneven development*—the tendency of some neighbourhoods, cities, or regions to grow and prosper while others stagnate and decline (Perry and Watkins, 1977). An example of this is the movement of middle- and upper-class people to the suburbs, which reduces the tax base of the city core. Conflict theorists argue that uneven development reflects inequalities of wealth and power in society. The problem not only affects areas in a state of decline but also produces external costs, even in "boom" areas, that are paid for by the entire community. Among these costs are increased pollution, traffic congestion, and rising rates of crime and violence. According to sociologist Mark Gottdiener these costs are "intrinsic to the very core of capitalism, and those who profit the most from development are not called upon to remedy its side effects" (1985: 214).

Gender Regimes in Cities Feminist perspectives have only recently been incorporated in urban studies (Garber and Turner, 1995). From this perspective, urbanization reflects the workings not only of the political economy but also of patriarchy. According to sociologist Lynn M. Appleton (1995), different kinds of cities have different *gender regimes*—prevailing ideologies of how women and men should think, feel, and act; how access to social positions and control of resources should be managed; and how relationships between men and women should be conducted. The higher density and greater diversity found in central cities serve as a challenge to the patriarchy found in the home and workplace in lower-density, homogeneous areas such as suburbs and rural areas because central cities offer a broader range of lifestyle choices, some of which do not involve traditional patriarchal family structures. For example, cities are more likely than suburbs to support a subculture of economically independent females. Thus the city may be a forum for challenging patriarchy; all residents who differ in marital status, paternity, sexual orientation, class, and/or race/ethnicity tend to live in close proximity to one another and may hold and act upon a common belief that both public and private patriarchy should be eliminated (Appleton, 1995).

Interactionist Perspectives: The Experience of City Life

Interactionists examine the *experience* of urban life. How does city life affect the people who live in a city? Some analysts feel cities create a positive social environment; others are cynical about the effect of urban living on the individual.

Simmel's View of City Life According to German sociologist Georg Simmel (1950/1902–1917), urban life is highly stimulating and it shapes people's thoughts and actions. Urban residents are influenced by the quick pace of city life and the pervasiveness of economic relations in everyday life. Due to the intensity of urban life, people become somewhat insensitive to events and individuals around them. When city life requires you to interact with hundreds of different people every day, you cannot become personally involved with each of them so most of your contacts will be impersonal. Urbanites are wary of one another because most interactions in the city are economic rather than social. Simmel suggests that attributes such as punctuality and exactness are rewarded but that friendliness and warmth in interpersonal relations are viewed as personal weaknesses. Some people act in a reserved way to cloak deeper feelings of distrust or dislike toward others. However, Simmel did not view city life as completely negative; he also pointed out that urban living could have a liberating effect on people because they had opportunities for individualism and autonomy (Flanagan, 1995).

Urbanism as a Way of Life Based on Simmel's observations on social relations in the city, early Chicago School sociologist Louis Wirth (1938) suggested that urbanization is a "way of life." *Urbanism* refers to the distinctive social and psychological patterns of life typically found in the city. According to Wirth, the size, density, and heterogeneity of urban populations typically result in an elaborate division of labour and in spatial segregation of people by race/ethnicity, social class, religion, and/or lifestyle. In the city, primary group ties largely are replaced by secondary relationships; social interaction is fragmented, impersonal, and often superficial ("Hello!" "Have a nice day."). Even though people gain some degree of freedom and privacy by living in the city, they pay a price for their autonomy, losing the group support and reassurance that comes from primary group ties.

From Wirth's perspective, people who live in urban areas are alienated, powerless, and lonely. A sense of community is obliterated and replaced by "mass society"—a large-scale, highly institutionalized

These photographs represent three of the ways people adapt to city life as described by Herbert Gans. Cosmopolites choose to live in the city to enjoy cultural facilities such as Toronto's Roy Thomson Hall. Ethnic villagers live in tightly knit neighbourhood enclaves, such as this Chinese neighbourhood in Richmond, British Columbia. Trapped residents can find no escape from the city, as exemplified by this homeless person in Toronto.

society in which individuality is supplanted by mass messages, faceless bureaucrats, and corporate interest.

Gans's Urban Villagers In contrast to Wirth's gloomy assessment of urban life, sociologist Herbert Gans (1982/1962) suggested that not everyone experiences the city in the same way. Based on research conducted in the west end of Boston, Gans concluded that many residents develop strong loyalties and a sense of community in central city areas that outsiders may view negatively. People make choices about the lifestyle they wish to lead based on their personal characteristics, the most important of which are social class and stage in the life cycle. According to Gans, there are five major categories of adaptation among urban dwellers. *Cosmopolites* are students, artists, writers, musicians, entertainers, and professionals who live in the city because they want to be close to its cultural facilities. *Unmarried* *people and childless couples* live in the city because they want to be close to work and entertainment. *Ethnic villagers* live in ethnically segregated neighbourhoods; some are recent immigrants who feel most comfortable within their own group. The *deprived* are poor individuals with dim future prospects; they have very limited education and few, if any, other resources. The *trapped* are urban dwellers who can find no escape from the city; this group includes persons left behind by the process of invasion and succession, downwardly mobile individuals who have lost their former position in society, older persons who have nowhere else to go, and individuals addicted to alcohol or other drugs. Transient people in the inner city are most likely to suffer the urban ills described by Wirth, but this is because of residential instability, and not simply an inevitable result of urbanization. Gans concluded that the city is a pleasure and a challenge for some urban dwellers and an urban nightmare for others.

GENDER AND CITY LIFE Do women and men experience city life differently? According to scholar Elizabeth Wilson (1991), some men view the city as sexual space in which women are categorized as prostitutes, lesbians, temptresses, or virtuous women in need of protection, based on their sexual desirability and accessibility. Wilson suggests that more affluent, dominant-group women are more likely to be viewed as virtuous women in need of protection by their own men or police officers. Cities offer a paradox for women: on the one hand, they offer more freedom than is found in comparatively isolated rural, suburban, and domestic settings; on the other, women may be in greater physical danger in the city. For Wilson, the answer to women's vulnerability in the city is not found in offering protection to them, but rather in changing people's perceptions so that they no longer treat women as sexual objects because of the impersonality of city life (Wilson, 1991).

Michelson (1994) has highlighted another dimension of the vulnerability of women in cities. Women with children are much more likely to be in the paid workforce than they were twenty years ago. When women were more likely to stay home, they spent much of their time in the company of immediate neighbours, and rarely ventured from their neighbourhoods at night without their husbands. Employed women have a much different city experience. Much of their time is now spent with people on the job and they are more often alone outside their immediate neighbourhoods at different hours.

For many women in this situation, travelling to and from work is perceived as dangerous. Michelson cites a Statistics Canada study showing that 80 percent of women fear entering parking garages and 76 percent fear using public transportation after dark. Women feel particularly vulnerable if they have to walk alone after dark because of work or school. Our cities have not yet adapted well to these major social changes in the lives of women.

DIVIDED INTERESTS: CITIES, SUBURBS, AND BEYOND

Since World War II, a dramatic population shift has occurred in North America as thousands of families have moved from cities to suburbs. Even though some people lived in suburban areas prior to the twentieth century, large-scale suburban development began in the 1950s. Postwar suburban growth was fuelled by the large baby boom families, aggressive land developers, inexpensive real estate and construction methods, better transportation, abundant energy, and liberalized mortgage policies (Jackson, 1985; Palen, 1995).

Regardless of its causes, mass suburbanization has created a territorial division of interests between cities and suburban areas (Flanagan, 1995). While many suburbanites rely on urban centres for their employment, entertainment, and other services, they pay their property taxes to suburban governments and school districts. While Canadian cities are very healthy compared with those in the United States and most other countries, they have not been immune to the problems of poverty, homelessness, unemployment, and urban sprawl. During the recession of the early 1990s Canadian cities were faced with cutting services or raising taxes at a time when the tax base already was shrinking because of migration to the suburbs. As services and urban infrastructures deteriorated, even more middle- and upper-class people moved out of cities, with some businesses following suit.

Montreal in particular has suffered from the doughnut effect. As people and industry have moved out of the central island of Montreal to suburban communities, the core has suffered. Urban

Montreal has the highest jobless rate of any major North American city, and rates of poverty, homelessness, and infant mortality are all considerably higher than the Canadian average. Despite these very real problems, Montreal is still a vibrant and safe place, and is far more livable than most American central cities. In fact, in the late 1990s the Washington-based group Population Action International ranked Montreal first in livability (tied with Melbourne and Seattle) among the world's 100 largest metropolitan areas.

The problems faced by Montreal and several of our other large cities are essentially political. Much of the decline of central cities is caused by a skewed tax system that drives businesses and middle-class residents out to the suburbs. The central cities must provide a wide range of services to their own residents as well as to those who commute downtown from the suburbs. Thus, business and residential property taxes are much higher downtown than in suburban areas. Business taxes in Montreal, for example, are 44 percent higher than in its surrounding municipalities and residential taxes are 30 percent higher (Lalonde, 1996).

POPULATION AND URBANIZATION IN THE FUTURE

In the twenty-first century, rapid global population growth is inevitable. Although death rates have declined in many developing nations, there has not been a corresponding decline in birth rates. Between 1985 and 2025, 93 percent of all global population growth will have occurred in Africa, Asia, and Latin America; 83 percent of the world's population will live in those regions by 2025 (Petersen, 1994).

Predicting changes in population is difficult. Natural disasters such as earthquakes, volcanic eruptions, hurricanes, tornados, floods, and so on obviously cannot be predicted. A cure for diseases caused by HIV may be found; however, HIV/AIDS cases may continue to increase and, as you have seen Chapter 11, other diseases may become epidemic in many parts of the world.

Whatever the impact of disease, developing nations will have an increasing number of people. While the world's population will *double*, the urban population will *triple* as people migrate from rural to urban areas in search of food, water, and jobs. Of all developing regions, Latin America is becoming the most urbanized; four megacities—Mexico City (20 million), Buenos Aires (12 million), Lima (7 million), and Santiago (5 million)—already contain more than half of this region's population and continue to grow rapidly. By 2010, Rio de Janeiro and São Paulo are expected to have a combined population of about 40 million people, who will be living in a 560-kilometre-long ***megalopolis*—a continuous concentration of two or more cities and their suburbs that have grown until they form an interconnected urban area** (Petersen, 1994).

One of the many effects of urbanization is greater exposure of people to the media. In the twenty-first century, increasing numbers of poor people in less developed nations will see images from the developed world that are beamed globally by news networks such as CNN. As futurist John L. Petersen (1994:119) notes, "For the first time in history, the poor are beginning to understand how relatively poor they are compared to the rich nations. They see, in detail, how the rest of the world lives and feel their increasing disenfranchisement." The impact this will have remains an open question.

The speed of social change means that areas that we currently think of as being relatively free from such problems will be characterized by depletion of natural resources and greater air and water pollution (see Ehrlich and Ehrlich, 1991). At the same time, if social and environmental problems become too great in one nation, members of the capitalist class may simply move to another country. For example, many affluent residents of Hong Kong acquired business interests and houses in the United States, Canada, and other countries before Hong Kong's reversion to China in 1997. As people become "world citizens" in this way, their lives are not linked to the stability of any one city or nation. However, this option is limited to only the wealthiest of citizens.

In a best-case scenario for the future, the problems brought about by rapid population growth in developing nations will be remedied by new technologies that make goods readily available to people. International trade agreements such as NAFTA (the North American Free Trade Agreement) and GATT (the General Agreement on Trade and Tariffs) will remove trade barriers and make it possible for all nations to engage fully in global trade. People in developing nations will benefit by gaining jobs and opportunities to purchase goods at lower prices. Of course, the opposite also may occur: people may be exploited as inexpensive labour, and their country's natural resources may be depleted as transnational corporations buy up raw materials without contributing to the long-term economic stability of the nation.

With regard to pollution in urban areas, some futurists predict that environmental activism will increase dramatically as people see irreversible changes in the atmosphere and experience first-hand the effects of environmental hazards and pollution on their own health and well-being. These environmental problems will cause a realization that overpopulation is a world problem, a problem that will be most apparent in the world's weakest economies and most fragile ecosystems. Futurists suggest that in this new century, we must "leave the old ways and invent new ones" (Petersen, 1994:340). What aspects of our "old ways" do you think we should discard? Can you help invent new ways?

CHAPTER REVIEW

What is demography?
Demography is the study of the size, composition, and distribution of the population.

What demographic processes result in population change?
Population change is the result of fertility (births), mortality (deaths), and migration.

What is the Malthusian perspective?
Over two hundred years ago, Thomas Malthus warned that overpopulation would result in poverty, starvation, and other major problems that would limit the size of the population.

What are the stages in demographic transition theory?
Demographic transition theory links population growth to four stages of economic development: (1) the preindustrial stage, with high birth and death rates, (2) early industrialization, with relatively high birth rates and a decline in death rates, (3) advanced industrialization and urbanization, with low birth and death rates, and (4) postindustrialization, with additional decreases in the birth rate coupled with a stable death rate.

What are the three functionalist models of urban growth?
Functionalists view urban growth in terms of ecological models. The concentric zone model sees the city as a series of circular areas, each characterized by a different type of land use; the sector model describes urban growth in terms of terrain and transportation routes; and the multiple nuclei model views cities as having numerous centres of development from which growth radiates.

What are the political economy/conflict perspectives on urban growth?
According to political economy models/conflict perspectives, urban growth is influenced by capital investment decisions, power and resource inequality, class and class conflict, and government subsidy programs.

How do interactionists view urban life?
Interactionist perspectives focus on how people experience urban life. Some analysts view the urban experience positively; others believe that urban dwellers become insensitive to events and people around them.

Key Terms

Internet Exercises

1. Visit the Statistics Canada page (**www.statcan.ca**) and find the section on Canadian Statistics. What information can you find about your own community? Now go to the section on the 1996 census. What information has recently been released from this census? How does it benefit you to have direct access to this type of data and information?
2. Many cities have now put themselves online. Using Lycos (**www.lycos.com**), search for your city and province. Many countries now have population data available on their Web sites. How is this information useful? Does your city have a Web site? If it does, what type of data does it contain and is this data useful? If not, what would you like it to contain?
3. For an interesting look at Canada's largest city, go to the Virtual Toronto Web Site at **www.ryerson.ca/vtoronto**. This site, which has been developed by the School of Applied Geography at Ryerson Polytechnic University, provides a digital atlas and a photo/video gallery. In addition to some technologically fascinating ways of showing us Toronto, the site contains a wealth of sociological information, including extensive population data. The site also has a Literary Landscapes section that includes representations of the female city and the ethnic city.

Net Links

For more Web links related to the topic of this chapter, see the Nelson sociology Web site: **www.sociologyessentials-2nded.nelson.com**.

Watch the world's population grow on the World Population Clock:

http://opr.princeton.edu:80/popclock

To look up demographic information on births, deaths, and infant mortality, go to the World Factbook at:

www.odci.gov/cia/publications/factbook

For the latest revision to world population estimates, go to:

www.undp.org/popin/#trends

Find out about Canada's immigration statistics at:

www.cic.gc.ca/english/index.html

Look under "reference" to find the latest year's statistics.

Questions for Critical Thinking

1. What impact does a high rate of immigration have on culture and personal identity in Canada?
2. If you were designing a study of growth patterns for the city in which you live (or one you know well), which theoretical model(s) would provide the most useful framework for your analysis?
3. What do you think everyday life in Canadian cities, suburbs, and rural areas will be like in 2020? Where would you prefer to live? What, if anything, does your answer reflect about the future of our cities?
4. What is the role of environmental scarcity as a cause of social conflict? How will this scarcity affect the security of developed countries?

Suggested Readings

These texts provide in-depth information on the topics in this chapter:

Roderic Beaujot. *Population Change in Canada: The Challenges of Policy Adaptation*. Toronto: McClelland and Stewart, 1991.

Leo Driedger. *The Urban Factor: Sociology of Canadian Cities*. Toronto: Oxford University Press, 1991.

Peter McGahan. *Urban Sociology in Canada* (3rd ed.). Toronto: Harcourt Brace, 1995.

Wayne W. McVey Jr. and Warren E. Kalbach. *Canadian Population*. Toronto: Nelson Canada, 1995.

The following books discuss global overpopulation and urban growth issues:

Paul Ehrlich and Anne Ehrlich. *The Population Explosion*. London: Hutchinson, 1990.

Thomas Homer-Dixon. *Environmental Scarcity and Global Security*. Foreign Policy Association, Headline Series, Number 300. Ephrata, Penn.: Science Press, 1993.

World Resources Institute. *World Resources 1996–97*. Washington: World Resources Institute, 1996.

INFOTRAC® COLLEGE EDITION

Either from the *Sociology In Our Times: The Essentials* Web site (**www.sociologyessentials-2nded.nelson.com**) or directly from your Web browser, you may access InfoTrac® College Edition, an online university library that includes over 600 popular and scholarly journals in which you can find articles related to the topics in this chapter.

GLOSSARY

absolute poverty A level of economic deprivation in which people do not have the means to secure the most basic necessities of life.

achieved status A social position that a person assumes voluntarily as a result of personal choice, merit, or direct effort.

ageism Prejudice and discrimination against people on the basis of age, particularly when they are older persons.

agents of socialization Those persons, groups, or institutions that teach people what they need to know in order to participate in society.

aggregate A collection of people who happen to be in the same place at the same time but have little else in common.

aging The physical, psychological, and social processes associated with growing older.

alienation A feeling of powerlessness and estrangement from other people and from oneself.

altruism Behaviour intended to help others and done without any expectation of personal benefit.

analysis The process through which data are organized so that comparisons can be made and conclusions drawn.

anomie Emile Durkheim's designation for a condition in which social control becomes ineffective as a result of the loss of shared values and a sense of purpose in society.

anticipatory socialization The process by which knowledge and skills are learned for future roles.

apartheid The policy of the South African government that required the separation of the races.

ascribed status A social position that is conferred on a person at birth or received involuntarily later in life.

assimilation A process by which members of subordinate racial and ethnic groups become absorbed into the dominant culture.

authoritarian leader A leader who makes all major group decisions and assigns tasks to group members.

authoritarian personality A personality type characterized by excessive conformity, submissiveness to authority, intolerance, insecurity, a high level of superstition, a propensity for stereotyping, and rigid thinking.

authoritarian political system A political system controlled by rulers who deny popular participation in government.

authority Power that people accept as legitimate rather than coercive.

bilateral descent A system of tracing descent through both the mother's and father's sides of the family.

body consciousness How a person perceives and feels about his or her body; it also includes an awareness of social conditions in society that contribute to this self-knowledge.

bourgeoisie (*or* capitalist class) Karl Marx's term for the class comprised of those who own and control the means of production.

bureaucracy An organizational model characterized by a hierarchy of authority, a clear division of labour, explicit rules and procedures, and impersonality in personnel matters.

bureaucratic personality A psychological construct that describes those workers who are more concerned with following correct procedures than they are with doing the job correctly.

capitalism An economic system characterized by private ownership of the means of production, from which personal profits can be derived through market competition and without government intervention.

capitalist class Class that consists of those who own the means of production.

case study An in-depth, multifaceted investigation of a single event, person, or social grouping.

caste system A system of social inequality in which people's status is permanently determined at birth based on their parents' ascribed characteristics.

casual crowd Relatively large gatherings of people who happen to be in the same place at the same time; if they interact at all, it is only briefly.

central city The densely populated centre of a metropolis.

charismatic authority Power legitimized on the basis of a leader's exceptional personal qualities.

chronological age A person's age based on date of birth.

church A large, bureaucratically organized religious organization that tends to seek accommodation with the larger society in order to maintain some degree of control over it.

civil disobedience Nonviolent action that seeks to change a policy or law by refusing to comply with it.

class The relative location of a person or group within a larger society, based on wealth, power, prestige, or other valued resources.

class conflict Karl Marx's term for the struggle between the capitalist class and the working class.

class system A type of stratification based on the ownership and control of resources and on the kinds of work people do.

cohabitation The sharing of a household by a couple who live together without being legally married.

cohort A category of people who are born within a specified period in time or who share some specified characteristic.

collective behaviour Relatively spontaneous, unstructured activity that is engaged in by a large number of people and that typically violates dominant group norms and values.

commonsense knowledge A form of knowing that guides ordinary conduct in everyday life.

complete observation Research in which the investigator systematically observes a social process but does not take part in it.

conflict perspective The sociological approach that views groups in society as engaged in a continuous power struggle for control of scarce resources.

conformity The process of maintaining or changing behaviour to comply with the norms established by a society, subculture, or other group.

conglomerate A combination of businesses in different commercial areas, all of which are owned by one holding company.

contingent work Part-time or temporary work.

control group Subjects in an experiment who are not exposed to the independent variable but later are compared to subjects in the experimental group.

conventional crowd Crowd made up of people who specifically come together for a scheduled event and thus share a common focus.

core nation According to world systems theory, a dominant capitalist centre characterized by high levels of industrialization and urbanization and a high degree of control over the world economy.

corporate crime An illegal act committed by corporate employees on behalf of the corporation and with its support.

corporation A large-scale organization that has legal powers (such as the ability to enter into contracts and buy and sell property) separate from its individual owner or owners.

correlation Exists when two variables are associated more frequently than could be expected by chance.

counterculture A group that strongly rejects dominant societal values and norms and seeks alternative lifestyles.

credentialism A process of social selection in which class advantage and social status are linked to the possession of academic qualifications.

crime Behaviour that violates criminal law and is punishable with fines, jail terms, and other sanctions.

criminology The systematic study of crime and the criminal justice system, including the police, courts, and prisons.

crowd A relatively large number of people who are in one another's immediate vicinity.

crude birth rate The number of live births per 1000 people in a population in a given year.

crude death rate The number of deaths per 1000 people in a population in a given year.

cult A religious group with practices and teachings outside the dominant cultural and religious traditions of a society.

cultural capital Pierre Bourdieu's term for people's social assets, including their values, beliefs, attitudes, and competencies in language and culture.

cultural imperialism The extensive infusion of one nation's culture into other nations.

cultural lag William Ogburn's term for a gap between the technical development of a society (material culture) and its moral and legal institutions (nonmaterial culture).

cultural relativism The belief that the behaviours and customs of a society must be viewed and analyzed within the context of its own culture.

cultural universals Customs and practices that occur across all societies.

culture The knowledge, language, values, customs, and material objects that are passed from person to person and from one generation to the next in a human group or society.

culture shock The disorientation that people feel when they encounter cultures radically different from their own.

democracy A political system in which people hold the ruling power, either directly or indirectly.

democratic leader A leader who encourages group discussion and decision making through consensus building.

demographic transition The process by which some societies have moved from high birth and death rates to relatively low birth and death rates as a result of technological development.

demography A subfield of sociology that examines population size, composition, and distribution.

denomination A large, organized religion characterized by accommodation to society but frequently lacking the ability or intention to dominate society.

dependency theory The perspective that global povery is at least partially attributable to the fact that low-income countries have been exploited by the high-income countries.

dependent variable A variable that is assumed to depend on or be caused by one or more other (independent) variables.

descriptive study Research that attempts to describe social reality or provide facts about some group, practice, or event.

developed nations Countries with highly industrialized economies, technologically advanced industrial, administrative, and service occupations, and relatively high levels of national and per capita (per person) income.

developing nations Countries undergoing transformation from agrarian to industrial economies.

deviance Any behaviour, belief, or condition that violates cultural norms.

differential association theory The proposition that individuals have a greater tendency to deviate from societal norms when they frequently associate with persons who are more favourable toward deviance than conformity.

diffusion The transmission of cultural items or social practices from one group or society to another.

disability A physical or health condition that stigmatizes or causes discrimination.

discovery The process of learning about something previously unknown or unrecognized.

discrimination Actions or practices of dominant group members (or their representatives) that have a harmful impact on members of a subordinate group.

domestic partnership A household partnership in which an unmarried couple lives together in a committed, sexually intimate relationship and is granted the same benefits as those accorded to married heterosexual couples.

dramaturgical analysis The study of social interaction that compares everyday life to a theatrical presentation.

dual-earner marriage A marriage in which both partners are in the labour force.

dyad A group consisting of two members.

dysfunctions A term referring to the undesirable consequences of any element of a society.

ecclesia A religious organization that is so integrated into the dominant culture that it claims as its membership all members of a society.

economy The social institution that ensures the maintenance of society through the production, distribution, and consumption of goods and services.

education The social institution responsible for the systematic transmission of knowledge, skills, and cultural values within a formally organized structure.

egalitarian family A family structure in which both partners share power and authority equally.

ego According to Sigmund Freud, the rational, reality-oriented component of personality that imposes restrictions on the innate pleasure-seeking drives of the id.

elder abuse A term used to describe physical abuse, psychological abuse, financial exploitation, and medical abuse or neglect of people age 65 or older.

elite model A view of society in which power in political systems is concentrated in the hands of a small group of elites and the masses are relatively powerless.

emigration The movement of people out of a geographic area to take up residency elsewhere.

empirical approach Research that attempts to answer questions through a systematic collection and analysis of data.

employment equity A strategy to eliminate the effects of discrimination and to make employment opportunities available to groups who have been excluded.

epidemics Sudden significant increases in the numbers of people contracting a disease.

ethnic group A collection of people who, as a result of their shared cultural traits and a high level of interaction, regard themselves, and are regarded as a cultural unit.

ethnic pluralism The coexistence of a variety of distinct racial and ethnic groups within one society.

ethnicity The cultural heritage or identity of a group based on factors such as language or country of origin.

ethnocentrism The belief in the superiority of one's own culture compared with that of others.

ethnography A detailed study of the life and activities of a group of people by researchers who may live with that group over a period of years.

experiment A research method involving a carefully designed test in which the researcher studies the impact of certain variables on subjects' attitudes or behaviour.

experimental group Subjects in an experiment who are exposed to the independent variable.

explanatory study Research that attempts to explain cause and effect relationships and to provide information on why certain events do or do not occur.

expressive leadership Group leadership that provides emotional support for members.

extended family A family unit composed of relatives in addition to parents and children who live in the same household.

fad A temporary but widely copied activity followed enthusiastically by large numbers of people.

false consciousness The term used by Karl Marx to indicate that people hold beliefs they think promote their best interests when those beliefs actually are damaging to their interests.

families we choose Social arrangements that include intimate relationships between couples and close relationships with other couples, and with other adults and children.

family A relationship in which people live together with commitment, form an economic unit and care for any young, and consider their identity to be significantly attached to the group.

fashion A currently valued style of behaviour, thinking, or appearance that is longer lasting and more widespread than a fad.

feminism The belief that all people—both women and men—are equal and that they should be valued equally and have equal rights.

feminist perspective The sociological approach that focuses on the significance of gender in understanding and explaining inequalities that exist between men and women in the household, in the paid labour force, and in the realms of politics, law, and culture.

feminization of poverty The trend in which women are disproportionately represented among individuals living in poverty.

fertility The actual level of childbearing for an individual or a population.

field research The study of social life in its natural setting: observing and interviewing people where they live, work, and play.

folkways Informal norms or everyday customs that may be violated without serious consequences within a particular culture.

formal organization A highly structured group formed for the purpose of completing certain tasks or achieving specific goals.

functional age A term used to describe observable individual attributes such as physical appearance, mobility, strength, coordination, and mental capacity that are used to assign people to age categories.

functionalist perspective The sociological approach that views society as a stable, orderly system.

gender The culturally and socially constructed meanings, beliefs, and practices associated with sex differences.

gender bias Behaviour that shows favouritism toward one gender over the other.

gender identity A person's perception of the self as female or male.

gender role Attitudes, behaviour, and activities that are socially defined as appropriate for each sex and are learned through the socialization process.

gender socialization The aspect of socialization that contains specific messages and practices concerning the nature of being female or male in a specific group or society.

generalized other George Herbert Mead's term for the child's awareness of the demands and expectations of the society as a whole or of the child's subculture.

global interdependence A relationship in which the lives of all people are intertwined closely and any one nation's problems are part of a larger global problem.

goal displacement A process that occurs in organizations when the rules become an end in themselves and organizational survival becomes more important than achievement of goals.

gossip Rumours about the personal lives of individuals.

government The formal organization that has the legal and political authority to regulate the relationships among members within a society and between the society and those outside its borders.

health The state of complete physical, mental, and social well-being.

health care Any activity intended to improve health.

hermaphrodite A person in whom sexual differentiation is ambiguous or incomplete.

heterosexism The belief that heterosexuality is the only valid form of sexual behaviour.

hidden curriculum The transmission of cultural values and attitudes, such as conformity and obedience to authority, through implied demands found in rules, routines, and regulations of schools.

homogamy The pattern of individuals marrying those who have similar characteristics, such as race/ethnicity, religious background, age, education, or social class.

homophobia An irrational fear and hatred of people who are not heterosexual.

hospice A homelike facility that provides supportive care for patients with terminal illnesses.

hypothesis In research studies, a tentative statement of the relationship between two or more concepts or variables.

id Sigmund Freud's term for the component of personality that includes all of the individual's basic biological drives and needs that demand immediate gratification.

ideal culture The values and standards of behaviour that people in a society profess to hold.

illegitimate opportunity structures Circumstances that provide an opportunity for people to acquire through illegitimate activities what they cannot achieve through legitimate channels.

immigration The movement of people into a geographic area to take up residency.

independent variable A variable that is presumed to cause or determine a dependent variable.

industrialization The process by which societies are transformed from dependence on agriculture and handmade products to an emphasis on manufacturing and related industries.

infant mortality rate The number of deaths of infants under 1 year of age per 1000 live births in a given year.

informal structure A term used to describe the aspect of organizational life in which participants' day-to-day activities and interactions ignore, bypass, or do not correspond with the official rules and procedures of the bureaucracy.

ingroup A group to which a person belongs and with which the person feels a sense of identity.

institutionalized racism A term used to describe the rules, procedures, and practices that directly and deliberately prevent minorities from having full and equal involvement in society.

instrumental leadership Group leadership that is goal or task oriented.

interactionist perspective The sociological approach that views society as the sum of the interactions of individuals and groups.

intergenerational mobility The social movement (upward or downward) experienced by family members from one generation to the next.

internal colonialism According to conflict theorists, a practice that occurs when members of a racial or ethnic group are conquered or colonized and forcibly placed under the economic and political control of the dominant group.

interview A research method using a data collection encounter in which an interviewer asks the respondent questions and records the answers.

intragenerational mobility The social movement (upward or downward) experienced by individuals within their own lifetime.

invasion The process by which a new category of people or type of land use arrives in an area previously occupied by another group or land use.

invention The process of reshaping existing cultural items into a new form.

job deskilling A reduction in the proficiency needed to perform a specific job that leads to a corresponding reduction in the wages paid for that job.

juvenile delinquency The violation of a law or the commission of a status offence by young people less than a specific age.

labelling theory The proposition that deviants are those people who have been successfully labelled as such by others.

labour union An organization of employees who join together to bargain with an employer or a group of employers over wages, benefits, and working conditions.

laissez-faire leader A leader who is only minimally involved in decision making and encourages group members to make their own decisions.

language A system of symbols that express ideas and enable people to think and communicate with one another.

latent functions Unintended functions that are hidden and remain unacknowledged by participants.

laws Formal, standardized norms that have been enacted by legislatures and are enforced by formal sanctions.

life chances Max Weber's term for the extent to which persons have access to important scarce resources.

life expectancy The average length of time a group of individuals of the same age will live.

looking-glass self Charles Horton Cooley's term for the way in which a person's sense of self is derived from the perceptions of others.

macrolevel analysis Sociological theory and research that focuses on whole societies, large-scale social structures, and social systems.

majority (dominant) group An advantaged group that has superior resources and rights in a society.

manifest functions Open, stated, and intended goals or consequences of activities within an organization or institution.

marginal job A position that differs from the employment norms of the society in which it is located.

marriage A legally recognized and/or socially approved arrangement between two or more individuals that carries certain rights and obligations and usually involves sexual activity.

mass A large collection of people who share an interest in a specific idea or issue but who are not in another's immediate physical vicinity.

mass behaviour Collective behaviour that takes place when people (who often are geographically separated from one another) respond to the same event in much the same way.

mass hysteria A form of dispersed collective behaviour that occurs when a large number of people react with strong emotions and self-destructive behaviour to a real or perceived threat.

master status A term used to describe the most important status a person occupies.

material culture A component of culture that consists of the physical or tangible creations (such as clothing, shelter, and art) that members of a society make, use, and share.

matriarchal family A family structure in which authority is held by the eldest female (usually the mother).

matriarchy A hierarchical system of social organization in which cultural, political, and economic structures are controlled by women.

matrilineal descent A system of tracing descent through the mother's side of the family.

means of production Karl Marx's term for tools, land, factories, and money for investment that form the economic basis of a society.

medicalization The process whereby an object or a condition becomes defined by society as a physical or psychological illness.

medicine An institutionalized system for the scientific diagnosis, treatment, and prevention of illness.

megalopolis A continuous concentration of two or more cities and their suburbs that have grown until they form an interconnected urban area.

meritocracy A hierarchy system in which all positions are rewarded based on people's ability and credentials.

metropolis One or more central cities and their surrounding suburbs that dominate the economic and cultural life of a region.

microlevel analysis Sociological theory and research that focuses on small groups rather than large-scale social structures.

migration The movement of people from one geographic area to another for the purpose of changing residency.

minority (subordinate) group A disadvantaged group whose members, because of physical or cultural characteristics, are subjected to unequal treatment by the dominant group and who regard themselves as objects of collective discrimination.

mob A highly emotional crowd whose members engage in, or are ready to engage in, violence against a specific target, which may be a person, a category of people, or physical property.

modernization theory A perspective that links global inequality to different levels of economic development and suggests that low-income economies can move to middle- and high-income economies by achieving self-sustained economic growth.

monarchy A political system in which power resides in one person or family and is passed from generation to generation through lines of inheritance.

monogamy Marriage between two partners, usually a woman and a man.

mores Strongly held norms with moral and ethical connotations that may not be violated without serious consequences in a particular culture.

mortality The incidence of death in a population.

multinational corporations Large companies that are headquartered in one country and have subsidiaries or branches in other countries.

new international division of labour theory Commodity is split into fragments that can be assigned to whichever part of the world can provide the most profitable combination of capital and labour.

nonmaterial culture A component of culture that consists of the abstract or intangible human creations of society (such as attitudes, beliefs, and values) that influence people's behaviour.

nonverbal communication The transfer of information between persons without the use of speech.

normative approach The use of religion, custom, habit, tradition, or authority to answer important questions.

norms Established rules of behaviour or standards of conduct.

nuclear family A family made up of one or two parents and their dependent children, all of whom live apart from other relatives.

objective Free from distorted subjective (personal or emotional) bias.

occupation A category of jobs that involve similar activities at different work sites.

occupational (*or* white-collar) crime A term used to describe illegal activities committed by people in the course of their employment or in dealing with their financial affairs.

oligopoly The situation that exists when several companies overwhelmingly control an entire industry.

organized crime A business operation that supplies illegal goods and services for profit.

outgroup A term used to describe a group to which a person does not belong and toward which the person may feel a sense of competitiveness or hostility.

panic A form of crowd behaviour that occurs when a large number of people react with strong emotions and self-destructive behaviour to a real or perceived threat.

participant observation A research method in which researchers collect systematic observations while being part of the activities of the group they are studying.

patriarchal family A family structure in which authority is held by the eldest male (usually the father).

patriarchy A hierarchical system of social organization in which cultural, political, and economic structures are controlled by men.

patrilineal descent A system of tracing descent through the father's side of the family.

pay equity Reflects the belief that wages ought to reflect the worth of a job, not the gender or race of the worker.

peer group A group of people who are linked by common interests, equal social position, and (usually) similar age.

peripheral nations According to world systems theory, nations that are dependent on core nations for capital, have little or no industrialization, and have uneven patterns of urbanization.

personal space The immediate area surrounding a person that the person claims as private.

perspective An overall approach to or viewpoint on some subject.

pluralist model An analysis of political systems that views power as widely dispersed throughout many competing interest groups.

polite racism A term used to describe an attempt to disguise a dislike of others through behaviour that appears to be nonprejudicial.

political party An organization whose purpose is to gain and hold legitimate control of government.

political socialization The process by which people learn political attitudes, values, and behaviour.

politics The social institution through which power is acquired and exercised by some people and groups.

polyandry The concurrent marriage of one woman with two or more men.

polygamy The concurrent marriage of a person of one sex with two or more members of the opposite sex.

polygyny The concurrent marriage of one man with two or more women.

population composition In demography, the biological and social characteristics of a population.

population pyramid A graphic representation of the distribution of a population by sex and age.

postindustrial economy An economy that is based on the provision of services rather than goods.

power According to Max Weber, the ability of people or groups to achieve their goals despite opposition from others.

power elite C. Wright Mills's term for a small clique composed of the top corporate, political, and military officials.

prejudice A negative attitude based on faulty generalizations about members of selected groups.

presentation of self Erving Goffman's term for people's efforts to present themselves to others in ways that are most favourable to their own interests or image.

prestige The respect or regard with which a person or status position is regarded by others.

preventive medicine Medicine that emphasizes a healthy lifestyle in order to prevent poor health before it occurs.

primary deviance A term used to describe the initial act of rule breaking.

primary group Charles Horton Cooley's term for a small, less specialized group in which members engage in face-to-face, emotion-based interactions over an extended period of time.

primary sector production The sector of the economy that extracts raw materials and natural resources from the environment.

primary sex characteristics The genitalia used in the reproductive process.

profane A term used to describe the everyday, secular, or "worldly," aspects of life.

profession A high-status, knowledge-based occupation.

proletariat (*or* working class) Karl Marx's term for those who must sell their labour because they have no other means to earn a livelihood.

propaganda Information provided by individuals or groups that have a vested interest in furthering their own cause or damaging an opposing one.

protest crowd Crowd that engages in activities intended to achieve specific political goals.

public opinion The political attitudes and beliefs communicated by ordinary citizens to decision makers.

punishment An action designed to deprive a person of things of value (including liberty) because of some offence the person is thought to have committed.

qualitative research Interpretive description (words) rather than statistics (numbers) is used to analyze underlying meanings and patterns of social relationships.

quantitative research The goal is scientific objectivity, and the focus is on data that can be measured numerically.

questionnaire A printed research instrument containing a series of items to which subjects respond.

race A term used by many people to specify groups of people distinguished by physical characteristics such as skin colour.

racial prejudice Beliefs that certain racial groups are innately inferior to others or have a disproportionate number of negative traits.

racism An organized set of beliefs about the innate inferiority of some racial groups, combined with the power to transform these ideas into practices that can deny or exclude equality of treatment on the basis of race.

rationality The process by which traditional methods of social organization, characterized by informality and spontaneity, gradually are replaced by efficiently administered formal rules and procedures (bureaucracy).

rational-legal authority Power legitimized by law or written rules and procedures. Also referred to as *bureaucratic authority*.

real culture The values and standards of behaviour that people actually follow (as contrasted with ideal culture).

reference group A term used to describe a group that strongly influences a person's behaviour and social attitudes, regardless of whether that individual is an actual member.

relative homelessness Being housed in a dwelling that fails to meet basic living standards.

relative poverty A level of economic deprivation in which people may be able to afford basic necessities but still are unable to maintain an average standard of living.

reliability In sociological research, the extent to which a study or research instrument yields consistent results.

religion A system of beliefs, symbols, and rituals, based on some sacred or supernatural realm, that guides human behaviour, gives meaning to life, and unites believers into a community.

representative sample A selection from a larger population that has the essential characteristics of the total population.

research method A strategy or technique for systematically conducting research.

resocialization The process of learning a new set of attitudes, values, and behaviours different from those in one's previous background and experiences.

respondent A person who provides data for analysis through an interview or questionnaire.

riot Violent crowd behaviour that is fuelled by deep-seated emotions but is not directed at one specific target.

rituals Regularly repeated and carefully prescribed forms of behaviour that symbolize a cherished value or belief.

role A set of behavioural expectations associated with a given status.

role conflict A situation in which incompatible role demands are placed on a person by two or more statuses held at the same time.

role exit A situation in which people disengage from social roles that have been central to their self-identity.

role expectation A term used to describe a group's or society's definition of the way a specific role ought to be played.

role performance How a person actually plays a role.

role strain The strain experienced by a person when incompatible demands are built into a single status that the person occupies.

role-taking The process by which a person mentally assumes the role of another person in order to understand the world from that person's point of view.

routinization of charisma A term for the process by which charismatic authority is succeeded by a bureaucracy controlled by a rationally established authority or by a combination of traditional and bureaucratic authority.

rumour An unsubstantiated report on an issue or subject.

sacred A term used to describe those aspects of life that are extraordinary or supernatural.

sample The people who are selected from the population to be studied.

sanction A reward for appropriate behaviour or a penalty for inappropriate behaviour.

scapegoat A person or group that is incapable of offering resistance to the hostility or aggression of others.

second shift Arlie Hochschild's term for the domestic work that employed women perform at home after they complete their workday on the job.

secondary analysis A research method in which researchers use existing material and analyze data that originally was collected by others.

secondary deviance A term used to describe the process whereby a person who has been labelled deviant accepts that new identity and continues the deviant behaviour.

secondary group A larger, more specialized group in which the members engage in more impersonal, goal-oriented relationships for a limited period of time.

secondary sector production The sector of the economy that processes raw materials (from the primary sector) into finished goods.

secondary sex characteristics The physical traits (other than reproductive organs) that identify an individual's sex.

sect A relatively small religious group that has broken away from another religious organization to renew what it views as the original version of the faith.

segregation A term used to describe the spatial and social separation of categories of people by race/ethnicity, class, gender, and/or religion.

self-concept The totality of our beliefs and feelings about ourselves.

self-fulfilling prophecy A situation in which a false belief or prediction produces behaviour that makes the originally false belief come true.

semiperipheral nations According to world systems theory, nations that are more developed than peripheral nations but less developed than core nations.

senile dementia A term for diseases, such as Alzheimer's, that involve a progressive impairment of judgment and memory.

sex A term used to describe the biological and anatomical differences between females and males.

sexism The subordination of one sex, usually female, based on the assumed superiority of the other sex.

sexual orientation A person's preference for emotional–sexual relationships with members of the opposite sex (heterosexuality), the same sex (homosexuality), or both sexes (bisexuality).

sick role Patterns of behaviour defined as appropriate for people who are sick.

significant others Those persons whose care, affection, and approval are especially desired and who are most important in the development of the self.

small group A collectivity small enough for all members to be acquainted with one another and to interact simultaneously.

social bond theory The proposition that the likelihood of deviant behaviour increases when a person's ties to society are weakened or broken.

social construction of reality The process by which our perception of reality is shaped largely by the subjective meaning that we give to an experience.

social control Systematic practices developed by social groups to encourage conformity and to discourage deviance.

social distance A term used to describe the extent to which people are willing to interact and establish relationships with members of racial and ethnic groups other than their own.

social facts Emile Durkheim's term for patterned ways of acting, thinking, and feeling that exist outside any one individual.

social gerontology The study of the social (nonphysical) aspects of aging.

social group A group that consists of two or more people who interact frequently and share a common identity and a feeling of interdependence.

social institution A set of organized beliefs and rules that establish how a society will attempt to meet its basic social needs.

social interaction The process by which people act toward or respond to other people.

social marginality The state of being part insider and part outsider in the social structure.

social mobility The movement of individuals or groups from one level in a stratification system to another.

social movement An organized group that acts consciously to promote or resist change through collective action.

social network A series of social relationships that link an individual to others.

social solidarity The state of having shared beliefs and values among members of a social group, along with intense and frequent interaction among group members.

social stratification The hierarchical arrangement of large social groups based on their control over basic resources.

social structure The stable pattern of social relationships that exist within a particular group or society.

socialism An economic system characterized by public ownership of the means of production, the pursuit of collective goals, and centralized decision making.

socialization The lifelong process of social interaction through which individuals acquire a self-identity and the physical, mental, and social skills needed for survival in society.

societal consensus A situation whereby the majority of members share a common set of values, beliefs, and behavioural expectations.

society A large social grouping that shares the same geographical territory and is subject to the same political authority and dominant cultural expectations.

sociological imagination C. Wright Mills's term for the ability to see the relationship between individual experiences and the larger society.

sociology The systematic study of human society and social interaction.

sociology of family The subdiscipline of sociology that attempts to describe and explain patterns of family life and variations in family structure.

special interest groups Political coalitions comprised of individuals or groups that share a specific interest that they wish to protect or advance with the help of the political system.

split labour market A term used to describe the division of the economy into two areas of employment: a primary sector or upper tier, composed of higher-paid (usually dominant group) workers in more secure jobs; and a secondary sector or lower tier, comprised of lower-paid (often subordinate group) workers in jobs with little security and hazardous working conditions.

state The political entity that possesses a legitimate monopoly over the use of force within its territory to achieve its goals.

status A socially defined position in a group or society characterized by certain expectations, rights, and duties.

status set A term used to describe all the statuses that a person occupies at a given time.

status symbol A material sign that informs others of a person's specific status.

stereotype An overgeneralization about the appearance, behaviour, or other characteristics of all members of a group.

stigma According to Erving Goffman, any physical or social attribute or sign that so devalues a person's social identity that it disqualifies that person from full social acceptance.

strain theory The proposition that people feel strain when they are exposed to cultural goals that they are unable to obtain because they do not have access to culturally approved means of achieving those goals.

street crime All violent crime, certain property crimes, and certain morals crimes.

subculture A group of people who share a distinctive set of cultural beliefs and behaviours that differ in some significant way from that of the larger society.

succession The process by which a new category of people or type of land use gradually predominates in an area formerly dominated by another group or activity.

superego Sigmund Freud's term for the human conscience, consisting of the moral and ethical aspects of personality.

survey A research method in which a number of respondents are asked identical questions through a systematic questionnaire or interview.

symbol Anything that meaningfully represents something else.

systemic racism Practices that have a harmful impact on subordinate group members even though the organizationally prescribed norms or regulations guiding these actions initially were established with no intent to harm.

taboo A more that is so strong that its violation is considered to be extremely offensive and even unmentionable.

terrorism The calculated unlawful use of physical force or threats of violence against persons or property in order to intimidate or coerce a government, organization, or individual for the purpose of gaining some political, religious, economic, or social objective.

theory A set of logically interrelated statements that attempts to describe, explain, and (occasionally) predict social events.

total institution Erving Goffman's term for a place where people are isolated from the rest of society for a set period of time and come under the control of the officials who run the institution.

totalitarian political system A political system in which the state seeks to regulate all aspects of people's public and private lives.

tracking The assignment of students to specific courses and educational programs based on their test scores, previous grades, or both.

traditional authority Power that is legitimized on the basis of long-standing custom.

transsexual A person who believes that he or she was born with the body of the wrong sex.

transvestite A male who lives as a woman or a female who lives as a man but does not alter the genitalia.

triad A group comprised of three members.

unemployment rate The percentage of unemployed persons in the labour force actively seeking jobs.

universal health care system System in which all citizens receive medical services paid for through taxation revenues.

urban sociology A subfield of sociology that examines social relationships and political and economic structures in the city.

urbanization The process by which an increasing proportion of a population lives in cities rather than in rural areas.

validity In sociological research, the extent to which a study or research instrument accurately measures what it is supposed to measure.

value A collective idea about what is right or wrong, good or bad, and desirable or undesirable in a particular culture.

value contradiction A situation in which values conflict with one another or are mutually exclusive.

variable In sociological research, any concept with measurable traits or characteristics that can change or vary from one person, time, situation, or society to another.

visible minority Refers to an official government category of nonwhite, non-Caucasian individuals.

wage gap A term used to describe the disparity between women's and men's earnings.

wealth The value of all of a person's or family's economic assets, including income, personal property, and income-producing property.

working class Consists of those who must sell their labour to the owners in order to earn enough money to survive.

world systems theory According to the world systems theory, the capitalist world economy is a global system divided into a hierarchy of three major types of nations—core, semiperipheral, and peripheral—in which upward or downward mobility is conditioned by the resources and obstacles that characterize the international system.

zero population growth The point at which no population increase occurs from year to year.

REFERENCES

Abella, Irving, and Harold Troper. 1982. *None Is Too Many*. Toronto: Lester and Orpen Dennys.

Aberle, David F. 1966. *The Peyote Religion Among the Navaho*. Chicago: Aldine.

Aberle, D.F., A.K. Cohen, A.K. Davis, M.J. Leng, Jr., and F.N. Sutton. 1950. "The Functional Prerequisites of Society." *Ethics*, 60(January):100–111.

Achilles, Rona. 1996. "Assisted Reproduction: The Social Issues." In E.D. Nelson and B.W. Robinson (eds.), *Gender in the 1990s*. Scarborough, Ont.: Nelson Canada, 346–364.

Active Health Report: The Active Health Report on Seniors. 1998. Ottawa: Minister of Supply and Services.

Adams, Michael. 1998. *Sex in the Snow*. Toronto: Penguin.

Adams, Owen B. 1990. "Divorce Rates in Canada." In C. McKie and K. Thompson (eds.), *Canadian Social Trends*. Toronto: Thompson Educational Publishing, 146–147.

Adams, Tom. 1991. *Grass Roots: How Ordinary People Are Changing America*. New York: Citadel Press.

Adler, Freda. 1975. *Sisters in Crime: The Rise of the New Female Criminal*. New York: McGraw-Hill.

Adler, Patricia A., and Peter Adler. 1994. *Constructions of Deviance: Social Power, Context, and Interaction*. Belmont, Cal.: Wadsworth.

Adler, Patricia, Steven J. Kless, and Peter Adler. 1995. "Socialization to Gender Roles: Popularity Among Elementary School Boys and Girls." In E.D. Nelson and B.W. Robinson (eds.), *Gender in the 1990s*. Scarborough, Ont.: Nelson, 119–141.

Adorno, Theodor W., Else Frenkel-Brunswick, Daniel J. Levinson, and R. Nevitt Sanford. 1950. *The Authoritarian Personality*. New York: Harper & Row.

Agger, Ben. 1993. *Gender, Culture, and Power: Toward a Feminist Postmodern Critical Theory*. Westport, Conn.: Praeger.

Aiello, John R., and S.E. Jones. 1971. "Field Study of Proxemic Behavior of Young School Children in Three Subcultural Groups." *Journal of Personality and Social Psychology*, 19:351–356.

Akyeampong, Ernest B. 1997. "The Labour Market: Year-End Review." *Perspectives on Labour Income*, (1997):16.

Albas, Cheryl, and Daniel Albas. 1988. "Emotion Work and Emotion Rules: The Case of Exams." *Qualitative Sociology*, 11(4):259–275.

———. 1989. "Aligning Actions: The Case of Subcultural Proxemics." *Canadian Ethnic Studies*, 21(2):74–81.

Albas, Daniel, and Cheryl Albas. 1988. "Aces and Bombers: The Post-Exam Impression Management Strategies of Students." *Symbolic Interaction*, 11(Fall):289–302.

———. 1992. "Love and Marriage." In K. Ishwaran (ed.), *Family and Marriage: Cross-Cultural Perspectives*. Toronto: Thompson Educational Publishing, 127–142.

Albert, Terry, and Gregory Williams. 1998. *The Economic Burden of HIV/AIDS in Canada*. Ottawa: Canadian Policy Research Networks.

Albrecht, Gary L. 1992. *The Disability Business: Rehabilitation in America*. Newbury Park, Cal.: Sage.

Alexander, Peter, and Roger Gill (eds.). 1984. *Utopias*. London: Duckworth.

Alix, Ernest K. 1995. *Sociology: An Everyday Life Approach*. Minneapolis: West Publishing.

Allahar, Anton. 1989. *Sociology and the Periphery: Theories and Issues*. Toronto: Garamond.

Allen, Tom C. 2000. *Someone to Talk To: Care and Control of the Homeless*. Halifax: Fernwood Publishing.

Allport, Gordon. 1958. *The Nature of Prejudice* (abridged ed.). New York: Doubleday/Anchor.

Altemeyer, Bob. 1981. *Right-Wing Authoritarianism*. Winnipeg, Manitoba: University of Manitoba Press.

———. 1998. *Enemies of Freedom: Understanding Right-Wing Authoritarianism*. San Francisco: Jossey-Bass.

Alwin, Duane, Philip Converse, and Steven Martin. 1985. "Living Arrangements and Social Integration." *Journal of Marriage and the Family*, 47:319–334.

Amott, Teresa, and Julie Matthaei. 1991. *Race, Gender, and Work: A Multicultural Economic History of Women in the United States*. Boston: South End Press.

Anderson, Elijah. 1990. *Streetwise: Race, Class, and Change in an Urban Community*. Chicago: University of Chicago Press.

———. 1994. "The Code of the Streets." *Atlantic Monthly* (May):80–94.

Anderson, Karen. 1996. *Sociology: A Critical Introduction*. Scarborough, Ont.: Nelson Canada.

Antonius, Andreas, and Robin Crowley. 1986. "The Ownership Structure of the Largest Canadian Corporations, 1979." *Canadian Journal of Sociology*, 11:253–268.

Anyon, Jean. 1980. "Social Class and the Hidden Curriculum of Work." *Journal of Education*, 162:67–92.

Appelbaum, R.P., and W.P. Chambliss. 1997. *Sociology* (2nd ed.). New York: Addison-Wesley Longman.

Appleton, Lynn M. 1995. "The Gender Regimes in American Cities." In Judith A. Garber and Robyne S. Turner (eds.), *Gender in Urban Research*. Thousand Oaks, Cal.: Sage, 44–59.

Archibald, Chris P. 1997. "HIV/AIDS—The New 'Great Teacher.'" *Canadian Journal of Public Health*, 88(January/February):11–12.

Armstrong, Pat. 1993. "Work and Family Life: Changing Patterns." In G.N. Ramu (ed.), *Marriage and the Family in Canada Today* (2nd ed.). Scarborough, Ont.: Prentice-Hall, 127–145.

Armstrong, Pat, and Hugh Armstrong. 1994. *The Double Ghetto: Canadian Women and Their Segregated Work*. Toronto: McClelland and Stewart.

———. 1996. *Wasting Away: The Undermining of the Canadian Health Care System*. Toronto: Oxford University Press.

Armstrong, Pat, Hugh Armstrong, Jacqueline Choiniere, Eric Mykhalovsky, and Jerry P. White. 1997. *Medical Alert: New Work Organizations in Health Care*. Toronto: Garamond Press.

Armstrong, Robin. 2000. "Mapping the Condition of First Nations Communities." *Canadian Social Trends*, vol. 3:28–32.

Arnup, Katherine. 1995. "We Are Family: Lesbian Mothers in Canada." In E.D. Nelson and B.W. Robinson (eds.), *Gender in the 1990s*. Scarborough, Ont.: Nelson Canada, 330–345.

Asch, Solomon E. 1955. "Opinions and Social Pressure." *Scientific American*, 193(5):31–35.

———. 1956. "Studies of Independence and Conformity: A Minority of One Against a Unanimous Majority." *Psychological Monographs*, 70(9) (Whole no. 416).

Atchley, Robert C. (ed.). 1994. *Social Forces and Aging*. Belmont, Cal.: Wadsworth.

Atwood, Margaret. 1987. "...the only position they've ever adopted toward us, country to country, has been the missionary position...." In Laurier LaPierre (ed.), *If You Love This Country*. Toronto: McClelland and Stewart, 17–23.

Audubon. 1994. "Issues in Focus: Issues for the September 1994 UN International Conference on Population and Development." *Audubon* (July/August):56–57.

Aulette, Judy Root. 1994. *Changing Families*. Belmont, Cal.: Wadsworth.

Axinn, William G., and Arland Thornton. 1992. "The Relationship Between Cohabitation and Divorce: Selectivity or Causal Influence?" *Demography*, 29(3):357–374.

Babbie, Earl. 1995. *The Practice of Social Research* (7th ed.). Belmont, Cal.: Wadsworth.

Backhouse, Constance, Roma Harris, Gillian Mitchell, and Alison Wylie. 1995. "The Chilly Climate for Faculty Women at Western: Postscript to the Backhouse Report." In the Chilly Collective (eds.), *Breaking Anonymity: The Chilly Climate for Women Faculty*. Waterloo, Ont.: Wilfrid Laurier University Press, 118–135.

Baker, Maureen. 1996. "Introduction to Family Studies: Cultural Variations." In M. Baker (ed.), *Families: Changing Trends in Canada*. Toronto: McGraw-Hill Ryerson, 3–32.

Baker, M., and Donna Lero. 1996. "Division of Labour: Paid Work and Family Structure." In M. Baker (ed.), *Families: Changing Trends in Canada*. Toronto: McGraw-Hill Ryerson, 78–103.

Baker, Robert. 1993. "'Pricks' and 'Chicks': A Plea for 'Persons.'" In Anne Minas (ed.), *Gender Basics: Feminist Perspectives on Women and Men*. Belmont, Cal.: Wadsworth, 66–68.

Balakrishnan, T.R., K. Vaninadha Rao, Evelyne Lapierre-Adameyk, and Karol J. Krotki. 1987. "A Hazard Model Analysis of the Covariates of Marriage Dissolution in Canada." *Demography*, 24(3):395–406.

Ballantine, Jeanne H. 1997. *The Sociology of Education: A Systematic Analysis* (4th ed.). Englewood Cliffs, N.J.: Prentice-Hall.

Ballara, Marcela. 1992. *Women and Literacy*. Prepared for the UN/NGO Group on Women and Development. Atlantic Highlands, N.J.: Zed Books.

Bandura, Albert. 1973. *Aggression: A Social Learning Analysis*. Englewood Cliffs, N.J.: Prentice-Hall.

Bane, Mary Jo. 1986. "Household Composition and Poverty: Which Comes First?" In Sheldon H. Danziger and Daniel H. Weinberg (eds.), *Fighting Poverty: What Works and What Doesn't*. Cambridge, Mass.: Harvard University Press.

Banner, Lois W. 1993. *In Full Flower: Aging Women, Power, and Sexuality*. New York: Vintage.

Barlow, Hugh D. 1987. *Introduction to Criminology* (4th ed.). Boston: Little, Brown.

Barlow, Maude. 1991. *Parcel of Rogues: How Free Trade Is Failing Canada*. Toronto: Key Porter Books.

Barnard, Chester. 1938. *The Functions of the Executive*. Cambridge, Mass.: Harvard University Press.

Baron, Dennis. 1986. *Grammar and Gender*. New Haven, Conn.: Yale University Press.

Baron, Stephen. 1994. *Street Youth and Crime: The Role of Labour Market Experiences*. Unpublished Ph.D. dissertation, University of Alberta.

Barrett, Stanley R. 1987. *Is God a Racist? The Right Wing in Canada*. Toronto: University of Toronto Press.

Barthel, Diane. 1988. *Putting on Appearances: Gender and Advertising*. Philadelphia: Temple University Press.

Basow, Susan A. 1992. *Gender Stereotypes and Roles* (3rd ed.). Pacific Grove, Cal.: Brooks/Cole.

Bates, Stephen. 1994. *Battleground: One Mother's Crusade, the Religious Right, and the Struggle for Our Schools*. New York: Owl/Henry Holt.

Baxter, J. 1970. "Interpersonal Spacing in Natural Settings." *Sociology*, 36(3):444–456.

Beare, Margaret. 1996a. *Criminal Conspiracies: Organized Crime in Canada*. Scarborough, Ont.: Nelson Canada.

———. 1996b. "Organized Crime and Money Laundering." In Robert A. Silverman, James J. Teevan, and Vincent F. Sacco (eds.), *Crime in Canadian Society* (5th ed.). Toronto: Harcourt Brace and Co., 187–245.

Beaujot, Roderic P., and Kevin McQuillan. 1982. *Growth and Dualism: The Demographic Development of Canadian Society*. Toronto: Gage.

Beaujot, Roderic. 1991. *Population Change in Canada: The Challenges of Policy Adaptation*. Toronto: Oxford University Press.

Beavis, Mary Ann, Nancy Klos, Tom Carter, and Christian Douchant. 1997. "Literature Review: Aboriginal Peoples and Homelessness." Canadian Mortgage and Housing Corporation. Available: www.cmhc-schl.gc.ca/Research/Homeless/F_aborig.html

Becker, Howard S. 1963. *Outsiders: Studies in the Sociology of Deviance*. New York: Free Press.

Beeghley, Leonard. 1996. *The Structure of Social Stratification in the United States* (2nd ed.). Boston: Allyn & Bacon.

Begin, Patricia. 1994. *Child Abuse*. Ottawa: Library of Parliamentary Research.

Belkin, Lisa. 1994. "Kill for Life?" *New York Times Magazine* (October 30):47–51, 62–64, 76, 80.

Bell, Inge Powell. 1989. "The Double Standard: Age." In Jo Freeman, *Women: A Feminist Perspective* (4th ed.). Mountain View, Cal.: Mayfield, 236–244.

Bellan, Ruben. 1978. *Winnipeg First Century: An Economic History*. Winnipeg: Queenston House Publishing.

Belsky, Janet. 1990. *The Psychology of Aging: Theory, Research, and Interventions* (2nd ed.). Pacific Grove, Cal.: Brooks/Cole.

Bendix, Reinhard. 1971. "Charismatic Leadership." In Reinhard Bendix and Guenther Roth (eds.), *Scholarship and Partisanship: Essays on Max Weber*. Berkeley: University of California Press, 170–187.

Benet, Sula. 1971. "Why They Live to Be 100, or Even Older, in Abkhasia." *The New York Times Magazine* (December 26):3, 28–29, 31–34.

Benokraitis, Nijole V. 1997. *Marriages and Families: Changes, Choices, and Constraints* (2nd ed.). Englewood Cliffs, N.J.: Prentice-Hall.

Benokraitis, Nijole V., and Joe R. Feagin. 1986. *Modern Sexism: Blatant, Subtle, and Covert Discrimination*. Englewood Cliffs, N.J.: Prentice-Hall.

———. 1995. *Modern Sexism: Blatant, Subtle, and Covert Discrimination* (2nd ed.). Englewood Cliffs, N.J.: Prentice-Hall.

Benson, Susan Porter. 1983. "The Customers Ain't God: The Work Culture of Department Store Saleswomen, 1890–1940." In Michael H. Frisch and Daniel J. Walkowitz, *Working Class America: Essays on Labor, Community, and American Society*. Urbana: University of Illinois Press, 185–211.

Berger, Bennett M. 1988. "Utopia and Its Environment." *Society* (January/February):37–41.

Berger, Peter. 1963. *Invitation to Sociology: A Humanistic Perspective*. New York: Anchor.

Berger, Peter, and Hansfried Kellner. 1964. "Marriage and the Construction of Reality." *Diogenes*, 46:1–32.

Berger, Peter, and Thomas Luckmann. 1967. *The Social Construction of Reality: A Treatise in the Sociology of Knowledge*. Garden City, N.Y.: Anchor Books.

Bergmann, Barbara R. 1986. *The Economic Emergence of Women*. New York: Basic Books.

Bernard, Jessie. 1982. *The Future of Marriage*. New Haven, Conn.: Yale University Press (orig. pub. 1973).

———. 1995. "The Good Provider Role: Its Rise and Fall." In E.D. Nelson and B.W. Robinson, *Gender in the 1990s*. Scarborough, Ont.: Nelson Canada, 156–171.

Berry, John W., W. Rudolf Kalin, and Donald M. Taylor. 1977. *Multiculturalism and Ethnic Attitudes in Canada*. Ottawa: Ministry of Supply and Services.

Berton, Pierre. 1987. "For the first time, Canadians have had to ask themselves what kind of people we are and what kind of people we want to be." In Laurier LaPierre (ed.), *If You Love This Country*. Toronto: McClelland and Stewart, 24–28.

Beyerstein, Barry. 1997. "Alternative Medicine: Where's the Evidence?" *Canadian Journal of Public Health*, 88 (May/June):149–150.

Biagi, Shirley. 1994. *Media/Impact: An Introduction to Mass Media* (2nd ed.). Belmont, Cal.: Wadsworth.

Bibby, Reginald W. 1987. *Fragmented Gods: The Poverty and Potential of Religion in Canada*. Toronto: Irwin.

———. 1995. *Mosaic Madness: The Potential and Poverty of Canadian Life*. Toronto: Stoddart.

———. 1995. *The Bibby Report: Social Trends Canadian Style*. Toronto: Stoddart.

———. 1996. "Fragmented Gods: Religion in Canada." In R. Brym (ed.), *Sociology in Question: Sociological Readings for the 21st Century*. Toronto: Harcourt Brace, 56–61.

———. 1998. "Religion." In Robert J. Brym (ed.), *New Society: Sociology for the 21st Century*. (2nd ed.). Toronto: Harcourt Brace, 128–152.

Bissoondath, Neil. 1994. *Selling Illusions: The Cult of Multiculturalism in Canada*. Toronto: Penguin.

Bittner, Egon. 1980. *Popular Interests in Psychiatric Remedies: A Study in Social Control*. New York: Ayer.

Blackford, Karen A. 1996. "Families and Parental Disability." In Marion Lynn (ed.), *Voices: Essays on Canadian Families*. Scarborough, Ont.: Nelson Canada, 161–163.

Blau, Peter M., and Marshall W. Meyer. 1987. *Bureaucracy in Modern Society* (3rd ed.). New York: Random House.

Blauner, Robert. 1972. *Racial Oppression in America*. New York: Harper & Row.

Blendon, Robert J., Karen Donelan, Cathy Schoen, Karen Davis, and Katherine Binns. 1998. *1998 Commonwealth Fund International Health Policy Survey*. New York: The Commonwealth Fund.

Bluestone, Barry, and Bennett Harrison.

1982. *The Deindustrialization of America*. New York: Basic Books.

Blumberg, Leonard. 1977. "The Ideology of a Therapeutic Social Movement: Alcoholics Anonymous." *Journal of Studies on Alcohol*, 38:2122–2143.

Blumer, Herbert G. 1946. "Collective Behavior." In Alfred McClung Lee (ed.), *A New Outline of the Principles of Sociology*. New York: Barnes & Noble, 167–219.

———. 1969. *Symbolic Interactionism: Perspective and Method*. Englewood Cliffs, N.J.: Prentice-Hall.

———. 1974. "Social Movements." In R. Serge Denisoff (ed.), *The Sociology of Dissent*. New York: Harcourt Brace Jovanovich, 74–90.

Bogardus, Emory S. 1925. "Measuring Social Distance." *Journal of Applied Sociology*, 9:299–308.

———. 1968. "Comparing Racial Distance in Ethiopia, South Africa, and the United States." *Sociology and Social Research*, 52(2):149–156.

Bolaria, B. Singh, and Rosemary Bolaria. 1994. "Inequality and Differential Health Risks of Environmental Degradation." In Bolaria and Bolaria (eds.), *Racial Minorities, Medicine and Health*. Halifax, N.S.: Fernwood, 85–97.

Bolaria, S. and P. Li. 1988. *Racial Oppression in Canada* (2nd ed.). Toronto: Garamond.

Boldt, Menno. 1993. *Surviving as Indians: The Challenge of Self-Government*. Toronto: University of Toronto Press.

Bonacich, Edna. 1972. "A Theory of Ethnic Antagonism: The Split Labor Market." *American Sociological Review*, 37:547–549.

———. 1976. "Advanced Capitalism and Black–White Relations in the United States: A Split Labor Market Interpretation." *American Sociological Review*, 41:34–51.

Bonger, Willem. 1969. *Criminality and Economic Conditions* (abridged ed.). Bloomington: Indiana University Press (orig. pub. 1916).

Bonner, Raymond. 1994. "Ethnic War Lacerates Former Soviet Resort Area." *New York Times* (June 8):A3.

Borchorst, A., and B. Siim. 1987. "Women and the Advanced Welfare State—A New Kind of Patriarchal Power?" In A. Showstack-Sasson (ed.), *Women and the State*. London: Hutchinson, 128–157.

Bordo, Susan. 1993. *Unbearable Weight: Feminism, Western Culture, and the Body*. Berkeley: University of California Press.

Bourdieu, Pierre, and Jean-Claude Passeron. 1990. *Reproduction in Education, Society and Culture*. Newbury Park, Cal.: Sage.

Bowles, Samuel. 1977. "Unequal Education and the Reproduction of the Social Division of Labor." In Jerome Karabel and A.H. Halsey (eds.), *Power and Ideology in Education*. New York: Oxford University Press, 137–153.

Bowles, Samuel, and Herbert Gintis. 1976. *Schooling in Capitalist America: Education and the Contradictions of Economic Life*. New York: Basic Books.

Boyd, Monica. 1992. "Gender, Visible Minority Status, and Immigrant Earnings Inequality: Reassessing an Employment Equity Premise." In V. Satzewich (ed.), *Deconstructing a Nation: Immigration, Multiculturalism, and Racism in Canada*. Halifax: Fernwood, 279–322.

———. 1995. "Gender Inequality: Economic and Political Aspects." In Robert J. Brym, *New Sociology: Sociology for the 21st Century*. Toronto, Harcourt Brace and Company.

Boyd, Monica, and Doug Norris. 1999. "The Crowded Nest: Young Adults at Home." *Canadian Social Trends* (Spring). Ottawa: Statistics Canada, 2–5.

Boyes, William, and Michael Melvin. 1994. *Economics* (2nd ed.). Boston: Houghton Mifflin.

Bradbury, Bettina. 1996. "The Social and Economic Origins of Contemporary Families." In Maureen Baker (ed.), *Families: Changing Trends in Canada*. Toronto: McGraw-Hill Ryerson, 55–103.

Branswell, Helen. 1998. "Canada Gets Failing Grade on Treatment of Its Poor." *Canadian Press*. (December 3).

Brantingham, Paul J., Shihing Mu, and Aruind Verma. 1995. "Patterns in Canadian Crime." In Margaret A. Jackson and Curt T. Griffiths (eds.), *Canadian Criminology*. Toronto: Harcourt Brace and Company, 187–245.

Braun, Denny. 1991. *The Rich Get Richer: The Rise of Income Inequality in the United States and the World*. Chicago: Nelson-Hall.

Braverman, Harry. 1974. *Labor and Monopoly Capital*. New York: Monthly Review Press.

Breault, K.D. 1986. "Suicide in America: A Test of Durkheim's Theory of Religious and Family Integration, 1933–1980." *American Journal of Sociology*, 92(3):628–656.

Briggs, Sheila. 1987. "Women and Religion." In Beth B. Hess and Myra Marx Ferree (eds.), *Analyzing Gender: A Handbook of Social Science Research*. Newbury Park, Cal.: Sage, 408–441.

Brint, Steven. 1994. *In an Age of Experts: The Changing Role of Professionals in Politics and Public Life*. Princeton, N.J.: Princeton University Press.

Brod, Harry (ed.). 1987. *The Making of Masculinities*. Boston: Allen & Unwin.

———. 1993b. "Slavery on Rise in Brazil, As Debt Chains Workers." *New York Times* (May 23):3.

Brooke, James. 1993b. "Slavery on Rise in Brazil, As Debt Chains Workers." *New York Times* (May 23):3.

Brooks-Gunn, Jeanne. 1986. "The Relationship of Maternal Beliefs About Sex Typing to Maternal and Young Children's Behavior." *Sex Roles*, 14:21–35.

Brunet, Robin. 1993. How to Lose Friends and Influence the Media. *Alberta Report/Western Report* (July 19):16.

Bryant, Heather. 1990. *The Infertility Dilemma: Reproductive Technologies and Prevention*. Ottawa: Canadian Advisory Council on the Status of Women.

Brym, Robert J. (ed.). 1996. *Society in Question: Sociological Readings for the 21st Century*. Toronto: Harcourt Brace and Company.

Buchignani, Norman, Doreen M. Indra, and Ram Srivastiva. 1985. *Continuous Journey: A Social History of South Asians in Canada*. Toronto: McClelland and Stewart.

Buckler, Grant. 1996. "Inet '96: Canadian Minister Calls Global Internet a Priority." *Newsbytes News Network*. (July 1).

Bumpass, Larry, James E. Sweet, and Andrew J. Cherlin. 1991. "The Role of Cohabitation in Declining Rates of Marriage." *Journal of Marriage and the Family*, 53:913–927.

Bunis, William K., Angela Yancik, and David Snow. 1996. "The Cultural Patterning of Sympathy Toward the Homeless and Other Victims of Misfortune." *Social Problems* (November):387–402.

Burch, Thomas K., and Ashok K. Madan. 1986. *Union Formation and Dissolution: Results from the 1984 Family History Survey*. Ottawa: Statistics Canada.

———. 1987. *Union Formation and Dissolution: Results from the 1984 Family History Survey*. Ottawa: Statistics Canada.

Burgess, Ernest W. 1925. "The Growth of the City." In Robert E. Park and Ernest W. Burgess (eds.), *The City*. Chicago: University of Chicago Press, 47–62.

Burke, Mary Anne, Susan Crompton, Alison Jones, and Katherine Nessner. 1994. "Caring for Children." In Craig McKie and K. Thompson (eds.), *Canadian Social Trends*, vol. 2. Toronto: Thompson Educational Publishing Inc.

Burman, Patrick. 1988. *Killing Time, Losing Ground: Experiences of Unemployment*. Toronto: Wall and Thompson.

Burnham, Walter Dean. 1983. *Democracy in the Making: American Government and Politics*. Englewood Cliffs, N.J.: Prentice-Hall.

Burns, Tom. 1992. *Erving Goffman*. New York: Routledge.

Burr, Chandler. 1997. "The AIDS Exception: Privacy versus Public Health." *The Atlantic Monthly* (June):57–67.

Burros, Marian. 1994. "Despite Awareness of Risks, More in U.S. Are Getting Fat." *New York Times* (July 17):1, 8.

Burt, Martha R. 1992. *Over the Edge: The Growth of Homelessness in the 1980s*. New York: Russell Sage Foundation.

Busby, Karen. 1999. "LEAF and Pornography: Litigating on Equality and Sexual Representations." In Nick Lansen and Brian Burtch (eds.), *Law in Society: A Canadian Reader*. Toronto: Harcourt Brace.

Busch, Ruth C. 1990. *Family Systems: Comparative Study of the Family*. New York: P. Lang.

Butler, Robert N. 1975. *Why Survive? Being Old in America*. New York: Harper & Row.

Byrne, John A. 1993. "The Horizontal Corporation: It's About Managing Across, Not Up and Down." *Business Week* (December 20):76–81.

Cable, Sherry, and Charles Cable. 1995. *Environmental Problems, Grassroots Solutions: The Politics of Grassroots Environmental Conflict*. New York: St. Martin's Press.

Cahill, Spencer E. 1986. "Language Practices and Self Definition: The Case of Gender Identity Acquisition." *Sociological Quarterly*, 27(September):295–312.

Calliste, Agnes. 1987. "Sleeping Car Porters in Canada: An Ethically Submerged Split Labour Market." *Canadian Ethnic Studies*, 19:1–20.

———. 1993/94. "Race, Gender, and Canadian Immigration Policy: Blacks from the Carribbean, 1900–1932." *Journal of Canadian Studies*, 28(4):131–148.

Callwood, June. 1995. *Trial Without End*. Toronto: Albert A. Knopf.

Campaign 2000. 1998. *Report Card 1998*. Toronto: Campaign 2000. Available: www.campaign2000.ca/main_htm

Canada Mortgage and Housing Corporation. 1998. "Survey of Canadians' Attitudes Toward Homelessness." Available: www.cmhc.schl.gc.ca/Research/Homeless/F_public.html

Canadian Centre for Justice Statistics, 1991–1993. *Homicide Survey*. Ottawa: Statistics Canada.

Canadian Committee on Women in Engineering. 1992. "More Than Just Numbers: Report of the Canadian Committee on Women in Engineering." Fredericton: Faculty of Engineering, University of New Brunswick.

Canadian Council on Social Development. 1996. *The Progress of Canada's Children: 1998 Highlights*. Ottawa: Canadian Council on Social Development.

Canadian Institute for Health Information. 2000. "Facts and Figures." Available: www.cihi.ca/facts/fac.htm

Canadian Institute of Child Health. 1994. *The Health of Canada's Children* (2nd ed.). Ottawa: Canadian Institute of Child Health.

Canadian Press. 1997. "Health-Care Bill Falls, Report Says." *Winnipeg Free Press* (August 12):A14.

Canadian Public Health Association. 1997. "Position Paper on Homelessness and Health." Available: www.cpha.ca/cpha.docs/homeless.eng.html

Cancian, Francesca M. 1992. "Feminist Science: Methodologies That Challenge Inequality." *Gender & Society*, 6(4):623–642.

Canetto, Silvia Sara. 1992. "She Died for Love and He for Glory: Gender Myths of Suicidal Behavior." OMEGA, 26(1):1–17.

Cantor, Muriel G., and Joel M. Cantor. 1992. *Prime-Time Television: Content and Control* (2nd ed.). Newbury Park, Cal.: Sage.

Cantril, Hadley. 1941. *The Psychology of Social Movements*. New York: Wiley.

Carrier, James G. 1986. *Social Class and the Construction of Inequality in American Education*. New York: Greenwood Press.

Carter, Kevin L. 1993. "Black Women Are Getting a Bad Rap in Popular Culture." *Austin American-Statesman* (October 11):B7.

Carter, Stephen L. 1994. *The Culture of Disbelief: How American Law and Politics Trivializes Religious Devotion*. New York: Anchor/Doubleday.

Castells, Manuel. 1977. *The Urban Question*. London: Edward Arnold (orig. pub. 1972 as *La Question Urbaine*, Paris).

Castles, Stephen. 1995. "Trois Siècles de Dépopulation Amerindienne." In L. Normandeau and V. Piche (eds.), *Les Populations Amerindienne et Inuit du Canada*. Montreal: Press de l'Université de Montréal.

Cavender, Gray. 1995. "Alternative Theory: Labeling and Critical Perspectives." In Joseph F. Sheley (ed.), *Criminology: A Contemporary Handbook* (2nd ed.). Belmont, Cal.: Wadsworth, 349–371.

Central Intelligence Agency. 1998. *World Factbook*. Available: http://odco.gov/cia/publications/factbook

Chafetz, Janet Saltzman. 1984. *Sex and Advantage: A Comparative, Macro-Structural Theory of Sex Stratification*. Totowa, N.J.: Rowman & Allanheld.

———. 1989. "Marital Intimacy and Conflict: The Irony of Spousal Equality." In Jo Freeman (ed.), *Women: A Feminist Perspective* (4th ed.). Mountain View, Cal.: Mayfield, 149–156.

Chagnon, Napoleon A. 1992. *Yanomamo: The Last Days of Eden*. New York: Harcourt Brace Jovanovich (rev. from 4th ed., *Yanomamo: The Fierce People*, by Holt, Rinehart & Winston).

Chalfant, H. Paul, Robert E. Beckley, and C. Eddie Palmer. 1994. *Religion in Contemporary Society* (3rd ed.). Itasca, Ill.: Peacock.

Chambliss, William J. 1969. *Crime and the Legal Process*. Toronto: McGraw-Hill.

———. 1973. "The Saints and the Roughnecks." *Society*, 11:24–31.

Chandler, Tertius, and Gerald Fox. 1974. *3000 Years of Urban History*. New York: Academic Press.

Chard, Jennifer. 1995. "Factfinder on Crime and the Administration of Justice in Canada." *Juristat*, 15(10). Ottawa: Canadian Centre for Justice Statistics.

Cheal, David. 1991. *Family and the State of Theory*. Toronto: University of Toronto Press.

———. 1996. "Stories About Stepfamilies." In *Growing Up in Canada*. Human Resources Development. Ottawa: Statistics Canada.

Chen, M. and N. Zhou. 1994. "The Portrayal of Older People in Canadian Advertisements: Regular vs. Specialized Magazines." In V. Marshall and B. McPherson (eds.), *Aging: Canadian Perspectives*. Petersborough, Ont.: Broadview, 206–18.

Chernin, Kim. 1981. *The Obsession: Reflections on the Tyranny of Slenderness*. New York: Harper & Row.

Childe, V. Gordon. 1957. "Civilization, Cities, and Towns." *Antiquity* (March):210–213.

Chossudovsky, Michel. 1997. *The Globalization of Poverty*. Penang: Third World Netwook.

Church, Elizabeth. 1996. "Kinship and Stepfamilies." In Marion Lynn (ed.), *Voices: Essays on Canadian Families*. Scarborough, Ont.: Nelson Canada, 81–106.

Church Council on Justice and Corrections. 1996. *Satisfying Justice*. Ottawa: Church Council on Justice and Corrections.

Churchill, Ward. 1994. *Indians Are Us? Culture and Genocide in Native North America*. Monroe, Maine: Common Courage Press.

"Citizen's Forum on Canada's Future: Report to the People and Government of Canada." 1991. Ottawa: Privy Council Office.

Citizenship and Immigration Canada. 1999. *Facts and Figures, 1998: Immigration Overview*. Ottawa: Citizenship and Immigration Canada.

Clark, Warren. 1998. "Religious Observance: Marriage and the Family." *Canadian Social Trends* (Fall). Ottawa: Statistics Canada, 2–7.

Clark, Wayne. 1997. "School Leavers Revisited." *Canadian Social Trends* (Winter). Cat. no. 11-008-XPE. Ottawa: Statistics Canada, 10–12.

Clement, Wallace and Daniel Drache. 1978. *A Practical Guide to Canadian Political Economy*. Toronto: James Lorimer and Company.

Clement, Wallace and Glen Williams. 1989. *The New Canadian Political Economy*. Kingston: McGill-Queen's University Press.

Cloward, Richard A., and Lloyd E. Ohlin. 1960. *Delinquency and Opportunity: A Theory of Delinquent Gangs*. New York: Free Press.

CNN. 1994. "Both Sides: School Prayer." (November 26).

Coakley, Jay J. 1994. *Sport in Society: Issues and Controversies* (5th ed.). St. Louis: Times Mirror/Mosby.

Cohen, Leah Hager. 1994. *Train Go Sorry: Inside a Deaf World*. Boston: Houghton Mifflin.

Cohen, Marjorie Griffin. 1993. "Capitalist Development, Industrialization, and Women's Work." In Graham S. Lowe and Harvey J. Krahn (eds.), *Work in Canada*. Scarborough, Ont.: Nelson Canada, 142–144.

Colby, David C., and Timothy E. Cook. 1991. "Epidemics and Agendas: The Politics of Nightly News Coverage of AIDS." *Journal of Health Politics, Policy and Law*, 16(2):215–249.

Coles, Gerald. 1987. *The Learning Mystique: A Critical Look at "Learning Disabilities."* New York: Pantheon.

Coles, Robert. 1979. *Work, Mobility, and Participation: A Comparative Study of American and Japanese Industry*. Berkeley: University of California Press.

Collins, Patricia Hill. 1989. "The Social Construction of Black Feminist Thought." *Signs*, 14:745–773.

———. 1990. *Black Feminist Thought: Knowledge, Consciousness, and the Politics of Empowerment*. London: HarperCollins Academic.

Collins, Randall. 1971. "A Conflict Theory of Sexual Stratification." *Social Problems*, 19(1):3–21.

———. 1982. *Sociological Insight: An Introduction to Non-Obvious Sociology*. New York: Oxford University Press.

Collins, Sharon M. 1989. "The Marginalization of Black Executives." *Social Problems*, 36:317–331.

Colombo, John Robert. 1996. *The Canadian Global Almanac: A Book of Facts*. Toronto: Macmillan.

Coltrane, Scott. 1989. "Household Labor and the Routine Production of Gender." *Social Problems*, 36:473–490.

Comack, Elizabeth. 1996. "Women and Crime." In R. Linden (ed.), *Criminology: A Canadian Perspective* (3rd ed.). Toronto: Harcourt Brace, 139–175.

———. 1996b. *Women in Trouble*. Halifax: Fernwood Publishing.

———. 2000. "Women and Crime." In R. Linden (ed.), *Criminology: A Canadian Perspective* (4th ed.). Toronto: Harcourt Brace.

Comfort, Alex. 1976. "Age Prejudice in America." *Social Policy*, 7(3):3–8.

Condry, Sandra McConnell, John C. Condry, Jr., and Lee Wolfram Pogatshnik. 1983. "Sex Differences: A Study of the Ear of the Beholder." *Sex Roles*, 9:697–704.

Connelly, Patricia M., and Martha MacDonald. 1990. *Women and the Labour Force*, Cat. no. 98–25. Ottawa: Minister of Supply and Services.

Conrad, Peter, and Joseph W. Schneider. 1992. *Deviance and Medicalization: From Badness to Sickness*. Philadelphia: Temple University Press.

Cook, Alice H., Val R. Lorwin, and Arlene Kaplan Daniels. 1992. *The Most Difficult Revolution: Women and Trade Unions*. Ithaca, N.Y.: Cornell University Press.

Cook, Ramsay. 1995. *Canada, Quebec and the Uses of Nationalism* (2nd ed.). Toronto: McClelland and Stewart.

Cook, Sherburn F. 1973. "The Significance of Disease in the Extinction of the New England Indians." *Human Biology*, 45:485–508.

Cook, Shirley J. 1969. "Canadian

Narcotics Legislation, 1908–1923. A Conflict Model Interpretation." *Canadian Review of Sociology and Anthropology,* 6(1):36–46.

Cookson, Peter W., Jr., and Caroline Hodges Persell. 1985. *Preparing for Power: America's Elite Boarding Schools.* New York: Basic Books.

Cooley, Charles Horton. 1922. *Human Nature and Social Order.* New York: Scribner (orig. pub. 1902).

———. 1962. *Social Organization.* New York: Schocken Books (orig. pub. 1909).

Coontz, Stephanie. 1992. *The Way We Never Were: American Families and the Nostalgia Trap.* New York: Basic Books.

Corelli, R. 1996. "Winter of Discontent." *Maclean's* (February 5):46–48.

Corliss, Richard. 1993. "Who's Bad?" *Time* (September 6):54–56.

Corr, Charles A., Clyde M. Nabe, and Donna M. Corr. 1994. *Death and Dying, Life and Living.* Belmont, Cal.: Brooks/Cole.

Corsaro, William A. 1992. "Interpretive Reproduction in Children's Peer Cultures." *Social Psychology Quarterly,* 55(2):160–177.

Coser, Lewis A. 1956. *The Functions of Social Conflict.* Glencoe, Ill.: Free Press.

Coutts, Jane. 1997. "Medicare Gives Poor a Better Chance." *The Globe and Mail* (August 1).A1.

Craig, Steve. 1992. "Considering Men and the Media." In Steve Craig (ed.), *Men, Masculinity, and the Media.* Newbury Park, Cal.: Sage, 1–7.

Crawford, Susan. 1993. "A Wink Here, a Leer There: It's Costly." *New York Times* (March 28):F17.

Creese, Gillian, and Brenda Beagan. 1999. "Gender at Work: Seeking Solutions for Women's Equality." In Curtis, James, Edward Grabb, and Neil Guppy (eds.), *Social Inequality in Canada: Patterns, Problems, and Policies.* Scarborough: Prentice Hall, 199–221.

Crichton, Anne, Ann Robertson, Christine Gordon, and Wendy Farrant. 1997. *Health Care: A Community Concern?* Calgary: University of Calgary Press.

Crichton, Michael. 1994. *Disclosure.* New York: Knopf.

Cunningham, J., and J.K. Antill. 1995. "Current Trends in Non-Marital Cohabitation: In Search of POSSLQ." In J.T. Wood and S. Duck (eds.), *Under-studied Relationships: Off the Beaten Track.* Thousand Oaks, Cal.: Sage, 148–172.

Curtis, Bruce, D.W. Livingston, and Harry Smaller. 1992. *Stacking the Deck: The Streaming of Working Class Kids in Ontario Schools.* Toronto: Our Schools/Our Selves Education Foundation.

Curtis, James E., and Ronald D. Lambert. 1994. "Culture." In R. Hagedorn (ed.), *Sociology* (5th ed.). Toronto: Holt Rinehart and Winston, 57–86.

Curtis, James E., Edward Grabb, and Neil Guppy. 1999. *Social Inequality in Canada: Patterns, Problems, Policies* (3rd ed.), Scarborough, Ont.: Prentice Hall.

Cyrus, Virginia. 1993. *Experiencing Race, Class, and Gender in the United States.* Mountain View, Cal.: Mayfield.

Dahl, Robert A. 1961. *Who Governs?* New Haven, Conn.: Yale University Press.

Dahrendorf, Ralph. 1959. *Class and Class Conflict in an Industrial Society.* Stanford, Cal.: Stanford University Press.

Daly, Kathleen, and Meda Chesney-Lind. 1988. "Feminism and Criminology." *Justice Quarterly,* 5:497–533.

Daly, Mary. 1973. *Beyond God the Father.* Boston: Beacon.

Darley, John M., and Thomas R. Shultz. 1990. "Moral Rules: Their Content and Acquisition." *Annual Review of Psychology,* 41:525–556.

Darnton, John. 1993. "Western Europe Is Ending Its Welcome to Immigrants." *New York Times* (August 10):A1, A6.

Das Gupta, Tania. 1995. "Families of Native Peoples, Immigrants, and People of Colour." In Nancy Mandell and Ann Duffy (eds.), *Canadian Families: Diversity, Conflict and Change* (2nd ed.). Toronto: Harcourt Brace, 141–174.

Davis, F. James. 1991. *Who Is Black?* University Park: Pennsylvania State University Press.

———. 1992. *Fashion, Culture, and Identity.* Chicago: University of Chicago Press.

Davis, Kingsley. 1940. "Extreme Social Isolation of a Child." *American Journal of Sociology,* 45(4):554–565.

———. 1949. *Human Society.* New York: Macmillan.

Davis, Kingsley, and Judith Blake. 1956. "Social Structure and Fertility: An Analytical Framework." *Economic Development and Cultural Change,* 4(April):211–235.

Davis, Kingsley, and Wilbert Moore. 1945. "Some Principles of Stratification." *American Sociological Review,* 7(April):242–249.

Dean, L.M., F.N. Willis, and J.N. la Rocco. 1976. "Invasion of Personal Space as a Function of Age, Sex and Race." *Psychological Reports,* 38(3) (pt. 1): 959–965.

Deaux, Kay, and Mary E. Kite. 1987. "Thinking About Gender." In Beth B. Hess and Myra Marx Ferree (eds.), *Analyzing Gender: A Handbook of Social Science Research.* Newbury Park, Cal.: Sage, 92–117.

DeKeseredy, Walter S. 1996. "Patterns of Family Violence." In Maureen Baker (ed.), *Families: Changing Trends in Canada.* Whitby, Ont.: McGraw-Hill Ryerson, 249–272.

DeKeseredy, Walter S., and Ronald Hinch. 1991. *Woman Abuse: Sociological Perspectives.* Toronto: Thompson Educational Publishing.

DeKeseredy, Walter S., and Katherine Kelly. 1995. "Sexual Abuse in Canadian University and College Dating Relationships: The Contribution of Male Peer Support." *Journal of Family Violence,* 10(1):41–53.

Derber, Charles. 1983. *The Pursuit of Attention: Power and Individualism in Everyday Life.* New York: Oxford University Press.

Desai, Sabra. 1994. "But You Are Different: In Conversation with a Friend." In Carl E. James and Andrew Shadd (eds.), *Talking About a Difference.* Toronto: Between the Lines, 191–198.

Dollard, John, Neal E. Miller, Leonard W. Doob, O.H. Mowrer, and Robert R. Sears. 1939. *Frustration and Aggression.* New Haven, Conn.: Yale University Press.

Domhoff, G. William. 1970. *The Higher Circles.* New York: Random House.

———. 1978. *The Powers That Be: Processes of Ruling Class Domination in America.* New York: Random House.

———. 1983. *Who Rules America Now? A View for the '80s.* Englewood Cliffs, N.J.: Prentice-Hall.

———. 1990. *The Power Elite and the State: How Policy Is Made in America*. New York: Aldine De Gruyter.

Doob, Anthony, and Julian V. Roberts. 1983. *An Analysis of the Public's View of Sentencing*. Ottawa: Department of Justice Canada.

Doyle Driedger, Sharon. 1998. "Divorce." *Maclean's* (April 20):39–44.

Driedger, Leo. 1982. "Attitudes of Winnipeg University Students Towards Immigrants of European and Non-European Origin." *Prairie Forum*, vol. 2:213–225.

Driedger, Leo, and Richard A. Mezoff. 1981. "Ethnic Prejudice and Discrimination in Winnipeg High Schools." *Canadian Journal of Sociology*, 6(1):1–17.

Driedger, Sharon Doyle. 1997. "Radical Responses." *Maclean's* (July 28):46–47.

Dubowitz, Howard, Maureen Black, Raymond H. Starr, Jr., and Susan Zuravin. 1993. "A Conceptual Definition of Child Neglect." *Criminal Justice and Behavior*, 20(1):8–26.

Duffy, A.D. 1988. "Struggling with Power: Feminist Critiques of Family Inequality." In N. Mandell and A. Duffy (eds.), *Restructuring the Canadian Family: Feminist Perspectives*. Toronto: Butterworths, 111–139.

Duffy, Ann, and Nancy Mandell. 1996. "Poverty in Canada." In Robert J. Brym (ed.), *Society in Question: Sociological Readings for the 21st Century*. Toronto: Harcourt Brace and Company, 96–104.

Duffy, Mike. 1992. "How Life Should Be? TV's Families, Then and Now, Reflect the Ideals of a Society." *Austin American-Statesman* (October 25):5.

Dumas, Jean. 1997. *Report on the Demographic Situation in Canada, 1988*. Cat. no. 91-209. Ottawa: Statistics Canada.

Dunning, Paula. 1997. *Education in Canada: An Overview*. Toronto: Canadian Education Association. Available at: www.acea.ca/trends.htm

Durkheim, Emile. 1933. *Division of Labor in Society*. Trans. George Simpson. New York: Free Press (orig. pub. 1893).

———. 1947. *The Elementary Forms of the Religious Life*. New York: Free Press (orig. pub. 1912).

———. 1956. *Education and Sociology*. Trans. Sherwood D. Fox. Glencoe, Ill.: Free Press.

———. 1964a. *The Rules of Sociological Method*. Trans. Sarah A. Solovay and John H. Mueller. New York: Free Press (orig. pub. 1895).

———. 1964b. *Suicide*. Trans. John A. Sparkling and George Simpson. New York: Free Press (orig. pub. 1897).

Durning, Alan. 1993. "Life on the Brink." In William Dan Perdue (ed.), *Systemic Crisis: Problems in Society, Politics, and World Order*. Fort Worth: Harcourt Brace: 274–282.

Durrant, Joan, and Linda Rose-Krasnor. 1995. *Corporal Punishment: Research and Policy Recommendations*. Ottawa: Family Violence Prevention Division of Health Canada and the Department of Justice.

Dyck, Rand. 1996. *Canadian Politics: Critical Approaches* (2nd ed.). Scarborough, Ont.: Nelson Canada.

Dye, Thomas R., and Harmon Zeigler. 1993. *The Irony of Democracy: An Uncommon Introduction to American Politics* (9th ed.). Belmont, Cal.: Wadsworth.

Dyson, Michael Eric. 1993. "Be Like Mike? Michael Jordan and the Pedagogy of Desire." In Michael Eric Dyson, *Reflecting Black: African-American Cultural Criticism*. Minneapolis: University of Minnesota Press, 64–75.

Ebaugh, Helen Rose Fuchs. 1988. *Becoming an EX: The Process of Role Exit*. Chicago: University of Chicago Press.

Eccles, Jacquelynne S., Janis E. Jacobs, and Rena D. Harold. 1990. "Gender Role Stereotypes, Expectancy Effects, and Parents' Socialization of Gender Difference." *Journal of Social Issues*, 46:183–201.

Economic Council of Canada. 1991. *New Faces in the Crowd: Economic and Social Impacts, Immigration*. Ottawa: Economic Council of Canada.

The Economist. "The Anti-Management Guru." (May 4).

Eder, Donna. 1985. "The Cycle of Popularity: Interpersonal Relations Among Female Adolescents." *Sociology of Education*, 58(July):154–165.

Eder, Donna, and Stephen Parker. 1987. "The Cultural Production and Reproduction of Gender: The Effect of Extracurricular Activities on Peer Group Culture." *Sociology of Education*, 60:200–213.

Edsall, Thomas Byrne, with Mary D. Edsall. 1992. *Chain Reaction: The Impact of Race, Rights, and Taxes on American Politics*. New York: Norton.

Edwards, Harry. 1973. *Sociology of Sport*. Homewood, Ill.: Dorsey.

Ehrenreich, Barbara, and Annette Fuentes. 1981. "Life on the Global Assembly." *Ms.* (January):52–59.

Ehrlich, Paul R. 1971. *The Population Bomb* (2nd ed.). New York: Sierra Club/Ballantine Books.

Ehrlich, Paul R., and Anne H. Ehrlich. 1991. *The Population Explosion*. New York: Touchstone/Simon & Schuster.

Ehrlich, Paul R., Anne H. Ehrlich and Gretchen C. Daily. 1995. *The Stork and the Plow: An Equity Answer to the Human Dilemma*. Connecticut: Yale University Press.

Eichler, Margrit. 1981. "The Inadequacy of the Monolithic Model of the Family." *Canadian Journal of Sociology*, 6: 367–388.

———. 1988a. *Families in Canada Today* (2nd ed.). Toronto: Gage.

———. 1988b. *Nonsexist Research Methods: A Practical Guide*. Boston: Allen & Unwin.

———. 1996. "The Impact of New Reproductive and Genetic Technologies on Families." In Maureen Baker (ed.), *Familes: Changing Trends in Canada*. Toronto: McGraw-Hill Ryerson, 104–108.

———. 1997. *Family Shifts: Families, Policies and Gender Equality*. Don Mills, Ont.: Oxford University Press.

Eitzen, D. Stanley, and Maxine Baca Zinn. 1995. *In Conflict and Order: Understanding Society* (7th ed.). Boston: Allyn & Bacon.

Eldridge, N.S., and L.A. Gilbert. 1990. "Correlates of Relationship Satisfaction in Lesbian Couples." *Psychology of Women Quarterly*, 14:43–62.

Elkin, Frederick, and Gerald Handel. 1989. *The Child and Society: The Process of Socialization* (5th ed.). New York: Random House.

Elliott, D.S., and A. Ageton. 1980. "Reconciling Differences in Estimates of Delinquency." *American Sociological Review*, 45(1):95–110.

Elliott, Jean Leonard, and Augie Fleras. 1990. "Immigration and the Canadian Ethnic Mosaic." In Peter Li (ed.), *Race and Ethnic Relations in Canada*. Toronto: Oxford University Press.

Elliott, Jennifer A. 1994. *An Introduction to Sustainable Development: The Developing World*. London and New York: Routledge.

Elliott, Stuart. 1993. "Advertising: The Homeless Give an Anthem New Meaning for the Holidays." *New York Times* (December 24):C14.

Engels, Friedrich. 1972. *The Origins of the Family, Private Property, and the States*. Ed. Eleanor Burke Leacock. New York: International.

Epstein, Cynthia Fuchs. 1988. *Deceptive Distinctions: Sex, Gender, and the Social Order*. New Haven, Conn.: Yale University Press.

Epstein, Ethan B. 1996. "Workers and the World Economy." *Foreign Affairs*, 75(May/June):16–37.

Epstein, Rachel. 1996. "Lesbian Families." In Marion Lynn (ed.), *Voices: Essays on Canadian Families*. Scarborough, Ont.: Nelson Canada, 109–130.

Erikson, Eric H. 1963. *Childhood and Society*. New York: Norton.

Erikson, Kai T. 1962. "Notes on the Sociology of Deviance." *Social Problems*, 9:307–314.

Eron, Leonard. 1987. "The Development of Aggressive Behavior from the Perspective of a Developing Behaviorism." *American Psychologist*, 42:435–442.

Esbensen, Finn-Aage, and David Huizinga. 1993. "Gangs, Drugs, and Delinquency in a Survey of Urban Youth." *Criminology*, 31(4):565–589.

Essed, Philomena. 1991. *Understanding Everyday Racism*. Newbury Park, Cal.: Sage.

Etzioni, Amitai. 1975. *A Comparative Analysis of Complex Organizations: On Power, Involvement, and Their Correlates* (rev. ed.). New York: Free Press.

Evans, Glen, and Norman L. Farberow. 1988. *The Encyclopedia of Suicide*. New York: Facts on File.

Evans, John, and Alexander Himelfarb. 1996. "Counting Crime." In Rick Linden (ed.), *Criminology: A Canadian Perspective* (3rd ed.). Toronto: Harcourt Brace and Company, 61–94.

Evans, Peter B. and John D. Stephens. 1988. "Development and the World Economy." In Neil J. Smelser (ed.), *Handbook of Sociology*. Newbury Park: Sage, 739–773.

Fagot, Beverly I. 1984. "Teacher and Peer Reactions to Boys' and Girls' Play Styles." *Sex Roles*, 11:691–702.

Fallon, Patricia, Melanie A. Katzman, and Susan C. Wooley. 1994. *Feminist Perspectives on Eating Disorders*. New York: Guilford Press.

Faludi, Susan. 1991. *Backlash: The Undeclared War Against American Women*. New York: Crown.

Farb, Peter. 1973. *Word Play: What Happens When People Talk*. New York: Knopf.

Farley, Christopher John. 1993a. "Today Los Angeles, Tomorrow ... " *Time* (July 26):49.

Farley, John E. 1992. *Sociology* (2nd ed.). Englewood Cliffs, N.J.: Prentice-Hall.

Fawcett, G. 1996. *Living With Disability in Canada: An Economic Portrait*, Cat. no. SDDP-020-10-96-E. Ottawa: Canadian Council on Social Development.

Feagin, Joe R. 1991. "The Continuing Significance of Race: Antiblack Discrimination in Public Places." *American Sociological Review*, 56(February):101–116.

Feagin, Joe R., and Clairece Booher Feagin. 1996. *Racial and Ethnic Relations* (5th ed.). Englewood Cliffs, N.J.: Prentice-Hall.

———. 1997. *Social Problems: A Critical Power-Conflict Perspective* (5th ed.). Englewood Cliffs, N.J.: Prentice-Hall.

Feagin, Joe R., Anthony M. Orum, and Gideon Sjoberg (eds.). 1991. *A Case for the Case Study*. Chapel Hill: University of North Carolina Press.

Feagin, Joe R., and Robert Parker. 1990. *Building American Cities: The Urban Real Estate Game* (2nd ed.). Englewood Cliffs, N.J.: Prentice-Hall.

Feagin, Joe R., and Hernan Vera. 1995. *White Racism: The Basics*. New York: Routledge.

Featherstone, Mike (ed.). 1990. *Global Culture: Nationalism, Globalization and Modernity*. Newbury Park, Cal.: Sage.

Fennell, Tom. 1993. "What's Wrong at School?" *Maclean's* (January 11):28–34.

Fennema, Elizabeth, and Gilah C. Leder (eds.). 1990. *Mathematics and Gender*. New York: Teachers College Press.

Ferrell, Keith. 1997. *Truth, Lies, and the Internet*. CNET (October 9). Available: www.cnet.com/content/Features/Dlife/Truth/index.html

Festinger, Leon, A. Pepitone, and T. Newcomb. 1952. "Some Consequences of Deindividuation in a Group." *Journal of Abnormal and Social Psychology*, 47:382–389.

Findlay, Deborah A., and Leslie J. Miller. 1994. "Through Medical Eyes: The Medicalization of Women's Bodies and Women's Lives." In B. Singh Bolaria and Harley D. Dickinson (eds.), *Health, Illness and Health Care in Canada* (2nd ed.). Toronto: Harcourt Brace, 276–306.

Finn Paradis, Lenora, and Scott B. Cummings. 1986. "The Evolution of Hospice in America Toward Organizational Homogeneity." *Journal of Health and Social Behavior*, 27:370–386.

Firestone, Shulamith. 1970. *The Dialectic of Sex*. New York: Morrow.

Fisher, Luke. 1994. "A Holy War Over Holidays." *Maclean's* (August 12):26.

Fisher, Mary. 1993. "Tap Moral Courage to Mold Opinions." *Masthead*, 45(3):27–30.

Fisher-Thompson, Donna. 1990. "Adult Sex-Typing of Children's Toys." *Sex Roles*, 3:291–303.

Flanagan, William G. 1995. *Urban Sociology: Images and Structure* (2nd ed.). Needham Heights, Mass.: Allyn & Bacon.

Fleras, Augie, and Jean Leonard Elliott. 1992. *Multiculturalism in Canada*. Scarborough, Ont.: Nelson.

———. 1996. *Unequal Relations: An Introduction to Race, Ethnic and Aboriginal Dynamics in Canada* (2nd ed.). Scarborough, Ont.: Prentice Hall.

Florida, Richard, and Martin Kenney. 1991. "Transplanted Organizations: The Transfer of Japanese Industrial Organization to the U.S." *American Sociological Review*, 56(3):381–398.

Ford, Clyde W. 1994. *We Can All Get Along: 50 Steps You Can Take to Help End Racism*. New York: Dell.

Fox, Bonnie. 1989. *From Culture to Power: The Sociology of English Canada*. Toronto: Oxford University Press.

Frank, Andre Gunder. 1969. *Latin America: Underdevelopment or Revolution?* New York: Monthly Review Press.

———. 1981. *Reflections on the World Economic Crisis*. New York: Monthly Review Press.

Frankl, Razelle. 1987. *Televangelism: The Marketing of Popular Religion*. Carbondale: Southern Illinois University Press.

Fraser, Sylvia. 1987. *My Father's House: A Memoir of Incest and Healing*. Toronto: Doubleday.

Freedman, Lisa. 1985. "Wife Assault." In Connie Bugerman and Margie Wolfe (eds.), *No Safe Place: Violence Against Women and Children*. Toronto: Women's Press, 41–59.

Freidson, Eliot. 1970. *Profession of Medicine*. New York: Dodd, Mead.

———. 1986. *Professional Powers*. Chicago: University of Chicago Press.

Frideres, James S. 1993. *Native Peoples in Canada: Contemporary Conflicts* (4th ed.). Scarborough, Ont.: Prentice Hall.

Friedman, Thomas. 1998. "The Global Neighbourhood." *Winnipeg Free Press* (July 20):A10.

Fulton, E. Kaye, and Ian Mather. 1993. "A Forest Fable." *Maclean's* (August 16):20.

Gabor, Thomas. 1994. *Everybody Does It: Crime by the Public*. Toronto: University of Toronto Press.

Gailey, Christine Ward. 1987. "Evolutionary Perspectives on Gender Hierarchy." In Beth B. Hess and Myra Marx Ferree (eds.), *Analyzing Gender: A Handbook of Social Science Research*. Newbury Park, Cal.: Sage, 32–67.

Galloway, Gloria. 1999. "Number of Racist Canadians Falling." *National Post*. Online. Retrieved March 1, 1999.

Gamson, William. 1990. *The Strategy of Social Protest* (2nd ed.). Belmont, Cal.: Wadsworth.

Gans, Herbert. 1982. *The Urban Villagers: Group and Class in the Life of Italian Americans* (updated and expanded ed.; orig. pub. 1962). New York: Free Press.

Garber, Judith A., and Robyne S. Turner. 1995. "Introduction." In Judith A. Garber and Robyne S. Turner (eds.), *Gender in Urban Research*. Thousand Oaks, Cal.: Sage, x–xxvi.

Garcia Coll, Cynthia T. 1990. "A Message to a Future Child About the Danger of Gangs." *Austin American-Statesman* (August 17):A6.

Gardner, Carol Brooks. 1989. "Analyzing Gender in Public Places: Rethinking Goffman's Vision of Everyday Life." *American Sociologist*, 20(Spring):42–56.

Garson, Barbara. 1989. *The Electronic Sweatshop: How Computers Are Transforming the Office of the Future into the Factory of the Past*. New York: Penguin.

Gaskell, Jane S., and Arlene Tigar McLaren (eds.). 1987. *Women and Education: A Canadian Perspective*. Calgary: Detselig.

Gatehouse, Jonathon. 1999. *The National Post* (May 19):A1.

Gaylin, Willard. 1992. *The Male Ego*. New York: Viking/Penguin.

Gecas, Viktor. 1982. "The Self-Concept." In Ralph H. Turner and James F. Short, Jr. (eds.), *Annual Review of Sociology, 1982*. Palo Alto, Cal.: Annual Reviews, 1–33.

Gee, Ellen M. 1994. "What Is Family?" In R. Hagedorn (ed.), *Sociology*. Toronto: Harcourt Brace, 369–398.

———. 1995. "Contemporary Diversities." In Nancy Mandell and Ann Duffy (eds.), *Canadian Families: Diversity, Conflict and Change*. Toronto: Harcourt Brace and Company, 79–109.

Geertz, Clifford. 1966. "Religion as a Cultural System." In Michael Banton (ed.), *Anthropological Approaches to the Study of Religion*. London: Tavistock, 1–46.

Gelles, Richard J., and Murray A. Straus. 1988. *Intimate Violence: The Definitive Study of the Causes and Consequences of Abuse in the American Family*. New York: Simon & Schuster.

Gelman, David. 1993. "The Violence in Our Heads." *Newsweek* (August 2):48.

"General Facts on Sweden." 1988. *Fact Sheets on Sweden*. Stockholm: The Swedish Institute.

Gerber, Linda. 1990. "Multiple Jeopardy: A Socio-Economic Comparison of Men and Women Among the Indian, Métis, and Inuit Peoples of Canada." *Canadian Ethnic Studies*, 22(3):22–34.

Gereffi, Gary. 1994. "The International Economy and Economic Development." In Neil J. Smelser and Richard Swedberg (eds.), *The Handbook of Economic Sociology*. Princeton, NJ: Princeton University Press, 206–233.

Gershenkron, Alexander. 1962. *Economic Backwardness in Historical Perspective*. Cambridge: Harvard University Press.

Gerson, Kathleen. 1993. *No Man's Land: Men's Changing Commitment to Family and Work*. New York: Basic Books.

Gerstel, Naomi, and Harriet Engel Gross. 1995. "Gender and Families in the United States: The Reality of Economic Dependence." In Jo Freeman (ed.), *Women: A Feminist Perspective* (5th ed.). Mountain View, Cal.: Mayfield, 92–127.

Ghosh, Ratna, and Rabindra Kanungo. 1992. *South Asian Canadians: Current Issues in the Politics of Culture*. Montreal: Shastri Indo-Canadian Institute.

Gibbs, Nancy. 1994. "Home Sweet School." *Time* (October 31):62–63.

Gibson, Malcolm D. 1994. "AIDS and the African Press." *Media, Culture, & Society*, 16(2):349–357.

Giddens, Anthony. 1996. *Introduction to Sociology* (2nd ed.). New York: W.W. Norton & Co.

Gilbert, Dennis, and Joseph A. Kahl. 1993. *The American Class Structure: A New Synthesis* (4th ed.). Belmont, Cal.: Wadsworth.

Gilbert, S.N. and B. Orok. 1993. "School Leavers." In *Canadian Social Trends*, Cat no. 11–008E. Ottawa: Statistics Canada, 2–7.

Gilder, George F. 1986. *Men and Marriage*. New York: Pelican.

Gilligan, Carol. 1982. *In a Different Voice: Psychological Theory and Women's Development*. Cambridge, Mass.: Harvard University Press.

Gilligan, Carol, Janie V. Ward, and Jill M. Taylor (eds.). 1988. *Mapping the Moral Domain: A Contribution of Women's Thinking to Psychological Theory and Education*. Cambridge, Mass.: Harvard University Press.

Gillis, A.R. 1995. "Urbanization." In Robert J. Brym (ed.), *New Society: Sociology for the 21st Century*. Toronto: Harcourt Brace and Company, 13.1–13.40.

Gilmore, David D. 1990. *Manhood in the Making: Cultural Concepts of Masculinity*. New Haven, Conn.: Yale University Press.

Gilmour, Glenn A. 1994. *Hate-Motivated Violence* (May). Ottawa: Research Section, Department of Justice.

Glastris, Paul. 1990. "The New Way to Get Rich." *U.S. News & World Report* (May 7):26–36.

Glenn, Norval D. 1991. "The Recent Trend in Marital Success in the United States." *Journal of Marriage and the Family*, 53:261–270.

Goffman, Erving. 1956. "The Nature of Deference and Demeanor." *American Anthropologist*, 58:473–502.

———. 1959. *The Presentation of Self in Everyday Life*. Garden City, N.Y.: Doubleday.

———. 1961. *Asylums: Essays on the Social Situation of Mental Patients and Other Inmates*. Chicago: Aldine.

———. 1963a. *Behavior in Public Places: Notes on the Social Structure of Gatherings*. New York: Free Press.

———. 1963b. *Stigma: Notes on the Management of Spoiled Identity*. Englewood Cliffs, N.J.: Prentice-Hall.

———. 1967. *Interaction Ritual: Essays on Face to Face Behavior*. Garden City, N.Y.: Anchor Books.

Goldberg, Robert A. 1991. *Grassroots Resistance: Social Movements in Twentieth Century America*. Belmont, Cal.: Wadsworth.

Golden, Carla. 1987. "Diversity and Variability in Women's Sexual Identities." In The Boston Lesbian Psychologies Collective (eds.), *Lesbian Psychologies*. Urbana: University of Illinois Press, 18–34.

Gonzales, David. 1994. "Frenzied Passengers, Their Hair and Clothes in Flames, Flee Burning Train." *New York Times* (December 22):A12.

Goode, William J. 1959. "The Theoretical Importance of Love." *American Sociological Review*, 24:39–47.

———. 1960. "A Theory of Role Strain." *American Sociological Review*, 25:483–496.

———. 1976. "Family Disorganization." In Robert K. Merton and Robert Nisbet (eds.), *Contemporary Social Problems* (4th ed.). New York: Harcourt Brace Jovanovich, 511–554.

Goodman, Peter S. 1996. "The High Cost of Sneakers." *Austin American-Statesman* (July 7):F1, F6.

Gordon, David. 1973. "Capitalism, Class, and Crime in America." *Crime and Delinquency*, 19:163–186.

Gordon, Milton. 1964. *Assimilation in American Life: The Role of Race, Religion, and National Origins*. New York: Oxford University Press.

Gordon, Robert M., and Jacquelyne Nelson. 1993. *Census '93: The Report of the 1993 Census of Provincial Correctional Centres in British Columbia*. Victoria: Ministry of the Solicitor General.

Gorey, Kevin, Eric J. Holowaty, Gordon Fehringer, Ethan Laukkanen, Agnes Moskowitz, David J. Webster, and Nancy Richter. 197. "An International Comparison of Cancer Survival: Toronto, Ontario, and Detroit, Michigan, Metropolitan Areas." *American Journal of Public Health*, 87:1156–1163.

Gorlick, Carolyne A. 1995. "Divorce: Options Available, Constraints Forced, Pathways Taken." In Nancy Mandell and Ann Duffy (eds.), *Canadian Families: Diversity, Conflict and Change*. Toronto: Harcourt Brace and Company, 211–234.

Gottdiener, Mark. 1985. *The Social Production of Urban Space*. Austin: University of Texas Press.

Gouldner, Alvin W. 1970. *The Coming Crisis of Western Sociology*. New York: Basic Books.

Gower, David. 1990. "Employment Opportunities of Disabled Canadians." In Craig McKie and Keith Thompson (eds.), *Canadian Social Trends*. Toronto: Thompson Educational Publishers, 218–220.

Grant, Karen. 1993. "Health and Health Care." In Peter S. Li and B. Singh Bolaria (eds.), *Contemporary Sociology: Critical Perspectives*. Toronto: Copp-Clark Pitman, 394–409.

Gray, Paul. 1993. "Camp for Crusaders." *Time* (April 19):40.

Green, Donald E. 1977. *The Politics of Indian Removal: Creek Government and Society in Crisis*. Lincoln: University of Nebraska Press.

Greenberg, Edward S., and Benjamin I. Page. 1993. *The Struggle for Democracy*. New York: HarperCollins.

Greenhouse, Steven. 1994. "State Department Finds Widespread Abuse of World's Women." *New York Times* (February 3):A1.

Greenspan, Edward. 1982. "The Role of the Defence Lawyer in Sentencing." In Craig L. Boydell and Ingrid Connidis (eds.), *The Canadian Criminal Justice System*. Toronto: Holt, Rinehart and Winston, 200–210.

Greenwald, John. 1993. "Japan: How the Miracle Finally Ended." *Time* (December 13):34–35.

Gregg, Allan, and Michael Posner. 1990. *The Big Picture: What Canadians Think About Almost Everything*. Toronto: McFarlane, Walter and Ross.

Griffiths, Curt T., and Simon N. Verdun-Jones. 1994. *Canadian Criminal Justice* (2nd ed.). Toronto: Harcourt Brace and Company.

Gross, Larry. 1993. *Contested Closets: The Politics and Ethics of Outing*. Minneapolis: University of Minnesota Press.

Grover, K.J., C.S. Russell, W.R. Schumm, and L.A. Paff-Bergen. 1985. "Mate Selection Processes and Marital Satisfaction." *Family Relations*, 34(3):383–386.

Gunn, R., and R. Linden. 1994. "The Processing of Child Sexual Abuse Cases." In J. Roberts and R.M. Mohr (eds.), *Confronting Sexual Assault: A Decade of Legal and Social Change*. Toronto: University of Toronto Press.

Guppy, Neil. 1984. "Access to Higher Education in Canada." *Canadian Journal of Higher Education*, 14:79–93.

———. 1995. "Education and Schooling." In L. Tepperman, J.E. Curtis, and R.J. Richardson (eds.), *Sociology*. Toronto: McGraw-Hill Ryerson, 450–478.

Haas, J., and W. Shaffir. 1995. "Giving Medical Students a Cloak of Competence." In L. Tepperman and James Curtis (eds.), *Everyday Life*. Toronto: McGraw-Hill Ryerson.

Hadden, Jeffrey K., and Anson Shupe. 1988. *Televangelism: Power and Politics on God's Frontier*. New York: Holt.

Hadden, Jeffrey K., and Charles K. Swann. 1981. *Prime Time Preachers: The Rising Power of Televangelism*. Reading, Mass.: Addison-Wesley.

Hagan, John, and Bill McCarthy. 1992. "Streetlife and Delinquency." *British Journal of Sociology*, 43(4):533–561.

Hagedorn, Robert. 1983. *Sociology* (2nd ed.). Toronto: Holt Rinehart and Winston.

Halberstadt, Amy G., and Martha B. Saitta. 1987. "Gender, Nonverbal Behavior, and Perceived Dominance: A Test of the Theory." *Journal of Personality and Social Psychology*, 53:257–272.

Hall, Edward. 1966. *The Hidden Dimension*. New York: Anchor/Doubleday.

H.A.L.S. *Health and Activity Limitation Survey*. 1991. Cat. no. 82-554. Ottawa: Statistics Canada.

Hamill, Pete. 1993. "How to Save the Homeless—and Ourselves." *New York* (September 20):34–39.

Hamilton, Allen C., and C. Murray Sinclair. 1991. *Report of the Aboriginal Justice Inquiry of Manitoba*, Winnipeg: Queen's Printer, vol. 1. Winnipeg: Queen's Printer.

Hamilton, Roberta. 1988. "Women, Wives and Mothers." in *Reconstructing the Canadian Family: Feminist Perspectives*. Toronto: Butterworths, 3–26.

Hamper, Ben. 1992. *Rivethead: Tales from the Assembly Line*. New York: Warner Books.

Hansen, Liane. 1995. "Internet and Cyberspace—Farther Away Than You Think." *Sunday National Public Radio* (November 12):Weekend Edition.

Harding, Jim. 1993. "Ecology and Social Change." In Peter S. Li and B. Singh Bolaria (eds.), *Sociology: Critical Perspectives*. Toronto: Copp Clark Pitman, 439–466.

Hardy, Melissa A., and Lawrence E. Hazelrigg. 1993. "The Gender of Poverty in an Aging Population." *Research on Aging*, 15(3):243–278.

Harlow, Harry F., and Margaret Kuenne Harlow. 1962. "Social Deprivation in Monkeys." *Scientific American*, 207(5):137–146.

———. 1977. "Effects of Various Mother-Infant Relationships on Rhesus Monkey Behaviors." In Brian M. Foss (ed.), *Determinants of Infant Behavior*, vol. 4. London: Methuen, 15–36.

Harman, Lesley. 1989. *When a Hostel Becomes a Home: Experiences of Women*. Toronto: Garamond Press.

———. 1995. "Family Poverty and Economic Struggles." In Nancy Mandell and Ann Duffy (eds.), *Canadian Families: Diversity, Conflict and Change*. Toronto: Harcourt Brace and Company, 235–269.

Harman, Robin. 1998. "Digital Third Worlds and Barriers to Internet Access." *Cybersociology*, 3 (August 7). Available: http://hometown.aol.com/Cybersoc/issue3.html

Harris, Anthony R. 1991. "Race, Class, and Crime." In Joseph F. Sheley (ed.), *Criminology: A Contemporary Handbook*. Belmont, Cal.: Wadsworth, 94–119.

Harris, Chauncey D., and Edward L. Ullman. 1945. "The Nature of Cities." *Annals of the Academy of Political and Social Sciences* (November):7–17.

Harris, Debbie. 1991. "Violence Against Women in Universities." *Canadian Women's Studies*, 11(4):35–41.

Harris, Marvin. 1974. *Cows, Pigs, Wars, and Witches*. New York: Random House.

———. 1985. *Good to Eat: Riddles of Food and Culture*. New York: Simon & Schuster.

Hartmann, Heidi. 1976. "Capitalism, Patriarchy, and Job Segregation by Sex." *Signs: Journal of Women in Culture and Society*, 1(Spring):137–169.

———. 1981. "The Unhappy Marriage of Marxism and Feminism." In Lydia Sargent (ed.), *Women and Revolution*. Boston: South End Press.

Hartnagel, Timothy F. 2000. "Correlates of Crime." In R. Linden (ed.), *Criminology: A Canadian Perspective* (4th ed.). Toronto: Harcourt Brace, 95–137.

Hatfield, Elaine. 1995. "What Do Women and Men Want From Love and Sex?" In E.D. Nelson and B.W. Robinson (eds.), *Gender in the 1990s*. Scarborough, Ont.: Nelson Canada, 257–275.

Hatkoff, T.S., and T.E. Laswell. 1979. "Male–Female Similarities and Differences in Conceptualizing Love." In M. Cook and G. Wilson (eds.), *Love and Attraction: An International Conference*. New York: Pergamon Press.

Hauchler, Ingomar, and Paul M. Kennedy (eds.). 1994. *Global Trends: The World Almanac of Development and Peace*. New York: Continuum.

Hauser, Christine. 1996. "Canada Promises Tough Stand Against Child Labour." *Reuters* (January 13).

Hauser, Robert M., and David L. Featherman. 1976. "Equality of Schooling: Trends and Prospects." *Sociology of Education*, 49:99–120.

Haviland, William A. 1993. *Cultural Anthropology* (7th ed.). Orlando, Fla.: Harcourt Brace Jovanovich.

Health Canada. 1994. *Suicide in Canada: Update on the Report of the Task Force on Suicide in Canada*. Ottawa: Health Programs and Services Branch.

———. 1997. *For the Safety of Canadian Children and Youth: From Injury Data to Preventative Measures*, Cat. no. H39-412/1997E. Ottawa: Health Programs and Services Branch.

Health Statistics Division. 2000. *How Healthy Are Canadians?* Ottawa: Statistics Canada.

Heilbroner, Robert. 1985. *The Nature and Logic of Capitalism*. New York: W.W. Norton and Company.

Heinrichs, Daniel. 1996. *Caring for Norah*. Winnipeg: Daniel Heinricks Publishing.

Hendley, Nate. 1998. "Passing the Puck on Child Sex Abuse?" *Eye Magazine* (October 1):10.

Henley, Nancy. 1977. *Body Politics: Power, Sex, and Nonverbal Communication*. Englewood Cliffs, N.J.: Prentice-Hall.

Henry, Frances, and Effie Ginzberg. 1984. *Who Gets Work: A Test of Racial Discrimination in Employment*. Toronto: Urban Alliance on Race Relations and the Social Planning Council of Toronto.

Henry, Frances, Carol Tator, Winston Mattis, and Tim Rees. 1995. *The Colour of Democracy: Racism in Canadian Society*. Toronto: Harcourt Brace and Company.

———. 1996. "The Victimization of Racial Minorities in Canada. In Robert J. Brym (ed.), *Society in Question: Sociological Readings for the 21st Century*. Toronto: Harcourt Brace and Company, 133–144.

Henslin, James M., and Adie Nelson. 1996. *Sociology: A Down to Earth Approach: Canadian Edition*. Scarborough, Ont.: Allyn and Bacon.

Hernandez, Debra Gersh. 1994. "AIDS Fades: The Epidemic Swells But Reporters Complain Editors Have Lost Interest." *Editor & Publisher*, 127(34):16–18.

Heshka, Stanley, and Yona Nelson. 1972. "Interpersonal Speaking Distances as a Function of Age, Sex, and Relationship." *Sociometry*, 35(4):491–498.

Hesse-Biber, Sharlene. 1996. *Am I Thin Enough Yet? The Cult of Thinness and the Commercialization of Identity*. New York: Oxford University Press.

Hettne, Bjorn. 1995. *Development Theory and the Three Worlds* (2nd ed.). Essex: Longman.

Heywood, Leslie. 1998. *Pretty Good for a Girl*. New York: The Free Press.

Hiller, Harry H. 1991. *Canadian Society: A Macro Analysis*. Scarborough, Ont.: Prentice Hall.

———. 1995. "Culture." In L. Tepperman, J.E. Curtis, and R.J. Richardson (eds.), *The Social World* (3rd ed.). Toronto: McGraw-Hill Ryerson, 81–113.

The Hindu. 1998. "The Idea of Human Development." (October 25):25.

Hirsch, Paul M. 1972. "Processing Fads and Fashions: An Organization-Set Analysis of Cultural Industry Systems." *American Journal of Sociology*, 77:639–659.

Hirschi, Travis. 1969. *Causes of Delinquency*. Berkeley: University of California Press.

Hochschild, Arlie Russell, with Ann Machung. 1989. *The Second Shift: Working Parents and the Revolution at Home*. New York: Viking/Penguin.

Hodgson, Doug. 1989. "The Legal and Public Policy Implications of Human Immunodeficiency Virus Antibody Testing in New Zealand." In *Legal Implications of AIDS*. Auckland: Legal Research Foundation, 39–95.

Hodson, Randy, and Robert E. Parker. 1988. "Work in High Technology Settings: A Review of the Empirical Literature." *Research in the Sociology of Work*, 4:1–29.

Hodson, Randy, and Teresa A. Sullivan. 1990. *The Social Organization of Work*. Belmont, Cal.: Wadsworth.

Hoffnung, Michele. 1995. "Motherhood: Contemporary Conflict for Women." In Jo Freeman (ed.), *Women: A Feminist Perspective* (5th ed.). Mountain View, Cal.: Mayfield, 162–181.

Holland, Dorothy C., and Margaret A. Eisenhart. 1981. *Women's Peer Groups and Choice of Career*. Final report for the National Institute of Education. ERIC ED 199 328. Washington, D.C.

———. 1990. *Educated in Romance: Women, Achievement, and College Culture*. Chicago: University of Chicago Press.

Holmes, Mark. 1998. *The Reformation of Canada's Schools: Breaking the Barriers to Parental Choice*. Montreal: McGill–Queen's University Press.

Homer-Dixon, Thomas. 1993. *Environmental Scarcity and Global Security*. Foreign Policy Association, Headline Series, no. 300. Ephrata, Penn.: Science Press.

hooks, bell. 1994. *Outlaw Culture: Resisting Representations*. New York: Routledge.

Hoover, Kenneth R. 1992. *The Elements of Social Scientific Thinking*. New York: St. Martin's Press.

Hoyt, Homer. 1939. *The Structure and Growth of Residential Neighborhoods in American Cities*. Washington, D.C.: Federal Housing Administration.

Huesmann, L. Rowell, Leonard Eron, Eric Dubow, and E. Seebauer. 1987. "Television Viewing Habits in Childhood and Adult Aggression." *Child Development*, 58:357–367.

Hughes, Colin. 1995. "Child Poverty Campaign 2000 and Child Welfare Practice: Working to End Child Poverty in Canada." *Child Welfare*, 74:70–79.

Hughes, Everett C. 1945. "Dilemmas and Contradictions of Status." *American Journal of Sociology*, 50:353–359.

Human Resources Development Canada. 1999. *The HRDC Strategic Policy Web Site*. Available: www.hrdc-drhc.gc.ca/stratpol/home.shtml

Humphrey, Derek. 1993. *Lawful Exit: The Limits of Freedom for Help in Dying*. Junction City, Ore.: Norris Lane Press.

Hunter, Floyd. 1953. *Community Power Structure*. Chapel Hill, N.C.: University of North Carolina Press.

Hurst, Charles E. 1992. *Social Inequality: Forms, Causes, and Consequences*. Boston: Allyn & Bacon.

Huston, Aletha C. 1985. "The Development of Sex Typing: Themes from Recent Research." *Developmental Review*, 5:2–17.

Hyde, Mary, and Carol La Prairie. 1987. "American Police Crime Prevention." Working paper. Ottawa: Solicitor General.

Innis, Harold. 1984. *The Fur Trade in Canada*. Toronto: The University of Toronto Press (orig. pub. 1930).

Institute National d'Etudes Demographiques. 1995. From Julie DaVanzo and David Adamson. 1997. "Russia's Demographic 'Crisis': How Real Is It?" *Rand Issue Paper*, July 1997. Santa Monica: Rand Center for Russian and Eurasian Studies.

Ip, Greg. 1996. "Shareholders vs. Job Holders." *The Globe and Mail* (March 23):B1.

Jackson, Beth E. 1993. "Constructing Adoptive Identities: The Accounts of Adopted Adults." Unpublished masters thesis, University of Manitoba.

Jackson, Kenneth T. 1985. *Crabgrass Frontier: The Suburbanization of the United States*. New York: Oxford University Press.

Jain, H. 1985. *Anti-Discrimination Staffing Policies: Implications of Human Rights Legislation for Employees and Trade Unions*. Ottawa: Secretary of State.

JAMA (The Journal of the American Medical Association). 1994. "Heterosexually Acquired AIDS—United States, 1993" (from the Centers for Disease Control and Prevention). *JAMA*, 271(13):975–977.

James, Carl E. 1995. *Seeing Ourselves: Exploring Race, Ethnicity and Culture*. Toronto: Thompson Educational Publishing.

James, Carl E., and Adrienne Shadd (eds.). 1994. *Talking About Difference: Encounters in Culture, Language and Identity*. Toronto: Between the Lines.

Jankowski, Martin Sanchez. 1991. *Islands in the Street: Gangs and American Urban Society*. Berkeley: University of California Press.

Janofsky, Michael. 1993. "Race and the American Workplace." *New York Times* (June 20):F1, F6.

Jary, David, and Julia Jary. 1991. *The Harper Collins Dictionary of Sociology*. New York: HarperPerennial.

Jenish, D'Ancy. 1992. "Prime Time Violence." *Maclean's*, 105(12–07):40–45.

Jenkinson, Edward B. 1979. *Censors in the Classroom: The Mind Benders*. Carbondale: Southern Illinois University Press.

Johnson, Claudia. 1994. *Stifled Laughter: One Woman's Story About Fighting Censorship*. Golden, Col.: Fulcrum.

Johnson, Dirk. 1994. "Equal Loads, Not Pay for Nonunion Drivers." *New York Times* (April 10):10.

Johnson, Earvin "Magic," with William Novak. 1992. *My Life*. New York: Fawcett Crest.

Johnson, Holly. 1996a. *Dangerous Domains: Violence Against Women in Canada*. Scarborough, Ont.: Nelson Canada.

———. 1996b. "Violence Against Women: A Special Topic Survey." In Robert A. Silverman, James J. Teevan, and Vincent F. Sacco (eds.), *Crime in Canadian Society* (5th ed.). Toronto: Harcourt Brace and Company, 210–221.

Joshi, Vijay. 1993. "In Asia, Millions Lose Childhood to Work." *Austin American-Statesman* (September 6):C30.

Jung, John. 1994. *Under the Influence: Alcohol and Human Behavior*. Pacific Grove, Cal.: Brooks/Cole.

Kaihla, Paul. 1991. "Terror in the Streets." *Maclean's* (March 25):78–21.

———. 1994. "Sex and the Law." *Maclean's* (October 24):30.

Kallen, Evelyn. 1991. "Ethnicity and Human Rights in Canada: Constitutionalizing a Hierarchy of Minority Rights." In Peter Li (ed.), *Race and Ethnic Relations in Canada.* Toronto: Oxford University Press, 77–97.

Kanter, Rosabeth Moss. 1977. *Men and Women of the Corporation*. New York: Basic Books.

———. 1983. *The Change Masters*. New York: Simon and Schuster.

———. 1983. *The Change Masters: Innovation and Entrepreneurship in the American Corporation*. New York: Simon & Schuster.

———. 1985. "All That Is Entrepreneurial Is Not Gold." *Wall Street Journal* (July 22):18.

Kaplan, David E., and Alec Dubro. 1987. *Yakuza: The Explosive Account of Japan's Criminal Underworld*. New York: Collier.

Kappeler, Victor E., Mark Blumberg, and Gary W. Potter. 1996. *The Mythology of Crime and Criminal Justice* (2nd ed.). Prospect Heights: Waveland Press.

Karp, David A., and William C. Yoels. 1976. "The College Classroom: Some Observations on the Meanings of Student Participation." *Sociology and Social Research*, 60:421–439.

Kaspar, Anne S. 1986. "Consciousness Re-evaluated: Interpretive Theory and Feminist Scholarship." *Sociological Inquiry*, 56(1):30–49.

Katz, Michael B. 1989. *The Undeserving Poor: From the War on Poverty to the War on Welfare*. New York: Pantheon.

Kauppinen-Toropainen, Kaisa, and Johanna Lammi. 1993. "Men in Female-Dominated Occupation: A Cross-Cultural Comparison." In Christine L. Williams (ed.), *Doing "Women's Work": Men in Nontraditional Occupations*. Newbury Park, Cal.: Sage, 91–112.

Kayal, Philip M. 1993. *Bearing Witness: Gay Men's Health Crisis and the Politics of AIDS*. Boulder, CO: Westview Press.

Keegan, Victor. 1996. "A World Without Bosses—Or Workers." *The Globe and Mail* (August 24):D4.

Keller, James. 1994. "I Treasure Each Moment." *Parade Magazine* (September 4):4–5.

Kelly, Liz. 1988. *Surviving Sexual Violence*. Minneapolis: University of Minnesota Press.

Kelman, Steven. 1991. "Sweden Sour? Downsizing the 'Third Way.'" *New Republic* (July 29):19–23.

Kemp, Alice Abel. 1994. *Women's Work: Degraded and Devalued*. Englewood Cliffs, N.J.: Prentice-Hall.

Kendall, Diana, and Joe R. Feagin. 1983. "Blatant and Subtle Patterns of Discrimination: Minority Women in Medical Schools." *Journal of Intergroup Relations* (Summer):21–27.

Kendall, Diana, Jane Lothian Murray and Rick Linden. *Sociology in Our Times* (2nd ed.). Scarborough: ITP Nelson.

Kennedy, Paul. 1993. *Preparing for the Twenty-First Century*. New York: Random House.

Kenyon, Kathleen. 1957. *Digging Up Jericho*. London: Ernest Benn.

Kersten, Joachim. 1993. "Street Youths, *Bosozoku*, and *Yakuza:* Subculture Formation and Societal Reactions in Japan." *Crime & Delinquency*, 39(3):277–295.

Kettle, John. 1998. "Women Snap Up Prime Jobs." *The Globe and Mail* (March 19).

Kidron, Michael and Ronald Segal. 1995. *The State of the World Atlas*. New York: Penguin.

Kilbourne, Jean. 1994. "Still Killing Us Softly: Advertising and the Obsession with Thinness." In Patricia Fallon, Melanie A. Katzman, and Susan C. Wooley (eds.), *Feminist Perspectives on Eating Disorders*. New York: Guilford, 395–454.

Killian, Lewis. 1984. "Organization, Rationality, and Spontaneity in the Civil Rights Movement." *American Sociological Review*, 49:770–783.

Kimmel, Michael S., and Michael A. Messner. 1992. *Men's Lives* (2nd ed.). New York: Macmillan.

King, James. 1997. *The Life of Margaret Laurence*. Toronto: Alfred A. Knopf.

Kinsella, Warren. 1994. *Web of Hate: The Far-Right Network in Canada*. Toronto: HarperCollins.

Kirby, Sandra, and Kate McKenna. 1989. *Experience, Research, and Social Change: Methods from the Margins*. Toronto: Garamond.

Kirby, S.L., and A. Robinson. 1998. *Lesbian Struggle for Human Rights in Canada: Report to the Secretary of State on the Status of Women*. Ottawa.

Kirkpatrick, P. 1994. "Triple Jeopardy: Disability, Race and Poverty in America." *Poverty and Race*, 3:1–8.

Kitano, Harry, and Iris Chi. 1986–87. "Asian Americans and Alcohol Use." *Alcohol Health and Research World*, 11:42–46.

Kitano, Harry, Iris Chi, Siyon Rhee, C.K. Law, and James E. Lubben. 1992. "Norms and Alcohol Consumption: Japanese in Japan, Hawaii, and California." *Journal of Studies on Alcohol*, 53(1):33–39.

Kitcher, Brigitte, Andrew Mitchell, Peter Clutterbuck, and Marvyn Novick. 1991. *Unequal Futures: The Legacies of Child Poverty in Canada*. Toronto: Child Poverty Action Group and the Social Planning Council of Metropolitan Toronto.

Klein, Alan M. 1993. *Little Big Men: Bodybuilding Subculture and Gender Construction*. Albany: SUNY Press.

Klockars, Carl B. 1979. "The Contemporary Crises of Marxist Criminology." *Criminology*, 16:477–515.

Kluckhohn, Clyde. 1961. "The Study of Values." In Donald N. Barrett (ed.), *Values in America*. South Bend, Ind.: University of Notre Dame Press, 17–46.

Knox, Paul L., and Peter J. Taylor (eds.). 1995. *World Cities in a World-System*. Cambridge: Cambridge University Press.

Knudsen, Dean D. 1992. *Child Maltreatment: Emerging Perspectives*. Dix Hills, N.Y.: General Hall.

Kohlberg, Lawrence. 1969. "Stage and Sequence: The Cognitive-Developmental Approach to Socialization." In David A. Goslin, *Handbook of Socialization Theory and Research*. Chicago: Rand McNally, 347–480.

———. 1981. "The Philosophy of Moral Development: Moral Stages and the Idea of Justice." *Essays on Moral Development*, vol. 1. San Francisco: Harper & Row.

Kohn, Melvin L., Atsushi Naoi, Carrie Schoenbach, Carmi Schooler, and Kazimierz M. Slomczynski. 1990. "Position in the Class Structure and Psychological Functioning in the

United States, Japan, and Poland." *American Journal of Sociology*, 95:964–1008.

Kolata, Gina. 1993. "Fear of Fatness: Living Large in a Slimfast World." *Austin American-Statesman* (January 3):C1, C6.

Korten, David C. 1996. *When Corporations Rule the World*. West Hartford, Conn.: Kumarian Press.

Kosmin, Barry A., and Seymour P. Lachman. 1993. *One Nation Under God: Religion in Contemporary American Society*. New York: Crown.

Kozol, Jonathan. 1988. *Rachael and Her Children: Homeless Families in America*. New York: Fawcett Columbine.

———. 1991. *Savage Inequalities: Children in America's Schools*. New York: Crown.

Krahn, Harvey J. 1995a. "Non-Standard Work on the Rise." *Perspectives on Labour and Income* (Winter). Ottawa: Statistics Canada, 35–42.

———. 1995b. "Social Stratification." In Robert J. Brym, *New Society for the 21st Century*. Toronto: Harcourt Brace and Company, 2.1–2.31.

Krahn, Harvey J., and Graham S. Lowe. 1998. *Work, Industry, and Canadian Society* (3rd ed.). Scarborough, Ont.: Nelson Canada.

———. 1996. *New Forms of Management and Work in Society in Question: Sociological Readings for the 21st Century*. Toronto: Harcourt Brace and Company.

Krysan, Maria, and Reynolds Farley. 1993. "Racial Stereotypes: Are They Alive and Well? Do They Continue to Influence Race Relations?" Paper presented at the annual meeting of the American Sociological Association, Miami Beach, Florida, August 16.

Kübler-Ross, Elisabeth. 1969. *On Death and Dying*. New York: Macmillan.

Kurtz, Lester. 1995. *Gods in the Global Village: The World's Religions in Sociological Perspective*. Thousand Oaks, Cal.: Sage.

Lalonde, Michelle. 1996. "The Mayor's Vision." *The Montreal Gazette* (May 4).

Lam, Andrew. 1995. "Beyond Clayoquot Sound." *Earth Island Journal* (June):24.

Lamanna, Marianne, and Agnes Riedmann. 1997. *Marriages and Families: Making Choices and Facing Change* (6th ed.). Belmont, Cal.: Wadsworth.

Land, Helen. 1994. "AIDS and Women of Color." *Families in Society: The Journal of Contemporary Human Services*, 75(6):355–362.

Lane, Harlan. 1992. *The Mask of Benevolence: Disabling the Deaf Community*. New York: Vintage Books.

Lanford, Audri, and Jim Lanford. 1998. "Urban Legends: Don't Believe Everything You Read" in *Internet Scambusters*. Available: www.scambusters.org/Scambusters22.html

Langelan, Martha J. 1993. *Back Off! How to Confront and Stop Sexual Harassment and Harassers*. New York: Fireside/Simon & Schuster.

LaNovara, Pina. 1995. "Changes in Family Living." In E.D. Nelson and Augie Fleras (eds.), *Social Problems In Canada*. Scarborough, Ont.: Prentice Hall, 304–317.

Lapchick, Richard E. 1991. *Five Minutes to Midnight: Race and Sport in the 1990s*. Lanham, MD: Madison Books.

LaPierre, Laurier. 1987. ".... a blot on the map..." In Laurier LaPierre (ed.), *If You Love This Country*. Toronto: McClelland and Stewart, 241–243.

Lapsley, Daniel K. 1990. "Continuity and Discontinuity in Adolescent Social Cognitive Development." In Raymond Montemayor, Gerald R. Adams, and Thomas P. Gullota (eds.), *From Childhood to Adolescence: A Transitional Period?* (*Advances in Adolescent Development*, vol. 2). Newbury Park, Cal.: Sage.

Larson, Magali Sarfatti. 1977. *The Rise of Professionalism: A Sociological Analysis*. Berkeley: University of California Press.

Lasch, Christopher. 1977. *Haven in a Heartless World*. New York: Basic Books.

Latouche, Serge. 1992. "Standard of Living." In Wolfgang Sachs (ed.), *The Development Dictionary*. Atlantic Highlands, NJ: Zed Books, 250–263.

Laumann, Edward O., John H. Gagnon, Robert T. Michael, and Stuart Michaels. 1994. *The Social Organization of Sexuality*. Chicago: University of Chicago Press.

Lavigne, Yves. 1987. *Hell's Angels: Taking Care of Business*. Toronto: Ballantine Books.

Law Reform Commission of Canada. 1974. *The Native Offender and the Law*. Ottawa: Information Canada.

Le Bon, Gustave. 1960. *The Crowd: A Study of the Popular Mind*. New York: Viking (orig. pub. 1895).

Lee, Sharon M. 1993. "Racial Classifications in the U.S. Census: 1890–1990." *Ethnic and Racial Studies*, 16 (1):75–94.

Leenaars, Antoon A. 1988. *Suicide Notes: Predictive Clues and Patterns*. New York: Human Sciences Press.

——— (ed.). 1991. *Life Span Perspectives of Suicide: Time-Lines in the Suicide Process*. New York: Plenum Press.

Leenaars, Antoon A., Susan Wenckstern, Isaac Sakinofsky, Ronald J. Dyck, Michael J. Kral, and Roger C. Bland. 1998. *Suicide in Canada*. Toronto: University of Toronto Press.

Lefrançois, Guy R. 1993. *The Lifespan* (4th ed.). Belmont, Cal.: Wadsworth.

Lehmann, Jennifer M. 1994. *Durkheim and Women*. Lincoln: University of Nebraska Press.

Lemert, Edwin M. 1951. *Social Pathology*. New York: McGraw-Hill.

Lengermann, Patricia Madoo, and Ruth A. Wallace. 1985. *Gender in America: Social Control and Social Change*. Englewood Cliffs, N.J.: Prentice-Hall.

Lenski, Gerhard. 1966. *Power and Privilege: A Theory of Social Stratification*. New York: McGraw-Hill.

Lenski, Gerhard, Jean Lenski, and Patrick Nolan. 1991. *Human Societies: An Introduction to Macrosociology* (6th ed.). New York: McGraw-Hill.

Leonard, Margaret A., and Stacy Randell. 1992. "Policy Shifts in the Massachusetts Response to Family Homelessness." In Padraig O'Malley, *Homelessness: New England and Beyond: New England Journal of Public Policy, Special Issue*. (May):483–497.

Lerner, Gerda. 1986. *The Creation of Patriarchy*. New York: Oxford University Press.

Lester, David. 1992. *Why People Kill Themselves: A 1990s Summary of Research Findings of Suicidal Behavior* (3rd ed.). Springfield, Ill.: Thomas.

Lester, David, and Margot Tallmer (eds.). 1993. *Now I Lay Me Down: Suicide in the Elderly*. Philadelphia: Charles Press.

Leventman, Paula Goldman. 1981. *Professionals Out of Work*. New York: Free Press.

Levin, Jack, and Jack McDevitt. 1993. *Hate Crimes: The Rising Tide of Bigotry and Bloodshed*. New York: Plenum Press.

Levin, William C. 1988. "Age Stereotyping: College Student Evaluations." *Research on Aging*, 10(1):134–148.

LeVine, Steve. 1997. "How to Amuse Rich Russians: Odds on the Horses." *New York Times* (October 15):A4.

Levitt, Kari. 1970. *Silent Surrender: the Multinational Corporation in Canada*. Toronto: Macmillan of Canada.

Levy, Janice C., and Eva Y. Deykin. 1989. "Suicidality, Depression, and Substance Abuse in Adolescence." *American Journal of Psychiatry*, 146(11):1462–1468.

Leyton, Elliott. 1979. *The Myth of Delinquency: An Anatomy of Juvenile Nihilism*. Toronto: McClelland and Stewart.

Lewis, Paul. 1996. "World Bank Moves to Cut Poorest Nations Debts." *The New York Times*, (March 16):17–18.

Lewis-Thornton, Rae. 1994. "Facing AIDS." *Essence* (December):64–130.

Li, Peter S. (ed.). 1990. *Race and Ethnic Relations in Canada*. Toronto: Oxford University Press.

Liebow, Elliot. 1993. *Tell Them Who I Am: The Lives of Homeless Women*. New York: Free Press.

Lightle, Juliana, and Betsy Doucet. 1992. *Sexual Harassment in the Workplace: A Guide to Prevention*. Los Altos, Cal.: Crisp Publications.

Linden, Rick. 1994. "Deviance and Crime." In Lorne Tepperman, James E. Curtis, and R.J. Richardson (eds.), *The Social World* (3rd ed.). Whitby, Ont.: McGraw-Hill Ryerson, 188–226.

Linden, Rick, and Cathy Fillmore. 1981. "A Comparative Study of Delinquency Involvement." *Canadian Review of Sociology and Anthropology* 18:343–361.

Linton, Ralph. 1936. *The Study of Man*. New York: Appleton-Century-Crofts.

Lipovenko, Dorothy. 1997. "Geriatric Dementia to Triple by 2031." *The Globe and Mail* (June 11):A6.

Lippa, Richard A. 1994. *Introduction to Social Psychology*. Pacific Grove, Cal.: Brooks/Cole.

Lips, Hilary M. 1989. "Gender-Role Socialization: Lessons in Femininity." In Jo Freeman (ed.), *Women: A Feminist Perspective* (4th ed.). Mountain View, Cal.: Mayfield, 197–216.

———. 1993. *Sex and Gender: An Introduction* (2nd ed.). Mountain View, Cal.: Mayfield.

Livingston, D.W., and Meg Luxton. 1995. "Gender Consciousness at Work: Modification of the Male Breadwinner Norm Among Steelworkers and Their Spouses." In E.D. Nelson and B.W. Robinson (eds.), *Gender in the 1990s*. Scarborough, Ont.: Nelson Canada, 172–200.

Lochhead, Clarence, and Richard Shillington. 1996. *A Statistical Profile of Urban Poverty*. Ottawa: Canadian Council of Social Development.

Lofland, John. 1993. "Collective Behavior: The Elementary Forms." In Russell L. Curtis, Jr., and Benigno E. Aguirre (eds.), *Collective Behavior and Social Movements*. Boston: Allyn & Bacon, 70–75.

London, Kathryn A. 1991. "Advance Data Number 194: Cohabitation, Marriage, Marital Dissolution, and Remarriage: United States 1988." U.S. Department of Health and Human Services: Vital and Health Statistics of the National Center, January 4.

Lorber, Judith. 1994. *Paradoxes of Gender*. New Haven, Conn.: Yale University Press.

Lorch, Donatella. 1993. "With 9% HIV Infection Rate, Uganda Is a Nation of Orphans." *Austin American-Statesman* (March 7):D4.

Loseke, Donileen. 1992. *The Battered Woman and Shelters: The Social Construction of Wife Abuse*. Albany: SUNY Press.

Lott, Bernice. 1994. *Women's Lives: Themes and Variations in Gender Learning* (2nd ed.). Pacific Grove, Cal.: Brooks/Cole.

Lowe, Graham S. 1999. "Labour Markets, Inequality, and the Future of Work." In Curtis, James, Edward Grabb and Neil Guppy (eds.), *Social Inequality in Canada: Patterns, Problems, and Policies*. Scarborough: Prentice Hall, 113–128.

Lummis, C. Douglas. 1992. "Equality." In Wolfgang Sachs (ed.), *The Development Dictionary*. Atlantic Highlands, N.J.: Zed Books, 38–52.

Lupul, M.R. 1988. "Ukrainians: The Fifth Cultural Wheel in Canada." In Ian H. Angus (ed.), *Ethnicity in a Technological Age*. Edmonton: Canadian Institute of Ukrainian Studies, University of Alberta, 177–192.

Luxton, Meg. 1980. More Than a Labour of Love. Toronto: Women's Press.

———. 1995. "Two Hands for the Clock: Changing Patterns of Gendered Division of Labour in the Home." In E.D. Nelson and B.W. Robinson (eds.), *Gender in the 1990s*. Scarborough, Ont.: Nelson Canada, 288–301.

Lynn, Marion (ed.). 1996. *Voices: Essays on Canadian Families*. Scarborough, Ont.: Nelson Canada.

Lynn, Marion, and Eimear O'Neill. 1995. "Families, Power, and Violence." (Eds.) *Canadian Families: Diversity, Conflict and Change*. Toronto: Harcourt Brace and Company, 271–305.

Lyons, John. 1998. "The Way We Live: Central Plains." *Winnipeg Free Press* (June 7):B3.

Maccoby, Eleanor E., and Carol Nagy Jacklin. 1987. "Gender Segregation in Childhood." *Advances in Child Development and Behavior*, 20:239–287.

MacDonald, Kevin, and Ross D. Parke. 1986. "Parental-Child Physical Play: The Effects of Sex and Age of Children and Parents." *Sex Roles*, 15:367–378.

Macionis, J., Juanne Nancarrow Clarke, and Linda M. Gerber. 1994. *Sociology*. Scarborough, Ont.: Prentice Hall.

Mack, Raymond W., and Calvin P. Bradford. 1979. *Transforming America: Patterns of Social Change* (2nd ed.). New York: Random House.

Mackie, Marlene. 1995. "Gender in the Family: Changing Patterns." In Nancy Mandell and Ann Duffy (eds.), *Canadian Families: Diversity, Conflict, and Change* (2nd ed.). Toronto: Harcourt Brace, 17–43.

MacKinnon, Catherine. 1979. *Sexual Harassment of Working Women: A Case of Sex Discrimination*. New Haven, Conn.: Yale University Press.

Maclean's. 1996. "What People Are Saying." (December 2).

Maggio, Rosalie. 1988. *The Non-Sexist Word Finder: A Dictionary of Gender-Free Usage*. Boston: Beacon.

Malinowski, Bronislaw. 1922. *Argonauts of the Western Pacific*. New York: Dutton.

———. 1964. "The Principle of Legitimacy: Parenthood, the Basis of Social Structure." In Rose Laub Coser (ed.), *The Family: Its Structure and*

Functions. New York: St. Martin's Press (orig. pub. 1929).

Man, Guida. 1996. "The Experience of Middle-Class Women in Recent Hong Kong Chinese Immigrant Families in Canada." In Marion Lynn (ed.), *Voices: Essays on Canadian Families*. Toronto: Nelson Canada, 271–300.

Mandell, Nancy, and Julianne Momirov. 1999. "Family Histories." In Nancy Mandell and Ann Duffy (eds.), *Canadian Families: Diversity, Conflict, and Change* (2nd ed.). Toronto: Harcourt Brace, 17–43.

Mann, Patricia S. 1994. *Micro-Politics: Agency in a Postfeminist Era*. Minneapolis: University of Minnesota Press.

Mansfield, Alan, and Barbara McGinn. 1993. "Pumping Irony: The Muscular and the Feminine." In Sue Scott and David Morgan (eds.), *Body Matters: Essays on the Sociology of the Body*. London: Falmer Press, 49–58.

Mao, Y., B.W. Moloughney, R. Semenciw, and H. Morrison. 1992. "Indian Reserve and Registered Indian Mortality in Canada." *Canadian Journal of Public Health*, 83:350–353.

Marble, Michelle. 1995. "Eating Disorders Awareness Week: February 6–12, 1995." *Women's Health Weekly* (February 6):12.

Marchak, Patricia. 1975. *Ideological Perspectives on Canadian Society*. Toronto: McGraw-Hill.

Marcil-Gratton, Nicole. 1993. "Growing Up with a Single Parent, a Transitional Experience? Some Demographic Measurements." In J. Hudson and B. Galaway (eds.), *Single Parent Families with Perspectives on Research and Policy*. Toronto: Thompson Educational Publishing.

Marger, Martin N. 1997. *Race and Ethnic Relations: American and Global Perspectives* (2nd ed.). Belmont, Cal.: Wadsworth.

Markoff, John. 1997. "To Gullible, Net Offers Many Traps." *New York Times* (March 28): A12.

———. 2000. "Napster Debate About More Than Music." *The Globe and Mail* (May 9):B14.

Marks, Peter. 1994. "Buttafuoco Keeps Life in Spotlight." *New York Times* (March 25):A13.

Marriott, Michael. 1993. "Harsh Rap Lyrics Provoke Black Backlash." *New York Times* (August 15):1, 16.

Marsden, Lorna, and Brenda Robertson. 1991. *Children in Poverty: Toward a Better Future*. Ottawa: Standing Committee on Social Affairs, Science, and Technology.

Marshall, Gordon (ed.). 1994. *The Concise Oxford Dictionary of Sociology*. New York: Oxford University Press.

Marshall, Katherine. 1990. "Women in Professional Occupations: Progress in the 1980s." In Craig McKie and Keith Thompson (eds.), *Canadian Social Trends*. Toronto: Thompson Educational Publishers, 109–112.

———. 1995. "Dual Earners: Who's Responsible for Housework?" In E.D. Nelson and B.W. Robinson, *Gender in the 1990s*. Scarborough, Ont.: Nelson Canada, 302–308.

Marshall, Susan E. 1989. "Keep Us on a Pedestal: Women Against Feminism in Twentieth-Century America." In Jo Freedman (ed.), *Women: A Feminist Perspective* (4th ed.). Mountain View, Cal.: Mayfield, 567–580.

———. 1994. "True Women or New Women? Status Maintenance and Antisuffrage Mobilization in the Gilded Age." Paper presented at the American Sociological Association 89th Annual Meeting, Los Angeles.

Martin, Carol L. 1989. "Children's Use of Gender-Related Information in Making Social Judgments." *Developmental Psychology*, 25:80–88.

Martin, James G., and Clyde W. Franklin. 1983. *Minority Group Relations*. Columbus, Ohio: Charles E. Merrill Publishing.

Martin, Nick. 1996. "Aboriginal Speech Dying." Winnipeg Free Press (March 29):A8.

Martin, Teresa Castro, and Larry L. Bumpass. 1989. "Recent Trends in Marital Disruption." *Demography*, 26:37–51.

Martineau, Harriet. 1962. *Society in America* (edited, abridged). Garden City, N.Y.: Doubleday (orig. pub. 1837).

Martinussen, John. 1997. *Society, State and Market: A Guide to Competing Theories of Development*. Halifax: Fernwood Books.

Marx, Karl. 1967. *Capital: A Critique of Political Economy*. Friedrich Engels (ed.). New York: International Publishers (orig. pub. 1867).

Marx, Karl, and Friedrich Engels. 1967. *The Communist Manifesto*. New York: Pantheon (orig. pub. 1848).

Mason Lee, Robert. 1991. *Death and Deliverance*. Toronto: Macfarlane Walter and Ross.

———. 1998. "I'll Be Home for Christmas." *The Globe and Mail* (December 24):A1.

Matas, David. 1995. "A Valuable Survey of Canadian Race Controversies." *The Globe and Mail* (July 8):C8.

Maynard, Rona. 1987. "How Do You Like Your Job?" *The Globe and Mail Report on Business Magazine* (November): 120–25.

McBride, Eve. 1985. "Rules for a Fine Marriage Simply a Matter of Space." *Toronto Star* (June 1).

McCall, George J., and Jerry L. Simmons. 1978. *Identities and Interactions: An Explanation of Human Associations in Everyday Life*. New York: Free Press.

McCarroll, Thomas. 1993. "New Star Over Asia." *Time* (August 9):53.

McCormick, Chris. 1995. *Constructing Danger: The Misrepresentation of Crime in the News*. Halifax: Fernwood Publishing.

McDaniel, Susan, and Erica Roosmalen. 1985. "Sexual Harassment in Canadian Academe: Explorations of Power and Privilege." *Atlantis* 17(1):3–19.

McDaniel, S.A. 1994. *Family and Friends*. Ottawa: Statistics Canada.

———. 1991. "Feminist Scholarship in Sociology: Transformation from Within." *Canadian Journal of Sociology*, 16:303–312.

McDonald, Marci. 1994. "The New Spirituality." *Maclean's* (October 10):44–48.

McEachern, William A. 1994. *Economics: A Contemporary Introduction*. Cincinnati: South-Western.

McElroy, Ann, and Patricia K. Townsend. 1989. *Medical Anthropology in Ecological Perspective* (2nd ed.). Boulder, Col.: Westview Press.

McGuigan, Cathleen. 1993. "Michael's World." *Newsweek* (September 6):34–39.

McGuire, Meredith B. 1992. *Religion: The Social Context* (2nd ed.). Belmont, Cal.: Wadsworth.

———. 1997. *Religion: The Social Context* (4th ed.). Belmont, Cal.: Wadsworth.

McKenzie, Roderick D. 1925. "The Ecological Approach to the Study of the Human Community." In Robert Park, Ernest Burgess, and Roderick D. McKenzie, *The City*. Chicago: University of Chicago Press.

McLanahan, Sara, and Karen Booth. 1991. "Mother-Only Families." In Alan Booth (ed.), *Contemporary Families: Looking Forward, Looking Backward*. Minneapolis: National Council on Family Relations, 405–428.

McPhail, Clark. 1971. "Civil Disorder Participation: A Critical Examination of Recent Research." *American Sociological Review*, 36:1058–1073.

———. 1991. *The Myth of the Maddening Crowd*. New York: Aldine de Gruyter.

McPhail, Clark, and Ronald T. Wohlstein. 1983. "Individual and Collective Behavior within Gatherings, Demonstrations, and Riots." In Ralph H. Turner and James F. Short, Jr. (eds.), *Annual Review of Sociology*, vol. 9. Palo Alto, Cal.: Annual Reviews, 579–600.

McPherson, Barry D. 1998. *Aging as a Social Process: An Introduction to Individual and Population Aging*. Toronto: Harcourt Brace.

McPherson, J. Miller, and Lynn Smith-Lovin. 1982. "Women and Weak Ties: Differences by Sex in the Size of Voluntary Organizations." *American Journal of Sociology*, 87(January):883–904.

———. 1986. "Sex Segregation in Voluntary Associations." *American Sociological Review*, 51(February): 61–79.

McQuaig, Linda. 1993. *The Wealthy Banker's Wife: The Assault on Equality in Canada*. Toronto: Penguin.

McQuillan, Kevin, and Marilyn Belle. 1999. "Who Does What? Gender and the Division of Labour in Canadian Households." In Curtis, James E., Edward Grabb, and Neil Guppy (eds.), *Social Inequality in Canada: Patterns, Problems, and Policies* (3rd ed.). Scarborough, Ont.: Nelson Canada.

McVey, Wayne W., and Warren Kalbach. 1995. *Canadian Population*. Scarborough, Ont.: Nelson Canada.

Mead, George Herbert. 1934. *Mind, Self, and Society*. Chicago: University of Chicago Press.

Medved, Michael. 1992. *Hollywood vs. America: Popular Culture and the War on Traditional Values*. New York: HarperPerennial.

Mental Medicine. 1994. "Wealth, Health, and Status." *Mental Medicine Update*, 3(2):7.

Merton, Robert King. 1938. "Social Structure and Anomie." *American Sociological Review*, 3(6):672–682.

———. 1968. *Social Theory and Social Structure* (enlarged ed.). New York: Free Press.

Miall, Charlene. 1986. "The Stigma of Involuntary Childlessness." *Social Problems*, 33(4):268–282.

Michael, Robert T., John H. Gagnon, Edward O. Laumann, and Gina Kolata. 1994. *Sex in America*. Boston: Little, Brown.

Michelson, William H. 1994. "Cities and Urbanization." In Lorne Tepperman, James Curtis, and R.J. Richardson (eds.), *The Social World* (3rd ed.). Toronto: McGraw-Hill, 672–709.

Mihorean, Steve, and Stan Lipinski. 1992. "International Incarceration Patterns, 1980–1990." *Jusistat*, 12(3). Ottawa: Statistics Canada.

Milgram, Stanley. 1963. "Behavioral Study of Obedience." *Journal of Abnormal and Social Psychology*, 67:371–378.

———. 1974. *Obedience to Authority*. New York: Harper & Row.

Miller, Casey, and Kate Swift. 1993. "Who Is Man?" In Anne Minas, *Gender Basics: Feminist Perspectives on Women and Men*. Belmont, Cal.: Wadsworth, 68–75.

Mills, C. Wright. 1959. *The Power Elite*. Fair Lawn, N.J.: Oxford University Press.

Mintz, Laurie B., and Nancy E. Betz. 1986. "Sex Differences in the Nature, Realism, and Correlates of Body Image." *Sex Roles*, 15:185–195.

Misztal, Barbara A. 1993. "Understanding Political Change in Eastern Europe: A Sociological Perspective." *Sociology*, 27(3):451–471.

Mitchell, Alana. 1999. "Home Schooling Goes AWOL." *The Globe and Mail* (February 2):A1, A7.

Mitchell, Catherine. 1995. "Expert Takes a Swipe at Spanking." *Winnipeg Free Press* (November 23).

Mollison, Andrew. 1992. "Study: Sexual Harassment Crosses Global Boundaries." *Austin American-Statesman* (December 1):A2.

Molotch, Harvey, and Marilyn Lester. 1974. "News as Purposive Behavior: On the Strategic Use of Routine Events, Accidents and Scandals." *American Sociological Review*, 39:101–112.

Moody, Harry R. 1994. *Aging: Concepts and Controversy*. Thousand Oaks, Cal.: Pine Forge Press.

Moog, Carol. 1990. *Are They Selling Her Lips? Advertising and Identity*. New York: Morrow.

Moore, Patricia, with C.P. Conn. 1985. *Disguised*. Waco, Tex.: Word Books.

Moore, Wilbert E. 1968. "Occupational Socialization." In David A. Goslin (ed.), *Handbook on Socialization Theory and Research*. Chicago: Rand McNally, 861–883.

Moorhead, Caroline (ed.). 1992. *Betrayal: A Report on Violence Toward Children in Today's World*. New York: Doubleday.

Moreau, Joanne. 1994. "Employment Equity." In Craig McKie and Keith Thompson (eds.), *Canadian Social Trends*, vol. 2. Toronto: Thompson Educational Publishers, 147–49.

Morgan, S. Philip, Diane N. Lye, and Gretchen A. Condran. 1988. "Sons, Daughters, and the Risk of Marital Disruption." *American Journal of Sociology*, 94(1):110–129.

Murdock, George P. 1945. "The Common Denominator of Cultures." In Ralph Linton (ed.), *The Science of Man in the World Crisis*. New York: Columbia University Press, 123–142.

Murphy, Emily F. 1922. *The Black Candle*. Toronto: Thomas Allan.

Mydans, Seth. 1997. "Its Mood Dark as the Haze, Southeast Asia Aches." *New York Times* (October 26): 3.

Nader, George A. 1976. *Cities of Canada*, vol. 2. *Profiles of Fifteen Metropolitan Centres*. Toronto: Macmillan of Canada.

Naeyaert, Kathleen. 1990. *Living with Sensory Loss: Vision*. Ottawa: National Advisory Council on Aging.

Nancarrow Clarke, Juanne. 1996. *Health, Illness, and Medicine in Canada*. Toronto: Oxford University Press.

National Council of Welfare. 1998. *Poverty Profile 1996*. Ottawa: Minister of Supply and Services Canada.

———. 1999. *Poverty Profile 1997*. Ottawa: Minister of Supply and Services Canada.

———. 1996. *Poverty Profile 1994*. Ottawa: Minister of Supply and Services Canada.

National Council on Crime and Delinquency. 1969. *The Infiltration into Legitimate Business by Organized Crime*. Washington, D.C.: National Council on Crime and Delinquency.

National Safety Council. 1992. *Accident Facts: 1992 Edition*. Chicago: National Safety Council.

Nelson, E.D. and Barrie W. Robinson. 1999. *Gender in Canada*. Scarborough: Prentice Hall.

Nemeth, Mary, Sharon Doyle Driedger, John DeMont, and Adrienne Webb. 1994. "Body Obsession." *Maclean's* (February 5):44.

Nemeth, Mary, Nora Underwood, and John Howse. 1993. "God Is Alive." *Maclean's* (April 12):32–36.

Nessner, Katherine. 1994. "Profile of Canadians with Disabilities." In Craig McKie (ed.), *Canadian Social Trends*. Toronto: Thompson Educational Publishing Company, 121–124.

Nett, Emily M. 1993. *Canadian Families: Past and Present* (2nd ed.). Toronto: Butterworths.

Nettler, Gwynn. 1984. *Explaining Crime* (3rd ed.). Toronto: McGraw-Hill.

Newman, David M. 1995. *Sociology: Exploring the Architecture of Everyday Life*. Thousand Oaks, Cal.: Pine Forge Press.

Ng, Edward. 1994. "Children and Elderly People: Sharing Public Income Resources." In Craig McKie (ed.), *Canadian Social Trends*. Toronto: Thompson Educational Publishing Company, 249–252.

Niebuhr, H. Richard. 1929. *The Social Sources of Denominationalism*. New York: Meridian.

Nielsen, Joyce McCarl. 1990. *Sex and Gender in Society: Perspectives on Stratification* (2nd ed.). Prospects Heights, Ill.: Waveland Press.

Norland, J.A. 1994. *Profile of Canada's Seniors*. Cat. no. 96-312E. Scarborough, Ont.: Statistics Canada and Prentice Hall.

Norris, Mary Jane. 1998. "Canada's Aboriginal Languages." *Canadian Social Trends* (Winter): 8–16.

Northcott, Herbert C. 1982. "The Best Years of Your Life." *Canadian Journal on Aging* 1:72–78.

———. 1994. "Alternative Health Care in Canada." In B. Singh Bolaria and Harley D. Dickinson (eds.), *Health, Illness, and Health Care in Canada*. Toronto: Harcourt Brace, 487–503.

Novak, Mark. 1993. *Aging and Society: A Canadian Perspective*. Scarborough, Ont.: Nelson Canada.

———. 1995. "Successful Aging." In *Aging and Society: A Canadian Reader*. Scarborough, Ont.: Nelson Canada.

———. 1997. *Aging and Society* (3rd ed.). Toronto: ITP Nelson.

Oakes, Jeannie. 1985. *Keeping Track: How High Schools Structure Inequality*. New Haven, Conn.: Yale University Press.

Obbo, Christine. 1993. "HIV Transmission: Men Are the Solution." In Stanlie M. James and Abena P.A. Busia (eds.), *Theorizing Black Feminisms: The Visionary Pragmatism of Black Women*. New York: Routledge, 160–181.

O'Brien, Carol-Anne, and Lorna Weir. 1995. "Lesbians and Gay Men Inside and Outside Families." In Nancy Mandell and Ann Duffy (eds.), *Canadian Families*. Toronto: Harcourt Brace and Company, 111–139.

O'Connell, Helen. 1994. *Women and the Family*. Prepared for the UN-NGO Group on Women and Development. Atlantic Highlands, N.J.: Zed Books.

Odendahl, Teresa. 1990. *Charity Begins at Home: Generosity and Self-Interest Among the Philanthropic Elite*. New York: Basic Books.

Oderkirk, Jillian. 1994. "Parents and Children Living with Low Incomes." In C. McKie (ed.), *Canadian Social Trends*, vol. 2. Toronto: Thompson Educational Publishing Company, 237–242.

Oderkirk, Jillian, and Clarence Lochhead. 1995. "Lone Parenthood: Gender Differences." In E.D. Nelson and B.W. Robinson (eds.), *Gender in the 1990s*. Scarborough, Ont.: Nelson Canada, 397–405.

Ogburn, William F. 1966. *Social Change with Respect to Culture and Original Nature*. New York: Dell (orig. pub. 1922).

Oliver, Michael. 1990. *The Politics of Disablement: A Sociological Approach*. New York: St. Martin's Press.

Orbach, Susie. 1978. *Fat Is a Feminist Issue*. New York: Paddington.

O'Reilly-Fleming, Thomas. 1993. *Down and Out in Canada: Homeless Canadians*. Toronto: Canadian Scholar's Press.

Ortner, Sherry B., and Harriet Whitehead (eds.). 1981. *Sexual Meanings: The Cultural Construction of Gender and Sexuality*. Cambridge, Mass.: Cambridge University Press.

Osterman, Cynthia. 1995. "Rising Child Poverty in World Worries Health Experts." *Reuters* (May 30):2.

O'Sullivan, Chris. 1993. "Fraternities and the Rape Culture." In Emile Buchwald et al. (eds.), *Transforming a Rape Culture*. Minneapolis: Milkweed Ltd.

Overall, Christine. 1991. "Reproductive Technology and the Future of the Family." In Jean E. Veevers (ed.), *Continuity and Change in Marriage and the Family*. Toronto: Holt, Rinehart and Winston, 466–477.

Owen, Bruce. 1996. "Harrassment Ends in Firings." In *Winnipeg Free Press* (March 23).

Page, Charles H. 1946. "Bureaucracy's Other Face." *Social Forces*, 25 (October):89–94.

Palen, J. John. 1995. *The Suburbs*. New York: McGraw-Hill.

Pammett, Jon H. 1993. "Tracking the Votes." In Alan Frizell et al. (eds.), *The Canadian General Election of 1993*. Ottawa: Carleton University Press.

Panitch, Leo, and Donald Swartz. 1993. *Assault on Trade Union Freedoms* (2nd ed.). Toronto: Garamond.

Parenti, Michael. 1994. *America Besieged*. San Francisco: City Lights.

Park, Robert E. 1915. "The City: Suggestions for the Investigation of Human Behavior in the City." *American Journal of Sociology*, 20:577–612.

———. 1928. "Human Migration and the Marginal Man." *American Journal of Sociology*, 33.

———. 1936. "Human Ecology." *American Journal of Sociology*, 42:1–15.

Park, Robert E., and Ernest W. Burgess. 1921. *Human Ecology*. Chicago: University of Chicago Press.

Parker, Robert Nash. 1995. "Violent Crime." In Joseph F. Sheley, *Criminology: A Contemporary Handbook* (2nd ed.). Belmont, Cal.: Wadsworth, 169–185.

Parkinson, C. Northcote. 1957. *Parkinson's*

Law and Other Studies in Administration. New York: Ballantine Books.

Parkinson, Gary, and Robert Drislane. 1996. *Exploring Sociology*. Toronto: Harcourt Brace.

Parrish, Dee Anna. 1990. *Abused: A Guide to Recovery for Adult Survivors of Emotional/Physical Child Abuse*. Barrytown, N.Y.: Station Hill Press.

Parsons, Talcott. 1951. *The Social System*. Glencoe, Ill.: Free Press.

———. 1955. "The American Family: Its Relations to Personality and to the Social Structure." In Talcott Parsons and Robert F. Bales (eds.), *Family, Socialization and Interaction Process*. Glencoe, Ill.: Free Press, 3–33.

Passell, Peter. 1994. "'Bell Curve' Critics Say Early I.Q. Isn't Destiny." *New York Times* (November 9):B10.

Patros, Philip G., and Tonia K. Shamoo. 1989. *Depression and Suicide in Children and Adolescents: Prevention, Intervention, and Postvention*. Boston: Allyn & Bacon.

Patterson, Christopher, and Elizabeth Podnieks. 1995. "A Guide to the Diagnosis and Treatment of Elder Abuse." In Mark Novak (ed.), *Aging and Society: A Canadian Reader*. Scarborough, Ont.: Nelson Canada.

Patterson, Naomi. 1998. "Old Dogs Must Learn New Tricks in the Modern Era." *SeniorNet* (Winter/Spring). Available: www/seniornet.org/newsline/olddogs.ht ml

Philbeck, Joyce. "Seniors and the Internet." *Cybersociology* (2). Available: www.socio.demon.co/uk/magazine/ magazine.html

PBS. 1992. "Sex, Power, and the Workplace."

Pearce, Diana. 1978. "The Feminization of Poverty: Women, Work, and Welfare." *Urban and Social Change Review*, 11(1/2):28–36.

Pearson, Judy C. 1985. *Gender and Communication*. Dubuque, Iowa: Brown.

Pelzer, Dave. 1995. *A Child Called "It"*. Deerfield Beach, Fla.: Health Communications.

Peplau, Letita Anne. 1991. "Lesbian and Gay Relationships." In John C. Gonsiorek and James D. Weinrich (eds.), *Homosexuality: Research Implications for Public Policy*. Newbury Park, Cal.: Sage.

Perrow, Charles. 1986. *Complex Organizations: A Critical Essay* (3rd ed.). New York: Random House.

Perry, David C., and Alfred J. Watkins (eds.). 1977. *The Rise of the Sunbelt Cities*. Beverly Hills, Cal.: Sage.

Perry-Jenkins, Maureen, and Ann C. Crouter. 1990. "Men's Provider Role Attitudes: Implications for Household Work and Marital Satisfaction." *Journal of Family Issues*, 11:136–156.

Peter, Karl A. 1987. *The Dynamics of Hutterite Society*. Edmonton: University of Alberta Press.

Peter, Laurence J., and Raymond Hull. 1969. *The Peter Principle: Why Things Always Go Wrong*. New York: Morrow.

Peters, John F. 1985. "Adolescents as Socialization Agents to Parents." *Adolescence*, 20 (Winter):921–933.

Peters, Linda, and Patricia Fallon. 1994. "The Journey of Recovery: Dimensions of Change." In Patricia Fallon, Melanie A. Katzman, and Susan C. Wooley (eds.), *Feminist Perspectives on Eating Disorders*. New York: Guilford Press, 339–354.

Petersen, John L. 1994. *The Road to 2015: Profiles of the Future*. Corte Madera, Cal.: Waite Group Press.

Pheasant, Valerie Bedassigae. 1994. "My Mother Used to Dance." In Carl E. James and Adrienne Shadd (eds.), *Talking about Difference*. Toronto: Between the Lines, 35–40.

Philips, Bruce. 1998. *Privacy Commissioner, 1997–98 Annual Report*. Ottawa: The Privacy Commissioner of Canada.

Philp, Margaret. 1997. "Poverty Crusade Gets Personal." *The Globe and Mail* (September 20):A1.

Piaget, Jean. 1954. *The Construction of Reality in the Child*. Trans. Margaret Cook. New York: Basic Books.

Picard, André. 1996. "Québécois Voices." *The Globe and Mail* (June 13):A21.

Pietilä, Hilkka and Jeanne Vickers. 1994. *Making Women Matter: The Role of the United Nations*. Atlantic Highlands, NJ: Zed Books.

Pillard, Richard C., and James D. Weinrich. 1986. "Evidence of Familial Nature of Male Homosexuality." *Archives of General Psychiatry*, 43(8):800–812.

Pinderhughes, Dianne M. 1986. "Political Choices: A Realignment in Partisanship Among Black Voters?" In James D. Williams (ed.), *The State of Black America 1986*. New York: National Urban League, 85–113.

Pineo, Peter C., and John Porter. 1979. "Occupational Prestige in Canada." In James E. Curtis and William G. Scott (eds.), *Social Stratification in Canada* (2nd ed.), 205–220.

Piot, Peter. 1997. "Why It Is Folly to Feel at All Complacent about AIDS." *The Globe and Mail* (July 24):A15.

Podnieks, Elizabeth. 1989. *A National Survey on Abuse of the Elderly in Canada: Preliminary Findings*. Toronto: Ryerson Polytechnical Institute.

Polakow, Valerie. 1993. *Lives on the Edge: Single Mothers and Their Children in the Other America*. Chicago: University of Chicago Press.

Pomice, Eva. 1990. "Madison Avenue's Blind Spot." In Karin Swisher (ed.), *The Elderly: Opposing Viewpoints*. San Diego: Greenhaven Press, 42–45.

Ponting, J.R. 1997. *First Nations in Canada: Perspectives on Opportunity, Empowerment and Self-Determination*. Toronto: McGraw-Hill Ryerson.

Pope, Carl E. 1995. "Juvenile Justice in the Next Millennium." In John Klofas and Stan Stojkovic (eds.), *Crime and Justice in the Year 2010*. Belmont, Cal.: Wadsworth, 267–280.

Popoff, Wilfred. 1996. "One Day You're Family; the Next Day You're Fired." *The Globe and Mail* (March 14):A22.

Porter, John. 1965. *The Vertical Mosaic*. Toronto: University of Toronto Press.

Porter, J., M. Porter, and B. Blishen. 1982. *Stations and Callings: Making It Through the School System*. Toronto: Methuen.

Posterski, Donald C. and Irwin Barker. 1993. *Where's a Good Church?* Winfield, B.C.: Wood Lake Books.

Presthus, Robert. 1978. *The Organizational Society*. New York: St. Martin's Press.

Puette, William J. 1992. *Through Jaundiced Eyes: How the Media View Organized Labor*. Ithaca, N.Y.: ILR Press/Cornell University.

Queen, Stuart A. and David B. Carpenter. 1953. *The American City*. New York: McGraw-Hill.

Quinney, Richard. 1974. *Critique of the Legal Order*. Boston: Little, Brown.

———. 1979. *Class, State, and Crime*. New York: McKay.

———. 1980. *Class, State, and Crime* (2nd ed.). New York: Longman.

Rabinowitz, Fredric E., and Sam V. Cochran. 1994. *Man Alive: A Primer of Men's Issues*. Pacific Grove, Cal.: Brooks/Cole.

Raboy, Marc. 1992. "Canadian Broadcasting, Canadian Nationhood: Two Concepts, Two Solitudes, and Great Expectations." In H. Holmes and D. Taras (eds.), *Seeing Ourselves: Media Power and Policy in Canada*. Toronto: Harcourt Brace Jovanovich, 156–187.

Radcliffe-Brown, A.R. 1952. *Structure and Function in Primitive Society*. New York: Free Press.

Raffalli, Mary. 1994. "Why So Few Women Physicists?" *New York Times Supplement* (January):Sect. 4A, 26–28.

Ramu, G.N. 1984. "Family Background and Perceived Marital Happiness: A Comparison of Voluntary Childless Couples and Parents." *Canadian Journal of Sociology*, 9:47–67.

———. 1993. *Marriage and the Family in Canada Today* (2nd ed.). Scarborough, Ont.: Prentice Hall.

Rankin, Robert P., and Jerry S. Maneker. 1985. "The Duration of Marriage in a Divorcing Population: The Impact of Children." *Journal of Marriage and the Family*, 47 (February):43–52.

Reckless, Walter C. 1967. *The Crime Problem*. New York: Meredith.

Reich, Robert. 1993. "Why the Rich Are Getting Richer and the Poor Poorer." In Paul J. Baker, Louis E. Anderson, and Dean S. Dorn (eds.), *Social Problems: A Critical Thinking Approach* (2nd ed.). Belmont, Cal.: Wadsworth, 145–149. Adapted from *The New Republic*, May 1, 1989.

Reiman, Jeffrey H. 1979. *The Rich Get Richer and the Poor Get Prison*. New York: Wiley.

Reinharz, Shulamit. 1992. *Feminist Methods in Social Research*. New York: Oxford University Press.

Reinisch, June. 1990. *The Kinsey Institute New Report on Sex: What You Must Know to Be Sexually Literate*. New York: St. Martin's Press.

Reissman, C.K. 1983. "Women and Medicalization: A New Perspective." *Social Policy*, 14:3–18.

Renzetti, Claire M., and Daniel J. Curran. 1992. *Women, Men, and Society*. Boston: Allyn & Bacon.

———. 1995. *Women, Men, and Society* (3rd ed.). Boston: Allyn & Bacon.

Reskin, Barbara F., and Irene Padavic. 1994. *Women and Men at Work*. Thousand Oaks, Cal.: Pine Forge Press.

Richardson, C. James. 1996. "Divorce and Remarriage in Families." In Maureen Baker (ed.), *Changing Trends in Canada*. Toronto: McGraw-Hill Ryerson, 215–248.

Richardson, John G., and Carl H. Simpson. 1982. "Children, Gender and Social Structure: An Analysis of the Content of Letters to Santa Claus." *Child Development*, 53:429–436.

Richardson, Laurel. 1993. "Inequalities of Power, Property, and Prestige." In Virginia Cyrus (ed.), *Experiencing Race, Class, and Gender in the United States*. Mountain View, Cal.: Mayfield, 229–236.

Richardson, R. Jack. 1990. Economic Concentration and Social Power in Contemporary Canada." In J. Curtis and L. Tepperman (eds.), *Images of Canada: The Sociological Tradition*, 341–351.

Richer, Stephen. 1988. "Equality to Benefit from Schooling: The Issue of Educational Opportunity." In D. Forcese and S. Richer (eds.), *Social Issues: Sociological Views of Canada*. Toronto: Prentice Hall, 262–286.

Richer, Stephen, and Lorne Weir. 1995. *Beyond Political Correctness: Toward the Inclusive University*. Toronto: University of Toronto Press.

Richler, Mordecai. 1991. "A Reporter at Large." *The New Yorker* (September 23):40–92.

———. 1992. *Oh Canada! Oh Quebec!* Toronto and New York: Knopf, 1.

Rifkin, Jeremy. 1995. *The End of Work*. New York: G.P. Putnam's Sons.

Riggs, Robert O., Patricia H. Murrell, and JoAnne C. Cutting. 1993. *Sexual Harassment in Higher Education: From Conflict to Community*. ASHE-ERIC Higher Education Reports, Washington, D.C.: George Washington University, 93–2.

Risman, Barbara J. 1987. "Intimate Relationships from a Microstructural Perspective: Men Who Mother." *Gender & Society*, 1:6–32.

Ritzer, George. 1993. *The McDonaldization of Society: An Investigation into the Changing Character of Contemporary Social Life*. Thousand Oaks, Cal.: Pine Forge Press.

Roberts, Julian. 1995. *Disproportionate Harm: Hate Crime in Canada*. Ottawa: Department of Justice.

Roberts, Keith A. 1995. *Religion in Sociological Perspective*. Belmont, Cal.: Wadsworth.

Roberts, Lance, and Rodney Clifton. 1990. "Multiculturalism in Canada: A Sociological Perspective." In Peter Li (ed.), *Race and Ethnic Relations in Canada*. Toronto: Oxford University Press, 120–147.

Robertson, Ian. 1977. *Sociology*. New York: Worth Publishers.

———. 1989. *Sociology: A Brief Introduction*. New York: Worth.

Robertson, Roland. 1992. *Globalization: Social Theory and Global Culture*. Newbury Park, Cal.: Sage.

Robinson, Ann, and Sandra Kirby. 1997. "Lesbian Struggles for Human Rights in Canada." Report to the Secretary of State on the Status of Women, Research Department, March 31, 1997.

Robinson, David, Frank J. Porporino, William A. Millson, Shelley Trevethan, and Barry McKillop. 1998. "A One-Day Snapshot of Inmates in Canada's Adult Correctional Facilities." *Juristat*, 18(8). Ottawa: Statistics Canada.

Rodgers, Kain, and Rebecca Kong. 1996. "Crimes Against Women and Children in the Family." In Leslie Kennedy and Vincent Sacco (eds.), *Crime Counts: A Criminal Event Analysis*. Scarborough, Ont.: Nelson Canada, 115–132.

Rogers, Harrell R. 1986. *Poor Women, Poor Families: The Economic Plight of America's Female-Headed Households*. Armonk, N.Y.: Sharpe.

Rollins, Judith. 1985. *Between Women: Domestics and Their Employers*. Philadelphia: Temple University Press.

Romaniuc, Anatole. 1994. "Fertility in Canada: Retrospective and Prospective." In Frank Trovato and Carl F. Grindstaff (eds.), *Perspectives on Canada's Population*. Toronto: Oxford University Press, 214–229.

Roof, Wade Clark. 1993. *A Generation of Seekers: The Spiritual Journeys of the Baby Boom Generation*. San Francisco: HarperSanFrancisco.

Ropers, Richard H. 1991. *Persistent Poverty: The American Dream Turned Nightmare*. New York: Plenum.

Rosenburg, Michael. 1995. "Ethnic and Race Relations." In L. Tepperman, J.E.

Curtis, and R.J. Richardson (eds.), *Sociology*. Toronto: McGraw-Hill Ryerson, 302–344.

Rosenhan, D.L. 1973. "On Being Sane in Insane Places." *Science*, 179(January): 250–58.

Rosenthal, Naomi, Meryl Fingrutd, Michele Ethier, Roberta Karant, and David McDonald. 1985. "Social Movements and Network Analysis: A Case Study of Nineteenth-Century Women's Reform in New York State." *American Journal of Sociology*, 90:1022–1054.

Rosenthal, Robert. 1969. "Empirical versus Degreed Validation of Clocks and Tests." *American Educational Research Journal*, 6 (November):689–691.

Rosnow, Ralph L., and Gary Alan Fine. 1976. *Rumor and Gossip: The Social Psychology of Hearsay*. New York: Elsevier.

Ross, David. 1998. *Child Poverty in Canada: Recasting the Issue*. Ottawa: Canadian Council on Social Development.

Ross, David P., E. Richard Shillington, and Clarence Lochhead. 1994. *The Canadian Fact Book on Poverty*. Ottawa: Canadian Council on Social Development.

———. 1997. "Does Family Income Affect the Healthy Development of Children?" *Perception* (21)1:1–5. Ottawa: Canadian Council on Social Development.

Ross, Rupert. 1996. *Returning to the Teachings: Exploring Aboriginal Justice*. Toronto: Penguin Books.

Rossi, Alice S. 1992. "Transition to Parenthood." In Arlene Skolnick and Jerome Skolnick (eds.), *Family in Transition*. New York: HarperCollins, 453–463.

Rossi, Peter H. 1989. *Down and Out in America: The Origins of Homelessness*. Chicago: University of Chicago Press.

Rossides, Daniel W. 1986. *The American Class System: An Introduction to Social Stratification*. Boston: Houghton Mifflin.

Rostow, Walt W. 1971. *The Stages of Economic Growth: A Non-Communist Manifesto* (2nd ed.). Cambridge: Cambridge University Press (orig. pub. 1960).

———. 1978. *The World Economy: History and Prospect*. Austin, Tex.: University of Texas Press.

Roth, Nicki. 1993. *Integrating the Shattered Self: Psychotherapy with Adult Incest Survivors*. Northvale, N.J.: Jason Aronson.

Rothman, Robert A. 1993. *Inequality and Stratification: Class, Color, and Gender* (2nd ed.). Englewood Cliffs, N.J.: Prentice-Hall.

Rowe, Patricia. 1992. "Child Abuse Telecast Floods National Hotline." *Children Today*, 21(2):11.

Rowley, Storer H. 1994. "Conference Condemns Mutilation of Female Genitals." *Austin American-Statesman* (September 11):A9.

Royal Commission on Aboriginal Peoples. 1995. *Choosing Life: Special Report on Suicide Among Aboriginal Peoples*. Ottawa: Canada Communications Group Publishing.

Rubin, Lillian B. 1976. *Worlds of Pain: Life in the Working-Class Family*. New York: Basic Books.

Russell, Diana E.H. 1986. *The Secret Trauma: Incest in the Lives of Girls and Women*. New York: Basic Books.

Rutherford, Leanna. 1998. "An Anorexic's Recovery." *Canadian Living* (October):107–110.

Rutstein, Nathan. 1993. *Healing in America*. Springfield, Mass.: Whitcomb.

Sadker, David, and Myra Sadker. 1985. "Is the OK Classroom OK?" *Phi Delta Kappan*, 55:358–367.

———. 1986. "Sexism in the Classroom: From Grade School to Graduate School." *Phi Delta Kappan*, 68:512–515.

Sadker, Myra, and David Sadker. 1984. *Year 3: Final Report, Promoting Effectiveness in Classroom Instruction*. Washington, D.C.: National Institute of Education.

———. 1994. *Failing at Fairness: How America's Schools Cheat Girls*. New York: Scribner.

Safilios-Rothschild, Constantina. 1969. "Family Sociology or Wives' Family Sociology? A Cross-Cultural Examination of Decision-Making." *Journal of Marriage and the Family*, 31(2):290–301.

Samovar, Larry A., and Richard E. Porter. 1991a. *Communication Between Cultures*. Belmont, Cal.: Wadsworth.

———. 1991b. *Intercultural Communication: A Reader* (6th ed.). Belmont, Cal.: Wadsworth.

Sanger, David E. 1994. "Cutting Itself Down to Size: Japan's Inferiority Complex." *New York Times* (February 6):E5.

Sass, Robert. 1986. "Workplace Health and Safety: Report from Canada." *International Journal of Health Services*, 16:565–582.

Satzewich, Vic. 1991. "Social Stratification: Class and Racial Inequalities." In B. Singh Bolaria (ed.), *Issues and Contradictions in Canadian Society*. Toronto: Harcourt Brace, 91–107.

Saunders, Eileen, 1999. "Theoretical Approaches to the Study of Women." In Curtis, James, Edward Grabb, and Neil Guppy (eds.), *Social Inequality in Canada: Patterns, Problems and Policies*. Scarborough: Prentice Hall, 168–185.

Schafer, A. 1998. *Down and Out in Winnipeg and Toronto: The Ethics of Legislating Against Panhandling*. Ottawa: Caledon Institute of Social Policy.

Schaefer, Richard T. 1993. *Racial and Ethnic Groups*. New York: HarperCollins.

———. 1995. *Race and Ethnicity in the United States*. New York: HarperCollins.

Schellenberg, G., and David P. Ross. 1997. *The Changing Nature of Part-Time Work*. Ottawa: The Canadian Council on Social Development.

Schemo, Diana Jean. 1996. "Indians in Brazil, Estranged from Their Land, Suffer an Epidemic of Suicide." *New York Times* (August 25):7.

Schmetzer, Uli. 1992. "Across Asia, Slave Trade Prospers—Often for Child Labor of Sex." *Austin American-Statesman* (February 22):J1, J7.

Schmidt, William E. 1993. "A Churchill Draws Fire with Remark on Race." *New York Times* (June 1):A2.

Schur, Edwin M. 1965. *Crimes Without Victims: Deviant Behavior and Public Policy*. Englewood Cliffs, N.J.: Prentice-Hall.

———. 1983. *Labeling Women Deviant: Gender, Stigma, and Social Control*. Philadelphia: Temple University Press.

Scott, Joan W. 1986. "Gender: A Useful Category of Historical Analysis." *American Historical Review*, 91(December):1053–1075.

Searles, Neil. 1995. *Physician Assisted Suicide in Manitoba*. Manitoba Association of Rights and Liberties.

Seid, Roberta P. 1994. "Too 'Close to the Bone': The Historical Context for Women's Obsession with Slenderness." In Patricia Fallon, Melanie A. Katzman, and Susan C. Wooley (eds.), *Feminist Perspectives on Eating Disorders*. New York: Guilford Press, 3–16.

Sengoku, Tamotsu. 1985. *Willing Workers: The Work Ethic in Japan, England, and the United States*. Westport, Conn.: Quorum Books.

Shadd, Adrienne. 1991. "Institutionalized Racism and Canadian History: Notes of a Black Canadian." In Ormond McKague (ed.), *Racism in Canada*. Saskatoon: Fifth House, 1–5.

———. 1994. "Where Are You Really From?" In Carl E. James and Adrienne Shadd (eds.), *Talking About Difference*. Toronto: Between the Lines Press, 9–15.

Shakin, Madeline, Debra Shakin, and Sarah Hall Sternglanz. 1985. "Infant Clothing: Sex Labeling for Strangers." *Sex Roles*, 12:955–964.

Shapiro, Joseph P. 1993. *No Pity: People with Disabilities Forging a New Civil Rights Movement*. Toronto: Time Books/Random House.

Shapiro, Susan P. 1990. "Collaring the Crime, Not the Criminal: Reconsidering the Concept of White-Collar Crime." *American Sociological Review*, 55:346–365.

Sharman, Monica, and James Tulloch. 1997. "Commentary: Unfinished Business." In *Progress of Nations 1996*. New York: United Nations.

Sheley, Joseph F. 1991. *Criminology: A Contemporary Handbook*. Belmont, Cal.: Wadsworth.

Shenon, Philip. 1994. "China's Mania for Baby Boys Creates Surplus of Bachelors." *New York Times* (August 16):A1, A4.

Sherman, Suzanne (ed.). 1992. "Frances Fuchs and Gayle Remick." In *Lesbian and Gay Marriage: Private Commitments, Public Ceremonies*. Philadelphia: Temple University Press, 189–201.

Shillington, E. Richard. 1991. "Estimates of Native Child Poverty: Census 1986." In *Children in Poverty: Toward a Better Future*. Ottawa: Standing Senate Committee on Social Affairs, Science, and Technology.

Shils, Edward A. 1965. "Charisma, Order, and Status." *American Sociological Review*, 30:199–213.

Shilts, Randy. 1988. And the Band Played On: Politics, People, and the AIDS Epidemic. New York: Penguin.

Shisslak, Catherine M., and Marjorie Crago. 1994. "Toward a New Model for the Prevention of Eating Disorders." In Patricia Fallon, Melanie A. Katzman, and Susan C. Wooley (eds.), *Feminist Perspectives on Eating Disorders*. New York: Guilford Press, 419–437.

Shkilynyk, Anastasia M. 1985. *A Poison Stronger Than Love: The Destruction of an Ojibwa Community*. New Haven: Yale University Press.

Shor, Ira. 1986. *Culture Wars: School and Society in the Conservative Restoration 1969–1984*. Boston: Routledge & Kegan Paul.

Shorto, Russell. 1991. "Made-in-Japan Parenting," *Health*, 54(June):56–57.

Sikorsky, Robert. 1990. "Highway Robbery: Canada's Auto Repair Scandal." *Reader's Digest* (February):55–63.

Silverman, Robert, and Leslie Kennedy. 1993. *Deadly Deeds: Murder in Canada*. Scarborough, Ont.: Nelson Canada.

Silverstein, Louise B. 1991. "Transforming the Debate About Child Care and Maternal Employment." *American Psychologist*, 46:1025–1032.

Simmel, Georg. 1904. "Fashion." *American Journal of Sociology*, 62 (May 1957):541–558.

———. 1950. *The Sociology of Georg Simmel*. Trans. Kurt Wolff. Glencoe, Ill.: Free Press (orig. written 1902–1917).

Simon, David R., and D. Stanley Eitzen. 1993. *Elite Deviance* (4th ed.). Boston: Allyn & Bacon.

Simons, Marlise. 1993a. "Homeless Find a Spot in France's Heart." *New York Times* (December 9):A4.

———. 1993b. "Prosecutor Fighting Girl-Mutilation." *New York Times* (November 23):A4.

Simons, Rita James. 1975. *Women and Crime*. Washington, D.C.: U.S. Government Printing Office.

Simpson, Sally S. 1989. "Feminist Theory, Crime, and Justice." *Criminology*, 27:605–632.

Singer, Bennett L., and David Deschamps (eds.). 1994. *Gay and Lesbian Stats*. New York: New Press.

Sjoberg, Gideon. 1965. *The Preindustrial City: Past and Present*. New York: Free Press.

Skocpol, Theda, and Edwin Amenta. 1986. "States and Social Policies." In Ralph H. Turner and James F. Short, Jr. (eds.), *Annual Review of Sociology*, 12:131–157.

Smandych, Russell. 1985. "Marxism and the Creation of Law: Re-Examining the Origins of Canadian Anti-Combines Legislation." In Thomas Fleming (ed.), *The New Criminologies in Canada: State, Crime and Control*. Toronto: Oxford University Press, 87–99.

Smelser, Neil J. 1988. "Social Structure." In Neil J. Smelser (ed.), *Handbook of Sociology*. Newbury Park, Cal.: Sage, 103–129.

Smith, Adam. 1976. *An Inquiry into the Nature and Causes of the Wealth of Nations*. Roy H. Campbell and Andrew S. Skinner (eds.). Oxford, England: Clarendon Press (orig. pub. 1776).

Smith, Dorothy. 1974. "Women's Perspective as a Radical Critique of Sociology." *Sociological Inquiry* (44):7–13.

———. 1985. "Women, Class and Family." In Varda Burstyn and Dorothy Smith (eds.), *Women, Class and the State*. Toronto: Garamond.

———. 1987. *The Everyday World as Problematic: A Feminist Sociology*. Toronto: University of Toronto Press.

Smith, Michael D. 1996. "Patriarchal Ideology and Wife Beating." In Robert J. Brym (ed.), *Society in Question: Sociological Readings for the 21st Century*. Toronto: Harcourt Brace, and Company.

Smyke, Patricia. 1991. *Women and Health*. Atlantic Highlands, NJ: Zed Books.

Snider, Laureen. 1988. "Commercial Crime." In Vincent F. Sacco (ed.), *Deviance, Conformity and Control in Canadian Society*. Scarborough, Ont.: Prentice Hall, 231–283.

Snow, David A., and Leon Anderson. 1993. *Down on Their Luck: A Case Study of Homeless Street People*. Berkeley: University of California Press.

Snyder, Benson R. 1971. *The Hidden Curriculum*. New York: Knopf.

Sokoloff, Natalie. 1992. *Black Women and White Women in the Professions*. New York: Routledge.

South, Scott J., Charles M. Bonjean, Judy Corder, and William T. Markham. 1982. "Sex and Power in the Federal

Bureaucracy." *Work and Occupations*, 9(2):233–254.

Spencer, Metta. 1993. *Foundations of Modern Sociology* (6th ed.). Scarborough, Ont.: Prentice Hall.

Stackhouse, John. 1996. "Disenfranchised Asian Youth Rage Against Those in Driver's Seat." *The Globe and Mail* (July 31):A7.

———. 1999. "Foreign Aid Cuts Assailed for Harming Children." *The Globe and Mail* (February 23):A1, A12.

Stamler, Rodney T. 1996. "Organized Crime." In Rick Linden (ed.), *Criminology: A Canadian Perspective* (3rd ed.). Toronto: Harcourt Brace and Company, 423–457.

Stanley, Alessandra. 1994. "Sexual Harassment Thrives in the New Russian Climate." *New York Times* (April 17):1, 7.

Stark, Rodney. 1992. *Sociology* (4th ed.). Belmont, Cal.: Wadsworth.

Starr, Paul. 1982. *The Social Transformation of Medicine: The Rise of a Sovereign Profession and the Making of a Vast Industry*. New York: Basic Books.

Statham, Anne, Laurel Richardson, and Judith A. Cook. 1991. *Gender and University Teaching: A Negotiated Difference*. Albany: SUNY Press.

Statistics Canada. 1990. *General Social Survey*. Ottawa: Ministry of Supply and Services.

———. 1991. *1991 Census of Canada, Profile of Census Metropolitan Areas and Census Agglomerations*, Part A. Cat. no. 93–337. Ottawa: Minister of Industry, Science, and Technology.

———. 1991b. *Population by Religion, 1991 Census*, Canadian Statistics. Cat. no. 93-319-XPB. Ottawa: Minister of Supply and Services.

———. 1992. *Labour Force Annual Averages*. Ottawa: Ministry of Industry, Science, and Technology. Minister of Supply and Services.

———. 1994a. *Women in the Labour Force*. Ottawa: Minister of Industry, Science, and Technology.

———. 1994b. *Violence Against Women Survey*. Ottawa: Minister of Industry, Science, and Technology.

———. 1995a. *Canada at a Glance*. Ottawa: Minister of Supply and Services.

———. 1995b. *General Social Survey*. Ottawa: Minister of Supply and Services.

———. 1996a. *The Daily* (April 24). Ottawa: Minister of Supply and Services.

———. 1996b. *The Daily* (May 9). Ottawa: Minister of Supply and Services.

———. 1996c. "Births and Deaths." *The Daily* (May 24). Ottawa: Minister of Supply and Services.

———. 1996d. *Canada at a Glance*. Cat. no. 93–319. Ottawa: Minister of Supply and Services.

———. 1996e. *General Social Survey*. Ottawa: Minister of Supply and Services.

———. 1996f. "Percentage Distribution of Total Income of Families and Unattached Individuals by Quintiles, Canada.

———. 1951–1996. *"Income Distributions by Size in Canada 1996."* Cat. no. 13-207-XPB. Ottawa: Centre for International Statistics of the Canadian Council on Social Development.

———. 1996g. "1996 Census: Visible Minority Population." Ottawa: Minister of Supply and Services.

———. 1997a. "Breast Cancer Mortality and Mammography." *The Daily* (July 28). Ottawa: Minister of Supply and Services.

———. 1997b. "Who Cares? Caregiving in the 1990s." *The Daily* (August 19). Ottawa: Minister of Supply and Services.

———. 1997c. "1996 Census: Marital Status, Common-law Unions and Families." *The Daily* (October 14). Cat. no. 11-001E.

———. 1997d. "1996 Census: Mother Tongue, Home Language and Knowledge of Languages." *The Daily* (December 2). Ottawa: Minister of Supply and Services. Available: www.statcan.ca/Daily/English/971202/d971202.htm

———. 1998a. *Report on the Demographic Situation in Canada*, 1997. Ottawa: Statistics Canada.

———. 1998b. "Marriages and Divorce." *The Daily* (January 29). Available: www.statcan.ca:80/Daily/English/980129/d980129.htm

———. 1998c. "1996 Census: Education, Mobility and Migration." *The Daily* (April 14). Ottawa: Minister of Supply and Services.

———. 1998d. "1996 Census: Ethnic Origins, Visible Minorities." *The Daily* (February 17). Ottawa: Minister of Supply and Services.

———. 1998e. "1996 Census: Sources of Income Earning and Total Income, and Family Income." *The Daily* (May 12). Ottawa: Minister of Supply and Services.

———. 1998f. "Ten Most Frequent Jobs for Women in Canada, 1996." *The Daily* (March 17). Ottawa: Minister of Supply and Services.

———. 1999a. "Earnings of Men and Women, 1998." Cat. no. 13-217-XPB. Ottawa: Minister of Supply and Services.

———. 1999b. "Union Statistics." *The Daily* (August 24). Ottawa: Statistics Canada.

———. 1999c. "Vital Statistics Compendium." *The Daily* (November 25). Ottawa: Minister of Supply and Services.

———. 1999d. "Marriages." *The Daily* (October 28). Ottawa: Minister of Supply and Services.

———. 2000a. Labour Force Update: An Overview of the 1999 Labour Market. Volume 4, Number 1 (Winter). 71-005-XPB. Ottawa: Statistics Canada.

———. 2000b. "Health Reports: How Healthy Are Canadians?" *The Daily* (March 31). Ottawa: Statistics Canada.

———. 2000c. "Income Levels, Income Inequality, and Low Income Among the Elderly." *The Daily* (March 6). Ottawa: Minister of Supply and Services.

———. 2000d. "Canadian Social Trends: The Changing Face of Conjugal Relationships." *The Daily* (March 16). Ottawa: Minister of Supply and Services.

Statutes of Canada, 1910 c.27.

Stein, Peter J. 1976. *Single*. Englewood Cliffs, N.J.: Prentice-Hall.

——— (ed.). 1981. *Single Life: Unmarried Adults in Social Context*. New York: St. Martin's Press.

Steinbacher, Roberta, and Helen Bequaert Holmes. 1987. "Sex Choice: Survival and Sisterhood." In Gena Corea et al. (eds.), *Man-Made Women: How New Reproductive Technologies Affect Women*. Bloomington: Indiana University Press, 52–63.

Steinmetz, Suzanne K. 1987. "Elderly Victims of Domestic Violence." In Carl D. Chambers, John H. Lindquist, O.Z. White, and Michael T. Harter, (eds.),

The Elderly: Victims and Deviants. Athens: Ohio University Press, 126–141.

Stevenson, Harold W., and James W. Stigler. 1992. *The Learning Gap: Why Our Schools Are Failing and What We Can Learn from Japanese and Chinese Education*. New York: Summit Books.

Stewart, Abigail J. 1994. "Toward a Feminist Strategy for Studying Women's Lives." In Carol E. Franz and Abigail J. Stewart (eds.), *Women Creating Lives: Identities, Resilience, and Resistance*. Boulder, Col.: Westview, 11–35.

Stier, Deborah S., and Judith A. Hall. 1984. "Gender Differences in Touch: An Empirical and Theoretical Review." *Journal of Personality and Social Psychology*, 47(2):440–459.

Stolker, Paula B. 1992. "Weigh My Job Performance, Not My Body: Extending Title VII to Weight-Based Discrimination." *New York Law School Journal of Human Rights*, 10(1):223–250.

Stout, Cam. 1994. "Common Law: A Growing Alternative." In C. McKie (ed.), *Canadian Social Trends*, vol. 2. Toronto: Thompson Educational Publishing, 179–182.

Strike, Carol. 1994. "AIDS into the 1990's." In *Canadian Social Trends*, 2. Toronto: Thompson Educational Publishing, 111–112.

Sum Quod Sum Foundation. 1997. *A Report on the Needs Assessment of Senior Gays and Lesbians*. Winnipeg: Sum Quod Sum Foundation Inc.

Sumner, William G. 1959. *Folkways*. New York: Dover (orig. pub. 1906).

Sutherland, Edwin H. 1939. *Principles of Criminology*. Philadelphia: Lippincott.

———. 1949. *White Collar Crime*. New York: Dryden.

Swidler, Ann. 1986. "Culture in Action: Symbols and Strategies." *American Sociological Review*, 51 (April):273–286.

Tait, Heather. 1999. "Educational Achievement of Young Aboriginal Adults." *Canadian Social Trends*. Spring 1999, Statistics Canada Cat. no. 11-008: 6–10.

Takaki, Ronald. 1993. *A Different Mirror: A History of Multicultural America*. Boston: Little, Brown.

Tannen, Deborah. 1990. *You Just Don't Understand: Women and Men in Conversation*. New York: Morrow.

———. 1993. "Commencement Address, State University of New York at Binghamton." Reprinted in *Chronicle of Higher Education* (June 9):B5.

———. 1995. "Wears Jump Suit. Sensible Shoes. Uses Husband's Last Name." In E.D. Nelson and B.W. Robinson (eds.), *Gender in the 1990s: Images, Realities, and Issues*. Scarborough, Ont.: Nelson Canada, 3–7.

Tanzer, Andrew. 1996. "The Pacific Century." *Forbes* (July 15):108–113.

Tavris, Carol. 1993. *The Mismeasure of Woman*. New York: Touchstone.

Taylor, Payl. 1997. "Fatal Viruses Return with a Vengeance." *The Globe and Mail* (April 12):A1.

The Economist. 1997. "The Anti-Management Guru." (May 4).

Thomas, D. 1992. *Criminality Among the Foreign Born: Analysis of Federal Prison Population*. Ottawa: Immigration and Employment Canada.

Thomas, William I., and Dorothy Swaine Thomas. 1928. *The Child in America*. New York: Knopf.

Thompson, Becky W. 1994. *A Hunger So Wide and So Deep: American Women Speak Out on Eating Problems*. Minneapolis: University of Minnesota.

Thomson, Elizabeth, and Ugo Colella. 1992. "Cohabitation and Marital Stability: Quality or Commitment?" *Journal of Marriage and the Family*, 54:259–267.

Thornberry, T.P., and M. Farnworth. 1982. "Social Correlates of Criminal Involvement." *American Sociological Review*, 47(4):505–518.

Thorne, Barrie, Cheris Kramarae, and Nancy Henley. 1983. *Language, Gender, and Society*. Rowley, Mass.: Newbury House.

Thornton, Russell. 1984. "Cherokee Population Losses During the Trail of Tears: A New Perspective and a New Estimate." *Ethnohistory*, 31:289–300.

Tidwell, Gary L. 1993. *Anatomy of a Fraud: Inside the Finances of the P.T.L. Ministries*. New York: Wiley.

Tilly, Charles (ed.). 1975. *The Formation of National States in Western Europe*. Princeton, N.J.: Princeton University Press.

Timpson, Joyce. 1995. "Four Decades of Literature on Native Canadian Child Welfare: Changing Themes." *Child Welfare*, 74:525.

Tomasevski, Katarina. 1993. Prepared on behalf of the UN-NGO Group on Women and Development. *Women and Human Rights*. Atlantic Highlands, N.J.: Zed Books.

Tong, Rosemarie. 1989. *Feminist Thought: A Comprehensive Introduction*. Boulder, Col.: Westview Press.

Troeltsch, Ernst. 1960. The Social Teachings of the Christian Churches, vols. 1 and 2. Trans. O. Wyon. New York: Harper (orig. pub. 1931).

Trovato, Frank. 1994. "Mortality Trends in Canada." In B. Singh Bolaria and Harley D. Dickinson (eds.), *Health, Illness, and Health Care in Canada*. Toronto: Harcourt Brace, 22–64.

Tucker, Robert C. (ed.). 1979. *The Marx-Engels Reader* (2nd ed.). New York: Norton.

Tumin, Melvin. 1953. "Some Principles of Stratification: A Critical Analysis." *American Sociological Review*, 18 (August):387–393.

Turner, Jonathan, Leonard Beeghley, and Charles H. Powers. 1995. *The Emergence of Sociological Theory* (3rd ed.). Belmont, Cal.: Wadsworth.

Turner, Ralph H., and Lewis M. Killian. 1993. "The Field of Collective Behavior." In Russell L. Curtis, Jr., and Benigno E. Aguirre (eds.), *Collective Behavior and Social Movements*. Boston: Allyn & Bacon, 5–20.

Twenhofel, Karen. 1993. "Do You Diet?" In Leslea Newman (ed.), *Eating Our Hearts Out: Personal Accounts of Women's Relationship to Food*. Freedom, Cal.: Crossing Press.

UNAIDS. 1998. "New World AIDS Day Report Finds Global HIV Infections Increased 10% in 1998." Available: www.unaids.org/highband/press/wadep98.html

UNICEF. 1997. *Progress of Nations 1996*. New York: United Nations.

United Nations. 1997. "Global Change and Sustainable Development: Critical Trends. "United Nations Department for Policy Coordination and Sustainable Development. Posted Online.

United Nations. 1998. *Revision of the World's Population Estimates and Projections*. New York: United Nations Population Division.

United Nations Development Programme. 1996. *The Human Development Report, 1996*. Cary, North Carolina: Oxford

University Press.

———. 1997. *The Human Development Report, 1997*. Cary, North Carolina: Oxford University Press.

———. 1998. *The Human Development Report, 1998*. Cary, North Carolina: Oxford University Press.

———. 1999. *Human Development Report, 1999*. New York: Oxford University Press.

United Nations DPCSD. 1997. "Report of Commission on Sustainable Development, April 1997." New York: United Nations Department for Policy Coordination and Sustainable Development. Posted Online.

Ursel, Jane. 1992. *Private Lives, Public Policy: 100 Years of State Intervention in the Family*. Toronto: Women's Press.

———. 1993. "Family and Social Policies." In G.N. Ramuy (ed.), *Marriage and the Family in Canada Today* (2nd ed.). Scarborough Ont.: Prentice-Hall, 146–165.

Vallières, Pierre. 1971. *White Niggers of America*. Toronto: McClelland and Stewart.

Van Biema, David. 1993a. "But Will It End the Abortion Debate?" *Time* (June 14):52–54.

Vanier Institute of the Family. 1994. *Profiling Canadian Families*. Ottawa: Vanier Institute of the Family.

———. 1998. "Families: Change and Continuity." Available: www.cfcefc.ca/docs 00000329.htm

Vaughan, Diane. 1985. "Uncoupling: The Social Construction of Divorce." In James M. Henslin (ed.), *Marriage and Family in a Changing Society* (2nd ed.). New York: Free Press, 429–439.

Veblen, Thorstein. 1967. *The Theory of the Leisure Class*. New York: Viking (orig. pub. 1899).

Veevers, Jean E. 1980. *Childless by Choice*. Toronto: Butterworths.

———. 1991. *Continuity and Change in Marriage and Family*. Toronto: Holt, Rinehart and Wilson.

Verburg, Peter. 1994. *The Alberta Report*.

Vetter, Harold J., and Gary R. Perlstein. 1991. *Perspectives on Terrorism*. Pacific Grove, Cal.: Brooks/Cole.

Vigil, James. 1990. "Cholos and Gangs: Culture Change and Street Youth in Los Angeles." In Ronald C. Huff (ed.), *Gangs in America*. Newbury Park, Cal.: Sage.

Vito, Gennaro F., and Ronald M. Holmes. 1994. *Criminology: Theory, Research and Policy*. Belmont, Cal.: Wadsworth.

Volpe, R. 1989. *Poverty and Child Abuse: A Review of Selected Literature*. Toronto: Institute for the Prevention of Child Abuse.

Wachtel, Andy. 1994. *Child Abuse and Neglect. A Discussion Paper and Overview of Topically Related Projects*. Ottawa: The Circle.

Wagner, Elvin, and Allen E. Stearn. 1945. *The Effects of Smallpox on the Destiny of the American Indian*. Boston: Bruce Humphries.

Waldram, James B., D. Ann Herring, and T. Kue Young. 1995. *Aboriginal Health in Canada: Historical, Cultural, and Epidemiological Perspectives*. Toronto: University of Toronto Press.

Waldron, Ingrid. 1994. "What Do We Know About the Causes of Sex Differences in Mortality? A Review of the Literature." In Peter Conrad and Rochelle Kern (eds.), *The Sociology of Health and Illness: Critical Perspectives*. New York: St. Martin's Press, 42–54.

Walker, Lawrence J. 1989. "A Longitudinal Study of Moral Reasoning." *Child Development*, 60:157–166.

Wallace, Harvey. 1996. *Family Violence: Legal, Medical, and Social Perspectives. Boston:* Allyn and Bacon.

Wallerstein, Immanuel. 1979. *The Capitalist World Economy*. Cambridge: Cambridge University Press.

———. 1984. *The Politics of the World Economy*. Cambridge, England: Polity Press.

———. 1991. *Unthinking Social Science: The Limits of Nineteenth Century Paradigms*. Cambridge, England: Polity Press.

Wannell, Ted, and Nathalie Caron. 1996. The Gender Earnings Gap Among Recent Postsecondary Graduates, 1984–92, Cat. no. 68 #11F0G19MPE. Ottawa: Statistics Canada.

Ward, Margaret. 1998. *The Family Dynamic: A Canadian Perspective* (2nd ed.). Scarborough: ITP Nelson.

Ward, Mike. 1996. "Firm Fined $6,000 After Man Killed in Unsafe Workplace." *Winnipeg Free Press* (March 7).

Waters, Malcolm. 1995. *Globalization*. London: Routledge.

Watson, Tracey. 1987. "Women Athletes and Athletic Women: The Dilemmas and Contradictions of Managing Incongruent Identities." *Sociological Inquiry*, 57(Fall):431–446.

Weber, Max. 1963. *The Sociology of Religion*. Trans. E. Fischoff. Boston: Beacon Press (orig. pub. 1922).

———. 1968. *Economy and Society: An Outline of Interpretive Sociology*. Trans. G. Roth and G. Wittich. New York: Bedminster Press (orig. pub. 1922).

———. 1976. *The Protestant Ethic and the Spirit of Capitalism*. Trans. Talcott Parsons. Introduction by Anthony Giddens. New York: Scribner (orig. pub. 1904–1905).

Weeks, John R. 1992. *Population: An Introduction to Concepts and Issues* (5th ed.). Belmont, Cal.: Wadsworth.

Weigel, Russell H., and P.W. Howes. 1985. "Conceptions of Racial Prejudice: Symbolic Racism Revisited." *Journal of Social Issues*, 41:124–132.

Weinfeld, Morton. 1995. "Ethnic and Race Relations." In R. Brym (ed.), *New Society: Sociology for the 21st Century*. Toronto: Harcourt Brace and Company, 4.1–4.29

Weinraub, Bernard. 1994. "Scarier Than Dinosaurs: The Sexes." *New York Times* (January 5):B1.

Weiss, Meira. 1994. *Conditional Love: Parents' Attitudes Toward Handicapped Children*. Westport, Conn.: Bergin & Garvey.

Weitz, Rose. 1995. *A Sociology of Health, Illness, and Health Care*. Belmont, Cal.: Wadsworth.

———. 1996. *The Sociology of Health, Illness, and Health Care: A Critical Approach*. Belmont, Cal.: Wadsworth.

Weitzman, Lenore J. 1985. *The Divorce Revolution*. New York: Free Press.

Wendell, Susan. 1995. "Toward a Feminist Theory of Disability." In E.D. Nelson and B.W. Robinson (eds.), *Gender in the 1990s*. Scarborough, Ont.: Nelson Canada, 455–465.

Weston, Kath. 1991. *Families We Choose: Lesbians, Gays, Kinship*. New York: Columbia University Press.

Weston, Marianne, and Bonnie Jeffery. 1994. "AIDS: The Politicizing of a Public Health Issue." In B. Singh Bolaria and Harley D. Dickinson (eds.), *Health, Illness, and Health Care in Canada* (2nd ed.). Toronto: Harcourt Brace and Company, 721–738.

Westrum, Ron. 1991. *Technologies and Society: The Shaping of People and*

Things. Belmont, Cal.: Wadsworth.

Whitaker, Reg. 1991. *Double Standard: The Secret Story of Canadian Immigration*. Toronto: Lester and Orpen Dennys.

Whitaker, Barbara. 1997. "Earning It; If You Can't Beat Dilbert, Hire Him." *New York Times* (June 29):C12.

White, James. 1987. "Premarital Cohabitation and Marital Stability in Canada." *Journal of Marriage and the Family*, 49:641–647.

White, Ralph K., and Ronald Lippitt. 1953. "Leader Behavior and Member Reaction in Three 'Social Climates.'" In Dorwin Cartwright and Alvin Zander (eds.), *Group Dynamics*. Evanston, Ill.: Row, Peterson, 586–611.

———. 1960. *Autocracy and Democracy: An Experimental Inquiry*. Westport, Conn.: Greenwood Press.

White, Ryan, and Anne Marie Cunningham. 1992. *Ryan White: My Own Story*. New York: Signet/Penguin.

Whyte, William H., Jr. 1988/43. *The Organization Man*. Garden City, N.Y.: Anchor.

Wickett, Ann. 1989. *Double Exit: When Aging Couples Commit Suicide Together*. Eugene, Ore.: Hemlock Society.

Wieler, Joseph M. 1986. "The Role of Law in Labour Relations." In Ivan Bernier and Andree Lojoie (eds.), *Labour Law and Urban Law in Canada*. Toronto: University of Toronto Press.

Williams, Christine L. 1989. *Gender Differences at Work*. Berkeley: University of California Press.

——— (ed.). 1993. *Doing "Women's Work": Men in Nontraditional Occupations*. Newbury Park, Cal.: Sage.

Williams, Robin M., Jr. 1970. *American Society: A Sociological Interpretation* (3rd ed.). New York: Knopf.

Wilson, David (ed.). 1997. "Globalization and the Changing U.S. City." *Annals of the American Academy of Political and Social Sciences*, 551 (May).

Wilson, Elizabeth. 1991. *The Sphinx in the City: Urban Life, the Control of Disorder, and Women*. Berkeley: University of California Press.

Wilson, Everett K., and Hanan Selvin. 1980. *Why Study Sociology? A Note to Undergraduates*. Belmont, Cal.: Wadsworth.

Winn, Maria. 1985. *The Plug-in Drug: Television, Children, and the Family*. New York: Viking.

Wirth, Louis. 1938. "Urbanism as a Way of Life." *American Journal of Sociology*, 40:1–24.

———. 1945. "The Problem of Minority Groups." In Ralph Linton (ed.), *The Science of Man in the World Crisis*. New York: Columbia University Press, 38.

Wiseman, Jacqueline. 1970. *Stations of the Lost: The Treatment of Skid Row Alcoholics*. Chicago: University of Chicago Press.

Wishart, Cynthia. 1993. "Workplace Harassment." In Graham S. Lowe and Harvey J. Krahn (eds.), *Work in Canada*. Scarborough, Ont.: Nelson Canada.

Wolf, Daniel. 1996. "A Bloody Biker War." *Maclean's* (January 15):10–11.

Wolf, Naomi. 1990. *The Beauty Myth: How Images of Beauty Are Used Against Women*. New York: Morrow.

———. 1994. "Hunger." In Patricia Fallon, Melanie A. Katzman, and Susan C. Wooley (eds.), *Feminist Perspectives on Eating Disorders*. New York: Guilford Press, 94–111.

Wolfe, David A. 1987. *Child Abuse: Implications for Child Development and Psychopathology*. Newbury Park, Cal.: Sage.

Wolfe, Jeanne M. 1992. "Canada's Livable Cities." *Social Policy*, 23:56–63.

Women for Economic Survival. 1984. *Women and Economic Hard Times: A Record*. Victoria: Women for Economic Survival and the University of Victoria.

Women Working Worldwide (eds.). 1991. *Common Interests: Women Organizing in Global Electronics*. London: Women Working Worldwide.

Women's Action Coalition (eds.). 1993. *WAC Stats: The Facts About Women* (2nd ed.). New York: New Press.

Wong, Sandra L. 1991. "Evaluating the Content of Textbooks: Public Interests and Professional Authority." *Sociology of Education*, 64:11–18.

Wood, Chris Caragata. 1994. "The Legacy of Sue Rodriquez." *Maclean's* (February 28):22.

Wood, Darryl S., and Curt T. Griffiths. 1996. "Patterns of Aboriginal Crime." In Robert A. Silverman, James J. Teevan, and Vincent F. Sacco (eds.), *Crime in Canadian Society* (5th ed.). Toronto: Harcourt Brace and Company, 222–223.

Wood, Julia T. 1994. *Gendered Lives: Communication, Gender, and Culture*. Belmont, Cal.: Wadsworth.

Wooden, Wayne S. 1995. *Renegade Kids, Suburban Outlaws: From Youth Culture to Delinquency*. Belmont, Cal.: Wadsworth.

Wooley, Susan C. 1994. "Sexual Abuse and Eating Disorders: The Concealed Debate." In Patricia Fallon, Melanie A. Katzman, and Susan C. Wooley (eds.), *Feminist Perspectives on Eating Disorders*. New York: Guilford Press, 171–211.

Wordsworth, Araminta. 2000. "Medical Bills Main Culprit in Bankruptcies: U.S. Study." *National Post* (April 27):A1, A8.

World Bank. 1996. *World Development Report 1996: From Plan to Market*. New York: Oxford University Press for the World Bank.

World Health Organization/Global Programme on AIDS. 1998. "Asian Business Leaders Crucial in Fight Against AIDS." Press release. WHO/32, April 14.

Wotherspoon, Terry. 1994. "Colonization, Self-Determination, and the Health of Canada's First Nations Peoples." In B. Singh Bolaria and Rosemary Bolaria (eds.), *Racial Minorities, Medicine and Health*. Halifax: Fernwood Publishing, 247–267.

Wresch, William. 1996. *Disconnected: Haves and Have-Nots In The Information Age*. New Brunswick: Rutgers University Press.

Wright, Erik Olin, Karen Shire, Shu-Ling Hwang, Maureen Dolan, and Janeen Baxter. 1992. "The Non-Effects of Class on the Gender Division of Labor in the Home: A Comparative Study of Sweden and the U.S." *Gender & Society*, 6(2):252–282.

Wu, Z. 1995. "The Stability of Cohabitation Relationships: The Role of Children." *Journal of Marriage and the Family*, 57:231–236.

Wylie, Alison. 1995. "The Contexts of Activism on 'Climate' Issue." In the Chilly Collective (eds.), *Breaking Anonymity: The Chilly Climate for Women Faculty*. Waterloo, Ont.: Wilfrid Laurier University Press, 29–60.

Yinger, J. Milton. 1960. "Contraculture and Subculture." *American Sociological Review*, 25 (October):625–635.

———. 1982. *Countercultures: The Promise and Peril of a World Turned Upside Down*. New York: Free Press.

Young, T.R. 1997. Posting on the TEACHSOC listserve (March 27), and e-mail correspondence with the author.

Zavella, Patricia. 1987. *Women's Work and Chicano Families: Cannery Workers of the Santa Clara Valley*. Ithaca, N.Y.: Cornell University Press.

Zelizer, Viviana. 1985. *Pricing the Priceless Child: The Changing Social Value of Children*. New Haven, Conn.: Yale University Press.

Zimbardo, Philip G. 1970. "The Human Choice: Individuation, Reason, and Order versus Deindividuation, Impulse, and Chaos." In W.J. Arnold and D. Levine (eds.), *Nebraska Symposium on Motivation, 1969*. Lincoln: University of Nebraska Press.

Zipp, John F. 1985. "Perceived Representativeness and Voting: An Assessment of the Impact of 'Choices' vs. 'Echoes.'" *The American Political Science Review*, 60(3):738–759.

Zuboff, Shoshana. 1988. *In the Age of the Smart Machine*. New York: Basic Books.

Zukewich Ghalam, Nancy. 1994. "Women in the Workplace." In Craig McKie (ed.), *Canadian Social Trends*, vol. 2. Toronto: Thompson Educational Publishing, 141–145.

Zuravin, Susan J. 1991. "Research Definitions of Childhood Physical Abuse and Neglect: Current Problems." In Raymond H. Starr, Jr. and David A. Wolfe (eds.), *The Effects of Child Abuse and Neglect*. London: Guilford Press, 100–128.

Zurcher, Louis A. 1983. *Social Roles: Conformity, Conflict, and Creativity*. Beverly Hills, Cal.: Sage.

INDEX

PHOTO CREDITS

p. 3, Izzy Schwartz/PhotoDisc; **p. 4,** G. Reekie/Canada Wide; **p. 7,** Phyllis Picardi/Stock, Boston; **p. 7,** Chapman & Parry/The Image Works; **p. 9,** Al Harvey; **p. 10,** AP/Wide World Photos; **p. 10,** The Granger Collection, New York; **p. 11,** The Bettmann Archive; **p. 11,** The Bettmann Archive; **p. 12,** The Granger Collection, New York; **p. 12,** The Granger Collection; **p. 13,** Al Harvey; **p. 14,** /Ward Perrin/CP Picture Archive; **p. 15,** Margrit Eichler, New York; **p. 19,** CP Picture Archive; **p. 20,** Ward Perrin/CP Picture Archive; **p. 27,** *At the Café*, E. Degas, Musée d'Orsay, Paris/Giraudon/Art Resource, NY AR 5483/PEC 7214; **p. 27,** Ruben Sprich/Reuters/CORBIS; **p. 28,** Sestini Agency/ Gamma Liaison; **p. 31,** Bob Kalman/The Image Works; **p. 32,** Peter Arkell/Zuma Images; **p. 37,** Kevin Frayer/CP Picture Archive; **p. 40,** Al Harvey; **p. 40,** Antonio Suarez/Zuma Images; **p. 40,** Ira Kirschenbaum/ Stock, Boston; **p. 41,** Dinodia Picture/The Image Works; **p. 41,** Lee Celano/SIPA Press; **p. 41,** Mark Richards/PhotoEdit; **p. 43,** Hans Deryk/ CP Picture Archive; **p. 43,** Robert Galbraith/CP Picture Archive; **p. 52,** Elliot Erwitt/Magnum Photos; **p. 54,** Ken Gigliotti/Winnipeg Free Press; **p. 55,** The Bettmann Archive; **p. 57,** Victor Englebert/ Photo Researchers; **p. 58,** Dave Buston/CP Picture Archive; **p. 61,** Moe Doiron/CP Picture Archive; **p. 61,** Jim Wilkes/CP Picture Archive; **p. 62,** Karen Kasmauski/Matrix; **p. 67,** Peter Bregg/CP Picture Archive; **p. 68,** James R. Holland/Stock, Boston; **p. 68,** Paul Fusco/Magnum Photos; **p. 71,** Bill Bachmann/The Image Works; **p. 72,** Photo 20–20; **p. 75,** Bob Daemmrich/Stock, Boston; **p. 75,** Richard Hutching/Photo Researchers; **p. 75,** Bob Daemmrich Photo/The Image Works; **p. 80,** Al Harvey; **p. 81,** Al Harvey; **p. 83,** Mike Sturk/CP Picture Archive; **p. 85,** Canadian Armed Forces; **p. 88,** Miro Vintoniv/Stock, Boston; **p. 92,** Tony Freeman/PhotoEdit; **p. 95,** Fred Chartrand/CP Picture Archive; **p. 101,** Phill Snel/CP Picture Archive; **p. 102,** Gabor Demjen/ Stock, Boston; **p. 106,** Andrew Wallace/CP Picture Archive; **p. 106,** Frank Gunn/CP Picture Archive; **p. 108,** Dick Hemingway; **p. 109,** Le Duc/Monkmeyer Press; **p. 113,** Kevin Frayer/CP Picture Archive; **p. 113,** Fred Chartrand/CP Picture Archive; **p. 116,** Paul Chiasson/CP Picture Archive; **p. 118,** Lindsay Hebberd/Woodfin Camp & Associates; **p. 118,** Eastcott/Momatiuk/Woodfin Camp & Associates; **p. 118,** Misha Erwitt/Magnum Photos; **p. 122,** Ryan Remiorz/CP Picture Archive; **p. 123,** Shaney Komulainen/CP Picture Archive; **p. 129,** CP Picture Archive; **p. 131,** Bruno Barbey/Magnum Photos; **p. 137,** PhotoDisc; **p. 138,** The Granger Collection, New York; **p. 141,** Ted Grant/Canadian Sport Images; **p. 142,** Luisa Salerno; **p. 147,** Bob Daemmrich/Stock, Boston; **p. 147,** Bob Daemmrich/Stock, Boston; **p. 147,** Ed Lallo/Liason International; **p. 148,** Bob Daemmrich Photo/ The Image Works; **p. 150,** Jean Marc Geloux/Gamma Liaison; **p. 153,** Richard Drew/AP/Wide World Photos; **p. 153,** D. Sorey/Gamma Liaison; **p. 159,** Mark Duncan/AP/Wide World Photos; **p. 159,** Reuters/CORBIS; **p. 165,** Paul Chiasson/CP Picture Archive; **p. 166,** CP Picture Archive; **p. 170,** L. Terry/Gamma Liaison; **p. 178,** Frank Gunn/CP Picture Archive; **p. 178,** The Northern Miner; **p. 187,** Mike Cassese/Canada Wide; **p. 190,** Bryan Kelsen/Gamma Liaison; **p. 197,** Keith Brofsky/PhotoDisc; **p. 199,** CP Picture Archive; **p. 213,** Gilles Mingasson/Gamma Liaison; **p. 221,** Chuck Stoody/CP Picture Archive; **p. 225,** John Maier, Jr./The Image Works; **p. 228,** Sygma/ CORBIS; **p. 229,** Alison Wright/The Image Works; **p. 231,** John Gaps III/AP/CP Picture Archive; **p. 233,** Macduff Everton/The Image Works; **p. 236,** Lauren Goodsmith/The Image Works; **p. 239,** Superstock; **p. 241,** Beth A. Keiser/AP/; **p. 249,** Kevin Frayer/CP Picture Archive; **p. 250,** Mark Duncan/CP Picture Archive; **p. 259,** J.Y. Rabeuf/The Image Works; **p. 260,** Paul Henry/CP Picture Archive; **p. 262,** Alistair Grant/CP Picture Archive; **p. 264,** Warren Todd/Canada Wide; **p. 267,** Lyn Hancock; **p. 269,** Al Harvey; **p. 277,** Jonathan Nourok/PhotoEdit; **p. 281,** Thomas Hoepker/Magnum; **p. 282,** Imperial War Museum; **p. 282,** Herman Kokojan/Black Star; **p. 287,** Claus Meyer/Black Star; **p. 287,** Judah Passow/JB Pictures/The Image Works; **p. 287,** George Holton/Photo Researchers; **p. 287,** The Bettmann Archive; **p. 290,** Barbara Campbell/Liaison International; **p. 297,** Michael Grecco/Stock, Boston; **p. 297,** T. Vogel/Rapho/Photo Researchers; **p. 300,** Alan Dorrow/JB Pictures/The Image Works; **p. 309,** Eraldo Peres/AP/ CP Picture Archive; **p. 318,** CP Picture Archive; **p. 319,** CP Picture Archive/Michael Lea/CP Picture Archive/Bruce Edwards/CP Picture Archive; **p. 321,** Patrick Guis/Gamma Liaison; **p. 324,** UN/DPI Photo; **p. 325,** Jeff DeBooy/CP Picture Archive; **p. 328,** Joe Bryska/Winnipeg Free Press; **p. 330,** Tim Clark/CP Picture Archive; **p. 337,** Paul Chiasson/CP Picture Archive; **p. 339,** Saun Best/Reuters; **p. 341,** AP/CP Picture Archive; **p. 341,** Betty Press/Woodfin Camp; **p. 341,** Cary Wolinsky/Stock, Boston; **p. 343,** CP Picture Archive; **p. 344,** Tom Hanson/CP Picture Archive; **p. 347,** Jacques Boissinot/CP Picture Archive; **p. 348,** Tom Hanson/CP Picture Archive; **p. 350,** Jacques Boissinot/CP Picture Archive; **p. 350,** Wayne Glowacki/CP Picture Archives; **p. 352,** NAC PA-051479; **p. 352,** Sylvie Paulin/CP Picture Archive; **p. 352,** Rich Chard/Maclean's; **p. 355,** The Bettmann Archive; **p. 358,** Mike Yamashita/Woodfin Camp; **p. 359,** Louis Psihoyos/Matrix; **p. 362,** I. Ka-Tai/Woodfin Camp & Associates; **p. 371,** CP Picture Archive; **p. 372,** Wayne Cuddington/CP Picture Archive, **p. 375,** Shackman/Monkmeyer; **p. 375,** Syndicated Features/The Image Works; **p. 383,** The Bettmann Archive; **p. 386,** Haruyoshi Yamaguchi/ Sygma/CORBIS; **p. 388,** Robert Brenner/PhotoEdit; **p. 396,** Dana Schuerholz/Impact Visuals; **p. 403,** Richard Lautens/CP Picture Archive; **p. 404,** Stephen Shames/Matrix; **p. 408,** A. Stawicki/Toronto Star; **p. 409,** Robert McElroy/Woodfin Camp; **p. 409,** Luisa Salerno; **p. 413,** Jon Burbank/The Image Works; **p. 416,** Bob Daemmrich/Stock, Boston; **p. 419,** John Zich/AP/Wide World Photos; **p. 420,** Mark O'Neill/ Canada Wide; **p. 431,** Andrew Vaughn/CP Picture Archive; **p. 432,** NAC PA-122657; **p. 435,** Betty Press/Woodfin Camp; **p. 436,** Luisa Salerno; **p. 437,** David Guttenfelder/CP Picture Archive; **p. 437,** Rikard Lama/CP Picture Archive; **p. 450,** Dick Hemingway; **p. 453,** P. Power/The Toronto Star; **p. 456,** George Crallé/Canada Wide; **p. 456,** Norm Betts/Canada Wide; **p. 456,** Bayne Stanley/Canada Wide

COPYRIGHT ACKNOWLEDGMENTS

p. 1: Extracted from *A Life of Margaret Laurence* by James King. Copyright © 1997. Reprinted by permission of Alfred A. Knopf Canada, a division of Random House of Canada Limited. **pp. 18–19:** Markoff, 1997; and Young, 1997 (used with permission from T.R. Young. Director, The Red Feather Institute for Advanced Studies in Sociology.) **pp. 35–37:** From *Returning to the Teachings: Exploring Aboriginal Justice* by Rupert Ross. Copyright © 1996 by the University of Saskatchewan. Reprinted by permission of Penguin Books Canada Ltd. **pp. 46–47:** Excerpts from *The Citizen's Forum on Canada's Future: Report to the People and Government of Canada, 1991*. Source Privy Council Office. Reproduced with the permission of the Minister of Public Works and Government Services, 1996. **pp. 50–51:** Trish Snyder and Terri Foxman, "The Global Marketing Hall of Shame," *Canadian Inflight Magazine* (July, 1998): 42–50. **p. 52:** From Shadd, Adrienne (1994) "Where are You Really from?" in Carl E. James and Adrienne Shadd (eds.) *Talking About Difference*. Toronto: Between the Lines, p. 11. Reprinted by permission. **p. 53:** "Ethnic Origins, 1996," adapted with permission from "Total Population by Ethnic Categories and Sex, for Canada, Provinces, Territories and Census Metropolitan Areas, 1996 Census," Cat. No. 930026XDB96002; "Household Income, 1995," adapted with permission from the Statistics Canada website at www.statcan.ca/english/census96/may12/t6can.htm. **p. 56:** Excerpt from *Yanomamo: The Last Days of Eden* by Napoleon A. Chagnon, copyright © 1992 by Harcourt, Inc., reprinted by permission of the publisher. **p. 65:** Pelzer, Dave. 1995. *A Child Called "It"*. Deerfield Beach, Fla.: Health Communications. **pp. 90–91:** Heinrichs, Daniel, 1996. *Caring for Norah*. Winnipeg: Daniel Heinricks Publishing. **pp. 90–91:** From *Old Dogs Must Learn New Tricks in the Modern Era* by Naomi Patterson © 1998. Reprinted with permission of the author. **pp. 93–94:** Moore, Patricia, with C.P. Conn. 1985. *Disguised*. Waco, TX: Word Books. **p. 99:** From O'Reilly-Fleming, Thomas. 1993. *Down and Out in Canada: Homeless Canadians*. Toronto: Canadian Scholar's Press, p. 56. Reprinted by permission. **pp. 110–111:** Schafer, A. (1998) *Down and Out in Winnipeg and Toronto: The Ethics of Legislating Against Panhandling*. Ottawa: Caledon Institute of Social Policy (August). **p. 115:** Source: Snow and Anderson, 1993; and Bunis, Yancik, and Snow, 1996. **p. 135:** Milgram, Stanley. 1963. "Behavioural Study of Obedience." *Journal of Abnormal and Social Psychology*. **p. 150:** PBS, 1992b. **pp. 156–157:** DILBERT Reprinted by permission of United Feature Syndicate, Inc. **p. 163:** From Kaihla, Paul. 1991. "Terror in the Streets." *Maclean's* (March 25): 18–21. Reprinted by permission. **pp. 169–170:** From *The Myth of Delinquency* (pp. 240–241) by Elliott Leyton, 1979. Used by permission of Oxford University Press. **pp. 170–171:** From Wolf, Daniel. 1996. "A Bloody Biker War." *Maclean's* (January 15): 10–11. Reprinted by permission. **pp. 172–173:** Kaplan, David E. and Alec Dubro. 1987. *Yakuza: The Explosive Account of Japan's Criminal Underworld*. New York: Collier. **p. 183:** "Percentages of Adults Charged by Sex, 1998," from *Juristat*, Cat. No. 85-0XPE, Vol. 19, No. 9. 1999. **p. 186:** Provincial Crime Rates per 100 000 Population, from *Juristat*, Cat. No. 85-XPE, Vol. 9, No. 9. 1999. **pp. 192–193:** Philips, Bruce. 1998. Privacy Commissioner, 1997–98 *Annual Report. Ottawa: The Privacy Commissioner of Canada*. **p. 195:** From O'Reilly-Fleming, Thomas. 1993. *Down and Out in Canada: Homeless Canadians*. Toronto: Canadian Scholar's Press, p. 56. Reprinted by permission. **p. 207:** Statistics Canada, from Income Distribution by Size in Canada, Cat. No. 13-207; Centre for International Statistics at the Canadian Council on Social Development, Statistics Canada, Income Distributions by Size in Canada, 1996, Cat. No. 13-207XPB. **p. 208:** Centre for International Statistics at the Canadian Council on Social Development using data from Statistics Canada, Income Distributions by Size in Canada, 1996, Cat. No. 13-207-XPB. **p. 212:** National Council of Welfare, 1999. Poverty Profile, 1997. Ottawa: Minister of Supply and Services, Fall 1999. Reproduced with the permission of the Minister of Public Works and Government Services Canada, 2000. **pp. 216–217:** Poverty Profile, 1994, Table 4, Poverty Profile, 1996, Poverty Rates by Family Types, Health Canada. Reproduced with permission of the Minister of Public Works and Government Services Canada, 1999. **p. 223:** Lummis, C. Douglas. 1992. "Equality" in Wolfgang Sachs (ed.), *The Development Dictionary*, Atlantic Highlands, NJ: Zed Books, p. 50. **p. 226:** From *Human Development Report 1998* by United Nations Development Program. Copyright © 1998 by the United Nations Development Program. Used by permission of Oxford University Press, Inc. **pp. 226–227:** *The Hindu*, "The Idea of Human Development." Reprinted by permission. **p. 231:** Chossudovsky, Michel. 1997. *The Globalization of Poverty*. Penang: Third World Network. p. 33. **p. 234:** From *Human Development Report 1998* by United Nations Development Program. Copyright © 1998 by the United Nations Development Program. Used by permission of Oxford University Press, Inc. **p. 235:** From *Human Development Report 1998* by United Nations Development Program. Copyright © 1998 by the United Nations Development Program. Used by permission of Oxford University Press, Inc. **p. 247:** From Shadd, Adrienne, 1994. "Where are You Really from?" in Carl E. James and Adrienne Shadd (eds.) *Talking About Difference*. Toronto: Between the Lines, pp. 35–36. **p. 253:** Statistics Canada, "Single and Multiple Origin Responses, 1996 Census." Adapted from "The Nation Series Package No. 6: Ethnic Origin and Visible Minority Population," Cat. No. 93F0026XDB9600. **pp. 256–267:** Doug Collins, quotations from various articles in the *North Shore News*, North Vancouver, BC. **p. 261:** From *My Life* by Earvin "Magic" Johnson with William Novak © 1992, Random House, Inc. Reprinted with permission. **p. 266:** Statistics Canada, "1996 Census: Ethnic Origins, Visible Minorities," *The Daily*, Cat. No. 11-001, February 17, 1998. **p. 268:** From *Seeing Ourselves: Exploring Race, Ethnicity and Culture* by Carl E. James. 1995. Toronto: Thompson Educational Publishing. **p. 270:** Statistics Canada, "1996 Census: Immigration and Citizenship," adapted from Cat. No. 11-001. November 4, 1997, p. 3. **p. 271:** Statistics Canada, "1996 Census: Visible Minority Population." **p. 275:** Reprinted by permission of the author. **p. 278:** Edwin M. Schur, *Labeling Women Deviant: Gender, Stigma, and Social Control* © 1983. Temple University Press. Reprinted by permission, The McGraw-Hill Companies. **p. 281:** Klein, (1983): 273. **p. 286:** Adapted from Judith Lorber, *Paradoxes of Gender* © 1994. Yale University Press. Reprinted by permission. **p. 288:** Tomasevski (1993): 85. **p. 291:** Reprinted with permission from "Do You Diet" by Karen Twenhofel in *Eating Our Hearts Out* edited by Leslea Newman © 1993. Published by The Crossing Press, Freedom, CA 95019. **p. 293:** Susan Bordo, *Unbearable Weight: Feminism, Western Culture, and the Body* © 1993 The Regents of the University of California. **p. 295:** Prepared by the Centre for International Statistics. © The Vanier Institute. 1996 figures from Akveampoing. **p. 296:** Statistics Canada

(1996) The Labour Force: Annual Averages, 1996. Cat. No. 13-217. **p. 298:** Statistics Canada (1996) Earnings of Men and Women in 1996, Cat. No. 13-217. **p. 299:** Statistics Canada, General Social survey, Cat. No. 11-612. **p. 307:** Lewis-Thornton, Rae. 1994. *Essence* (December): p. 63. **p. 310:** UNAIDS. www.UNAIDS.org. **pp. 314–315:** From *Ryan White: My Own Story* by Ryan White and Ann Marie Cunningham. Copyright © 1991 by Jeanne White and Ann Marie Cunningham. Used by permission of Dial Books for Young Readers, a division for Penguin Putnam Inc. **p. 322:** Statistics Canada, *Report on Canadian Health and Disability Survey*, Cat. No. 82-555. **p. 322:** Keller, James. 1994. "I Treasure Each Moment." *Parade Magazine* (September 4):4–5. **p. 323:** Wendell, Susan. 1995. "Toward a Feminist Theory of Disability." In E.D. Nelson and B.W. Robinson (eds.), *Gender in the 1990s*. Scarborough, Ont: Nelson Canada, 458. **pp. 325–326:** Armstrong, Pat, Hugh Armstrong, Jacqueline Choiniere, Eric Myhalovsky, and Jerry P. White, 1997. *Medical Alert: New Work Organizations in Health Care*. Toronto: Garamond Press, p. 72. **p. 329:** Gerard Anderson, *Highlights of the 1998 Multinational Comparisons of Health Care*. New York, NY: The Commonwealth Fund, 1998. **p. 330:** Beyerstein, Barry, 1997. "Alternative Medicine: Where's the Evidence?" *Canadian Journal of Public Health*, 88 (May/June): 149–150. **p. 337:** From *If you Love This Country*, edited by Laurier La Pierre © 1987. Reprinted by permission of McClelland & Stewart, *The Canadian Publishers*. Reprinted by permission of Elsa Franklin. **p. 338:** From *America Besieged* by Michael Parenti. © 1994. San Francisco: City Lights. **pp. 360–361:** From *The End of Work* by Jeremy Rifkin, © 1995. New York: G.P. Putnam's Sons. **p. 369:** Mason Lee (1998): A1. **p. 376:** Statistics Canada, "Canadian Families: Diversity and Change," Cat. No. 12F0061XFE. **p. 384:** Statistics Canada "Families: Number, Type and Structure," Cat. No. 93-312; and "Families: Social and Economic Characteristics," Cat. No. 93-320. **p. 387:** Statistics Canada, *The Daily*, October 23, 1998. Cat. No. 11-001. **p. 390:** Overall, Christine (1991) "Reproductive Technology and the Future of the Family," in Jean E. Veevers, *Continuity and Change in Marriage and the Family*. Toronto: Harcourt Brace. **p. 393:** Statistics Canada, *The Daily*, October 14, 1997. **p. 407:** Fisher, Luke. 1994. "A Holy War Over Holidays," August 12, 1994, p. 26. Reprinted by permission of Maclean's Magazine. **p. 411:** Statistics Canada. 1998. 1996 Census: Sources of income, earnings, and total income, and family income. *The Daily* (May 12, 1998). **p. 413:** Reprinted with permission, The Toronto Star Syndicate. **pp. 414–415:** Dunning, Paula. 1997. *Education in Canada: An Overview*. Toronto: Canadian Education Association. **p. 418:** National Opinion Research Center, General Social Survey (1989): 156–159. **p. 424:** Vanier Institute of the Family, 1994. 1996 figures from Statistics Canada, General Social Survey, Cat. No. 11-612. **p. 435:** 1880 data: Statistics Canada (1991) Mortality—Summary List of cases, 1991, Cat. No. 84-209; 1996 data: Nichols, Mark (1999) "Men's Health," *Maclean's* February 22, 1999. **p. 438:** Reproduced with the permission of the Minister of Public Works and Government Services Canada, 2000. **p. 439:** Reproduced with the permission of the Minister of Public Works and Government Services Canada, 2000. **p. 442:** From *Population: An Introduction to Concepts and Issues*, 6th ed. by J.R. Weeks © 1996. Reprinted by permission of Wadsworth Publishing, a division of International Thomson Publishing. **pp. 444–445:** Castles, Stephen. 1995. "Trois Siècles de Dépopulations Amerindienne" in L. Normandeau and V. Piche (eds.) *Les Populations Amerindienne et Inuit du Canada*. **p. 446:** Statistics Canada, from Population Projections for Canada, Provinces and Territories, 1984–2006. Cat. No. 91-520; and from 1961 Census Bulletin 1.2-2. **p. 449:** From *The PreIndustrial City: Past and Present* by Gideon Sjoberg © 1965, Free Press: New York. **p. 452:** Adapted from Harris and Ullman, 1945.

NOTES

NOTES

NOTES

NOTES

NOTES

To the owner of this book

We hope that you have enjoyed *Sociology In Our Times: The Essentials*, Second Canadian Edition (ISBN 0-17-616889-3), and we would like to know as much about your experiences with this text as you would care to offer. Only through your comments and those of others can we learn how to make this a better text for future readers.

School ________________ Your instructor's name ______________________

Course ___________ Was the text required? _______ Recommended? _____

1. What did you like the most about *Sociology In Our Times: The Essentials*?

____

____

____

2. How useful was this text for your course?

____

____

____

3. Do you have any recommendations for ways to improve the next edition of this text?

____

____

____

4. In the space below or in a separate letter, please write any other comments you have about the book. (For example, please feel free to comment on reading level, writing style, terminology, design features, and learning aids.)

____

____

____

____

Optional

Your name ______________________________ Date __________________

May Nelson Thomson Learning quote you, either in promotion for *Sociology In Our Times: The Essentials*, or in future publishing ventures?

Yes _______ No _______

Thanks!

You can also send your comments to us via e-mail at **college@nelson.com**

PLEASE TAPE SHUT. DO NOT STAPLE.

TAPE SHUT

TAPE SHUT

FOLD HERE

MAIL POSTE

Canada Post Corporation
Société canadienne des postes
Postage paid
if mailed in Canada
Business Reply
Port payé
si posté au Canada
Réponse d'affaires
0066102399 01

NELSON
THOMSON LEARNING™

0066102399-M1K5G4-BR01

TAPE SHUT

TAPE SHUT

NELSON THOMSON LEARNING
HIGHER EDUCATION
PO BOX 60225 STN BRM B
TORONTO ON M7Y 2H1